National Conference
on

"ADVANCED COMPUTING APPLICATIONS IN CIVIL ENGINEERING"

(ACACE-2018)

National Conference on

ADVANCED COMPUTING APPLICATIONS IN CIVIL ENGINEERING

(ACACE-2018)

20 - 21 April, 2018

Editors

Prof. V. Bhikshma

Prof. P. Raja Sekhar

Dr. K. L. Radhika

Dr. K. Shashikanth

Mrs. S.V.S.N.D.L. Prasanna

Organized by

Department of Civil Engineering
University College of Engineering (A), Osmania University,
Hyderabad - 500007, Telangana State

Sponsored by

TEQIP – III

VSSUT, Burla, Odisha

Published by

BS Publications, Hyderabad

Disclaimer

The Publisher and Organizers do not claim any responsibility for the accuracy of the data, statements made, and opinions expressed by authors. The authors are solely responsible for the contents published in the paper.

Published by

BS Publications

A unit of **BSP Books Pvt. Ltd.**

4-4-309/316, Giriraj Lane, Sultan Bazar,
Hyderabad - 500 095
Phone : 040 - 23445688, 23445600
e-mail : info@bspbooks.net
www.bspbooks.net

ISBN: 978-93-87593-22-0 (Paperback)

Prof. S. RAMACHANDRAM
Vice-Chancellor

OSMANIA UNIVERSITY
(University with Potential for Excellence)
Hyderabad – 500 007, Telangana
Re-accredited by NAAC with A+ Grade

Tel: +91-40-27098048 / 088, +91-40-27682364 / 221 • Fax: +91-40-27098003 / 704 • email: vc@osmania.ac.in, vcosmania@gmail.com

April 12, 2018

MESSAGE

I am happy to learn that the Department of Civil Engineering, University College of Engineering, Osmania University, Hyderabad in association with Veer Surendra Sai University of Technology, Burla, Odisha is organizing Two Day National Conference on **"Advanced Computing Applications in Civil Engineering (ACACE – 2018)"** funded under TEQIP – III during April 20-21, 2018 and is bringing out the Conference Proceedings to mark the occasion.

I compliment the Principal, Faculty, Staff, Research Scholars and Students of the Department of Civil Engineering for their initiative in organizing this event. I highly value such scholarly events which promote healthy interaction and proactive academic culture in the college.

The theme you have chosen for the National Conference is of topical significance and academic relevance. Civil Engineering is the basic branch of Engineering which can provide basic infrastructure such as Buildings, Highways, Railways, Bridges, Dams and Hydro Power plants to any developing country.

I am sure that the use of latest computing applications in Civil Engineering will enhance the quality of life for the present and future generations. This National Conference will provide a forum for deliberation on various issues pertaining to the theme and come out with useful insights for Indian Construction Industry.

I wish the National Conference all success.

[PROF. S. RAMACHANDRAM]

Dr. Ch. Gopal Reddy
M.Sc., Ph.D.
Professor of Physics
&
Registrar

OSMANIA UNIVERSITY
Hyderabad – 500 007, T.S. INDIA
Tel. (O) : +91-40-27098043
+91-40-27682363
Mobile : +91-98665 06129
Fax. : +91-40-27090020
Email : registrar@osmania.ac.in

Date: 12-04-2018

MESSAGE

I am happy to know that Department of Civil Engineering, University College of Engineering, Osmania University is organizing Two Day National Conference on **"Advanced Computing Applications in Civil Engineering (ACACE-2018)"** during 20-21 April, 2018 being sponsored by TEQIP-III.

The major themes such as Computational Methods, Innovative Modeling Techniques, Analysis of Structures, Finite Element Analysis, Advanced Modeling Applications in Climate Change. Environmental Modeling, Computational Fluid Dynamics (CFD), etc., of the conference cover the recent trends in the field of Civil Engineering.

I am sure that the participants of National Conference will focus on the exchange of information, innovations, new discoveries and research outcomes to evolve ways and means to address the practical challenges being faced in the field of Civil Engineering.

I hope that the National Conference provide a better stage to the scientists, research scholars and PG students to discuss their research contributions with the participants of different Universities / scientific institutions all over India.

My hearty congratulations and warmest wishes to the Head, Department of Civil Engineering and Organizing Committee (ACACE-2018) of the conference.

I wish the conference a great success.

PROF. CH. GOPAL REDDY

Prof. P. Laxminarayana
M.E., Ph.D. (Mech. Engg.)
Dean, Faculty of Engineering
University College of Engineering
Osmania University, Hyderabad – 500007
Ph: No: 040-27087493, 27682252
Email: deanenggon@gmail.com

MESSAGE

It gives me immense pleasure to know that Department of Civil Engineering is organizing two days National Conference on **Advanced Computing Applications in Civil Engineering** during 20-21 April, 2018 on the occasion of **Osmania University Centenary celebrations.** The conference provides the common platform for the academicians, Engineers Researchers and scientists to share and discuss on the current research work in the computational domain and seek solutions to the emerging problems of the society. I am sure the conference gives an opportunity for the delegates to share latest technical know-how in the fields of Advanced Computing Applications in Civil Engineering.

I am very hopeful that the deliberations that take place during these two days of the conference would yield fruitful results which will be helpful to the society in general and to the Researchers and Faculty members in particular

I Congratulate the Organizing Teams of ACACE-2018 and wish them a grand success.

PROF. P. LAXMINARAYANA

Prof. S. SAMEEN FATIMA
MS, PhD
PRINCIPAL

UNIVERSITY COLLEGE OF ENGINEERING
(AUTONOMOUS)
OSMANIA UNIVERSITY
HYDERABAD – 500 007, TELANGANA
(O) 040-27098254
(O) 040-27682384

MESSAGE

I am pleased to note that Department of Civil Engineering is organizing a two day National Conference on Advanced Computing Applications in Civil Engineering during 20-21 April, 2018 on the occasion of Osmania University Centenary celebrations. Centenary celebrations of OU are marked with various events such as International and National conferences/workshops/Symposium.

I deeply appreciate our oldest and energetic Department of Civil Engineering in conducting conferences in frontier and advanced fields of Engineering. The field of computing has been a fascinating field especially for Engineers and has attracted considerable attention across various disciplines of Engineering including Civil Engineering. Most of the significant developments that took place in the last few decades are no doubt from computational fields. The present theme for the conference is apt and provides improved solutions for complex problems.

I wish the organizing committee of ACACE a grand success

Prof. S. Sameen Fatima

DEPARTMENT OF CIVIL ENGINEERING
UNIVERSITY COLLEGE OF ENGINEERING (A)
OSMANIA UNIVERSITY, HYDERABAD – 7, T.S.
Phone : +91-40-27097125 Fax : +: +91-40-27090317
Website: www.osmania.ac.in/uceou.edu

Centenary Celebrations
1917-2017

MESSAGE

I am very happy that two day National Conference on ***"Advanced Computing Applications in Civil Engineering (ACACE-2018)"*** is being scheduled in the Department of Civil Engineering, during 20-21 April 2018. It is a very good platform to share the knowledge of interdisciplinary research n Civil Engineering particularly in Model analysis and computational techniques. This conference has a special significance because it is being conducted during the centenary celebrations in Osmania Univesity, Hyderabad, India. A deep research discussion and deliberations are possible in this conference as the different areas are merged together to showcase the research output. As the world is moving towards computerization and globalization, an interdisciplinary research among the various disciplines of Engineering is the need of the hour. A good collaborative research and the newer modeling approaches enhances the quality of research output.

I am sure this conference would provide new directions and dimensions in computational field particularly in Civil Engineering discipline. I congratulate all the team members of this conference for their dedicated work and invaluable contribution for the success of this conference.

With best wishes

Prof. V. Bhikshma
M.Tech, Ph.d (Structural Engineering
Head, Department of Civil Engineering
University College of Engineering (A)

Phone : 040-27097125
Fax : 040-27090317

DEPARTMENT OF CIVIL ENGINEERING
UNIVERSITY COLLEGE OF ENGINEERING (AUTONOMOUS)
OSMANIA UNIVERSITY, HYDERABAD - 500 007 (T.S.)

Dr. M. Anjaneya Prasad Ph D (IITM)
Professor & Chair-Person BOS (A)
Civil Engineering Department
Osmania University, Hyderabad - 7

MESSAGE

I am delighted to note that the Department of Civil Engineering is organizing TWO day National Level Conference on Advanced Computing Applications in Civil Engineering (ACACE-2018) during 20-21 April 2018 with the support of TEQIP-III.

Computer applications and modeling have become very much essential for any field of Engineering to effectively address the issues and challenges in research and also in various engineering applications in view of rapid developments that are taking place globally. The themes for topics of the conference were aptly selected to focus on various Civil Engineering applications to provide better solutions.

I am sure that the deliberations of the conference will be very much useful for research scholars and academia.

I am very happy to be associated with the conference and I also extend my GOOD WISHES for the success of the conference.

Dr. M. Anjaneya Prasad

MESSAGE FROM THE ORGANIZING COMMITTEE

The Department of Civil Engineering, University College of Engineering of Osmania University pleased to organize the National Conference on "***Advanced Computing Applications in Civil Engineering (ACACE-2018)***" in Association with VSSUT, Burla, Odisha (TEQIP III Mentee Institution) as part of ***Centenary Celebrations of OSMANIA UNIVERSITY*** during 20-21, April, 2018.

We take pride in conduct of the conference in the backdrop of OU celebrating its 100th year of its existence. OU has made significant contributions in the higher education field in the state of Telangana for the upliftment of its society in terms of social, modern, cultural, economic domains. Osmania University continues to score big in ratings and rankings, which are done by various institutions every year. In the recent UK-based Times Higher Education Rankings, Osmania University figured in the top 1,000 universities of the world.

The world of computing has seen tremendous growth in the recent past. The themes such as Innovative Modeling techniques, FEM, Multicriterion Decision Making (MCDM), Evolutionary Algorithms, Advanced modeling applications in Climate change, Soft Computing applications etc. reflects rapidly growing multidisciplinary fields that uses advanced computing capabilities to understand and solve complex problems. The response to the conference is overwhelming and we complement the Authors for publishing their research papers in the conference. Further, the papers presented in the conference would be published in the UGC recognized Journal for larger audience after thorough peer review process as a Special Issue in the ***International Journal of Emerging Technology and Advanced Engineering (IJETAE)*** (UGC approved open access online journal). We express our sincere gratitude to key note speakers for sparing valuable time and resources. Committee conveys special thanks to National Advisory committee, Organizing Committee and other subcommittees and Student Volunteers for their active involvement in the conduct of conference.

The organizing committee expresses profound thanks to TEQIP –III for their sponsorship and continued patronage of the programs conducted in the Department of Civil Engineering.

We hope that the deliberations and discussions in the Two Day National conference will promote useful and fruitful interactions among participants thus help in understanding of the latest developments.

ORGANIZING COMMITTEE

CHIEF PATRON

Hon'ble **Prof. S. Ramachandram**
Vice-Chancellor
Osmania University

PATRONS

Prof. Bibhuti Bushan Pati
Vice-Chancellor
VSSUT
Burla, Odisha

Prof. S. Sameen Fatima
Principal
University College of
Engineering (A), Osmania University

Prof. P. Laxminarayana
Dean
Faculty of Engineering
Osmania University

CHAIRPERSON

Prof. V. Bhikshma
Professor & Head
Civil Engineering Department
University College of Engineering, OU

ADVISORY COMMITTEE

Prof. V.S.S. Kumar
Prof. M. Kumar
Prof. N. Suresh Kumar
Prof. M. Gopal Naik
Prof. M. A. Prasad
Prof. T. Sambaiah
Prof. Sanjay Kumar Patro VSSUT, Burla
Prof. P. K. Pradhan VSSUT, Burla

ORGANIZING COMMITTEE

Dr. M. V. S. Sridhar
Dr. D. Rupesh Kumar
Dr. D. Rajasekhar Reddy
Dr. R. Srinivasa Kumar
Mrs. D. Annapurna
Mrs. P. Anuradha
Mr. R. Rajendar
Mrs. A. Ushasree
Mr. L. Ajay Kumar

CONFERENCE SECRETARY

Prof. P. Raja Sekhar

CONVENORS

Dr. K.L. Radhika
Dr. K. Shashikanth
Mrs. S.V.S.N.D.L. Prasanna

NATIONAL ADVISORY COMMITTEE

Prof. D. Nagesh Kumar, IISc , Bangalore

Prof. V.V. Srinivas, IISc, Bangalore

Prof. T.I. Eldho, IITB, Mumbai

Prof. Subimal Ghosh, IITB Mumbai

Prof. Subhankar Karmarkar, IITB Mumbai

Prof. K.V. L. Subramaniam, IIT Hyderabad

Prof. Pradeep Kumar Ramancharla, IIIT-Hyderabad

Prof. N.V. Ramana Rao, Director, NIT Warangal

Prof. N. Umamahesh, NIT Warangal

Prof. D. Ramaseshu, NIT Warangal

Prof. C.S.R.K. Prasad, NIT Warangal

Prof. G. Rajesh Kumar, NIT Warangal

Prof. P. Rathish Kumar, NIT Warangal

Prof. Srinivas Raju, BITS, Hyderabad

Prof. N. Murali Krishna, Retd. Professor, OU

Prof. M. R. Madhav, Retd. Professor, IITK

Prof. G.V. Rao, Retd. Professor, IITD

Prof. B. L. P. Swamy, Vasavi Engg College

Prof. P. Jagannadha Rao, ACE, Hyderabad

Prof. P. SubbaRao, JNTUK

Prof. G. N. Pradeep Kumar, SVU

Prof. D.S.R.K. Murthy, AU

LOCAL ORGANIZING COMMITTEES

A. SPONSORSHIP & FINANCE COMMITTEE

Prof. V. Bhikshma	Chairperson
Prof. P. Rajasekhar	Org. Secretary
Dr. K.L.Radhika	Conveners
Dr. K. Shashikanth	Conveners
Ms. SVSNDL. Prasanna	Conveners

B. TECHNICAL COMMITTEE

Prof. M. Kumar	Chairperson
Dr. M.V.S. Sreedhar	Member
Dr. D. Rajasekhar Reddy	Member
Ms. D. Annapurna	Member
Mr. R. Rajendar	Member
Mr. J. Karunakar	M.E Scholar
Ms. Navyasri	M.E Scholar
Ms. P. Swathipriya	M.E Scholar
Mr. Naresh	M.E Scholar
Mr. B. Srinivas Naik	CED Staff
Mr. Vinay	CED Staff

C. PRINTING, PUBLISHING, PHOTOGRAPHY & MEDIA COMMITTEE

Prof. N. Suresh Kumar	Chairperson
Dr. M.V.S. Sreedhar	Member
Dr. R. Srinivas Kumar	Member
Ms. Divya Shankar	M.E Scholar
Mr. Yaseen	M.E Scholar

D. STAGE ORGANISATION (INAUGURAL & VALEDICTORY) COMMITTEE

Prof. M. Gopal Naik	Chairperson
Ms. D. Annapurna	Member
Ms. P. Anuradha	Member
Mr. L. Ajay Kumar	Member
Ms. G. Sravani	M.E Scholar
Mr. D. Sainath	M.E Scholar
Ms. Divya Shankar	M.E Scholar
Ms. Manisha	M.E Scholar

E. REGISTRATION COMMITTEE

Prof. M. A. Prasad	Chairperson
Mr. L. Ajay Kumar	Member
Ms. A. Ushasree	Member
Mr. J. Karunakar	M.E Scholar
Ms. Alekhya	M.E Scholar
Ms. K. Sravya	M.E Scholar
Ms. A. Urmila	M.E Scholar

F. REFRESHMENT & FOOD COMMITTEE

Prof. T. Sambaiah	Chairperson
Dr. D. Rajasekhar Reddy	Member
Dr. R. Srinivas Kumar	Member
Mr. Ch. Nagaphaneendra	M.E Scholar
Mr. V. Naveen	M.E Scholar
Mr. Abhilesh	M.E Scholar
Mr. Mohd. Saber	CED Staff
Mr. Ch. Balraj	CED Staff

G. TRANSPORTATION COMMITTEE

Dr. D. Rupesh Kumar	Chairperson
Dr. R. Srinivas Kumar	M.E Member
Mrs. A. Ushasree	M.E Member
Mr. P. Shravan	Scholar
Md. Leesan	Scholar

H. INVITATION PRINTING & DISTRIBUTION COMMITTEE

Dr. D. Rupesh Kumar	Chairperson
Mr. Shravan	M.E Scholar
Mr. Akhil	M.E Scholar
Mr. Sai Teja	M.E Scholar

PREFACE

With pleasure, we the organizing committee members bring out the proceedings of the Papers presented in the National Conference on "***Advanced Computing Applications in Civil Engineering - ACACE-2018***". The conference is being conducted as part of the ongoing Centenary Celebrations of Osmania University. Osmania University was established by HEH VII Nizam, Mir Osman Ali Khan through Firman to develop the then Princely State Hyderabad in educational, modern, secular, cultural fields and impart quality education, making it the first university in the country to provide education in native and Urdu language.

The world of computing has been a fascinating field especially for Engineers and continuous to grow by leaps and bounds. Computers and allied technologies have taken the world by storm. Engineers have always been smart in adopting these new exciting developments for their disciplines. Civil Engineers are always in the forefront in utilizing these technologies for the development mankind and provided enormous opportunities to new budding Civil Engineers.

Computational modeling has been an intense research domain in the recent past and enabled to solve complex problems of Civil Engineering. The conventional method of computing relies mostly on analytical/empirical relations which are time consuming when posed with real life problems. To study, model and analyze such complex problems, advanced computer based solutions are most sought after. The soft computing and advanced modeling tools have been used extensively in research and Development works. These techniques have been inspired by the reasoning, intuition, consciousness and wisdom possessed by human beings. The fields such as Finite Difference Method (FDM), Finite Element Method (FEM), and Boundary Element Method (BEM) etc are the most widely used numerical techniques to solve intricate problems in various disciplines such as Structural Engineering, Water Resources Engineering, Geotechnical Engineering, Transportation Engineering etc. The Soft computing tools viz. ANN, Fuzzy logic, ANFYS etc are also applied to various disciplines of Civil Engineering. Further, they provide powerful tools to carry out numerical simulation studies. ACACE Provides common platform to the Scientists, Engineers, Technocrats, Researchers to discuss, deliberate and share current research work and seek solutions to the emerging problems facing the Civil Engineering field. The response to the conference has been overwhelming from the various organizations especially from the researchers.

We sincerely express our thanks to National Advisory committee, Organizing committee and Local organizing committee for their active involvement in the conduct of conference. We profusely thank all Keynote speakers, Chairpersons and Co-chairpersons of various technical sessions for accepting our invitation to conduct proceedings of the conference. We are grateful to GAR Corporation

Private Limited, TEQIP-III, and Theme Ambience Infrastructure Pvt. Ltd. for sponsoring the conference.

We are happy to see many young researchers for their enthusiastic participation and presentation of their research work. These conferences provide a window for young researchers to exhibit their work and get further help in their work. We hope that the deliberations and discussions in the Two Day National conference will promote useful and fruitful interactions among participants thus help in understanding of the latest developments.

Conveners

Dr. K. L. Radhika

Dr. K. Shashikanth

Mrs. SVSNDL Prasanna

Organizing Secretary

Prof. P. Raja Sekhar

02:00 - 03:00 pm	**Keynote Addresses – IV** [Water Resources Engineering] ***Imaging Preferential Pathways in Fractured Granites Using ERT-Tracer Experiments And Numerical Simulations*** **Dr. K. B. V. N. Phanindra, Indian Institute of Technology Hyderabad**
03:00 - 04:00pm	**Technical Session – III** **[*Stream: COMPUTATIONAL TECHNIQUES IN WATER RESOURCE ENGINEERING*]** **Chair:** Prof. Y. Ellam Raj, AVINET, Ibrahimpatnam. **Co-Chair:** Dr. G. Sravan Kumar, Vasavi College of Engineering

PAPER ID	TITLE OF THE PAPER
201	Estimating Runoff Using SCS Curve Number Method *Zeenat Ara, Mohammad Zakwan*
202	Daily River flow Modeling using Artificial Neural Networks *C. S. V. Subrahmanya Kumar, G.K.Viswanadh*
203	Performance Evaluation of Daily Sediment Yield Transport Model Using Artificial Neural Networks *C. S.V. Subrahmanya Kumar, G.K.Viswanadh*
204	Assessment and Evaluation of Groundwater Quality due to Landfill Leachate Using Fuzzy Logic *C. S. V. Subrahmanya Kumar, G.K.Viswanadh*
206	Indian Summer Monsoon Rainfall Extremes projections using Block Maxima Approach under Climate Change *K. Shashikanth, M. Prashanthi*
207	ANFYS Model for Reservoir Operation *Saraswathi H, M. A. Prasad*
208	Temperature Projections from GCMs using Quantile Remapping Method *K. Shashikanth, Rajsekhar Reddy, M. Anjaneya Prasad*
209	Water Distribution Network Model Using EPANET *M. Anjaneya Prasad, K. Shashikanth, M. Redya Naik, M. Narender Reddy*

Two Day National Conference on

ADVANCED COMPUTING APPLICATIONS IN CIVIL ENGINEERING [ACACE -2018]

20 – 21 April, 2018

Programme Schedule

Day – 1: Friday [20.04.2018]

08:30 - 10:00 am	**Registration**
10:00 - 11:30 am	**Inauguration**
11:45 - 01:00 pm	**Keynote Lecture – I** [Structural Engineering] ***Numerical Modeling of Hybrid FRP Strengthened Short Concrete Columns Under Eccentric Compression*** **Prof. S. Suriya Prakash, IIT Hyderabad**
02:00 - 03:30pm	**Keynote Lecture – II** [Structural Engineering] ***Interval Finite Element Analysis of Thin Plates*** **Prof. M. V. Rama Rao, Vasavi College of Engineering, Hyderabad**
03:45 - 05:45 pm	**Technical Session – I** [***Stream: FINITE ELEMENT ANALYSIS***] **Chair**: Prof. Sreenivasa Sarma, CBIT **Co-Chair**: Prof. Manohar, MES, Saidabad

PAPER ID	TITLE OF THE PAPER
111	Structural Behavior of Four Legged Transmission Line Tower Under Tornado loading *Darshan Kumar R. Rana, V. R. Panchal*
113	Effect of Multi-Support Excitation on Cable Stayed Suspension Hybrid Bridge *Parthi K. Patel, V. R. Panchal*
117	A Three Dimensional Non-Linear Finite Element Modelling of Top-Seat Angle Connection *D. R. Panchal, H. D. Devani*
118	Analysis of Composite Laminated Plate Using FEM *Nethravathi C, Sreenivasa M. B.*

119	Evaluation of Response Reduction Factor of Aircraft Hangar Constructed by Double Layer Grid System *Satish N. Prajapati, Vijay R. Panchal, Jignesh A. Amin*
122	Analytical Study on Two- Way Rectangular RC Slab with Opening at Different Locations *Katrodiya Daxesh, G. Chauhan Neha, H. Chauhan Ritesh*
124	A Study on Retrofitting of RCC Industrial Building *B. Santhosh Reddy, D. Rupesh Kumar, K. Chaithanya Varada Prasasd*
129	Application of 3D Printing for Building Prototype Model of Osmania University Arts College – A Case Study *L. Siva Rama Krishna, Aravind Reddy G, Bhaskar Sudhakanth V, SriramVenkatesh*
130	Development of Artificial Neural Network Model for Geo-polymer Concrete *G. Sushma, D. Annapurna*
131	Effect of Slope Combination on Dynamic Analysis of RCC Chimney – Height 310m *K. Chaithanya Varada Prasad, P. Anuradha, K. L. Radhika, B. Santhosh Reddy*
132	Development of Mathematical Model for Geo-Polymer Concrete *Prof. V. Bhikshma,T. Naveen Kumar*
133	A Comparative Study on Seismic Analysis of Irregular Framed Structure with Bare Frame, Open Ground Storey and In-filled Frame *Sirigiri Sowmya, K. L. Radhika,*
134	A Study on Skew Effect of Prestressed Concrete Bridges *Rupesh Kumar D, Venkateswarlu R*

Day – 2 : Saturday [21.04.2018]

10:00 - 11:30 am	**Keynote Lecture – III** [Civil Engineering] ***Moving Beyond Finite Elements: Towards Meshless Isogeometric Analysis*** **Prof. Amirtham Rajagopal, IIT, Hyderabad.**
11:45 - 01:00 pm	**Technical Session – II** [***Stream: SEISMIC ANALYSIS***] **Chair:** Prof. N. Murali Krishna, C V R College of Engineering, Ibrahimpatnam **Co-Chair:** Prof. Hamraj, MJCET

PAPER ID	**TITLE OF THE PAPER**
103	A Seismic Design of Building-Equipment System Using Conical Friction Pendulum Isolator *Meet M. Joshi, V. R. Panchal, D. P. Soni*

04:15 - 05:15pm	**Technical Session – IV** [***Stream: EMERGING TRENDS IN TRANSPORTATION ENGINEERING & CONSTRUCTION MANAGEMENT***] **Chair:** Prof. Mir Iqbal Faheem, Deccan College of Engineering **Co-Chair:** Prof. S. S. V. Chalam, CBIT
PAPER ID	**TITLE OF THE PAPER**
301	Evaluation of Performance Of Isolated Signalized Intersections and Design of a Coordinated Signal System by using VISSIM Software *R. Srinivasa Kumar, K. Vinay Kumar*
303	Evaluation of the effect of Aggregate Gradation and Binder Parameters on Bituminous Mix Rutting *D. Rajashekar Reddy*
302	A Case study of Mode Choice Analysis in Hyderabad City *S. Ramesh Kumar, M. Kumar, C. S. V Subramanya Kumar, Praveen*
401	Project Success Analysis of Contractor Organization Attributes using Regression Model *Balla Bhavani Shankar, Asem Ali Ahmed Alshahethi, K. L. Radhika*
402	Factors Affecting Cost Estimation: A Case from Yemen Construction Projects *Asem Ali Ahmed Alshahethi, Balla Bhavani Shankar, K. L. Radhika*
403	A Comparative Study of Different Contractor Selection Methods *S.V.S.N.D.L. Prasanna, Kalithkar Rakesh*

CONTENTS

KEYNOTES

STREAM I: STRUCTURAL ENGINEERING

STREAM II: WATER RESOURCES ENGINEERING

STREAM III: TRANSPORTATION ENGINEERING AND CONSTRUCTION ENGINEERING MANAGEMENT

Keynotes

Numerical Modeling of Hybrid FRP Strengthened Short Concrete Columns under Eccentric Compression

Chellapandian M[1], Suriya Prakash S[2], Akanshu Sharma[3]

[1, 2] *Department of Civil Engineering, Indian Institute of Technology, Hyderabad, India.*
[3] *Institute of Construction Materials, University of Stuttgart, Stuttgart, Germany*

Abstract
The paper deals with the numerical modelling of short columns under uniaxial eccentric compression. The objective of this study is to develop a non-linear microplane based model for evaluating the behavior of hybrid fiber reinforced polymer (FRP) strengthened columns under eccentric compression in terms of initial and post cracking stiffness, peak load, ultimate displacement and failure type. This study includes modelling three series of specimens namely (i) plain concrete columns (PC), (ii) control reinforced concrete (RC) column and (iii) hybrid FRP strengthened column which is a combination of near surface mounting (NSM) and external bonding (EB). The numerical results are compared with the experimental observations which are documented in the companion paper of authors [1]. Results reveal that the developed numerical model was able to predict the overall load – displacement behavior and failure mode in an accurate sense.

***Keywords*: Hybrid Strengthening; Microplane based Approach; Numerical Modelling; Short Columns.**

I. INTRODUCTION

Reinforced Concrete (RC) columns are the key load bearing elements in a structure which often requires strengthening due to various reasons like (i) decrease in load carrying capacity of the structure (ii) additional service requirements (iii) change in the type of load (iv) natural/man-made disasters. Presence of significant amount of bending due to eccentricity can lead to reduction in strength, ductility and lead to sudden brittle failure. In such cases, strengthening of columns is essential to meet the design requirements. Strengthening of RC columns using FRP has been extensively studied by many researchers [2-5]. Moreover, modelling of RC elements using commercial finite element (FE) software has been carried out in the past. However, the accuracy of finite element predictions reduces due to cracking and associated brittleness. Moreover, FE models based on the continuum mechanics cannot represent the discontinuity. This study focuses on using a microplane based modeling approach for predicting the overall behavior of short columns under uniaxial eccentric compression.

II. MICROPLANE BASED MODELING OF CONCRETE

Microplane based modelling approach uses material characterisation represented by the relation between stress and strain components in the planes of various orientations. In this approach, the tensorial invariants are assumed to be located in an imaginary plane known as microplane[6-7]. The overall response can be calculated by superimposing all the components from the microplane i.e., the numerical integration over a number of microplane gives the macroscopic strain tensor which can be further integrated to determine the stress components (Fig. 1). More details of microplane based modeling can be found elsewhere [8-9].

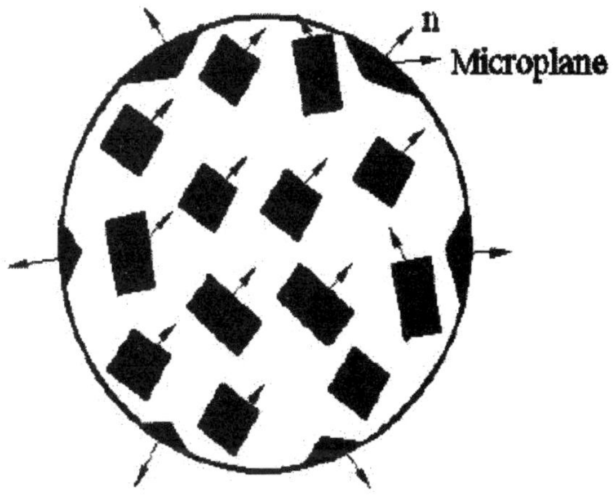

(i) Integration Points in a Sphere

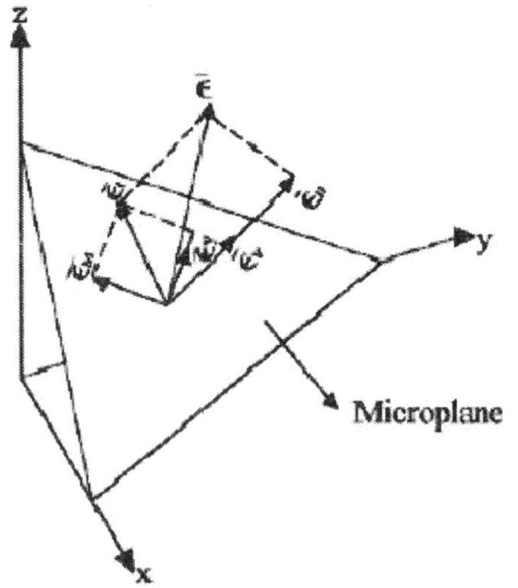

(ii) Strain Tensor in Microplane

Fig. 1: Representation of microplane based modeling of concrete

III. MATERIAL PROPERTIES AND MODELING INPUTS

FE models are developed using a pre-processor FEMAP and the developed models are analysed using FE program MASA. Nonlinear behavior of concrete in tension and compression are given as input in the developed FE model. The stress-strain properties of steel obtained from the coupon test results are used in the modeling. In the case of FRP laminates, the behavior of the material is assumed linear elastic until rupture and the same is used for modeling. For modeling of FRP fabric, the properties of epoxy and fibers are defined separately which combines together to provide the composite properties. Mesh size of 25 mm is chosen from the mesh convergence study. Concrete is modeled using three dimensional eight node solid elements. Two node truss element is used to model the steel reinforcements. CFRP laminates are modeled as a two node rod element (truss element with bond definitions) in which the interface bond properties are defined. CFRP fabric is modeled as a three-dimensional solid element representing epoxy in which the carbon fibers are embedded as a one-dimensional truss element.

IV. RESULTS AND DISCUSSION

The numerical load –displacement behavior is compared with the test results and shown in Fig. 2. The developed FE model is able to predict the overall behavior in an accurate sense. The difference in peak strength for all the specimens are found to be less than 2% when compared to the experiments. Plain columns had sudden failure at a strain corresponding to its peak strength. Control RC column (CP) had a better peak strength and post-peak predictions. Hybrid strengthened specimens had improvement in peak strength and ductility by 46% and 64% respectively. The detailed experimental observations can be found elsewhere [1]. The failure mode observed for control column is compared with the experimental observation and shown in Fig. 3. The model had initial tension cracks after which the failure occurred near peak load due to severe crushing of concrete in the compression face (Fig. 3).

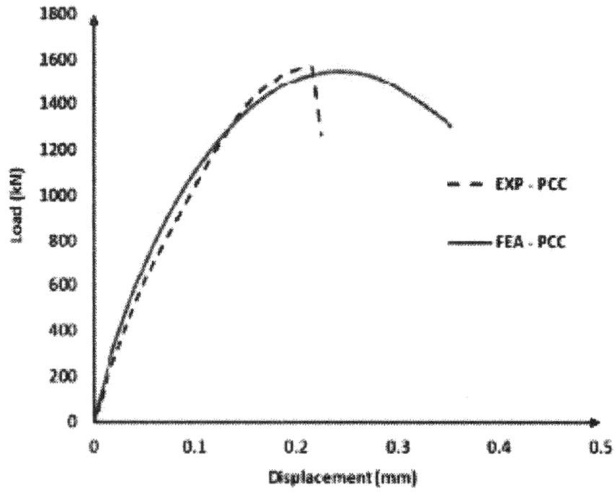

(i) Plain Concrete Column

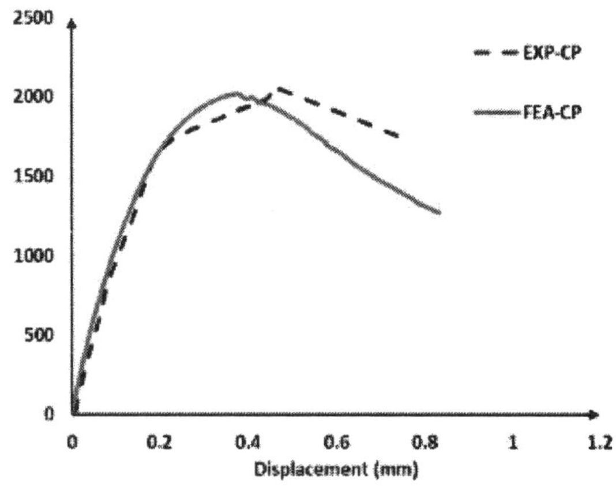

(ii) Reinforced Concrete Column

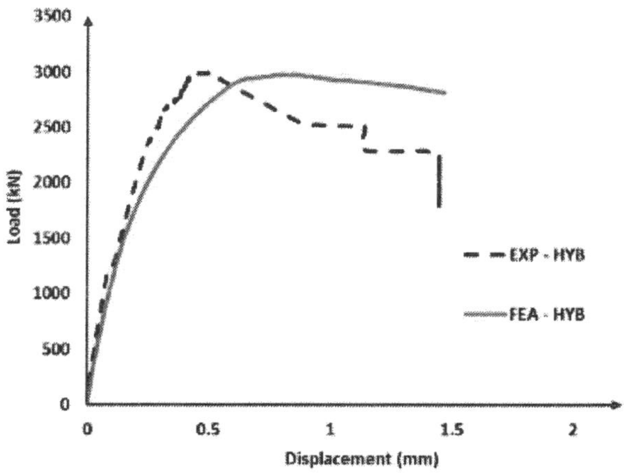

(iii) Hybrid Strengthened Column

Fig. 2 Overall Load - Displacement Comparison of Short Columns

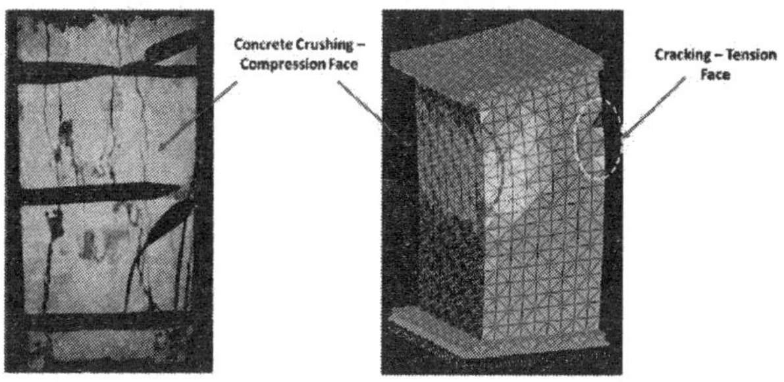

Fig. 3 Failure Mode Comparison of Control RC Column (CP)

V. SUMMARY

- The microplane based nonlinear finite element model developed in this study effectively captured the overall response of short columns under eccentric compression loading.
- Failure mode of columns are effectively captured using the developed numerical model.
- Hybrid FRP strengthened specimens had better performance in terms of improving the overall peak strength and ductility. The failure occurred due to rupture of FRP fabric in the compression face.

References

[1] Chellapandian M, Prakash SS and Rajagopal A. Analytical and finite element studies on hybrid FRP strengthened RC column elements under axial and eccentric compression. Composite Structures 2018; 184: 234-248.

[2] Chellapandian M, Prakash SS and Sharma A. Strength and ductility of innovative hybrid NSM reinforced and FRP confined short RC columns under axial compression. Composite Structures Elsevier 2017; 176: 205 - 216.

[3] Maaddawy T, Sayed M and Magid BA. Effect of cross sectional shape and loading condition on performance of reinforced concrete members confined with carbon fiber reinforced polymers. Materials and design 2013; 31: 2330-2341.

[4] Barros JAO, Varma RK, Sena-Cruz, M and Azevedo AFM. Near surface mounted FRP strips for the flexural strengthening of RC columns - experimental and numerical research Engineering Structures 2008; 30(12): 3412-3425.

[5] Jain S, Chellapandian M and Prakash SS. Emergency repair of severely damaged reinforced concrete column elements under axial compression: an experimental study. Construction and Building Materials 2017; 155: 751-761.

[6] Gambarelli S, Nistico N and Ozbolt J. Numerical analysis of compressed concrete columns confined with CFRP: Microplane-based approach. Composites Part B: Engineering, 2014; 67: 303-312.

[7] Ozbolt J, Li Y-J and Kozar I. Microplane model for concrete with relaxed kinematic constraint. International Journal of Solids and Structures 2001; 38: 2683–711.

[8] Ozbolt J. MASA – Macroscopic Space Analysis. Internal Report, Institute für Werkstoffe im Bauwesen, University ät Stuttgart, Germany; 1998.

[9] Ozbolt J, Mestrovic D, Li Y-J and Eligehausen R. Compression failure – beams made of different concrete types and sizes. ASCE Journal of Structural Engineering, 2000; 126(2): 200–209.

Interval Finite Element Analysis of Thin Plates

M. V. Rama Rao[1], Rafi L. Muhanna[2] and Robert L. Mullen[3]
[1]Vasavi College of Engineering, Hyderabad-500 031 INDIA.
[2]School of Civil and Environmental Engineering, Georgia Institute of Technology Atlanta, GA 30332-0355, USA.
[3]School of Civil and Environmental Engineering, University of South Carolina, GA 30332-0355, USA

dr.mvrr@gmail.com, rafi.muhanna@gtsav.gatech.edu, rlm@cec.sc.edu

I. Introduction

Plates play a major role in several important structures viz. ships, pressure vessels, and other structural components. Thus it is important to understand their structural behaviour and possible conditions of failure especially under conditions of uncertainty. The structural behaviour of thin plates in bending depends on several important factors including load, stiffness characteristics of plate and support conditions. The problem of plate bending is one of the oldest in the theory of elasticity and is discussed in several textbooks (Reddy,2007). On the other hand, structural analysis without considering uncertainty in loading or material properties leads to an incomplete understanding of the strucural performance. Structural analysis using interval variables has been used by several researchers to incorporate uncertainty into structural analysis (Muhanna, R. L. and Mullen, R. L. 1995, Muhanna and Mullen, 2001, Pownuk, 2004 and Neumaier and Pownuk 2007).

To the authors' knowledge, applications of interval methods for the analysis of plates with uncertainty of load and material properties do not exist anywhere in literature. In view of this, we present an initial investigation into the application of interval finite element methods to problems of bending of thin plates. Usually, derived quantities in Interval Finite Element Method (IFEM) such as stresses and strains have additional overestimation in comparison with primary quantities such as displacements. This issue has plagued displacement-based IFEM for quite some time. The recent development of mixed/hybrid IFEM formulation by the authors (Rama Rao, Mullen and Muhanna, 2011) is capable of simultaneous calculation of interval strains and displacements with the same accuracy.

This work presents the application of interval finite element methods to the analysis of thin plates. Uncertainty is considered in both the applied load and Young's modulus as explained in section 2. Examples are finally presented and discussed. In the present study a rectangular plate is analysed different type of edge conditions of such as clamped and simply supported edge conditions and the deformations are obtained.

II. Linear Interval Finite Element Method

Finite element method is one of the most common numerical methods for solving differential and partial differential equations with enormous applications in different fields of science and engineering. Interval finite element methods have been developed to handle the analysis of systems for which uncertain parameters are M. V. Rama Rao, Rafi L. Muhanna and Robert L. Mullen described as intervals. A variety of solution techniques have been developed for IFEM. In the present work, an element-by-element (EBE) technique is utilized for element assembly (Muhanna and Mullen, 2001; Zhang, 2005). Then a mixed/hybrid formulation is incorporated to simultaneously calculate the interval strains and displacements (Rama Rao, Mullen and Muhanna, 2011). The iterative scheme that is developed by Neumaier and Pownuk (Neumaier and Pownuk, 2007) has been used for the solution of the linear interval system of equations. The solution includes displacements, strains, and forces simultaneously with the same high level of accuracy.

III. Finite Element Model of the Plate

Thin plates are characterized by a structure that is bounded by upper and lower surface planes that are separated by a distance h as shown in Figure 1. The x-y coordinate axes are located on the neutral plane of the plate (the "in-plane" directions) and the z-axis is normal to the x-y plane. In the absence of in-plane loading, the neutral plane is at the midpoint through the thickness. In the present work, it will be assumed that the thickness of plate h is a constant. Consequently, the location of the x-y axes will lie at the mid-surface plane (z=0).

In most plate applications, the external loading includes distributed load normal to the plate (z direction), concentrated loads normal to the plate, or in-plane tensile, bending or shear loads applied to the edge of the plate. Such loading will produce deformations of the plate in the x, y, z coordinate directions which in general can be characterized by displacements u(x, y, z) , v(x, y, z) and w(x, y, z) in the x, y and z directions, respectively.

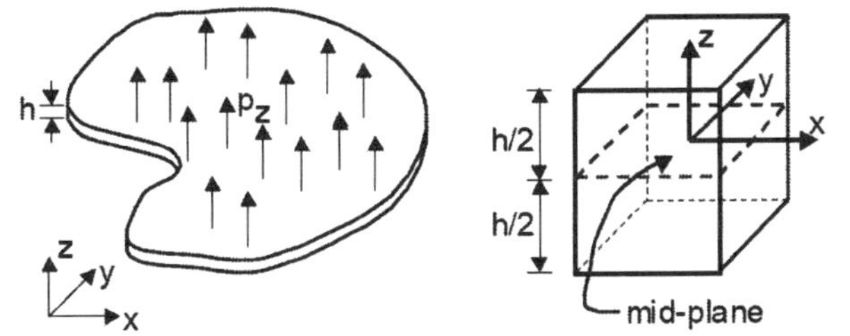

Figure 1 Geometry of thin plate

The plate is discretized into rectangular ACM (Adini-Clough-Melosh) plate elements. The ACM element is a non-conforming element with 12 degrees of freedom (3 degrees of freedom at each of the four nodes). Degrees of freedom at each node (i) are the transverse displacement and normal rotation about each axis, wt, $\theta_{xi} = \frac{\partial w_i}{\partial y}$ and $\theta_{yi} = \frac{\partial w_i}{\partial x}$, as illustrated in Figure 2. Note that θ_{yi} is a vector in the negative y direction.

Node "1" is selected at the lower left comer of the plate (x=-a, y=-b) and that the nodes are numbered 1,2,3,4 in counterclockwise direction around the plate. We assume that the plate dimensions are given by 2a and 2b as shown in Figure 1 and that the x-y coordinate system is located at the center of plate. The 12 degrees of freedom are arranged in the vector of generalized nodal displacements {d} as:

$$\{d\}^T = \{w_1 \quad \theta_{x1} \quad \theta_{y1} \quad w_2 \quad \theta_{x2} \quad \theta_{y2} \quad w_3 \quad \theta_{x3} \quad \theta_{y3} \quad w_4 \quad \theta_{x4} \quad \theta_{y4}\}^T$$

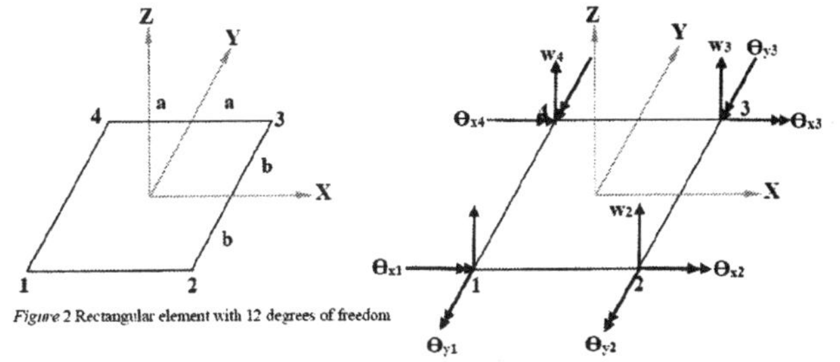

Figure 2 Rectangular element with 12 degrees of freedom

3.1. STIFFNESS MATRIX AND FORCE VECTOR OF THE ACM PLATE ELEMENT

We assume that w(x, y) is some function over the plate geometry as follows:

$$w(x,y) = a_1 + a_2x + a_3y + a_4x^2 + a_5xy + a_6y^2 + a_7x^3 + a_8x^2y + a_9xy^2 + a_{10}y^3 + a_{11}x^3y + a_{12}xy^3$$

We obtain

$$w(x,y) = \lfloor N(x,y) \rfloor [\Phi]^{-1}\{d\}$$

Where {a}and {d} are vector of unknown coefficients and vector of generalized nodal displacements for the element respectively.

From the moment-curvature relationship, we obtain

$$\begin{Bmatrix} M_x \\ M_y \\ M_{xy} \end{Bmatrix} = [D]\begin{Bmatrix} \kappa_x \\ \kappa_y \\ \kappa_{xy} \end{Bmatrix} = [D][B][\Phi]^{-1}\{d\} \text{ where } [D] = \frac{Eh^3}{12(1-\nu^2)}\begin{bmatrix} 1 & \nu & 0 \\ \nu & 1 & 0 \\ 0 & 0 & \frac{(1-\nu)}{2} \end{bmatrix}$$

The stiffness matrix $[K^{(e)}]$ is given as

$$[K^{(e)}] = [\Phi^{-1}]^T \left(\int_{-a}^{a}\int_{-b}^{b} [B]^T[D][B]dxdy \right) [\Phi^{-1}]$$

and the nodal force vector for the plate element $\{p^{(e)}\}$ is given as:

$$\{p^{(e)}\} = [\Phi^{-1}]^T \left(\int_{-a}^{a}\int_{-b}^{b} p_z \lfloor N(x,y) \rfloor^T dxdy \right)$$

IV. Interval Finite Element Model of the Plate

An element-by-element (EBE) technique is utilized for element assembly as outlined in section 2. Interval uncertainty is considered in pressure z p and Young's modulus of the plate E. Accordingly, the stiffness matrix and the force vector of the plate element are rewritten, denoting interval quantities in boldface, as follows:

$$\left[\boldsymbol{K}^{(e)}\right]=\int_{-a}^{a}\int_{-b}^{b}\left[B\Phi^{-1}\right]^{T}\left[\boldsymbol{D}\right]\left[B\Phi^{-1}\right]dxdy$$

and

$$\left\{\boldsymbol{P}^{(e)}\right\}=\left[\Phi^{-1}\right]^{T}\left(\int_{-a}^{a}\int_{-b}^{b}\boldsymbol{p}_{z}\left[N(x,y)\right]^{T}dxdy\right)$$

The decomposition for the element stiffness matrix $[K^{(e)}]$ is expressed as

$$[\boldsymbol{K}]=[A][\boldsymbol{D}][A]^{T}$$

When each plate element is subjected to an interval pressure p_z, the corresponding interval force vector {P} for the structure can be defined as:

$$\{\boldsymbol{P}\}_{n\times 1}=\begin{Bmatrix}\boldsymbol{P}_{1}^{(e)}\\ \boldsymbol{P}_{2}^{(e)}\\ \boldsymbol{P}_{3}^{(e)}\\ \cdots\end{Bmatrix}=[M]_{n\times m}[\boldsymbol{\delta}]_{m\times 1}$$

where n is the number of degrees of freedom for the structure and m is the number of elements.

The current interval formulation is based on the Element-By-Element (EBE) finite element technique (Muhanna and Mullen, 2001, Rama Rao, Mullen and Muhanna, 2011).

We obtain

$$\left(\begin{pmatrix}\boldsymbol{0} & C^{T} & B_{1}^{T} & 0\\ C & 0 & 0 & 0\\ B_{1} & 0 & 0 & -I\\ 0 & 0 & -I & 0\end{pmatrix}+\begin{bmatrix}A\\0\\0\\0\end{bmatrix}[\boldsymbol{D}][A\ \ 0\ \ 0\ \ 0]\right)\begin{pmatrix}\boldsymbol{U}\\ \lambda_{1}\\ \lambda_{2}\\ \kappa\end{pmatrix}=\begin{pmatrix}\boldsymbol{P}_{C}\\0\\0\\0\end{pmatrix}+\begin{Bmatrix}M\\0\\0\\0\end{Bmatrix}\{\delta\}$$

where λ_1 and λ_2 are vectors of Lagrange Multipliers. The solution of the above equation will provide the values of interval displacements U (primary unknowns) as well as interval values of $\{\lambda_1\}$, $\{\lambda_2\}$ and {K} (secondary unknowns) with the same level of sharpness (Rama Rao, Mullen and Muhanna ,2011). The vector of interval moments {M} can be obtained from the vector of interval curvatures {κ} as

$$\begin{Bmatrix}\boldsymbol{M}_{x}\\ \boldsymbol{M}_{y}\\ \boldsymbol{M}_{xy}\end{Bmatrix}=[\boldsymbol{D}]\begin{Bmatrix}\boldsymbol{\kappa}_{x}\\ \boldsymbol{\kappa}_{y}\\ \boldsymbol{\kappa}_{xy}\end{Bmatrix}=\frac{\boldsymbol{E}h^{3}}{12(1-\nu^{2})}\begin{bmatrix}1 & \nu & 0\\ \nu & 1 & 0\\ 0 & 0 & \frac{(1-\nu)}{2}\end{bmatrix}\begin{Bmatrix}\boldsymbol{\kappa}_{x}\\ \boldsymbol{\kappa}_{y}\\ \boldsymbol{\kappa}_{xy}\end{Bmatrix} \quad (43)$$

The applicability of the procedure outlined above is illustrated by solving numerical examples in the next section.

V. Example Problems

A thin rectangular plate with clamped edges is chosen to illustrate the applicability of the present approach to handle uncertainty in load and material properties in case of thin plate problems. These examples are chosen to demonstrate the ability of the current approach to obtain sharp bounds to the displacements and forces even in the presence of large number of interval variables. The material and geometric properties of the plate are given in Table 1 below.

Table 1 Properties of rectangular plate and discretization scheme

Length Lx	2.0 m	Applied Pressure p_z	14.0×10^3 Pa
Width Ly Thickness	3.0 m 0.025 m	Number of divisions along x-axis Number of divisions along y-axis	nx ny
Young's modulus	210 GPa	Notation for discretization scheme	$nx\times ny$
Poisson's ratio ν	0.3		

Figures 1 presents the variation of the lower and upper bounds of the interval displacement w_z along the length and width of the plate respectively. Figure 2 presents the variation of the lower and upper bounds of the slope θ_x along the width of the plate. Figure 3 presents the variation of the lower and upper bounds of the slope θ_y along the length of the plate.

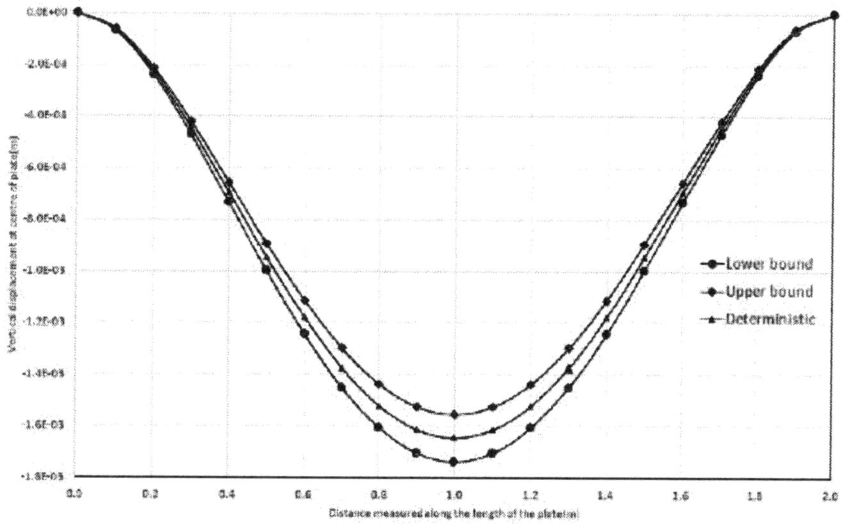

Clamped plate- variation of vertical displacement along the length of the plate with 10% uncertainty of load and 1% uncertainty of E

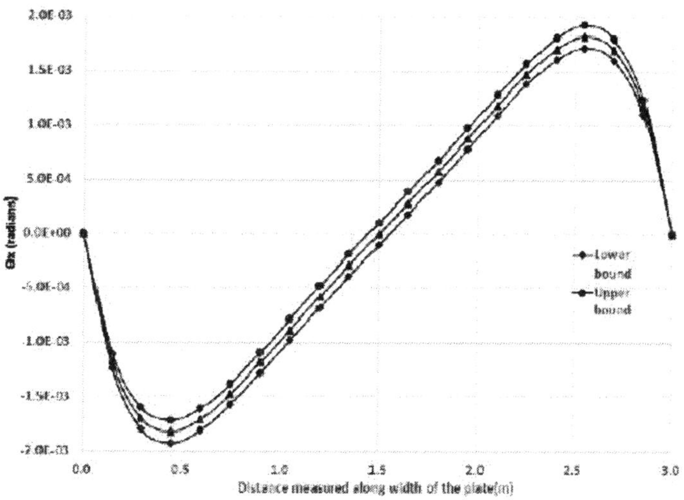

Clamped plate- variation of θ_x along the width of the plate with 10% uncertainty of load and 1% uncertainty of E

M. V. Rama Rao, Rafi L. Muhanna and Robert L. Mullen

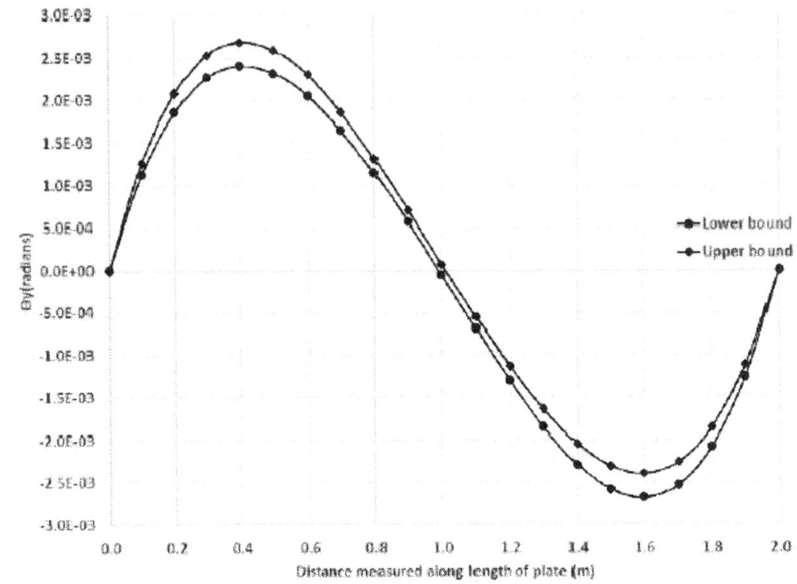

Clamped plate- variation of θ_y along the length of the plate with 10% uncertainty of load and 1% uncertainty of E

VI. CONCLUSION

A linear Interval Finite Element Method (IFEM) for structural analysis of thin plates is presented. Uncertainty in the applied load and Young's modulus is represented as interval numbers. Results are also computed using combinatorial solution and Monte Carlo simulations as appropriate. Example problems illustrate the applicability of the present approach to the problem of predicting the structural behavior of thin plates in the presence of uncertainties.

References

[1] Moore, R., E, 1966. Interval Analysis, Prentice-Hall, Englewood Cliffs, N.J. Muhanna, R. L. & Mullen, R. L. 1995. Development of Interval Based Methods for Fuzziness in Continuum Mechanics. In Proceedings of ISUMA-NAFIPS'95: 17-20 September, 1995. IEEE.

[2] Muhanna, R. L. & Mullen, R. L. 2001. Uncertainty in Mechanics Problems—Interval-Based Approach, Journal of Engineering Mechanics 127 (6): 557–566.

[3] Muhanna, R. L., Zhang, H., & Mullen, R. L. 2007. Interval finite element as a basis for generalized models of uncertainty in engineering mechanics. Reliable Computing, 13(2), 173–194.

[4] Neumaier, A., 1990. Interval methods for systems of equations, Cambridge University Press.

[5] Neumaier, A. & Pownuk, A. 2007. Linear Systems with Large Uncertainties, with Applications to Truss Structures, Reliable Computing, 13(2): 149-172.

[6] Pownuk, A., 2004. Efficient method of solution of large scale engineering problems with interval parameters." Proc. NSF workshop on reliable engineering computing (REC2004), R. L. Muhanna and R. L. Mullen, eds., Savannah, GA, USA.

[7] Rama Rao, M. V., Mullen, R. L., Muhanna, R. L., 2011, "A New Interval Finite Element Formulation With the Same Accuracy in Primary and Derived Variables", International Journal of Reliability and Safety, Vol. 5, Nos. 3/4.

[8] Zhang, H. 2005. Nondeterministic Linear Static Finite Element Analysis: An Interval Approach. Ph.D. Dissertation, Georgia Institute of Technology, School of Civil and Environmental Engineering.

Moving Beyond Finite Elements: Towards Meshless Isogeometric Analysis

AmirthamRajagopal

Associate Professor, Department of Civil Engineering, Indian Institute of Technology, Hyderabad.

Abstract: Finite element method has been a powerful numerical tool for various applications. However standard finite elements are all of C0 continuouslagrangian elements. These possess only displacement continuity whereas the derivatives of displacements are disconitnious. This leads to errors in finite element solution. An approach to overcome these errors is via a adaptive finite element analysis procedure. For certain class of problems where reproducing a particular field is of interest, like for instance in fracture mechanics problems, the standard finite elements have been extended to include additional terms of approximation which are referred to as the enrichment functions and has lead to the development of extended finite element method. For applications such as phase transitions, material interfaces, standard finite elements do not have smoother approximations. Hence there has been developments in meshfee methods. These have been extended to include modeling of geometry as well as field variable and are called as isogeomteric methods. The talk will focus on the progress in research in these directions and numerical examples will be presented to demonstrate the progress.

Imaging Preferential Pathways in Fractured Granites using ERT-Tracer Experiments and Numerical Simulations

KBVN Phanindra

Department of Civil Engineering, Indian Institute of Technology Hyderabad

Extended Abstract

I. INTRODUCTION

Fractured geologic media pose formidable challenges to hydrogeologists due to the strenuous mapping of fracture-matrix system and quantification of flow and transport processes. Fracture characterization under controlled laboratory conditions using rock block experiments has been successfully developed and validated by many researchers. However, at field scale, the intricacy in the manipulation of conditions has resulted in large uncertainties in the estimation of fracture zone properties. Field based methodologies for fracture characterization include: classical pumping tests, cross-hole tomographic tests, geophysical methods, and geochemical tracer tests. The choice of a field technique in solitary or in combination to map fracture geometry is primarily governed by the intended use and availability of resources. This study is aimed to demonstrate the application of tracer-ERT studies coupled with numerical simulations in mapping the sub-surface heterogeneity and preferential flow paths at sub-basin scale in a fractured granitic aquifer.

II. METHODOLOGY

Series of natural gradient saline tracer experiments were performed from a depth window of 18 to 22 m (that correspond to major yielding fracture) in an injection well located inside the IIT Hyderabad campus. Prior to the tracer injection, a baseline scenario is established by: i) performing surface ERT along two sections that are transverse to flow gradient, ii) measuring electrochemical properties of groundwater drawn from multiple depths using a discrete level sampler, and iii) plotting electrical and fluid resistivity logs at the monitoring wells. Dipole-dipole configuration with a spread of 160 m and electrode spacing of 4 m was employed during ERT surveys with data quality improved by considering stacking, reciprocal measurements, resolution indicators, and geophysical logs. Temporal changes in electrical properties (that were used to highlight preferential flow paths) were assessed by carrying independent data inversion on the elapsed ERT datasets and subtracting from the background inverted image, using a non-dimensional salinity indicator, viz. percentage change in resistivity (*pc*) given by:

$$pc = \left(\frac{\rho_o - \rho_t}{\rho_o} \right) \times 100$$

where, ρ_o and ρ_t respectively are the pixel-to-pixel resistivity values for the background image and the image lagged by time 't'. To ascertain the dominant flow and transport processes of the study area, we used the experimental results and numerically simulated the aquifer system using HydroGeoSphere (HGS) software. Two numerical conceptualizations viz., equivalent porous model (EPM) and dual continuum model (DCM) were considered in this study.

III. RESULTS AND DISCUSSION

Temporal changes in resistivity resulting from tracer movement along the two ERT sections are presented in Figure 1. Two dominant flow zones, one per section are largely contributing to the groundwater flow. This concludes that, weathered to fractured rock conditions prevail in the region. The dominant flow zone imaged in ERT-1 exists between chainages 80 m to 110 m (aligned at 80.71° to 96.9° with injection well 'IW') and between depths 22 m to 29 m. Additionally, two discrete, disconnected high resistivity anomalies indicating the presence of conductive fractures were noticed at a depth of 28 m and chainages of 60 m and 120 m respectively. The dominant flow zone imaged in ERT-2 exists between chainages 65 m to 120 m (aligned at 55.26° to 120.23° with IW) and between depths 22 m to 30 m. The temporal shift in peak intensity from ERT-1 to ERT-2 is in accordance with local hydraulic gradient. Results conclude that tracer-

ERT tests can effectively capture the flow characteristics of weathered to fractured granitic formations. The peak tracer concentration was observed 6:30 and 7:00 hours after tracer injection at the two sections, lower than the time taken by a fluid particle to reach under natural gradient conditions. This might be due to a high transverse dispersion. After about 23:00 hours of injection, the average *pc* at the two ERT sections is just above the cutoff value, confirming the subsidence of the injected tracer.

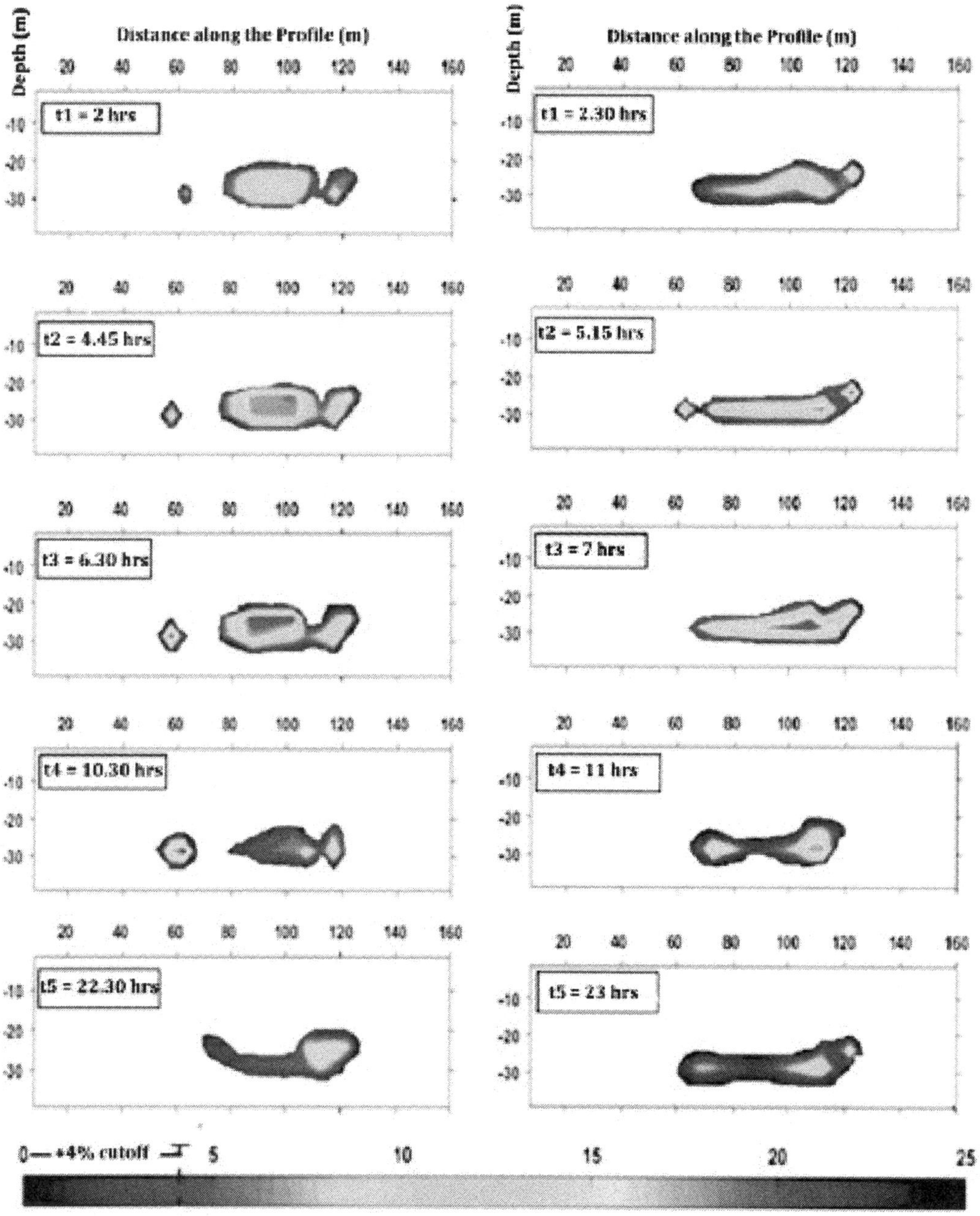

Figure 1 Tracer movement inferred via dynamic changes in resistivity along ERT-1 (left) and ERT-2 (right) sections. X-axis represents the chainage in m and Y-axis represents the depth below ground surface in m

Numerical simulations were performed using a rectangular domain of 200 m x 300 m with a thickness of 40 m. HGS was used to simulate the dispersion of solute in a uniform and steady subsurface water flow field. Steady state flow condition was achieved by injecting the tracer at a very low rate (2.78×10^{-4} m^3/s) to avoid disturbance to natural flow field. Numerical results conclude that, EPM has significantly underestimated and delayed the peak tracer concentration that might be due to averaging of hydraulic and solute properties. In contrast, DPM has slightly overestimated with an early peak time concentration. This might be due to high fracture porosity and high mass transfer coefficient. Statistically, DCM performed better (R^2 = 0.82, NSE = 0.815, RMSE = 64.6 mg/l) to EPM approach (R^2 = 0.57, NSE = -0.755, RMSE = 199 mg/l) in simulating migration of a conservative tracer considering advection and dispersion mechanisms. This

concludes that considering a dual continuum approach to simulate flow and transport processes is reliable for analysing the response of aquifer system to various external stresses specific to the study area. Even though this conclusion is not surprising in general, this paper highlights the need for a paradigm shift in modeling the fractured aquifers of central and southern India, by accounting for the largescale spatial variability in the sub-surface system.

IV. CONCLUSION

This study elucidates the applicability of field scale tracer-ERT experiments coupled with numerical simulations to delineate preferential flow and transport paths in a weathered to the fractured granitic aquifer. ERT was able to capture the preferential flow paths inferred via a decrease in resistivity in the time-lapse images. Two dominant flow zones, one per section confirms the existence of a highly weathered to fractured aquifer within the study area. Results of field experiments were further utilized to evaluate two mathematical conceptualizations (EPM and DCM) that apply to fractured aquifers. Results of numerical analysis suggest that DCM simulated tracer breakthrough curves are in agreement with geochemical samplings at the monitoring well locations, and hence suggested for the study region.

References

[1] Cassiani, G., Bruno, V., Villa, A., Fusi, N. and Binley, A.M., 2006. A saline trace test monitored via time-lapse surface electrical resistivity tomography. *Journal of Applied Geophysics*, 59(3), pp.244-259.

[2] Huang, Y., Yu, Z., Zhou, Z., Wang, J. and Guo, Q., 2013. Modeling Flow and Solute Transport in Fractured Porous Media at Jinping I-Hydropower Station, China. *Journal of Hydrologic Engineering*, 19(9), p.05014007.

[3] Robert, T., Caterina, D., Deceuster, J., Kaufmann, O. and Nguyen, F., 2012. A salt tracer test monitored with surface ERT to detect preferential flow and transport paths in fractured/karstified limestones. *Geophysics*, 77(2), pp.B55-B67.

[4] Vijay, Sreeparvathy, BVN P Kambhammettu, SR Peddinti and PSL, Sarada. (2018). Application of ERT, saline tracer and numerical studies to delineate preferential paths in fractured granites. Groundwater. 10.1111/gwat.12663.

Stream I: Structural Engineering

Analysis of Dome for Different Pulse Loading History of Blast Load

Mohammed Sahal M. Kazi[1], Dipali Y. Patel[2]

[1] *Post Graduate Student (Structural Engineering), Department of Civil Engineering, Chandubhai S. Patel Institute of Technology, Charotar University of Science and Technology, Changa, Gujarat, India*
[2] *AssistantProfessor, Departmentof Civil Engineering, Chandubhai S. Patel Institute of Technology, Charotar University of Science and Technology, Changa, Gujarat, India*

[1]sahalkazi151@yahoo.com
[2]dipalipatel.cv@charusat.ac.in

***Abstract*— Different types of loads are Dead load, Wind load, Snow load etc. are acting on dome structure during its entire life period. Due to increasing number of terrorist attacks, it is very important to analyze and design dome structure to be safer against the blast load. The dome structure can be subjected to any arbitrary pulse but for our benefit it is assumed to have some specific shape. But till date very less research has been established on the analytical study of arbitrary pulses. In this study, blast pressure is calculated as per IS: 4991 – 1968. Using this blast pressure different pulses are converted in form of time vs. acceleration. Pulses are converted in C sharp and different pulse time history is applied on the dome structure. This modeling of dome structure is done in SAP2000. Generating maximum stresses and acceleration are studied from different pulse time history acting on dome structure and also studied which type of pulse shape is more critical.**

Key Words*— Dome structure; Blast load; Pulse time history; C sharp; Acceleration; Stresses.

I. INTRODUCTION

Dome - It may be defined as a thin shell generated by the revolution of a regular curve about one of its vertical axes. The pre-eminence of domes is in their strength and stiffness that they stand without support of columns. The shape of the dome depends upon the type of the curve and the direction of theaxis of revolution. The dome area of shell may be spherical, parabolic or elliptical, covering circular or polygonal.The stresses in the dome are generally membrane compressive stresses in major part of the shell except circumferential tensile stresses near the edge.The domes are one of the most efficient shapes in the world. It is lightest structure to cover up the circular shape.

Figure 1 Dome structure

Pulse activity - Due to blast, air pressure generate on a structure above ground level is basically a single pulse and can frequently idealize by simple shapes.

Numbers of researchers have acquired thedynamic characteristics of large reinforced concrete domes.Tahaseen et al. [1] has studied on Reinforced Cement Concrete (RCC) dome design. The analysis and design of RCC domes were clearly explained and after the analysis and design, we get the hoop reinforcement in a dome, meridional reinforcement and ring beam reinforcement. The dynamic response of shell under the blast loading using the finite element program conclude that the dome structure under blast loading are sensitive to the TNT equivalent weights of explosive and the rise-span ratio of the reticulated shell.Lam and Mendis[2] have worked on the parametric study involving time-history analysis of cantilevered wall models. They have analysed to the structure based on pre-defined pressure function to study basic trends.This study is the identification of the direct relationship between the corner period and the clearing time for the blast. The model has been designed and assessment of cantilevered walls for its performance under blast load is carried out. Also, numerical solution of conversion of pressure into acceleration is given.

II. Modeling and Analysis

(A) Analysis of dome by pulse time history

<u>Dome structure data</u>

Diameter (D) = 13.7 m
Height (H) = 6.85 m
Radius (R)= 6.85 m
Thickness (t) = 0.15 m
Dome type = Spherical

<u>Material property</u>

Weight per unit volume (Concrete) = 25 kN/m^3

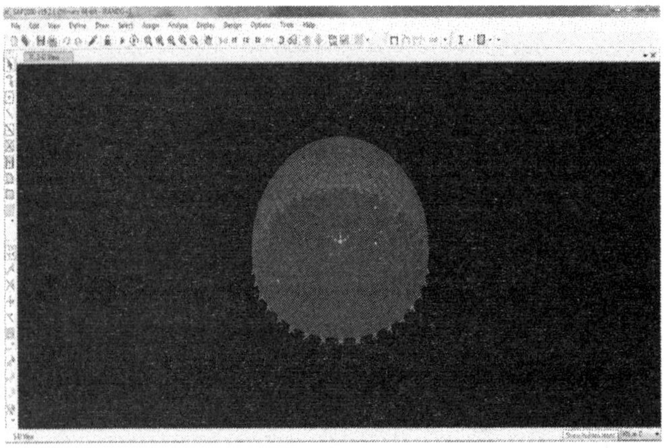

Figure 2 3D model in sap 2000 version19

(B) Steps to be followed to check the effect of different pulse ondome structure

1. Calculate the blast pressure as per IS 4991- 1968.
2. Convert pulse (Time vs. Pressure) in form of pulse time history (Time vs. Acceleration).
3. Apply that pulse time history on the dome structure.
4. Analysis of dome by different pulse time history.

<u>(1) Calculation of blast pressure</u>

- Calculation of blast pressure as per IS: 4991 – 1968

Blast parameters due to the detonation of 0.1tonne explosive are evaluated on a above structure, situated at 30 m from ground zero.

- As per IS 4991-1968

Blast Pressure = 33 kN/m^2

<u>(2) Blast pressure in form of acceleration</u>

Structure Data

Blast load = 33 kN/m^2
Area = 295 m^2
Total mass = 110 Tonne
Total blast load = 33 x 295 = 9735 kN

Acceleration = (total blast load / total mass)

= (9735 / 110)

= 88.5 m / sec^2

<u>(3) Idealized pulse of blast loading</u>

1. Rectangular Pulse
2. First-Half Triangular Pulse
3. Half Cycle Cosine Pulse
4. Full Cycle Cosine Pulse
5. Half + and Half – Triangular Pulse
6. Half Lower Arrow Pulse
7. Half Upper Arrow Pulse
8. Triangular and Inverse Triangular Pulse
9. Pulse no.10

Shape of pulses are as follows:

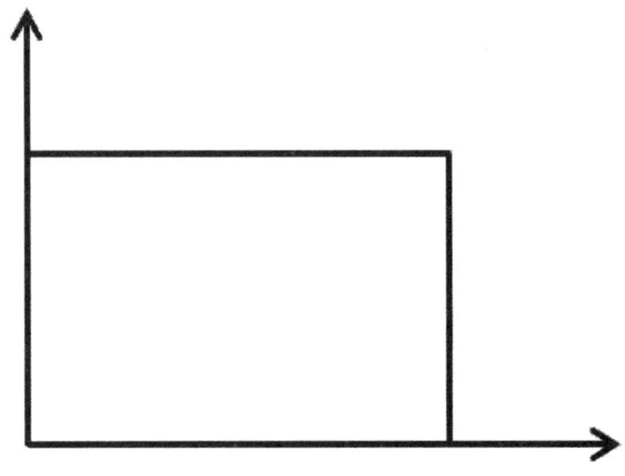

Figure 3 Rectangular pulse

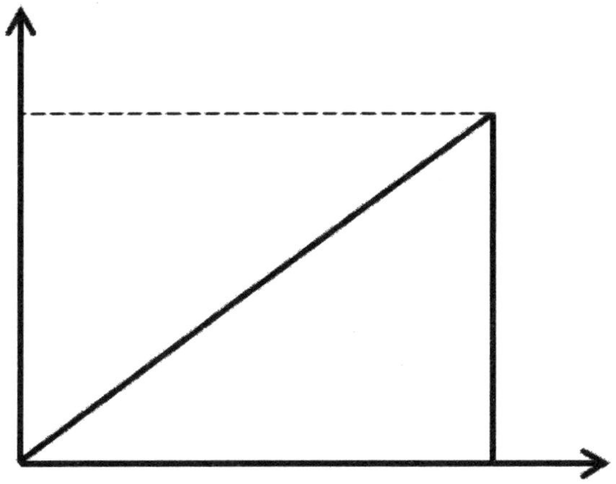

Figure 4 First-half triangular pulse

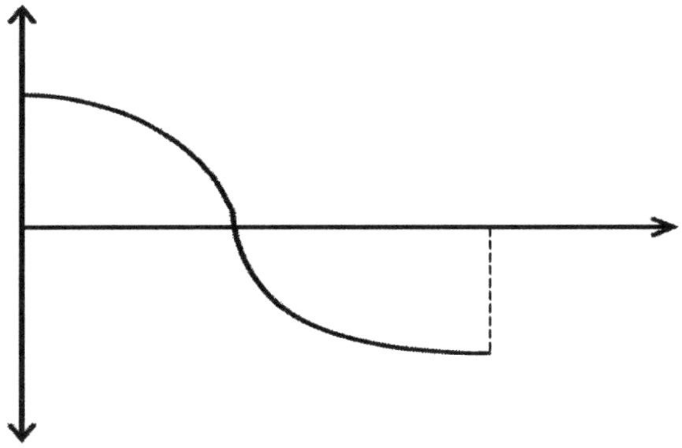

Figure 5 Half cycle cosine pulse

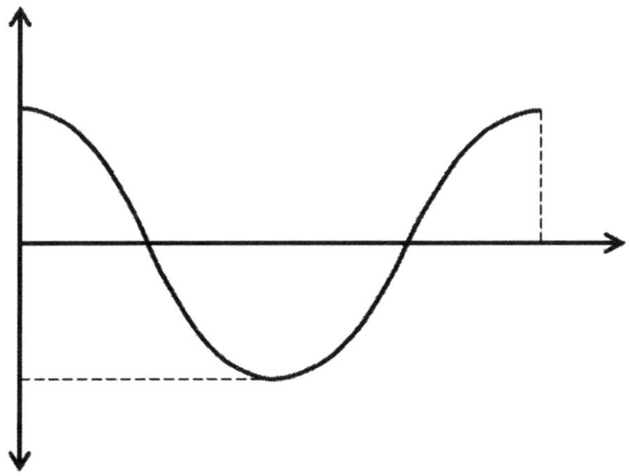

Figure 6 Full cycle cosine pulse

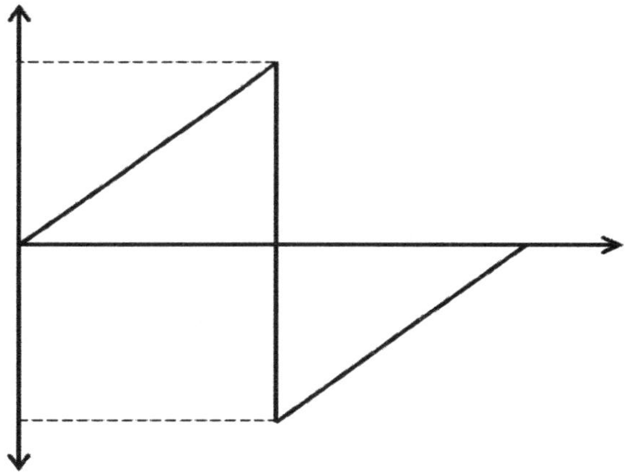

Figure 7 Half + and half – triangular pulse

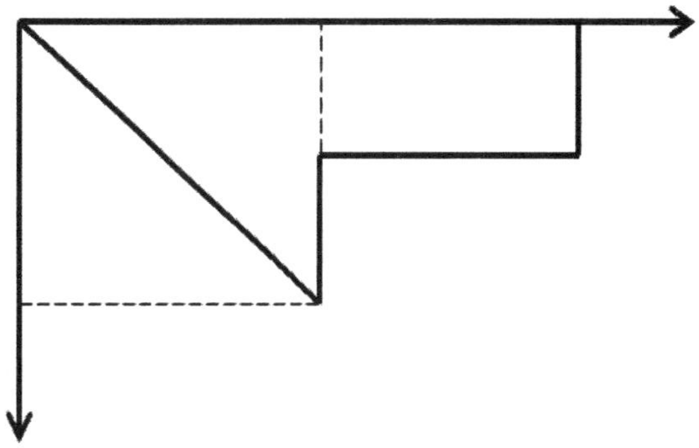

Figure 8 Half-lower arrow pulse

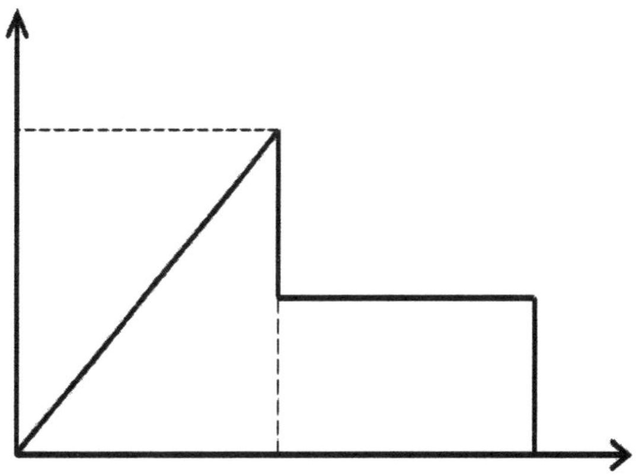

Figure 9 Half - upper arrow pulse

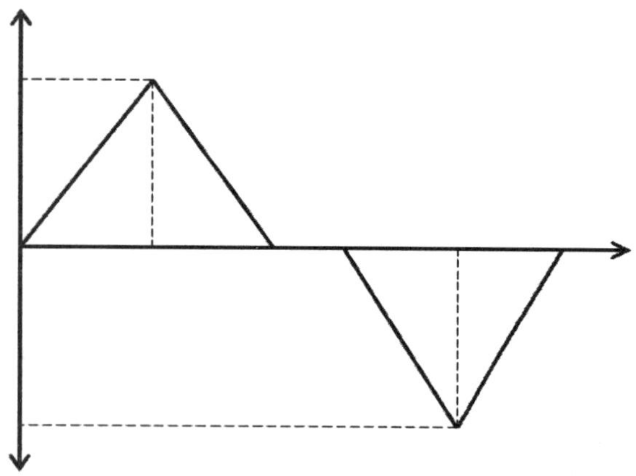

Figure 10 Triangular and inverse triangular pulse

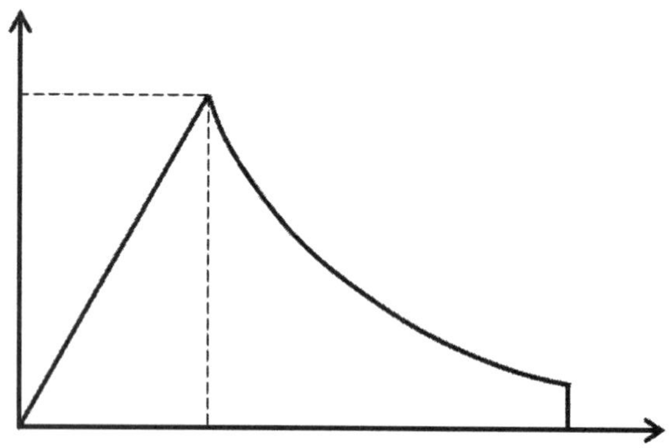

Figure 11 Pulse no.10

-Procedure to develop different blast pulse in form of time vs. acceleration.

To develop pulse, program has been made using C sharp. This is made in two phases. In first phase from Fig. 12 using parameters such as Force, Pulse Duration, Time Step Then Pulse time history data are generated in form of pressure.

Develop rectangular pulse

- Force (Blast pressure) = 9735 kN
- Initial pulse duration = 0 second
- Final pulse duration = 2 second
- Time step = 0.005 second
- Pulse type = Rectangular Pulse

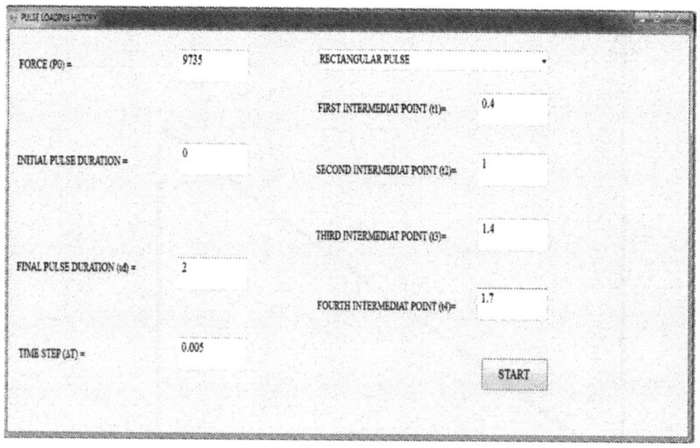

Figure 12 Input parameter to develop pulse

In second phase of this program, from fig. 13 using parameter such as Mass (m) then pulse loading history is generated in form of time vs. acceleration.

- Mass = 110 Tonne

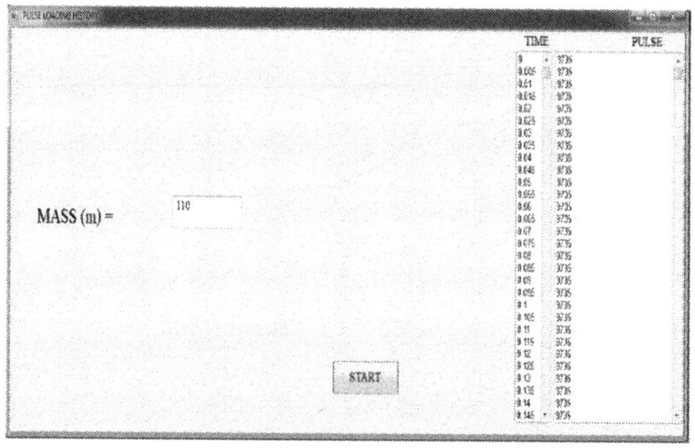

Figure 13 Input mass of dome to developed pulse

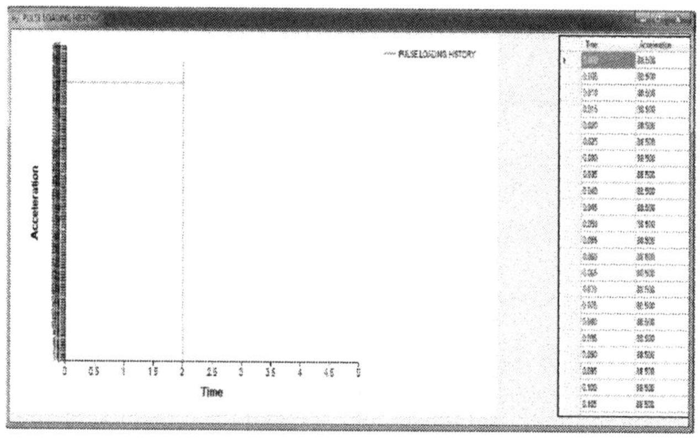

Figure 14 Rectangular pulse loading history

-This is the rectangular pulse of blast loading in form of time vs. acceleration. Some other different pulse develops in program using C sharp are following.

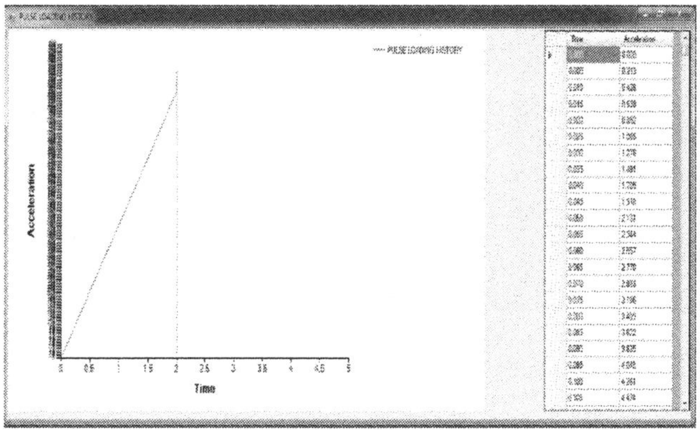

Figure 15 First-half triangular pulse loading history

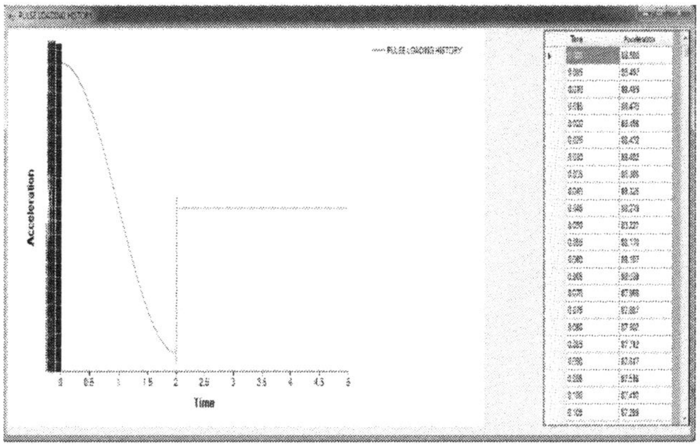

Figure 16 Half cycle cosine pulse loading history

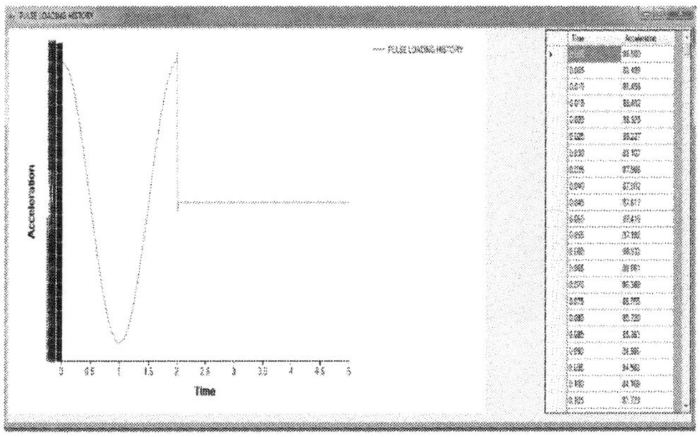

Figure 17 Full cycle cosine pulse loading history

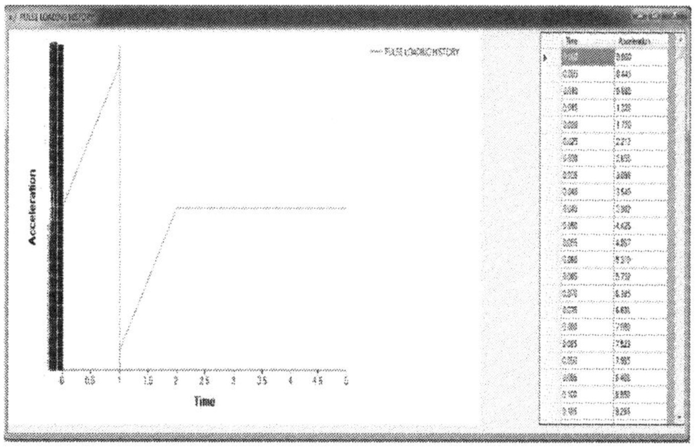

Figure 18 Half + and half – triangular pulse loading history

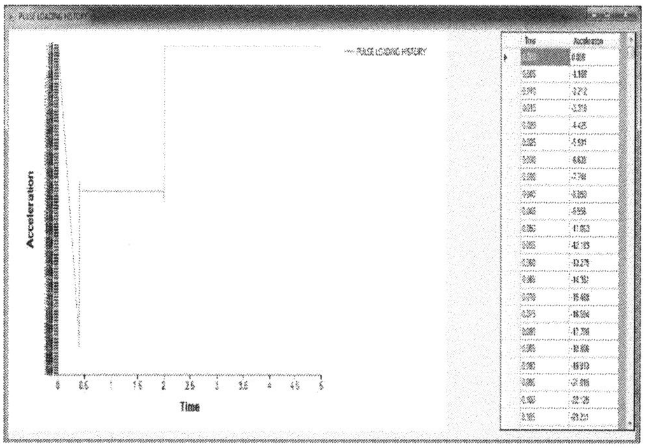

Figure 19 Half lower arrow pulse loading history

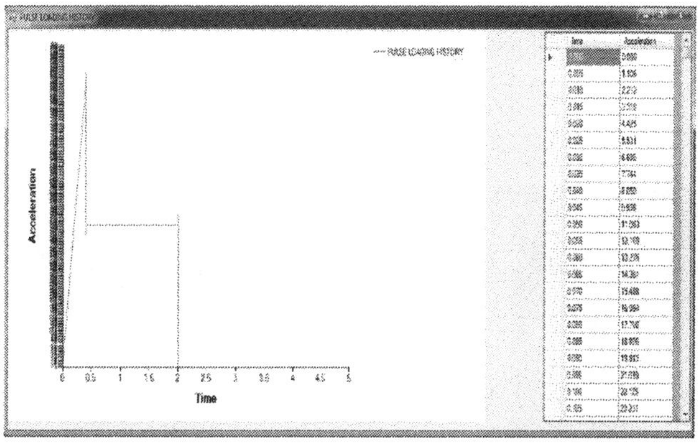

Figure 20 Half upper arrow pulse loading history

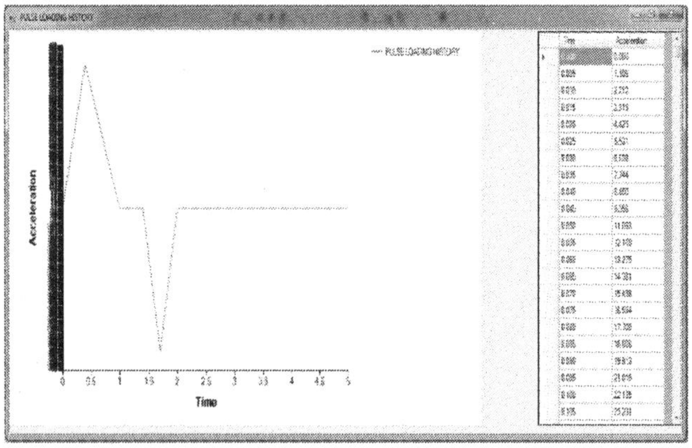

Figure 21 Triangular and inverse triangular pulse loading history

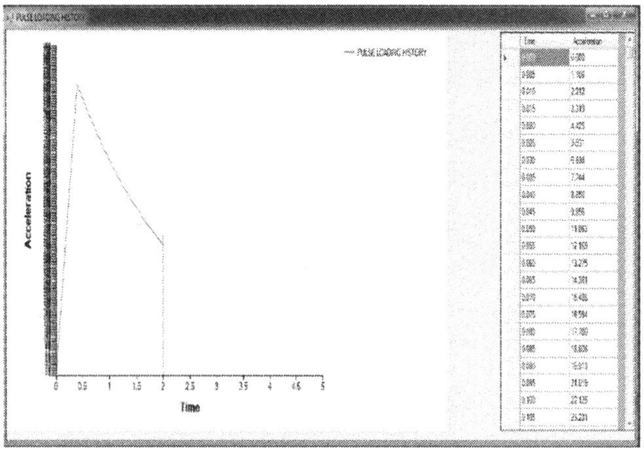

Figure 22 Pulse no.10 loading history

These are the pulse of blast loading in form of time vs. acceleration (Time history).

-Apply that pulse time history on the dome structure in SAP 2000.

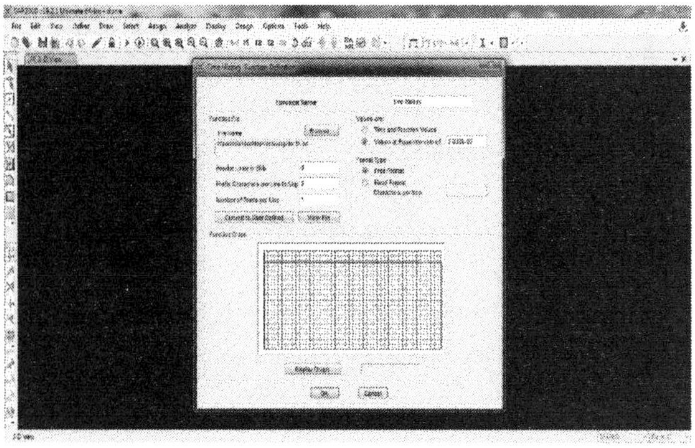

Figure 23 Rectangular pulse time history

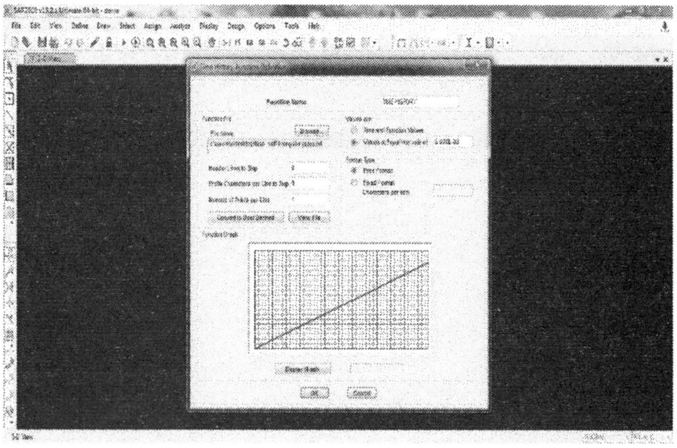

Figure 24 First-half triangular pulse time history

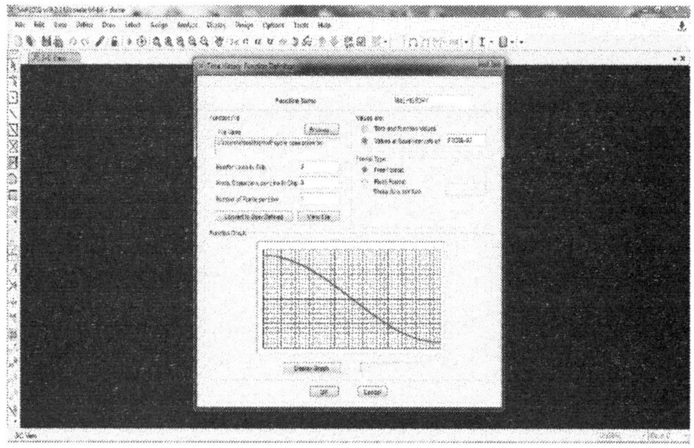

Figure 25 Half cycle cosine pulse time history

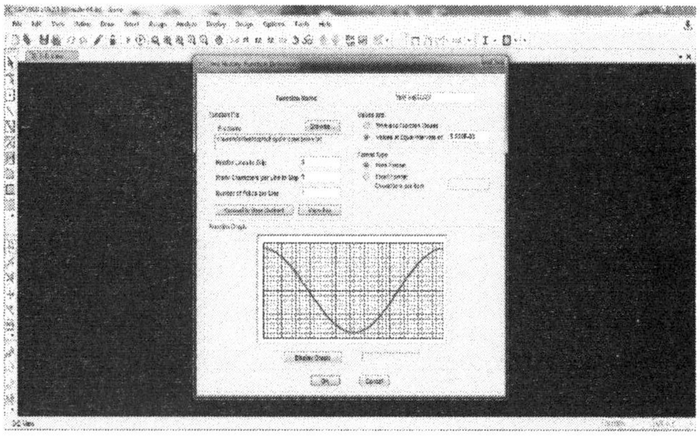

Figure 26 Full cycle cosine pulse time history

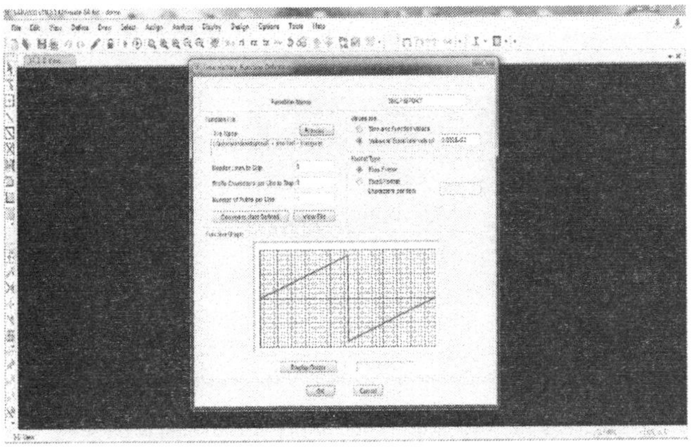

Figure 27 Half + and half – triangular pulse time history

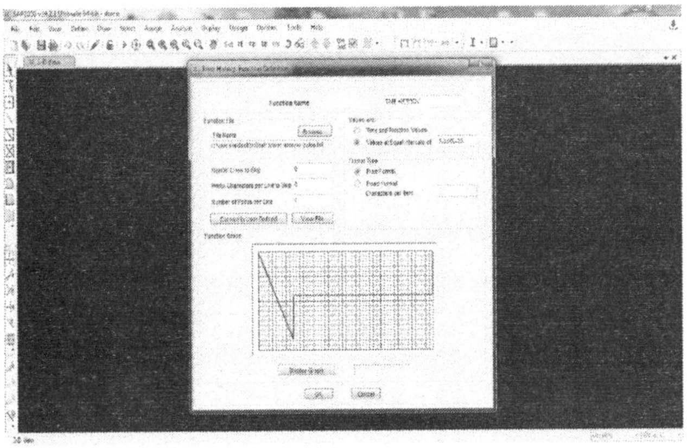

Figure 28 Half lower arrow pulse time history

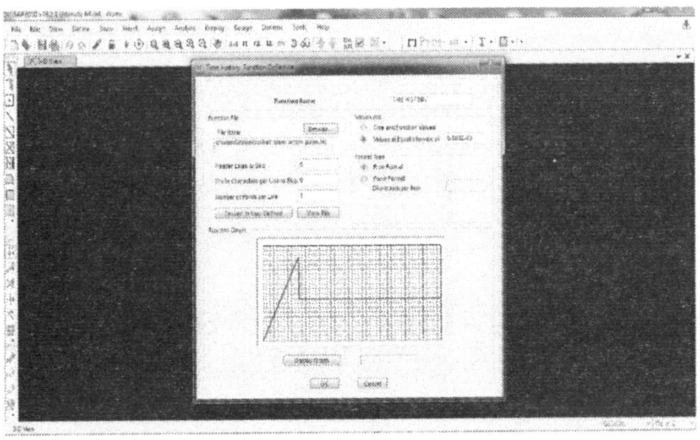

Figure 29 Half upper arrow pulse time history

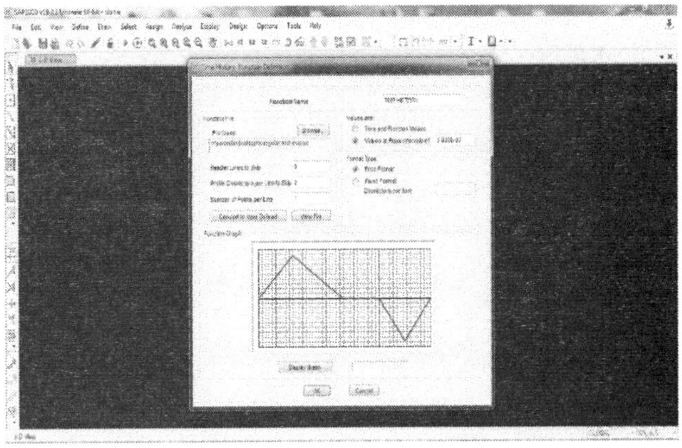

Figure 30 Triangular and inverse triangular pulse time history

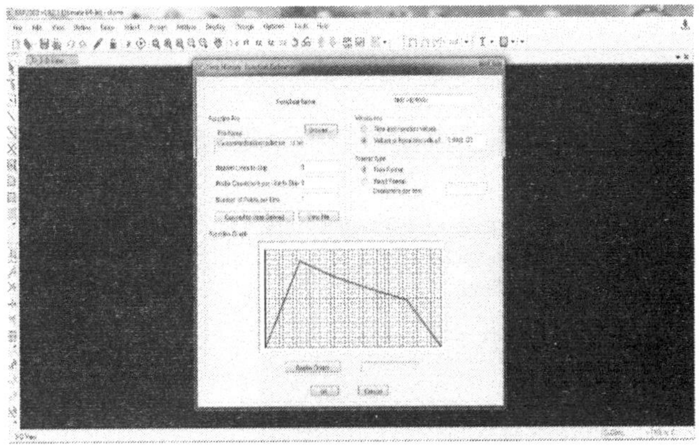

Figure 31 Pulse no.10-time history

III. Analytical Results

These different pulse time histories are applied on the dome structure. After the analyzing following are the results generated in form of maximum acceleration and stresses.

(A) Maximum acceleration of domestructure under the different pulse time history are following:

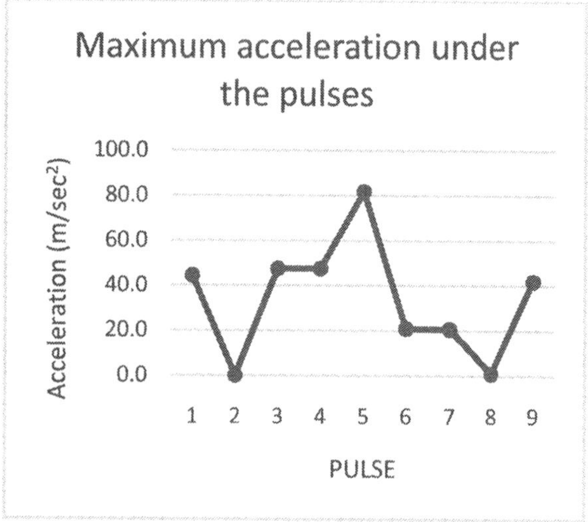

Figure 32 Maximum acceleration graph

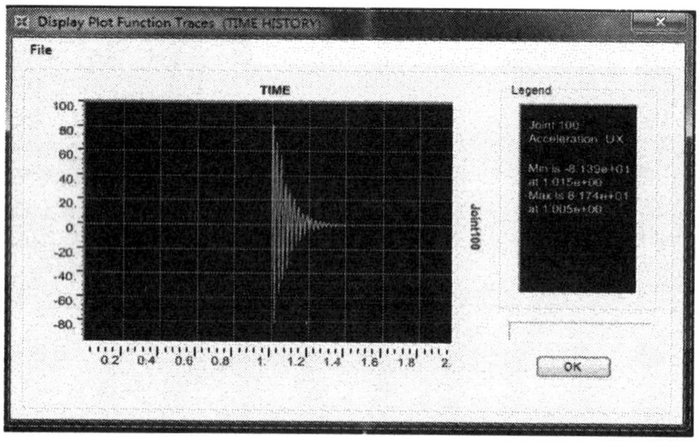

Figure 33 Maximum acceleration of half + and half – triangular pulse

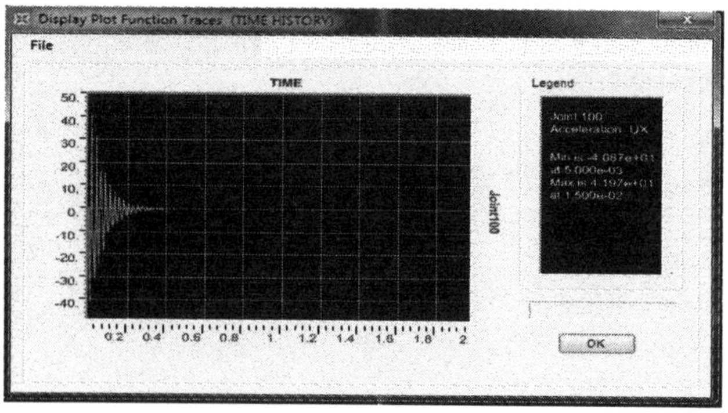

Figure 34 Average acceleration of pulse no.10

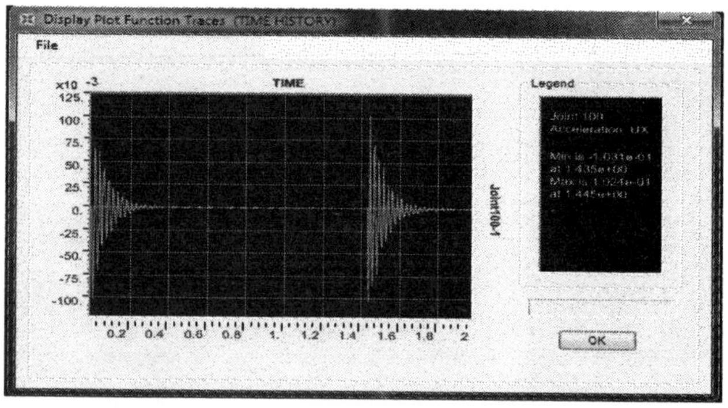

Figure 35 Lowest acceleration of first-half triangular pulse

(B) Maximum compression stresses (Hoop stresses or circumferential stresses)of Dome Structure Under the effect of Different Pulse Time History are following:

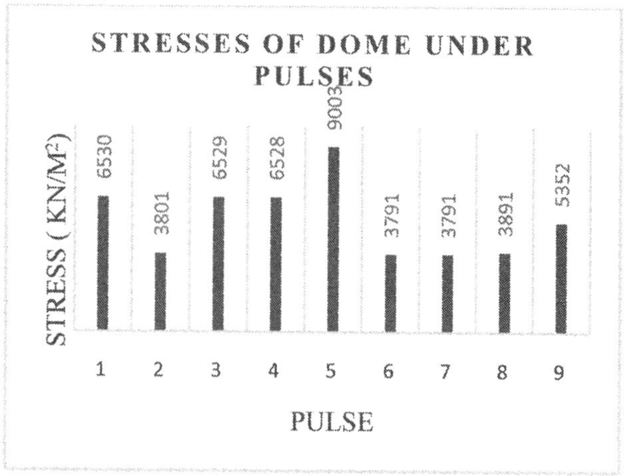

Figure 36 Maximum circumferential stressesgraph

(C) Maximum meridional compression of dome structure under the effect of different Pulse time history are following:

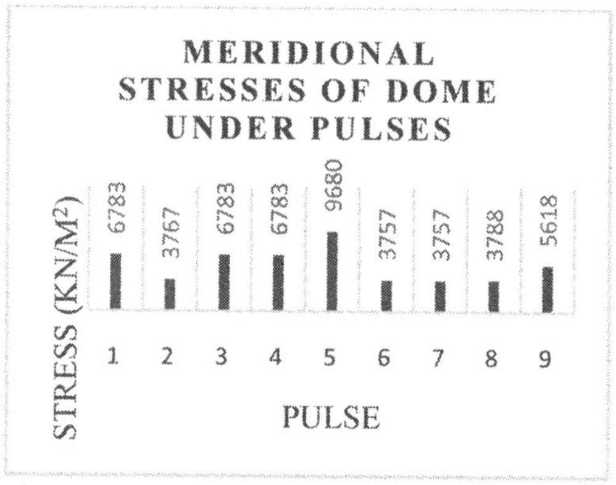

Figure 37 Maximum Meridional Stresses graph

IV. Conclusion

Different nine shapes of pulse loading have been analyzed for blast load of 0.1 tonne explosion on dome structure. The following conclusions have been derived after the analysis.

1. The results of lower arrow pulse and upper arrow pulse are found to be similar as the pulse shapes are similar by considering horizontal axis as a plane of symmetry. Also, for half cycle cosine pulse and full cycle cosine pulsethe results are similar as the pattern of pulse shape is same.
2. After the analysis of dome structure under different nine pulse history, the maximum acceleration developed is 81.7 m/sec^2 due to half + and half – triangular Pulse for 0.1 tonne explosive at the distance of 30 m.
3. The maximum compression stress (Hoop stress or circumferential stress) developed is 9.00 MPa due to and half + and half - triangular Pulse for 0.1 tonne explosive on dome structure at the distance of 30 m and it exceeds the permissible limit of 8.5 MPa as per IS 456:2000. Stresses for other eight pulses are within the permissible limit as per IS 456: 2000, table 21.
4. After the analysis, the maximum meridional compression stress developed is 9.6 MPa due to half + and half - triangular Pulse for 0.1 tonne explosive weight and it exceeds the permissible limit. Stresses for remaining pulse are in permissible limit as per IS 456: 2000, table 21.
5. Half + and half – triangular pulse is the most critical shape for loading in which the stresses and acceleration are maximum.

References

[1] Nelson Lam and priyan Mendis(2004), 'Response spectrum solution for blast loading' Electronic Journal of Structural Engineering, volume 4, pp.28-44.

[2] J.A.Abdalla and A.S.Mohammed(2008),'Dynamic characteristics of large reinforced concrete domes' The 14th World Conference on Earthquake Engineering, Beijing, China.

[3] Galawezh Saber and Ghaedan Hussein (2013), 'Analysis and optimum design of curved roof structures' 2nd International Balkans Conference on Challenges of Civil Engineering, BCCCE, pp.23-25.

[4] Euripidis Mistakidis (2014), 'Construction of the steel dome of the multipurpose al-sadd sports hall in Doha, Qatar'AKTOR S.A.P.O. Box 37108, Doha, Qatar.

[5] Ms. M.A.Jain(2016),'Parametric Study of Dome' International Journal for Scientific Research & Development, vol. 4, pp. 1669-1671 Panchal, V. R. and Jangid, R. S. (2007), 'Variable friction pendulum system for seismic isolation of liquid storage tanks', Nuclear Engineering and Design, Vol. 238, pp. 1304-1315.

[6] Manav Patel and Dr. V. R. Panchal(2017), 'Development of shock spectra for different pulse shapes using C sharp' International Conference on Research and Innovations in Science, Engineering & Technology, pp. 418-423.

[7] Anuj Chandiwala (2014), 'Analysis and Design of Steel Dome Using Software' International Journal of Research in Engineering and Technology, Eissn: 2319-1163, pissn:2321-7308, pp.35-39.

[8] Anil Kumar (2014), 'Effect of damping on shock spectra of impulse loads' International Journal of Scientific & Engineering Research, Volume 5, Issue 5, ISSN 2229-5518, pp.78-85.

A Seismic Design of Building-Equipment System using Conical Friction Pendulum Isolator

Meet M. Joshi[1], V. R. Panchal[2], D. P. Soni[3]

[1] *Post Graduate Student (Structural Engineering), M. S. Patel Department of Civil Engineering, Chandubhai S. Patel Institute of Technology, Charotar University of Science and Technology, Changa, Gujarat, India*

[2] *Professor and Head, M. S. Patel Department of Civil Engineering, Chandubhai S. Patel Institute of Technology, Charotar University of Science and Technology, Changa, Gujarat, India*

[3] *Professor and Head of Civil Engineering Department, SardarVallabhbhai Patel Institute of Technology, Vasad, Gujarat, India*

[1]meetj2608@gmail.com
[2]vijaypanchal.cv@charusat.ac.in
[3]devesh18@gmail.com

***Abstract*— In this study, building-equipment system is analyzed to determine its response under six different near-fault ground excitations. Governing equation of motion for building-equipment system is solved using Newmark's linear acceleration method. Seismic response of building-equipment system isolated with Conical Friction Pendulum Isolator (CFPI) is compared with the seismic response of building-equipment system isolated with Variable Frequency Pendulum Isolator (VFPI) in order to find the effectiveness of CFPI. The equipment displacement and equipment acceleration are developed and discussed in the study. It is observed that VFPI is found quite effective in base isolation of building-equipment system as compared to CFPI.**

***Keywords*—Base isolation; Building-equipment system; CFPI; Near-fault ground excitations;.**

I. Introduction

Base isolation technique has been proven to be an effective method to resist the structure from devastating effect of earthquake ground motions. In base isolation system, foundation of the structure is kept isolated from structure using flexible layer (or isolator) which results in detachment of super structure from the earth surface. Thus it protects the structure from damaging effects of earthquake excitations. Due to the flexibility of isolator, time period of the isolator becomes longer than the time period of structure. Time period of isolator governs the fundamental time period of isolated structure. Time period of the isolator is relatively long compared to those containing significant earthquake ground motions. Hence, isolator helps in avoiding resonance condition in the structure. From various literatures, it is proved that base isolation technique is efficient to minimize devastating effects of the earthquake on the structures. Sliding base isolators incorporates isolation and energy dissipation in single unit. Such isolation system effectively controls the vibration of structures occurring from ground excitation and it behaves independently from amplitude and frequency of ground excitations. In recent times, development of base isolation is focused on the use of frictional type of base isolation systems as it is very effective for large range of frequency input. There are various types of friction isolation systems like Pure Friction (PF), Friction Pendulum System (FPS), Triple Friction Pendulum System (TFPS), Variable Frequency Pendulum Isolator (VFPI) and Conical Friction Pendulum Isolator (CFPI).

Mrunal and Sinha [1] conducted study on multi-storey building with equipment isolated with FPS, PF and VFPI. In this study, they proved that VFPI is effective as compared to the FPS and PF. Lu et al. [2] studied sliding bearings with variable curvatures for near-fault ground motions. From the study results shows that VFPI and CFPI have better isolation effectiveness than FPS. Ismail et al. [3] studied performance of structure-equipment system isolated using roll-n-cage (RNC) isolation bearing system. The results depict that RNC isolator is effective in controlling the structure-equipment system behavior under wide variety of earthquakes.

In this study, CFPI-isolated multi-storey building with equal mass at each floor and top light equipment with 1% of floor mass is considered. Different near fault ground motions are used to determine the equipment acceleration, equipment displacement and recoverable energy of CFPI-isolated building. Comparison of VFPI and CFPI has been made. Newmark's linear acceleration method is used to solve the equation of motion.

II. Concept of CFPI

Among various types of isolators, FPS is a sliding type of isolator. It has simple geometry and is better in re-centering mechanism as well as for dissipation of energy. But, in FPS there is spherical sliding surface which generates constant isolation frequency and that frequency may cause resonance problem under strong long-period earthquakes. To overcome this problem, fully passive adaptive system introduced such as CFPI.

Due to variable curvature, CFPI has adaptive isolation stiffness which is continuously changing with respect to isolator displacement. In sliding isolator with variable curvature, the designer gets freedom of designing by varying restoring force and stiffness of isolator. Sliding surface of CFPI is similar to FPS up to d_b after that it starts becoming tangent to the spherical surface. The parameter d_b and R are important for defining the geometry of CFPI isolator. In the CFPI, following equations are used to define the geometry of the sliding surface Shaikhzadeh and Karamoddin [4].

$$d_b = 0.1\,R \tag{1}$$

$$y(x) = \begin{cases} R - \sqrt{R^2 - x^2} & ; \ |x| \le d_b \\ c_1 + c_2(|x| - d_b) ; & d_b < |x| \end{cases} \tag{2}$$

where,

$$c_1 = R - \sqrt{R^2 - d_b^2} \tag{3}$$

$$c_2 = \frac{d_b}{\sqrt{R^2 - d_b^2}} \tag{4}$$

In the above equations, R represents curvature radius at the center of the sliding curve and horizontal displacement of the isolator is denoted as x. The frequency of the isolator can be calculated by approximate formula as:

$$\omega_b = \sqrt{g\ddot{y}(x)} \tag{5}$$

After substituting $y(x)$ from Equation (2) in Equation (5) and taking second order derivative, it is concluded that $\omega_b(x) = 0$ for $x > d_b$. This shows that, when the isolation displacement exceeds d_b, isolation system possess no predominant frequency. When the isolator displacement exceeds d_b, the restoring force becomes constant and isolator frequency becomes zero after d_b. Figure 1 shows geometry of CFPI.

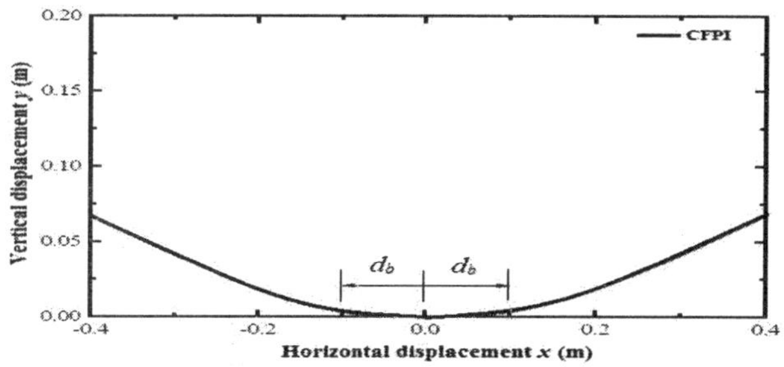

Figure 1 Geometry of CFPI [5]

III. Governing Equation Of Motion

The governing equation of motion for building-equipment system is considered as follows

$$[M]\{\ddot{x}\} + [C]\{\dot{x}\} + [K]\{x\} = -[M]\{r\}\{\ddot{x}_b + \ddot{x}_g\} \tag{6}$$

where, $[M]$ denote mass, $[C]$ depicts damping and $[K]$ is stiffness matrices, having size of $N \times N$; $\{r\} = \{1,1,\ldots,1\}^T$ is influence coefficient vector; $\ddot{x}_g$ is the ground acceleration; $\ddot{x}_b$ denote acceleration of base mass with respect to the ground.

$$F_b = k_b\, x_b + F_x \tag{7}$$

where, F_b is restoring force, F_x is frictional force, k_b is isolator stiffness and x_b is isolator displacement.

The CFPI can be subjected (before sliding) to the limiting frictional force *(Q)*, which is given by,

$$Q = \mu W \tag{8}$$

where, μ is the coefficient of friction of CFPI. W is the weight of the building.

k_b of CFPI is designed in such a way that certain value of isolation period T_b is obtained; which is given by

$$T_b = 2\pi\sqrt{\frac{M}{k_b}} \tag{9}$$

The maximum time interval for equation solution is taken as 0.02/500 sec i.e., $\Delta t = 0.00004$ sec.

IV. Numerical Study

In this study, CFPI-isolated single-storey building and five-storey building with equal mass is considered. Also, light equipment with 1% of floor mass is considered at top. Figures 1& 2 show the single storey-building and five-storey building with equipment isolated using CFPI. Tables I & II show the building properties and different earthquake ground motions, respectively. Building-equipment system response quantities under consideration are the acceleration of equipment, equipment displacement and recoverable energy.

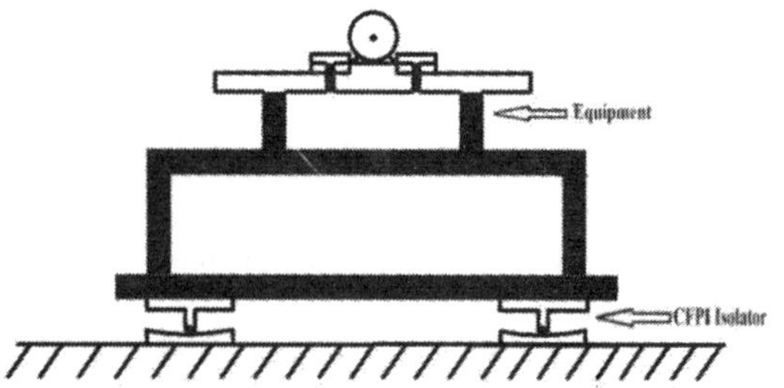

Figure 2 Single storey building with equipment isolated using CFPI

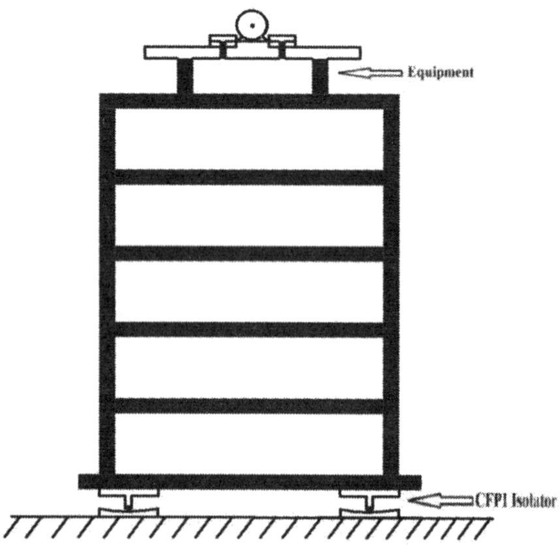

Figure 3 Five storey building with equipment isolated using CFP

TABLE I
BUILDING AND EQUIPMENT PROPERTIES

Lumped mass for each floor	60080 kg
Storey stiffness for each floor	11260 kN/m
Equipment mass	1% of floor mass
Damping ratio of building	5%
Damping ratio of equipment	5%
Fundamental time period of building	0.5 sec
Ratio of mass to base mass	1.0
Equipment frequency	3.85 Hz

TABLE II
ISOLATER PROPERTIES

Coefficient of friction	0.02
Base isolation time period	2.0 sec

TABLE III
CHARACTERISTICS OF EARTHQUAKES IN THE STUDY

Near Fault Ground excitations	Normal component		
	PGD (cm)	PGV (cm/s)	PGA (g)
Imperial Valley, 1979 (El Centro #5) (EQ 11)	76.5	98	0.37
Imperial Valley, 1979 (El Centro #7) (EQ 21)	49.1	113	0.46
Northridge, 1994 (Newhall) (EQ 31)	38.1	119	0.72
Landers, 1992 (Lucerne Valley) (EQ 41)	230	136	0.71
Northridge, 1994 (Rinaldi) (EQ 51)	39.1	175	0.89
Northridge, 1994 (Sylmar) (EQ 61)	31.1	122	0.73

V. RESULTS AND DISCUSSION

Figures 4-9 show the time variation of equipment acceleration, equipment displacement and recoverable energy of building-equipment system of single storey building isolated using VFPI and CFPI whereas Figures 10-15 show the time variation of equipment acceleration, equipment displacement and recoverable energy of building-equipment system of five storey isolated building using VFPI and CFPI. Table IV shows the peak response value of building-equipment system isolated using the VFPI and CFPI.

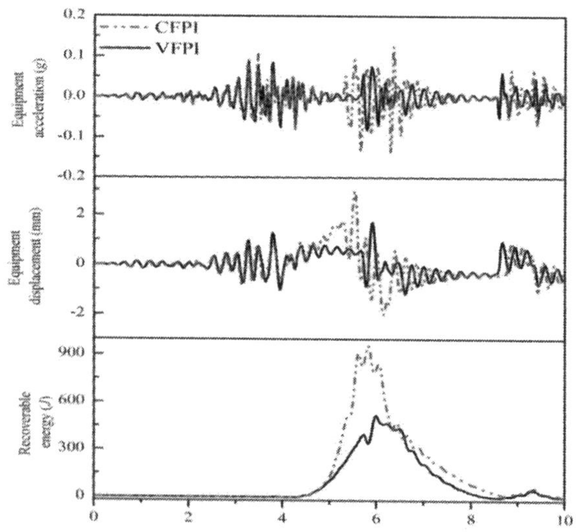

Imperial Valley, 1979 (EI-Centro Array #5)

Figure 4 Time vs. equipment acceleration, equipment displacement and recoverable energy of single storey building-equipment system isolated with CFPI (T_b =2.0 Sec, μ= 0.02) and VFPI (T_I =2.0 Sec, μ= 0.02, d= 0.1m)

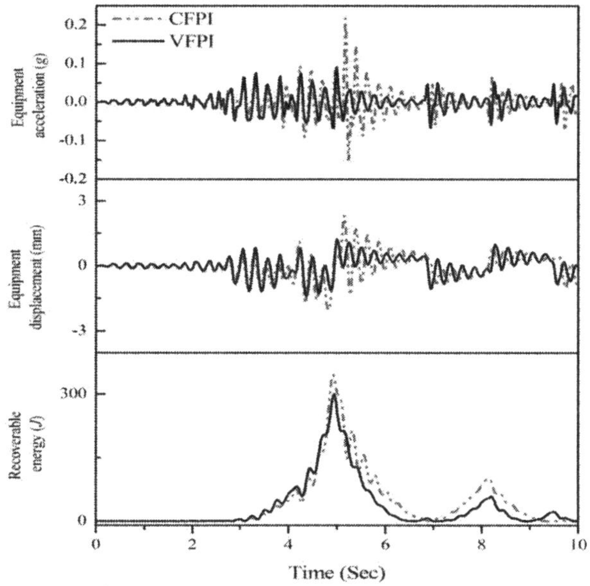

Imperial Valley, 1979 (EI-Centro Array #7)

Figure 5 Time vs. equipment acceleration, equipment displacement and recoverable energy of single storey building-equipment system isolated with CFPI (T_b =2.0 Sec, μ= 0.02) and VFPI (T_I =2.0 Sec, μ= 0.02, d= 0.1m)

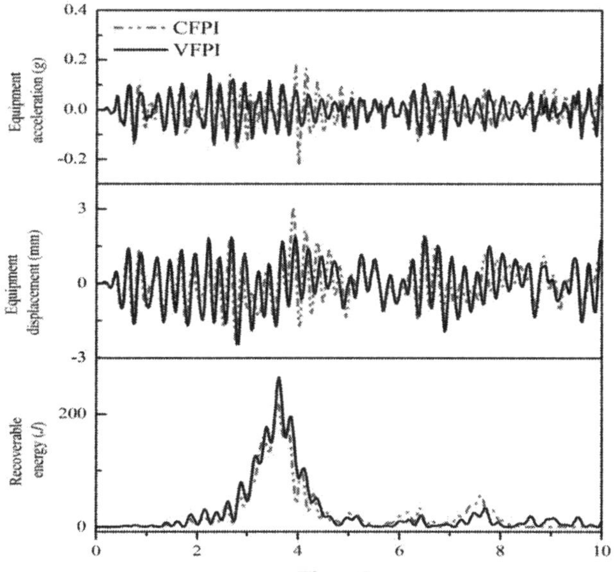

Northridge, 1994 (Newhall)

Figure 6 Time vs. equipment acceleration, equipment displacement and recoverable energy of single storey building-equipment system isolated with CFPI (T_b =2.0 Sec, μ= 0.02) and VFPI (T_I =2.0 Sec, μ= 0.02, d= 0.1m)

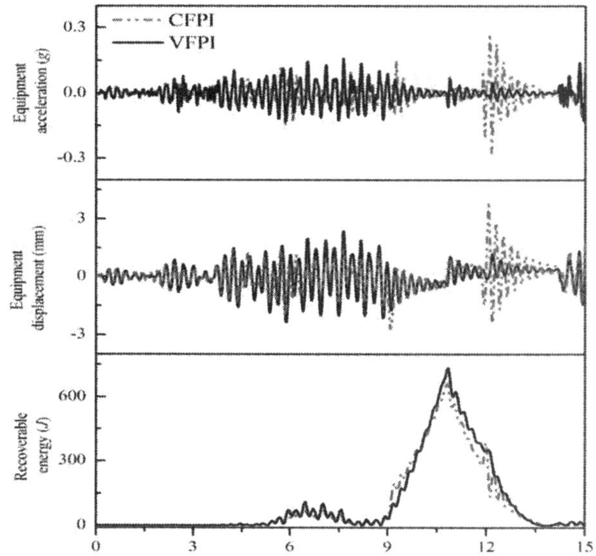

Landers, 1992 (Lucerne Valley)

Figure 7 Time vs. equipment acceleration, equipment displacement and recoverable energy of single storey building-equipment system isolated with CFPI (T_b =2.0 Sec, μ= 0.02) and VFPI (T_I =2.0 Sec, μ= 0.02, d= 0.1m)

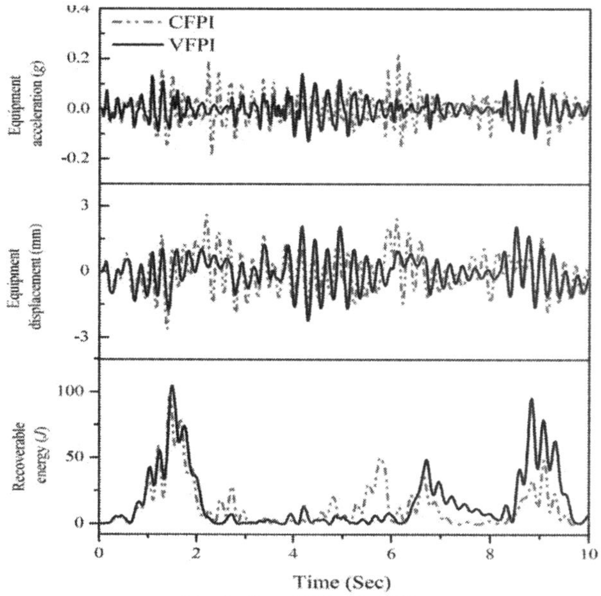

Northridge, 1994 (Rinaldi)

Figure 8 Time vs. equipment acceleration, equipment displacement and recoverable energy of single storey building-equipment system isolated with CFPI (T_b =2.0 Sec, μ= 0.02) and VFPI (T_I =2.0 Sec, μ= 0.02, d= 0.1m)

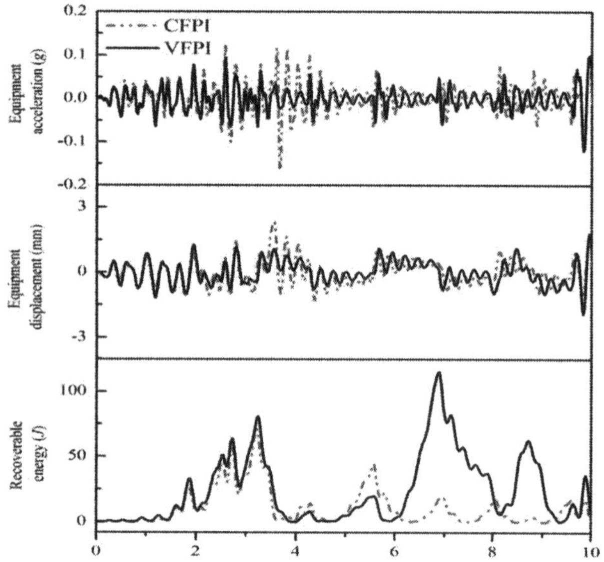

Northridge, 1994 (Sylmar)

Figure 9 Time vs. equipment acceleration, equipment displacement and recoverable energy of single storey building-equipment system isolated with CFPI (T_b =2.0 Sec, μ= 0.02) and VFPI (T_l =2.0 Sec, μ= 0.02, d= 0.1m)

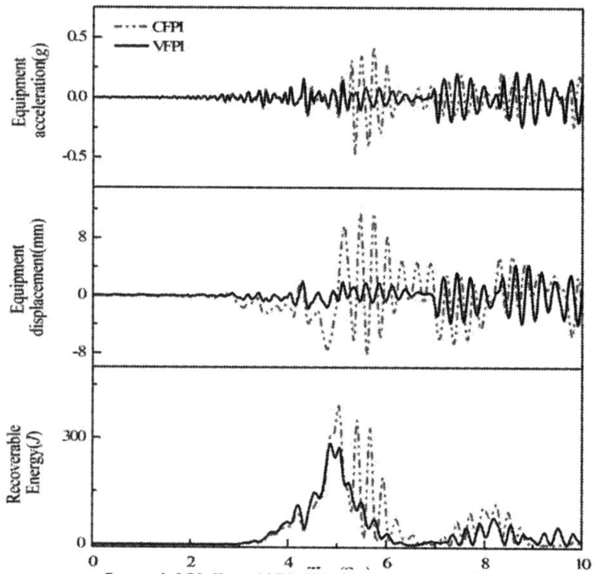

Imperial Valley, 1979 (EI-Centro Array #7)

Figure 11 Time vs. equipment acceleration, equipment displacement and recoverable energy of five storeybuilding-equipment system isolated with CFPI (T_b =2.0 Sec, μ= 0.02) and VFPI (T_l =2.0 Sec, μ= 0.02, d= 0.1m)

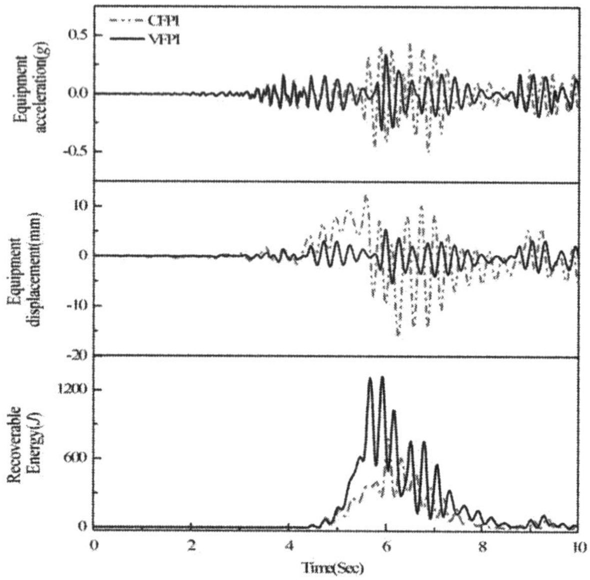

Imperial Valley, 1979 (EI-Centro Array #5)

Figure 10 Time vs. equipment acceleration, equipment displacement and recoverable energy of five storeybuilding-equipment system isolated with CFPI (T_b =2.0 Sec, μ= 0.02) and VFPI (T_l =2.0 Sec, μ= 0.02, d= 0.1m)

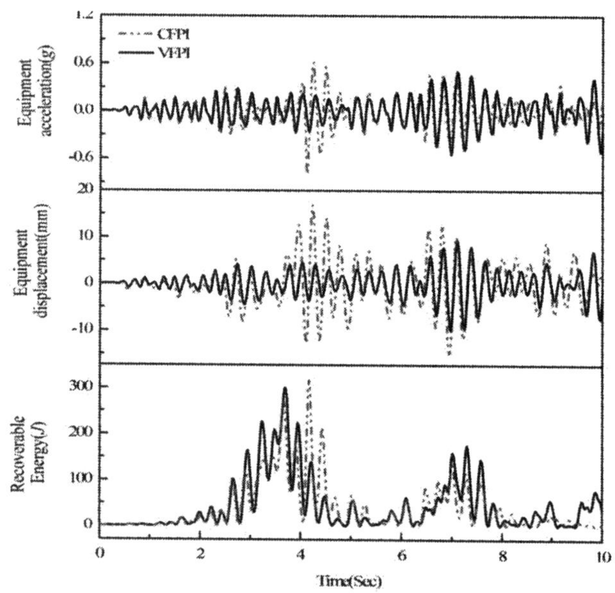

Northridge, 1994 (Newhall)

Figure 12 Time vs. equipment acceleration, equipment displacement and recoverable energy of five storey building-equipment system isolated with CFPI (T_b =2.0 Sec, μ= 0.02) and VFPI (T_l =2.0 Sec, μ= 0.02, d= 0.1m)

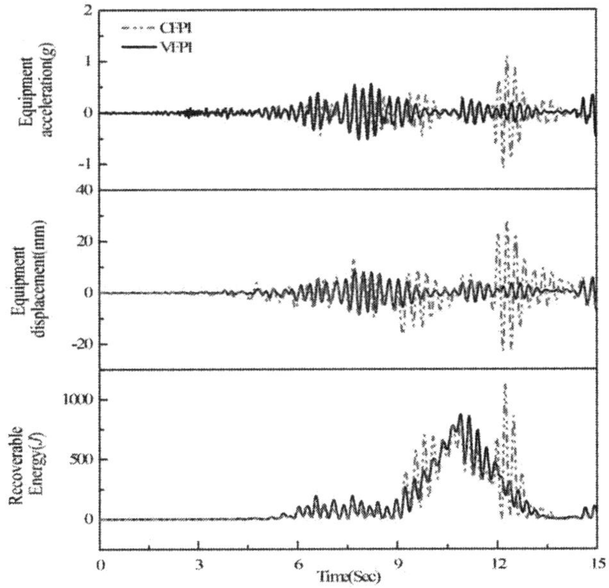

Landers, 1992 (Lucerne Valley)

Figure 13 Time vs. equipment acceleration, equipment displacement and recoverable energy of five storey building-equipment system isolated with CFPI (T_b =2.0 Sec, μ= 0.02) and VFPI (T_l =2.0 Sec, μ= 0.02, d= 0.1m)

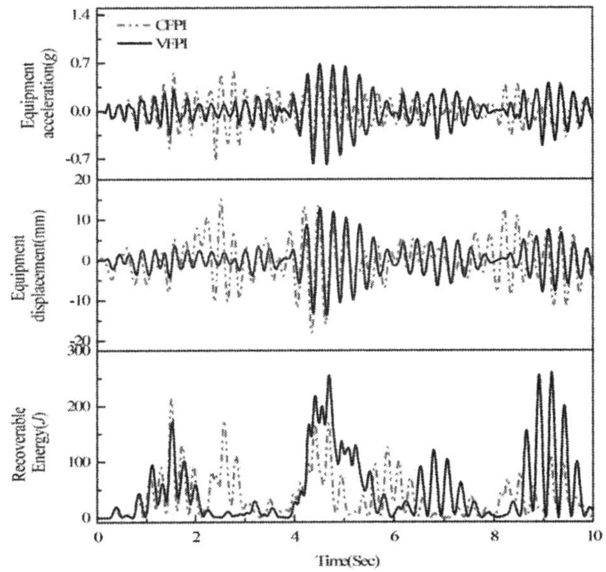

Northridge, 1994 (Rinaldi)

Figure 14 Time vs. equipment acceleration, equipment displacement and recoverable energy of five storey building-equipment system isolated with CFPI (T_b =2.0 Sec, μ= 0.02) and VFPI (T_l =2.0 Sec, μ= 0.02,d = 0.1m)

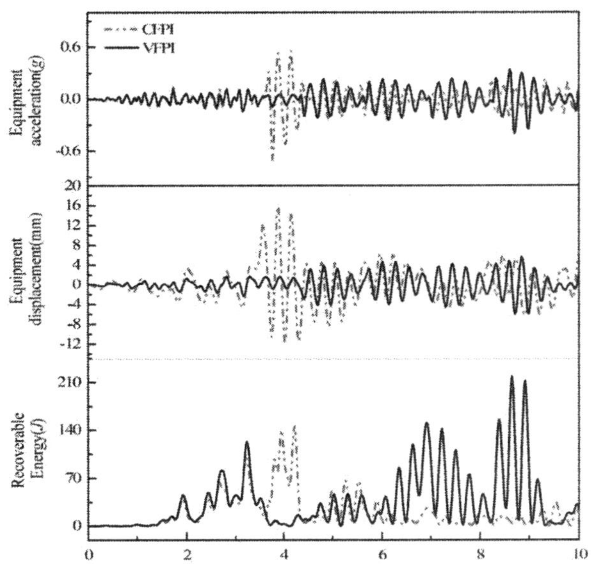

Northridge, 1994 (Sylmar)

Figure 15 Time vs. equipment acceleration, equipment displacement and recoverable energy of five storey building-equipment system isolated with CFPI (T_b =2.0 Sec, μ= 0.02) and VFPI (T_l =2.0 Sec, μ= 0.02, d = 0.1

TABLE IV
PEAK RESPONSE QUANTITIES OF BUILDING-EQUIPMENT SYSTEM ISOLATED BY CFPI AND VFPI

Earthquake ground motion	Recording Station	Isolator	N = 1			N = 5		
			Equipment acceleration (g)	Equipment displacement (mm)	Recoverable energy (J)	Equipment acceleration (g)	Equipment displacement (mm)	Recoverable energy (J)
Imperial Valley, 1979	El Centro Array #5	CFPI	0.136	2.989	957.840	0.495	16.005	1321.510
		VFPI	0.140	2.510	517.920	0.344	5.510	777.090
Imperial Valley, 1979	El Centro Array #7	CFPI	0.218	2.340	346.190	0.487	11.550	393.410
		VFPI	0.193	2.748	301.340	0.285	4.590	285.120
Northridge, 1994	Newhall	CFPI	0.224	3.086	219.640	0.788	16.930	316.920
		VFPI	0.164	2.674	265.180	0.540	9.880	300.190
Landers, 1992	Lucerne Valley	CFPI	0.276	3.877	660.320	1.100	28.040	1119.300
		VFPI	0.166	2.578	734.290	0.550	9.120	872.000
Northridge, 1994	Rinaldi	CFPI	0.221	2.964	98.196	0.727	18.070	213.780
		VFPI	0.140	2.084	104.790	0.779	13.750	260.940
Northridge, 1994	Sylmar	CFPI	0.163	2.33	70.66	0.710	15.890	146.240
		VFPI	0.164	2.73	114.84	0.397	6.038	218.950

VI. CONCLUSIONS

In this study, building-equipment system is analyzed to determine its response under six different near-fault ground excitations. Single-storey building-equipment system and five-storey building-equipment system isolated using CFPI and VFPI are taken in this study. The equipment displacement, equipment acceleration and recoverable energy are developed and discussed in the study.

Conclusions derived from the above study are as follows:

1. In case of VFPI isolated building-equipment system, equipment acceleration and equipment displacement are less than that of CFPI isolated building-equipment system under most of the earthquake ground motions.
2. From the above study, it is evident that equipment acceleration and equipment displacement increases when studied for five storey building-equipment system as compare to that of a single storey building-equipment system isolated using CFPI and VFPI, where there is little increase observed in recoverable energy for five storey building as compared to that of a single storey building.
3. In case of VFPI isolated building-equipment system, recoverable energy is less than that of CFPI isolated building-equipment system under most of the earthquake ground motions.
4. From the above results, it is observed that VFPI is more effective than CFPI.

References

[1] Murnal, P. and Sinha, R. (2004), 'Aseismic design of structure – equipment systems using variable frequency pendulum isolator', Nuclear Engineering and Design, Vol. 231, pp. 129-139.

[2] Lu, L.(2004), 'Near-fault seismic isolation using sliding bearings with variable curvatures', 13th World conference on earthquake engineering, Canada.

[3] Ismail, M., Rodellar, J. and Ikhouane, F. (2009), 'Performance of structure-equipment system with a novel roll-n-cage isolation bearing' Computers and structures, Vol. 87, pp. 1631-1643.

[4] Ali, A.S. and Abbas, K. (2015), 'Parametric study of Conical friction pendulum isolator under near-fault ground motions', 10th International congress on civil engineering, Iran.

[5] Malu, G. and Mrunal, P. (2012), 'Comparative study of sliding isolation system for low frequency ground motion', 15th World Conference on Earthquake Engineering, Portugal.

Study on Plain Surface with Wave Type Configuration Bar Reinforced Concrete Frame Subjected to Lateral Loads

JaymeshV. Soni[1], Vijay R. Panchal[2], Nirpex A. Patel[3]

[1] *Post Graduate Student (Structural Engineering), M. S. Patel Department of Civil Engineering, Chandubhai S. Patel Institute of Technology, Charotar University of Science and Technology, Changa, Gujarat, India*

[2] *Professor and Head, M. S. Patel Department of Civil Engineering, Chandubhai S. Patel Institute of Technology, Charotar University of Science and Technology, Changa, Gujarat, India*

[3] *Assistant Professor, M. S. Patel Department of Civil Engineering, Chandubhai S. Patel Institute of Technology, Charotar University of Science and Technology, Changa, Gujarat, India*

[1]jaimeshsoni13@gmail.com
[2]vijaypanchal.cv@charusat.ac.in
[3]nirpexpatel.cv@charusat.ac.in

***Abstract*— The purpose of this study is to investigate the behaviour of concrete frame reinforced with Plain Surface with Wave Type Configuration (PSWC) bar under application of lateral loads. In this study, Finite Element (FE) 3D model of Reinforced Concrete (RC) frame is developed using ABAQUS for quasi-static solution. Concrete Damage Plasticity (CDP) is developed for M-30 grade concrete used for RC frame. Displacement based loading condition is applied. A finite element analysis is carried out for PSWC-bar with different pitch distances and offsets. In order to find effectiveness of PSWC-bar RC frame, a comparison is made with conventional bar RC frame under lateral loads. It is observed that application of PSWC-bar as a reinforcement improves the performance of RC frame compared to conventional bar.**

***Keywords*—CDP; Conventional bar; FEA;Lateral load;Offset;Pitch;PSWC-bar;RC frame.**

I. Introduction

Reinforcement play an important role in contributing strength to structure. It strengthens the tension zone of the structure. Earlier traditional bars with plain surface were used as reinforcement. Conventional bar had high strength as compared to traditional bar, but it had surface protrusion because of lugs. Recent studies found that reinforced concrete structure withconventional bar as reinforcement has shorter life span as compared to structure reinforced with traditional bar. This led to invention of plain surface with wave type configuration (PSWC) bar. As it was mainly invented to substitute conventional bar as it increased the life span of the structure [1, 2]. Previous study showed thatthe use of PSWC-bar as reinforcement in beam as well as column and beam-column junction as reinforcement increased flexural load-carrying capacity and axial load-carrying capacity and moment resisting capacity of the structure [3-5].

In this study, analysis of Reinforced Concrete (RC) frame with PSWC-bar is conducted to compute the displacement and load carrying capacity of RC frame. For this study, PSWC- bar used with different pitches and offsets. Offset is the distance between central axis of the bar and the highest point of the curvature that is provided to the bar. Pitch distance is entire length of the wave formed in PSWC –bar.The objective of this study is to compare the effectiveness of conventional bar with PSWC-bar (with different pitches and offsets).

II. Validation And Modeling

3D non-linear model of RC frame is developed using ABAQUS for validation work. Figure 1 shows RC frame model reinforced with conventional bar.The size of beam is 300×400 mm with 4nos.20mm at top and bottom and stirrup of 10 @150mm. The size of column is 300×400 mm with 4nos.20 mm and stirrup of 10 mm @125mm. Grade of concrete is M30. Table I & II show the nonlinear material properties of concrete and steel bar. For concrete, the concrete damage plasticity model is developed.

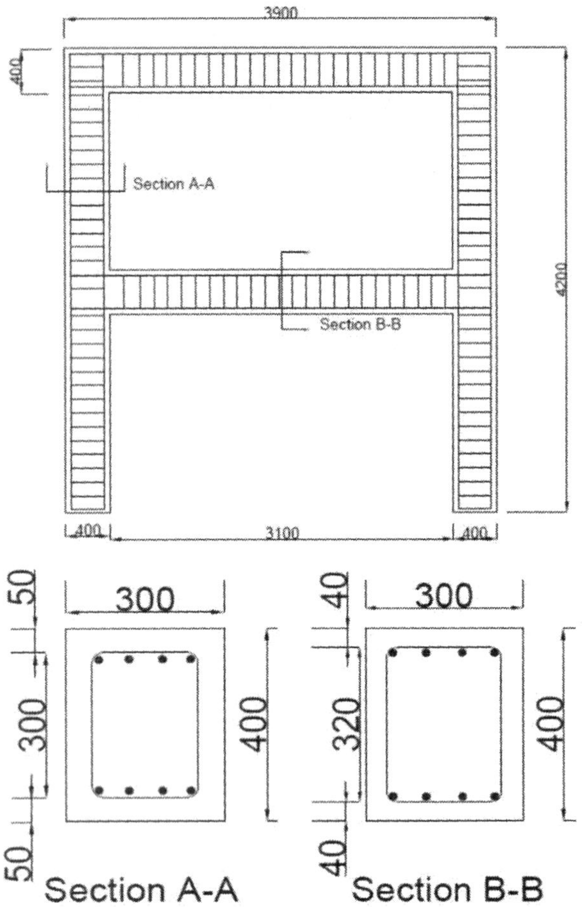

Figure 1. Structural detailing of RC frame utilized for finite simulation

TABLE I
CDP PARAMETERS

k_c	σ_{b0}/σ_{c0}	ϵ	μ	f_{ck}(N/mm^2)
0.7	1.16	0.1	0	30

TABLE II
MATERIAL PROPERTIES OF MAIN BAR AND STIRRUPS

Modulus of elasticity (N/mm^2)	210×10^3
Poisson's ratio	0.3
Density (ton/mm^3)	7.85×10^{-6}
Plasticity parameter (main reinforcement -20 mm ϕ)	
Yield stress (N/mm^2)	Plastic strain
370	0
395	0.0001
418	0.0012
349	0.004
Plasticity parameter (stirrups - 10 mm ϕ)	
Yield stress (N/mm^2)	Plastic strain
334.56	0
454.33	0.0695

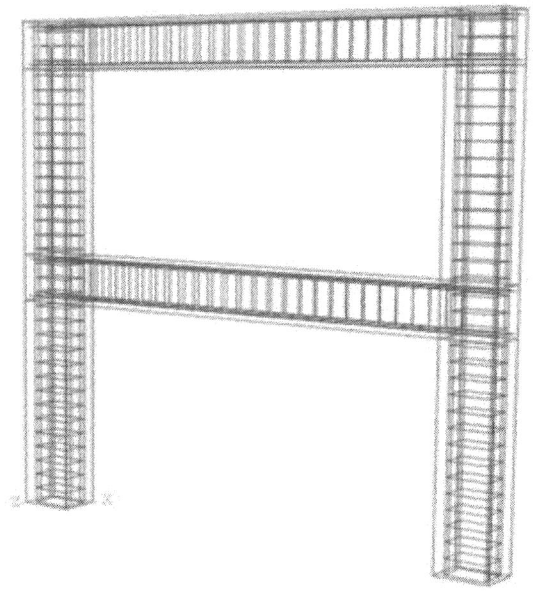

Figure 2. Model of RC frame developed in ABAQUS

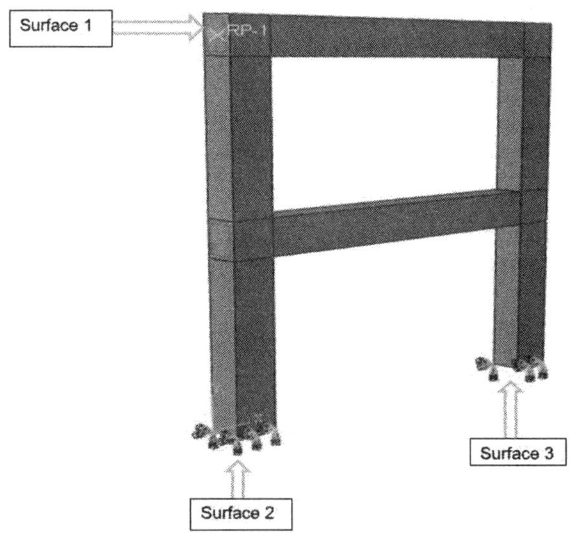

Figure 3. Boundary condition and displacement application

Fixed boundary condition is applied on surface-2 and surface-3. Static general displacement is applied up to 120 mm at the reference point (RP-1) which is tied to the free end surface-1 in the horizontal direction as shown in Figure 3.

The analytical result is very close to the result obtained by Francisco et al. [6], the error is 0.15% shown in Figure 4.

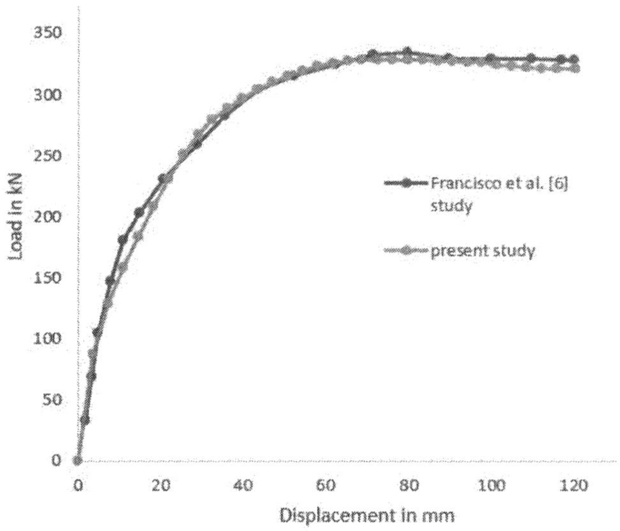

Figure 4. Comparison of Load Vs displacement graph

III. PSWC-BAR AND MODELING DETAILS

Rebar with lugs are corroded faster as compared to plain surface bar. Therefore, Kar invented PSWC-bar[1].

PSWC-bar with 16mm, 18mm, 20 mm and 22 mm offset with 240mm, 300 mm, 360 mm and 420 mm pitch distance is shown in Figures 5 to 8. Concrete frame is reinforced with PSWC-bar with different offsets and pitch distances.

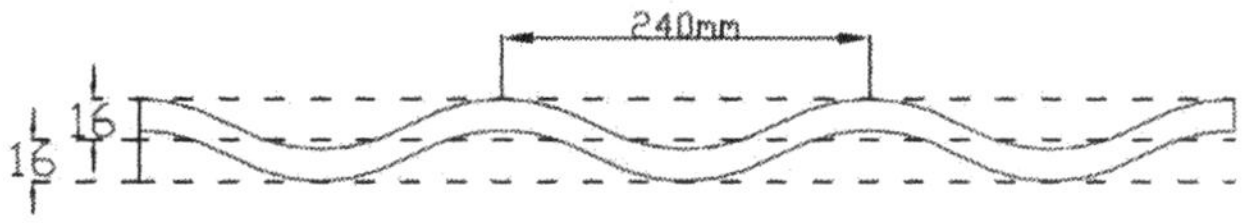

Figure 5. PSWC-bar with 16 mm offset and 240 mm pitch distance

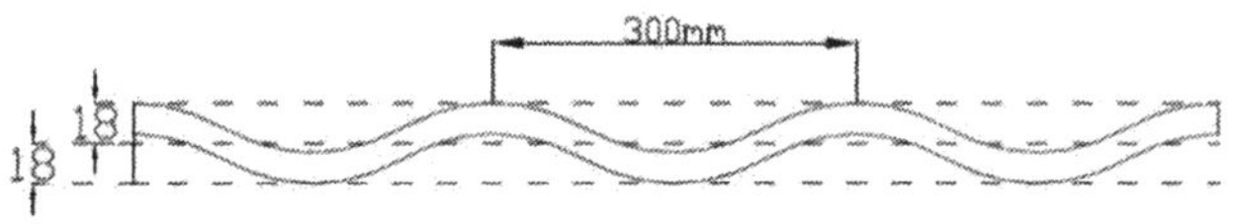

Figure 6. PSWC-bar with 18 mm offset and 300 mm pitch distance

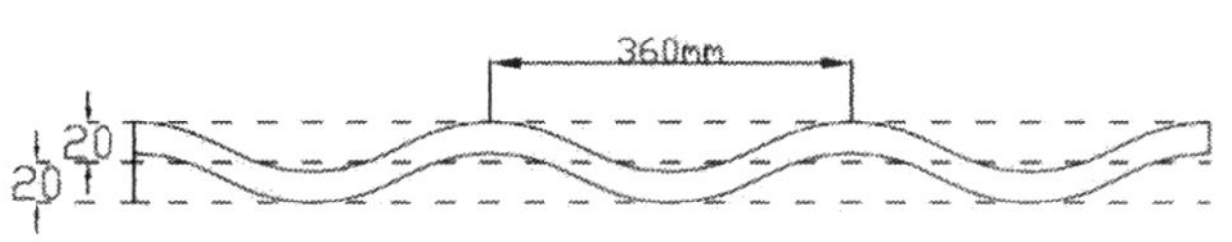

Figure 7. PSWC-bar with 20 mm offset and 360 mm pitch distance

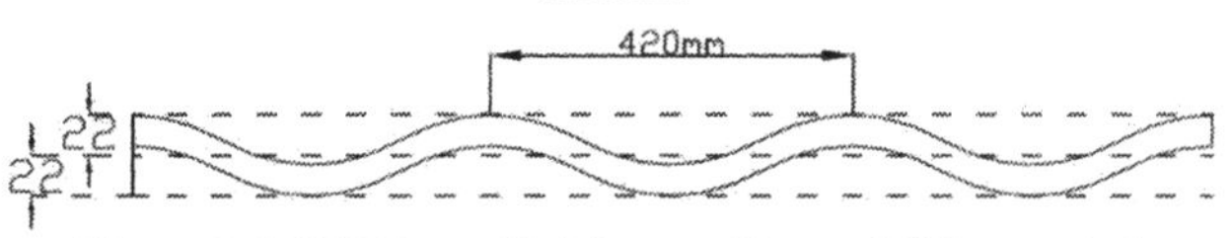

Figure 8. PSWC-bar with 22 mm offset and 420 mm pitch distance

PSWC-bar with five different offsets and four different pitches are used as reinforcement in concrete frame for this study.

Models with PSWC-bar as reinforcement are created with various pitch distances and offsets.Total 20 models with PSWC-bar are developed.

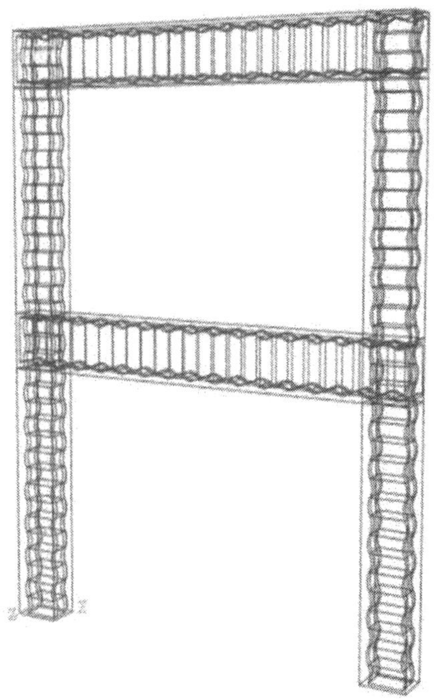

Figure 9. Model concrete frame with PSWC-bar as reinforcement

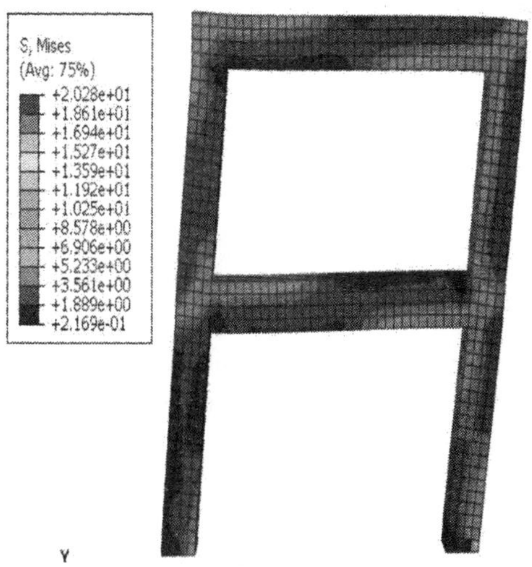

Figure 10. Stresses developed in concrete at 120 mm displacement

Parts like concrete frame, PSWC-bar and stirrups as a reinforcement for beam as well as column are created. All the parts are assembled as shown in Figure 9 with a replacement of conventional bar as per structural details as shown in Figure 1.

An embedded region constraint allows to embed the model within a "host" region of the model or within the whole model. In this case, concrete is host region and steel is embedded region. Embedded region defines interaction between different sections working together in entire model.

The effect of stress on RC frame and also on reinforcement is shown in Figures 10 & 11. Load vs displacement graph for all 4 different pitches and 5 different offsets are plotted.

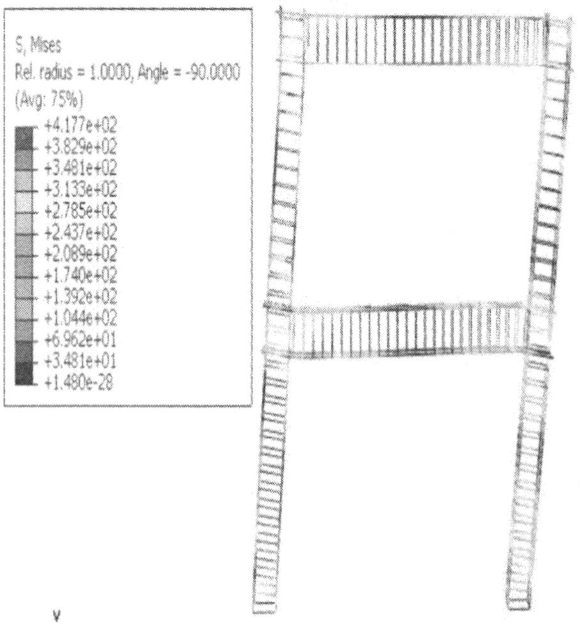

Figure 11. Stresses developed in reinforcement at 120 mm displacement

After performing analysis of all models in ABAQUS, the comparison of conventional bar with PSWC-bar with different pitches and offsets is shown in Figures 12 to 15.

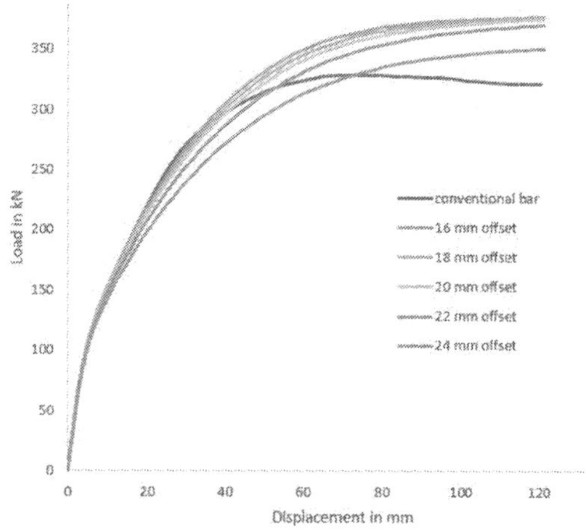

Figure 12. Load vs displacement graph of PSWC-bar RC frame with different offsets with 240 mm pitch and conventional bar

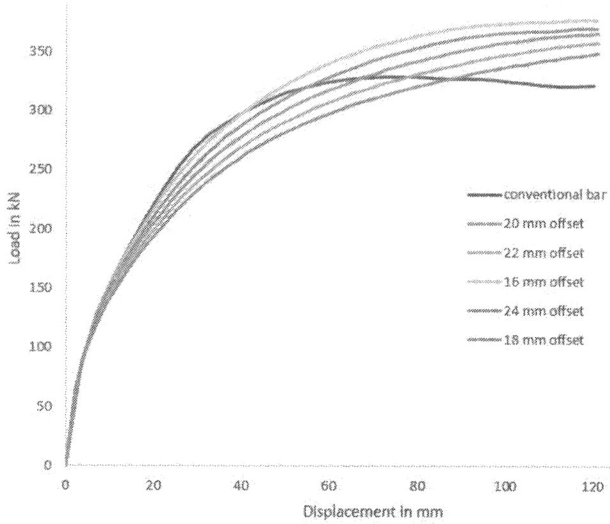

Figure 13. Load vs displacement graph of PSWC-bar RC frame with different offsets with 300 mm pitch and conventional bar

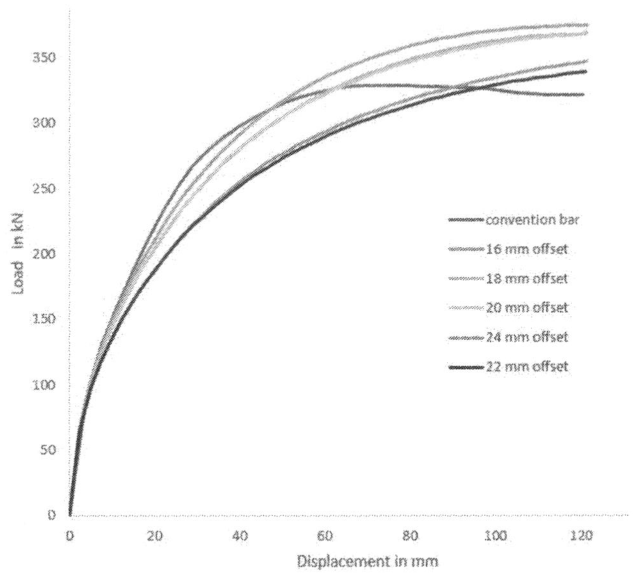

Figure 14. Load vs displacement graph of PSWC-bar RC frame with different offsets with 360 mm pitch and conventional bar

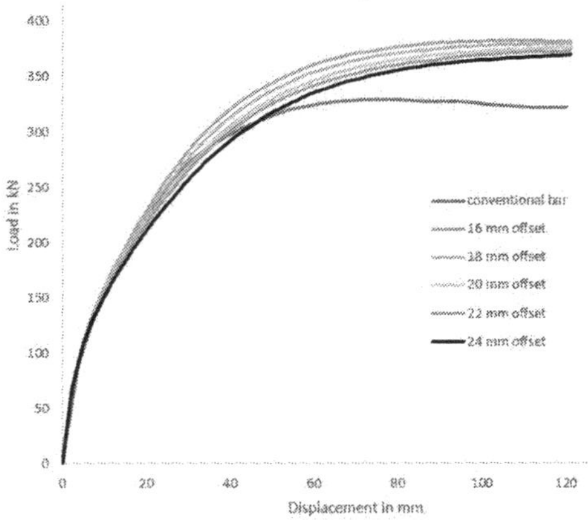

Figure 15. Load vs displacement graph of PSWC-bar RC frame with different offsets with 420 mm pitch and conventional bar

TABLE III
LOAD CARRYING CAPACITY DATA OF DIFFERENT PITCHES DISTANCE RELATED TO OFFSETS

Pitch (mm)	Offset				
	16 (mm)	18 (mm)	20 (mm)	22 (mm)	24 (mm)
	Load (kN)				
240	374.6	368.6	367.8	339	346.9
300	377.1	370.1	365.5	357.8	348.8
360	377.5	376.8	375.7	370.6	350.8
420	382.4	379.7	376.3	373.3	369.5

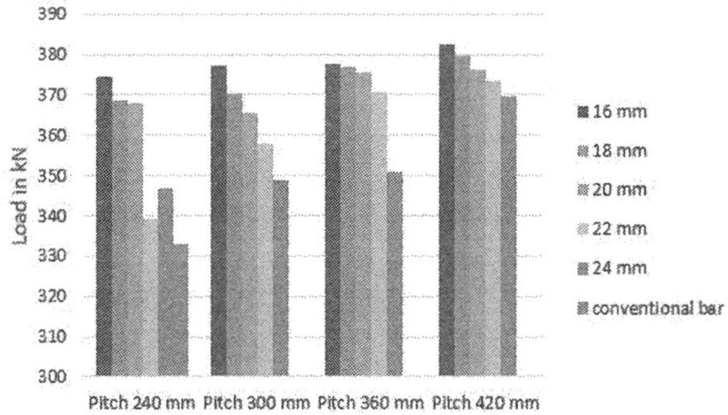

Figure 16. Load carrying capacity of PSWC- bar RC frame with different pitch distance related to offsets

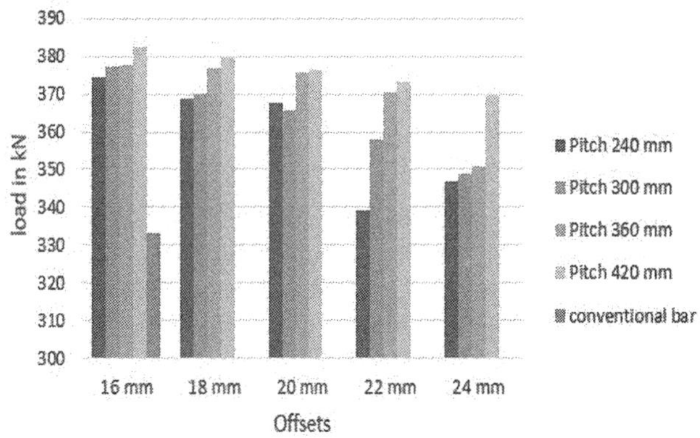

Figure 17. Load carrying capacity of different offsets related to pitch

Load carrying capacity data and graph of different pitches distance related to different offsets is shown in Tables III & IV and Figures 16 & 17.

Percentage increment in the load carrying capacity of PSWC-RC frame with different pitches and offsets compared to conventional bar is described in Table V. The observation shows that the different pitches with 16 mm offset gives 14% to 16% increments in load carrying capacity compared to conventional bar.

TABLE IV
LOAD CARRYING CAPACITY DATA OF DIFFERENT OFFSETS RELATED TO PITCHES

Offsets (mm)	Pitch 240 mm	Pitch 300 mm	Pitch 360 mm	Pitch 420 mm
	Load (kN)			
16	374.666	377.175	377.539	382.429
18	368.666	370.175	376.842	379.754
20	367.829	365.596	375.706	376.306
22	339.03	357.815	370.624	373.306
24	346.932	348.804	350.867	369.523

TABLE V
PERCENTAGE VARIATION IN LOAD CARRYING CAPACITY OF CONCRETE FRAME REINFORCED WITH PSWC-BAR WITH DIFFERENT PITCH AND OFFSET TO CONVENTIONAL BAR

Models		PSWC-bar Offset (mm)				
		16	18	20	22	24
Pitch (mm)	240	14%	12%	12%	3%	5%
	300	15%	13%	11%	9%	6%
	360	15%	15%	14%	13%	7%
	420	16%	15%	14%	14%	12%

IV. CONCLUSIONS

Using ABAQUS, the PSWC-bar RC frame is analyzed with different pitches and offsets. A comparison is made between load carrying capacity of PSWC-bar RC frame and conventional bar RC frame in order to find the effectiveness of PSWC-bar in RC frame. The conclusion derive from this comparative study are as follows.

1) Enhancement is observed in load carrying capacity of concrete frame reinforced with PSWC-bar for adopted all offsets with varying in pitch distance 240 mm, 300 mm, 360 mm & 420 mm.
2) Decrement is observed in load carrying capacity of concrete frame reinforced with PSWC-bar for all adopted pitch distance with varying offset16 mm, 18 mm, 20 mm, 22 mm& 24 mm.
3) Area under the curve of load vs displacement graph for PSWC- bar with different offsets & pitch distances is higher as compared to conventional bar. It indicates improvement in behaviour of entire RC frame.

References

[1] Kar, Anil K., (2010)"Rebar for Durable Concrete Constructions", New Building Materials & construction world; Vol. 39, pp. 59-65.

[2] Kar, A. K., and Vij, S. K., (2009) "Enhancing the Life Span of Concrete Bridges," New Building Materials & Construction World, Vol. 15, pp. 114-156.

[3] Varu, R., (2014) "Study on C-bar as reinforcement in column", M. Tech thesis, Nirma University, Ahmedabad.

[4] Patel, N. A., (2015) "Study on PSWC-Bar as Reinforcement for Beams", M. Tech thesis, Nirma University, Ahmedabad.

[5] Patel, A.R., Panchal, V. R., Chauhan, N., and Patel, N. A., (2017)"Analytical Study on PSWC-bar as Reinforcement in RCC Beam-Column Junction", M. Tech thesis.

[6] Francisco, L. A., Bashar, A., Sergio, O., (2014) "Numerical Simulation of RC Frame Testing with Damaged Plasticity Model. Comparison with Simplified Model", Second European Conference on Earthquake Engineering and Seismology, Istanbul

Seismic Response of Elevated Liquid Storage Steel Tanks Isolated by Polynomial Friction Pendulum Isolator

Uday H. Handiwala[1], V. R. Panchal[2]

[1] *Post Graduate Student (Structural Engineering), M S Patel Department of Civil Engineering, Chandubhai S. Patel Institute of Technology, Charotar University of Science and Technology, Changa, Gujarat, India*

[2] *Professor and Head, M S Patel Department of Civil Engineering, Chandubhai S. Patel Institute of Technology, Charotar University of Science and Technology, Changa, Gujarat, India*

[1]udayhandiwala@gmail.com
[2]vijaypanchal.cv@charusat.ac.in

***Abstract*—In this study, seismic behaviour of two elevated liquid storage steel tanks (slender and broad) isolated with PFPI located at top of tower is investigated under six different near-fault ground excitations. Seismic response of elevated tank isolated with Polynomial Friction Pendulum Isolator (PFPI) is compared with Variable Curvature Friction Pendulum System(VCFPS) in order to find the adequacy of PFPI. The consistent fluid mass of the elevated tank is lumped mass known as impulsive, convective and rigid masses. Governing equation of motion of elevated liquid storage tank is solved using Newmark's linear acceleration method. It is concluded that PFPI is quite effective in reducing isolator displacement as compared to VCFPS, and VCFPS is considerably effective in reducing base shear, convective displacement, impulsive displacement and tower displacement compared to PFPI.**

***Keywords*—Base isolation; Elevated liquid storage tank; Near-fault ground excitations; PFPI.**

I. Introduction

As per current scenario, earthquake is one of the main reason of destruction to life and property. Liquid storage tanks are very useful structure in industries and nuclear power plants. Tanks are used to store various liquids, and they may be corrosive or low-temperature (e.g., CNG) substances, so the storage tanks weight is varying with time due to change in the level of liquid. There have been many examples of failures of liquid storage tanks due to seismic events like (Northridge earthquake, 1994; Kobe earthquake, 1995; Chi-Chi earthquake, 1999; Bhuj earthquake, 2001). Causes behind the failure of tanks are (i) tank wall is buckled because of excessive generation of compressive stresses in the tank wall, (ii) uplift of anchorage system and (iii) failure of piping system. Failures of tanks not only alter necessary infrastructure as well as cause fires or ecological sullying when there are combustible materials or breaks of dangerous chemicals. So, it is crucial to protect the tanks against the intense earthquake events. Throughout the years, base-isolation has been perceived as one of the best options for ensuring safety of tanks against serious earthquake tremors. Base-isolation is passive earthquake protective system in which tank is uncoupled from the surface of earth by providing specially designed isolators between the super structure and foundation.

The elevated liquid storage steel tanks are horizontally flexible however their failure against recent seismic events has grabbedsignificant attention of investigators. Shelton and Hampton [1], Shrimali and Jangid [2], Panchal and Jangid [3], Panchal et al. [4] explored seismic behavior of storage tanks and isolated tanks. According to few investigators, base isolated structure situated at near fault locations is more susceptible to the largepulse-like groundmotions. The seismic responses of tanks situated at near-fault locations are higher than those of structural system under far-field ground motions. As a result, very large isolators will berequired. Therefore, special concern in recent research work is to diminish the seismic response of elevated broad and slender tanks.

Lu et al. [5] suggested new kind of isolator called Polynomial Friction Pendulum Isolator (PFPI) which is similar to Friction Pendulum System (FPS). There have been so much study done on isolation of tanks described as above, still the study of elevated tank isolated by PFPI have not done yet.

In this study, the seismic analysis of tank isolated with PFPI is conducted to compute the displacement of isolator, impulsive displacement, convective displacement, tower displacement and base-shear for near-fault ground excitations. From these quantities of response, the relative isolator displacement is much important for designing of PFPI. The objective of the study is to compare the effectiveness of PFPI and VCFPS.

Six different near-fault ground excitations are used for this study. Table I shows the characteristics of near-fault excitations used for this study.

TABLE I
CHARACTERISTICS OF NEAR FAULT EXCITATIONS

	Normal component		
Near Fault Ground Excitations	PGD (cm)	PGV (cm/s)	PGA (g)
Imperial Valley,1979(EL Centro #5) (EQ 11)	76.5	98	0.37
Imperial Valley, 1979(EL Centro #7) (EQ 21)	49.1	113	0.46
Northridge, 1994 (Newhall) (EQ 31)	38.1	119	0.72
Landers, 1992 (Lucerne Valley) (EQ 41)	230	136	0.71
Northridge, 1994 (Rinaldi) (EQ 51)	39.1	175	0.89
Northridge, 1994 (Sylmar) (EQ 61)	31.1	122	0.73

II. MODELING AND IDEALIZING

Broad and Slender elevated liquid storage steel tanks are used for base isolation modelling. Figure 1 shows elevated tank isolated with PFPI. The contained liquid stored in tank is assumed as an inviscid, incompressible and has irrotational flow. At the time of earthquake, whole liquid mass of tank vibrates in three pattern such as convective or sloshing, impulsive and rigid mass. There are different modes in which convective and impulsive masses are vibrating but sloshing mode is considered first and then impulsive mode for response assumption. impulsive mass (m_i), Sloshing mass (m_c) and rigid mass (m_b) are lumped masses. The self-weight of steel tower structure and base mass is assumed as 10% and 5% of the liquid mass*(m)*, respectively. Four Degree freedom system is considered for the analysis. u_c, u_i, u_b and u_t are used to denote four degrees of freedom of the system, which indicates the absolute displacement of sloshing mass, impulsive mass, rigid mass and tower drift, respectively.

The different assumptions used for the system are as follows which is used by Panchal and Jangid [4]:

1. The self-weight of tank is neglected due to the fact that it's very small.
2. Damping ratio is assumed for damping coefficient of the motion of impulsive and convective masses.
3. Contribution of horizontal component of near-fault ground excitation in excitation of the structure is very much higher than that of vertical component. Hence, the impact of the vertical component may beneglected.

The convective, rigid and impulsive masses in terms of liquid mass, *m* is evaluated as

$$m_c = Y_c\, m \quad (1)$$

$$m_i = Y_i\, m \quad (2)$$

$$m_r = Y_r\, m \quad (3)$$

$$m = \pi R^2 H \rho_w \quad (4)$$

where Y_c, Y_i and Y_r are mass ratio; tank aspect ratio, $S=H/R$; H is height of liquid; R is tank radius; ρ_w is mass density of tank liquid.

For t_h/R = 0.004, the ratio of mass for different masses are evaluate as Shrimali and Jangid [2]

$$Y_c = 1.01327 - 0.87578\, S + 0.35708\, S^2 - 0.066925\, S^3 + 0.00439\, S^4 \quad (5)$$

$$Y_i = -0.15497 + 1.21716\, S - 0.62839\, S^2 - 0.14434\, S^3 - 0.0125\, S^4 \quad (6)$$

$$Y_r = -0.01599 + 0.86356\, S - 0.30941\, S^2 + 0.04083\, S^3 \quad (7)$$

The fundamental frequency of the convective mass (ω_c) and of impulsive mass (ω_i) are given by the following equations as

$$\omega_c = \sqrt{1.84 \frac{g}{R} \tan h\,(1.84S)} \quad (8)$$

$$\omega_i = \frac{P}{H}\sqrt{\frac{E}{\rho_s}} \quad (9)$$

where g denotes the acceleration due to gravity; R stands for radius of storage tank; E is elastic modulus; ρ_s is density of tank wall; and P expressed as

$$P = 0.037085 + 0.084302\, S - 0.05088\, S^2 + 0.012523\, S^3 - 0.0012\, S^4 \quad (10)$$

The stiffness and damping of convective and impulsive masses are as given below

$$k_c = m_c\omega_c^2 \tag{11}$$

$$k_i = m_i\omega_i^2 \tag{12}$$

$$k_t = \left(\frac{2\pi}{T_t}\right)^2 (M + 0.1m) \tag{13}$$

$$k_b = \left(\frac{2\pi}{T_b}\right)^2 M \tag{14}$$

$$c_c = 2\xi_c m_c \omega_c \tag{15}$$

$$c_i = 2\xi_i m_i \omega_i \tag{16}$$

$$c_t = 2\xi_t (M + 0.1m)\omega_t \tag{17}$$

where ξ_c and ξ_i denotes ratio of damping for convective and impulsive masses, respectively.

III. Concept of PFPI

In FPS system, the major problem observed is resonant [3]. PFPI is used to solve this problem of resonant. The only difference in PFPI and FPS is that in PFPI, the sliding surface has been made of an axially symmetric surface with a variable curvature where in FPS, sliding surface has been made of surface with constant curvature.

The advantage of this isolator is that it can handle long period pulse and decrease isolator drift and structural acceleration when compared to FPS. In the PFPI, following polynomial function is used to define the geometry of the sliding surface

$$y'(x) = \frac{u_r(x)}{P} = ax^5 + cx^3 + ex \tag{18}$$

$$y''(x) = \frac{k_r(x)}{P} = 5ax^4 + 3cx^2 + e \tag{19}$$

$$a = \frac{-k_0+k_1}{-5(D_1)^4}, \; c = \frac{2(-k_0+k_1)}{3(D_1)^2}, \; e = k_0 \tag{20}$$

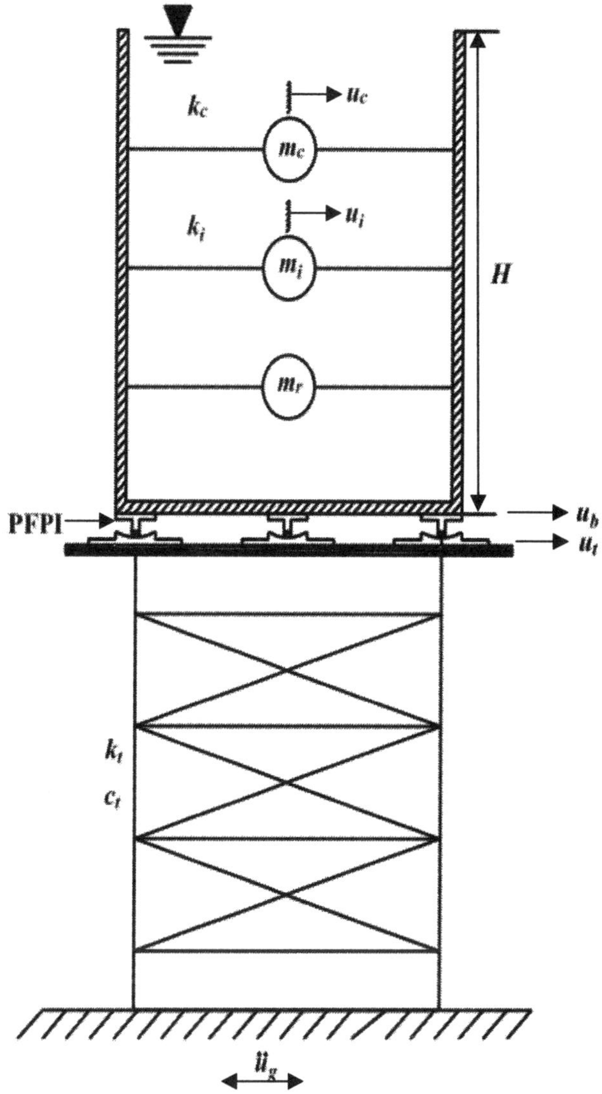

Figure 1 Mathematical modelling of elevated liquid storage tank isolated with PFPI located at the top of tower

where $y'(x)$ and $y''(x)$ are normalized restoring force and normalized isolator stiffness, respectively, with respect to vertical load P, $u_r(x)$ and $k_r(x)$ are restoring force and restoring stiffness, respectively. a, c and e are polynomial coefficients, k_0 is the normalized initial stiffness $x = 0$, k_1 is normalized isolated stiffness at $x = D_1$ and D_1 is defined as critical isolator drift.

In this type of isolator, there are two process parts in displacement which is shown in Figure 2. The softening and hardening sections were aimed to control the structural acceleration and isolator drift, respectively.

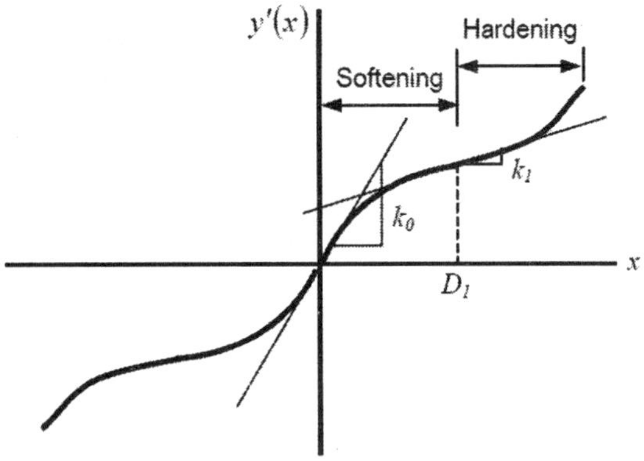

Figure 2 The normalized restoring force of a PFPI [3]

IV. Governing Equation of Motion

The governing equation of motion is explicit below in form of matrix:

$$[M]\{\ddot{x}\} + [C]\{\dot{x}\} + [K]\{x\} + \{F\} = -[M]\{r\}\ddot{u}_g \qquad (21)$$

Where $\{x\} = \{x_c, x_i, x_b, x_t\}^T$ is the relative displacement vector: $x_c = u_c - u_b$ is relative sloshing mass displacement, $x_i = u_i - u_b$ is relative impulsive mass displacement, $x_b = u_b - u_t$ is relative bearing displacement and $x_t = u_t - u_g$ is relative tower displacement; $\{r\}$ is influence co-efficient vector; $\ddot{u}_g$ is earthquake ground acceleration. In above equation $[M]$, $[C]$ and $[K]$ are mass, damping and stiffness matrix and they are explicit as

$$[M] = \begin{bmatrix} m_c & 0 & m_c & m_c \\ 0 & m_i & m_i & m_i \\ m_c & m_i & M & M \\ m_c & m_i & M & M + 2m_b \end{bmatrix}$$

$$[C] = \begin{bmatrix} c_c & 0 & 0 & 0 \\ 0 & c_i & 0 & 0 \\ 0 & 0 & 0 & 0 \\ 0 & 0 & 0 & c_t \end{bmatrix}$$

$$[K] = \begin{bmatrix} k_c & 0 & 0 & 0 \\ 0 & k_i & 0 & 0 \\ 0 & 0 & k_b & 0 \\ 0 & 0 & 0 & k_t \end{bmatrix}$$

$$\{r\} = \{0,0,0,1\}^T \qquad (22)$$

V. Comparative Study

The response of elevated broad and slender tanks isolated with PFPI and VCFPS at the top of tower for six different earthquake ground excitations is examined. The various essential parameters required todefine broad and slender liquid storage tank system are as follows which is taken from Panchal and Jangid [4].

TABLE II

Properties Of Elevated Liquid Storage Tank

Parameters	Tank	
	Broad	Slender
Damping ratio, ξ_c and ξ_i	0.5% and 2%	0.5% and 2%
Elastic modulus, E	200 GPa	200 GPa
Density of mass, ρ_s	7900 kg/m^3	7900 kg/m^3
Aspect ratio, S (H/R)	0.6	1.85
Tank height, H	14.6 m	11.3 m
Natural frequency, ω_c and ω_i	0.123 and 3.944 Hz	0.273 and 5.963 Hz
t_h/R	0.004	0.004

where t_h/R is ratio of thickness of wall of tank to radius.

The different response quantities are base-shear (F_b), isolator displacement (x_b), impulsive displacement (x_i), tower displacement (x_t) and convective displacement (x_c). Tower time period (T_t)is taken 0.5 sec and 1 sec. Two types of isolator are used for comparison of seismic response, i.e., (i) PFPI (T_b = 2.50 sec and μ = 0.02), the value of constant a, c and e are 81.25, -10.83 and 0.65 respectively. (ii) VCFPS (T_b = 2.50 sec and μ= 0.02).

Figures 3 & 5 show the graph of time verses different seismic response quantities of PFPI and VCFPS for broad tank and slender tank, respectively.

Figures 4 & 6 indicate the Hysteresis loop of PFPI and VCFPS for broad tank and slender tank, respectively.

Figures 3-6 demonstrate that there is decrease in isolator displacement and increase in other response quantities compared to VCFPS.

Tables III & IV shows the comparison of peak response quantities of non-isolated, PFPI and VCFPS for broad and slender tank, respectively.

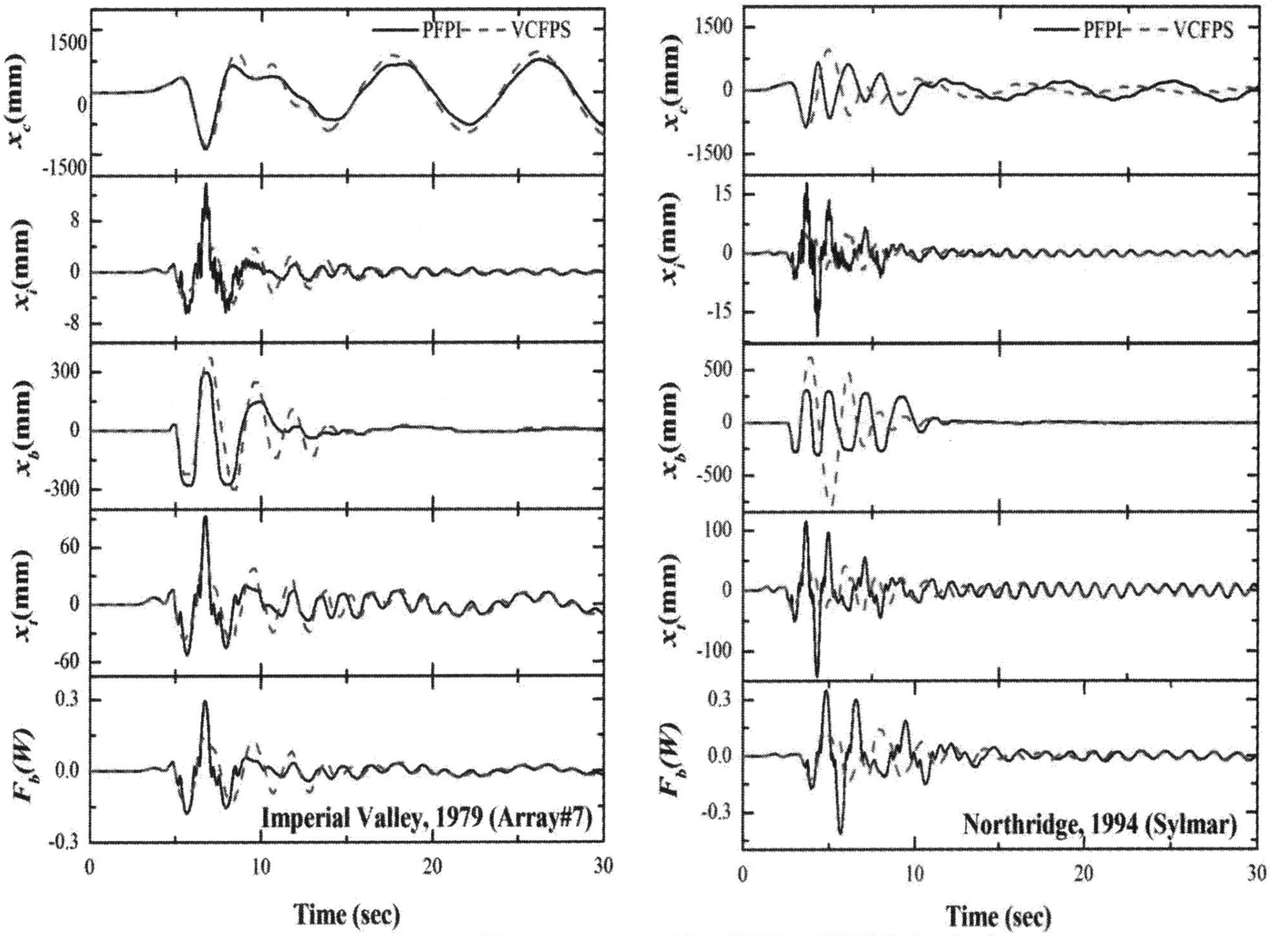

Figure 3 Graph f time verses different response quantities of PFPI and VCFPS for broad tank

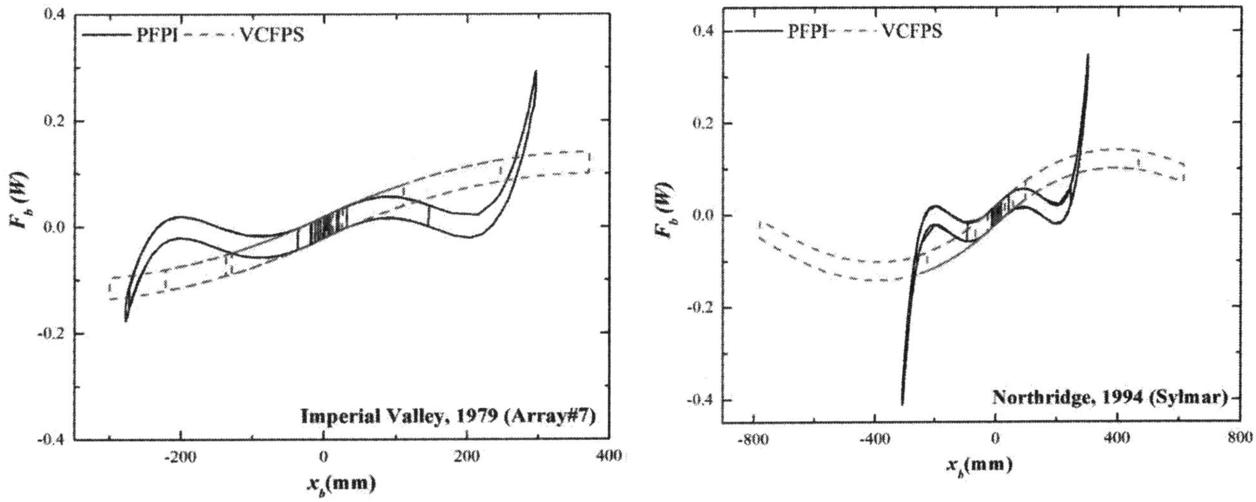

Figure 4 The hysteresis loop of PFPI and VCFPS of broad tank

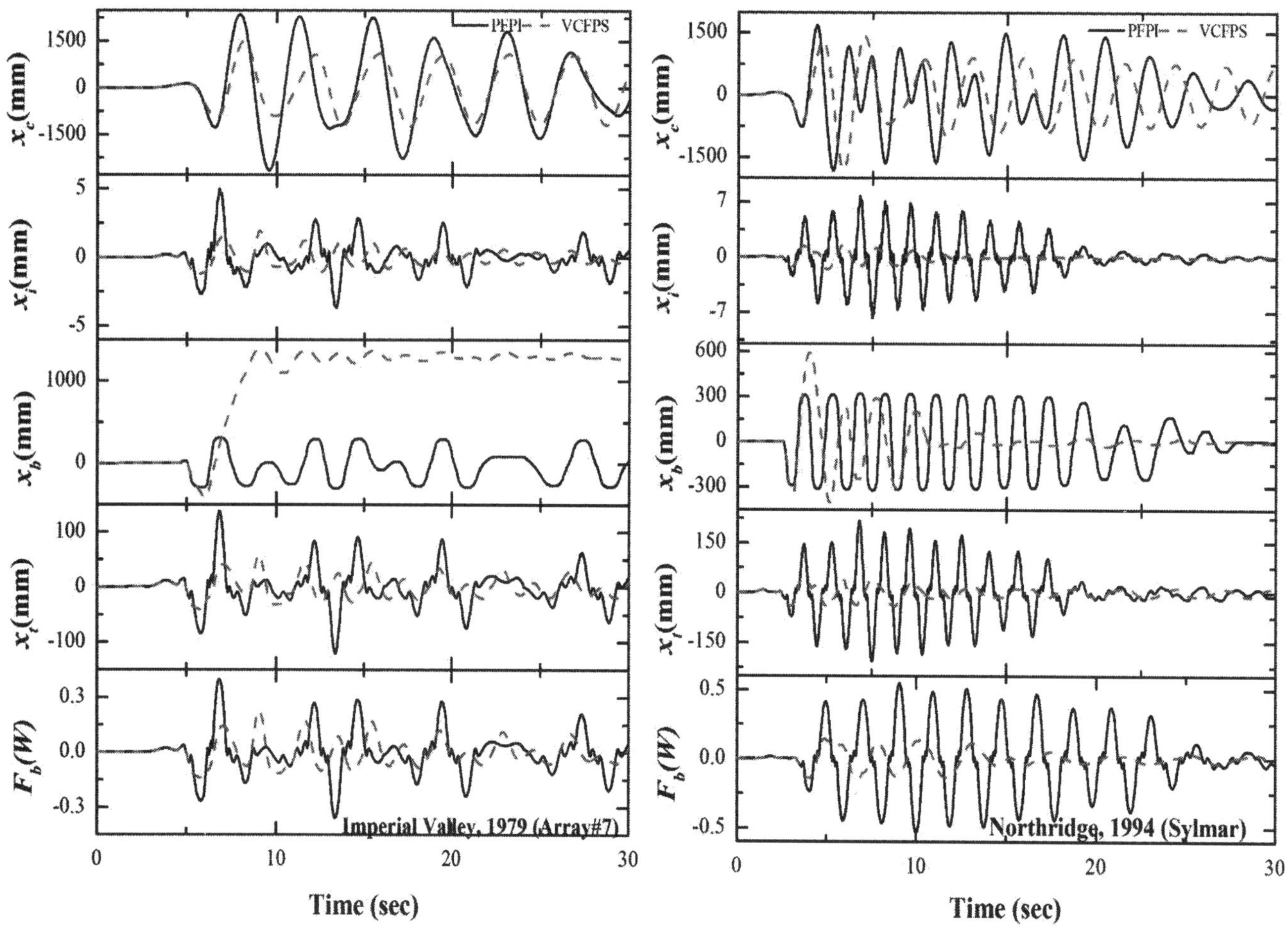

Figure 5 Graph of time verses different response quantities of PFPI and VCFPS for slender tank

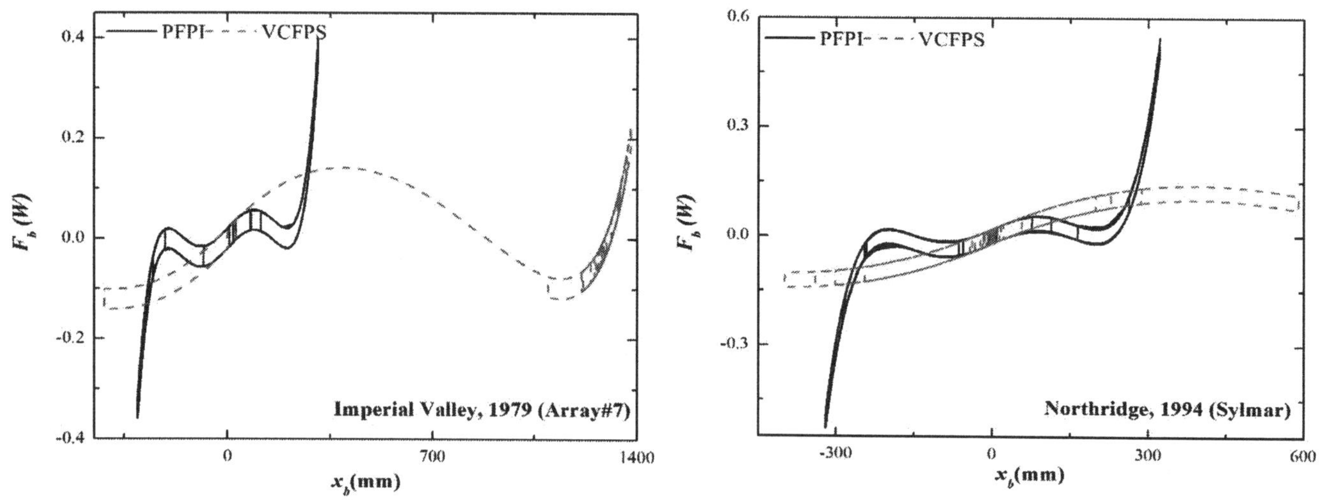

Figure 6 The hysteresis loop of PFPI and VCFPS of slender tank

TABLE III

COMPARISON OF PEAK RESPONSE QUANTITIES OF NON ISOLATED, PFPI AND VCFPS FOR BROAD TANK

Near Fault Ground Motions	Tank condition	T_t = 1.0 sec					T_t = 0.5 sec				
		x_c (mm)	x_i (mm)	x_b (mm)	x_t (mm)	F_b *(W)*	x_c (mm)	x_i (mm)	x_b (mm)	x_t (mm)	F_b *(W)*
Imperial Valley, 1979 (Array#5)	Non isolated	1333.55	8.96	-	76.17	0.31	1313.64	28.38	-	50.48	0.81
	PFPI	1662.60	9.22	284.61	64.72	0.21	1540.40	10.92	298.74	20.57	0.31
	VCFPS	1527.10	5.14	257.95	37.77	0.19	1524.60	5.00	305.19	9.17	0.14
Imperial Valley, 1979 (Array#7)	Non isolated	1107.05	25.98	-	223.47	0.90	1103.59	22.82	-	45.29	0.73
	PFPI	1364.10	13.76	296.07	92.55	0.29	1193.40	9.31	294.25	18.31	0.28
	VCFPS	1291.80	5.33	371.08	40.42	0.14	1267.50	4.90	399.83	9.53	0.14
Northridge, 1994 (Newhall)	Non isolated	731.54	32.03	-	270.83	1.09	562.35	35.79	-	68.53	1.11
	PFPI	863.11	6.22	272.43	43.68	0.15	750.50	6.51	282.18	13.11	0.20
	VCFPS	681.76	4.72	293.70	39.63	0.13	632.93	4.72	321.48	9.14	0.14
Landers, 1992 (Lucerne Valley)	Non isolated	1801.57	11.40	-	95.95	0.39	1802.04	15.31	-	28.14	0.45
	PFPI	1913.70	8.89	286.38	67.91	0.23	1579.70	15.30	316.30	31.90	0.48
	VCFPS	2036.80	4.73	269.86	39.06	0.13	2021.40	4.52	302.45	9.30	0.14
Northridge, 1994 (Rinaldi)	Non isolated	765.36	40.60	-	359.89	1.45	553.79	34.13	-	68.59	0.11
	PFPI	913.16	18.57	306.42	128.32	0.38	928.58	57.27	364.27	95.26	1.29
	VCFPS	764.15	5.11	421.91	40.03	0.14	726.48	5.00	457.22	9.42	0.14
Northridge, 1994 (Sylmar)	Non isolated	591.60	14.91	-	123.09	0.50	539.78	34.09	-	64.99	1.04
	PFPI	858.66	20.96	309.58	142.00	0.41	830.76	41.61	345.16	62.61	0.90
	VCFPS	959.87	4.99	780.73	40.70	0.14	926.30	5.30	775.85	9.58	0.14

TABLE IV

COMPARISON OF PEAK RESPONSE QUANTITIES OF NON ISOLATED, PFPI AND VCFPS FOR SLENDER TANK

Near Fault Ground Motions	Tank condition	T_t = 1.0 sec					T_t = 0.5 sec				
		x_c (mm)	x_i (mm)	x_b (mm)	x_t (mm)	F_b *(W)*	x_c (mm)	x_i (mm)	x_b (mm)	x_t (mm)	F_b *(W)*
Imperial Valley, 1979 (Array#5)	Non isolated	1776.75	6.11	-	197.07	0.79	1552.21	9.20	-	67.52	0.11
	PFPI	2702.40	4.62	305.83	128.22	0.38	2247.10	6.22	330.72	45.56	0.67
	VCFPS	1712.80	2.15	1388.10	69.50	0.26	1643.60	4.09	1421.80	28.71	0.46
Imperial Valley, 1979 (Array#7)	Non isolated	1689.50	76.99	-	218.92	0.88	1599.19	8.07	-	58.31	0.94
	PFPI	2645.60	5.00	308.06	137.92	0.40	1894.60	5.48	323.97	38.93	0.57
	VCFPS	1503.00	1.93	1379.80	60.27	0.23	1407.30	3.11	1412.40	24.76	0.40
Northridge, 1994 (Newhall)	Non isolated	1025.89	10.02	-	307.23	1.24	910.99	15.56	-	118.34	1.91
	PFPI	1868.30	2.63	289.90	77.41	0.25	929.99	4.28	313.55	30.06	0.45

Contd...

	VCFPS	1339.20	1.19	298.27	39.43	0.13	1292.20	1.13	324.77	9.36	0.14
Landers, 1992 (Lucerne Valley)	Non isolated	1495.51	2.39	-	79.21	0.32	1428.20	5.30	-	42.25	0.68
	PFPI	2542.70	4.47	307.98	137.26	0.40	2188.70	6.35	331.82	46.78	0.68
	VCFPS	1342.20	3.12	1407.70	96.37	0.37	1171.80	6.03	1451.80	45.92	0.74
Northridge, 1994 (Rinaldi)	Non isolated	1041.68	16.92	-	520.33	2.09	737.11	14.34	-	106.78	1.72
	PFPI	1672.70	5.97	315.15	173.87	0.47	1413.80	19.78	378.27	131.94	1.65
	VCFPS	1079.80	1.30	458.59	40.17	0.14	1011.00	1.31	488.13	9.64	0.14
Northridge, 1994(Sylmar)	Non isolated	1091.95	6.50	-	194.19	0.78	872.25	9.57	-	68.80	1.11
	PFPI	1820.90	7.72	321.16	217.08	0.55	1338.10	16.53	370.38	110.85	1.44
	VCFPS	1806.30	1.61	590.71	41.19	0.14	1667.50	1.50	636.49	9.75	0.14

VI. Conclusions

The elevated broad and slender liquid-storage tank ar eanalyzed to determine its responses under six different earthquake ground excitations with the help of Newmark's linear acceleration method. To examine the effectiveness of PFPI, the earthquake response of structure isolated with PFPI is compared with that of VCFPS. The conclusion derived from this comparative study are as follows:

1) The PFPI is more efficient in reducing the displacement of isolator of tank as compared to VCFPS.
2) The VCFPS is quite effective in reducing base shear, impulsive displacement, convective displacement and tower displacement as compared to PFPI.
3) For non-isolated condition, impulsive displacement, tower displacement and base shear increase but convective displacement is reduced as compared to PFPI and VCFPS.
4) For broad and slender tank as time period of tower structure increase, convective displacement and tower displacement increase and other response quantities decrease for PFPI.
5) In case of VCFPS for broad tank as time period of tower structure increase, convective displacement, impulsive displacement, and tower displacement increase and other response quantities decrease, while in case of slender tank as time period of tower increase convective displacement and tower displacement increase and other response quantities decrease.

References

[1] Shenton, H. W. and Hampton, F. P. (1999) 'Seismic response of isolated elevated water tanks', Journal of Structural Eng., Vol. 125, pp. 965-976.

[2] Shrimali, M. K. and Jangid, R. S. (2003) 'Earthquake response of isolated elevated liquid storage steel tanks', Journal of Constructional Steel Research, Vol. 59, pp. 1267-1288.

[3] Panchal, V. R. and Jangid, R. S. (2007), 'Variable friction pendulum system for seismic isolation of liquid storage tanks', Nuclear Engineering and Design, Vol. 238, pp. 1304-1315.

[4] Panchal, V. R., Soni, D. P. and Mistry, B. B. (2011) 'Double variable frequency pendulum isolator for seismic isolation of liquid storage tanks', Nuclear and Engineering and Design, Vol. 241, pp. 700-713.

[5] Lyan, Lu., Wang, J. and Hsu, C. (2006) 'Sliding isolation using variable frequency bearings for near-fault ground motions',International Conference on Earthquake Engineeringpp. 1-10.

[6] Panchal, V. R. and Jangid, R. S. (2012), 'Behavior of liquid storage tanks with VCFPS under near-fault ground motions', Structure and Infrastructure Engineering, Vol. 8, pp. 71-88.

Effect of Blast Loading on Pipe Rack for Varying Peak Overpressure

Aishwarya M. Sailor[1],Dipali Y. Patel[2], Anil Belani[3]

[1] *Postgraduate Student (Structural Engineering), Department of Civil Engineering, Chandubhai S. Patel Institute of Technology, Charotar University of Science and Technology, Changa, Gujarat, India*

[2] *Assistant Professor, Department of Civil Engineering, Chandubhai S. Patel Institute of Technology, Charotar University of Science and Technology, Changa, Gujarat, India*

[3] *Assistant General Manager, L&T Gulf Pvt. Ltd., Vadodara, Gujarat, India*

[1]aeny.sailor@gmail.com
[2]dipalipatel.cv@charusat.ac.in
[3]anilbelani@gmail.com

***Abstract*— Oil and Gas Plants are often exposed to Vapor Cloud Explosion (VCE). While blast overpressures are typically considered for closed buildings, wherever required, they are often ignored for open structures. One such type of structure, which has widespread presence in process plants is pipe-rack. With plants becoming more congested day by day, higher blast pressures are expected and ignoring them is not desirable.The work carried out, aims to study the behavior of a typical pipe-rack structure with and without the blast load. Various loads typically faced by process pipe-rack are considered. Further, the pipe-rack considered is analyzed and designed against pre-defined levels of peak overpressure corresponding to varying levels of equivalent TNT explosive weights. The performance of structure is critically assessed in terms of deflection; shear force, axial force and bending moment.The study highlights that open structures such as pipe-racks can no longer enjoy ignorance from blast loads acting on them and the same needs to be invariably considered.**

***Keywords*—Pipe rack structure, Blast analysis, Explosive weight, Peak overpressure, STAAD.Pro.**

I. Introduction

Pipe rack structure is the most important structure in the field of process industries and petrochemical refineries and so it is necessary to analyse and design in order to satisfy the different parameters of safety and economy [1]. Pipe rack is a structure whose basic geometry is like a portal frame having multi-tiers which are provided to support piping assembly, cable trays and (with) fin-fan coolers or without coolers. Pipe rack is the main artery of a process unit. It connects all equipment with lines that cannot run through adjacent areas.

Recently, the world is facing terrorist activities. Hence blast protection has become an important consideration for structural designers [3]. Normally, the conventional structures are not designed to resist the effect of blast load. Therefore, the conventional structures are more susceptible to damage from explosion because the design loads in many cases are significantly lower than those produced by explosion.

Structural design to resist the influence of accidental explosions, was recognised as one of the option available to attain the appropriate level of blast protection. The types of explosions which may occur in petrochemical plants can be classified into four basic types: vapour cloud explosions, vessel explosions, condensed phase explosions and dust explosions. Blast overpressures from vapour cloud explosions are specifically hard to compute because they tend to be directional, may come from numerous sources and vary with site conditions [2]. The preliminary objectives for provision of blast resistant design to the structure are: personal safety and financial consideration.

Kikaniet. al [6] has worked on comparative study of pipe rack structure with modular concept. They have worked on seismic analysis and wind analysis to observe the behaviour of the pipe-rack. AmolUnde and Dr.Potnis [7] had done analysis of structure under blast. They had checked the floor displacement by applying blast pressure time history on the structure. Here, attempt is made to perceive the effect of blast load on pipe-rack structure.

II. Modelling Of Pipe-Rack Structure

The considered geometry of pipe-rack is shown in Figure 1 and Figure 2. The considered parameters are as per TABLE I. The modelling of pipe-rack has been done using STAAD. Pro SS6.

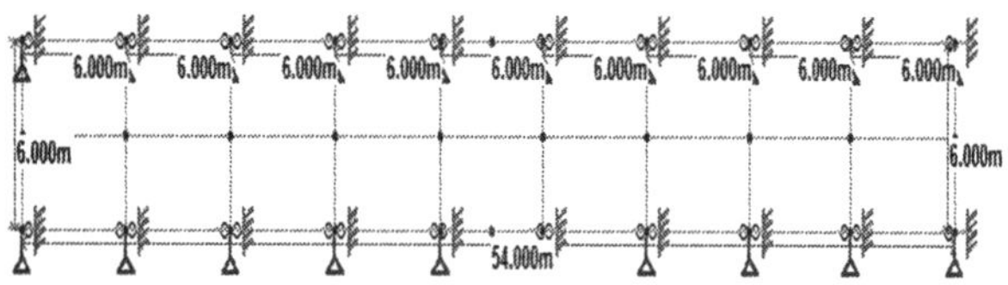

Figure 1 Top view of pipe rack

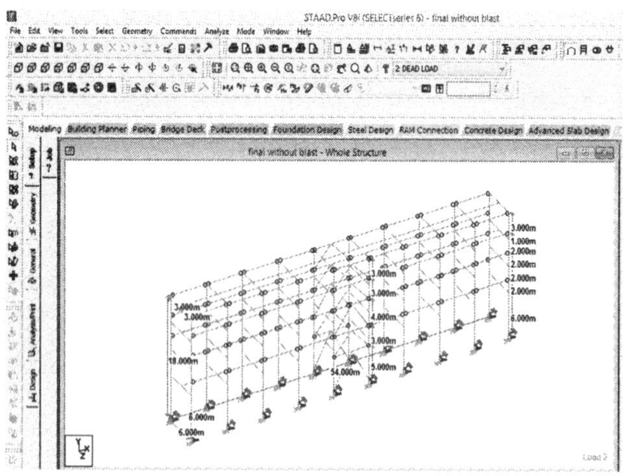

Figure 2 Model of pipe rack for the geometry of present study

Pipe-rack structure are generally subjected to pipe loads, cable tray loads, thermal friction load, thermal load, anchor load and wind load.

Bracings are provided as double angle and are defined as truss members in STAAD. Pro.

TABLE I
PARAMETER OF PIPE-RACK

S. No.	Description	Parametric value (m)
1	Height	18 (transverse tier @6m, 10m, 14m and 18m Longitudinal tier @8m, 12m and 15m)
2	Length	54 (9 bay @6m)
3	Width	6

The loadings applied on the pipe-rack structure are defined as follows:

Transverse tier (Applied as UDL)

- Pipe Erection P(E) = 150 kg/m^2
- Pipe Operating P(O) = 250 kg/m^2
- Pipe Testing P(T) = 350 kg/m^2
- Pipe Anchor-Friction force P(A-F) = 25 kg/m^2 (10% of pipe operating force)

Longitudinal tier (Applied at Center)

- Pipe Erection P(E) = 10 kN
- Pipe Operating P(O) = 15 kN
- Pipe Testing P(T) = 20 kN
- Pipe Anchor-Friction force P(A-F) = 1.5 kN (10% of pipe operating force)

TABLE II
DIFFERENT LOAD COMBINATIONS

Pipe Condition	Load Combination
Empty	DL + P(E)
	DL + P(E) ± WL
Operating	DL + P(O) ± T(A-F)
	DL + P(O) ± T(A-F) ± WL
	DL + P(O) ± T(A-F)
	DL + 0.8 [P(O) ± T(A-F) ± WL]
	DL + 0.8 [P(O) ± T(A-F)]
	0.9 [DL + P(O) ± T(A-F)] ± WL
	0.9 [DL + P(O) ± T(A-F)]
Test	DL + P(T)
	DL + P(T) ± 0.25WL
	DL + P(T)
Maintenance	DL + P(E)

Table II indicate the different load combination which are taken in account during the design of pipe rack for different pipe conditions and for maintenance.

The load combination DL + P(O) + BLAST is considered for analysis of pipe rack under blast load. The load on the transverse tier is applied as UDL while the load on longitudinal tier is applied as the point load. This applied load is shown in Figure 3.

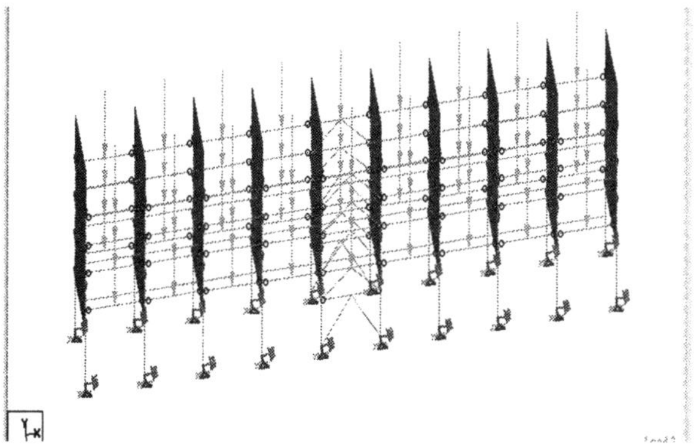

Figure 3 Application of pipe load on transverse and longitudinal tier

As per IS : 4991 – 1968, clause 10.2.1, pg. no. 31, the average dynamic yield stress of structural steels may be assumed to exceed the minimum specified static yield stress by 25 percent, which is considered in the design of pipe rack.

a) Wind Pressure:

The pipe-rack is assumed to be located at Vadodara, Gujarat. Wind load on pipe-rack has been calculated as per IS : 875 (Part 3) - 1987. The shielding factor is also multiplied by a wind load for subsequent frame as per IS : 875 (Part 3) – 1987,Clause 6.3.3.4, Pg. 46.

- **Design Wind Speed (V_z)**

TABLE III
DESIGN WIND SPEED

Height of tier (m)	V_b (m/sec)	K_1	K_2	K_3	$V_z = V_b K_1 K_2 K_3$ (m/sec)
6	44	1.07	0.88	1	41.43
8	44	1.07	0.88	1	41.43
10	44	1.07	0.88	1	41.43
12	44	1.07	0.904	1	42.56
14	44	1.07	0.928	1	43.69
15	44	1.07	0.94	1	44.26
18	44	1.07	0.964	1	45.39

The calculated design wind speed for different height is shown in Table III.

$V_z = V_b K_1 K_2 K_3$ (Clause 5.3, Pg. 8)

$V_b = 44$ m/sec
$K_1 = 1.07$
$K_2 =$ (As per Category 3 Class B)
$K_3 = 1$

- **Design Wind Pressure (P_z)**

$P_z = 0.6\ V_z^2$ (Clause 5.4, pg. 12)

TABLE IV shows the design wind pressure at different height of structure.

TABLE IV
DESIGN WIND PRESSURE

Height of tier (m)	$P_z = 0.6\ V_z^2$ (KN/m^2)
6	1.02987
8	1.02987
10	1.02987
12	1.0868
14	1.1453
15	1.17537
18	1.23615

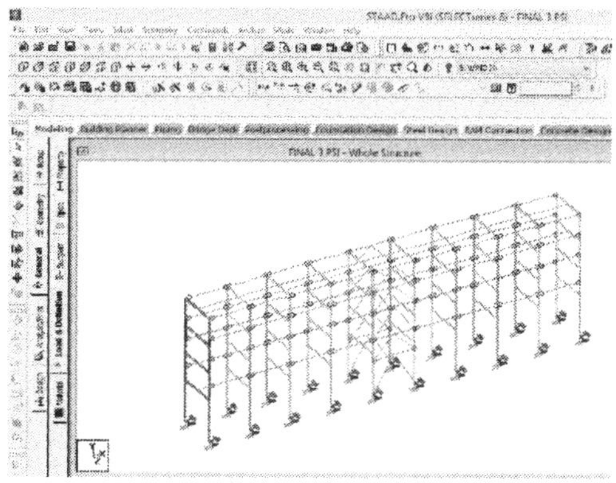

Figure 4 Application of wind load on pipe rack

b) Shielding Factor:

When there are more than two frames of similar geometry and spacing, the wind load on the third and subsequent frames should be taken as equal to that on the second frame.

The frame spacing ratio is equal to the distance, center to center of the frames, beams or girders divided by the least overall dimension of the frame, beam or girder measured at the right angles to the direction of the wind.

Calculation for transverse direction frame

$$\text{Spacing ratio} = \frac{(4*0.6*10) + (0.25*18*2)}{18*10} = 0.183$$

Calculation for longitudinal direction frame

$$\text{Spacing ratio} = \frac{(10*0.6*18) + (4*0.25*6)}{18*54} = 0.117$$

From Table 29 IS : 875 (Part 3) – 1987 pg. no 46

$\eta = 0.817$ for transverse direction frame

$\eta = 0.883$ for longitudinal direction frame

c) Blast Load

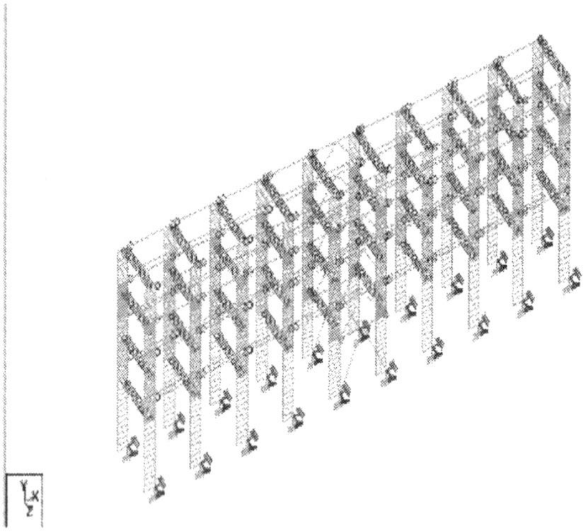

Figure 5 Application of blast load on pipe rack

Blast load is calculated for 1 psi explosion. The same has been calculated for 1.5 psi, 2 psi, 2.5 psi, 3 psi, 3.5 psi and 4 psi.

1 psi = 6894.76 N/m^2

Load acting on column ISWB 350 = load * exposed width

= 6.89476 * 0.350

= 2.413166 kN/m

Load acting on column ISWB 250 = load * exposed width

= 6.89476 * 0.250

= 1.72369 kN/m

III. Analysis Of Blast Load

It is considered that explosion is occurs in X+ direction of the structure and blast load is applied statically on the member of pipe-rack structure. Pipe-rack is designed for different explosive weight (i.e. 1 psi, 1.5 psi, 2 psi, 2.5 psi, 3 psi, 3.5 psi and 4 psi) and is compared with the pipe-rack without blast (W.B.) effect. TABLE V contain the different section properties used in the optimized design.

TABLE V
DIFFERENT SECTION USED IN THE OPTIMISED DESIGN OF PIPE RACK

Blast Load	Without Blast	1 psi	1.5 psi	2 psi	2.5 psi	3 psi	3.5 psi	4 psi
Column	ISWB350	ISWB400	ISWB400	ISWB450	ISWB500	ISWB550	ISWB600	ISWB600H
Transverse Beam	ISWB250	ISWB300	ISWB300	ISWB300	ISWB300	ISWB400	ISWB450	ISWB500
Longitudinal beam	ISWB250	ISMB300	ISWB300	ISWB300	ISWB350	ISMB600	ISWB600	ISWB600H
Secondary Beam	ISWB250	ISWB250	ISWB250	ISWB250	ISWB250	ISWB250	ISWB250	ISWB250
Bracings	ISA200X 100X10	ISA200X 150X10	ISA200X 150X12	ISA200X 150X18	ISA200X 200X20	ISA200X 200X25	ISA200X 200X25	ISA200X 200X25
Steel Weight	631.06kN	714.21kN	728.554kN	796.77kN	891.862kN	1204.35kN	1356.87kN	1490.77kN

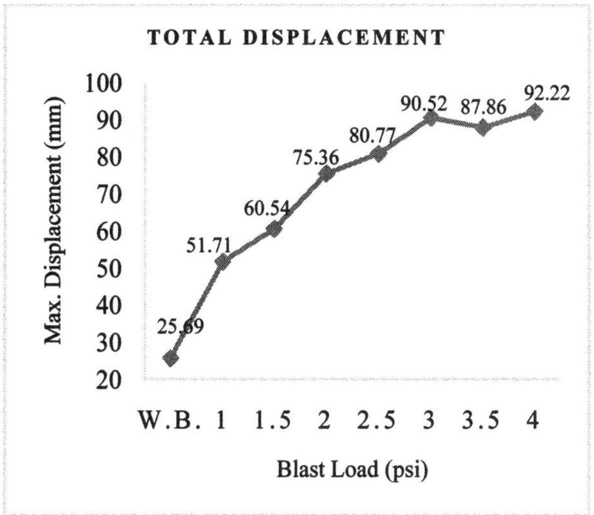

Figure 6 Maximum displacement for variable explosion

Total displacement of the structure increases with the increase in the weight of the blast on the structure. Maximum displacement in case of 4 psi is 92.224 mm which exceeds the maximum permissible limit of 90 (H/200) mm. The same is within permissible limit for 1 psi, 1.5 psi, 2 psi, 2.5 psi, 3 psi and 3.5 psi explosion.

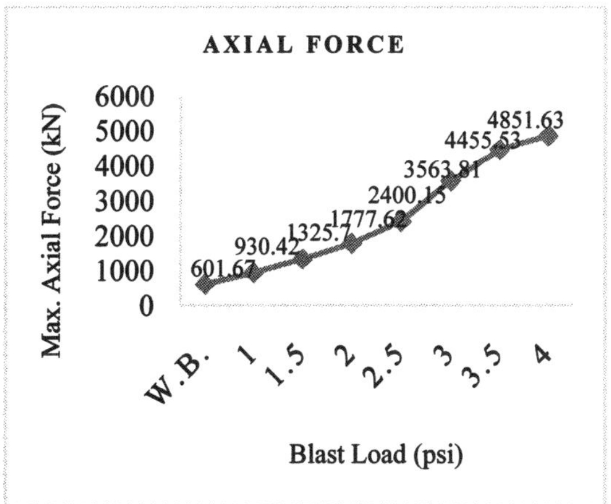

Figure 7 Maximum axial force for variable explosion

As the amount of blast load increases on the structure; to resist its effect on structure, higher section provision is necessary. Because of that, maximum axial force of the structure is increases with the increase in the weight of the blast on the structure.

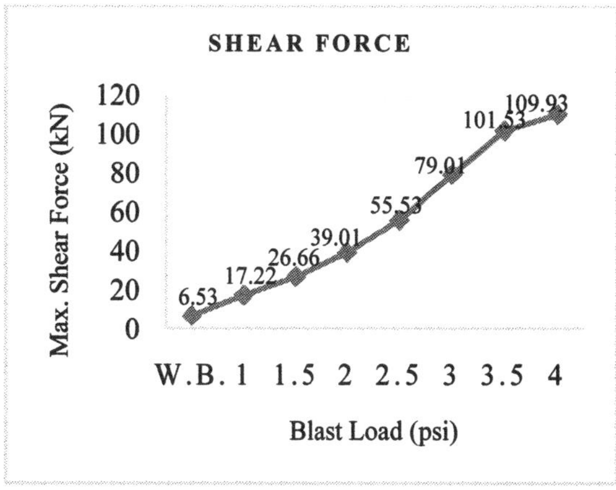

Figure 8 Maximum shear force for variable explosion

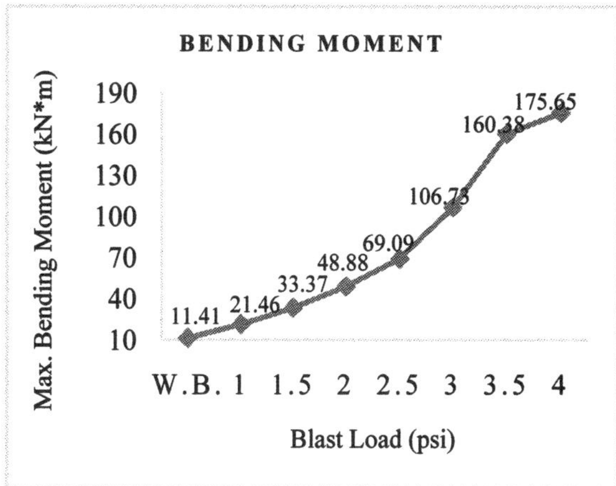

Figure 9 Maximumbending moment in Y direction for variable explosion

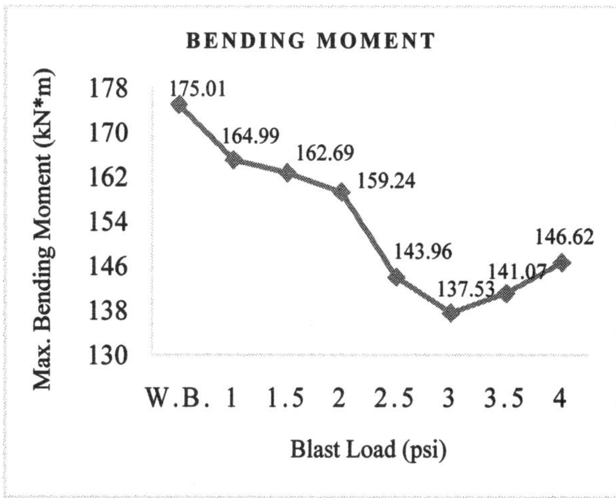

Figure 10 Maximum bending moment in Z direction for variable explosion

IV. Conclusions

The pipe rack structure having similar geometry is analyzed and designed for both with and without blast effect.

Results are proposed for both with and without blast load on pipe rack structure for parameters like maximum displacement, maximum axial force, maximums hear force and maximum bending moment. At the end of the study, total weight of the structure is summarized for different pipe rack structure to check the economical criteria.

From the analysis the following conclusions are derived:

1. After carrying out blast analysis of the pipe rack structure, result shows that critical forces are generated in the load case which contains blast load. Hence, blast forces are more dominant than general forces in the case of pipe rack structures, where blast loads are acting.
2. The percentage increase in displacement from 1 psi to 4 psi is 78.33 %.
3. The axial force, shear force and bending moment in transverse direction are 5 times, 6 times and 8 times higher as the blast pressure is increased from 1 psi to 4 psi.
4. At the end of analysis and design of pipe-rack structure exposed to blast, the results are compared with the design of pipe rack structure without blast effect. Comparatively higher values are found in various parameters like displacement, axial force, shear force and bending moment as the blast load increases on the structure. It shows that heavy sections of steel are required in the pipe rack under the explosion than the normal pipe rack structure.

References

[1] T. Ngo, P. Mendis, A. gupta and J. Ramsay (2007), "Blast Loading and Blast Effects on Structures-An Overview", EJSE Special Issue: Loading on Structures.

[2] HrvojeDraganic and Vladimir Sigmund (2012), "Blast loading On Structures", Technical Gazette, Vol. 19, pp: 643-652.

[3] ASCE (1999) – "Design of Blast resistant buildings in Petrochemical Facilities", American Society of Civil Engineers, Reston, Virginia.

[4] Ashit K. Kikani and Panchal. V. R. (2016), "Comparative study of Pipe rack structure with Modular concept and Normal Stick-Built approach using ASCE 7-02" Journal of Civil engineering and Environmental technology, Vol. 3, Issue 4.

[5] AmolUnde and Dr. Potnis, July 2013, "Blast Analysis of Structure" International journal of Engineering Research and Technology (IJERT), ISSN: 2278-0181, Vol. 2, Issue 7.

[6] IS: 4991 (1968) "Criteria for Blast Resistant Design of Structures for Explosions above Ground", Bureau of Indian standard, New Delhi.

[7] IS: 875 Part 3 (1987) "Code of Practice for Design Loads (Other than Earthquake) for Buildings and Structures", Bureau of Indian standard, New Delhi.

Seismic Response of Segmental Building using Resilient Friction Base Isolator

Yuvrajsinh H. Rathod[1], V. R. Panchal[2], D. P. Soni[3]

[1] *Post Graduate Student (Structural Engineering), M.S. Patel Department of Civil Engineering, Chandubhai S. Patel Institute of Technology, Charotar University of Science and Technology, Changa, Gujarat, India*

[2] *Professor and Head, M. S. Patel Department of Civil Engineering, Chandubhai S. Patel Institute of Technology, Charotar University of Science and Technology, Changa, Gujarat, India*

[3] *Professor, Civil Engineering Department, Sardar Vallabhai Patel Institute of Technology, Vasad, Gujarat, India*

[1]yuvi1845@gmail.com
[2]vijaypanchal.cv@charusat.ac.in
[3]devesh18@gmail.com

***Abstract*—Seismic response of segmental building with the use of Resilient Friction Base Isolator (R-FBI) under normal component of near-fault ground motions is investigated. The segmental building has 20 degrees of freedom and it is modelled as shear building. The response of segmental building is evaluated by the governing equation of motion using Newmark's method with the assumption that the variation of acceleration is linear through small time interval. To check the effectiveness of R-FBI, response of segmental building with Laminated Rubber Bearing (LRB) is compared with R-FBI. Based on the results, when segmental building is supported by R-FBI, response of segmental building is effectively reduced under near-fault ground motions.**

***Keywords* -Resilient Friction Base Isolator; Laminated Rubber Bearing; near-fault ground excitations; Base isolation; Segmental building.**

I. Introduction

Seismic design of structure is based on the concept of increasing the capacity of resistance of the structure. The effect of ground excitations can be reduced by providing braced frames, shear walls or moment-resistant frames in the structure. Although, these type of method generally result in inter storey drifts for flexible buildings and high floor accelerations for rigid buildings. Due to this, both structural and non-structural components of the building may suffer through relevant damages during the earthquake, also if the structure remains safe. This is not suitable for those type of buildings whose components are more precious or expensive than the buildings itself. There are many type of buildings or structures telecommunication centers, hospitals, fire stations, police stations are examples of facilities that contains valuable equipments and which should remain operational immediately after an earthquake shocks.

The results of an aftershocks on a structure depend on the dynamic properties of the structures and earthquake ground motions. The ductility design concept has been used over past decades for an earthquake resistant design of structures. Although, it has proved that the performance of the ductile structure during ground excitations to be undesirable and far below expectation. Based on structural concept, more effective techniques are desired to get structural safety and effectiveness against severe ground excitation.

The concept of base-isolation system is most effective alternative among all other structural control systems for earthquake engineering. Base-isolation is decoupling the building by minimum horizontal stiffness bearing between foundation and super structure. In simple words, it is a technology developed to reduce the destruction of structure during the earthquake. The natural time period of the conventional building is lower than base isolated building. Now as shown in response spectrum, this extensiveness of time period can minimize the pseudo-acceleration and hence, the earthquake generate forces in structure, but the buckling is increased.

In order to diminish above stated problems Pan et al. [1] has proposed a new concept in which superstructure is parted into several segments which contains specific storey are interconnected with vibration isolation system. Pan and Cui [2] has also studied the seismic response of various ground excitation on segmental building. Mostaghel and Khodaverdian [3] carried out work on dynamics of R-FBI to check the effectiveness of base isolation system in various conditions. Sanap et al. [4] studied the effectiveness of R-FBI system in ten storey Reinforced concrete building which is excited by four real ground motions. Lin et al. [5] has carried out numerical study to check the R-FBI system for non-uniform shear-beam structure under various conditions.

This study comprises the investigation of the seismic response of segmental building with R-FBI under the normal component of six near-field ground excitations as shown in Table I, In order to check the efficiency of R-FBI, Seismic response of segmental building with R-FBI is compared with segmental building with LRB. The response quantities of the study are the base storey displacement and absolute storey acceleration.

II. Explanation of R-FBI

R-FBI device has main components like a set of flat rings with central and peripheral rubber cores and cover plates of top and bottom. A layers of flat rings can slide with each other along the rubber cores. It is combination of friction damping and resiliency of rubber which is most advantage of this type of isolator. Rubber cores and flat rings of the system does not carry any type of vertical load. It is only deals with the sliding displacement of the system. The system provides parallel action of friction, restoring force and damping. R-FBI does not provide isolation against vertical ground motion.The bearing force of R-FBI system is,

$$F_x = c_b\dot{x}_b + k_b x_b + F_x \quad (1)$$

The paramaters of R-FBI, are (a) damping ratio ξ_b (b) friction coefficient μ and (c) isolation time period T_b. The ξ_b and T_b are evaluated from Equations (2) & (3), respectively.

$$\xi_b = \frac{c_b}{2M\omega_b} \quad (2)$$

$$T_b = 2\pi\sqrt{\frac{M}{k_b}} \quad (3)$$

where$M = (m_b + \sum_{j=i}^{N} m_j)$ is total mass of the building frequency; m_j is mass of the jth floor; and $\omega_b = \frac{2\pi}{T_b}$ is isolation.

III. Structural Modelling

The model of the segmental building as shown n Figure 1 is taken in the present investigation. The R-FBI is provided between each segment of the building and also between base and foundation of the same. The segmental building is the multi-degree-of- freedom model which is used in the seismic analysis of the building. It is modelled as a shear building, in which floors are rigid diaphragms and the axial displacement of columns can be omitted. So, only lateral displacement can be possible. For the ith storey, m_i and h_i are the lumped mass and storey height, respectively. The following formula is used to determine the lateral stiffness of the storey (k_i):

$$k_i = {12EI_j}/{h_i^3} \quad (4)$$

where I_j stands for the moment of inertia of all columns of the building at the ith level, and E represents Young's modulus. In the study of a segmental building, the isolation systems can be used as virtual storeys with a stated lateral stiffness k_{bi} and without a storey height.

D'Alembert's principle is used to initiate the equations of motion of the system. Let $x_{i(t)}$ be the horizontal deformation of the ith floor to the active base of the structure; the equations of motion can be formulated as below:

$$M\ddot{x}(t) + C\dot{x}(t) + Kx(t) = -M\{1\}\ddot{u}_g(t) \quad (5)$$

where *[M]*, *[K]*, and *[C]* are stated as mass matrices, stiffness matrices and damping matrices respectively.

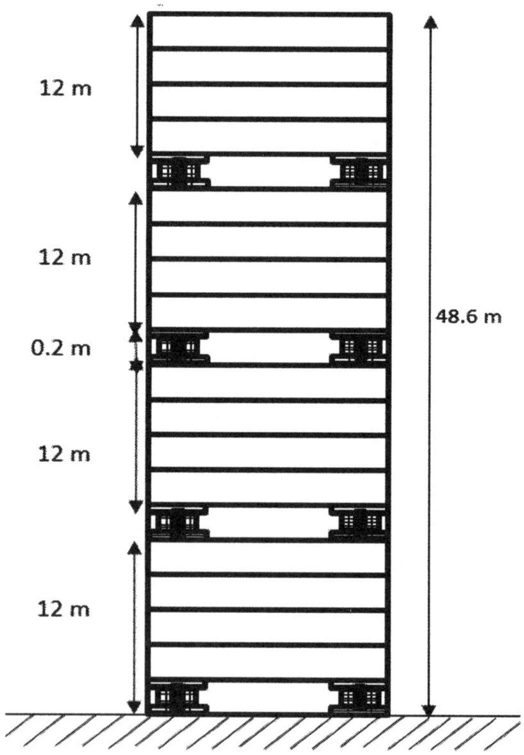

Figure 1. 16-storey segmental building isolated with R-FBI

IV. Numerical Study

Here, the building is of 16-storey with beam column frame structure. It is further organizes into four segments which are interrelated with the help of vibration isolation systems. The building is of 48.6 m height. The lateral stiffness of each segments differ with the height of the structure. It is a constant for all the storey in a segment, the stiffness of first segment is 2.4×10^9 N/m, then it minimizes to 1.29×10^9 N/m for the second segment and 6.76×10^8 N/m for the third segment, and finally becomes 3.15×10^8 N/m for the fourth segment. The lumped mass and mass of roof of each storey are 3.49×10^5 kg, and 1.39×10^5 kg respectively and the mass of base isolated raft is 2.52×10^5 kg. The modal damping ratio of the building is assumed as 5%. The each segment is of 12 m height as shown in Figure 1. Here, lateral stiffness of isolation system for base isolated building and segmental building are given in Table II (Pan and Cui [2]).

TABLE I
Description Of Near-Field Ground Excitations Utilized In This Investigation

Near-field ground excitation (Normal component)	Recording station	Time duration (sec)	Peak ground displacement (m)	Peak ground velocity (m/sec)	Peak ground acceleration(g)
Imperial Valley, California (15 October, 1979) (EQ 11)	El Centro Array #5	39.420	0.765	0.980	0.370
Imperial Valley, California (15 October, 1979) (EQ 21)	El Centro Array #7	36.900	0.491	1.130	0.460
Northridge, California (17 January, 1994) (EQ 31)	Newhall	60.000	0.381	1.190	0.720
Landers, California (28 June, 1992) (EQ 41)	Lucerne Valley	49.284	2.300	1.360	0.710
Northridge, California (17 January, 1994) (EQ 51)	Rinaldi	14.950	0.391	1.750	0.890
Northridge, California (17 January, 1994) (EQ 61)	Sylmar	60.000	0.311	1.220	0.730

TABLE II
Lateral Stiffness Of Isolation

	k_{b1} (10^8 N/m)	k_{b2} (10^8 N/m)	k_{b3} (10^8 N/m)	k_{b4} (10^8 N/m)
Segmental Building Model	1.51	2.76	0.57	3.15

V. Results and Discussion

A seismic response of segmental building isolated with R-FBI and LRB is investigated under component of near-fault ground motions.

Storey Displacement: A definite reduction in storey displacement can be observed in the segmental building using R-FBI system over LRB system for near-fault ground motions. Also, tabular comparison of maximum story displacement for both segmental building is shown in Table III. Average reduction of storey displacement is 57.14 % noticed in segmental building in near-fault ground motions. Plot of all maximum storey displacement for both the system are shown in Figure 2.

Storey Acceleration: Acceleration of segmental building using R-FBI and LRB is more or less similar at the base of the structure under near fault ground motion. Overall increase of acceleration is seen in the segmental building using R-FBI over LRB. Plot of absolute peak acceleration (m) for both the system is shown in Figure 3. Tabular comparison of peak acceleration of R-FBI system and LRB system is shown in Table IV. Average of storey acceleration is 59.25 % noticed in segmental building in near-fault ground motions.

Hysteretic Damping: Plots of hysteretic damping of R-FBI and LRB in segmental buildings are shown in Figure 4 under near-fault ground motions.

TABLE III
ISOLATOR DISPLACEMENT OF SEGMENTAL BUILDING USING R-FBI AND LRB AT BASE LEVEL

Type	Earthquake	R-FBI(mm)	LRB(mm)	Percentage %
Near faultground motion	EQ11	19.11	68.01	71.91
	EQ21	31.95	77.32	58.68
	EQ31	40.01	85.42	53.16
	EQ41	27.12	69.36	60.91
	EQ51	58.03	90.35	35.77
	EQ61	31.47	83.71	62.40
	Average			57.14

TABLE IV
TOP ABSOLUTE ACCELERATION OF SEGMENTAL BUILDING USING R-FBI AND LRB

Type	Earthquake	R-FBI (g)	LRB (g)	Percentage %
Near faultground motion	EQ11	0.81	0.42	90.71
	EQ21	0.79	0.46	72.08
	EQ31	0.98	0.75	30.54
	EQ41	1.02	0.65	57.51
	EQ51	1.36	0.77	76.99
	EQ61	0.79	0.62	27.68
	Average			59.25

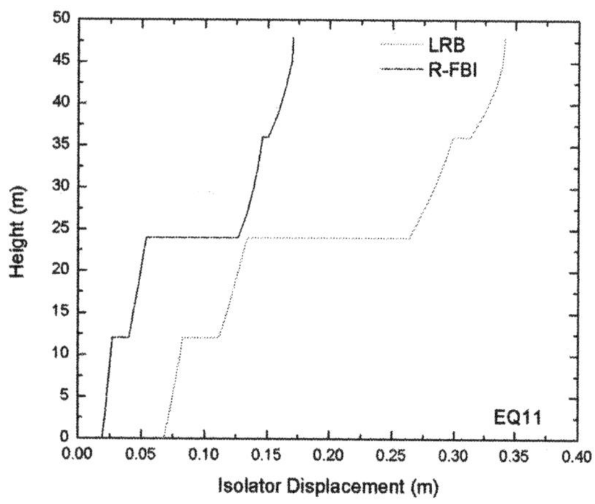

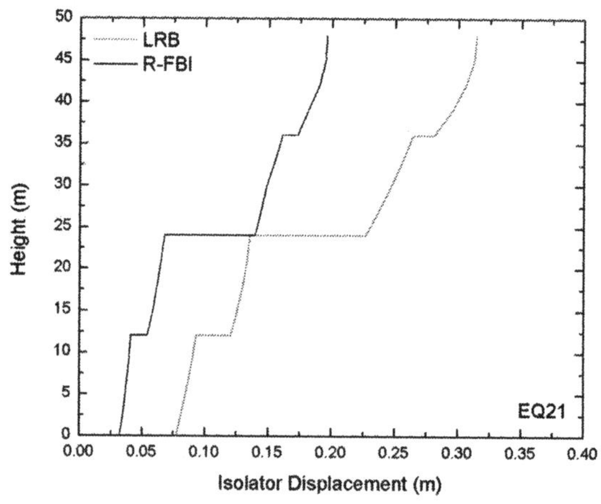

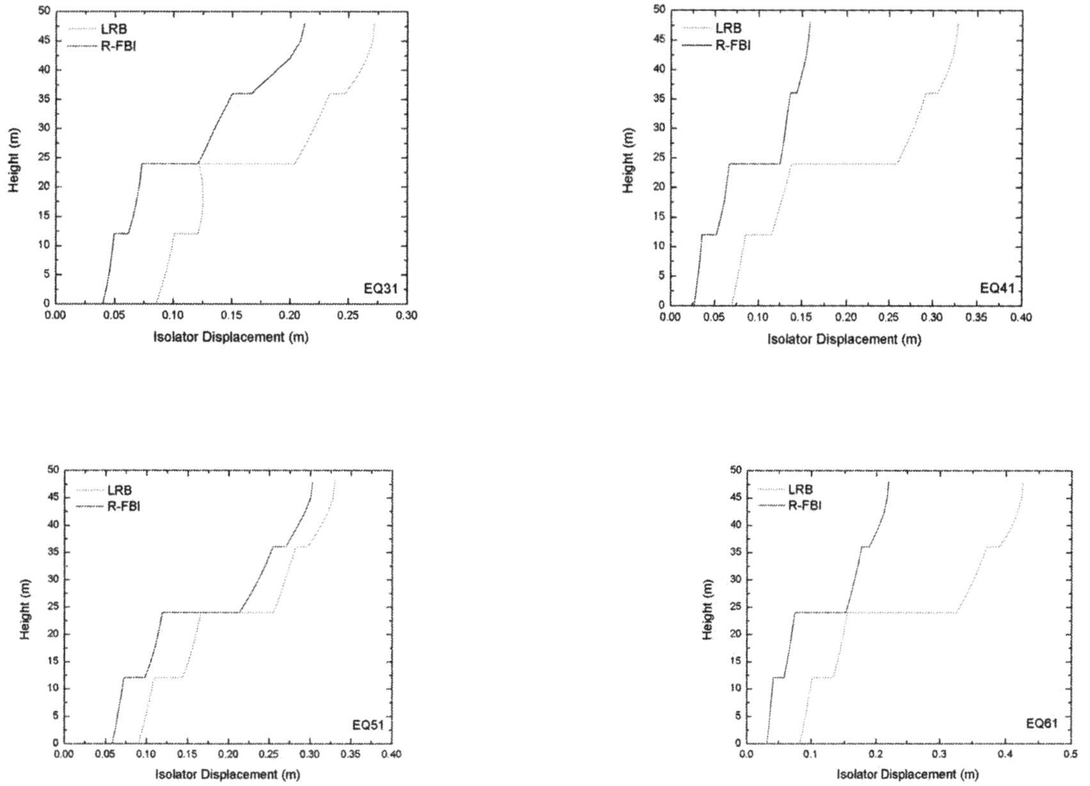

Figure 2 Comparison of isolator displacement of segmental building using R-FBI and LRB at base level

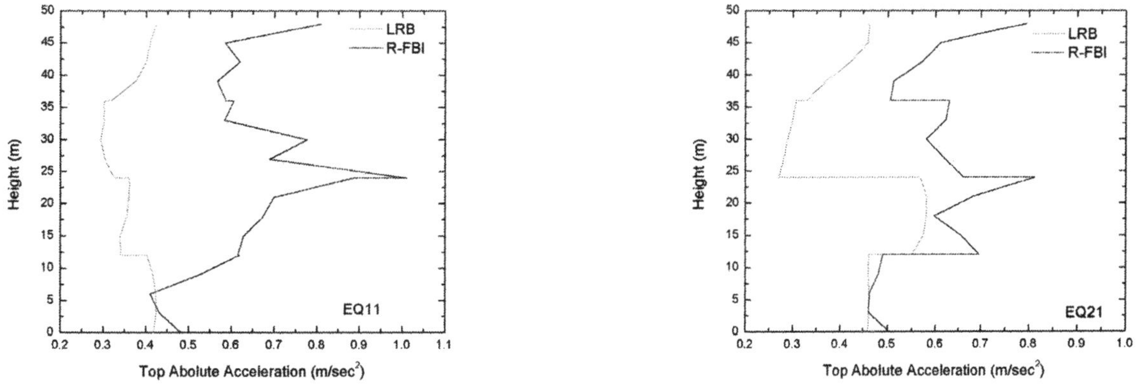

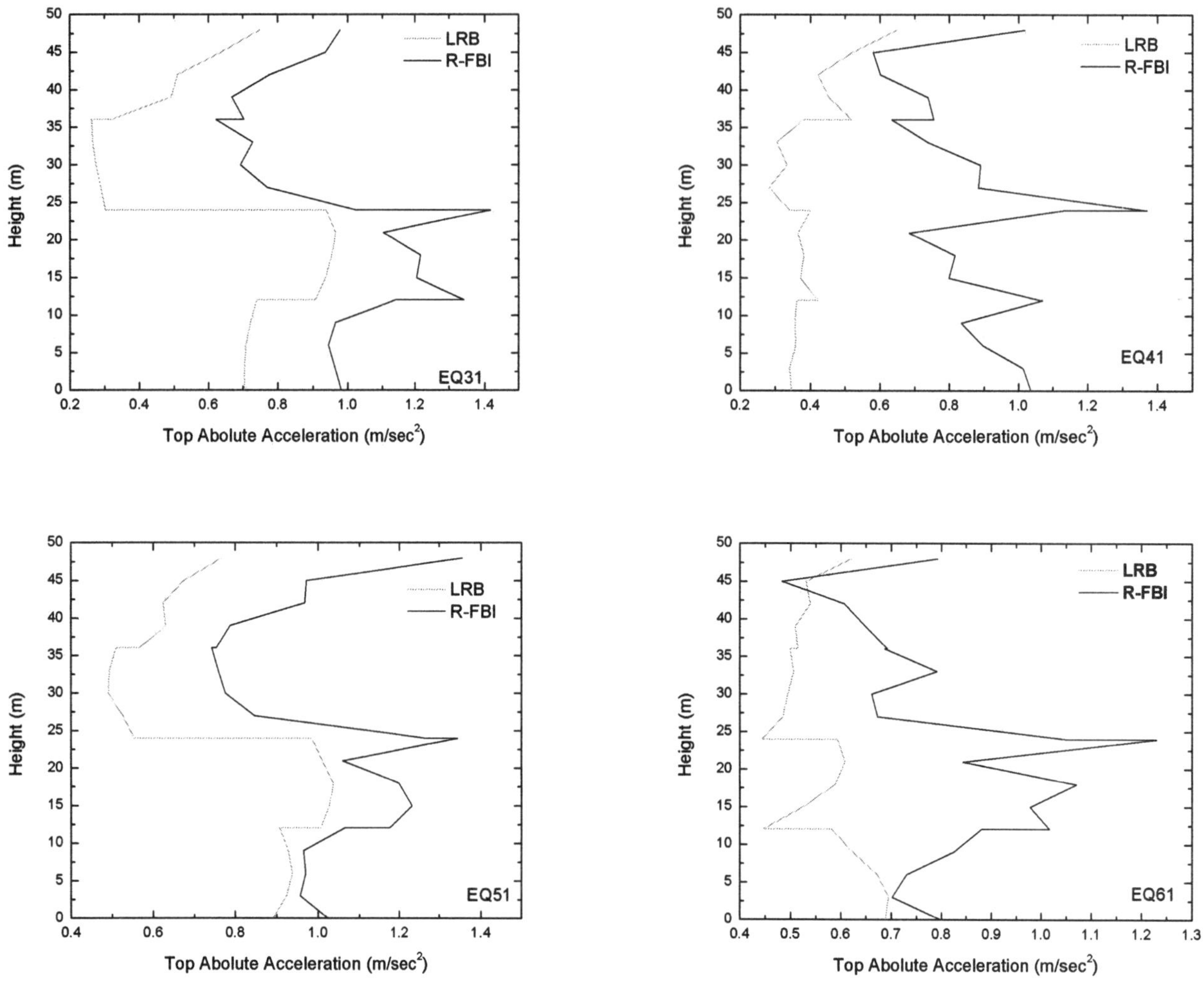

Figure 3 Comparison of top absolute acceleration of segmental building using R-FBI and LRB

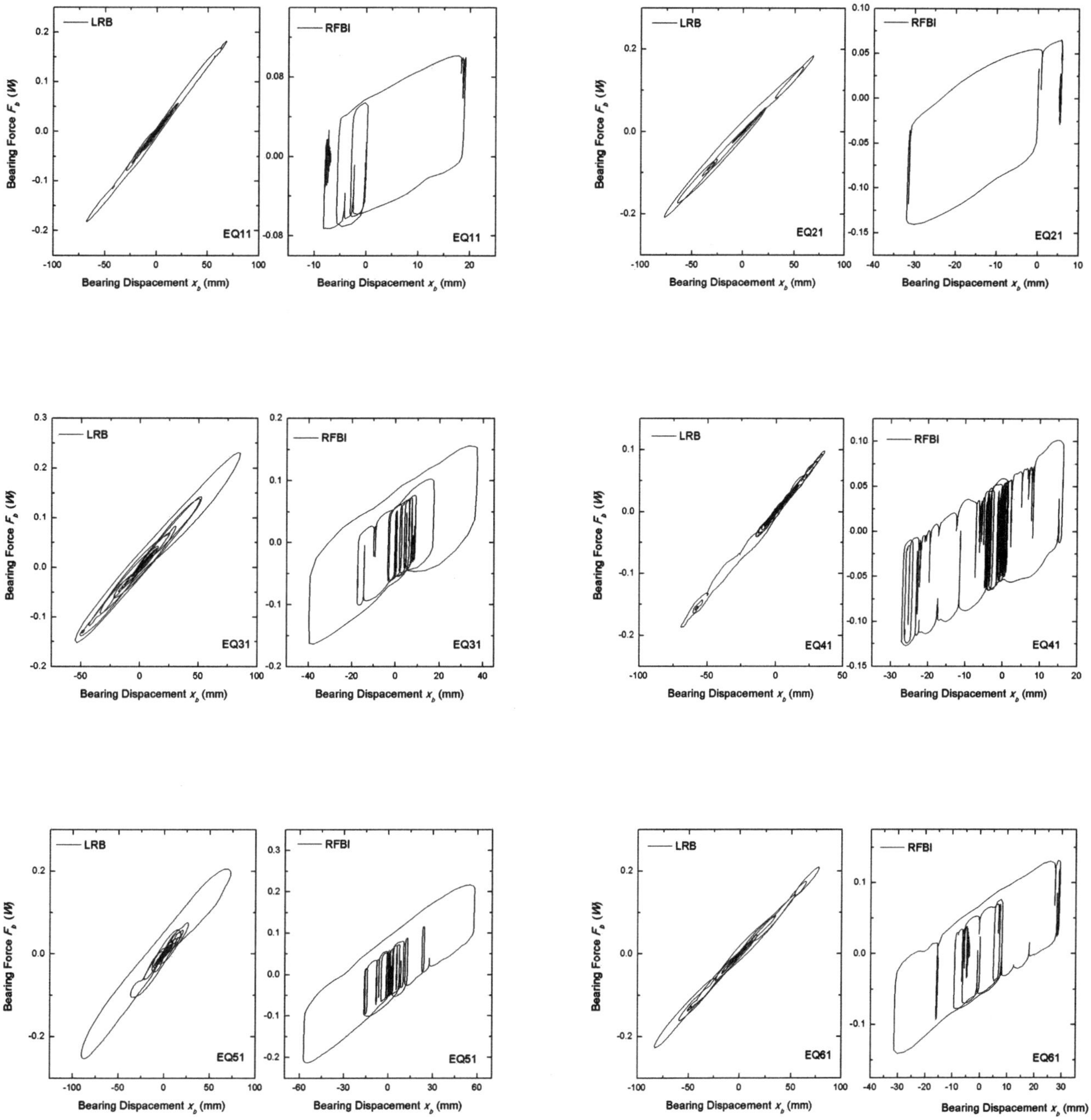

Figure 4 Hysteresis loop of R-FBI and LRB

VI. Conclusions

The segmental building has been analyzed by providing resilient friction base isolator and laminated rubber bearing at base and each segment under the near-field ground excitation. In order to check the efficiency of segmental building with isolation system, the seismic response obtained from the R-FBI system is compared with LRB system. In the above study, following conclusions are made:

1. A definite advantage of reduction in base displacement is obtained in the segmental building using R-FBI system over LRB for near fault ground motions.
2. Peak acceleration of segmental building using R-FBI system is at found more as compared to LRB under near fault ground motions.

References

[1] Pan, T.C., Ling, S.F. and Cui, W. (1995) "Seismic Response of Segmental Building" Earthquake Engineering and Structural Dynamics, vol. 24, pp. 1039-1048.

[2] Pan, T.C. and Cui, W. (1998) "Response of Segmental Buildings to Random Seismic Motions" ISET Journal of Earthquake Technology, vol. 35, pp. 105-112.

[3] Mostaghel, N. And Khodaverdian, M. (1987) "Dynamics of Resilient-Friction Base Isolator (R-FBI)" Earthquake Engineering and Structural Dynamics, Vol. 15, pp. 379-390.

[4] Sanap, S. B., Jadhao, P. D. and Dumne S. M. (2014) "Seismic Response Analysis of Isolated Building with Resilient Friction Base Isolator" International Journal of Scientific & Engineering Research, vol. 5, pp. 288-294.

[5] Lin Su., Goodarz, A. and Tadjbakhsh I. G. (1989) "Performance of Sliding Resilient-Friction Base-Isolation System" Journal of Structural Engineering, vol. 117, pp. 165-181.

Double Polynomial Friction Pendulum System for Seismic Isolation of Three Span Continuous Deck Bridge

Srushti S. Patel[1], V. R. Panchal[2], D.P. Soni[3], N. H. Chauhan[4]

[1] *Post Graduate Student (Structural Engineering), M.S. Patel Department of Civil Engineering, Chandubhai S. Patel Institute of Technology, Charotar University of Science and Technology, Changa, Gujarat, India*

[2] *Professor and Head, M. S. Patel Department of Civil Engineering, Chandubhai S. Patel Institute of Technology, Charotar University of Science and Technology, Changa, Gujarat, India*

[3] *Professor, Civil Engineering Department, Sardar Vallabhai Patel Institute of Technology, Vasad, Gujarat, India*

[4] *Assistant Professor, M. S. Patel Department of Civil Engineering, Chandubhai S. Patel Institute of Technology, Charotar University of Science and Technology, Changa, Gujarat, India*

[1]srushtipatel598@gmail.com
[2]vijaypanchal.cv@charusat.ac.in
[3]devesh18@gmail.com
[4]nehachauhan.cv@charusat.ac.in

***Abstract* - In this study, a three-span continuous deck bridge is seismically isolated by the Double Polynomial Friction Pendulum Isolator (DPFPI). Newmark's linear acceleration method is used to solvethe governing equations of motion of the bridge. In order to investigate the behaviour of the DPFPI, the response is obtained for six near-fault earthquake ground excitations. For the purpose of study, piers and deck of bridge are assumed as rigid. In order to check efficiency of DPFPI, seismic responses of the bridge isolated with DPFPI and Double Variable Frequency Pendulum Isolator (DVFPI) are compared. It is found that DVFPI is more efficient than DPFPI for seismic isolation of bridge. It is observed that efficiency of DPFPI can be achieved maximum by designing the topsurface with higher initial stiffness as compared to that of the bottom surface stiffness and keeping similar coefficient of friction for both top and bottom sliding surfaces, respectively.**

***Keywords* - DPFPI; DVFPI; continuous deck bridge; earthquake ground motions; base isolation.**

I. INTRODUCTION

Bridges are important for transportation network, and their collapse during an earthquake will affect lives of people as well as causes economic loss. And hence Base isolation technique has gained wide acceptance while designing of a bridge to ensure safety against the devastating effects of earthquake.

Kunde and Jangid [1] carried out various numerical and experimental studies which showed that seismic isolation of bridge is an effective technique for minimizing the effects of earthquake on bridges. Kunde and Jangid[2] studied mathematical models of bridge isolated by different seismic isolation techniques. They conducted parametric study considering different parameters like flexibility and rigidity of piers and deck. From the parametric study, they concluded that the isolated bridge having bridge deck and piers assumed as a rigid body is the most efficient. Panchal and Jangid [3] studied the seismic behaviour of bridge isolated by Variable Curvature Friction Pendulum System (VCFPS) and investigated influence of near-fault ground motions for base isolation of deck bridge. Soni et al. [4] conducted numerical study to find the effectiveness of DVFPI for seismic isolation of multi-span bridge under bi-lateral earthquake ground motions. Lu et al. [5] proposed and defined PFPI and conducted theoretical as well as experimental study for seismic isolation of building structure with PFPI which has variable stiffness. Saha et al. [6] studied the effect of six bi-lateral earthquake ground motions on benchmark highway bridge when isolated with PFPIs as well as conducted a parametric study to compare the efficiency of Friction Pendulum System (FPS) and Polynomial Friction Pendulum Isolator (PFPI) for base isolation. From this review, it is evident that few attempts have been made to study the seismic behaviour of bridges with isolators having variable stiffness nature.

To address above concern, the seismic response of bridge isolated with DPFPI is studied under six near-fault earthquake ground excitations. The specific objectives of the present study may be summarized as: (i) to study the performance of bridge isolated with DPFPI under near-fault ground excitations, (ii) to compare the seismic response of bridges isolated with DPFPI and DVFPI and (iii) to investigate the influence of crucial parameters on the seismic response of the bridge isolated with DPFPI by conducting a parametric study.

II. CONCEPT OF DPFPI

In FPS system, the major problem observed is of resonance and hence to solve this problem PFPI is developed [5]. The only difference in PFPI and FPS is that in PFPI, the sliding surface has been made a variable curvature while in FPS, sliding surface has a constant curvature.

The DPFPI consists of an articulated slider between two varying curvature sliding surfaces. Since sliding in DPFPI can happen on both surfaces, capacity of the DPFPI to absorb displacement is double than that of the PFPI. This main attribute of DPFPI makes it possible to overcome large sliding displacements that may occur due to severe earthquake ground excitations. Also, the designer can enhance the performance of DPFPI by varying coefficients of friction at top and bottom sliding surfaces separately as well as varying initial time periods of both the sliding surfaces respectively.

In DPFPI as similar to that of PFPI, following polynomial function is used to define the geometry of the sliding surface [5].

$$y'(x) = \frac{u_r(x)}{P} = ax^5 + cx^3 + ex \tag{2.1}$$

$$y''(x) = \frac{k_r(x)}{P} = 5ax^4 + 3cx^2 + e \tag{2.2}$$

$$a = \frac{-k_0 + k_1}{5(D_1)^4} c = \frac{2(-k_0+k_1)}{3(D_1)^2} e = k_0 \tag{2.3}$$

where $y'(x)$ and $y''(x)$ are normalized restoring force and normalized isolator stiffness, respectively, with respect to vertical load P,$u_r(x)$ and $k_r(x)$ are restoring force and restoring stiffness, respectively. a, c and e are polynomial coefficients, $k_0$is the normalized initial stiffness$x = 0$,k_1 is normalized isolated stiffness at $x = D_1$and D_1 is defined as critical isolator drift.

The values of three polynomial coefficients a, c and e are 81.25, -10.83 and 0.65, respectively and value for critical isolator drift D_1 is equal to 0.2 m.

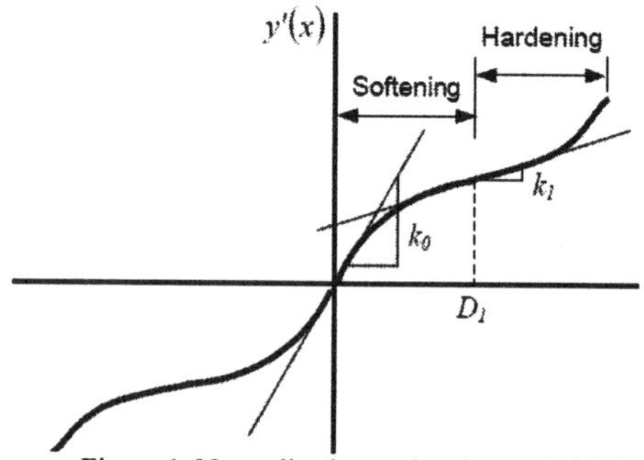

Figure 1: Normalized restoring force $y'(x)$ [5]

In this type of isolator, there are two process parts in displacement which is shown in Figure 1. The softening and hardening sections were aimed to control the structural acceleration and isolator drift, respectively.

III. GOVERNING EQUATION OF MOTION

The governing equation of motion for bridge modeled as two degree of freedom under single horizontal component of near fault ground excitation is expressed by:

$$m_d\left(\ddot{u_d} + \ddot{u_g}\right) + F_{b_1} = 0 \tag{3.1}$$

$$m_s\left(\ddot{u_s} + \ddot{u_g}\right) - F_{b_1} + F_{b_2} = 0 \tag{3.2}$$

where m_d is deck mass of bridge,m_s is mass of slider, $\ddot{u_d}$ is deck acceleration relative to ground,u_s is acceleration of slider relative to ground, $\ddot{u_g}$ is ground acceleration and F_{b_1}& F_{b_2} are the isolator forces acting at the top and bottom sliding surfaces respectively.

IV. MODELING AND IDEALIZING

Figure 2 represents the mathematical model and configuration of the three-span continuous bridge isolated with DPFPI at abutments and piers.

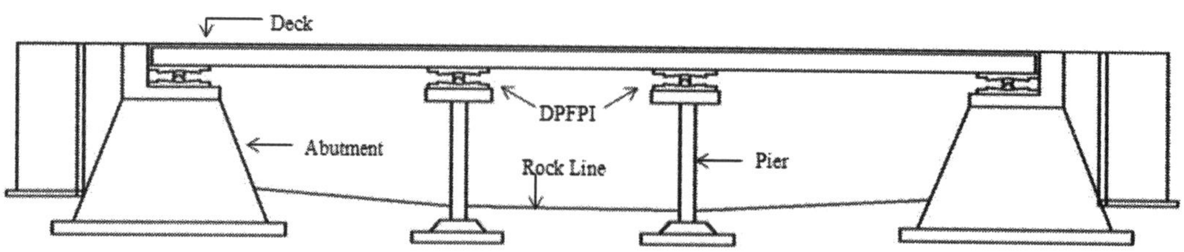

(a)

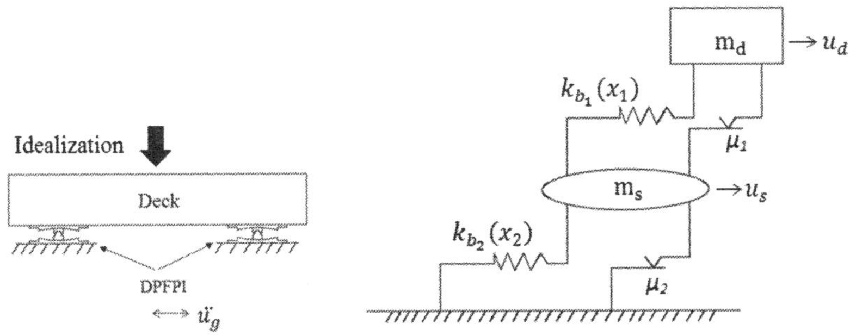

(b) (c)

Figure 2:(a) Configuration (b) idealization and (c) mathematical model ofthree span deck bridge isolated by the DPFPI

Following are the assumptions for the analysis of bridge:

1. The bridge piers and deck are assumed as rigid. This is based on the fact that in the isolated bridge, the flexibility is mainly concentrated in the isolation systems and bridge piers & deck behave almost as a rigid body.
2. The piers of the bridge are taken as rigidly fixed at the foundation level.
3. The bridge is rested on hard soil.
4. The DPFPI provided above the abutments and piers have the same dynamic characteristics.
5. Contribution of horizontal component of earthquake ground excitations is very much higher than that of vertical component. Hence, the impact of the vertical component may be neglected.

TABLE I
PROPERTIES OF BRIDGE

Properties	Pier	Deck
Length/height (m)	8	90
Young's modulus of elasticity (N/m^2)	20.67×10^9	20.67×10^9
Mass density (kg/m^3)	2.4×10^3	2.4×10^3
Moment of inertia (m^4)	0.64	2.08
Cross-sectional area (m^2)	4.09	3.57

V. COMPARATIVE STUDY

For the present study a three-span continuous deck bridge is considered. Detailed properties of bridge are shown in Table I [3].

Details of earthquake ground excitations considered for the study are shown in Table II.

TABLE II
CHARACTERISTICS OF EARTHQUAKES IN THE STUDY

Near-Fault Ground Excitations	PGD (cm)	PGV (cm/s)	PGA (g)
Imperial Valley, 1979 (Array #5)	76.5	98	0.37
Imperial Valley, 1979 (Array #7)	49.1	113	0.46
Northridge, 1994 (Newhall)	38.1	119	0.72
Landers, 1992 (Lucerne Valley)	230	136	0.71
Northridge, 1994 (Rinaldi)	39.1	175	0.89
Northridge, 1994 (Sylmar)	31.1	122	0.73

The behaviour of DPFPI is observed for four cases. Friction coefficient and geometry of isolator is selected such that initial combined time period T_c and equivalent friction μ_c for each case remains same. $T_c$and $\mu_c$of the DPFPI are calculated by:

$$T_c = \sqrt{T_1^2 + T_2^2}\mu_c = \frac{\mu_1 T_1^2 + \mu_2 T_2^2}{T_1^2 + T_2^2} \quad (5.1)$$

where T_1 and T_2 are the initial time period and μ_1 and μ_2 are the friction coefficient of top and bottom sliding surfaces, respectively.

TABLE III
PROPERTIES OF THE DPFPI DESIGN CASES

Cases	T_1 (sec)	T_2 (sec)	T_c (sec)	μ_1	μ_2	μ_c
A	1.000	2.000	2.236	0.032	0.040	0.036
B	1.580	1.580	2.236	0.036	0.036	0.036
C	1.580	1.580	2.236	0.032	0.040	0.036
D	1.000	2.000	2.236	0.036	0.036	0.036

VI. RESULTS AND DISCUSSION

The time histories of absolute deck acceleration, base shear and isolator displacement of three span deck bridge isolated with DPFPI and DVFPI under 1979 Imperial Valley (Array#5) Earthquake for the four DPFPI design cases are shown in Figure 3. Also as evident from the figure, there is a noticeable decrease in displacement of isolator of bridge isolated with DPFPI as compared to DVFPI.

The variation of base shear with respect to isolator displacement is known as hysteresis loop. Hysteresis loop of DPFPI and DVFPI subjected to 1979 Imperial Valley (Array#5) Earthquake are shown in Figure 4. The area of this loop represents the amount of energy dissipation. Hence, from this figure, it can be concluded that amount of energy dissipation is higher in case of DVFPI than that of DPFPI

The numerical values of peak responses of the bridge isolated by DPFPI and DVFPI under six near fault earthquake ground excitations are mentioned in Table IV. It is worth noting that isolator displacement of bridge isolated with DPFPI is reduced but at a cost of increase in pier base shear as compared to that of the bridge isolated by DVFPI.

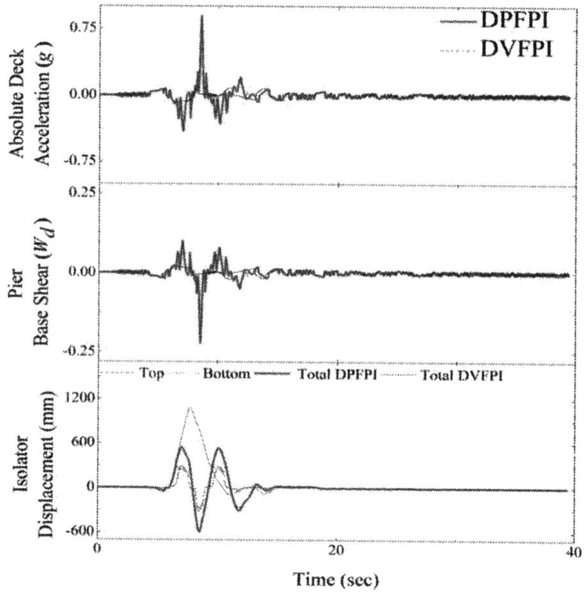

(a)

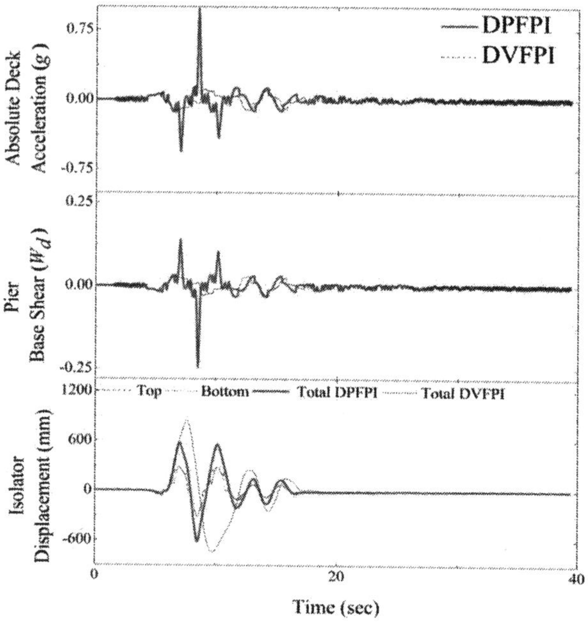

(b)

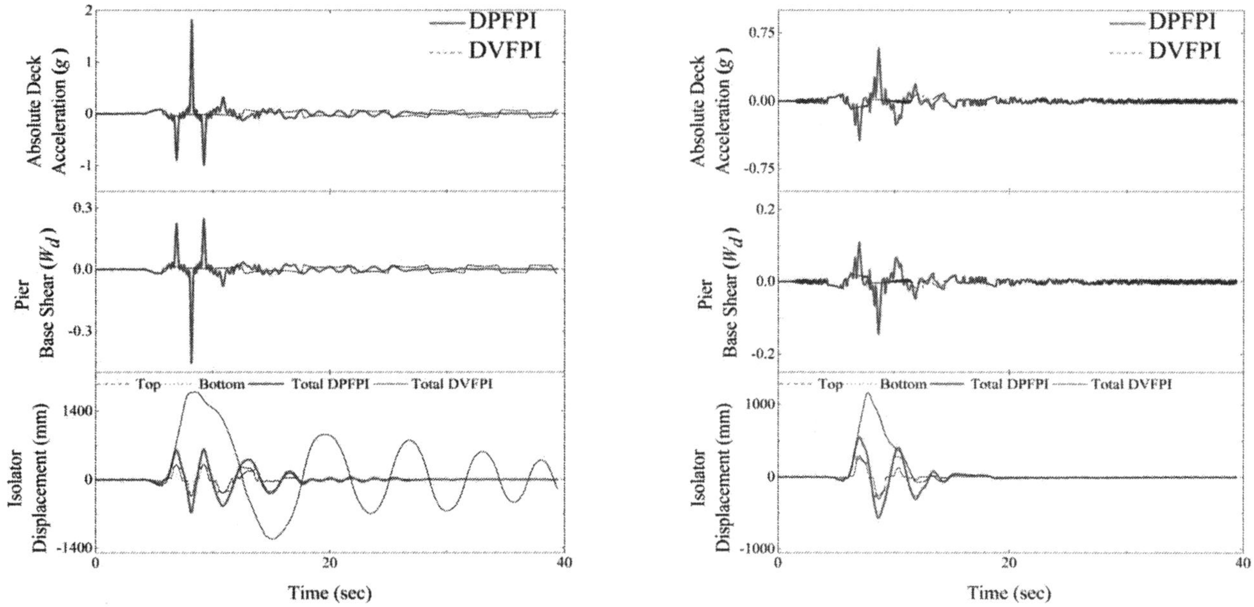

(c) (d)

Figure 3: Time Variation of absolute deck acceleration, pier base shear and isolator displacement at pier and abutments of the bridge isolated by DPFPI and DVFPI under 1979 Imperial Valley (Array#5) Earthquake (a)Case-A: $T_1 < T_2$, $\mu_1 < \mu_2$, (b) Case-B: $T_1 = T_2$, $\mu_1 = \mu_2$, (c) Case-C: $T_1 = T_2$, $\mu_1 < \mu_2$ and (d) Case-D:($T_1 < T_2$, $\mu_1 = \mu_2$)

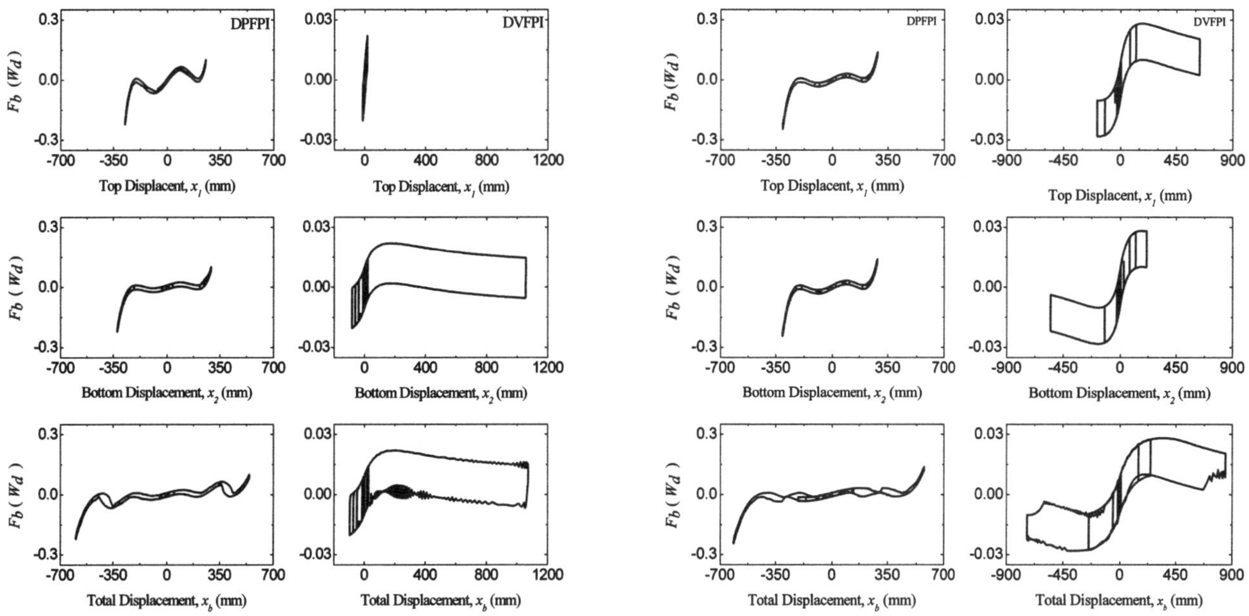

(a) (b)

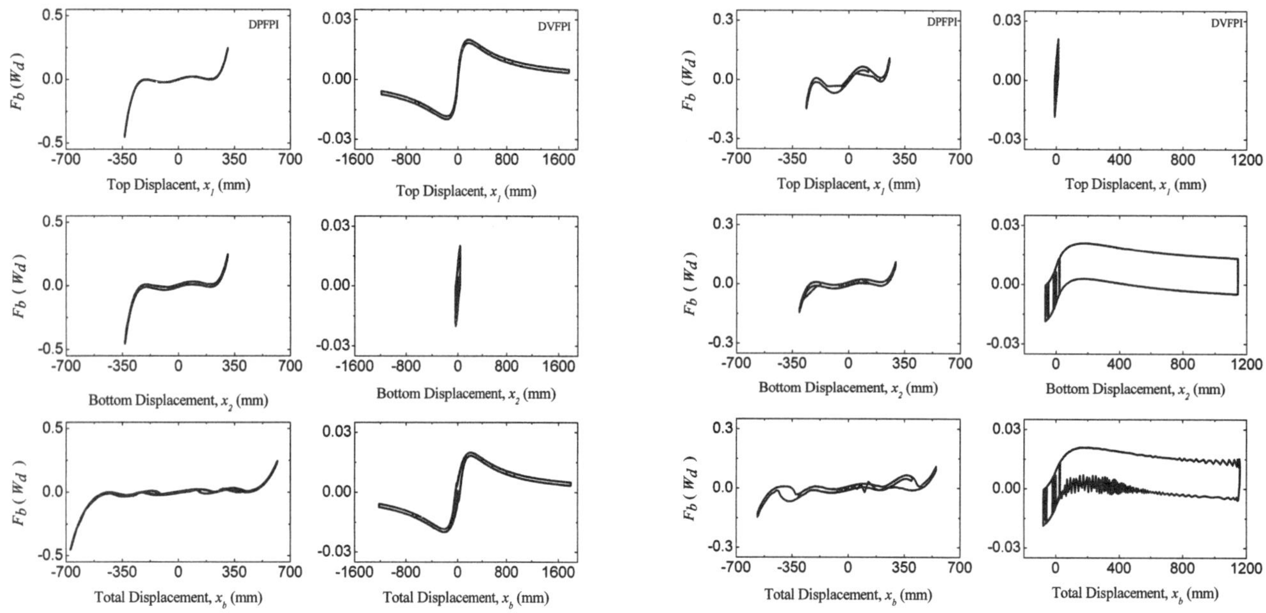

(c) (d)

Figure 4: Decomposed & overall force-displacement loop of the bridge isolated by DPFPI and DVFPI under 1979 Imperial Valley (Array#5) Earthquake (a) Case-A: $T_1 < T_2$, $\mu_1 < \mu_2$, (b) Case-B: $T_1 = T_2$, $\mu_1 = \mu_2$, (c) Case-C: $T_1 = T_2$, $\mu_1 < \mu_2$ and (d) Case-D:($T_1 < T_2$, $\mu_1 = \mu_2$)

TABLE IV

PEAK RESPONSES QUANTITIES OF BRIDGE ISOLATED BY DVFPI AND DPFPI

Earthquake	Case	Deck Acceleration (*g*)		Base Shear (W_d)		Isolator Displacement (mm)	
		DVFPI	DPFPI	DVFPI	DPFPI	DVFPI	DPFPI
1979 Imperial Valley (Array #5)	A	0.09	0.89	0.02	0.22	1072.50	597.77
	B	0.11	0.98	0.03	0.24	846.73	605.09
	C	0.08	1.82	0.02	0.45	1793.30	671.92
	D	0.08	0.58	0.02	0.15	1159.20	567.57
1979 Imperial Valley (Array #7)	A	0.09	0.98	0.02	0.24	796.20	605.09
	B	0.11	1.62	0.03	0.40	1002.50	659.99
	C	0.08	2.07	0.02	0.52	907.41	685.21
	D	0.08	0.80	0.02	0.20	818.36	589.75
1994 Northridge (Newhall)	A	0.09	0.26	0.02	0.07	382.67	361.61
	B	0.11	0.13	0.03	0.03	473.60	352.51
	C	0.08	0.51	0.02	0.13	1037.70	569.80
	D	0.09	0.26	0.02	0.07	381.42	354.49
1992 Landers (Lucerne Valley)	A	0.09	0.76	0.02	0.19	1949.50	585.75
	B	0.11	1.07	0.03	0.27	1564.30	624.00
	C	0.08	1.48	0.02	0.37	8759.40	652.63
	D	0.08	0.70	0.02	0.17	2138.80	579.98

Contd...

1994 Northridge (Rinaldi)	A	0.09	0.26	0.02	0.07	493.28	466.68
	B	0.11	0.13	0.03	0.03	486.04	481.01
	C	0.08	0.40	0.02	0.10	594.28	554.81
	D	0.08	0.27	0.02	0.07	506.91	477.16
1994 Northridge (Sylmar)	A	0.09	1.89	0.02	0.47	450.54	660.84
	B	0.11	0.31	0.03	0.08	585.48	536.32
	C	0.08	0.22	0.02	0.06	587.32	520.40
	D	0.08	1.73	0.02	0.43	460.90	652.82

VII. Conclusions

The bridge isolated with DPFPI is analyzed to determine seismic response under six different near fault ground motions. To examine the effectiveness of DPFPI, parametric study is carried out and seismic response quantities of DPFPI and DVFPI are compared.

From the study following conclusions are derived:

1. DVFPI is more efficient than DPFPI for seismic isolation of bridge.
2. Performance of DPFPI can be optimized by designing both the sliding surfaces with similar coefficient and higher initial stiffness of top surface as compared to that of bottom surface.
3. In bridge isolated with DPFPI, isolator displacement is reduced, and base shear is increased as compared to bridge isolated with DVFPI.
4. The total amount of energy dissipation is higher in case of bridge isolated with DVFPI than that of bridge isolated with DPFPI.

References

[1] Kunde, M. C. and Jangid, R. S. (2003), 'Seismic Behavior of Isolated Bridges: A State-of-the-art review', Electronic Journal of Structural Engineering, Vol. 3, pp. 140-170.

[2] Kunde, M. C. and Jangid, R. S. (2006), 'Effects of Pier and Deck Flexibility on the Seismic Response of Isolated Bridges', Journal of Bridge Engineering, Vol.11, pp. 109-121.

[3] Panchal, V. R. and Jangid, R. S. (2008), 'Seismic Isolation of Bridge Using Variable Curvature Friction Pendulum System', The14th World Conference on Earthquake Engineering, Beijing, China.

[4] Soni, D. P., Mistry, B. B. and Panchal, V. R. (2011), 'Seismic Isolation of Bridges with Variable Frequency Pendulum Isolator', Advances in Structural Engineering, Vol.15, pp. 185-203.

[5] Lu, L., Lee, T., Juang, S. and Yeh, S. (2013) 'Polynomial friction pendulum isolators (PFPIs) for building floor isolation: An experimental and theoretical study', Engineering Structures, Vol. 56, pp. 970-982.

[6] Saha, A., Saha, P. and Patro, S. (2017) 'Polynomial friction pendulum isolators (PFPIs) for seismic performance control of benchmark highway bridge', Earthquake Engineering and Engineering Vibration, Vol. 16, pp. 827-84.

Structural Behavior of Four Legged Transmission Line Tower Under Tornado Loading

Darshankumar R. Rana[1], V. R. Panchal[2]

[1] *Post Graduate Student (Structural Engineering), M. S. Patel Department of Civil Engineering, Chandubhai S. Patel Institute of Technology, Charotar University of Science and Technology, Changa, Gujarat, India*

[2] *Professor and Head,M. S. Patel Department of Civil Engineering, Chandubhai S. Patel Institute of Technology, Charotar University of Science and Technology, Changa, Gujarat, India*

[1]18merana@gmail.com
[2]vijaypanchal.cv@charusat.ac.in.

***Abstract*— Transmission line towers are generally used to carry and supply electricity from one place to another. As per records, out of total failure of tower, 60-80% of failure occurs because of High Intensity Wind Events such as tornado. Because of that, study of structural behaviour of transmission line tower under tornado loading is essential. In present study, a Computational Fluid Dynamics (CFD) model is developed using commercial program ANSYS Fluent to obtain wind data associated with tornado. A four legged suspension transmission line tower is modelled and studied under two sets of wind data of tornado in form of CFD wind data and wind velocity time history in STAAD Pro V8i. A comparison is made between the behaviour of tower under CFD wind data and wind velocity time history. The nodal displacement of transmission line tower at top node due to CFD wind data is found more than wind velocity time history. This difference in displacement could be due to the fact that analysis using CFD wind data considers loads on conductors and maximum value of velocity component.**

***Keywords*—ANSYS Fluent; Computational Fluid Dynamics;Structural Behaviour; Tornado; Transmission Line Tower.**

I. Introduction

Electricity is one of most important gifts which science has given to mankind. Electrical energy is one of the simplest type of energy as it is comparatively easy to transform in to other form of energy and distribute as well as preserve. This electricity is transmitted using two approach either overhead transmission lines or underground cables. Transmission line tower became most convenient option for distribution of electricity. Transmission line towers generally consist of 28 to 42 % of the cost of the transmission line which represents the importance of them. Failure of transmission line tower leads to economical as well as social damages. The high wind events such as tornado is one of main reasons of failure of transmission line tower. Because of that, study of the structural behaviour of transmission line tower under tornado loading is important.

There have been few studies on response of transmission line tower under high intensity events. Savory et al. [1] modelled tornado and microburst-induced wind loading to study nature of failure of a lattice transmission tower and checked the effects of the path of the event relative to tower. Ahmad and Ansari [2] studied the response of transmission line tower under tornado loads with help of STAAD pro software. The velocity and force time histories generated using Wen's formula were applied at different levels of tower and they observed number of mode shapes of tower and failure of tower. Hamada and Damatty [3] studied the behaviour of guyed transmission line tower under tornado loading which was obtained from a Computational Fluid Dynamics (CFD) model and they investigated variation of internal forces in tower members with respect to location of tornado.

In present study, a four legged suspension transmission line tower is modeled and analyzed under two types of wind data set of tornado. A CFD model is developed using commercial program ANSYS Fluent. This model is used to obtain wind data associated with tornado. The analysis of tower is carried out to obtain the response of transmission line tower under tornado loading using STAAD Pro. The same transmission line tower is analyzed under wind velocity time history wind data which was used by Ahmad and Ansari [2]. The comparison between these two analysed data has been made to study behaviour of tower under tornado.

II. Detailing of Tower

Figure 1 shows geometry of 400 kV four legged transmission line tower considered in the study. The total height of the transmission line tower is taken 38 m and width is taken 8 m after considering all required clearances and wind span length of tower is assumed as 400 m which was used by Panchal et al.[4].

Figure 1. Geometry of Transmission Line Tower

III. CFD Model

The domain used for the simulation of tornado is based on Ward-type Tornado Vortex Chamber (TVC). Figure 2 shows domain which is used for tornado simulation and different surface of domain.

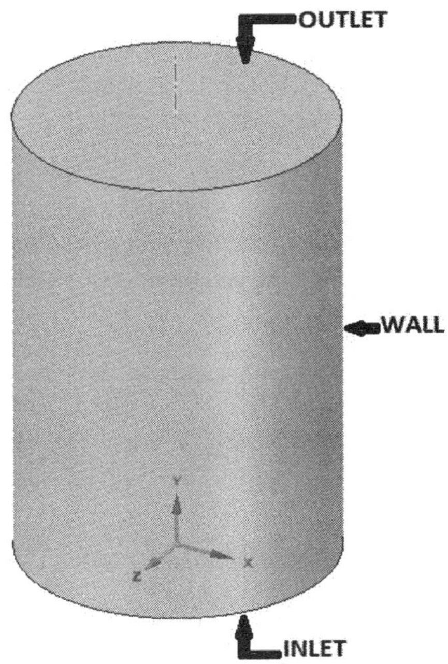

Figure 2. Used Domain and Surfaces of Domain

These surfaces of domain have different boundary conditions such as Enhance No Slip Wall function which is assumed for the walls. In this simulation, User Defined Function (UDF) is used. Inlet surface has a velocity-inlet boundary condition. With the help of UDF, the radial and tangential velocities are defined as well as the axial velocity is assumed as zero. The values of Turbulence Intensity (TI) at inlet surface and Turbulence Viscosity Ratio (TVR) are assumed as 10% and 10, respectively. The value of velocity is calculated with the help of same equations which were used by Natarajan and Hangan [5]. The radial velocity (V_r) and tangential velocity (V_t) are calculated as per Equations 1 &2:

$$V_r = V_0 \times \left(\frac{H}{H_0}\right) \quad (1)$$

where V_r is the radial velocity in m/sec, V_0 is the reference velocity and H_0 is reference height assumed as 0.25 m.

$$V_t = 2 \times S \times V_r \quad (2)$$

where V_t is the tangential velocity in m/sec, V_r is the radial velocity obtained from Equation 1 and S is the Swirl ratio assumed as 1.0.

In present study, domain meshing is carried out with fine sized meshing function. Figure 3 shows the meshing of domain carried out in ANSYS Fluent.

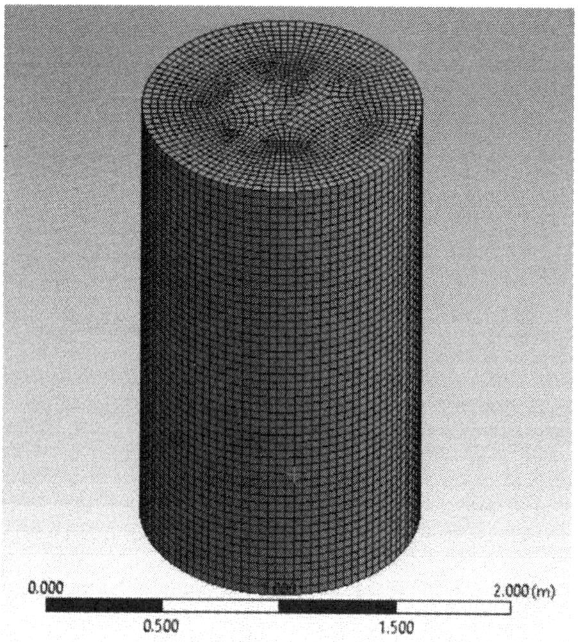

Figure 3. Meshing of Domain

This simulation is carried out in the steady state manner. Hence, change in velocity component value respect to time is not observed. Figures 4 & 5 show contours of tangential and radial velocity component on plane through the domain, respectively. Wind load acting on transmission line tower due to tornado loading is calculated with the help of the maximum value of velocity components obtained from developed CFD model as shown in Table I.

TABLE I
MAXIMUM VALUE OF VELOCITY COMPONENTS

S. No.	Velocity Component	Value (m/s)
1	Radial Velocity (V_r)	40.37
2	Tangential Velocity (V_t)	131.95

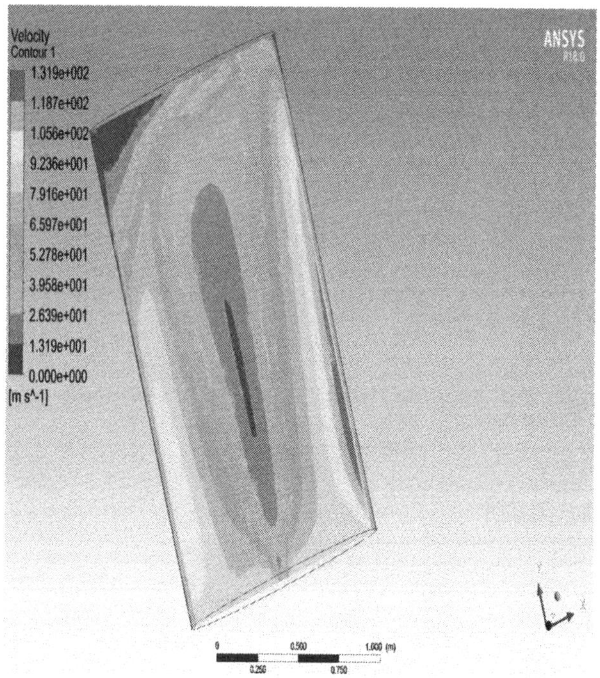

Figure 4. Contours of Tangential Velocity on Plane Through Domain

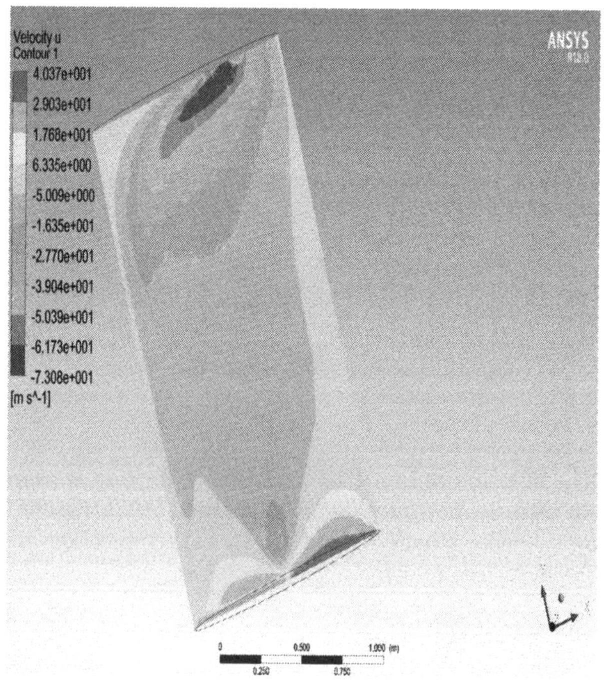

Figure 5. Contours of Radial Velocity on Plane Through The Domain

IV. Load Calculations and Analysis of Tower

Transmission line tower is divided into five different panels.The load acting on tower due to tornado load is calculated with help of panels. Horizontal loads acting on transmission line tower due to wind at any nodal point in certain direction can be calculated with the help of Equation 3 which was used by Hamada et al. [6]:

$$F_{wi} = \frac{1}{2} \times \rho_a \times (Z \times V)^2 \times G \times C_{dt} \times A \quad (3)$$

where

F_{wi}= Wind force acting on "i"direction in N
V = Tornado wind velocity component in m/sec
Z = Terrain factor taken equal to 1
ρ_a= Density of air in kg/m^3
C_{dt} = Drag coefficient calculated with help of solidity ratio
A = Total effective surface area of panel in mm^2
G = Gust response factor assumed as 1

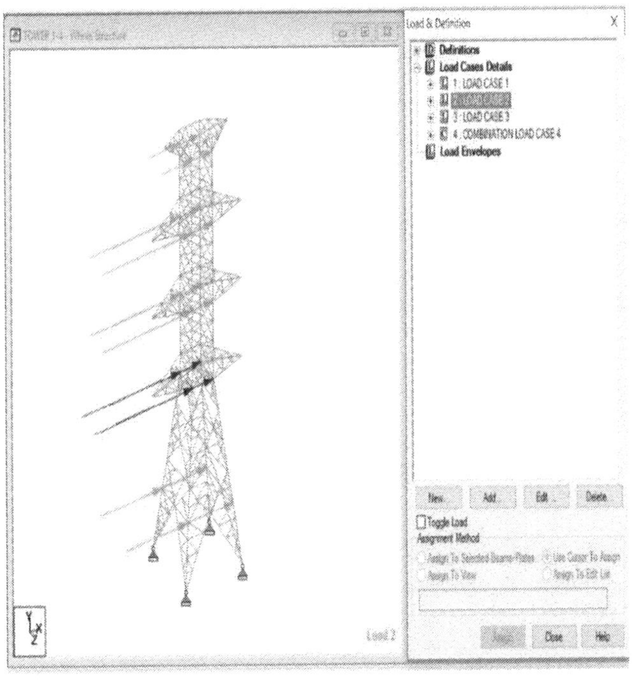

Figure 6. Load Applied on Tower in STAAD Pro V8i

The calculation of drag coefficient is carried out using I.S. 802 (Part 1/ Sec 1): 2015 [7]. The calculations of load acting on conductors and earth wire are also calculated with the help of Equation 3 where in area of panels A is replaced with product of diameter of wire and the span length of transmission line. The load acting on insulators are calculated with the help of same Equation 3 where in A is considered as half of the total area of string of insulators instead of effective area of panels. In present study, self-weights of earth wire, insulators and conductors are also considered as vertical loads acting on tower. The analysis of transmission line tower under calculated loadsis carried using commercial software STAAD Pro V8i. The same transmission line tower is studied under wind velocity time history data developed and used by Ahmad and Ansari [2] in STAAD Pro V8i. Figure 6 shows the loadsacting on transmission line tower in STAAD Pro V8i.

V. Results

The comparison has been made between the behaviour of four legged suspension transmission line tower under two different wind data of tornado. Tables II & III show the maximum nodal displacement in x direction which occurs at top of the tower and y direction which occurs at topmost cross arm of tower, respectively.

Figure 7 shows nodal displacement of tower in different direction due to two tornado wind data. Figures 8 & 9 show the nodal displacement of tower along the height due to wind velocity time history data and due to CFD wind data, respectively.

TABLE II

Nodal Displacements in X Direction in mm

Nodal displacements in x Direction (mm)	
Due to CFD wind data	Due to velocity time history data
270.853	197.460

TABLE III

Nodal Displacements in Y Direction in mm

Nodal displacements in y Direction (mm)	
Due to CFD wind data	Due to velocity time history data
67.977	55.813

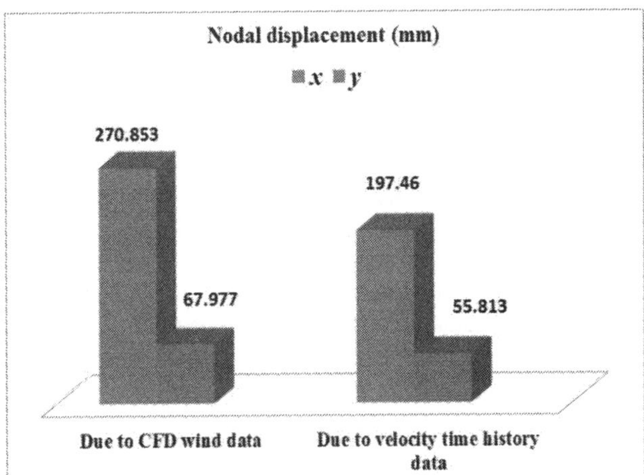

Figure 7. Nodal Displacement of Tower

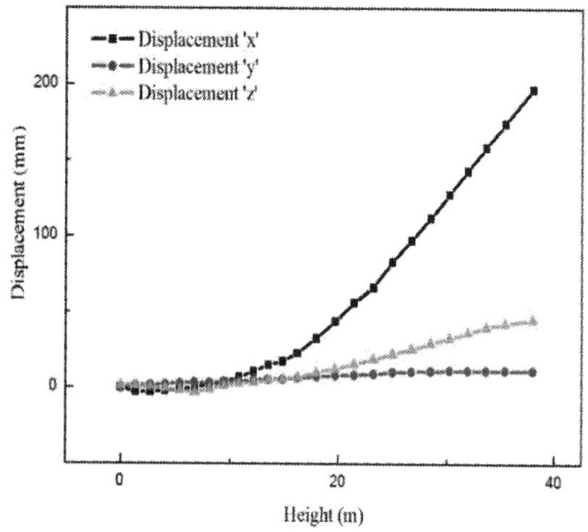

Figure 8.Nodal Displacements of Tower along Height due to Wind Velocity Time History Data

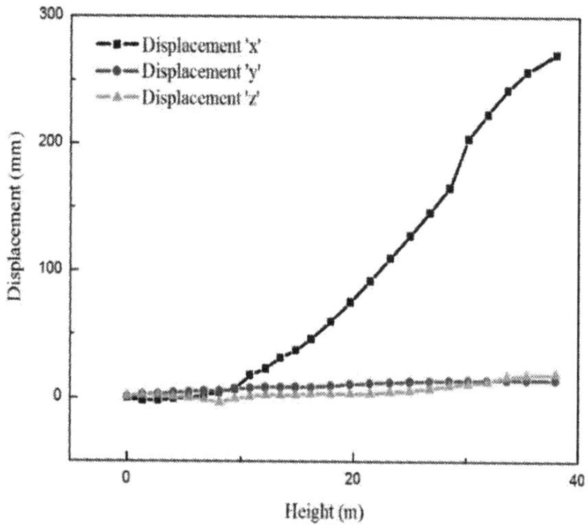

Figure 9. Nodal Displacements of Tower along Height due to CFD wind Data

VI. Conclusions

The four legged suspension transmission line tower is analyzed under tornado loading to study its responses and structural behavior of tower. The structural behavior of a four legged transmission line tower is studied under two tornado wind data in form of CFD wind data and wind velocity time history data and comparison between two studies has been made. The conclusions derived from this study are as follows:

1) The maximum nodal displacement due to CFD wind data is 37.17% more than maximum nodal displacement due to wind velocity time history data of tornado in x direction and maximum nodal displacement due to CFD wind data is 21.79% more than maximum nodal displacement due to wind velocity time history data of tornado in y direction.
2) The analysis of tower using CFD wind data is more efficient than wind velocity time history data because of consideration of loads due to conductors, insulators and earth wire.
3) The rapid increment is observed in value of nodal displacement in x direction after 12 m of height of tower due to tornado loading.
4) The tangential velocity could be one of important factors which affects the response and failure of transmission line tower under tornado loading.

References

[1] Savory, E., Gerard, A. R., Zinoddini, M., Toy, N. and Disney, P. (2001), 'Modeling of tornado and microburst-induced wind loading and failure of a lattice transmission tower', Engineering Structures, vol. 23, pp. 365-375.

[2] Ahmad, S. and Ansari, E. (2009), 'Response of transmission towers subjected to tornado loads', The Seventh Asia-Pacific Conference on Wind Engineering, Taipei, Taiwan.

[3] Hamada, A. and Damatty, A. A. (2011), 'Behaviour of guyed transmission line structures under tornado wind loading', Computers and Structures, vol. 89, pp. 986-1003.

[4] Panchal, H. S., Vyas, V. H. and Desai, H. G. (2016),'Comparative analysis of transmission line tower for different configuration using conventional angle section and closed hollow section', Journal of Civil Engineering and Environmental Technology, vol. 3, pp. 266-268.

[5] Natarajan, D. and Hangan, H.(2012), 'Large eddy simulations of translation and surface roughness effects on tornado-like vortices', Journal of Wind Engineering and Industrial Aerodynamics, vol.13, pp. 577-584.

[6] Hamada, A., Damatty, A. A., Hagan, H. and Shehata, A. Y.(2010), 'Finite element modelling of transmission line structures under tornado wind loading',Wind and Structures, vol.13, pp. 451-469.

[7] I.S. 802 (Part 1/ Sec 1): 2015, 'Use of Structural Steel in Overhead Transmission Line Towers'- code of practice [Third Revision], section 1: - Material and Loads.

Seismic Response of Liquid Storage Tank Isolated with Double Polynomial Friction Pendulum Isolator

Abdeali. K. Jiruwala[1], V. R. Panchal[2], D. P. Soni[3]

[1] Post Graduate Student (Structural Engineering), M. S. Patel Department of Civil Engineering, Chandubhai S. Patel Institute of Technology, Charotar University of Science and Technology, Changa, Gujarat, India
[2] Professor and Head,M. S. Patel Department of Civil Engineering, Chandubhai S. Patel Institute of Technology, Charotar University of Science and Technology, Changa, Gujarat, India
[3]Professor, Civil Engineering Department, SardarVallabhaiPatel Institute of Technology, Gujarat Technological University, Vasad, Gujarat, India

[1]abdeali.jiruwala@gmail.com
[2]vijaypanchal.cv@charusat.ac.in
[3]devesh18@gmail.com

Abstract—Seismic response of liquid storage tank isolated with double polynomial friction pendulum isolator (DPFPI) under near-fault ground excitation is investigated. The governing equation of motion is solved using Newmark's linear acceleration method. The geometry and friction coefficient of upper and lowersliding surfaces are different. To check the efficiency of DPFPI seismic response of the liquid storage tank are compared with that of double variable frequency pendulum isolator (DVFPI). It is found that DVFPI is more efficient than DPFPI. It was observed that working efficiency of the DPFPI can be made more effective by providing the upper sliding surface with high initial stiffness compared to the lower one and the friction coefficient of both sliding surfacesto be same.

Keywords—Base isolation; DPFPI; DVFPI; Liquid storage tank; Near-fault groundexcitations.

I. Introduction

Liquid storage tank are important structures since it plays important role in areas of industries, nuclear power plant and directly or indirectly connected to human and animal life. In the past earthquakes, there are many reports on the damage of liquid storage tank (Northridge earthquake, 1994; Chi-Chi earthquake, 1999; Bhuj earthquake, 2001). The main cause of failure of liquid storage tank occurs because of (i) uplift of anchorage structure (ii) Damage of piping structure (iii) buckling in tank wall.

For over thirty years, base isolation is proved to be the best technique to protect the structure from extreme earthquake. Kim and Lee [1], Panchal and Jangid [2], Jadhav and Jangid [3] have done many research to study the efficiency of liquid storage tank by applying base isolation technique. Lu et al. [4] proposed and defined polynomial friction pendulum isolator (PFPI) and conducted theoretical as well as experimental study for seismic isolation of building structure with PFPI which has variable stiffness.

TABLE I
CHARACTERISTICS OF SIX NEAR-FAULT GROUND EXCITATIONS

Near-Fault ground excitations	Normal component		
	PGD (cm)	PGV (cm/s)	PGA (g)
1979, Imperial Valley (El Centro Array #5)	76.5	98	0.37
1979, Imperial Valley (El Centro Array #7)	49.1	113	0.46
1994, Northridge (Newhall)	38.1	119	0.72
1992, Landers (Lucerne Valley)	230	136	0.71
1994, Northridge (Rinaldi)	39.1	175	0.89
1994, Northridge (Sylmar)	31.1	122	0.73

There are many studies done on single sliding bearing but only fewer studies are attempted towards double sliding bearing to examine the seismic performance of liquid storage tank. Double sliding bearing has come into picture for two reasons [5]:(a) displacement capacity of such isolator is double compared to traditional isolator and (b) at both sliding surfaces isolator geometry and friction coefficients can be varied for better performance. Based on these merits, numerous applications of the double friction pendulum system (DFPS)[5],the triple friction pendulum system (TFPS) [6] and the double variable frequency pendulum isolator (DVFPI) [7] have been found and has been designed and tested. The DFPS consists of two spherical sliding surfaces while DVFPI has two elliptical sliding surfaces, whereas DPFPI consist of two polynomial sliding surfaces.

The objective of the study is to find effectiveness of DPFPI by comparing seismic responses of the liquid storage tank isolated by DPFPI with that of DVFPI isolated by liquid storage tank under six different near-fault ground excitations as mentioned in Table I for four DPFPI design cases as mentioned in Table II.

II. Description of DPFPI

The DPFPI is an adaption of PFPI. The sliding surface of PFPI adopts the shape of polynomial with variable curvature [4]. The effectiveness of PFPI can be enhanced by adding second sliding surface which is known as DPFPI.As on both the surface sliding is possible the displacement capability of DPFPI is doubled as compared to PFPI. Hence, DPFPI can hold huge displacement produced by strong ground excitation. The main difference between the DVFPI and the DPFPI is in their shape. In DVFPI the shape of both sliding surfaces is elliptical but in DPFPI both sliding surfaces are polynomial. In DPFPI, following polynomial function is used to define the geometry of the sliding surface:

$$y'(x) = \frac{u_r(x)}{P} = ax^5 + cx^3 + ex \tag{1}$$

$$y''(x) = \frac{k_r(x)}{P} = 5ax^4 + 3cx^2 + e \tag{2}$$

Where $u_r(x)$ is restoring force, $k_r(x)$ is isolator stiffness, $y'(x)$ and $y''(x)$ is normalized restoring force and normalized isolator stiffness with respect to the vertical load P, respectively and a, c and e are the three polynomial coefficients.

The polynomial coefficients are replaced by three design parameters k_0, k_1 and D_1. The relation between design parameters and polynomial coefficients are as follows:

$$a = \frac{(-k_0 + k_1)}{-5(D_1)^4}, c = \frac{2(-k_0 + k_1)}{3(D_1)^2}, e = k_0 \tag{3}$$

where k_0 is the normalized initial isolator stiffness at $x = 0$, $k_1$is the normalized isolator stiffness at $x = D_1$ and D_1 is the critical isolator drift.

The curve shown in Figure 1 consist of mainly two sections, hardening and softening section.The hardening and softening sections were aimed to control the isolator drift and structural acceleration, respectively.

The lower and upper surface of the DPFPI which is defined by two parameters, friction coefficient and geometry of isolator are not equal. Both sliding surface of the DPFPI has the same initial combined time period and the friction coefficient defined by Soni et al. [8].

$$T_c = \sqrt{T_1^2 + T_2^2} \tag{4}$$

$$\mu_c = \frac{\mu_1 T_1^2 + \mu_2 T_2^2}{T_1^2 + T_2^2} \tag{5}$$

where T_c and μ_c are the initial combined time period and combined friction coefficient of the sliding surfaces respectively; T_2 and T_1 are the initial time period of lower and upper sliding surface respectively; μ_2 and μ_1 are the friction coefficient of the lower and upper sliding surface respectively.

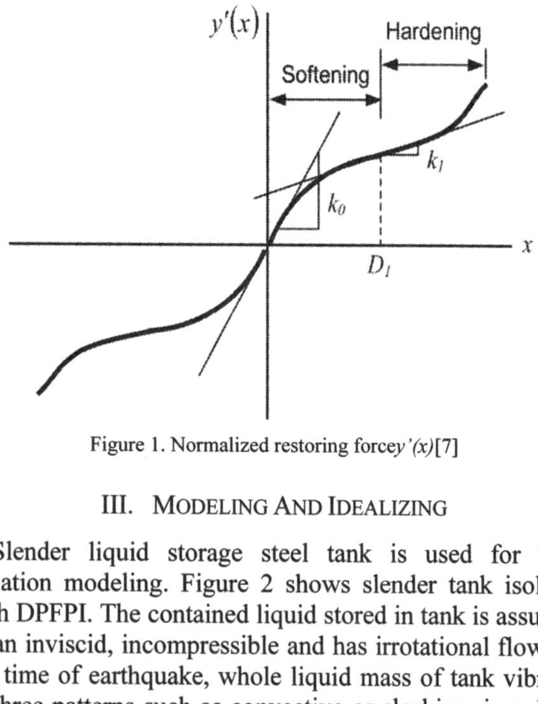

Figure 1. Normalized restoring force$y'(x)$[7]

III. Modeling And Idealizing

Slender liquid storage steel tank is used for base isolation modeling. Figure 2 shows slender tank isolated with DPFPI. The contained liquid stored in tank is assumed as an inviscid, incompressible and has irrotational flow. At the time of earthquake, whole liquid mass of tank vibrates in three patterns such as convective or sloshing, impulsive and rigid mass. A convective and impulsive mass vibrates in different modes but first convective mode is considered and then the impulsive mode is considered for response assumption. Impulsive mass (m_i), Sloshing mass (m_c) and rigid mass (m_r) are called lumped masses. Three-degree-of-freedom system is considered for the analysis, i.e., u_b, u_i and u_c, which indicates the absolute rigid, impulsive and sloshing displacement of masses, respectively.

The different assumptions which are used for the system are given as follows:

1. The tanks self-weight is neglected due to the fact that it's very small.
2. Damping ratio is assumed for damping coefficient of the motion of impulsive and convective masses.
3. The coefficient of friction of the DPFPI does not depend upon the relative velocity of sliding surfaces.
4. It is assumed that the slider of the isolator remains in contact with the sliding surfaces.

Mathematical modeling of ground rested liquid storage tank isolated by DPFPI is shown in Figure 2.

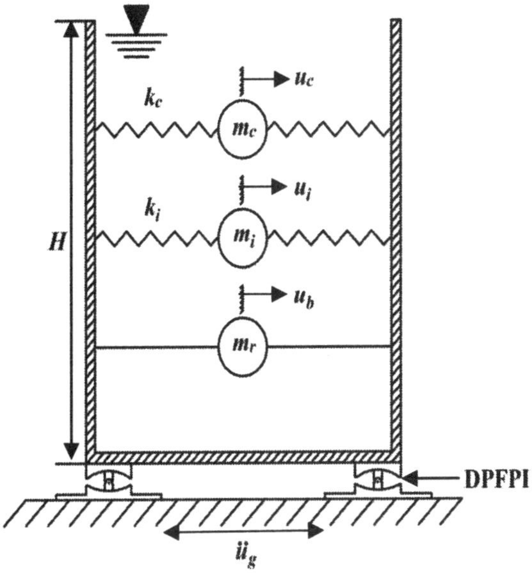

Figure 2.Mathematical modeling of ground rested liquid storage tank isolated by DPFPI

The m_c, m_i and m_r in relation to liquid mass, m and various mass ratios for t_h/R= 0.004 [9] are introduced as:

$$m_c = Y_c m \tag{6}$$

$$m_i = Y_i m \tag{7}$$

$$m_r = Y_r m \tag{8}$$

$$m = \pi R^2 H \rho_w \tag{9}$$

$$Y_c = 1.01327 - 0.87578 * S + 0.35708 * S^2 - 0.06692 * S^3 + 0.00439 * S^4 \tag{10}$$

$$Y_i = -0.15467 + 1.21716 * S - 0.62839 * S^2 + 0.14434 * S^3 - 0.0125 * S^4 \tag{11}$$

$$Y_r = -0.01599 + 0.86356 * S - 0.30941 * S^2 + 0.04083 * S^3 \tag{12}$$

where Y_c, Y_i and Y_r are the mass ratios; tank aspect ratio, $S=H/R$; ρ_w is denoted as the mass density of containing liquid; R is tank radius; H is liquid height.

Following equation shows the fundamental frequency of convective and impulsive mass, ω_c and ω_i, respectively:

$$\omega_c = \sqrt{1.84\left(\frac{g}{R}\right)\tanh(1.84S)} \tag{13}$$

$$\omega_i = \frac{P}{H}\sqrt{\frac{E}{\rho_s}} \tag{14}$$

where g is gravitational acceleration; E is the elastic modulus and ρ_s is tank wall density; and P is given by:

$$P = 0.037085 + 0.084302 * S - 0.05088 * S^2 + 0.012523 * S^3 - 0.0012 * S^4 \tag{15}$$

The damping and stiffness, equivalent with the impulsive and convective masses are introduced as:

$$c_c = 2\xi_c m_c \omega_c \tag{16}$$

$$c_i = 2\xi_i m_i \omega_i \tag{17}$$

$$k_c = m_c \omega_c^2 \tag{18}$$

$$k_i = m_i \omega_i^2 \tag{19}$$

where ξ_i and ξ_c denotes the ratio of damping corresponding to impulsive and sloshing mass, respectively.

The governing equation of motion is expressed as given below in matrix form for liquid storage tank with isolation:

$$[m]\{\ddot{x}\} + [c]\{\dot{x}\} + [k]\{x\} + \{F\} = -[m]\{r\}\ddot{u}_g \tag{20}$$

where $[m]$ is mass matrix, $[c]$ is damping matrix and $[k]$ is stiffness matrix; $\{x\} = \{x_c, x_i, x_b\}^T$; $x_c = u_c - u_b$ is convective mass displacement, $x_i = u_i - u_b$ is impulsive mass displacement in relation with bearing displacement and $x_b = u_b - u_g$ is bearing displacement in relation with the ground; $\{F\} = \{0, 0, F_x\}$ is the friction force vectors; $\{r\} = \{0,0,1\}^T$ is the influence coefficient vector; F_x is the frictional force in the DPFPI; $\ddot{u}_g$ is the seismic ground acceleration.

IV. Comparative Study

The response of slender tanks isolated with modified-DPFPI for six different earthquake ground excitations is examined. The various essential parameters required to define slender liquid storage tank system are as follows which is taken from Soni et al. [8].

1. Aspect ratio, S is 1.85;
2. Height, H is 11.3 m;
3. The natural frequency of impulsive mass (ω_i) and convective mass (ω_c) is 5.963and 0.273Hz;
4. Ratio of damping of impulsive mass (ξ_i) and sloshing mass (ξ_c) is 2% and 0.5%;
5. Elastic modulus, E is 200 *GPa*;
6. Density of mass, ρ_s is 7900 kg/m^3 and
7. Thickness of wall oftank to radius ratio, t_h/R is 0.004.

In Equation (3) the values of the three polynomial coefficients *a*, *c* and *e* are taken as 81.25, -10.83 and 0.65, respectively and value for critical isolator drift D_1 is equal to 0.2.

The different response quantities are base-shear (F_b), displacement of isolator (x_b), impulsive displacement (x_i) and convective displacement (x_c). Two types of isolatorsare

used for comparison of seismic response, i.e., (i) DVFPI, (ii) DPFPI. Both the isolator is investigated for four DPFPI design cases as mentioned in Table II.

Figure 3 describe the graph of different response quantities and Figure 4 describe the overall and decomposed force deformation loop of slender tank isolated with DPFPI and DVFPI subjected to the earthquake, 1979 Imperial Valley recorded at El Centro Array #5. Figures 3 & 4 demonstrate that there is a noticeable decrease in bearing displacement isolated with DPFPI as compared to DVFPI. Comparison of peak values of various response quantities of DPFPI and DVFPI are shown in Table III.

TABLE II
PROPERTIES OF FOUR DPFPI DESIGN CASES

Cases	T_1(sec)	T_2 (sec)	T_3 (sec)	μ_1	μ_2	μ_c
A	1.000	2.000	2.236	0.032	0.040	0.036
B	1.580	1.580	2.236	0.036	0.036	0.036
C	1.580	1.580	2.236	0.032	0.040	0.036
D	1.000	2.000	2.236	0.036	0.036	0.036

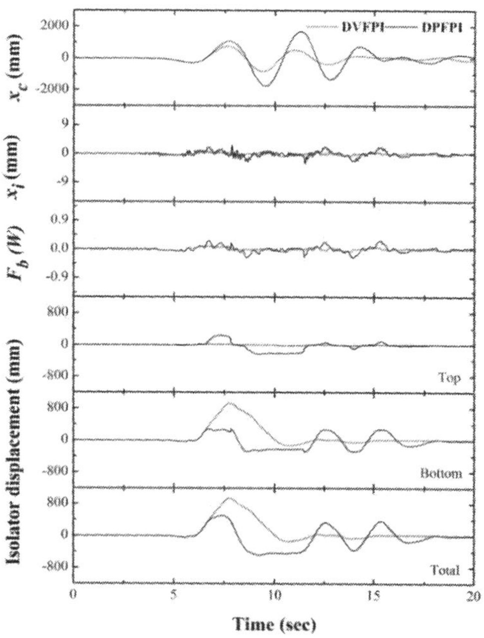

(a)

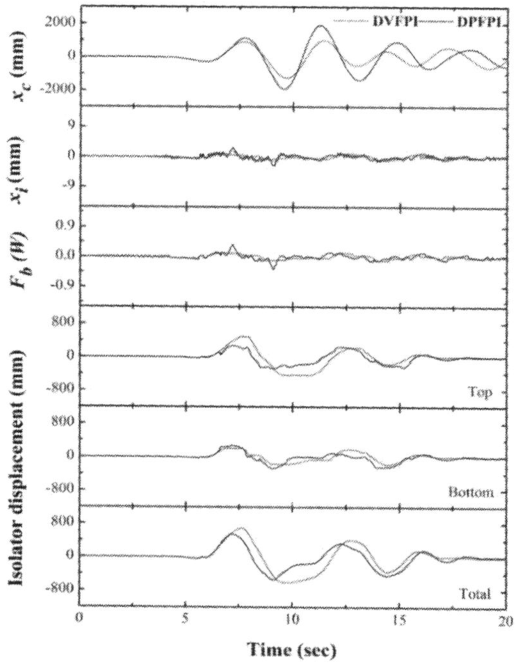

(b)

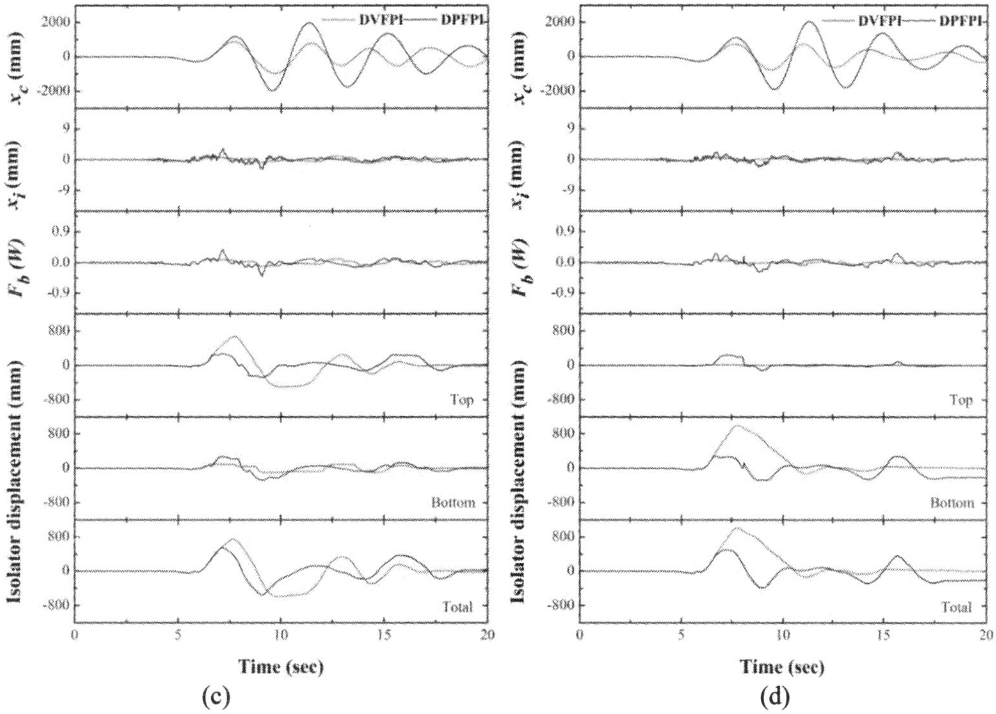

Figure 3. Graph of time versus different response quantities of slender tank isolated by DPFPI and DVFPI subjected to the earthquake, 1979 Imperial Valley, (Array #5):(a) Case A ($T_1<T_2$ and $\mu_1<\mu_2$); (b) Case B ($T_1 = T_2$ and $\mu_1=\mu_2$);(c) Case C ($T_1 = T_2$ and $\mu_1<\mu_2$); (d) Case D ($T_1<T_2$ and $\mu_1=\mu_2$).

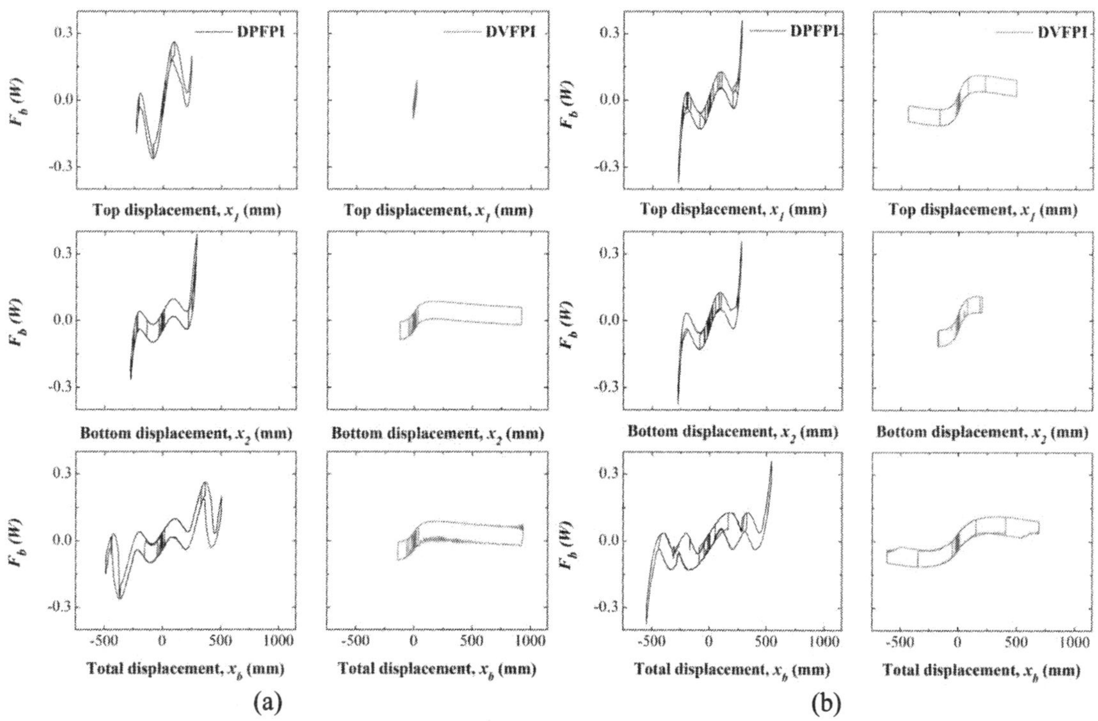

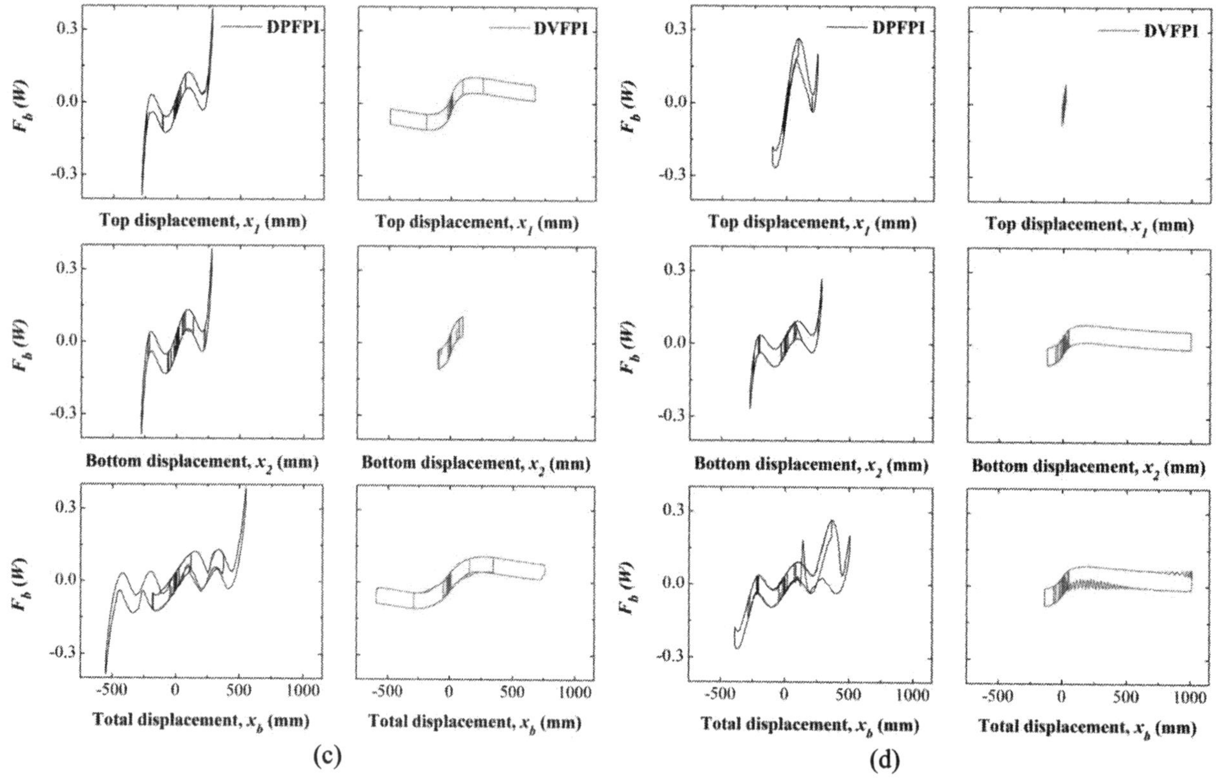

Figure 4. Overall and decomposed force-deformation loop of slender tank isolated by DPFPI and DVFPI subjected to the earthquake, 1979 Imperial Valley, (Array #5):(a) Case A ($T_1 < T_2$ and $\mu_1 < \mu_2$); (b) Case B ($T_1 = T_2$ and $\mu_1 = \mu_2$); (c) Case C ($T_1 = T_2$ and $\mu_1 < \mu_2$); (d) Case D ($T_1 < T_2$ and $\mu_1 = \mu_2$).

TABLE III

PEAK VALUES OF RESPONSE QUANTITIES OF LIQUID STORAGE SLENDER TANK ISOLATED BY DPFPI AND DVFPI UNDER SIX NEAR-FAULT GROUND EXCITATIONS

Earthquakes	Cases	x_c (mm)		x_i (mm)		F_b (W)		x_b (mm)	
		DPFPI	DVFPI	DPFPI	DVFPI	DPFPI	DVFPI	DPFPI	DVFPI
1979, Imperial Valley (El Centro Array #5)	A	1767.50	814.10	2.98	1.15	0.39	0.09	504.35	936.71
	B	1911.60	1249.30	2.80	1.23	0.37	0.11	547.93	689.78
	C	1961.40	972.63	3.17	1.14	0.39	0.11	550.17	758.82
	D	2028.10	783.16	2.21	1.15	0.27	0.08	505.70	1012.00
1979, Imperial Valley (El Centro Array #7)	A	2584.40	710.51	8.14	1.17	0.94	0.09	673.68	714.65
	B	2592.60	1287.40	8.02	1.28	0.96	0.11	677.34	757.89
	C	2573.00	1139.80	8.17	1.22	0.95	0.11	676.86	770.81
	D	2600.70	646.14	7.98	1.14	0.93	0.08	673.43	738.32
1994, Northridge (Newhall)	A	770.47	923.50	1.06	1.11	0.09	0.09	366.26	330.30
	B	709.56	1254.50	0.93	1.41	0.08	0.11	399.43	316.10
	C	647.95	1276.70	0.93	1.30	0.08	0.11	406.04	317.54
	D	770.90	934.07	1.23	1.01	0.09	0.08	365.97	343.42

Contd...

1992, Landers (Lucerne valley)	A	1822.20	942.46	6.26	1.20	0.76	0.09	652.95	1891.90
	B	1782.50	1091.50	6.05	1.34	0.71	0.11	648.20	1418.30
	C	1830.10	1052.20	6.68	1.15	0.79	0.11	657.95	1679.30
	D	1880.50	909.93	6.71	1.18	0.83	0.08	661.87	2070.00
1994, Northridge (Rinaldi)	A	539.34	814.10	1.17	1.15	0.10	0.09	498.35	936.71
	B	526.73	777.48	1.35	1.40	0.10	0.11	500.25	455.52
	C	535.63	761.61	1.24	1.34	0.10	0.11	502.56	456.63
	D	558.54	608.61	1.34	1.34	0.10	0.08	503.04	477.01
1994, Northridge (Sylmar)	A	1911.50	671.79	6.31	1.05	0.66	0.09	576.34	418.78
	B	1077.60	1110.10	2.48	1.29	0.24	0.11	521.32	502.96
	C	1131.80	1023.20	2.49	1.28	0.25	0.11	523.16	497.98
	D	1773.10	654.94	6.74	1.02	0.70	0.08	580.64	429.80

V. Conclusions

The isolated liquid storage slender tank has been analyzed by providing DPFPI at base under the near-fault ground excitation. To examine the efficiency of DPFPI, the earthquake response of structure isolated with DPFPI is compared with that of DVFPI. The conclusions derived from this comparative study are as follows:

1. The DPFPI is more efficient in reducing the displacement of isolator than DVFPI.
2. Sloshing displacement, impulsive displacement and base shear are increased after installation of DPFPI in tank as compared to DVFPI.
3. It was observed that working efficiency of the DPFPI can be made more effective by providing the upper sliding surface with high initial stiffness compared to the lower one and the friction coefficient of both sliding surfaces should be same.
4. The amount of energy dissipation is more in DVFPI as compared to DPFPI.

References

[1] Kim, N. S., and Lee, D. G. 1995. Pseudo dynamic test for evaluation of seismic performance of base-isolated liquid storage tanks, Engineering Structures, Vol. 17, pp. 198-208.

[2] Panchal, V. R., and Jangid, R. S. 2008. Variable friction pendulum system for seismic isolation of liquid storage tanks, Nuclear Engineering and Design, Vol. 238, pp. 1304-1315.

[3] Jadhav, M. B., and Jangid, R. S. 2006. Response of base-isolated liquid storage tanks to near fault motions, Structural Engineering and Mechanics, Vol.23, pp. 615-634.

[4] Lu, L., Lee, T., Juang, S., and Yeh, S. 2013. Polynomial friction pendulum isolators for building floor isolation: An experimental and theoretical study, Engineering Structures, Vol. 56, pp. 970-982.

[5] Fenz, D. M., and Constantinou, M. C. 2006. Behaviour of the double concave friction pendulum bearing, Earthquake Engineering and Structural Dynamics, Vol. 35, pp. 1403–1424.

[6] Fenz, D. M., and Constantinou, M. C. 2008. Spherical sliding isolation bearings with adaptive behavior, Theory Earthquake Engineering and Structural Dynamics, Vol. 37, pp. 163-183.

[7] Soni, D. P., Mistry, B. B., Jangid, R. S., and Panchal, V. R. 2010. Seismic response of the double variable frequency pendulum isolator, Structural Control and Health Monitoring, Vol. 18, pp. 450-470.

[8] Soni, D. P., Mistry, B. B., and Panchal, V. R. 2011. Double variable frequency pendulum isolator for seismic isolation of liquid storage tanks, Nuclear Engineering and Design, Vol. 241, pp. 700-713.

[9] Haroun, M.A. 1983. Vibration studies and test of liquid storage tanks, Earthquake Engineering and Structural Dynamics, Vol. 11, pp. 179-206.

Effect of Multi-Support Excitation on Cable Stayed Suspension Hybrid Bridge

Parth K. Patel[1], V. R. Panchal[2]

[1]*Post Graduate Student (Structural Engineering), Department of Civil Engineering, Chandubhai S. Patel Institute of Technology, Charotar University of Science and Technology, Changa, Gujarat, India*

[2]*Professor and Head, Department of Civil Engineering, Chandubhai S. Patel Institute of Technology, Charotar University of Science and Technology, Changa, Gujarat, India*

[1]pk_119@yahoo.com

[2]vijaypanchal.cv@charusat.ac.in

***Abstract*—The cable-stayed suspension hybrid bridge (CSSHB) is combination of two structural systems one is cable-stayed bridge, which provide more rigidity due to presence of tensed cable stays as a force resistance element and another is suspension bridge, which provide long span in bridge. So, combination of these two systems can be used to provide long span and higher stiffness in bridge. In this study, effect of multi-support excitations is investigated in cable-stayed suspension hybrid bridge (CSSHB) and also analyzed using non-linear time history in SAP2000 software. A comparison is made with the hybrid bridge without effect of multi-support excitation and hybrid bridge with effect of multi-support excitation and found that the acceleration of deck, displacement of deck and top pylon displacement of CSSHB is reduced as compared to without multi-support excitation.**

***Keywords*—Cable-stayed bridge, Suspension bridge, Cable-stayed suspension Hybrid Bridge, Multi-support excitation, SAP2000.**

I. Introduction

The function of bridge is to travel across large spans of land or largest mass of water, and to connect two far-off points, after all reducing the distance between them. The bridge design is depending on the nature of the land and the use of the bridge and also depends on the construction area of the bridge. There are different types of bridge are available like cable stayed bridge, beam bridge, truss bridge, arch bridge, etc. In suspension bridge, cables are providing between towers and that cables are known as suspension cables and also provide vertical cables or suspender cables are known as hangers that hold the deck. These cables are always in tension and carry the majority load and transfer the load on pylon. The idea of using chain or rope to support a bridge span will result in to the new attraction which is known as cable stayed bridge. The cable styed bridge is similar to suspension bridge. In this type of bridge, towers and deck are hold by cables, but its cables hold the deck by connecting it directly to the towers instead via suspender cables.

Now days, suspension and cable-stayed bridge are used for larger span bridge. cable-stayed bridge possess high rigidity tensioned cable whereas suspension bridge gives larger span. The bridge which will be constructed combining above two bridge will have longer span and higher stiffness and that type of bridge is known as Cable-Stayed Suspension Hybrid bridge (CSSHB).

II. Multi-support Excitation

It is important to perform dynamic analysis for the structures subjected to earthquake induced ground motions. The support induced vibrations cause deformations and stresses in the structural systems. There are two types of support excitations such as single-support excitation and multi-support excitation.

In single-support excitation, the same ground motion is considered at all supports point of a bridge such as pier and pylon of bridge. The supports move as one rigid base. The presence of spatial variation in ground motion leads to the different excitation at different support points of a bridge such as pier and pylon of the bridge which is known as multi-support excitation (MSE).

III. Literature Survey

Palheriya and Dabhekar [1] presented state-of-the-review on the analysis of the CSSHB.

Zhang et al. [2] carried out three-dimensional nonlinear aerodynamic stability analysis of cable stayed suspension hybrid bridge of 1400m span. They also carried out parametric study to find the influence of various design parameters on the aerodynamic stability of the bridge are analytically investigated.

Savaliya et al. [3] studied the nonlinear static analysis and modal time history analysis of cable-stayed suspension hybrid bridge in SAP2000 software. The time period of bridge for different mode shape were also presented.

Kartal and Soyluk [4] studied the effect of multi-support earthquake ground motions and traffic loadings on the dynamic behavior of a cable-stayed bridge. The results showed that the structural responses obtained for the multi-support earthquake excitation are usually larger than the responses determined for the traffic loading. They concluded that the combined effect of the multi-support earthquake ground motions and traffic loadings should be considered for the realistic design of cable-stayed bridges.

Li and Yang [5] investigated effects of multi-support excitation on seismic response of a long span prestressed concrete continuous rigid frame bridge. They considered local effect, passage effect as well as incoherence effect and in numerical simulation. They concluded that uniform seismic excitation is not able to control the seismic design for long span rigid framed bridge and influence of multi-support excitation must be considered for the rigid framed bridge.

Patel at al. [6] investigated response of TFPS-isolated cable-stayed bridge with multi-support excitation using SAP2000. They concluded that base shear and deck acceleration reduced and bearing displacement is increased under the MSE as compared to without MSE.

IV. Bridge Configurations

The bridge configuration is based on cable-stayed suspension hybrid bridge of Lingding Strait in China having pylon height 258.9 m, two side spans = 319 m and central span is 1400 m. The behavior of hybrid bridge is studied for delta-shaped pylon and effect of MSE is also investigated. The geometric configuration of CSSHB is shown in Figure 1.

A. Geometrical details:

- Main span = 1400 m
- Side Span = 319 m
- Height of Pylon = 258.9 m
- Dimension of tower's column = 6×5 m
- Transverse beam = 3.17×3.17 m
- Deck = Closed box concrete
- Girders = 36.8 m wide, 3.494 m high
- Delta-shaped pylon

The dimension of delta-shape pylon is shown in Figure 2.

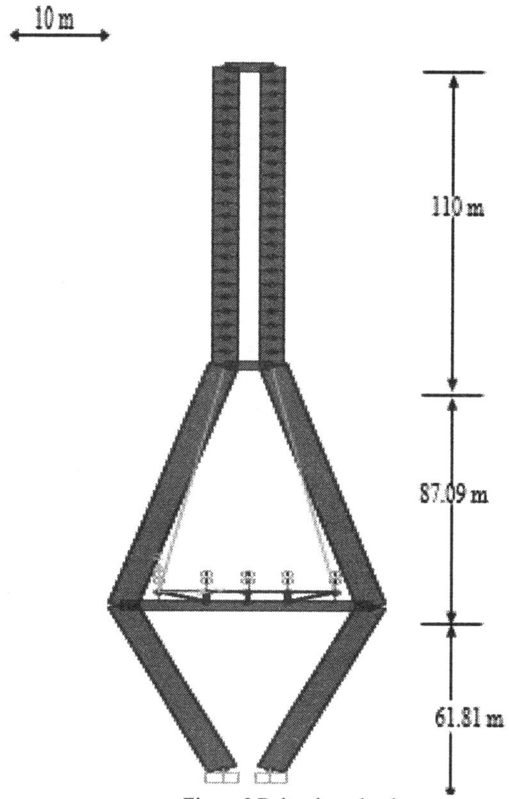

Figure 2 Delta-shaped pylon

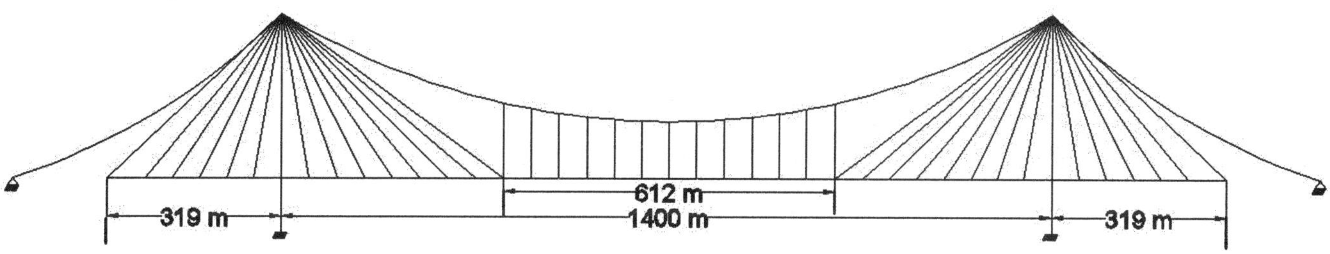

Figure 1 Geometric configuration of CSSHB

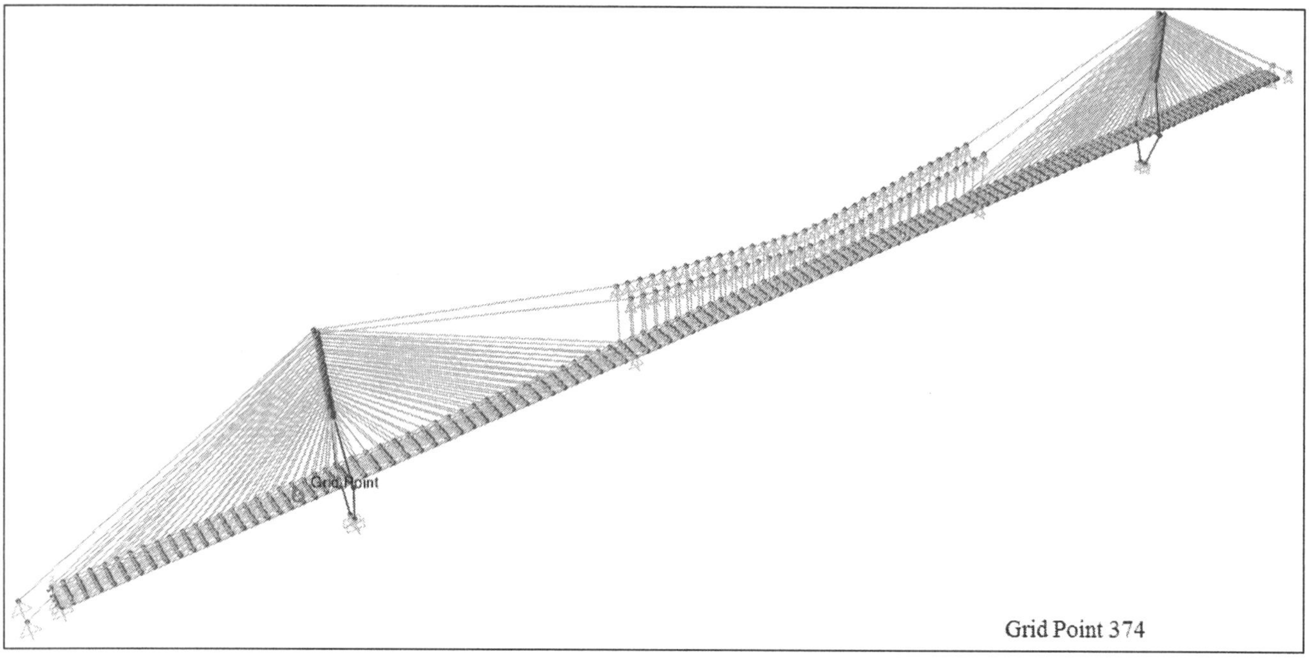

Figure 3 3D View of CSSHB

3D view of cable-stayed suspension hybrid bridge is shown in Figure 3. The deck section of hybrid bridge and longitudinal view of deck are shown in Figures 4 & 5.

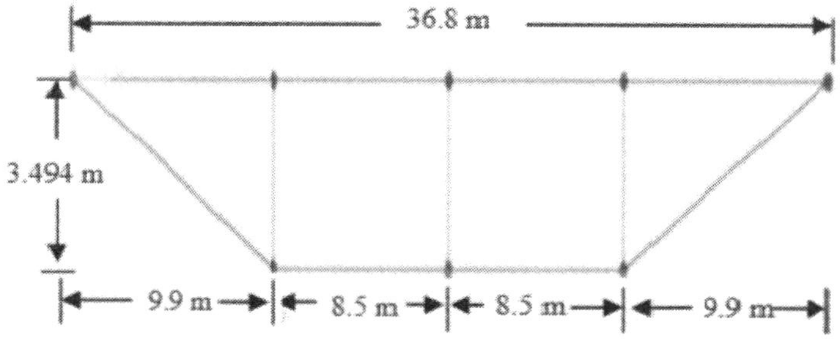

Figure 4 Deck section

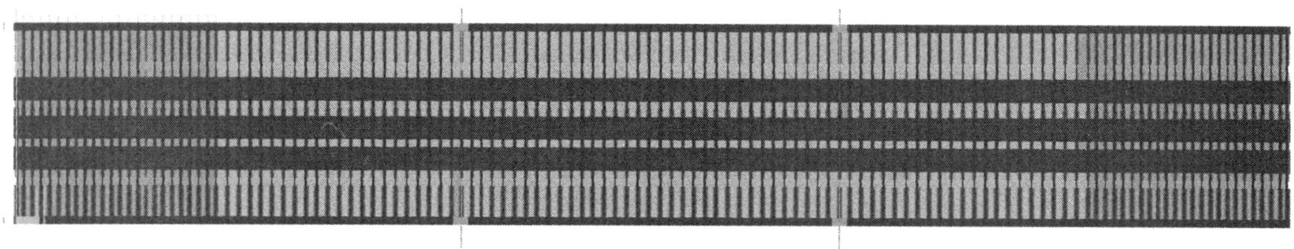

Figure 5 Longitudinal view of deck

TABLE I
MEMBER DETAILS

Members	*E* (MPa)	*A* (m^2)
Tower C	3.8×10^7	30
Tower TB	3.8×10^7	10
Main Cable CS	2×10^5	0.3167
Main Cable SS	2×10^5	0.3547
Hanger Cable	2×10^5	0.0064
Stayed cables	2×10^5	0.31

E-elastic modulus; *A*-area; *CS*-Cable stay; *SS*-Suspension side; *C*- tower's column; *TB*- tower's transverse beam.

V. ANALYSIS OF HYBRID BRIDGE

Nonlinear dynamic analysis is carried out to determine response of the CSSHB with and without MSE. The near fault ground motions used in the study are shown in Table II. The repose quantities of interest are deck displacement, deck acceleration & top pylon displacement.

TABLE II
GROUND MOTION DATA

Near Fault ground excitation	Normal component		
	PGD (cm)	PGV (cm/s)	PGA (*g*)
Imperial Valley, 1979 (El Centro #5)	76.5	98	0.37
Imperial Valley, 1979 (El Centro #7)	49.1	113	0.46
Northridge, 1994 (Newhall)	38.1	119	0.72
Northridge, 1994 (Sylmar)	31.1	122	0.73

Figures 6 and 7 show comparison of deck displacement of CSSHB with and without MSE.

Figures 8 and 9 show comparison of deck acceleration of CSSHB with and without MSE.

Figures 10 and 11 show comparison of top pylon displacement of CSSHB with and without MSE.

From the Figures 6-11, it is observed that all response quantities of interest are increased in case of CSSHB with MSE.Therefore, influence of multi-support excitation must be considered for the analysis of CSSHB.

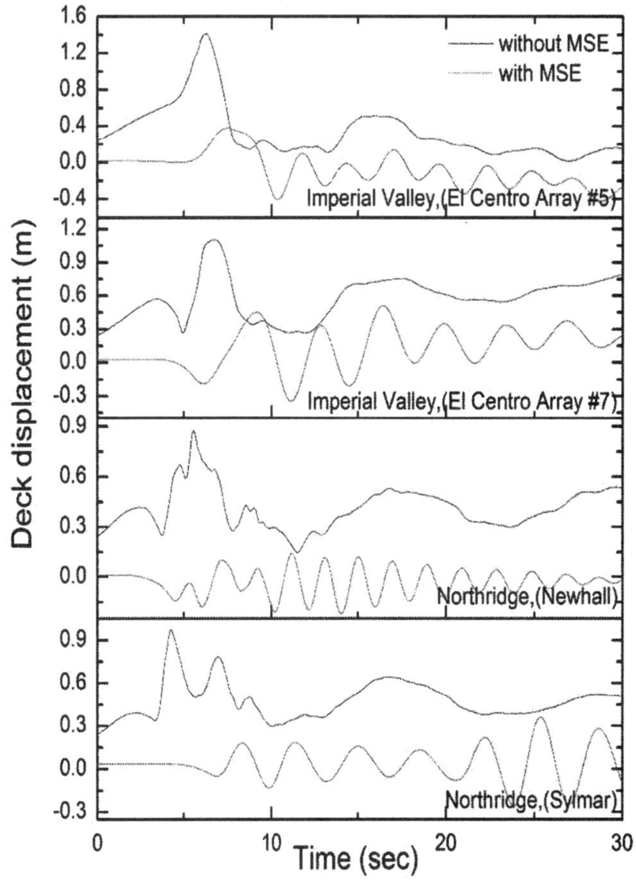

Figure 6 Comparison of deck displacement of CSSHB

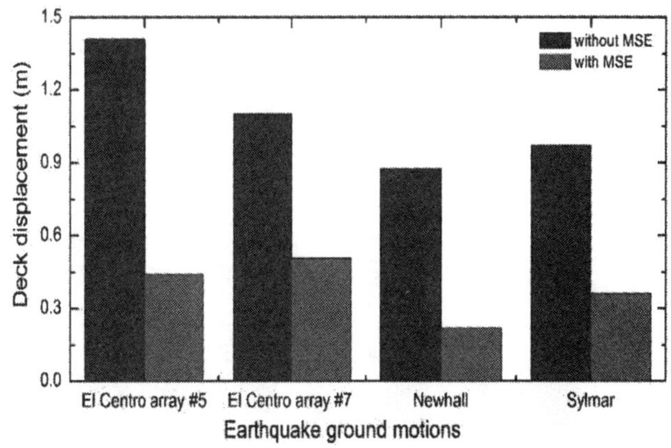

Figure 7 Comparison of deck displacement of CSSHB

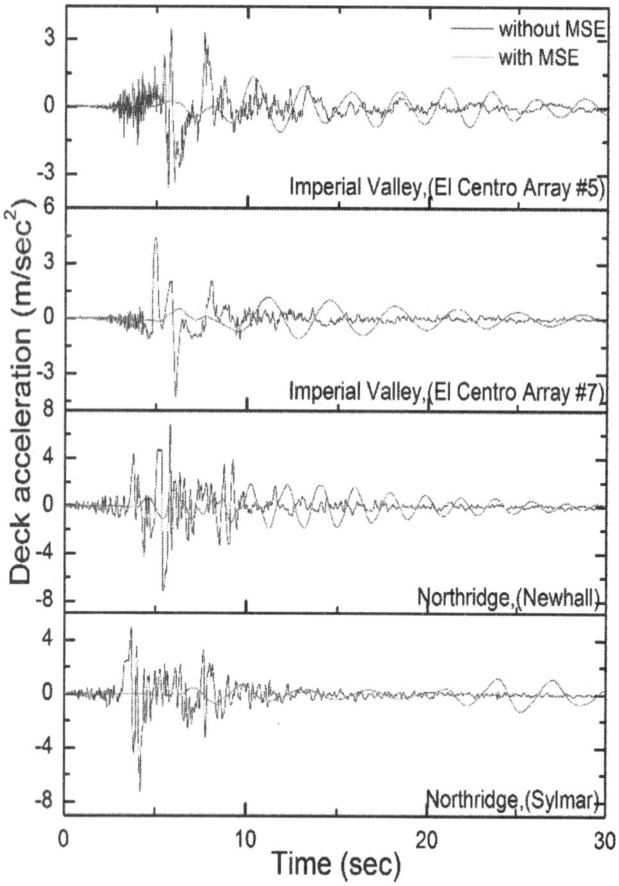

Figure 8 Comparison of deck acceleration of CSSHB

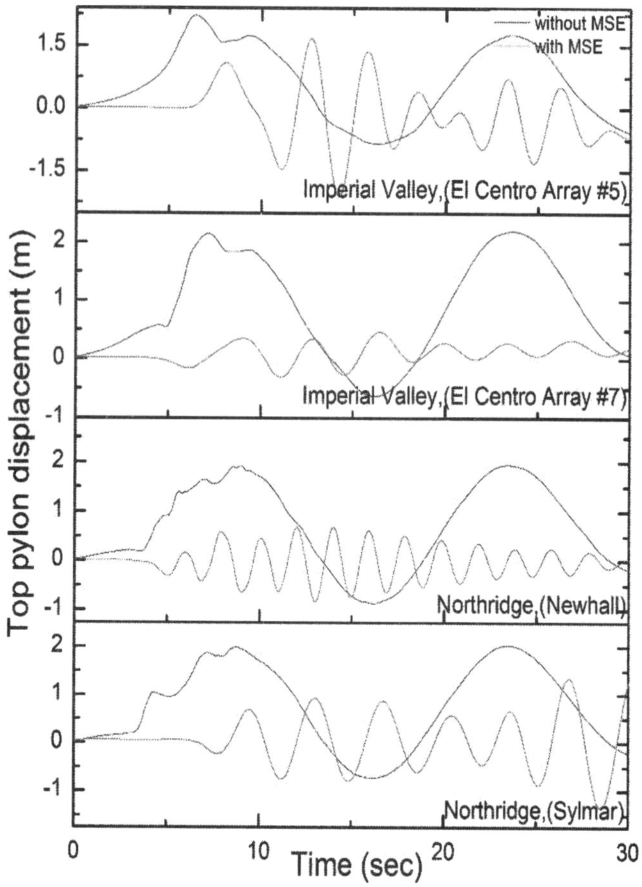

Figure 10 Comparison of top pylon displacement of CSSHB

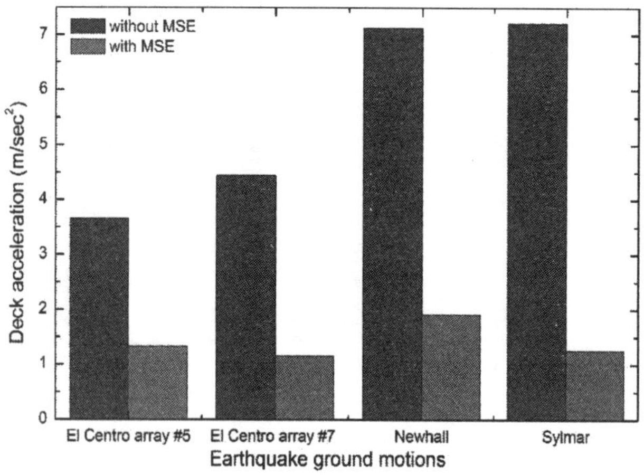

Figure 9 Comparison of deck acceleration of CSSHB

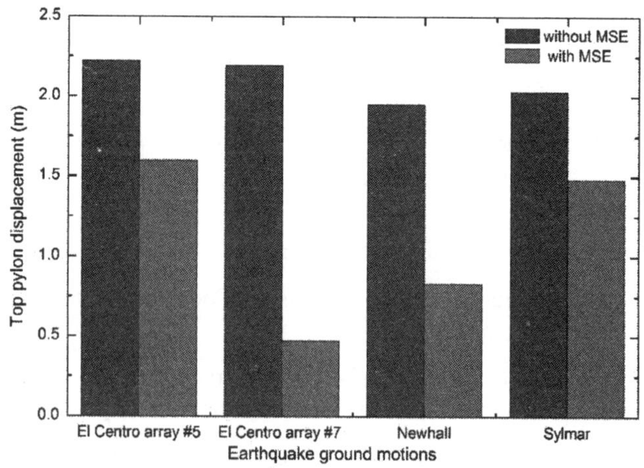

Figure 11 Comparison of top pylon displacement of CSSHB

TABLEIII
PEAK RESPONSE QUANTITIES OF CSSHB

Near-fault earthquake ground motion	Deck displacement (m) (Grid point 374)		Deck acceleration (m/sec^2) (Grid point 374)		Top pylon displacement (m) (Grid point 1253)	
	Without MSE	With MSE	Without MSE	With MSE	Without MSE	With MSE
Imperial Valley, 1979 (El Centro #5)	1.41	0.442	3.65	1.33	2.22	1.6
Imperial Valley, 1979 (El Centro #7)	1.1	0.506	4.44	1.15	2.19	0.470
Northridge, 1994 (Newhall)	0.874	0.220	7.13	1.91	1.95	0.829
Northridge, 1994 (Sylmar)	0.971	0.362	7.22	1.26	2.03	1.33

VI. CONCLUSIONS

In this study, seismic response of cable stayed suspension hybrid bridge (CSSHB) using multi-support excitation has been investigated using SAP2000. On the basis of results following conclusions may be drawn:

1. Deck displacement of CSSHB with multi-support excitation is less than that of CSSHB without multi-support excitation.
2. It is observed that deck acceleration of CSSHB with multi-support excitation is less than that of CSSHB without multi-support excitation.
3. It is also concluded that top pylon displacement of CSSHB is reduced for multi-support excitation as compared to without multi-support excitation.
4. As uniform seismic excitation is not able to control the seismic analysis of long span bridge, influence of multi-support excitation must be considered for the analysis of CSSHB.

References

[1] Palheriya, A. and Dabhekar, K. (2018), "Analysis of Hybrid Form of Cable Stayed and Suspension Bridge - A Review", International Journal of Innovations in Engineering and Science, Vol. 3, pp.16-19.

[2] Zhang, X. and Sun, B. (2004), "Aerodynamic stability of cable-stayed-suspension hybrid bridges", Journal of Zhejiang University Science, Vol.6A, pp. 869-874.

[3] Savaliya, G., Desai, A. and Vasanwala, S. (2015), "Static and dynamic analysis of cable-stayed suspension hybrid bridge & validation", International Journal of Advanced Research in Engineering and Technology, Vol. 6, pp. 91-98.

[4] Kartal, H. and Soyluk, K. (2012), "Dynamic Behavior of a Cable-Stayed Bridge under Earthquake and Traffic Loads" 10th International Congress on Advances in Civil Engineering. Middle East Technical University, Ankara, Turkey.

[5] Li, J. and Yang, Q. (2008), "Seismic responses analysis of long continuous rigid-framed bridge subjected to multi-support excitations" The 14th World Conference on Earthquake Engineering, Beijing, China.

[6] Patel, V., Panchal, V. and Soni, D. (2017), "Effect Of Multi-support Excitation On Seismic Behavior Of TFPS-isolated Cable Stayed Bridge" SIEICON International conference, Vadodara, India.

Performance of Channel and Tee Types of Shear Connector in Composite Slab with Steel Decking at Elevated Temperature

Bhaumik kumar I. Patel[1], V. R. Panchal[2], Nirpex A. Patel[3]

[1] Postgraduate Student (Structural Engineering), Department of Civil Engineering, Chandubhai S. Patel Institute of Technology, Charotar University of Science and Technology, Changa, Gujarat, India

[2] Professor and Head, Department of Civil Engineering, Chandubhai S. Patel Institute of Technology, Charotar University of Science and Technology, Changa, Gujarat, India

[3] Assistant Professor, Department of Civil Engineering, Chandubhai S. Patel Institute of Technology, Charotar University of Science and Technology, Changa, Gujarat, India

[1]bholu23395@gmail.com
[2]vijaypanchal.cv@charusat.ac.in
[3]nirpexpatel.cv@charusat.ac.in

***Abstract*—A 3-D non-linear finite element model of composite slab connected with steel beam with the help of Channel and Tee type shear connector with temperature distribution is developed in Abaqus/CAE. Concrete damaged plasticity model (CDP) for concrete. Analytical study is carried out to achieve quasi-static solution. Mechanical properties like elasto-plastic are used for all concrete and steel components. Thermal properties like specific heat, thermal expansion and thermal conductivity are used for all steel and concrete components. All elements assigned with appropriate material properties, loading and boundary conditions. Fire resistance capacity is analyzed with change in orientation 0°and 90° for Channel and Tee types of shear connector. Pre-failure behavior of Channel and Tee type shear connector under combination of fire and shear forces is analyzed. Stress, strain and deflection contours is mapped. In this study, Finite element analysis shows that shear capacity is increased in Channel and Tee types of connector compared to stud connector with elevated temperature.**

***Keywords*—Channel connector; Concrete damaged plasticity; Elevated temperature; Shear capacity; Tee connector.**

I. INTRODUCTION

Composite slab with profiled sheeting is the most general form of construction in now-a-days. Headed Stud, Channel and Tee shear connectors are used to transfer the lateral force from composite slab to steel beam. The shear capacity, slip and failure mode of the shear connectors relies on the several factors such as geometry of profiled sheeting, position of shear connectors in composite slab and number of connectors used in a rib of profiled sheeting [1]. It is recommended from various design codes and researchers that shear connectors are placed in central position.

Fire is a very complex phenomenon which can source serious structural damage. Fire can arise at any time in structures, and the protection of tenants and preserving the integrity of the structure are of leading preference. The response of a structural parts visible to fire is ruled by the rate heat, which is due to the mechanical properties of the material decrease as the temperature increases and similarly, the structural resistance of a member reductions with temperature increase.

When a steel beam and composite slab are exposed to fire, both the structural steel beam and concrete slab are uncovered to fire. On the other side, shear connectors are indirectly heated by heat transfer from the structural steel as showed in Figure 1. Fire will cause these parts to drop their mechanical strength with respect to the temperatures stretched. Though, the mechanical performance of composite slab uncovered to fire is much additional complex due to the dissimilar materials existing. The performance and strength of the shear connector are two of the main issues distressing the performance of a composite slab. Therefore, a 3D FE model of a push test using Abaqus/CAE is established to simulate the performance of Channel and Tee type shear connector at 0° and 90° orientation at elevated temperatures.

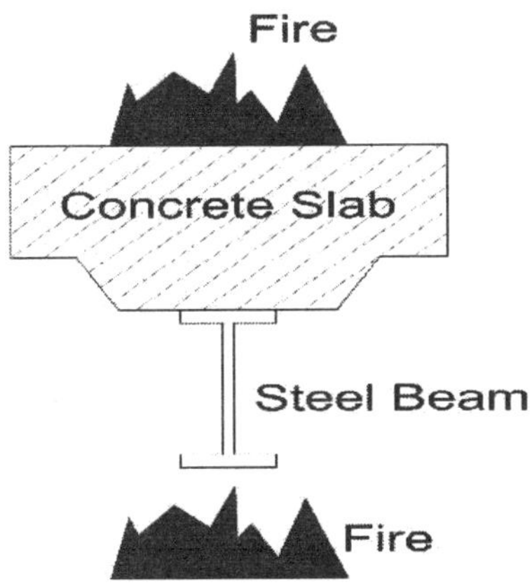

Figure 1. Push test on composite specimen subjected to fire

The general arrangement of push test is shown in Figure 1 Headed stud connector of 19×100 mm long is situated at the central side of the trough. Welding is provided through flange of steel beam having section of 254.6×14.2 mm to the deck. The depth of concrete slab is 125 mm [2].

II. Finite Element Model

A. General

A pre-processor 3D-nonlinear FE modal of composite slab is developed by using Abaqus/CAE software for the push test. For the quasi-static solution of FE model slow load application is used. For the analysis of the push test model suitable application of material, boundary conditions, constrain and contact interaction are specified. Figure 2 show the geometry of profile sheet and Figure 3 show the c/s elevation of Headed shear stud.

B. Geometry and Assembly

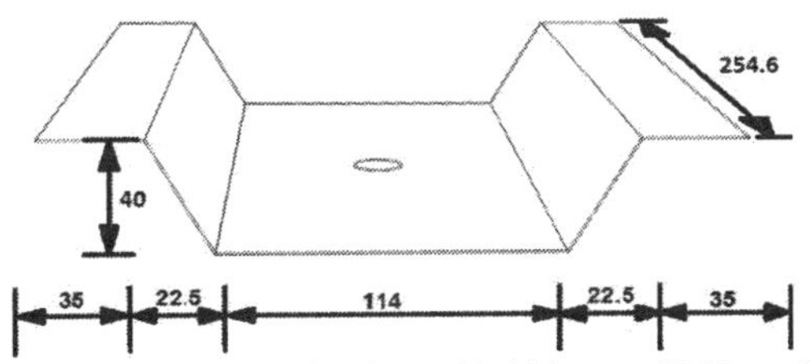

Figure 2. Geometry of profile sheet with thickness of 0.68 mm (All dimensions are in mm)

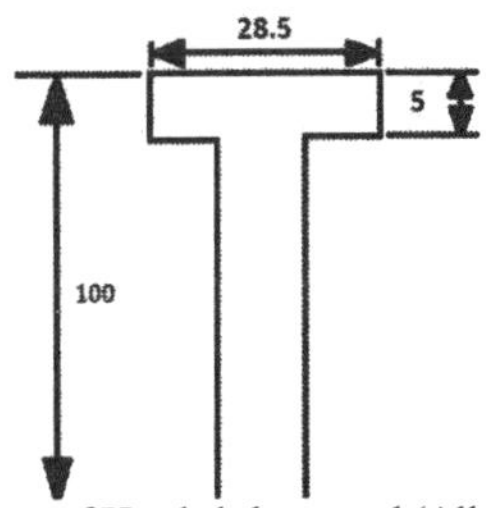

Figure 3. C/S elevation of Headed shear stud (All dimention are in mm)

The geometry of the push test is established by assuming a half symmetric at the center line of the steel beam web as shown in Figure 4 only the flange of beam is modeled and the web is ignored in modelling as geometry of the steel beam is not a part of interest. C3D8R 8-Node Brick type element meshing is applied to shear stud, concrete slab, profile sheet and steel beam.

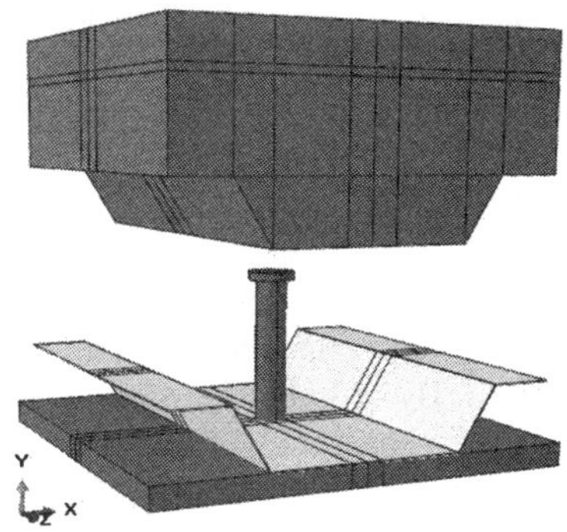

Figure 4. General arrangement of all component for FE analysis

C. Load application and boundary conditions

Loading surface and boundary conditions are provided as similar as study of Mirza and Uy [1] as shown in Figure 5. The surface of steel beam flange, concrete slab and profile sheet lying in same plane defined as surface 1 are prevented from translating at Z-axis. Bottom surface of steel beam flange is defined as surface 2 restrained from moving in Y-axis direction. Concrete slab defined as surface 3 and displacement is applied to positive X-direction.

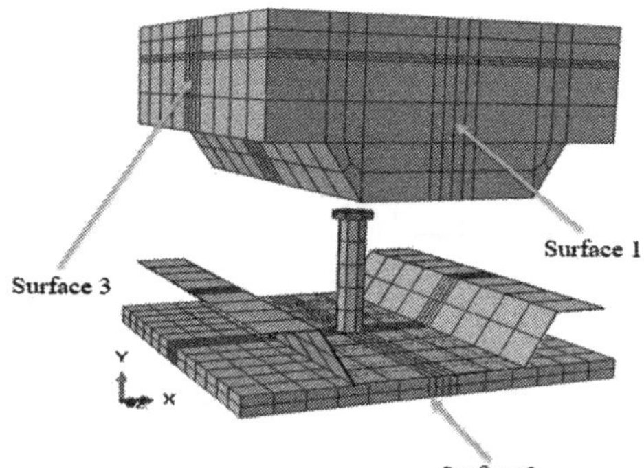

Figure 5. Loading and Boundary condition

D. *Contact interaction and Constraints*

All the parts are combined to form assembly and provided appropriate contact interaction and constraints. Contact interaction and constraints are as similar as defined in study of Mirza and Uy [1]. Surface to surface contact interaction is applied to concrete slab and profile sheet, concrete slab to Headed stud and profile sheet to steel beam flange. Tie constraint is provided between Headed stud to profile sheet and headed stud to steel beam flange.

E. *Validation*

FE model of push test for half symmetric portion developed in this study is verified with the analytical results Mirza and Uy [1]. Figure 6 show the FE stress results of Headed shear stud. The shear capacity, slip behavior and failure modes of Headed stud is investigated. Figure 7 show similarity in elasto-plastic behavior with error of 5.83% & 1.81% in ultimate load and relative slip respectively.

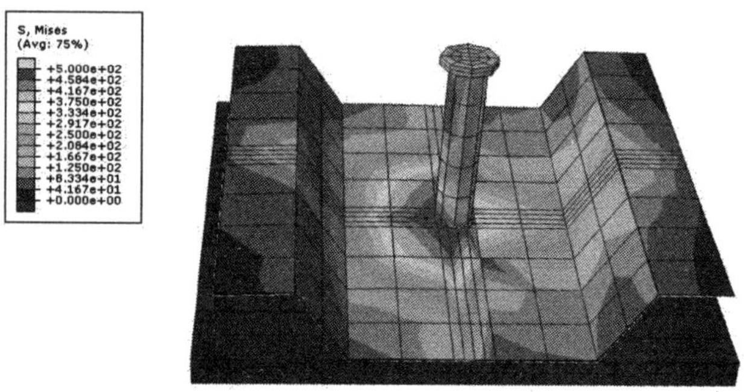

Figure 6. FE stress result of Headed Shear Stud

TABLE I
COMPARISON OF ANALYTICAL RESULTS

	Mirza and Uy [1]	Present study	Error (%)
Load (kN)	61.82	58.21	5.83
Slip (mm)	1.10	1.08	1.81

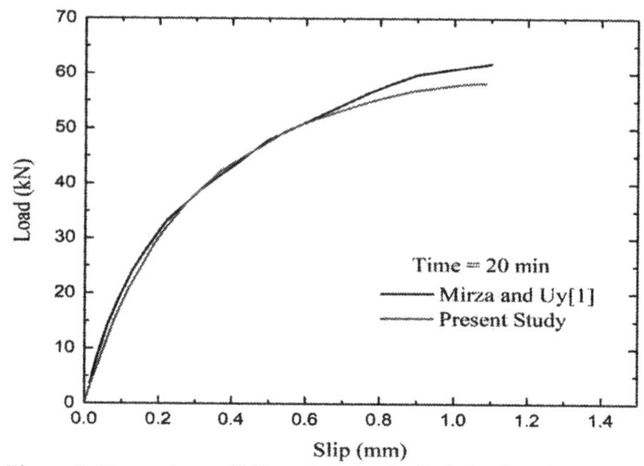

Figure 7. Comparison of FE analysis load–slip behavior of push test

III. PARAMETRIC STUDY

The FE model is generated in this study to analyze shear capacity, slip and failure modes of Headed stud connector, Channel connector and Tee connector with different orientation which are placed at center position of profile sheet [3]. The results obtained from FE analysis of shear connectors are as similar as analytical result of Mirza and Uy [1]. Further study on replacement of Headed shear stud with Channel and Tee connectors with different orientation is carried out to investigate relative shear capacity, slip and failure mode at elevated temperatures.

A. *Material property of concrete slab*

For the concrete slab, concrete damage plasticity model (CDP) is used. The behavior of concrete is defined in the terms of elasto-plastic properties for compressive & tensile strength of M 35.5 grade concrete. According to BS EN 1992-1-1 [4] provision, the elasto-plastic properties are defined. Density and poisson's ratio of concrete slab are taken as 2400kg/m^3 and 0.2 respectively and dilation angle is taken as 47°. According to BS EN 1992-1-1 [4] provision, the compression and tensile damage parameterare defined as shown in Figures 8 & 9.

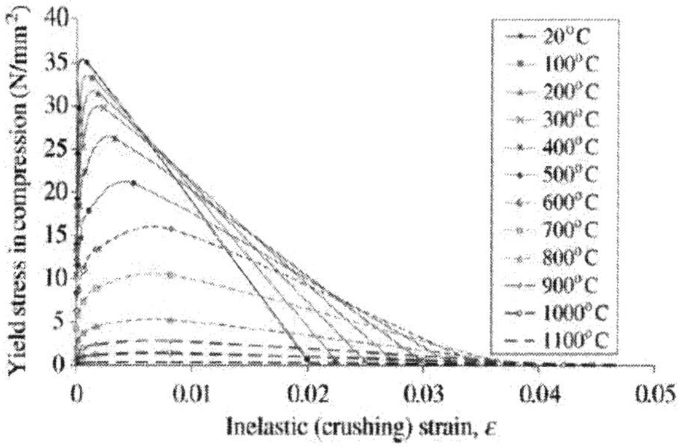

Figure 8. Yield stress Vs Crushing strain curve EC2 British Standard Institution [4]

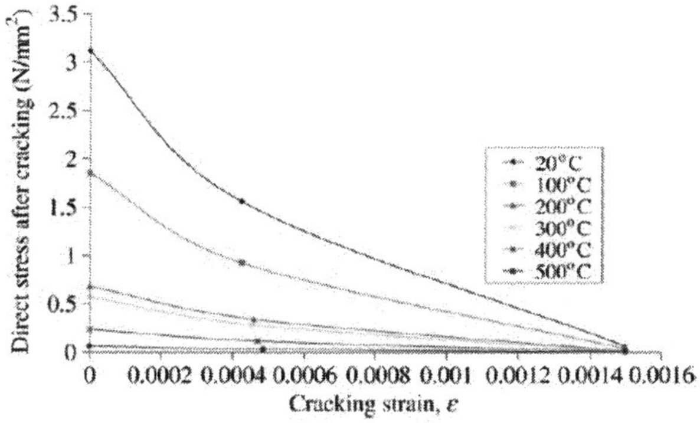

Figure 9. Cracking strain Vs Direct stress curve EC2 British Standard Institution [4]

B. Thermal material property of concrete slab

According to BS EN 1992-1-1 [4] provision, thermal properties of concrete slab, i.e., Specific heat, Thermal conductivity, Thermal expansion are shown in Figures 10-12 respectively.

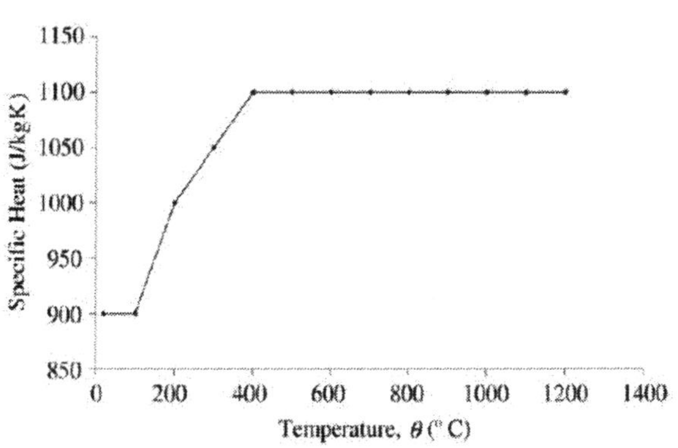

Figure 10. Specific heat for concrete EC2 British Standard Institution [4]

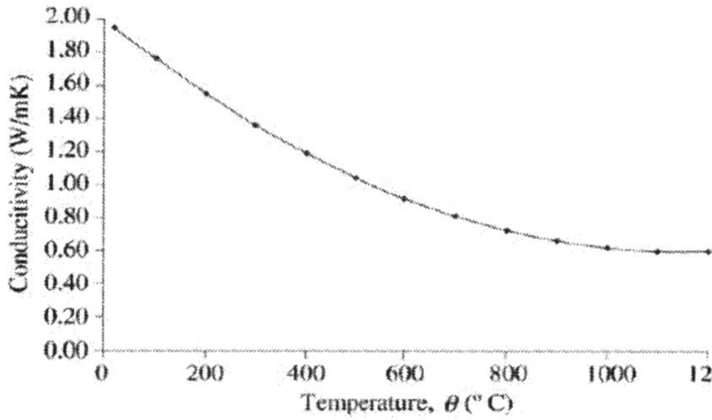

Figure 11. Thermal conductivity for concrete EC2 British Standard Institution [4]

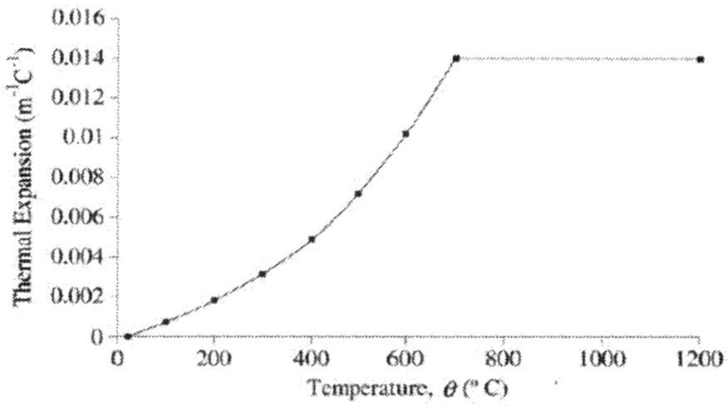

Figure 12.Thermal expansion for concrete EC2 British Standard Institution [4]

C. Material property for structural steel (profile sheet, steel beam, Tee and Channel connectors)

The modulus of elasticity of profile sheet, Tee and Channel connector is 200 GPa vary with the fire exposure time. According to BS EN 1993-1-1 [5] provision, yield stress for Tee and Channel connector and profile sheet is 500 MPa, and the density of all steel component is taken as 7800 kg/m^3.

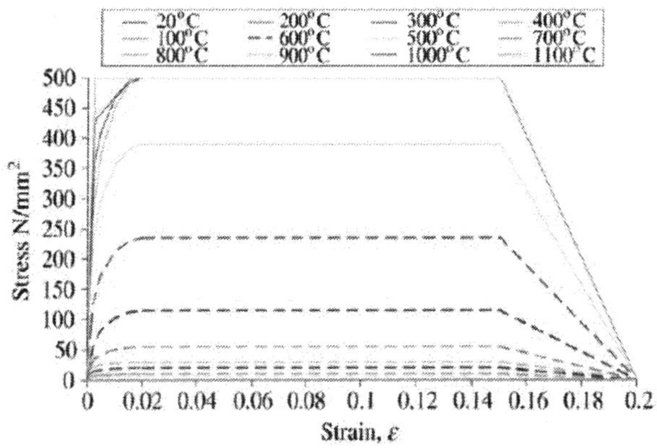

Figure 13. Stress-strainat elevated temperature for structural steel, EC3 British Standard Institution [5]

D. Thermal material property of structural steel

According to BS EN 1993-1-1 [5] provision, thermal properties of structural steel, i.e., Specific heat, Thermal conductivity, Thermal expansion are shown in Figures 14-16 respectively.

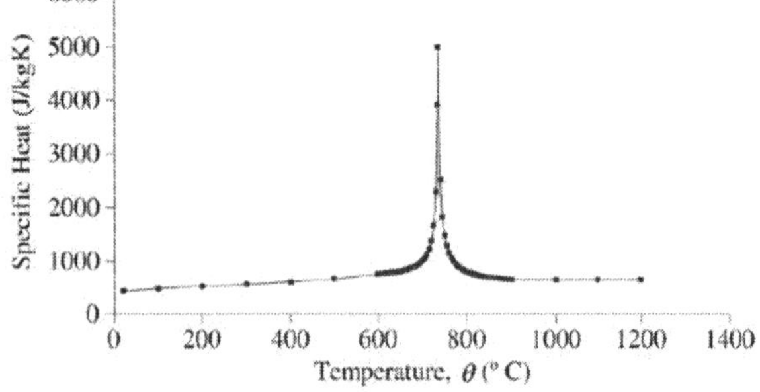

Figure 14. Specific heat for structural steel EC3 British Standard Institution [5]

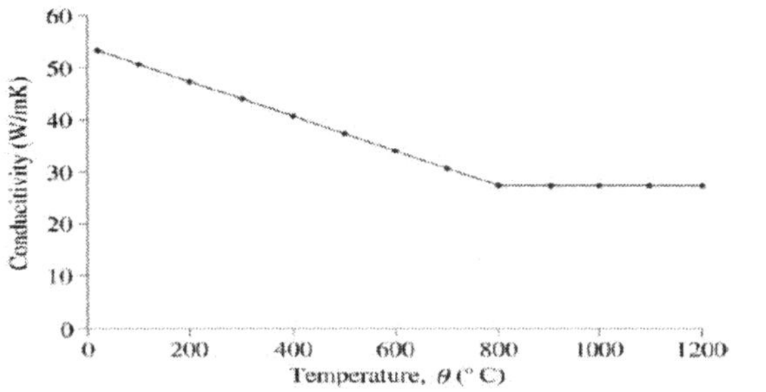

Figure 15. Thermal conductivity for structural steel EC3 British Standard Institution [5]

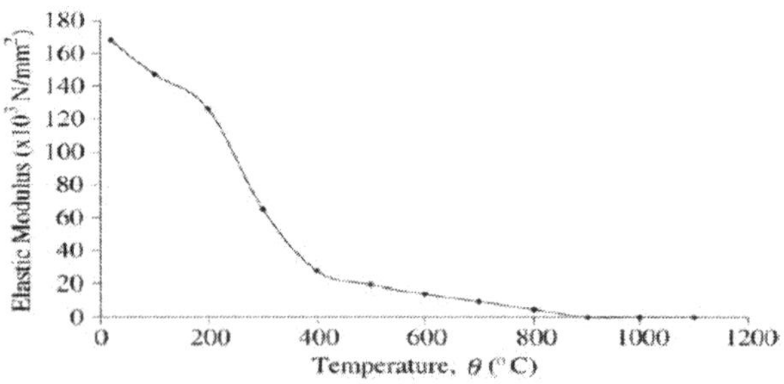

Figure 16. Thermal expansion for structural steel EC3 British Standard Institution [5]

E. Geometry of Channel and Tee connectors

Channel connector and Tee connector are developed using the FE software Abaqus/CAE. C/S elevation of Channel connector is as shown in Figure 17(a) and C/S top view of Tee type Channel connector is as shown in Figure 17(b) Channel connector are connected through profile sheet to steel beam flange where thickness of profile sheet is 0.68 mm and section of steel beam flange is 458×254.6×14.2 mm, similarly Tee connector is also connected to profile sheet and steel flange. The Concrete slab is provided with depth of 125 mm. C3D8R 8-Node Brick type element is used for meshing concrete slab, profile sheet, steel beam flange, Channel and Tee connector. Four models are developed with different orientation of Channel and Tee connectors with height of 100 mm as shown in Figures 18-21.

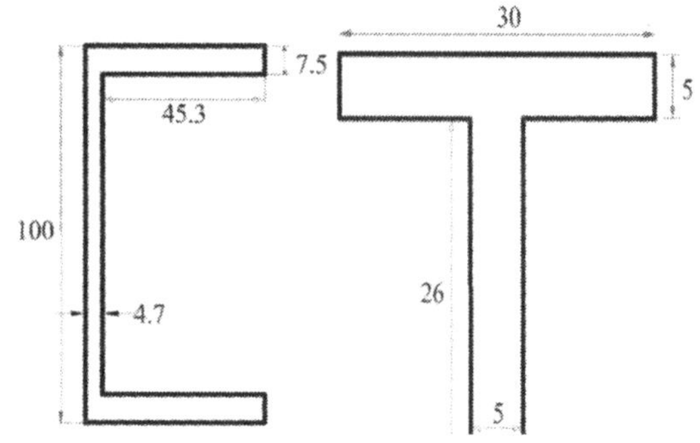

(a) (b)

Figure 17. Geometry of Channel Connector and Tee connectors (All dimensions are in mm)

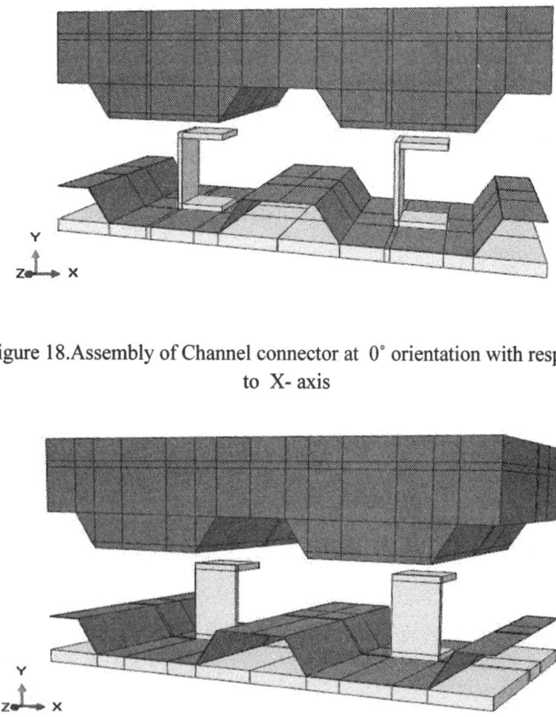

Figure 18.Assembly of Channel connector at 0° orientation with respect to X- axis

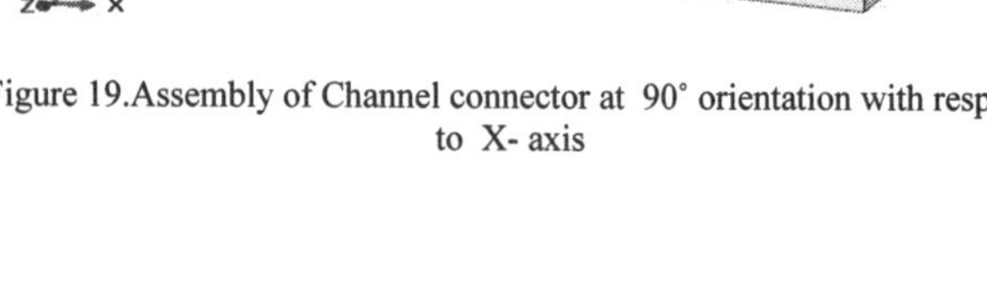

Figure 19.Assembly of Channel connector at 90° orientation with respect to X- axis

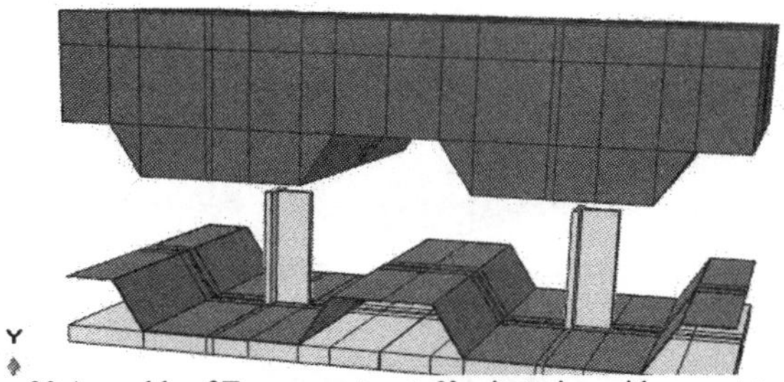

Figure 20.Assembly of Tee connector at 0° orientation with respect to X-axis

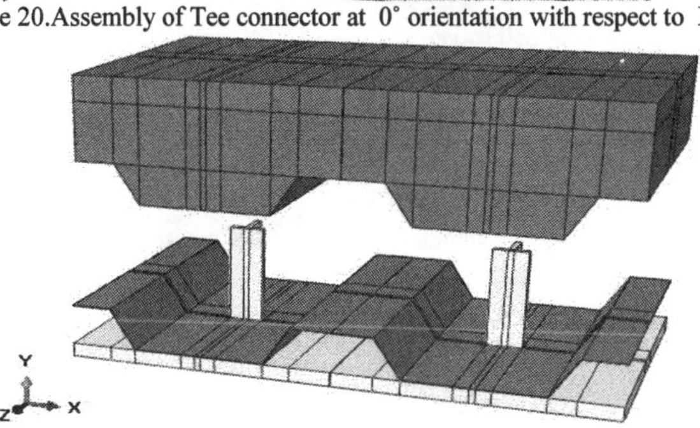

Figure 21.AssemblyofTee connector at 90° orientation with respect to X-axis

F. Contact interaction and Constraint

All the parts are combined to create assembly and assigned suitable contact interaction and constraints. Welding application is implemented in FE model by tying the surface of the profile sheet around Channel and Tee connector at its base, and the bottom surface of Channel and Tee connector tie constrain to the top surface of steel beam flange. Surface to surface contact is given between the concrete slab and profile sheet by using the contact pair algorithm, and same contact application for concrete slab to Channel connector and apart from Tee connector in second model. Frictional penalty coefficient is applied to profile sheet bottom and steel beam flange top is given as 0.5, and the normal behavior is given as "hard contact" to prevent the penetration in another object.

G. Loading and Boundary Conditions

Loading surface and boundary conditions for channel and Tee type shear connector same as Headed stud connector shown in Figure 5. The bottom surface of steel beam denoted as surface 2 is restrained in all direction. The surface 1 in which the nodes of profile sheet, steel beam and concrete slab are restrained to displace in Z direction. The push test is carried by applying displacement on the surface 3 of concrete in positive X direction with the help of smooth amplitude application with rate of 0.25 mm/sec for efficiency of the analysis results.

H. Analysis procedure

Analysis is consisting two step by step procedure structural [6] and temperature analysis respectively. Fire amplitude represent by the ISO834 [7] curve, gives average value of compartmental fire for small size which is define in ISO834 [7] shown in Figure 22.

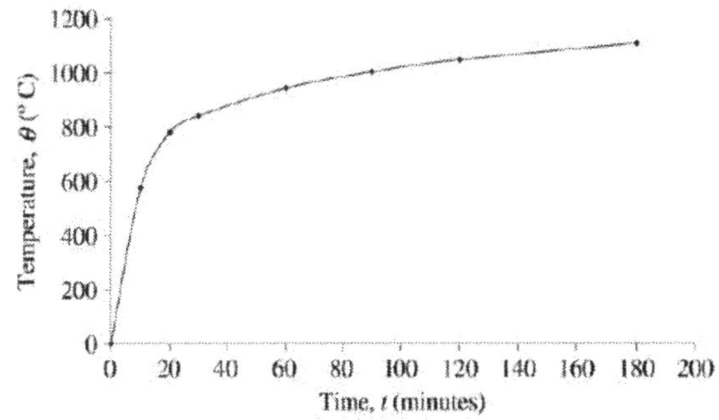

Figure 22. ISO834 Fire standard curve [7]

IV. Results And Discussion

Results are evaluated in terms of load v/s slip curve by replacing Headed stud with Channel and Tee connector at different orientations. Displacement is calculated on the node chosen from the opposite surface of the load applied. The analysis result for shear resistance per stud Mirza and Uy (2009) [1] is 84.25 kN at 1.25 mm slip. Shear resistance of Channel at 0° orientation is 152.21 kN with 1.259 mm slip and at 90° orientation is 136.7 kN with 1.253 mm slip. The analysis result for shear resistance of Tee at 0° orientation is 117.28 kN with 1.249 mm slip and at 90° orientation is 89.87 kN with 1.27 mm slip. Figures 23-26 show stress counters in Channel and Tee types of shear connector with 0° and 90° orientation at fire exposure time of 0, 20, 90, 180 minutes. Figures 27-28 show the load v/s displacement graph of Channel connector at 0° and 90° orientation at fire exposure time of 0, 20, 90 and 180 minutes. Figures 29-30show load v/s displacement graph of Tee connector at 0° and 90° orientation at fire exposure time of 0, 20, 90 and 180 minutes. Figures 31-34 show comparative graph of Headed stud, Channel and Tee types of shear connector at fire exposure time of 0, 20, 90 and 180 minutes.

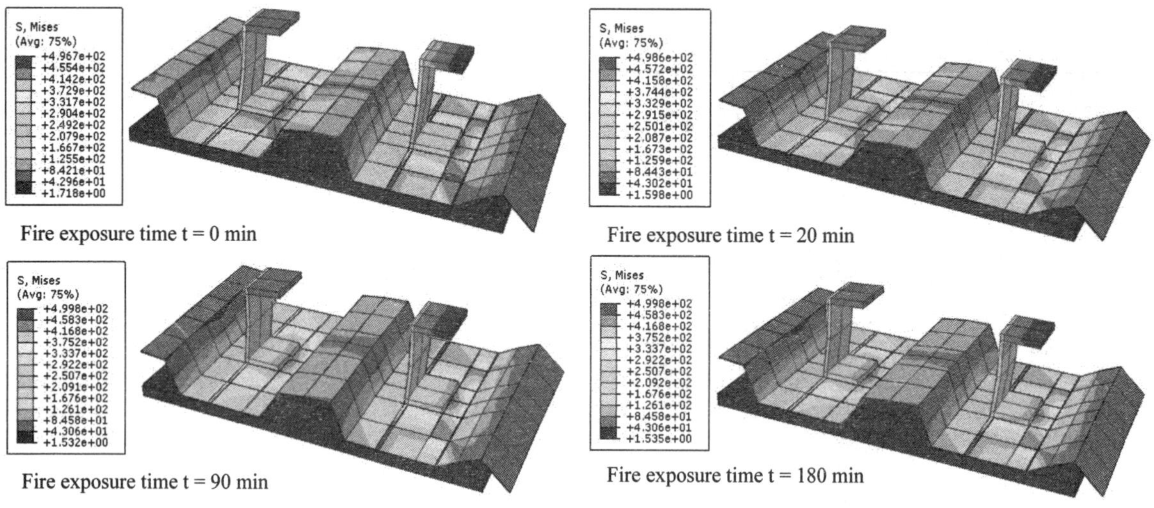

Figure 23. FE stress results of Channel connector at 0° orientation

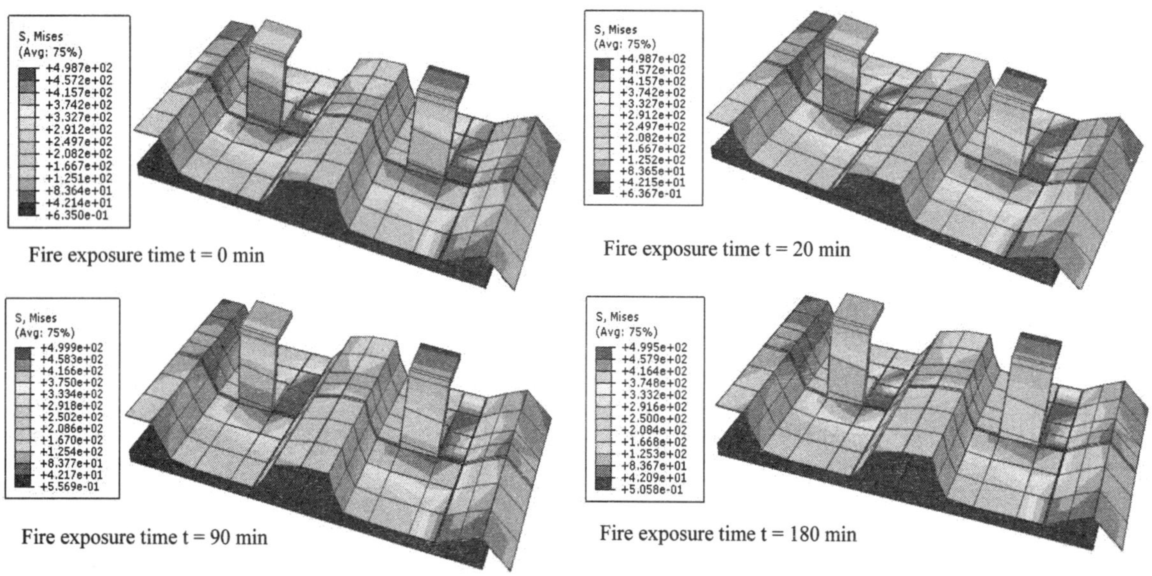

Figure 24. FE stress results of Channel connector at 90° orientation

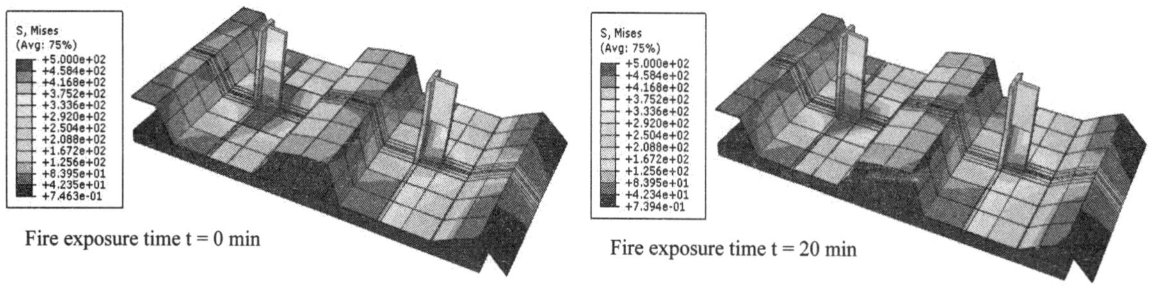

Figure25. (a) FE stress results ofTee connector at 0° orientation

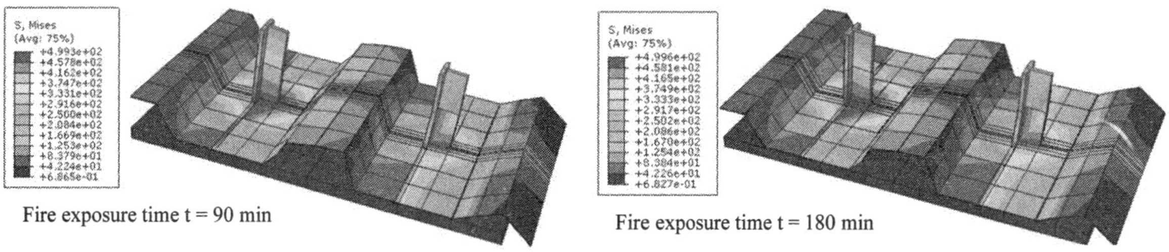

Figure 25.(b) FE stress results ofTee connector at 0˚ orientation

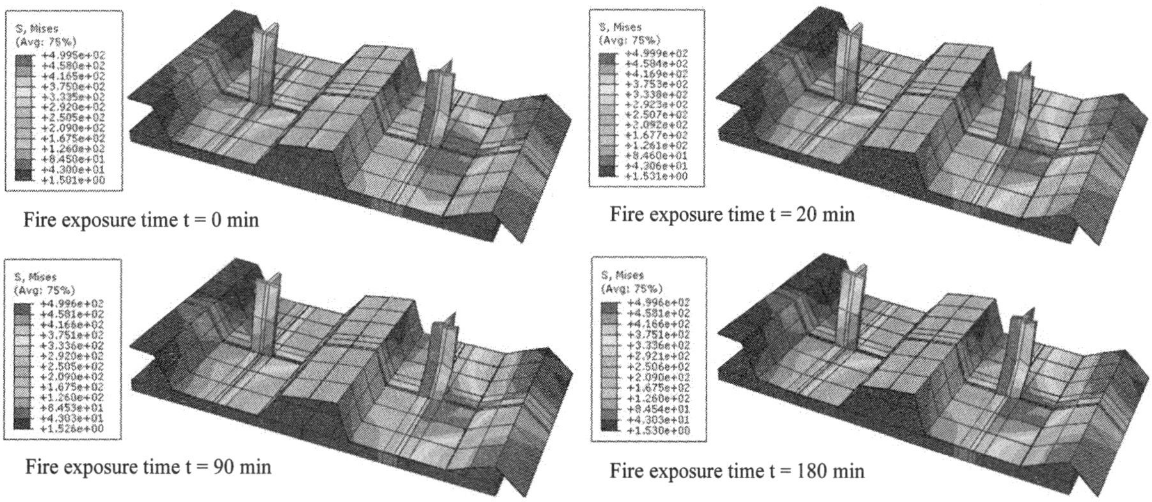

Figure 26. FE stress results of Tee connector at 90˚ orientation

Table II show values of load v/s displacement for all connectors at fire exposure time of 0, 20, 90, 180 minutes of fire. Table III show percentage increment in ultimate load carrying capacity of Channel and Tee types of shear connector with respect to Headed stud shear connector at different fire exposure time.

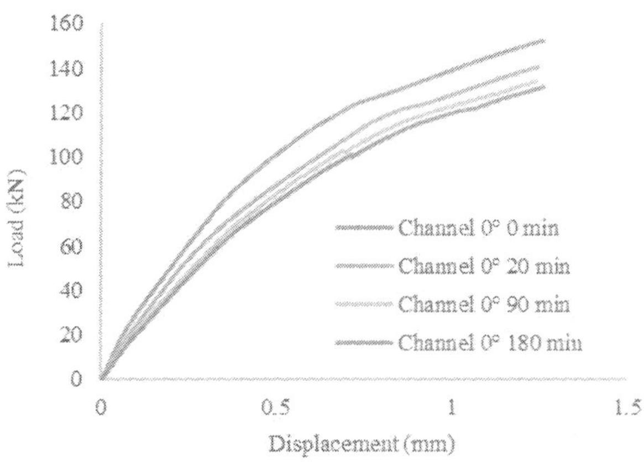

Figure 27. Comparison for Channel type shear connector with 0° orientation of push test with elevated temperature

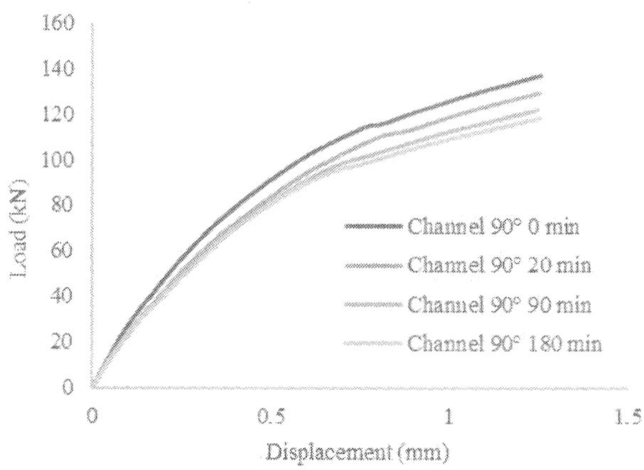

Figure 28.Comparison for Channel type shear connector with 90° orientation of push test with elevated temperature

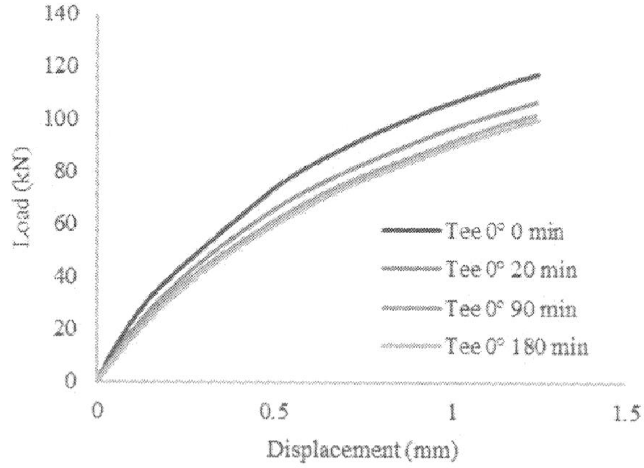

Figure 29.Comparison for Tee type shear connector with 0° orientation of push test with elevated temperature

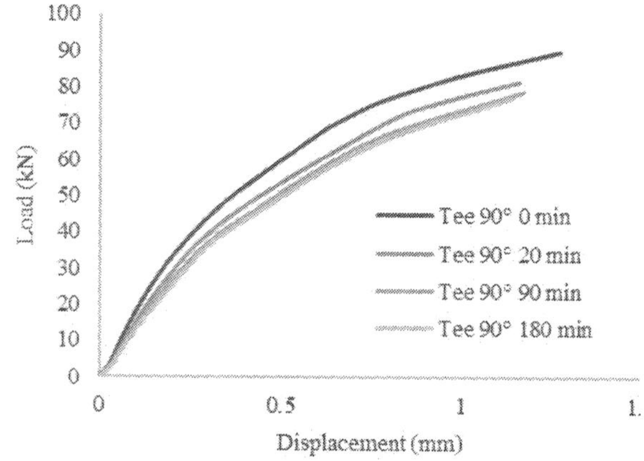

Figure 30.Comparison for Tee type shear connector with 90° orientation of push test with elevated temperature

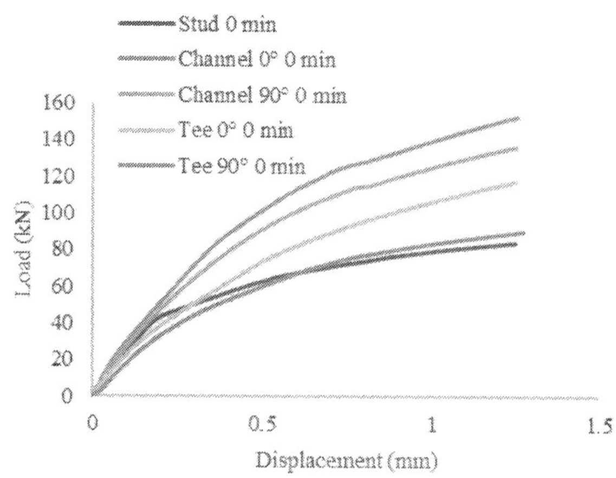

Figure 31. Comparison of push test of Channel, Tee & Stud type shear connectors for fire exposure time of 0 minute

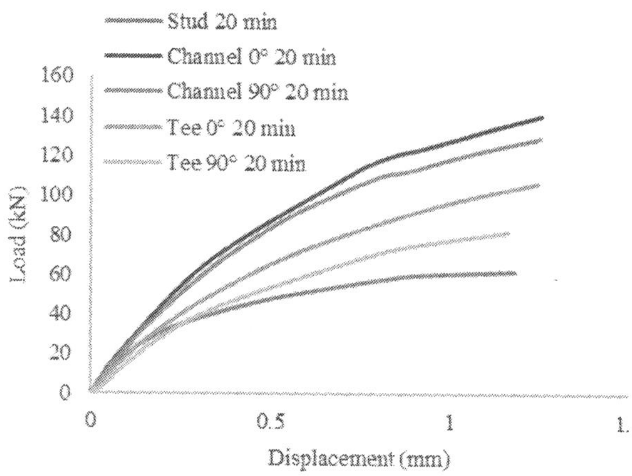

Figure 32. Comparison of push test of Channel, Tee & Stud type shear connectors for fire exposure time of 20 minutes

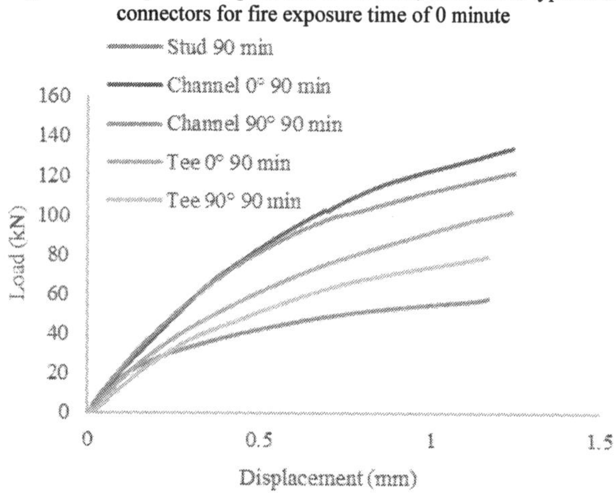

Figure 33. Comparison of push test of Channel, Tee & Stud type shear connectors for fire exposure time of 90 minutes

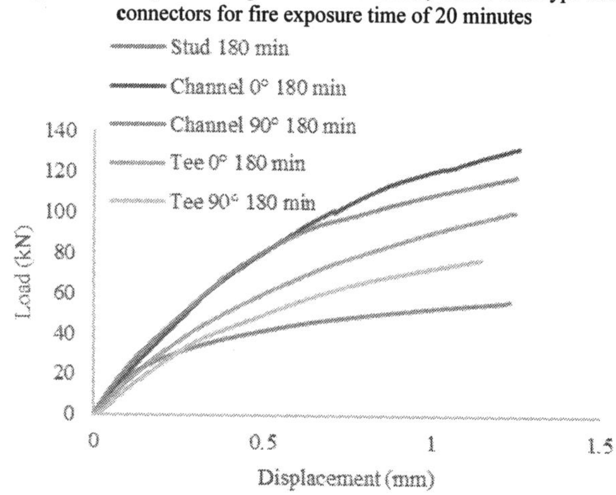

Figure 34. Comparison of push test of Channel, Tee & Stud type shear connectors for fire exposure time of 180 minutes

TABLE II

COMPARISON PUSH TEST OF CHANNEL, TEE & STUD TYPES OF SHEAR CONNECTOR FOR FIRE EXPOSURE TIME OF 0, 20, 90, 180 MINUTES RESPECTIVELY

Shear Connector	Orientation	Fire Exposure Time							
		0 minute		20 minutes		90 minutes		180 minutes	
		Ultimate Load (kN)	Relative Displacement (mm)	Ultimate Load (kN)	Relative Displacement (mm)	Ultimate Load (kN)	Relative Displacement (mm)	Ultimate Load (kN)	Relative Displacement (mm)
Stud[1]	---	84.25	1.25	61.82	1.18	58.17	1.17	56.35	1.23
Channel	0°	152.21	1.259	140.83	1.255	134.21	1.242	131.59	1.259
	90°	136.7	1.253	129.17	1.251	122.05	1.246	118.02	1.252
Tee	0°	117.28	1.249	106.95	1.244	102.05	1.239	100.21	1.248
	90°	89.87	1.27	81.71	1.16	79.06	1.17	77.14	1.14

TABLE III

PERCENTAGE INCREMENT IN ULTIMATE LOAD CARRYING CAPACITY OF CHANNEL AND TEE TYPES OF SHEAR CONNECTOR

Shear Connector	Orientation	Fire Exposure Time			
		0 minute	20 minutes	90 minutes	180 minutes
Channel	0°	80.66 %	127.80 %	130.72 %	133.52 %
	90°	62.26 %	108.94 %	109.81 %	109.44 %
Tee	0°	39.20 %	73.00 %	75.43 %	77.83 %
	90°	6.67 %	32.17 %	35.91 %	36.89 %

V. CONCLUSIONS

- According to analytical results, it is observed that shear capacity, slip and failure mode of Channel connector indicate its application to the structure shows better performance compared to Headed stud and Tee connector. As well as the Tee connector indicate its application to the structure shows better performance compared to only Headed stud connector with elevated temperature.
- Load v/s slip behaviour of Channel connector with 0° orientation indicates increment compared to Channel connector with 90° orientation at elevated temperature.
- Load v/s slip behaviour of Tee connector with 0° orientation indicates increment compared to Tee connector with 90° orientation at elevated temperature.
- Application of Channel connector with 0° orientation having highest energy absorption capacity among all types of shear connector at all different level of elevated temperature.

References

[1] O. Mirza, B. Uy (2009) "Behavior of headed stud shear connectors for composite steel–concrete beams at elevated temperatures", Journal of Constructional Steel Research, Vol. 65, pp: 662-674.

[2] E. Ellobody, B. Young (2006) "Performance of shear connection in composite beams with profiled steel Sheeting", Journal of Constructional Steel Research, Vol. 62, pp: 682-694.

[3] Yash Pandya, V. R. Panchal, Nirpex A. Patel (2017), "Study on shear capacity of different types of shear connectors in composite slab with steel decking", New Horizons in Civil Engineering, pp: 136-142.

[4] BS EN 1992-1-1 (2004). "Eurocode 2: Design of concrete structures: Part 1-1: General rules and rules for buildings". London: British Standards Institution.

[5] BS EN 1993-1-1 (2004). "Eurocode 3: Design of steel structures: Part 1-1: General rules and rules for buildings", London: British Standards Institution.

[6] BS EN 1994-1-1 (2004). "Eurocode 4: Design of composite steel and concrete structures: Part 1-1: General rules and rules for buildings", London: British Standards Institution.

[7] ISO834, "Fire resistance tests, Element of building construction", 1999-09-15.

A Three Dimensional Non-Linear Finite Element Modelling of Top-Seat Angle Connection

D.R. Panchal[1], H.D. Devani[2]

[1]*Assistant Professor, Department of Applied Mechanics, Faculty of Technology and Engineering, The Maharaja Sayajirao University of Baroda, Vadodara, Gujarat, India*

[2]*M.E. (Structural Engineering) Post Graduate Scholar, Department of Applied Mechanics, Faculty of Technology and Engineering, The Maharaja Sayajirao University of Baroda, Vadodara, Gujarat, India*

[1]drpanchal-appmech@msubaroda.ac.in
[2]hddevani@gmail.com

***Abstract*—Real behavior of steel beam to column connection in steel construction is not linear and it needs to be quantified. Assuming the connection to be pinned, overestimates the span moment and deflection while it underestimates the support moment. On the other side assuming it to be rigid, the reverse is true. In this paper, the non-linear behavior of top-seat angle beam to column connection, which is widely used in steel construction is numerically modelled. The focus of this study is to develop a sophisticated 3-D non-linear finite element model and to compare the results (moment-rotation curve) with existing experimental data from the relevant literature. A finite element software package *ABAQUS* has been adopted for this purpose, within which Newton-Raphson method is implemented to solve geometric, material and contact non-linearities. Contact problems being highly non-linear often lead to non-convergence of the solution and to avoid those 1-Dimensional beam elements (Beams in Space) with kinematic coupling are used to model bolts in this study. Results are compared with Experiments and they show close agreement with numerical modelling done in this study.**

***Keywords*—Bolt Modelling, Contact Non-linearity, Moment-Rotation, Semi-Rigid connection, Steel Connection.**

I. INTRODUCTION

Structural analysis of steel framework is usually carried out by assuming joints as either flexible (pinned) or fully rigid, in order to simplify calculations. Various experiments were doneto show that connections commonly considered as pinned or hinges often exhibit fairly significant rotational stiffness and strength and, connections considered as rigid can develop bending deformation. These behavioural features of connections can significantly influence the response of steel framework. From the point of assembly, rigid connections are those in which beams are directly welded to column flanges and pinned are those which have very little connection stiffness like single or double web angle or header plate connections. But connections which are fastened through bolts or rivets using various components like top and seat angles show non-linear behaviour and lie somewhere between the assumption of fully rigid and perfectly pinned condition and those are called semi-rigid connections.

These simple assumptions of either pinned or fully rigid connection used in common design routine are undoubtedly effective in analysing a large number of structures, but in many cases, the correct assessment of structural reliability requires the semi-rigid behaviour of joints to be accounted for. To quantify the semi-rigid behaviour of connections moment-rotation (M-θ) curves are used; as rotational deformation (θ) is the primary mode of distortion for any connection which is caused by in-plane bending moment (M). The modelling of M-θcurve of beam-to-column joints requires two steps to be accomplished. The primary step is to predict M-θcurve and second is to represent that curve mathematically, which intern is required to account for joint rotational behaviour in structural analysis. This study is aimed to predict M-θcurve and its non-linear behaviour, that is the first step.

Although the most accurate knowledge of the joint behavior is obtained through experimental tests, the Finite element method is chosen among various methods (empirical methods, analytical method, mechanical models) to predict moment-rotation curve due to the fact that experiments are too expensive for everyday design practice and also FEM provide low cost-effectiveness ratio compared to above methods. And also for developing simple prediction methods, the extensive parametric study is required and it can only be done by using FEM.

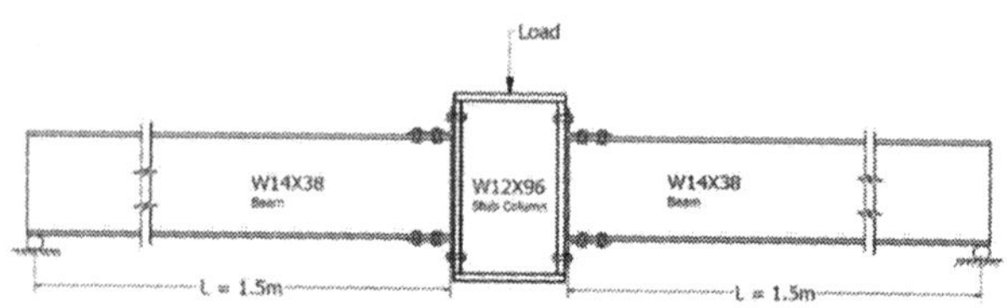

Fig.1 Experimental set-up used by A. Azizinamini (1982) [1]

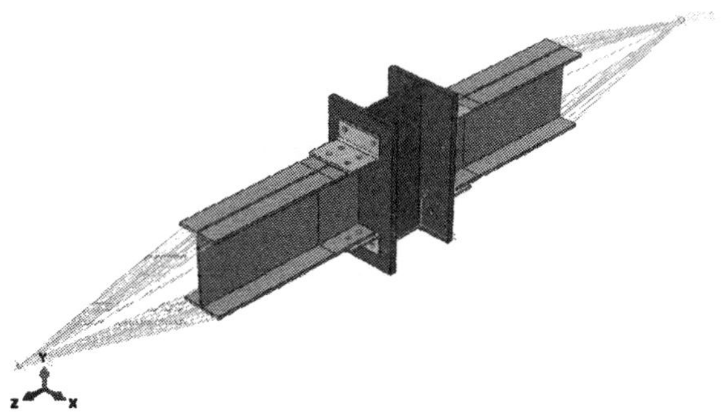

Fig.2. Reduced Beam Length of 750mm while loading point @1500mm

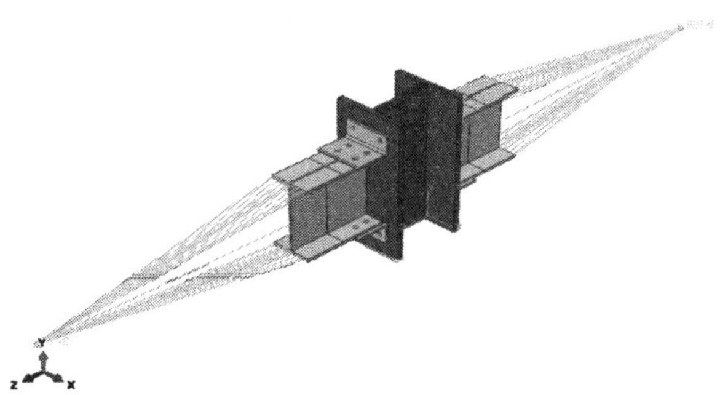

Fig.3. Reduced Beam Length of 375mm while loading point @1500mm

Ali Ahemad*et al.*[2] numerically modelled top-seat angle connection using *ABAQUS*, with small sliding contact formulation considering non-linear material behaviour, and shown that the bolt sustains additional tensile force due to prying action, bolt pretension increases the initial connection stiffness. A. Pirmoz*et al.*[3] used *ANSYS* to model connection and shown role of seat angle in a top-seat angle connection. Mohammad Jobaer Hasan et al. [4] modelled top-seat angle connection using *ABAQUS/CAE* and done a parametric study to predict the moment-rotation response of stainless steel connection.

All the above-mentioned researchers have modelled all the components with 3-D solid elements, even bolts. All of them have utilized benchmark experiment done by A. Azizinamini [1]. Also, they have used a quarter symmetric model of the connection. But the length of the beam was kept same as it was in the experiment that is 1500mm.The aim of this study is to develop a sophisticated 3-D non-linear finite element model of top-seat angle connection, with bolts modeled as beam elements, and with reduced beam length while keeping loading point same as earlier (with the help of kinematic coupling). The model used for this purpose is of A. Azizinamini [1].

II. Finite Element Modeling

Among various specimen tested by A. Azizinamini [1], two specimens namelyA1 and A2 are taken up for FE modelling and results are compared in terms of M-θ curve. A commercial general purpose finite element software package *ABAQUS/CAE* was adopted for this purpose. A full scale model was made at first and then beam length is reduced while keeping loading point same (using kinematic coupling) as of it was in the full-scale model, as shown in Figure-2 and Figure-3, which is explained further in following sections.

A. Test set-up and Geometry of the model:

Figure-1 shows the experimental set-up used by A. Azizinamini [1]. It can be seen that a set of two beam sections are attached to a centrally placed stub column. Figure-4 shows a typical top-seat angle bolted connection, for which required number and diameter of bolts and appropriate angle sections are chosen based on design principles and then after the top and bottom flanges of beams are connected to centrally placed stub column with those sections. Geometrical properties of various components used for this FE modelling are mentioned in Table-1. Length of stub column is arbitrarily taken as 700 mm and length of beam was as mentioned 1500 mm, 750mm (Half Beam) and 375mm (One fourth of total length) taken. Gap of 12mm was kept between column flange and beam.

Table 1Geometrical properties used in the current FE model (Reference A. Azizinamini (1982) [1])

Specimen	A1	A2
Column Section	W12X96	W12X96
Beam Section	W14X38	W14X38
Angle section	L6 X 4 X3/8	L6 X 4 X1/2
Length (L) in mm	203.2	203.2
Gauge (g) in mm	63.5	63.5
Bolt Spacing @ column flange (mm)	139.7	139.7
Bolt Spacing @ Beam flange (mm)	88.9	88.9

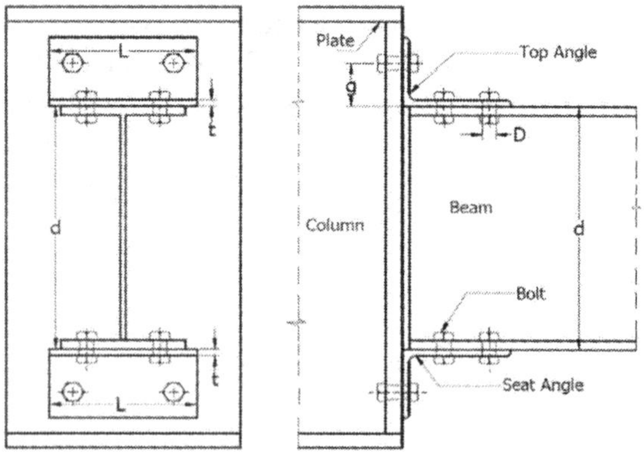

B. *Material Properties:*

Stress-Strain relationship for all the connection components used by A. Azizinamini[1] is represented by a bilinear material constitutive model with Von-Mises yield criterion (Classical metal plasticity in *ABAQUS/CAE*) and isotropic hardening rule. ASTM A36 grade of steel was used for beams, columns and angle sections and for bolts A325 was used. Material properties reported by A. Azizinamini[1] for all sections except bolt are mentioned in Table-2. For bolts, typical properties are taken from Mohammad Jobaer Hasan et al. [4] as it was not reported by A. Azizinamini[1].

Table 2 Material properties used in the current FE model

Material Properties	A1	A2
Yield stress angle(Mpa)	365	277
Yield stress bolt (Mpa)	636	636
Ultimate stress (Mpa)	550	530
Ultimate stress (Mpa)	830	830
Elongation at ultimate stress for angle	20%	20%
Elongation at ultimate stress for bolt	10%	10%
Modulus of elasticity E (Mpa)	206000	206000
Poisson's ratio	0.3	0.3

C. *Element selection and Mesh density:*

Mohammad Jobaer Hasan et al. [4] suggested that brick (Hexahedral) elements are more suitable to model continuum behaviour of bolted steel connections rather than standard shell elements. There were two families of elements used in this modelling of top-seat angle connection, namely three-dimensional solid continuum elements and structural elements (beams in space) [10].*ABAQUS/CAE*offers vast varieties of both types of elements. Between bricks and tetras, bricks are chosen due to first-order tetras are usually overly stiff, and extremely fine meshes are required to obtain accurate results[10].

Various types of linear (8-Noded elements, C3D8, C3D8H, C3D8R, C3D8I) and quadratic (20 Noded elements, C3D20, C3D20H, C3D20R) brick elements are available, Mohammad Jobaer Hasan et al. [4]compared all the above mentioned elements and came to conclusion that 8 Noded brick elements with incompatible modes are more suitable for modelling the connection. According to Mohammad Jobaer Hasan et al. [4].8-Noded brick element with reduced integration (1 G point) underestimates the connection resistance as they are not suitable for contact modelling due to their inherent deficiency and they show hourglassing (that is they deform without any resistance to load). On the other hand, C3D8 elements with full integration (8G points) are accurate in terms of constitutive law integration, but parasitic shear stresses (shear-locking) is a common problem for this kind of elements when bending dominated structure is modelled. C3D8I, 8 Noded elements with full integration (8G points) are first-order elements that are enhanced by incompatiblemodes to improve their bending behaviour. The primary effect of these modes is to eliminate the parasitic shearstresses that cause the response of the regular first-order displacement elements to be too stiff in bending. In addition, these modes eliminate the artificial stiffening due to Poisson's effect in bending. Because of the added internal degrees of freedom due to the incompatible modes (13 for C3D8I), these elements are somewhat more expensive than the regular first-order displacement elements; however, they are significantly more economical than second-order elements. The incompatible mode elements use full integration and, thus, have no hourglass modes[10].So C3D8I and C3D8R with enhanced hourglass control elements are chosen to mesh all the components except bolts, which are modelled with B31 Beams in space and discussed in upcoming section.

Mesh density is such chosen that, near the critical region that is near the beam column junction, seeding size is taken as 10mm and far away it is 40mm and 35 mm for beam section and column section respectively. Mohammad Jobaer Hasan et al. [4] carried out mesh sensitivity analysis and showed that 14,585 number of C3D8I elements are sufficient for the quarter symmetric model. Figure-6 shows the meshing done for this study.

D. Bolt Modelling:

Fastener joints can be difficult to analyse due to the many parameters and complex phenomena involved in the behaviour of the joints like friction, sliding, bolt hole deformation, contact, high local stress, non-linear material behaviour, bolt-pretension etc [5].Also,an explicit representationof the connection is not always needed as long as the essential features are adequately captured. The fastener can be modelled as either beam elements, connector elements, rigid elements, solid elements or spring elements. So, unlike *and* Ali Ahemad*et al. [2].*,A. Pirmoz*et al.[3], and* Mohammad Jobaer Hasan et al. [4],who have modelled bolts as solid elements, bolts in this study are modelled with beam elements namely beams in space (B31) with kinematic coupling constraint to reduce computational time and also to avoid convergence issue arising due to above mentioned reasons.

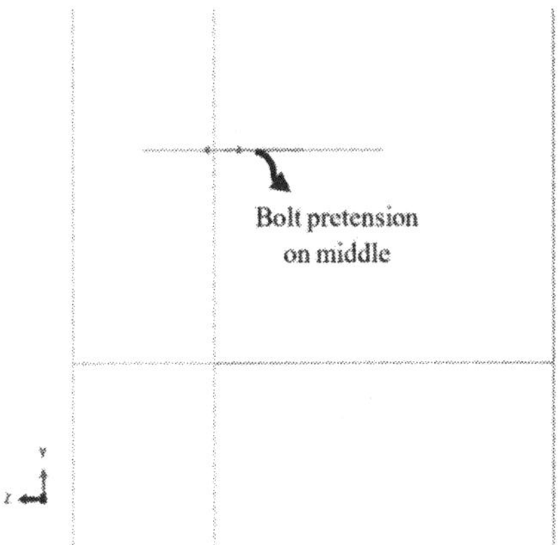

Figure 5 Bolt Pre-Tension of 173kN

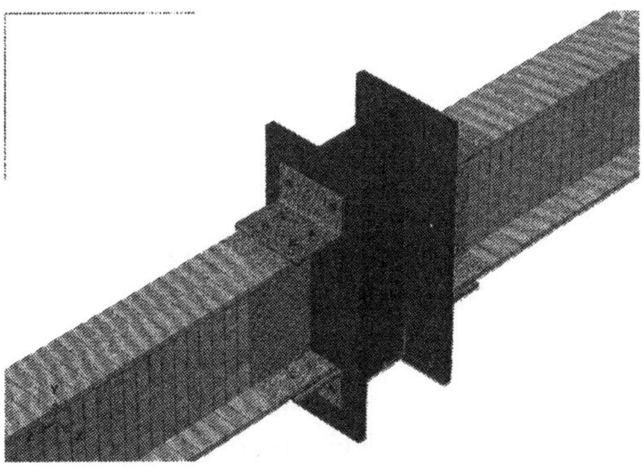

Figure-6 Mesh Pattern for connection model A1

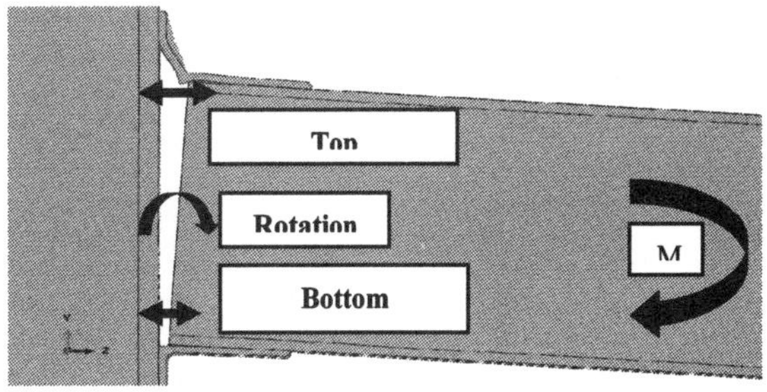

Figure 7 Top-Seat Angle connection after deformation

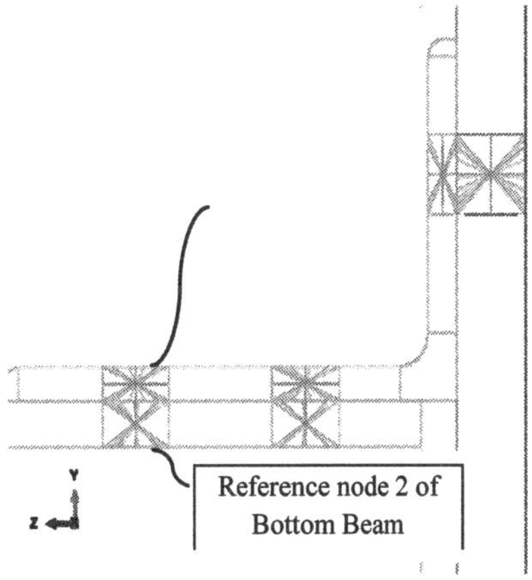

Figure-8 Kinematic Coupling for bolts

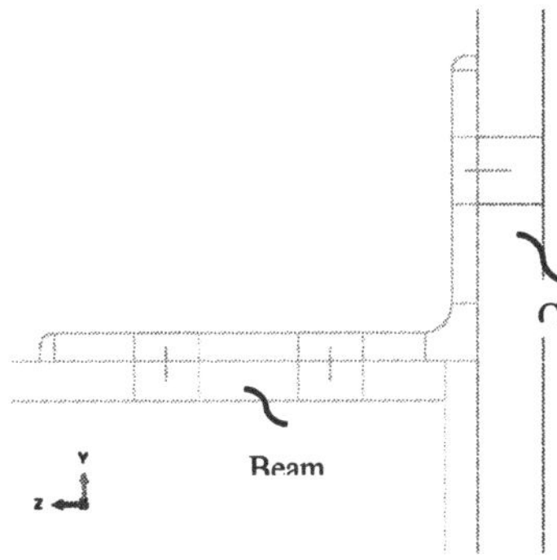

Figure-9 Length of Bolts as Beams

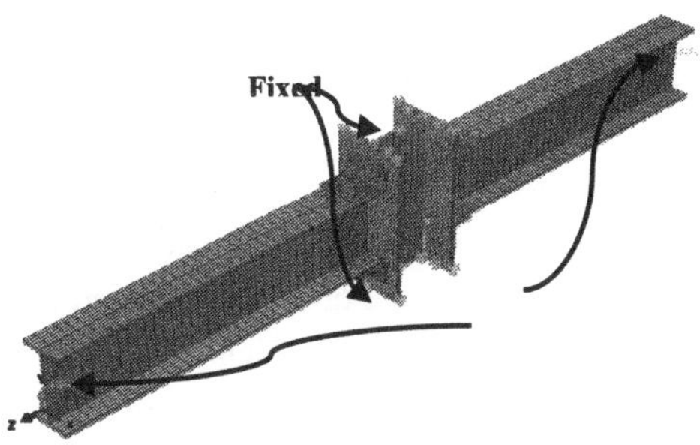

Figure-10 Boundary Conditions

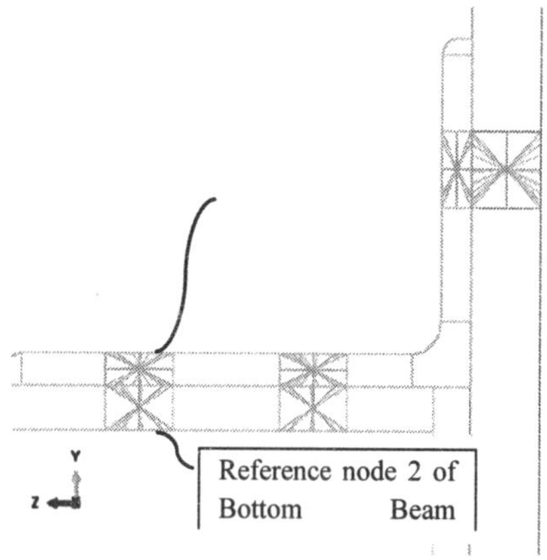

Figure-8 Kinematic Coupling for bolts

What kinematic coupling does is, limits the motion of a group of nodes (in this case nodes inside the bolt hole) to the rigid body motion defined by a reference node (node of beam element) [11] as shown in figure-8. Length of beam element (Figure 9) is such chosen that it divides full length of beam part into 3 equal length elements, and on the middle element bolt pretension is applied and nodes of remaining elements act as a reference node for kinematic coupling as shown in figure-8.

E. Loads and Boundary conditions:

Boundary conditions, as shown in Figure-10, top and the bottom face of column section are fixed, that is U1=U2=U3=0 (3-d elements have only translational dofs) are applied in the initial step. A. Azizinamini[1] did not mention the amount of bolt pretension force but only mentioned that bolts are tightened by an air wrench using the turn-of-the-nut method, so as it was suggested by Mohammad Jobaer Hasan et al. [4], in the second step that is pretension step, bolt load option is used within *ABAQUS/CAE*, with bolt pretension of 173kN and it was modified in the third step by "fixing at current length" (preventing it to propagate to the next step). In the third step, 50 mm displacement in the downward direction is applied at both cantilever ends of the beam sections.

For both steps, Static-General type of analysis procedure is used with non-linear geometry (nlgeom) option on, meaning Newton-Raphson method is used to solve this problem.Connection moment was determined by multiplying reaction force at cantilever end with its distance to the instantaneous centre of rotation, which is at the heel of seat angle as shown in Figure-7. Relative connection rotation is determined by subtracting bottom displacement from top displacement and dividing it by depth of the connecting beam, as shown in Figure-7.

F. Contact modelling:

Contact can be defined as "the interaction between bodies that have come to touch each other and exchange load and energy (heat and electric charge)". Material properties (e.g. modulus of elasticity) are not enough for modelling contact but surface properties like coefficient of friction etc. are needed. Contact problems are called "Highly non-linear problems", due to as the contact status is changing, stiffness matrix will change. It is very challenging for Newton Raphson solver to capture abrupt changes in contact status.Surface to surface based contact was used within *ABAQUS/CAE* to simulate contact between beam and column flanges to the surface of angle sectionswith a coefficient of friction as 0.3 [2] for tangential behaviour and hard contact with penalty approach for normal behaviour, considering beam and column flanges as masterand angle surface as slave (basedon mesh density and stiffness of connection member), with the finite sliding formulation.

G. Results and Discussion:

Results of FE model developed in this study with bolts as beam elements and Bolts as 3-D elements are compared by Moment-Rotation curve, with experiments of A. Azizinamini[1] and FE model of Mohammad Jobaer Hasan et al. [4]as shown in Figure-12. It can be seen that FE model developed in this study can predict moment-rotation curve with great accuracy within elastic range, also it can be seen that bolts with beam element perform almost equal to bolts with 3-D elements and that is why it can safely be used to model bolts in the bolted connections.

Figure-11 shows the result comparison for different length of beams (375mm, 750mm) to that of a full length of the beam, that is 1500mm. As it can be seen that results are same for half and a quarter length of the beam to that of full length of the beam. Note that by reducing length of the beam we are not taking any advantage of symmetry but it is an advantage of kinematic coupling option provided within *ABAQUS/CAE.* Figure-14 and 16 shows the displacement and stress contours developed in the current FE Model.

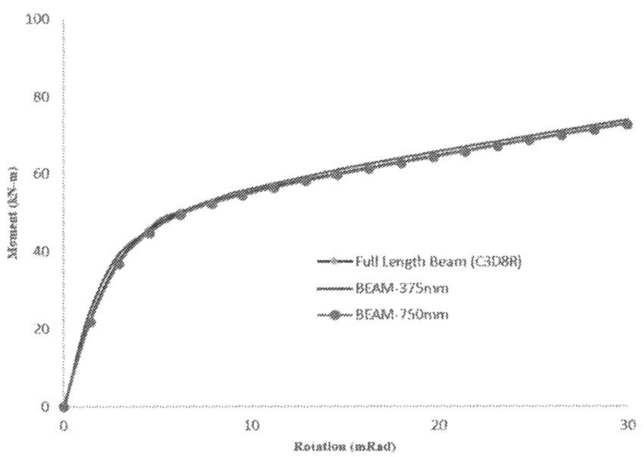

Beam

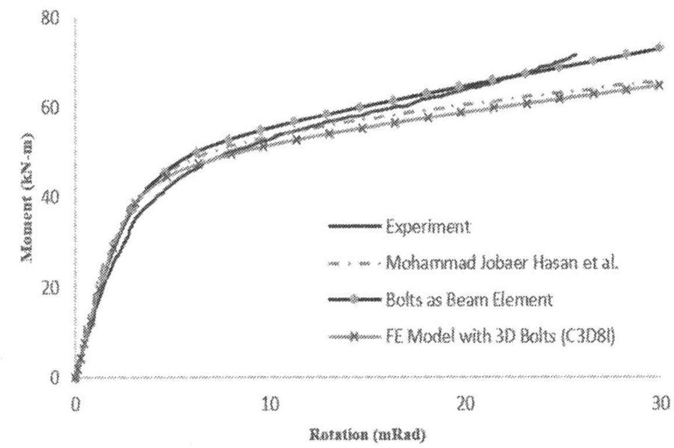

Figure 12 M-θ Curve for A1 Specimen

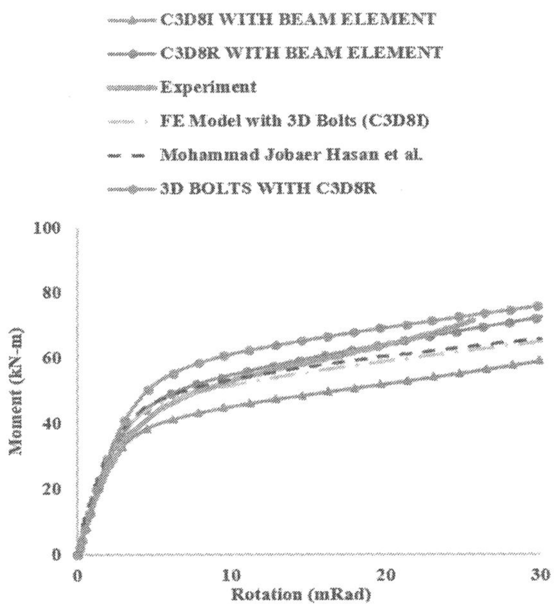

Figure 13 Comparison of M-θ Curve for Different Element Types

Figure-13 compares the C3D8I elements with C3D8R elements, and it can be seen that when whole model is made up of 3D elements, C3D8I element behaves well compared to C3D8R elements unlike when bolts are modelled as beam elements, in that case, C3D8R elements with enhanced hourglass control behaves well.

Figure-15 compares moment-rotation behaviour for A2 specimen. The behaviour of current FE model for A2 specimen with that of an experiment does not match exactly, but yes the nature of the curve is quite similar to that of an experimental one.

Although FE modelling done in this study predict the moment-rotation behavior of the top-seat angle connection with great accuracy, minor deviations are observed due to following reasons.

1. As it is known that plasticity data can influence the model behaviour to a great extent, in this modelling actual non-linear behaviour of material was not known; values were taken from literature available, which may cause variations in the results.
2. Bolt pretension force can also influence the moment-rotation response of the connection as it was shown by Mohammad Jobaer Hasan et al. [4]
3. Type of element, mesh density, the coefficient of friction, type of solver used, minimum and maximum increment size for Newton Raphson solver, contact formulation etc. all these things can influence the behaviour of moment rotation response of connection to a great extent.

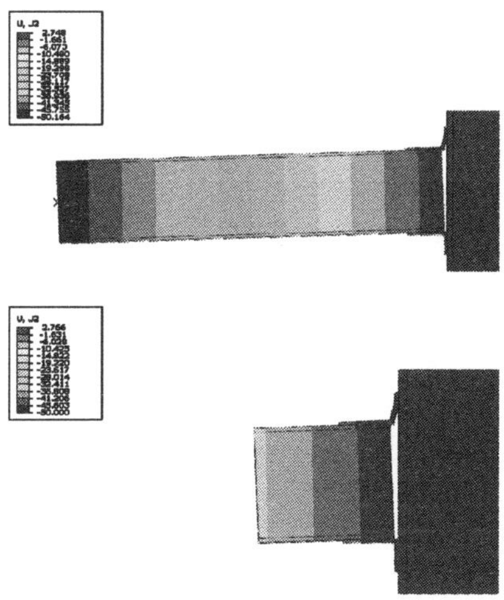

Figure- 14 Displacement Contour for Full and 1/4th Length of Beam

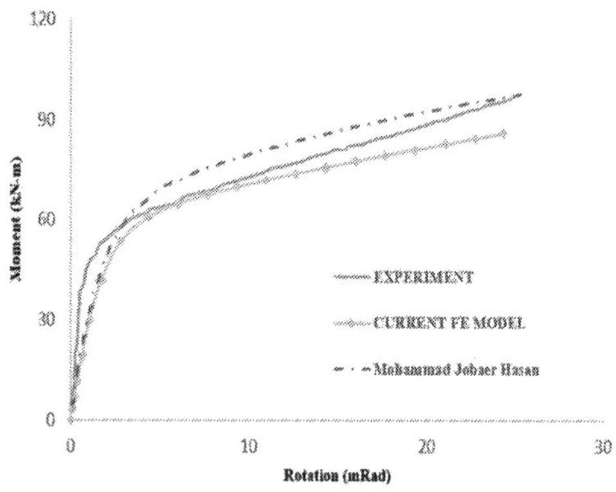

Figure 15 M-θ Curve for A2 Specimen

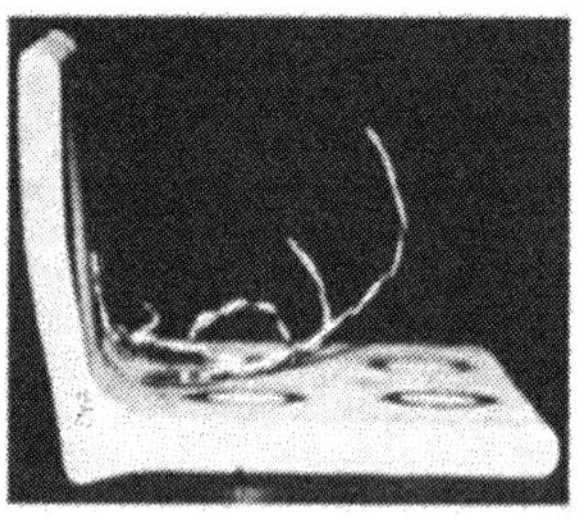

III. Conclusion

In this paper, a three-dimensional non-linear finite element model of top-seat angle connection is modelled and its moment-rotation response is compared with existing experimental data. It is shown that finite element method can surely be used to predict moment-rotation response of steel connection, which is necessary to design semi-rigid framework.

Further, it is also shown that using the kinematic coupling, almost three fourth of the total length of the beam can safely be eliminated (keeping loading point at the same distance) to reduce the total number of elements within the model which intern will decrease the total numbers of degrees of freedom in the model.

Beams in space (Beam elements) can be used to model bolts in the bolted connection rather than an explicit 3-D bolts, which will reduce the total no of elements and degrees of freedom in the model to a great extent, as well as it also eliminates convergence issue faced by Newton-Raphson solver while doing severe discontinuous iterations.

It is also shown that when a full connection is modelled with 3-D elements, that is bolts also with 3-D elements, C3D8I elements capture the continuum behaviour and moment-rotation response of connection quite well compared to C3D8R elements. But when bolts are modelled using beam elements, C3D8R elements with enhanced hourglass control is best suited to truly capture moment rotation response of the connection.

References

[1] A. Azizinamini, Monotonic Response of Semi-Rigid Beam to Column Connections, Msc Thesis, Department Of Civil Engineering, University Of South Carolina, Columbia (1982).

[2] Ali Ahemad, NorimitsuKishi, Ken-Ichi Matsuoka, And Masato Komuoro, Nonlinear Analysis On Prying Of Top-And Seat-Angle Connections (2001).

[3] A. Pirmoz, F. Danesh, The Seat Angle Role On Moment-Rotation Response of Bolted Angle Connections (2009), K. N. Toosi University of Technology, Tehran, Iran

[4] Mohammad Jobaer Hasan, Mahmud Ashraf, Brian Uy Moment-Rotation Behaviour of Top-Seat Angle Bolted Connections Produced from Austenitic Stainless Steel (2017), School of Engineering and Information Technology, The University of New South Wales, Canberra, Act 2610, Australia

[5] Alexandra Korolija, Master Thesis in Solid Mechanics, FE-Modeling of Bolted Joints in Structures (2012), Division of Solid Mechanics Department of Mechanical Engineering Linköping University 581 83 Linköping, Sweden.

Analysis of Composite Laminated Plate using Fem

Nethravathi C[1] *and Sreenivasa M B*[2]

[1]PG Scholar, Structural Engineering Department, V.T.U PG Studies, Mysuru, India
[2]Assistant Professor of Structural Engineering Department, V.T.U PG Studies, Mysuru, India.

Abstract— A numerical analysis using finite element method (FEM) has been carried out to study the buckling behavior of graphite/epoxy laminated composite plates subjected to inplane uniaxial and biaxial compression loadings .In the present study, the effect of aspect ratio, number of plies and fibre orientation on buckling behavior graphite/epoxy. The results shows that the buckling loads of a composite laminated plate subjected to inplane uniaxial compressive loading decreases by increasing the plate aspect ratio (β). It is seen that the number of plies,inplane loads and aspect ratio (β) have a substantial influence on buckling strength of composite laminated plate.

Key words : *buckling analysis, aspect ratio, boundary condition, number of plies, symmetrically laminated composite plate, uniaxial and biaxial compression loading.*

I. Introduction

The rapid development of technology in the field of "material science" has made structural components slender with less weight, superior specific strength and stiffness compared to conventional materials. These materials are widely used in many engineering applications like aerospace, spacecraft nuclear structures, offshore and marine structures. Many studies have showed that such structures fail not due to high stress but due to insufficient elastic stability of slender or thin walled members. This results made to focus more on the static stability and buckling characteristics of beam, column plate and shell type of structures. The ability of the structure to retain its equilibrium configuration under loading is termed as stability and when loading produces an abrupt change in shape of member it is termed as instability. About 200 years ago L. Euler a German scientist studied the first problem of elastic instability concerned to lateral buckling of compressed members. Wood and stone where the principal structural materials used in early days. Thus Euler's theory was not much used due to the bulkiness of the structural elements. Buckling property of many engineering structural elements under compressive loading has always been an important field of research.

Improvement in technology developed a combined structure by joining two or more different materials in macro level to meet the material requirement which is called as composite material.

1.1 Composite materials

A composite material is one in which two or more materials are combined to form a single structure with an identifiable interface. Composite materials have many advantages over conventional materials in structural performance with their superior strength to weight ratios as well as stiffness to weight ratios. Laminated composites are widely used in aerospace, automobiles and marine industries. Laminated composite are made up of plies (layers) each ply being composed of straight parallel fibres (e.g. glass, boron, graphite and carbon) embedded in and bonded together by a matrix material (e.g. epoxy resin, Polyether, ketone, nylon).

Composite Laminates have high stiffness and strength to weight ratios, superior fatigue response characteristics, facility to vary fibre orientation, material and stacking pattern, resistance to electro chemical corrosion and other superior material properties of composite. It requires better understanding of the structural behaviour and failure conditions for safe and more economical design .Laminated composite plate mainly fail in buckling due to presence of inplane loadings.

The orientation of the fibres and stacking sequence has a large effect on the deformation and stress throughout the laminate

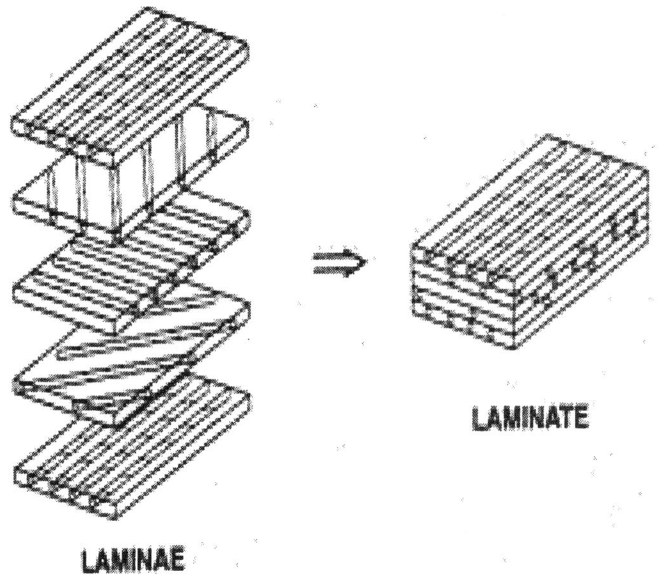

Fig. 1. Composite Laminates

1.1.1 Characteristics and Classification of composite plates:

1. Fibrous composite materials: consists of fibres in a matrix.
2. Laminated composite materials : consists of layers of various materials
3. Particulate composite materials : composed of particles in a matrix
4. Combination of some or all of the three.

1.1.2 General theory and classification of simple lamination type:

The following are the laminate arrangements which are most widely used and simply analyzed

1. **Parallel ply:** all plies at the same arbitrary orientation
2. **Unsymmetric cross ply:** all plies oriented at either 0° and 90°.
3. **Symmetric cross ply:** all plies orientated at either 0° or 90° and arranged symmetrically about the midplane.
4. **Alternating balanced angle ply:** Even number of plies oriented alternately at +θ and – θ.
5. **Symmetric balanced angle ply:** Even number of plies arranged symmetrically about the midplane with an equal number of plies oriented at +θ and at – θ.

1.2 PLATES

Plates are flat structural elements whose thickness is smaller than other dimensions and they are the most widely used slender structural elements subjected to both inplane and out of plane loadings.

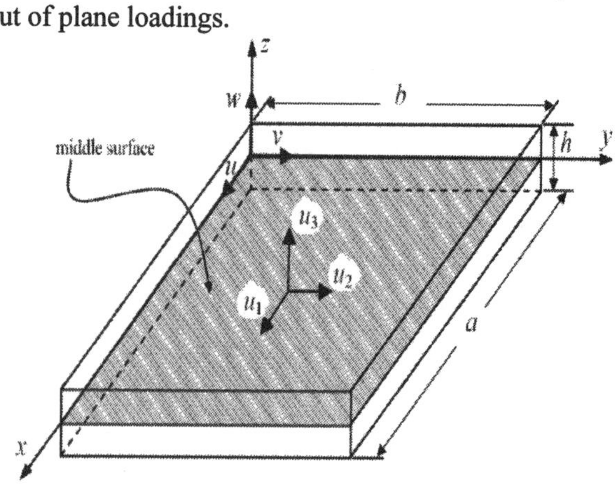

Fig. 2. Dimension, coordinate axes and displacement systems of Rectangular plate

Plates may be classified into three types :

- Thin plates with small deflection
- Thin plates with large deflection
- Thick plates

Thin plates with small deflection: If the ratio of thickness (h) to the smaller span length (a) shold be less than 0.05 and the deflection (w) in z-direction is less than thickness (t0 then the plates are considered as thin plates with small deflections.

Thin plates with large deflections: If the ratio of thikness (h) to smaller span length (a) should be less than 0.05 and the deflection (w) in z-direction is greater than thickness (t) then the plates to be considered as thin plates with large deflection

Thick plates : if the ratio of thickness 9t) to the smaller span length (a) is greater than 0.05, the plate to be considered as thick plates.

II. Objectives

To determine the Buckling strength of simply supported isotrophic plate with various aspect ratios when subjected to uniaxial and biaxial loads

1. Buckling strength of simply supported composite laminated plate for graphite epoxy, material with various aspect ratio and number of plies and different fibre orientation subjected to uniaxial and biaxial compression load

III. Geometry, Boundary Conditions and Material Properties

For complex geometrical and boundary conditions, analytical method are not so easily adaptable, so numerical methods like finite element method have been used. In this work, Eigen buckling analysis is used for predicting the buckling load of a rectangular composite plate through the use of finite element package ANSYS. The **SHELL 281** (8 noded shell element). The **SHELL 281** structural element is chosen from **ANSYS14.5** element library. **SHELL281** has 8 nodes with 6 degrees of freedom at each node, translation along x, y, z directions and rotations about nodal x, y and z-axes. **SHELL281** can be used for layered applications of a structural SHELL model up to 250 different layers ae permitted for application.

Table 3.1. Geometric boundary condition

Material	Material constants	
	Young's modulus (E)in N/mm^2	Poisson's ratio (μ)
Steel	210924	0.3

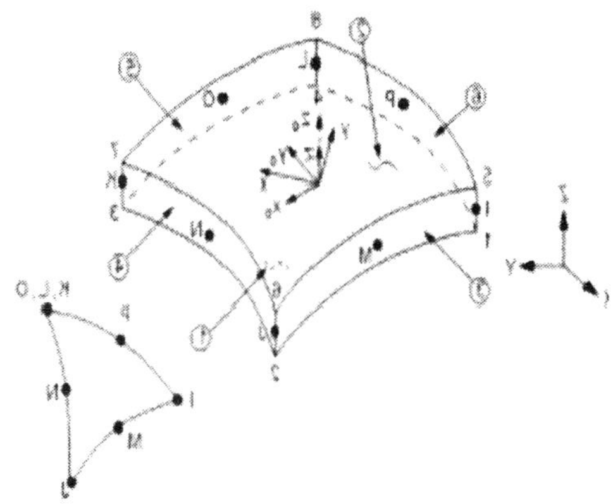

Fig. 3. SHELL 281 element (ANSYS element reference)

Table 3.2. Isotropic material constants

Boundary condition	Position of the edge	
Simply supported	U=w=θ_x=0 @ x=0 And w=θ_x=0@x=a	V=w= θ_y=0@y=0 And w= θ_y=0@y=-b

IV. Results and Discussions

Case 1: Critical buckling load (N_{cr}) for SSSS isotrophic unperforated plate

a. Uniaxial compression loading having thickness 8mm.:Table 4.1 gives the value of Critical buckling load for various aspect ratio(β) and fig 4.1 shows the variation of critical buckling load (N_{cr}), The critical buckling load of a plate having β=0.5 is approximately, 2, 1.28, 1 times higher than the buckling load of plate having β equal to 1.0,1.5 and 2 respectively.

Table 4.1. Critical buckling load N_{cr} for SSSS isotrophic unperforated plate with respect to aspect ratio (β) subjected to inplane uniaxial compression loading having thickness 8 mm.

a in mm	b in mm	Aspect ratio (β)	Critical Buckling load (N_{cr})
100	200	0.5	3768.3
200	200	1.0	1934.7
300	200	1.5	1515.7
400	200	2.0	1516.5

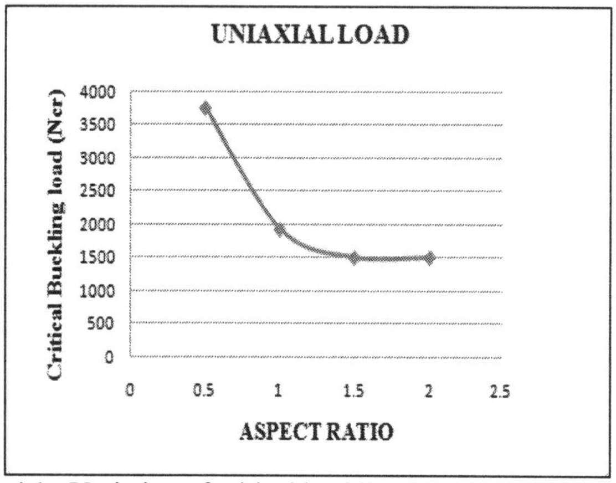

Fig 4.1 : Variation of critical buckling load N_{cr} for SSSS isotropic unperforated plate subjected to inplane Uniaxial load.

b. Biaxial compression loading having thickness 8mm.: Table 4.2 gives the value of critical buckling load (N_{cr}) for various aspect ratio(β) and fig 4.2 shows the variation of critical buckling load, The critical buckling load of a plate having β=0.5 is approximately 1.3,1.5 and 0.9 times higher than the buckling load of plate having β equal to 1.0,1.5 and 2 respectively.

Table 4.2 Critical buckling load N_{cr} for SSSS isotrophic unperforated plate with respect to aspect ratio(β) subjected to inplane biaxial compression loading having thickness 8mm.

a in mm	b in mm	Aspect ratio (β)	Critical Buckling load (N_{cr})
100	200	0.5	2343.3
200	200	1.0	1706.1
300	200	1.5	1185.6
400	200	2.0	1202.32

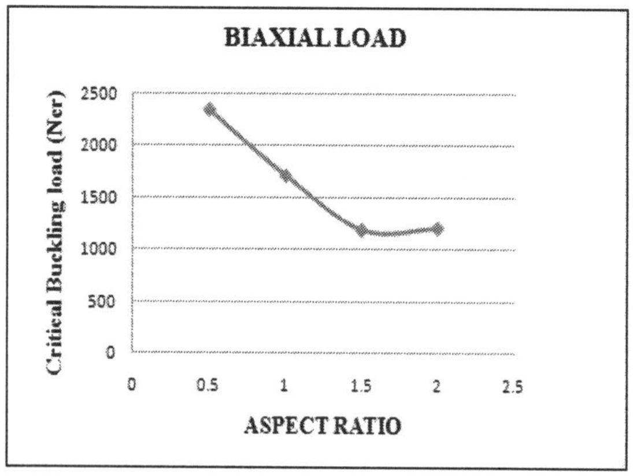

Fig 4.2. Variation of critical buckling load N_{cr} for SSSS isotropic unperforated plate subjected to inplane Biaxial load.

Case 2: critical buckling load(N_{cr}) fibre orientation $(0°/90°/-90°/0°)_s$ for graphite /epoxy Composite laminated plate

a. Uniaxial compression loading for 8 plies and 16 plies: Table 4.3 gives the buckling load (N_{cr}) for graphite /epoxy Composite laminated plate having various aspect ratio(β), fig 4.3 and fig 4.4 shows the the variation of critical buckling load (N_{cr}) for 8 plies and 16 plies. The critical buckling load(8 plies)of a plate having β=0.5 is approximately, 2, 2.1 and 1.8 times higher than the buckling load of plate having β equal to 1.0, 1.5 and 2 respectively and for 16 plies, critical buckling load (N_{cr}) having β=0.5 is approximately, and 13 times higher than the buckling load of plate having β equal to 1.0,1.5 and 2 respectively.

Table 4.3 : Critical buckling load (N_{cr}) for SSSS graphite/epoxy composite laminate plate with respect to aspect ratio (β) subjected to inplane uniaxial compression loading with fibre orientation (0°/90°/-90°/0°)

Aspect ratio (β)	a in mm	b in mm	Critical buckling load (N_{cr})	
			8 plies	16 plies
0.5	50	100	26.43	203.05
1.0	100	100	13.37	105.85
1.5	150	100	12.65	93.91
2.0	200	100	14.82	80.63

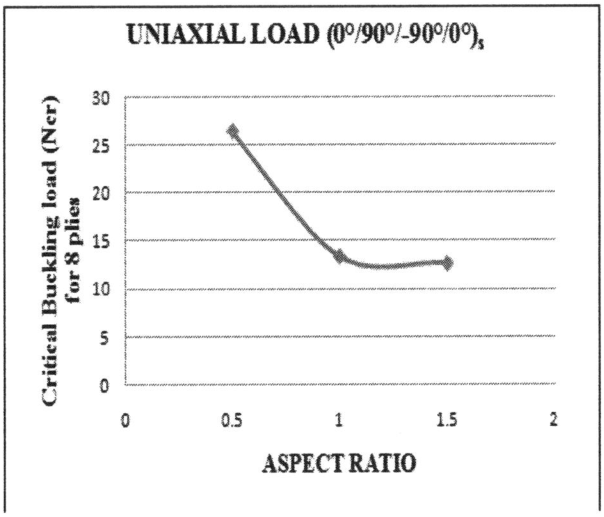

Fig 4.3 Variation of critical buckling load(N_{cr}) for 8 plies with fibre orientation $(0°/90°/-90°/0°)_s$ subjected to inplane Uniaxial compression loading

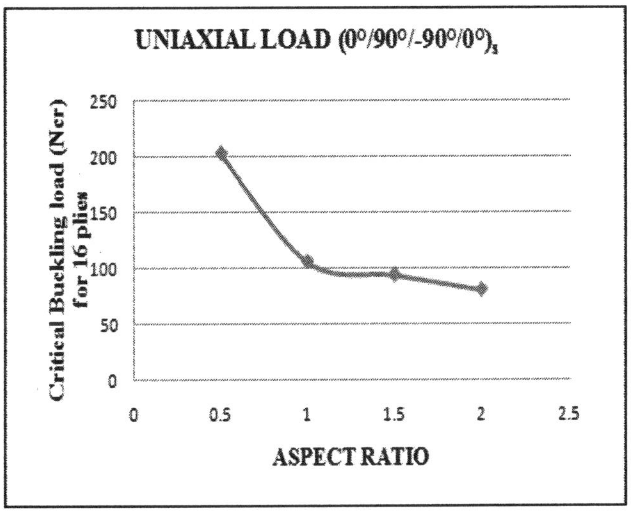

Fig. 4.4. Variation of critical buckling load (N_{cr}) for 16 plies with fibre orientation $(0°/90°/-90°/0°)_s$ subjected to inplane Uniaxial compression loading

b. **biaxial compression loading for 8 plies and 16 plies**: Table 4.4 gives critical buckling load (N_{cr}) for various aspect ratio(β), fibre orientation $(0°/90°/-90°/0°)_s$ and fig 4.5 and 4.6 variation of critical buckling load (N_{cr}). For 8 plies, critical buckling load of a composite laminated plate having β=0.5 is approximately 3.8,9 and 12.5 times higher than the buckling load of plate having β equal to 1.0,1.5 and 2 respectively. For 16 plies, The critical buckling load of a composite laminated plate having β=0.5 is approximately 2.9,1.8 and 2.2 times higher than the buckling load of plate having β equal to 1.0,1.5 and 2 respectively.

Table 4.4 Critical buckling load (N_{cr}) for SSSS graphite/epoxy composite laminate plate with respect to aspect ratio (β) subjected to inplane biaxial compression loading with fibre orientation $(0°/90°/-90°/0°)_s$

Aspect ratio (β)	a in mm	b in mm	Critical buckling load (N_{cr})	
			8 plies	16 plies
0.5	50	100	26.83	249.61
1.0	100	100	14.43	131.77
1.5	150	100	17.42	129.69
2.0	200	100	16.93	146.57

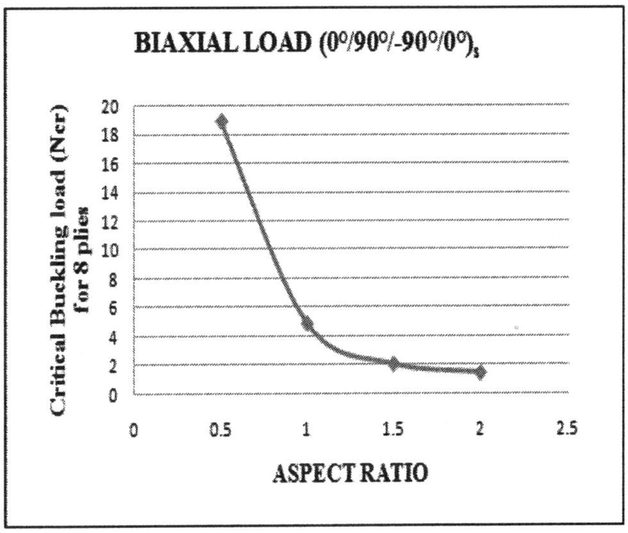

Fig. 4.5. Variation of critical buckling load(N_{cr}) for 8 plies with fibre orientation $(0°/90°/-90°/0°)_s$ subjected to inplane biaxial compression loading

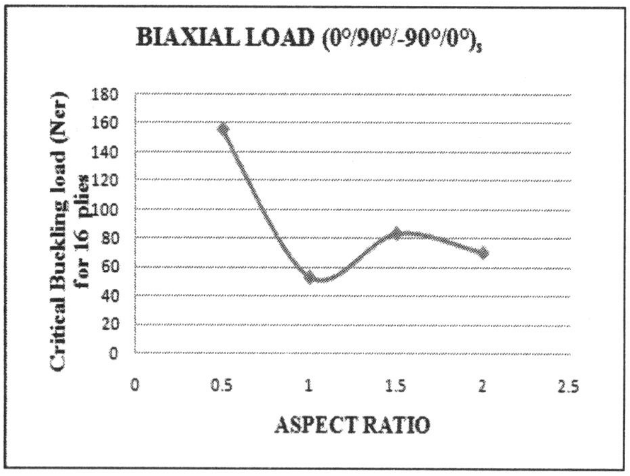

Fig. 4.6. Variation of critical buckling load(N_{cr}) for 16 plies with fibre orientation $(0°/90°/-90°/0°)_s$ subjected to inplane biaxial compression loading

Case 3: Critical buckling load (N_{cr}) for SSSS graphite/ epoxy composite laminate plate with fibre orientation $(0°/30°/-30°/90°)_s$

a. Uniaxial compression loading for 8 plies and 16 plies: Table 4.5 gives the value of Critical buckling load (N_{cr}) for various aspect ratio(β),fig 4.7 and fig 4.8 shows various aspect ratio(β).for 8 plies and 16 plies, The critical buckling load of a plate having β=0.5 is approximately,1.75,1.5 and 1.5 times higher than the buckling load of plate having β equal to 1.0,1.5 and 2 respectively. For 16 plies, . The critical buckling load of a plate having β=0.5 is approximately, 1.85,1.9 and 1.7 times higher than the buckling load of plate having β equal to 1.0,1.5 and 2 respectively.

Table 4.5 Critical buckling load (N_{cr}) for SSSS graphite/epoxy composite laminate plate with respect to aspect ratio (β) subjected to inplane uniaxial compression loading with fibre orientation $(0°/30°/-30°/90°)_s$

Aspect ratio (β)	a in mm	b in mm	Critical buckling load (N_{cr})	
			8 plies	16 plies
0.5	50	100	18.90	155.53
1.0	100	100	4.92	52.925
1.5	150	100	2.09	83.02
2.0	200	100	1.49	70.10

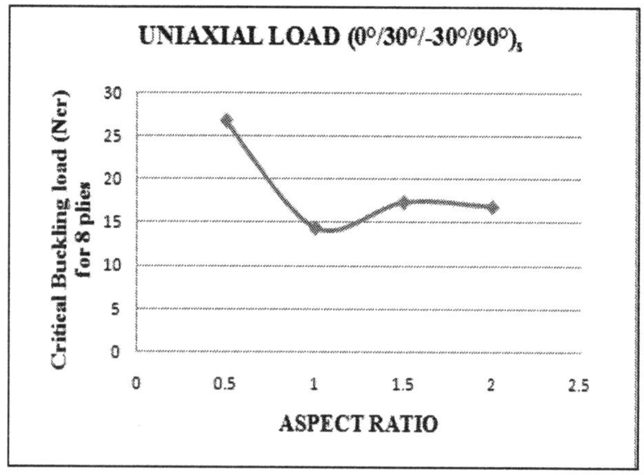

Fig. 4.7. Variation of critical buckling load (N_{cr}) for 8 plies with fibre orientation $(0°/30°/-30°/90°)_s$ subjected to inplane Uniaxial compression loading

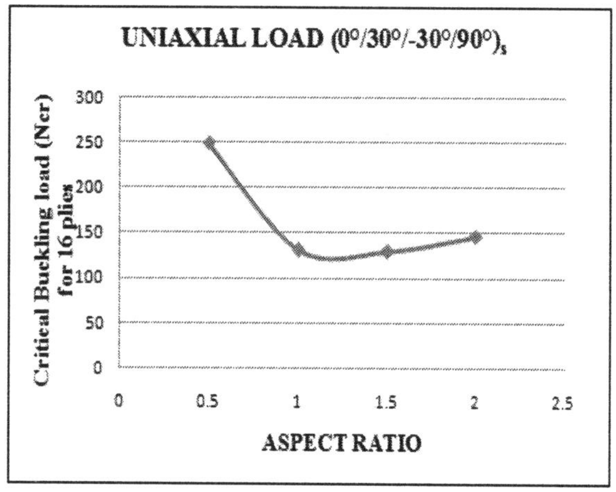

Fig. 4.8. Variation of critical buckling load(N_{cr}) for 16 plies with fibre orientation $(0°/30°/-30°/90°)_s$ subjected to inplane Uniaxial compression loading

b. Biaxial compression loading for 8plies and 16 plies: table 3.6 gives the value of Critical buckling load (N_{cr}) for various aspect ratio(β), fig 4.9 and fig 4.10 shows various aspect ratio(β) for 8 plies and 16 plies. The critical buckling load of a composite laminated plate having β=0.5 is approximately 2.8,2 and 2.1 times higher than the buckling load of plate having β equal to 1.0,1.5 and 2 respectively for 8 plies. The critical buckling load of a composite laminated plate having β=0.5 is approximately 3.1,1.7 and 1.5 times higher than the buckling load of plate having β equal to 1.0,1.5 and 2 respectively for 16 plies

Table 4.6: Critical buckling load (N_{cr}) for SSSS graphite/epoxy composite laminate plate with respect to aspect ratio (β) subjected to inplane biaxial compression loading with fibre orientation (0°/30°/-30°/90°)$_s$

Aspect ratio (β)	a in mm	b in mm	Critical buckling load (N_{cr})	
			8 plies	16 plies
0.5	50	100	19.34	202.09
1.0	100	100	6.98	65.88
1.5	150	100	9.84	119.32
2.0	200	100	9.45	136.97

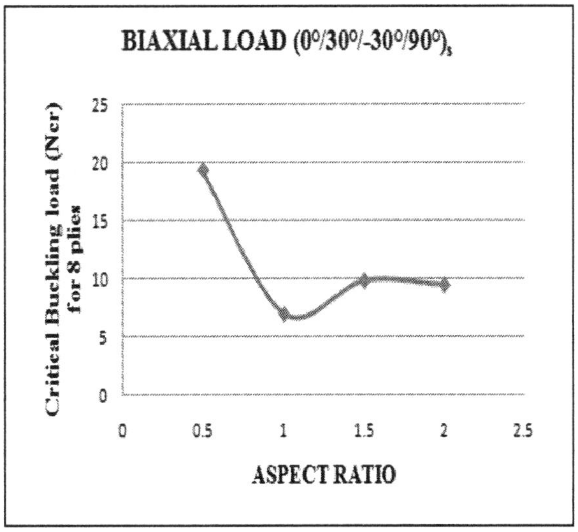

Fig. 4.9. Variation of critical buckling load(N_{cr}) for 8 plies with fibre orientation (0°/30°/-30°/90°)$_s$ subjected to inplane biaxial compression loading

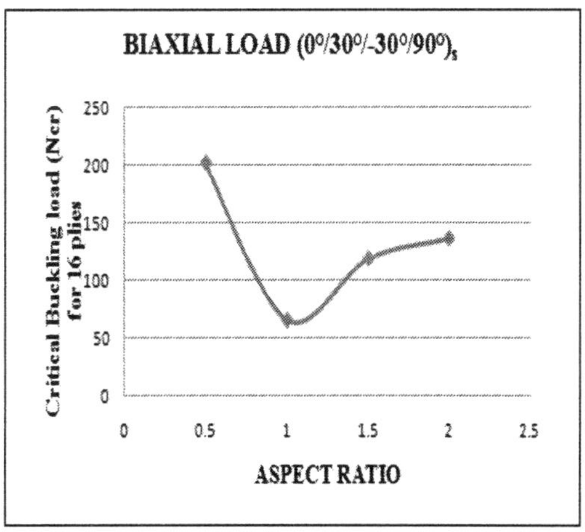

Fig. 4.10. Variation of critical buckling load (N_{cr}) for 16 plies with fibre orientation (0°/30°/-30°/90°)$_s$ subjected to inplane biaxial compression loading

V. Conclusion

This study considers the determination of critical buckling load of a composite laminated plate made up of Graphite-Epoxy with all round simply supported plate boundary condition.The considered laminated composite plate has varying aspect ratio(β) 0.5-2.0 and fibre orientation $(0°/90°/-90°/0°)_s$,$(0°/30°/-30°/90°)_s$.From the present work following conclusions are drawn.

1. For Isotrophic plate the critical buckling load is maximum at the plate aspect ratio β=0.5, and for β=1.0 to 2.0 the critical buckling load decreases about 31.8% under inplane uniaxial compression loading.

2. For Isotrophic plate the critical buckling load is maximum at the plate aspect ratio β=0.5, and for β=1.0 to 2.0 the critical buckling load decreases about 65-74% under inplane biaxial compression loading.

3. The buckling load is maximum for the plates having aspect ratio equal to 0.5 for all the fibre orientations.

4. The Critical buckling load of composite laminated plate for all the three fibre orientation having 8 and 16 plies subjected to inplane uniaxial compression loading is approximately 28% to 23% higher than the plate subjected to inplane biaxial loading for β=0.5-2.0 respectively.

REFERENCES

1. Abdulkareem AI Humdany and Emad Q.Hussein, "Theotical and numerical analysis for buckling of Antisymmetric simply supported laminated plate under Uniaxial loads", Journal of kerala university, 2012, vol.10, pp 149-160.

2. Eugenio Ruocco and Vincenzo Mallardo,"Buckling analysis of Levy type Orthotropic stiffened plate and shell based on different strain displacement model", International journal of non-liner mechanics, 2013, vol.50, pp 40-47.

3. Loptain. A.V and Morozov.E.V, "Buckling of SSCF rectangular orthotropic plates subjected to linearly varying in-plane loading", Composite structures, 2011, vol93, pp1900-1909.

4. Murmu. T and Pradhan. S.C, "Buckling of biaxial compressed orthotropic plates at small scales", Mechanics research communications, 2009, vol.36, pp933-938.

5. Priyanka Dhueveyana and Mittal.N.D, "Buckling behaviour of an orthotropic composite laminate using FEA"' International journal of scientific Engineering and Technology, 2012, vol.1, pp93-95.

Evaluation of Response Reduction Factor of Aircraft Hangar Constructed by Double Layer Grid System

Satish N. Prajapati[1], Vijay R. Panchal[2], Jignesh A. Amin[3]

[1] Post Graduate Student (Structural Engineering), Department of Civil Engineering, Chandubhai S. Patel Institute of Technology, Charotar University of Science and Technology, Changa, Gujarat, India

[2] Professor and Head, Department of Civil Engineering, Chandubhai S. Patel Institute of Technology, Charotar University of Science and Technology, Changa, Gujarat, India

[3] Professor and Head of Civil Engineering Department, Sardar Vallabhbhai Patel Institute of Technology, Vasad, Gujarat, India

[1]prajapatisatish848@gmail.com
[2]vijaypanchal.cv@charusat.ac.in
[3]jamin_svit@yahoo.com

***Abstract*—Themost of the seismic design codes used today integrate the nonlinear response of the structure by the provision of a proper response reduction factor 'R'. Higher value of R factor is adopted due to significant reduction in the base shear leading to more economical structure. As per IS 1893:2016 (Part-1), the value of R factor ranges from 3 to 5 for different moment resisting frames.But, it does not give any kind of information about the components of R factor. R factor depends on ductility factor, over strength factor, and redundancy factor which is calculated from the pushover curve, a plot of base shear v/s roof displacement. This study focuses on the estimation of actual value of R factor for aircraft hangar structure constructed with double layer grid which is designed for all the seismic zones. The grid is supported by the RCC columns of 12 m height on three sides of the perimeter. R factor is computed from the obtained pushover curve for all the seismic zones for the aircraft hangar.**

***Keywords*—Ductility factor; Nonlinear static pushover analysis; Over strength factor; Redundancy factor; Response reduction factor;**

I. Introduction

Earthquakes are one the most disastrous natural hazards that adversely affect life, property, livelihood and industry. The nonlinear response of the structure is not integrated in seismic design philosophy but its effect is integrated by using proper response reduction factor. *R* factor is an important seismic design tool, which describes the intensity of inelasticity predictable in the structural systems throughout an earthquake. During earthquake, large amount of horizontal and overturning forces are produced and it acts majorly on the mass of the structure.

We cannot design a structure for the actual intensity of earthquake taking cost considerations and also actual earthquake force is higher than the structure is designed for. Hence, IS codes introduced the response reduction factor '*R*' by which the base shear is decreased and the economy can be obtained with higher ductility. Kaushik et al. [1] had carried out pushover analysis in SAP2000 on four story RC frame with different framing conditions. Value of *R* factor ranges from 3 to 5 in IS 1893:2016 (Part-1) code which depends on the type of moment resisting frames but it does not give any information on what basis values of *R* factor is considered [2].

In the present study, *R* factor is computed for the aircraft hangar structure designed for all the seismic zones and comparison is made with the adopted value of *R* provided in seismic code. *R* factor is computed parameter wise to find out the effect of every parameters, i.e., over strength, ductility and redundancy. Here,*R* factor provided iscomputed from the pushover curve which is based on available literatures.

II. Concept of Response Reduction Factor

The concept of *R* factor depends on the observation that an efficiently detailed seismic frame can withstand large amount of inelastic deformation without collapse. The *R* factor is termed as "response reduction factor" in IS Code, "response modification factor" in ASCE Code and "behaviour factor" in Euro Code. *R* factor imitates the capacity of the structure to disperse energy by inelastic behaviour. This factor is utilized to decrease the design base shear forces in earthquake resistant design and stands for over strength, damping and energy dispersion capability of the structure. It can be easily understood from the Figure 1.

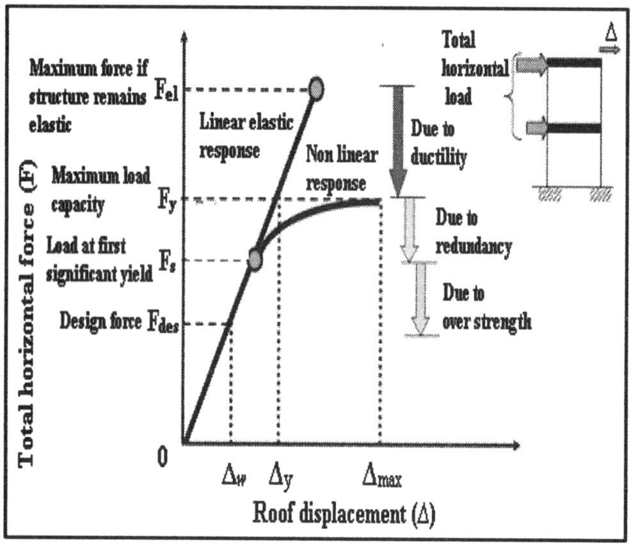

Figure 1 Concept of *R* factor [IS 1893 (Part-1) Draft code]

As per ATC-19, response reduction factor comprises of, over strength factor (R_S), ductility factor (R_μ), structural redundancy factor (R_R) and damping factor (R_ξ) [3]. In equation form, it is given by:

$$R = R_S \times R_\mu \times R_R \times R_\xi \tag{1}$$

III. Description of Aircraft Hangar Considered

The double layer grid aircraft hangar with RCC columns is analyzed and designed by using SAP2000 V19. The grid is supported by the perimeter RCC columns at three sides with one side kept open. The RCC columns of 12 m clear height are designed as per IS 456:2000 [4] and HYSD415 reinforcement bars are used in columns. Moreover, the distance between the neighboring columns is taken as 10 m. The design of double layer grid is done as per IS 800:2007 [5]. Hollow circular steel pipe sections of Fe345 are used in the design of double layer grid members. In this double layer grid, dimensions of top and bottom chord members are kept same, i.e., outer diameter of 0.2 m, inner diameter of 0.16 m with the thickness of 0.02 m are used. While the dimensions of diagonal members are kept lower than the top and bottom chord members, i.e., outer diameter of 0.15 m, inner diameter of 0.114 m with the thickness of 0.018 m are used. The distance between the top chord and bottom chord members is kept as 2 m with 45° angle is taken into consideration in this study.

In this study, the aircraft hangar structure is considered as special moment resisting frame hence value of *R* factor is taken as 5. The aircraft hangar is supposed to be located in zones II, III, IV, and V. As per IS seismic codes, we do not take seismic forces and wind loads simultaneously. Hence in this study, only seismic forces are taken into considerations.

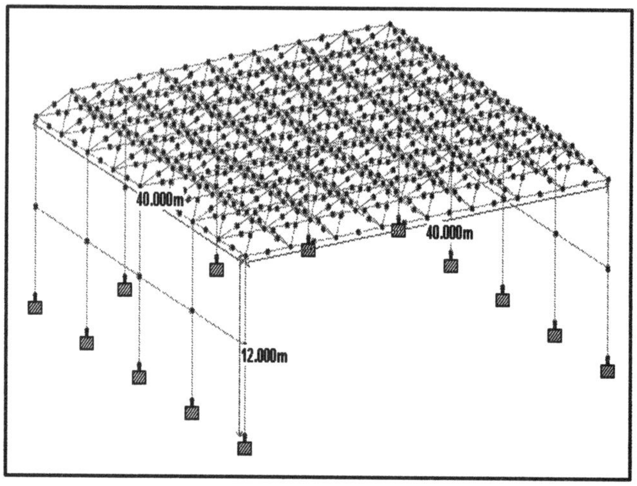

Figure 2 Aircraft hangar frame

For evaluation of *R* factor, only one single frame is considered from the aircraft hangar frame which is shown in Figure 2 and pushover analysis is performed on this frame. The description and various other parameters of the single frame are given in TablesI and II for all seismic zones.

TABLE I
DESCRIPTION OF AIRCRAFT HANGAR FOR ZONE II AND III

Parameters	Zones	
	Zone-II	Zone-III
Size of plan	40 × 10 m	40 × 10 m
Size of top layer grid	35 × 5 m	35 × 5 m
Size of bottom layer gird	40 × 10 m	40 × 10 m
Size of column	0.45 × 0.45 m	0.50 × 0.50 m
Size of tie beam	0.45 × 0.30 m	0.45 × 0.30 m
Reinforcement in column	12 – 20#	16 – 20#

Contd...

Reinforcement in tie beam	6 – 20#	6 – 20#
Grade of concrete	M20	M25
Height of tie beam	6 m	6 m
Soil type	Medium	Medium

TABLE II
DESCRIPTIONOF AIRCRAFT HANGAR FOR ZONE IV AND V

Parameters	Zones	
	Zone-IV	Zone-V
Size of plan	40 × 10 m	40 × 10 m
Size of top layer grid	35 × 5 m	35 × 5 m
Size of bottom layer gird	40 × 10 m	40 × 10 m
Size of column	0.60 × 0.60 m	0.60 × 0.60 m
Size of tie beam	0.45 × 0.30 m	0.45 × 0.30 m
Reinforcement in column	12 – 25#	16 – 25#
Reinforcement in tie beam	6 – 20#	6 – 20#
Grade of concrete	M25	M30
Height of tie beam	6 m	6 m
Soil type	Medium	Medium

IV. MODELLING AND ANALYSIS OF AIRCRAFT HANGAR

For the nonlinear static pushover analysis of aircraft hangar frame, SAP2000 V19 software is used. The RCC columns and tie beams are modelled as 3D frame elements. Columns are fixed at the bottom and damping ratio is assumed as 5% for all the models considered. In this frame, the members of the double layer grid are interconnected through the connecter and whole weight of the grid is supported by the columns. Also, this type of structure is vulnerable to be damaged during the earthquake because failure of one critical compression member leads to the failure of whole structure. Here, advantages of compressive nature of concrete and high strength, ductility, toughness, uniformity of steel are utilized in the frame. The frame considered for study is shown in Figure 3.

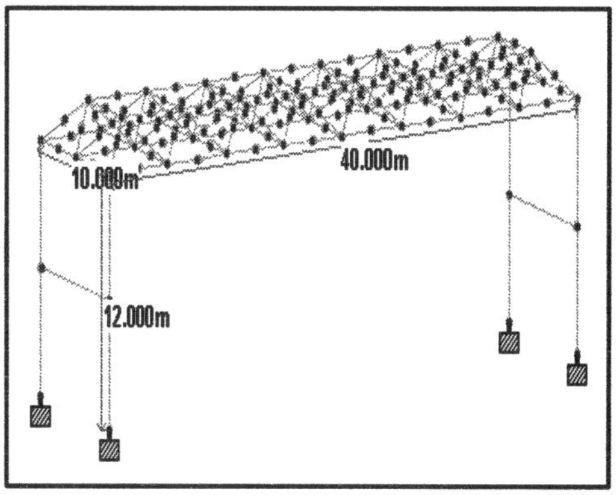

Figure 3 Single frame ofaircraft hangar

Nonlinear static analysis which is also known as pushover analysis is done to find out the capacity of a structure. By pushover analysis, pushover curve is obtained and is used to understand the nonlinear behaviour of structure which is subjected to lateral loads. Pushover analysis requires an expertise of moment curvature relationship, stress-strain model, material property, plastic hinge property, types of hinge, hinge length and its location. In the pipe sections of double layer grid, only axial hinges (P) are assigned and in tie beams only flexural hinges (M3) are assigned, while in the case of columns axial and biaxial moment hinges (P-M2-M3) are assigned as per FEMA-356 [6].

Live load of 18.75 kN is applied on the nodes of the top layer grid only and dead load of G.I. roof sheets of 3.375 kN is also applied to the double layer grid. Along with pushover load case, gravity load case is also defined in which dead load and 25% of live load is taken. Pushover load case starts after the gravity load case. Gravity load is applied as per force controlled procedure and the pushover load is applied as per the displacement controlled procedure. Earthquake load is applied according to IS 1893:2016 (Part-1). Lateral force is applied incrementally in the *x*-direction until the structure reaches its target displacement and the pushover curve is obtained. As per ATC-40[7], various performance levels of the structure are shown in Figure 4.

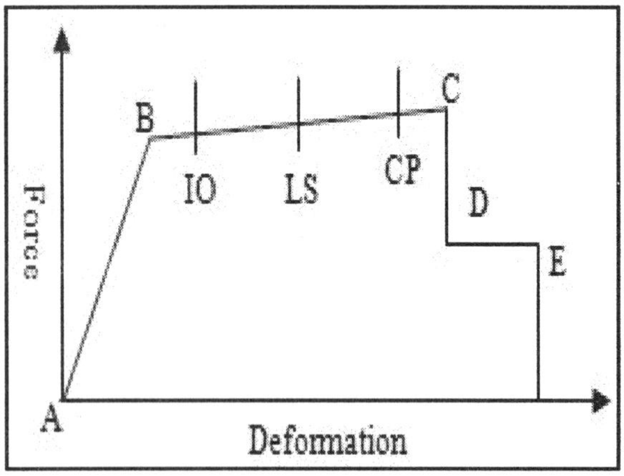

Figure 4 Performance levels of structure (ATC-40)

- Line AB shows the linear elastic range which represents operational level in which facility remains uninterrupted with minor damage.
- Line BC shows the strain hardening portion of the structure with 5-10% of initial slope. Line BC consists of three points, i.e., immediate occupancy (IO), life safety (LS), and collapse prevention (CP) and these points are knows as the nonlinear states of the hinges.
- Point C to D represents the sudden drop which shows the failure of the structural components and also that of the whole structure may occur. After point C, lateral loads are assumed as irresistible.
- Structure's capacity of resistance may be zero or pretended as 20% of the nominal strength from point D to E. In this stage, structure is not capable to resist lateral loads but it can resist the gravity loads.
- Point E represents the ultimate deformation capacity, after point E, structure is not allowed to deform because it cannot resist any type of gravity loads. Hence after point C response of the structure is not allowable.

V. Results

As given in ATC-19, R factor comprises of, over strength factor (R_S), ductility factor (R_μ), redundancy factor (R_R), and damping factor (R_ξ). But in this study, damping factor is neglected as damped and undamped natural frequencies are equal for the structure. Pushover curve is the plot between base shear v/s target displacement. Different pushover curves for all the seismic zones are shown in Figures 5 to 8 respectively. Bilinearisation of pushover curve is done by the equal area procedure and hence yield displacement and maximum displacement are obtained. Bilinearisation is represented by the blue line in the pushover curve.

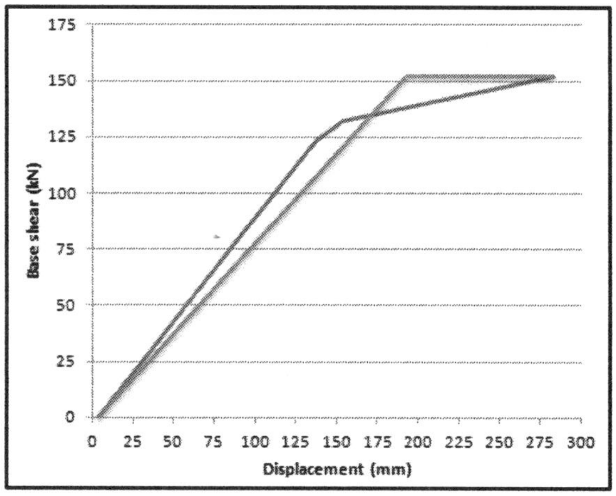

Figure 5 Pushover curve of aircraft hangar for zone-II

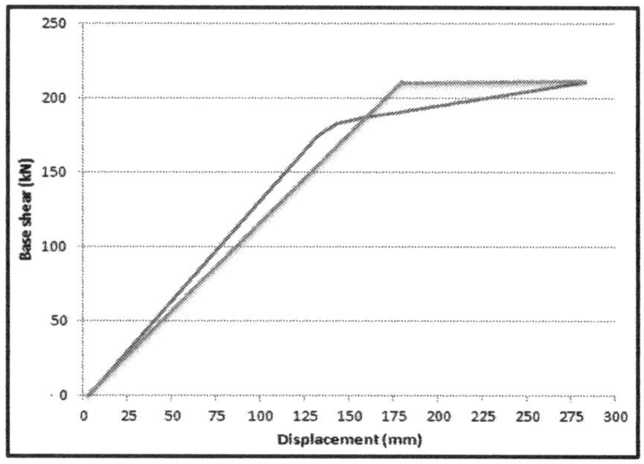

Figure 6 Pushover curve of aircraft hangar for zone-III

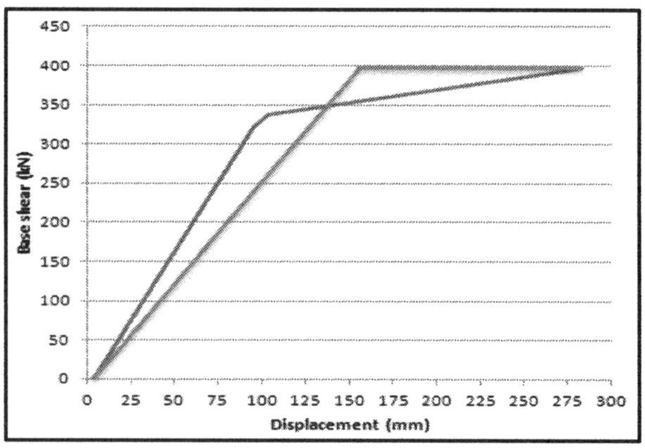

Figure 7 Pushover curve of aircraft hangar for zone-IV

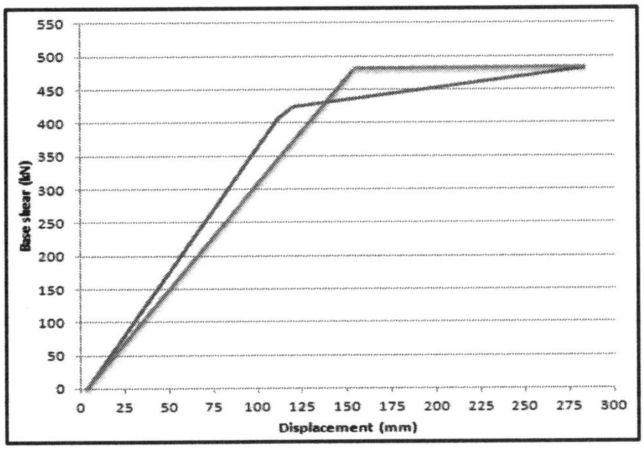

Figure 8 Pushover curve of aircraft hangar for zone-V

Calculation of R factor of aircraft hangar for zone-V is explained below:

A. Calculation of over strength factor

Maximum base shear obtained from pushover curve,

V_u= 481.947 kN

Design base shear obtained by earthquake calculation,

V_d= 125.18 kN

As per ATC-19, over strength factor is given by,

$R_S = V_u / V_d$= 481.947/125.18

R_S = 3.85

B. Calculation of ductility factor

Maximum displacement obtained from pushover curve,

Δm = 283.317 mm

Yield displacement obtained from pushover curve,

Δy = 155 mm

Displacement ductility ratio given in ATC-19,

$\mu = \Delta m/\Delta y$ = 283.317/155 = 1.83

Now, using equation of ductility factor which is given by Miranda and Bertero [8],

$R_\mu = \{(\mu\text{-}1/\Phi)+1\}$ (2)

$\Phi = 1+\{1/(12T\text{-}\mu T)\}\text{–}\{(1/5T)*exp[-2\{ln(T)\text{-}0.2)\text{^}2]\}$(3)

For medium soil,

T = 0.93 seconds (from pushover analysis)

Putting all these values in above Equation 3, we get,

Φ = 0.675

Now, putting value of Φ and μ in Equation 2, we get,

R_μ= 2.23

C. Calculation of redundancy factor

The value of redundancy factor is given by ATC-19 which is shown in Table III.

TABLE III
REDUNDANCY FACTORAS PER ATC-19

Lines of vertical seismic framing	Redundancy factor
2	0.71
3	0.86
4	1.00

So, R_R = 0.71

D. Calculation of response reduction factor R

Equation of R factor is given in Equation 1 wherein, damping factor is R_ξ is taken as 1.

So, $R = R_S \times R_\mu \times R_R$= 3.85 × 2.23 × 0.71 = 6.10

Now, Table IV shows the different values of factor with its components for all seismic zones.

TABLE IV
RESPONSE REDUCTION FACTOR FOR ALL SEISMIC ZONES

Parameters	Zones			
	Zone II	Zone III	Zone IV	Zone V
Over strength factor (R_S)	5.51	4.43	4.75	3.85
Ductility ratio (μ)	1.48	1.57	1.80	1.83
Ductility factor (R_μ)	1.72	1.78	2.16	2.23
Redundancy factor (R_R)	0.71	0.71	0.71	0.71
Response reduction factor (R)	6.73	5.60	7.29	6.10

VI. Conclusion

A detailed study is conducted here to obtain the appropriate values of R factor for aircraft hangar. The work described here consists of four models of aircraft hangar which are located in seismic zones II, III, IV and V with clear height of 14 m. The major outcomes of this study are summarized below:

1) Evaluation of R factor by exact analysis procedure will be helpful to do economical design of the structure.
2) The value of R factor for all the four models of aircraft hangar varies from 5.60 to 7.29 for all the seismic zones.
3) The actual value of R factor is taken lower in actual designs due to lack of ductile detailing as per codal provisions, poor workmanship, poor quality control, and irregularities in dimensions, etc.

References

[1] Kaushik, H., Rai, D. and Jain, S. (2009) 'Effectiveness of Some Strengthening Options for Masonry-In filled RC Frames with Open First Story', Journal of Structural Engineering, vol. 135, pp. 925-937.

[2] I.S. 1893 (2016) 'Indian Standard Criteria for Earthquake Resistant Design of Structures Part-1, General Provisions and Buildings', Bureau of Indian Standards, New Delhi, India.

[3] ATC 19 (1995), 'Structural Response Modification Factors Report', Applied Technology Council, Redwood City, California, USA.

[4] I.S. 456 (2000) 'Indian Standard Code of Practice for Plain and Reinforced Concrete', Bureau of Indian Standards, New Delhi, India.

[5] I.S. 800 (2007) 'Indian Standard Code of Practice for General Construction in Steel', Bureau of Indian Standards, New Delhi, India.

[6] FEMA 356 (2000), 'Prestandard and Commentary for the Seismic Rehabilitation of Buildings', Federal Emergency Management Agency, Washington, D.C., USA.

[7] ATC 40 (1996), 'Seismic Evaluation and retrofit of concrete buildings', Applied Technology Council, Redwood City, California, USA.

[8] Miranda, E. and Bertero, V.V. (1994), 'Evaluation of strength reduction factors for earthquake-resistant design', Earthquake Spectra, EERI, vol. 2, pp. 357-379.

An Energy Based Seismic Evaluation and Retrofit Strategy of Existing Reinforced Concrete (RC) Building by Energy Spectrum Method

K.J. Raval[1], V.R. Panchal[2], G.L. Rai[3], R.K. Sheth[4]

[1]Post Graduate Student(Structural Engineering), Department of Civil Engineering, Chandubhai S. Patel Institute of Technology, Charotar University of Science and Technology, Changa, Gujarat, India

[2]Professor and Head, Department of Civil Engineering, Chandubhai S. Patel Institute of Technology, Charotar University of Science and Technology, Changa, Gujarat, India

[3]Managing Director and CEO, Dhirendra Group of Company, Mumbai, Maharashtra, India

[4]Assistant Professor, Department of Civil Engineering, Dharmsinh Desai University, Nadiad, Gujarat, India

[1]raval12669@gmail.com
[2]vijaypanchal.cv@charusat.ac.in
[3]gr@dgc24.com
[4]rks.cl@ddu.ac.in

***Abstract*—Seismic evaluation is performed for existing Reinforced Concrete (RC) building. In this study an energy based seismic evaluation method is used for G+3 existing RC building located in Mumbai. Seismic evaluation by the energy spectrum evaluation method considers the desired maximum displacement value from the intersection point of energy demand and energy capacity curve. Demand and capacity curve obtained from the pushover curve by energy balance equation. Modelling and analysis has been done in SAP2000 software. Study compares the need of retrofitting to strengthening of columns of existing RC building by conventional method and energy spectrum method. Observation acquired from this study is that energy spectrum method can be considered as an efficient and easy tool of evaluation to predict approximate displacement demand and strengthening of columns of given building.**

***Keywords*—Energy based seismic evaluation; Energy spectrum; Pushover analysis; RC building; Retrofitting; Seismic demand.**

I. Introduction

Seismic forces are considered as the utmost severe forces on the surface of ground which cause instability and harm to structures. To resist the ground excitations, structures should have sufficient seismic strength and detailing requirements of Indian Standards. In present, there are many buildings which has lacking the seismic strength and specifying requirements of IS: 1893:2016, IS: 4326:2013 and IS: 13920:2016. In any Reinforced Concrete(RC) building, the structural elements should be designed and detailed in such a way that the applied forces and deflections are within the permissible limits. Seismic retrofitting is needed after the earthquake and design time period of structure to maintain a seismic performance and seismic strength. Seismic retrofitting is to modify the existing structure to achieve strength against seismic action, surface motion or failure of soil reason to earthquake. To adopt retrofit system, a performance established methodology can be used. The performance-based methodology classifies an aimed structure performance level for an expected earthquake intensity. To fulfil the required seismic retrofitting strategy and technique of existing building, proper seismic evaluation must be done first by suitable seismic evaluation method which plays the key role.

Presently for seismic analysis, elastic analysis method is used. Seismic analysis method of structure is characterised as seismic coefficient approach and dynamic analysis. Seismic coefficient methodology is an equivalent static analysis and dynamic analysis is characterised as response spectrum analysis for linear structures and time history analysis for linear and non-linear structures.

Possible seismic design approaches to satisfy the performance objective cover various elastic and inelastic analysis procedures.

Performance-Based Seismic Design (PBSD) has been generally utilized by the building and research group since the 1994 Northridge Earthquake. This earthquake may be one of the strongest earthquake in U.S. history. The objective of PBSD is an attempt to predict the structure with target seismic performance. PBPD is one of the PBSD method in which energy balance is used to evaluate performance.

II. Energy Spectrum Evaluation Method

A. Energy balance concept

Energy balance concept is the soul of a PBPD method. Early researchers have used this concept in a design to estimate the amount of plastic energy absorbed by the structure [1] and to calculate constant ductility inelastic design spectra [2]. Basic fundamental of an energy balance concept is illustrated in Fig. 1.

The energy calculated from monotonic load deformation response of inelastic system and energy computed from corresponding elastic system are equal. The energy balance equation for single degree of freedom system with elastic-plastic load deformation characteristic is given as follow [3],

$$E = \frac{1}{2}MS_v^2 = \frac{1}{2}V_yD_y + V_y\,(D_m - D_y) \tag{1}$$

Where E is energy; M is mass; S_v is pseudo velocity; V_y is yield strength; D_y is yield displacement; D_m is maximum inelastic displacement.

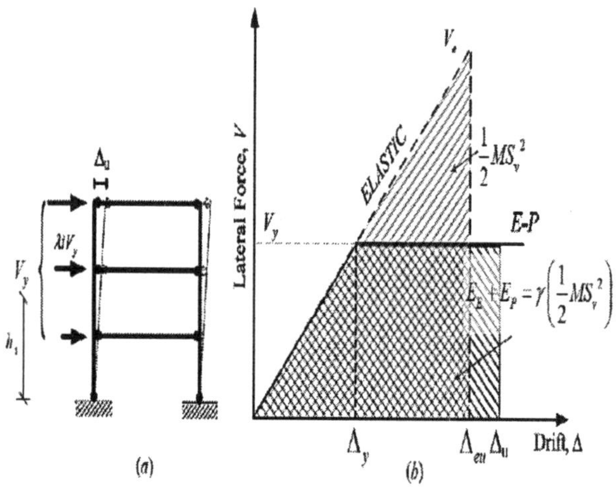

Fig. 1. Modified energy balance concept [4]

The energy balance equation given above is valid only for systems with period in the sensitive acceleration regions of the spectra. This equation is modified as that it can be used for all periods by multiplying energy factor, introduced by Lee & Goel [3]. So, the energy balance equation can be rewritten as: [5]

$$E_e + E_p = \gamma\left(\frac{1}{2}MS_v^2\right) = \frac{1}{2}\gamma M\left(\frac{T}{2\pi}\frac{S_a}{g}g\right)^2 \tag{2}$$

$$= \frac{1}{2}\gamma\left(\frac{W}{g}\right)\left(\frac{T}{2\pi}\frac{S_a}{g}g\right)^2 \tag{3}$$

where E_e denoted aselastic component of energy (work); E_p as plastic component of energy (work); T as fundamental period and S_a/gas pseudo spectral acceleration.

The energy modification factor (γ) is depends on the structural ductility and ductility reduction factor with the yield drift θ_y assumed as:

$$\gamma = \frac{(2\mu_s - 1)}{R_\mu^2} \tag{4}$$

Where μ_s is denoted as structural ductility and R_μ^2 as ductility reduction factor.

Evaluation of RC structure has a special problem because of their complex and pinched (degrading) hysteretic behaviour. Hence, for the RC structures the energy modification factor (γ^*) is used, which described as below:

$$\gamma^* = \frac{(2\mu_s^* - 1)}{R_\mu^{*2}} \tag{5}$$

where μ_s^* is modified structural ductility and R_μ^{*2} is ductility reduction factor for modified μ_s^* from the value of Table II.

To use this energy balance concept for evaluation process, the right-hand part of the equation can be used as energy demand for a given hazard level; E_d, and the left side part of the equation can be used as energy capacity of a given structural system, E_c. These quantities are differing with the displacement. Evaluation of desired maximum reference displacement can be obtained by solving the work-energy equation by analytical or graphically by constructing the two energy curves as a function of the reference displacement & by determining their intersection point [6]. The graphical method is more suitable as the two energy plots describe a comparable visual data of the capacity and demand as a function of displacement as described in Fig. 2.

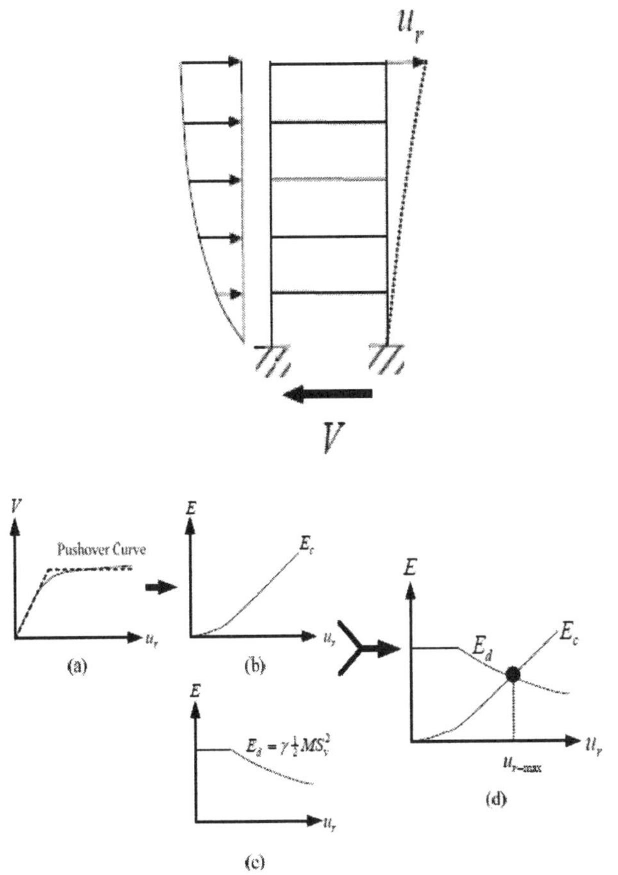

Fig. 2. (a) Pushover curve, (b) Energy displacement capacity diagram, (c) Energy demand diagram and (d) Determination of displacement demand [4]

To extend energy balance formulation for MDOF systems, the equivalent simple oscillator concept can be used. In equivalent simple oscillator, by assuming constant mode shapes afterward yielding and neglect the coupling between the modes [7], Leelataviwat et al. [4] stated that the energy demand of the nth mode of MDOF system can be calculated. Useful values for energy-based evaluation by energy spectrum concept are given inTablesI-III and Fig. 3.

TABLE I
ASSUMED DESIGN YIELD DRIFT RATIOS

Frame Type	RC	Steel			
Yield Drift Ratio, $\theta_y(\%)$	SMF	MF	EBF	STMF	CBF
	0.5	1	0.5	0.75	0.3

TABLE II
DUCTILITY REDUCTION FACTOR AND CORRESPONDING STRUCTURAL PERIOD RANGE

Period Range	Ductility Reduction Factor
$0 \leq T < \frac{T_1}{10}$	$R_\mu = 1$
$\frac{T_1}{10} \leq T < \frac{T_1}{4}$	$R_\mu = \sqrt{2\mu_s - 1}\left(\frac{T_1}{4T}\right)^{2.513\log\left(\frac{1}{\sqrt{2\mu_s-1}}\right)}$
$\frac{T_1}{4} \leq T < T_1'$	$R_\mu = \sqrt{2\mu_s - 1}$
$T_1' \leq T < T_1$	$R_\mu = \frac{T\mu_s}{T_1}$
$T_1 \leq T$	$R_\mu = \mu_s$

Note:$T_1 = 0.57\ sec,\ T_1' = T_1\left(\frac{\sqrt{2\mu_s-1}}{\mu_s}\right) sec$

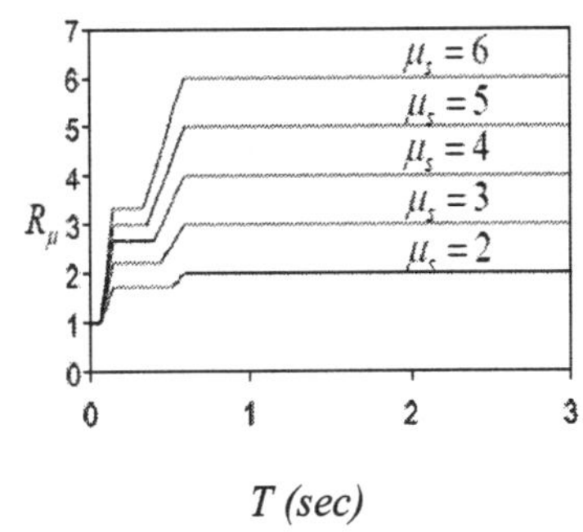

(a)

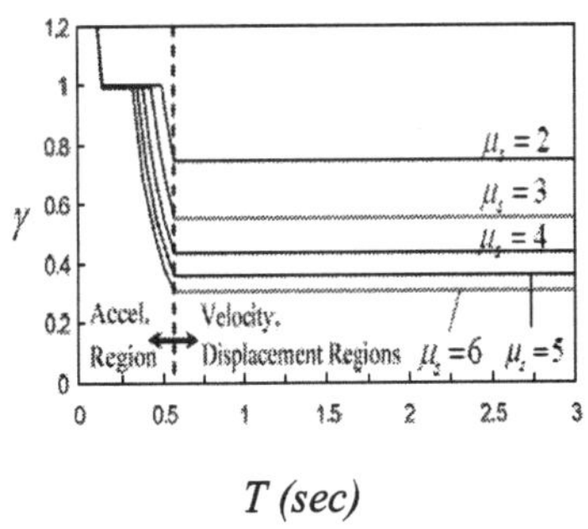

(b)

Fig. 3. (a) Idealized inelastic spectra, (b) Energy modification factor inelastic spectra [4]

TABLE III
VALUES OF C_2 FACTOR, FUNCTION OF R AND T

	$0.2 \leq T < 0.4$	$0.4 \leq T \leq 0.8$	$0.8 \leq T$
$R = 3.0 \sim 6.0$	$3.0 - 7.5(T - 0.2)$	$1.5 - 1.0(T - 0.4)$	$1.1 - 0.045(T - 0.8)$
$R = 2.0$	$2.5 - 6.5(T - 0.2)$	$1.1 - 0.077(T - 0.4)$	

B. Design base shear by energy balance equation

The evaluation of design base shear by energy balance concept is described below as in term of a design base shear coefficient[4].

$$\frac{V_b}{W} = \frac{-\alpha + \sqrt{\alpha^2 + 4\gamma\left(\frac{S_a}{g}\right)^2}}{2} \tag{6}$$

where α is a dimensionless parameter given by,

$$\alpha = \left(\sum_{i=1}^{n} \lambda_i h_i\right) * \frac{\theta_p 8\pi^2}{T^2 g} \tag{7}$$

In which, λ_i is proportioning factor of equivalent lateral force at floor level i, h_i is height of the building at floor level i, θ_p is the plastic component of the target drift ratio

C. Strengthening of columns by FRP strategy of retrofitting

To increase strength, ductility of elements or building as a whole and stiffness, retrofitting is carried out. Retrofitting strategies are classified as local and global retrofitting. Local retrofitting strategies includes strengthening of beam, column, beam to column joint, wall and foundation where as global strategies includes addition of infill wall, shear wall, steel bracing and reduction of irregularities.

III. MODELLING DETAILS OF EXISTING RC BUILDING

An existing G+3 RC building is considered to compare the seismic analysis between force-based analysis approach and an energy based seismic evaluation approach with applied retrofitting strategy.

The general details of existing G+3 RC building is shown in Tables IV-VII.

TABLE IV
THE GENERAL DETAILS OF EXISTING RC BUILDING

Structure type	**RC regular frame**
Horizontal floor system	Beams and slab
Use of building	Commercial
Number of storey	G+3
Concrete Grade	M15
Grade of steel	Fe415
Zone factor	IV
Type of soil	Medium
Importance factor	1
Response reduction factor	5

TABLE V
SECTION DETAILS

Types of member	**Section details (*mm*)**
Beams	300 ×600
Columns	300×300
	600×600
	230 × 450
	230 ×550
	230 ×680
	230 ×840
	680 (Circular)
Slab thickness	200

TABLE VI
DIMENSION DETAILS

Dimension Type	**Dimension details**
Overall length in x direction (m)	35.54
Overall length in y direction (m)	28.357

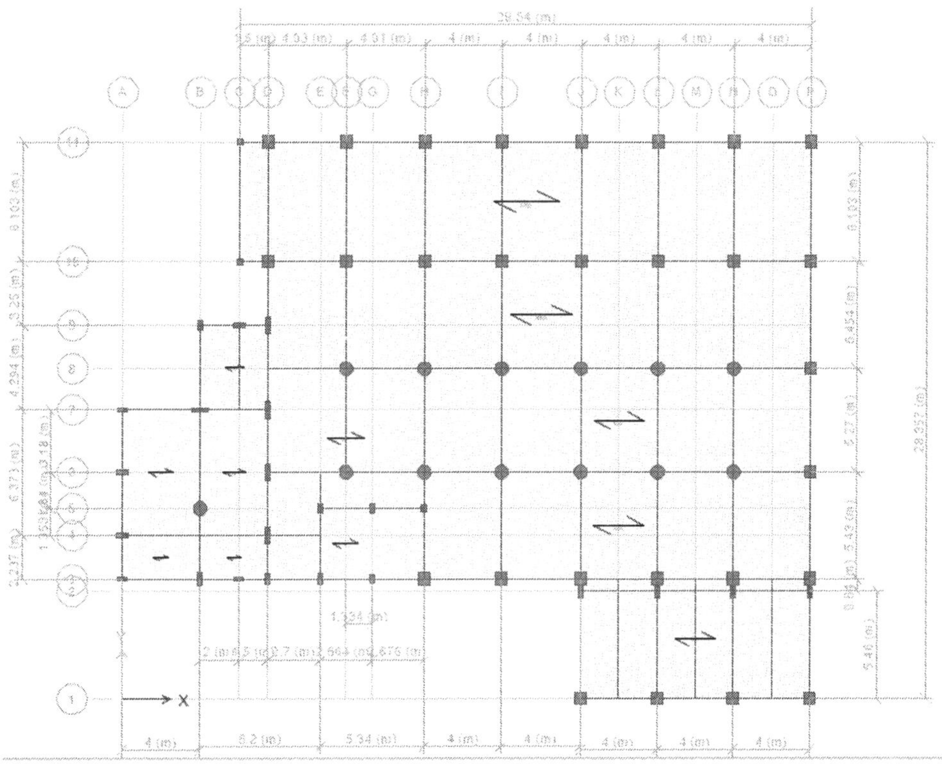

Fig. 4. Plan arrangement of G+3 RC building

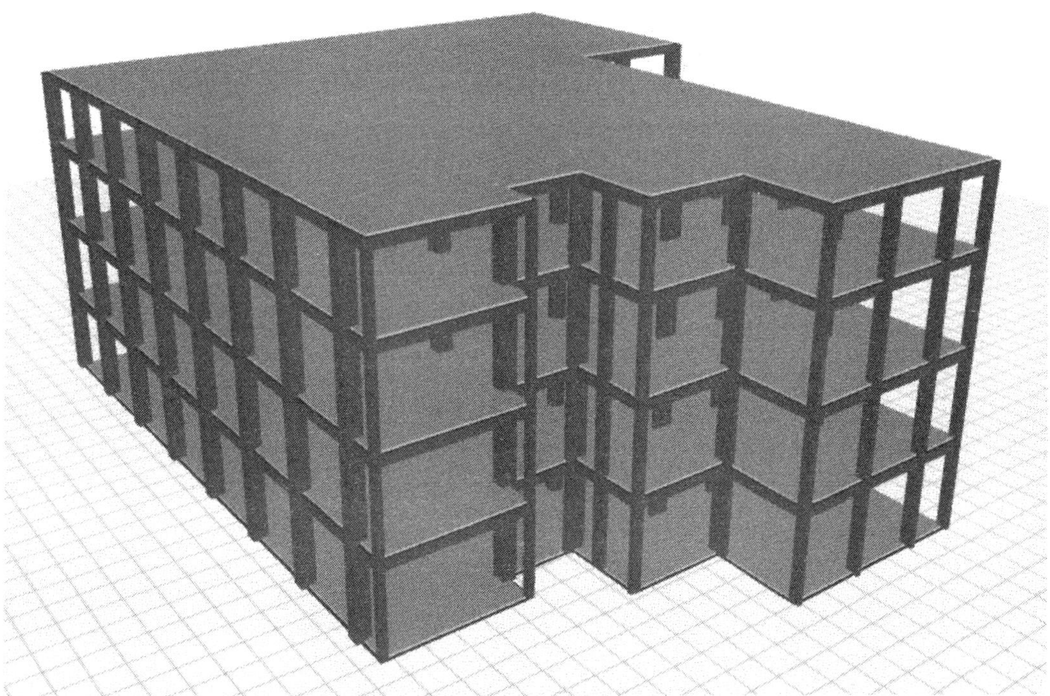

Fig. 5. 3D modelling of G+3 RC building

TABLE VII
HEIGHT DETAIL OF G+3 RC BUILDING

Storey	Height (m)	Elevation (m)
4	3.66	16.34
3	4.26	12.68
2	4.16	8.42
1	4.26	4.26
Base	-	0

IV. RESULTS AND DISCUSSION

Analysis of the existing RC building is done as per IS: 456:2000 and IS: 1893:2016 using SAP2000 software. Energy capacity and demand curves (Fig. 7) are obtained using energy balance concept after bilinearization of pushover curves in x and y directions (Fig. 6). The peak roof displacement in x and y directions are obtained from the intersection point of demand and capacity curves for both directions (Fig 7). Comparison of performance point for maximum displacement by energy spectrum and ATC-40 capacity spectrum obtained from SAP2000 is shown in Table VIII.

TABLE VIII
PERFORMANCE POINT FOR MAXIMUM DISPLACEMENT

	x – direction (m)	y – direction (m)
ATC – 40 Capacity spectrum	0.044	0.053
Energy balance concept	0.041	0.051

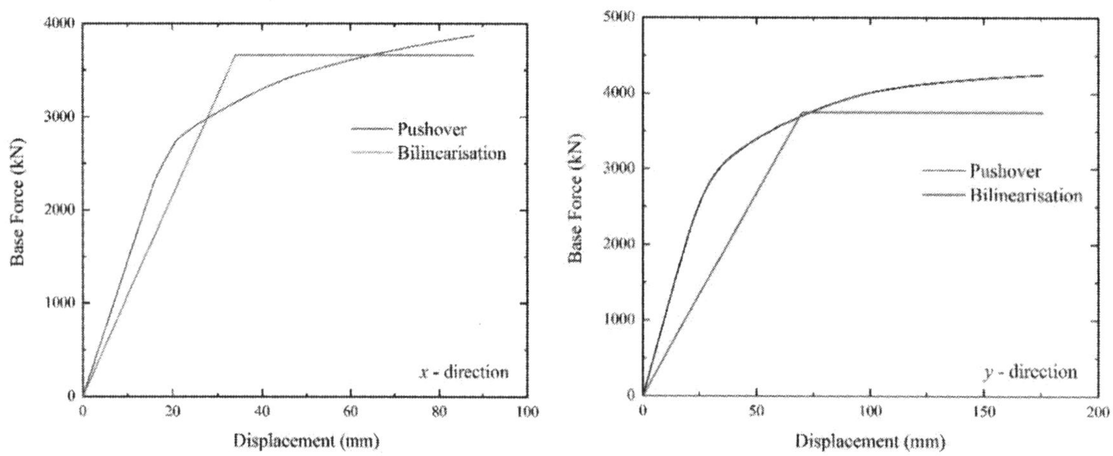

Fig. 6. Bilinearization of pushover curve in x and y directions

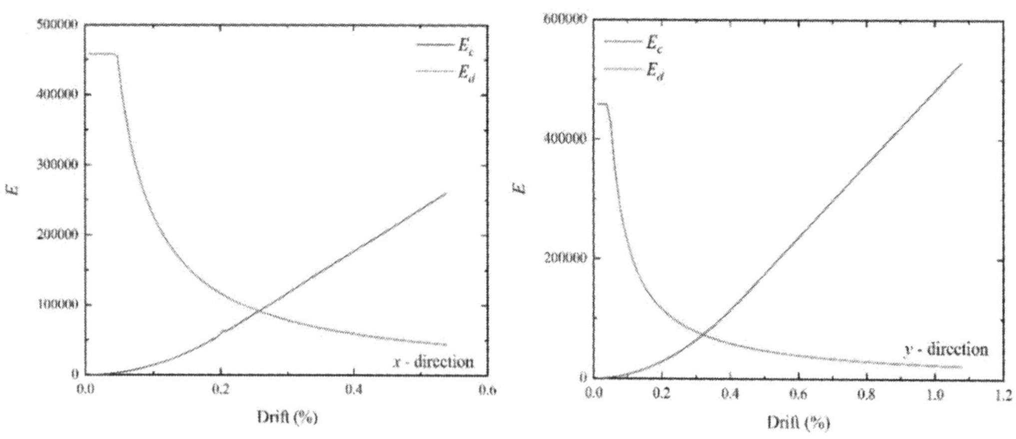

Fig. 7. Energy capacity and demand curve in x and y directions

TABLE IX.
LATERAL FORCE DISTRIBUTION

x– direction					*y* - direction				
Storey	Lateral forces		Unit base shear		Storey	Lateral forces		Unit base shear	
	FBD (kN)	Energy balance concept (kN)	FBD	Energy balance concept		FBD (kN)	Energy balance concept (kN)	FBD	Energy balance concept
4	1948.67	769.10	0.43	0.34	4	1948.67	897.12	0.43	0.34
3	1664.62	762.27	0.36	0.33	3	1664.62	862.21	0.36	0.33
2	763.60	508.29	0.17	0.22	2	763.60	569.18	0.17	0.22
1	195.46	253.27	0.04	0.11	1	195.46	282.38	0.04	0.11

Table IX shows the values of lateral forces and unit base shear at each storey level by force-based method and energy balance concept in *x* and *y* directions. Its graphical illustration is described in Figs.8-11 in *x* and *y* directions respectively. Due to difference in designed base shear by both methods, demand of ground floor columns for increased axial forces are different.

A retrofitting strategy is applied to columns which are failed due to axial load only. A retrofitting of ground floor columns in existing RC building is done by Fiber Reinforced Polymer (FRP) ply, which isshown in Table X. Column failure are classified from the Demand Capacity Ratio (DCR). If DCR is greater than or equal to 1 then column is considered as fail, otherwise it is considered as safe. A retrofitting of members is done as per IITK-GSDMA guidelines and ACI 440.2R-08 [8].

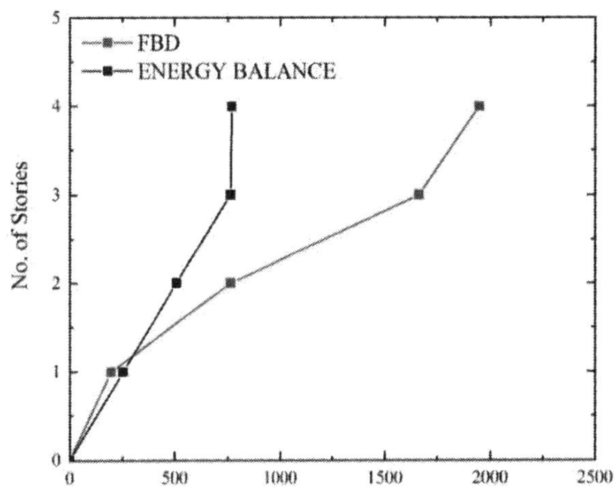

Fig. 8. Lateral force distribution, *x* - direction

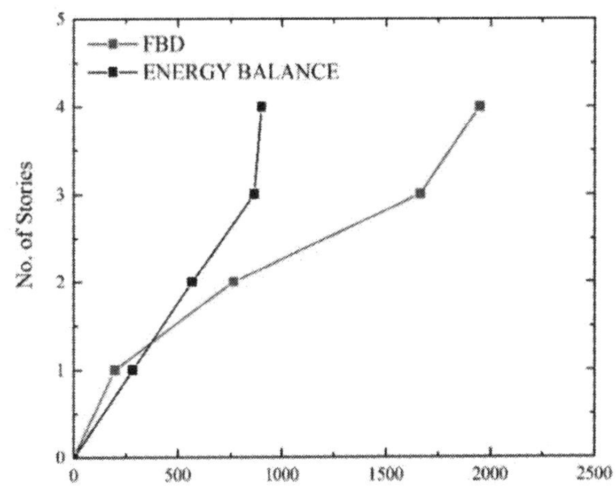

Fig. 9. Lateral force distribution, *y* - direction

TABLE X.
STRENGTHENING OF COLUMNS WITH FRP PLY

Size (mm)	ID no.	DCR	FRP Plies(no.)	DCR	FRP Plies(no.)
230 × 680	943	1.07	1	0.69	0
600 × 600	977	1.14	1	0.94	0
300 × 300	1004	1.33	1	1.30	1
600 × 600	1040	1.33	1	1.33	1
230 × 840	1052	1.36	1	1.36	1
600 × 600	1056	1.57	1	1.57	1
230 × 840	1094	1.18	1	1.03	1
300 × 300	1108	2.67	3	2.40	2
600 × 600	1112	1.28	1	1.28	1
600 × 600	1140	1.97	1	1.97	1
300 × 300	1145	2.49	3	2.14	2
600 × 600	1178	1.13	1	1.13	1
			16		**12**

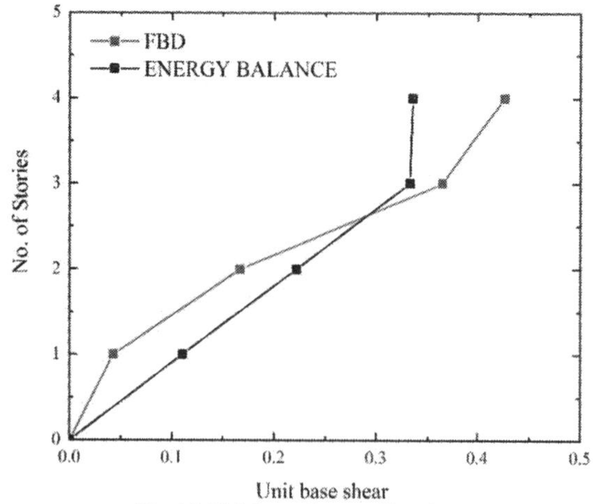

Fig. 10. Unit base shear, *x*-direction

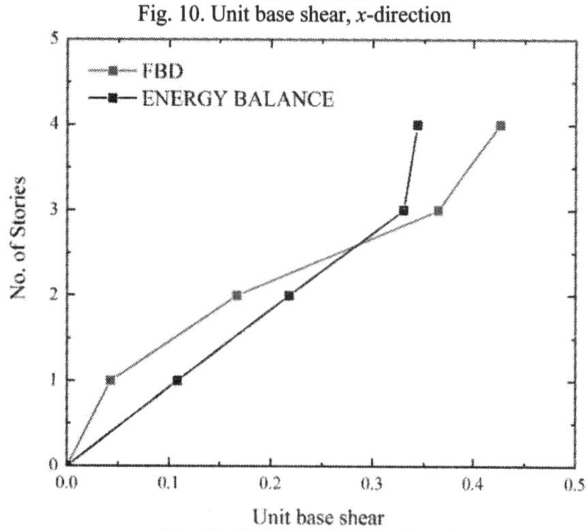

Fig. 11. Unit base shear, *y*-direction

V. CONCLUSION

Study compares the target peak displacement by performance point of energy spectrum and performance point of ATC-40 capacity spectrum by SAP2000. Another study is evaluate the difference of axial force demand due to applied design lateral forces by both the method to strengthening of columns with the FRP technique. The study concludes that;

1). Performance point for maximum displacement by energy spectrum is less than ATC-40 capacity spectrum (SAP2000).

2). Evaluated design base shear isless from energy balance concept than force-based design method.

3). Number of ground floor columns which failed due to increase in axial force evaluated by energy balance concept is less than evaluated by Force-Based Design (FBD) method.

4). Requirement of retrofitting as per demand capacity ratio is less for applied lateral forces evaluated from energy balance concept than the Force-Based Design (FBD) method.

References

[1] George, W. H. 1956. Limit Design of Structures to Resist Earthquakes, *World Conference on Earthquake Engineering,* vol. 5, pp. 1-11.

[2] Newmark, N. M., Hall, W. J. 1982. Earthquake Spectra and Design, *Earthquake Engineering Research Institute,* El Carrito, CA.

[3] Lee, S. S., Goel, S. C. 2001. Report on Performance-Based Design of Steel Moment Frames Using Target Drift and Yield Mechanism, *Department of Civil and Environmental Engineering,* University of Michigan, Ann Arbor, Michigan City Indiana, United States of America.

[4] Leelataviwat, S., Saewon, W., Goel, S. C. 2008. An Energy-Based Method for Seismic Evaluation of Structures, *14th World Conference of Earthquake Engineering,* Beijing, China.

[5] Liao, W. C., Goel S. C. 2012. Performance-Based Plastic Design and Energy-Based Evaluation of Seismic Resistant RC Moment Frame, *Journal of Marine Science and Technology,* vol. 20, pp. 304-310.

[6] Liao, W. C. 2010. Ph.D. Thesis on Performance Based Plastic Design of Earthquake Resistant Reinforced Concrete Moment Frames, The University of Michigan, Michigan, United States of America.

[7] Goel, S. C. 2009. Performance Based Plastic Design (PBPD) Method for Earthquake-Resistant Structures: An Overview, *The Structural Design of Tall and Special Building,* vol. 19, pp. 115-137.

[8] ACI 440.2R-08, (2008) Guide for The Design and Construction of Externally Bonded FRP Systems for Strengthening Concrete Structures, American Concrete Institute, Michigan City Indiana, United States of America.

[9] IS 1893 (2016), Indian Standard Criteria for Earthquake Resistant Design of Structures Part-1, General Provisions and Buildings, Bureau of Indian Standards, New Delhi, India.

[10] IS 456 (2000), Plain and Reinforced Concrete-Code of Practice, Bureau of Indian Standards, New Delhi, India.

[11] IS 4326 (2013), Earthquake Resistant Design and Construction of Buildings-Code of Practice, Bureau of Indian Standards, New Delhi, India.

[12] IS 13920 (2016), Ductile Detailing of Reinforced Concrete Structures Subjected to Seismic Forces-Code of Practice, Bureau of Indian Standards, New Delhi, India.

Analytical Study on Two-Way Rectangular RC Slab with Opening at Different Locations

Katrodiya Daxesh G.[1], Chauhan Neha H.[2], Chauhan Ritesh L.[3]

[1] *Post Graduate Student (Structural Engineering), M.S. Patel Department of Civil Engineering, Chandubhai S. Patel Institute of Technology, Charotar University of Science and Technology, Changa, Gujarat, India*
[2]*Assistant Professor,M. S. Patel Department of Civil Engineering, Chandubhai S. Patel Institute of Technology, Charotar University of Science and Technology, Changa, Gujarat, India*
[3] *Consulting Structural Engineer, Arcon Civil Project Consultants, Surat, Gujarat, India*

[1]daxeshkatrodiaya17@gmail.com
[2]nehachauhan.cv@charusat.ac.in
[3]info@arconconsultants.com

***Abstract* — Two-way rectangular RC slab contain opening of considerable size for ducts, pipes and other services. Such opening in slab disturbs the load transfer path. Yield line theory is used to analyze uniformly loaded two-way slab with opening at different locations. In this study seven different positions of opening are considered: the slab central, the center of short span, the center of long span, the center of two opposite short span, the center of two opposite long span, the two central, the center of short span and long span. The ratio of the size of opening to span of slab (k/L) is kept same for all locations of opening. The sizes of opening from 0.1 to 0.5 of the span of slab are considered. Nine boundary conditions of slab are considered and the effects of openings for different type of boundary conditions were studied over different locations of opening. Equation for bending moment of RC slab having an opening at different location also derived in this study.**

***Keywords:*Two-way slab; Reinforced concrete; Yield line theory; Opening;Bending moment.**

I. INTRODUCTION

Reinforced concrete slab carries pipe, ducts and other services through opening of considerable size at different location over slab. Due to this kind of opening, the load transfer gets disturb. Therefore, we need to consider such provision in slabs during the analysis and design.

Akinyele [1] carried out Comparison of computer based yield line theory with elastic theory and finite element methods for solid slabs. The result of analysis shows that for two-way slab yield line theory is conservative for all conditions. They also conclude that yield line theory has been safe and economical compare to elastic method and finite element methods. MortezaFadaee et al. [2] presented a Design of two-way slab subjected to concentrated load using Plastic Method (Yield Line Method). In this research paper, they develop equation for moment coefficient, which depends on location of concentrated load, span and different boundary condition. From this study, they conclude that plastic method which is appropriate method for designing such RC slab for different edge condition. Islam et al. [3] presented an equation for limit design of uniformly loaded rectangular slab with opening at various locations like central opening, corner opening, at center of short side and at center of long side opening. They conclude that using this other can develop design equation and charts for uniformly loaded two-way slab with opening of various positions. From this review it is evident that the yield line theory is an approach for determining the ultimate load capacity of reinforced concrete slabs subjected to any kind of loading and having different boundary conditions. There are many simplified methods for calculating the bending moment, deflection and shear force but the most design of RC member are based on elastic analysis. The most practical method is plastic method. The plastic method is also known as yield line method. The ultimate bending moment of such slabs may be determine using the yield line theory.

To address above concern, the yield line theory for reinforced concrete two-way slab with different boundary conditions by considering opening is developed. For knowing the effectiveness of openings different locations and different boundary conditions are considered.

II. CONCEPT OF YIELD LINE THEORY

An advanced ultimate load method, which provides realistic value of failure load of reinforced concrete slab based on inelastic behavior of structure to failure, is known as yield line theory. The yield line theory is not restricted by complexities of shape, support conditions and load combinations. The coefficients in Annex D-1 of IS 456:2000 [4] to work out the bending moment for the design of two-way slabs are based on inelastic analysis. In addition to that, the code also recommends the use of yield line theory for slab analysis as per Clause 24.4, IS 456:2000 [4].

III. Methodology

Over time, there have been several analytical methods that have been used in the analysis of slabs. In this paper virtual work method is used for analysis of slab having opening at different location and different boundary conditions.

The boundary conditions considered for the study are as follows:

Type 1: Interior Panels (All Edges Fixed)
Type 2: One Short Edge Discontinuous
Type 3: One Long Edge Discontinuous
Type 4: Two Adjacent Edge Discontinuous
Type 5: Two Short Edges Discontinuous
Type 6: Two Long Edges Discontinuous
Type 7: One Long Edge Continuous
Type 8: One Short Edge Continuous
Type 9: All Edges Discontinuous

Seven different positions of opening for the slab having all edges fixedare considered as shown in Figure 1 to Figure 7. At central opening, opening at the center of a short span, opening at center of a long span, opening at center of two opposite short span, opening at center of two opposite long span, two central opening, opening at center of a short span and long span are the seven different positions of opening considered for the analysis.

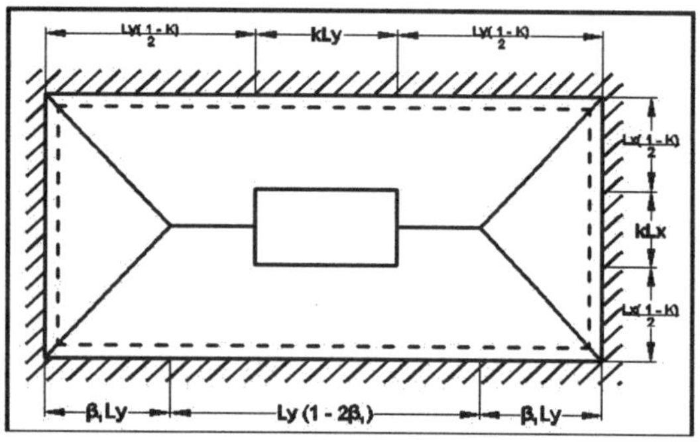

Figure 1: RC slab having central opening

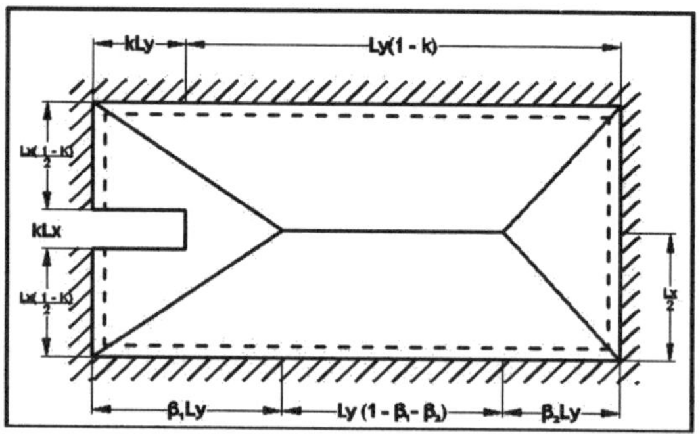

Figure 2: RC slab having opening at center of short span

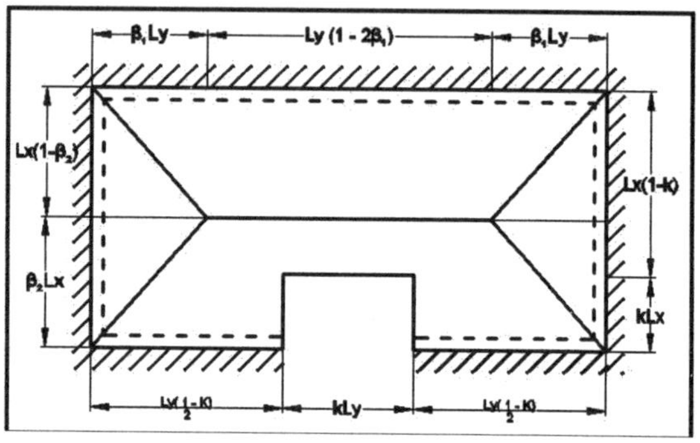

Figure 3: RC slab having opening at center of long span

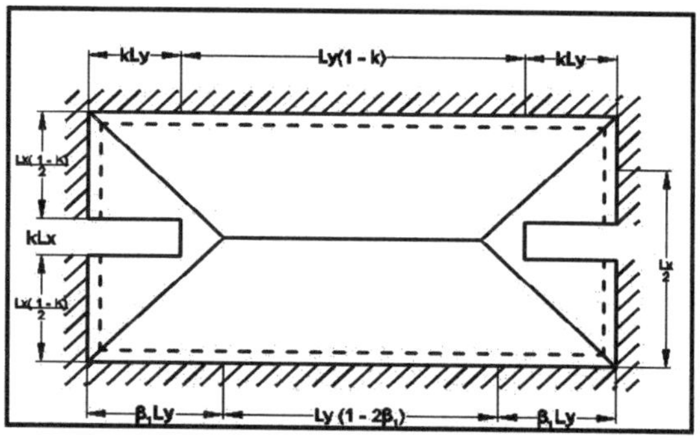

Figure 4: RC slab having opening at center of two opposite short span

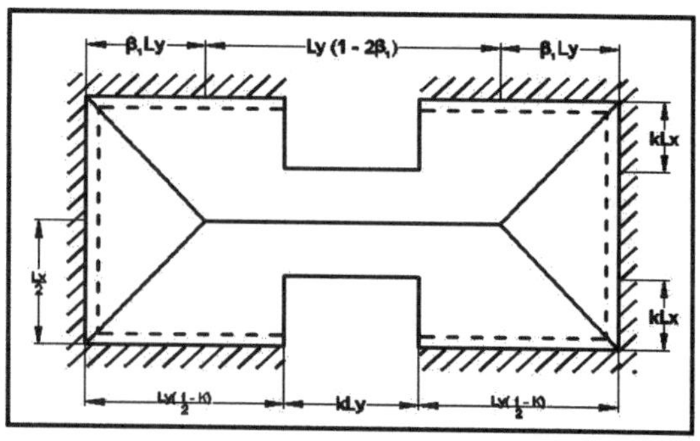

Figure 5: RC slab having opening at center of two opposite long span

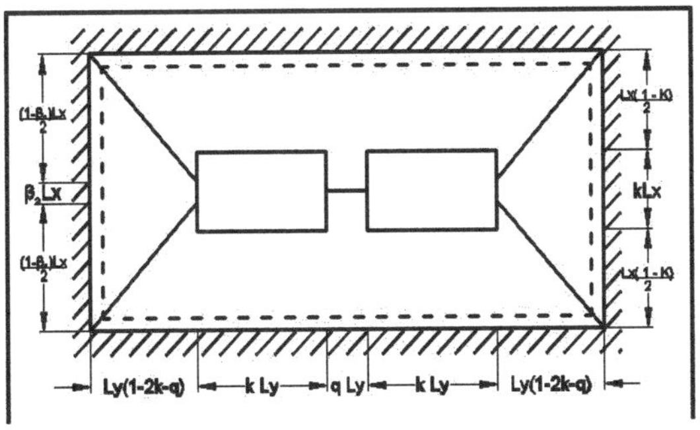

Figure 6: RC slab having two central opening

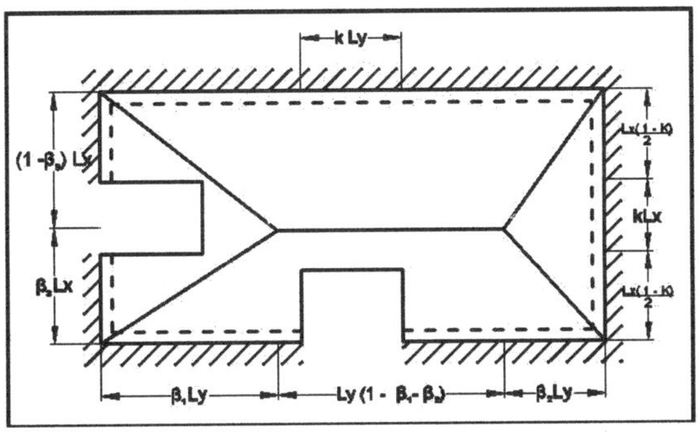

Figure 7: RC slab having opening at center of short span and long span

For the present study location type is given for different location of slab opening as per Table I.

TABLE I
LOCATION TYPE FOR DIFFERENT LOCATION OF OPENING

Location of Opening	Location Type
Slab having central opening	1
Slab having opening at center of short span	2
Slab having opening at center of long span	3
Slab having opening at center of two opposite short span	4
Slab having opening at center of two opposite long span	5
Slab having two central opening	6
Slab having opening at center of short span and long span	7

A. Conditions for each cases

Different cases involve two similar values and two variable values for analysis. Seven different locations of opening in slab as describe in Table I and span ratio 1.5 remain similar for all the cases. Size of opening from 0.1 to 0.5 of each span and different boundary conditions for slab is variable terms for each cases of analysis.

1) Case 1.1:

This case includes uniformly loaded two-way slabs with all edges fixed and having opening at seven different locations for the value of similar span ratio as 1.5 for all and the size of opening is considering for this case as 0.1 of short span and long span.

TABLE II
CONDITION FOR EACH CASES

Case No.	Type of Slab	Span Ratio (Ly/Lx)	Location of Opening (Location Type)	Size of Opening (k)
Case 1.1	1	1.5	1	0.1
			2	
			3	
			4	
			5	
			6	
			7	

Similarly, case 1.2 to 1.9 is defined for different type of slab 2 to 9 respectively but other conditions are remaining same as case 1.1. Case 2.1 to 2.9, 3.1 to 3.9, 4.1 to 4.9 and 5.1 to 5.9, these all case includes similar conditions as of case 1.1 to 1.9 but the size of opening for this case as 0.2. 0.3, 0.4 and 0.5 of short span and long span respectively.

IV. RESULTS AND DISCUSSION

Uniformly loaded two-way slab having opening at different location and different boundary conditions are analyzed using yield line theory. From this study, the equation of bending moment for such slab can be derived for each boundary condition.

Following are the assumptions for the analysis of two-way slab having opening at different location and different boundary condition.

1. The slab will be considered to be reinforced orthotropically by steel in both x & y directions.
2. Absence of top steel over discontinuous edge.

The Equations (4.1) to (4.7) are derived by virtual work method to find bending moment of reinforced concrete slab having openings at different locations for slab having all edges fixed.

A. Central opening

$$m_y = \frac{WL_x^2}{12}\left[\frac{3\beta_1\left(1-2k^2+k^3\right)-2\beta_1^2}{2r\beta_1\left(1+r'-k\right)+\alpha^2\left(1+r'\right)}\right] \tag{4.1}$$

B. Opening at short span

$$m_y = \frac{wL_x^2\beta_1\beta_2\left[3\left(1-k^2\right)-\beta_1-\beta_2\right]}{6\left[4r\beta_1\beta_2\left(1+r'\right)+\alpha^2\beta_1\left(1+r'\right)+\alpha^2\beta_2\left(1+r'-kr'\right)\right]} \tag{4.2}$$

C. Opening at long span

$$m_y = \frac{wL_x^2}{6}\frac{\beta_1\beta_2\left(1-\beta_2\right)\left[3-2\beta_1-3k^2\right]}{\begin{bmatrix} r\beta_1+rr'\beta_1\beta_2+rr'\beta_1\left(1-\beta_2\right)\left(1-k\right) \\ +2\alpha^2\beta_2\left(1-\beta_2\right)\left(1+r'\right) \end{bmatrix}} \tag{4.3}$$

D. Opening at center of two opposite short span

$$m_y = \frac{wL_x^2}{12}\frac{\beta_1\left[3-2\beta_1-6k^2\right]}{\left[2r\beta_1\left(1+r'\right)+\alpha^2\left(1+r'-kr'\right)\right]} \tag{4.4}$$

E. Opening at center of two opposite long span

$$m_y = \frac{wL_x^2}{12}\frac{\beta_1\left[3-2\beta_1-6k^2\right]}{\left[2r\beta_1\left(1+r'-kr'\right)+\alpha^2\left(1+r'\right)\right]} \tag{4.5}$$

F. Two central opening

$$m_y = \frac{wL_x^2}{24}\frac{\left(1-\beta_2\right)\left(1-2k-q\right)\begin{bmatrix}\left(1-2k-q\right)\left(2+\beta_2\right) \\ +6k\left(1-k\right)+3q\end{bmatrix}}{\begin{bmatrix} r\left(1-2k-q\right)^2+rq\left(1-\beta_2\right)\left(1-2k-q\right) \\ +rr'\left(1-2k-q\right)+\alpha^2\left(1-\beta_2\right)\left(1-\beta_2+r'\right) \end{bmatrix}} \tag{4.6}$$

G. Opening at center of short span and long span

$$m_y = \frac{wL_x^2}{6}\frac{\beta_1\beta_2\beta_3\left(1-\beta_3\right)\left[3-\beta_1-\beta_2-6k^2\right]}{\begin{bmatrix} r\beta_1\beta_2+rr'\beta_1\beta_2\beta_3+rr'\beta_1\beta_2\left(1-k\right)\left(1-\beta_3\right) \\ +\alpha^2\beta_3\left(1-\beta_3\right)\beta_1\left(1+r'\right)+\alpha^2\beta_3\left(1-\beta_3\right)\beta_2\left(1+r'-kr'\right) \end{bmatrix}} \tag{4.7}$$

Similarly, the bending moment equation for other boundary conditions as described in previous section can be find out using virtual work method. The result obtained from performed analysis are given in Table III. The numerical values in Table III depicts the bending moment in *x* and *y* direction of two-way slab having opening at different location for different boundary conditions.

TABLE III
BENDING MOMENT OF TWO-WAY SLAB FOR CASE 1.1

Case No.	Location of Opening	Bending Moment (kNm)			
		Mx (+ve)	Mx (-ve)	My (+ve)	My (-ve)
Case 1.1	1	10.893	14.488	7.262	9.658
	2	10.784	14.343	7.189	9.561
	3	10.857	14.44	7.238	9.627
	4	10.739	14.283	7.159	9.521
	5	10.992	14.619	7.328	9.746
	6	11.147	14.826	7.431	9.883
	7	10.808	14.375	7.205	9.583

For other cases, the bendimg moment of short span (M*x*) is represented in a graphical representation as shown in Figures 8 to 16.

Figure 8 represent result value of positive bending moment in *x* direction for case 1.1 to 5.1. From this graph, it seems that there is a very small variation in bending moment for case 1.1, 2.1, 3.1 and 5.1 having different location of opening. But there is more variation in bending moment for slab having two central opening and opening at center of two opposite short span compare to other location of opening for case 4.1. For case 4.1, provision of opening in this particular type of slab at any location will be created. The appropriate place for provision of opening in this type of slab is at two central opening.

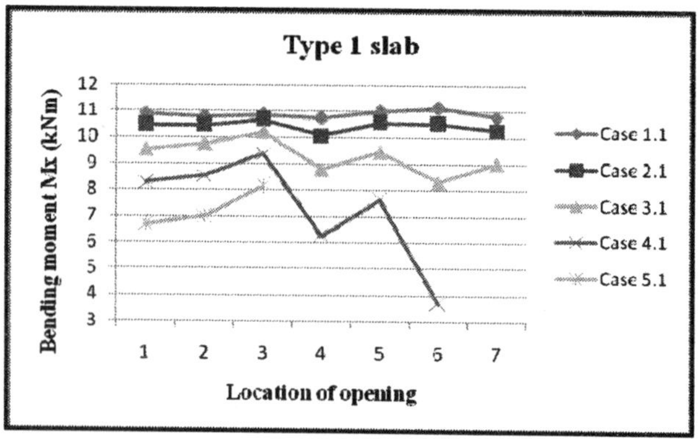

Figure 8: Bending moment (M*x*) of type 1 slab for case 1.1 to 5.1

Figure 9 shows result value of positive bending moment in x direction for case 1.2 to 5.2. From this graph, analysis of case 1.2, 2.2 and 3.2 leads to result that there is similar behavior of bending moment for different location of opening as of case 1.1, 2.1 and 3.1. But there is more variation in bending moment for slab having two central opening and opening at center of two opposite short span compare to other location of opening for case 4.2. It is similar kind of behavior as of case 4.1 discussed in Figure 8.

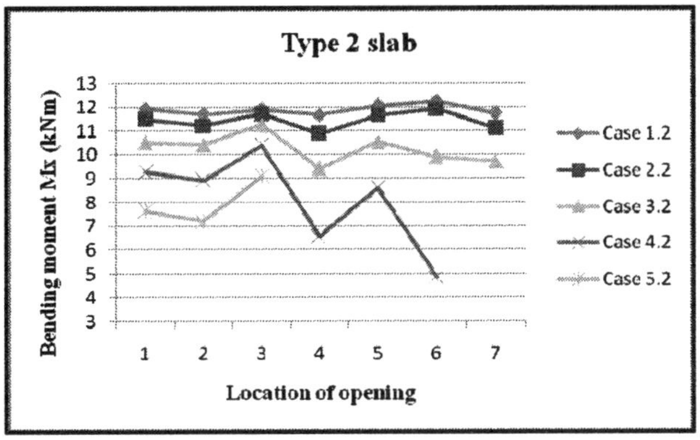

Figure 9: Bending moment (Mx) of type 2 slab for case 1.2 to 5.2

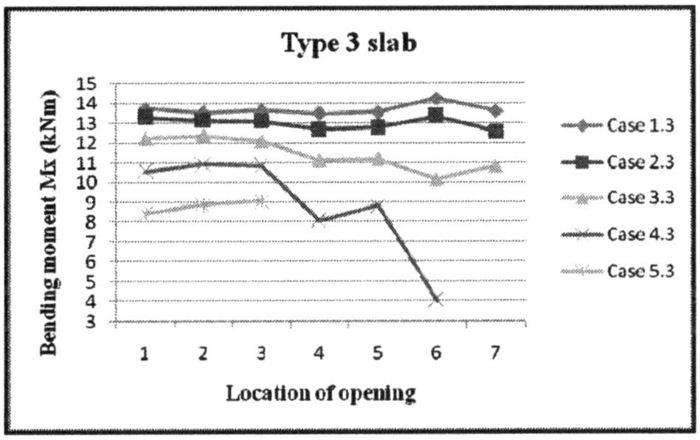

Figure 10: Bending moment (Mx) of type 3 slab for case 1.3 to 5.3

Figure 10 shows the results value of positive bending moment in x direction for case 1.3 to 5.3. From this graph, analysis of case 1.3, 2.3, 3.3 and 5.3 leads to result that there is similar behavior of bending moment for different location of opening as of case 1.1, 2.1 and 3.1 as discuss in Figure 8. Analysis of case 4.3 leads to the result that the variation in bending moment for slab remains very small for all location of opening except for two central opening and opening at center of two opposite short edges. Large opening in the slab (case 4.3) at any location does not affect the total bending moment in any axis but there is a large variation in bending moment of slab having two central opening and opening at center of two opposite short edges.

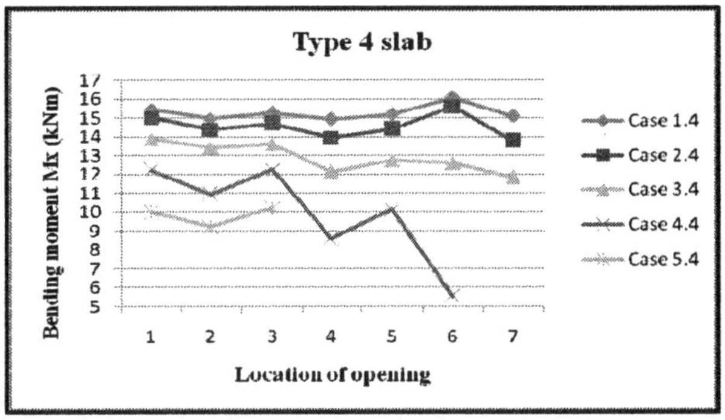

Figure 11: Bending moment (Mx) of type 4 slab for case 1.4 to 5.4

Figure 11 shows the results value of positive bending moment in x direction for case 1.4 to 5.4. Analysis of case 3.4 leads to result that there is similar behavior of bending moment for different location of opening as of case 1.1, 2.1 and 3.1. But analysis of case 1.4 and 2.4 leads to result that there is very small variation in bending moment for slab having different location of opening except for two central opening so that provision of opening in this particular type of slab at any location will be created except two central opening. For case 4.4, it is similar kind of behavior as of case 4.1 discussed in Figure 8.

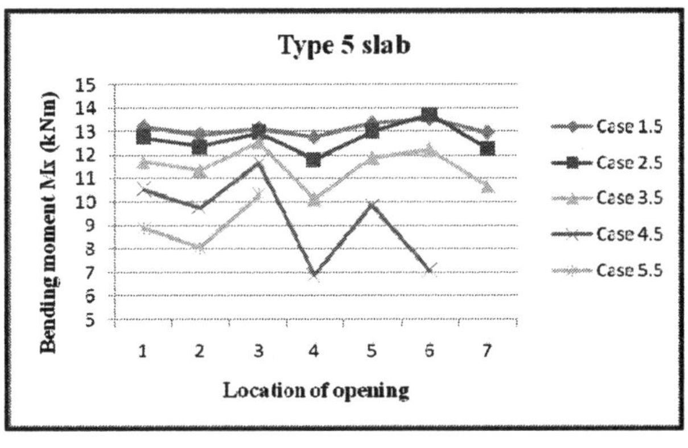

Figure 12: Bending moment (Mx) of type 5 slab for case 1.5 to 5.5

Figure 12 illustrates the results value of positive bending moment in x direction for case 1.5 to 5.5. From this graph, it seems that there is very small variation in bending moment for case 1.5, 2.5 and 3.5 having different location of opening. The appropriate place for provision of opening in this type of slab is at two central opening. From graph of case 4.5, it is similar kind of behavior as of case 4.1 discuss in Figure 8.

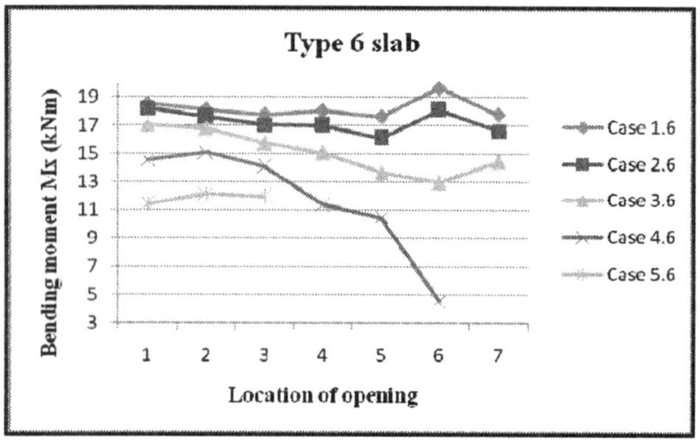

Figure 13: Bending moment (M*x*) of type 6 slab for case 1.6 to 5.6

Figure 13 illustrates the results value of positive bending moment in x direction for case 1.6 to 5.6. Analysis of case 1.6 and 2.6 leads to result that there is very small variation in bending moment for slab having different location of opening except for two central opening so that provision of opening in this particular type of slab at any location will be created except two central opening. But analysis of case 3.6 leads to result that there is very small variation in bending moment for slab having different location of opening except for opening at center two opposite long edges and two central opening. Analysis of case 5.6 leads to result that there is very small variation in bending moment of slab having opening at different location. So that provision of opening in this particular type of slab at any location will be created.

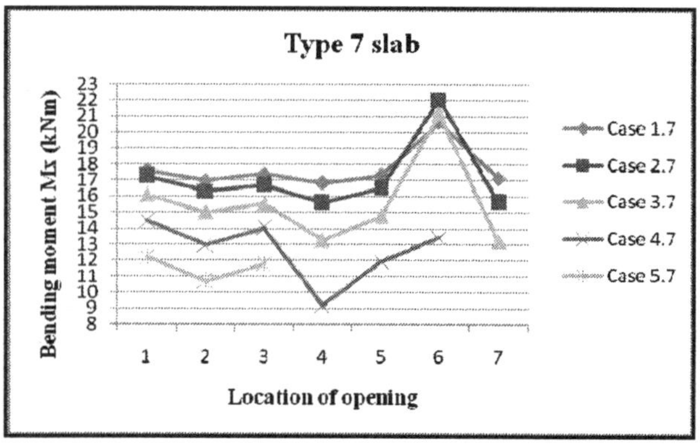

Figure 14: Bending moment (M*x*) of type 7 slab for case 1.7 to 5.7

Figure 14 shows the results value of positive bending moment in x direction for case 1.7 to 5.7. Analysis of case 1.7, 2.7 and 3.7 leads to results that there is very small variation in bending moment of slab having opening at different location except for two central opening. From graph of case 4.7, it seems that there is very small variation in bending moment of slab having different location of opening except opening at center of two opposite short edges. Graph of case 5.7 behavior is a similar kind of behavior as of case 5.6 discussed in Figure 13.

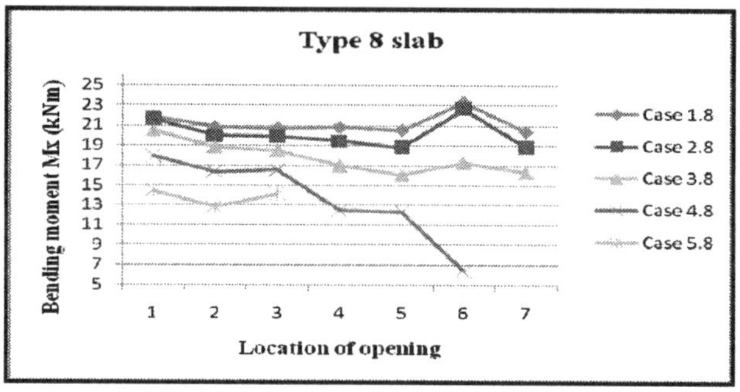

Figure 15: Bending moment (M*x*) of type 8 slab for case 1.8 to 5.8

Figure 15 illustrates the results value of positive bending moment in x direction for case 1.8 to 5.8. From graph of case 1.8, 2.8 and 3.8, it is similar kind of behavior as of case 1.7, 2.7 and 3.7 discuss in Figure 14. Graph of case 4.8 showing similar kind of behavior as of case 4.6 discussed in Figure 13.

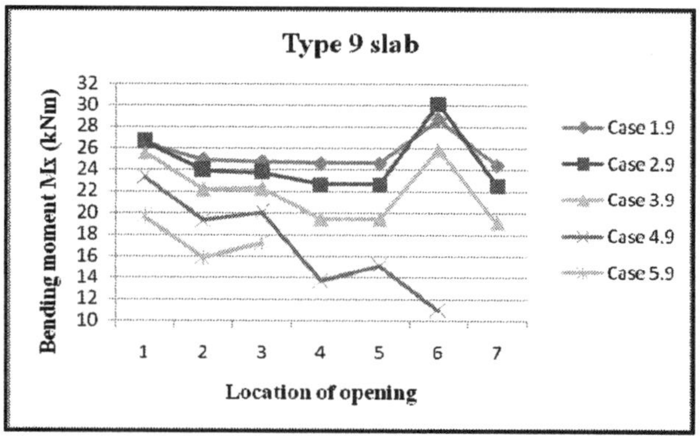

Figure 16: Bending moment (M*x*) of type 9 slab for case 1.9 to 5.9

Figure 16 contains results value of positive bending moment in x direction for case 1.9 to 5.9. From graph type 9 slab, it seems that there is similar kind of behaviour as of type 8 slab discuss in Figure 15.

V. CONCLUSIONS

The uniformly loaded two-way slab having opening at different location can be analyzed using yield line theory for different boundary conditions. From the analysis, the equation for bending moment in x & y directions can be derive so that one can analyzed such slab having different size and location of opening. In order to study effectiveness of opening for different location and boundary conditions, the equation of bending moment are used.

From the study following conclusions are derived:

1. From analysis of case 1.1 to 1.5 and case 2.1 to 2.3, the variation in bending moment about both x and y axis for small opening in slab remain very small for all cases of opening except for opening at corner. Provision of opening in this particular type of slab at any location can be created.
2. From analysis of case 1.6 to 1.9, the variation in bending moment about both x and y-axis for small opening in slab remain very small for all cases of opening except for two central opening. And there is very low bending moment in slab having opening at corner and at two opposite corner. Provision of opening in this particular type of slab at any location can be created except slab with two central opening.
3. From analysis of case 2.4 to 2.6, Provision of opening in this particular type of slab at any location will be created. The appropriate place for provision of opening in this particular type of slab is at center of two opposite long edge and at corner.
4. Analysis of case 2.7 to 2.9 leads to the result that the variation in bending moment about both x and y-axis for small opening in slab remain very small for all cases of opening except for two central opening. Provision of opening in this particular type of slab at any location can be created except slab with two central opening.
5. Analysis of case 3.1 to 3.3 leads to the result that the variation in bending moment about both x and y-axis for small opening in slab remain very small for all cases of opening except for opening at centre of two opposite long edges. Provision of opening in this particular type of slab at any location can be created. The appropriate place for provision of opening in this particular type of slab is opening at center of two opposite long edge.
6. Analysis of case 3.7 to 3.9 leads to the result that the variation in bending moment about both x and y-axis for small opening in slab remain very small for all cases of opening except for two central opening. Provision of opening in this particular type of slab at any location can be created except slab with two central opening.
7. The overall conclusion for slab having small opening is to provide opening at any location except slab with opening at two central opening (Location Type 6). Thus, the appropriate location for small opening in this type of slab is at any location. The best place for opening is at corner (Location Type 9).
8. Analysis of case 4.1 to 4.9 leads to the result that the variation in bending moment about both x and y-axis for opening in slab remain small for all cases of opening except for two central opening. The appropriate place for provision of opening in this type of slab is at two central opening. Similarly analysis of case 5.1 to 5.6 suggests that the appropriate place for provision of opening in this type of slab is at any location except for opening at corner (Location Type 9).
9. Analysis of case 5.7 to 5.9 leads to the result that the variation in bending moment about both x and y-axis for opening in slab remain small for all cases of opening. But the appropriate location for provision of opening in this type of slab is at center of short edge compares other location.
10. The overall conclusion for slab having large opening is to provide opening at any location except for opening at corner (Location Type 9). Thus, the appropriate location for large opening in this type of slab is at two central opening (Location Type 6).

References

[1] Akinyele, J. O. (2011). 'Compression of computer based yield line theory with elastic theory and finite element method for solid slab.' International Journal of Engineering and Technology, vol. 3, pp. 1-5.

[2] Fadaee, M., Iranmanesh, A. and Fadaee, M. J. (2013). 'A simplify method for designing RC Slab under concentrated loading.' International Journal of Engineering and Technology, vol.5.

[3] Islam, I. And Park, R. (1971) 'Yield line analysis of two-way reinforced concrete slab with opening.' The structural engineer, vol. 49.

[4] IS 456:2000, 'Plain and Reinforced Concrete - code of practice.

A Study on Retrofitting of RCC Industrial Building

B. Santhosh Reddy[1], D. Rupesh Kumar[2], K. Chaithanya Varada Prasasd[3]

[1,3]*Master's scholar, Civil Engineering Department, University College of Engineering (A), Osmania University, Hyderabad–500007, T.S., India*

[2]*Associate Professor, Civil Engineering Department, University College of Engineering (A), Osmania University, Hyderabad–500007, T.S., India*

[1]santhoshreddy6446@gmail.com
[2]rkdhondy@gmail.com
[3]chaithanyavarada@gmail.co

***Abstract*—This work deals with the various principles of retrofitting of structures. The latest techniques in retrofitting of structures are discussed. Reinforced cement concrete repair techniques like jacketing, shotcrete method (guniting) and form and pump methods that can be carried out are explained well. Strengthening of columns and footings using jacketing repair technique is explained in detail with a case study. An industrial building is selected for case study that was constructed a decade back with the past codes and a model is generated in STAAD.Pro. The change in the loading due to extra machinery is calculated. For bearing the extra loading the building is retrofitted in the columns and footings. The design values for retrofitting is being manually calculated and checked in STAAD.Pro by generating a model and analyzing it for the loadings calculated. Cost analysis is also done for RCC, FRP and SFRC jacketing techniques and compared to find the economical technique. In the present study RCC jacketing is used as it is cheaper than the FRP jacketing and gives more carpet area compared to SFRC jacketing.**

***Keywords*—RCC Jacketing, shotcrete, guniting, FRP jacketing,SFRC jacketing.**

I. Introduction

Major structures like buildings, dams and bridges are subjected to severe loading and their performance is likely to change with time. RCC is the most widely used and versatile construction material possessing several advantages. Very often one comes across with some defect in concrete due to errors in the design construction activities or due to environmental impacts. The defects may manifest themselves in the form of cracks, spalling of concrete, exposure of reinforcement, excessive deflections or other signs of distress. To prevent this kind of calamities rehabilitation of the structure can be done at the initial stages of damage.

Retrofitting can generally be classified in two categories: Global and the local. The global retrofitting technique targets the seismic resistance of the building. It includes adding of infill wall, adding of shear wall, adding of steel bracings and base isolation. Adding of infill wall in the ground storey is a viable option to retrofit buildings with soft storey. Shear walls can be introduced in a building with flat slabs or flat plates. A new shear wall should be provided with an adequate foundation. Steel braces can be inserted in frames to provide lateral strength, stiffness, ductility, and to improve energy dissipation. These can be provided in the exterior frames with least disruption of the building use. Local retrofitting technique targets the seismic resistance of a member. The local retrofit technique includes the concrete, steel or Fibre reinforced polymer Jacketting to the structural members like beams, columns, beam column joint, foundation. Concrete jacketing involves adding.

The need to retrofit and rehabilitate a structure may arise at any time from the beginning of the construction phase until the end of the service life.

During the construction phase, it may occur because of:

i. Design errors
ii. Deficient concrete production
iii. Bad execution processes.

During the service life, it may arise on account of:

i. An earthquake
ii. An accident, such as collisions, fire, explosions
iii. Situations involving changes in the structure functionality
iv. The development of more demanding code requirements.

With all these errors the design life of the structure is decreased. This can be observed visually sometimes by formation of cracks. Proper study has to be made during the initial stages and proper retrofitting technique should be used to reduce the losses.

The jacketing is the widely used rehabilitation technique for strengthening the elements. In jacketing reinforce cement concrete (RCC) jacketing, Fibre reinforced polymer (FRP) jacketing and Steel fibre reinforced concrete (SFRC) jacketing techniques are popular. The details of these jacketing techniques are described briefly in the report.

II. Literature Review

PranayRanjan et al. [1] discusses design of RCC, FRP and SFRC jacketing of failed columns of a G+3 storey existing building and compares suitability of three methods of retrofitting.

Uma Shankar et al. [2] describes a case study to seismically upgrade a seven storey non-ductile concrete framed building of early nineties. Fiber-reinforced polymer (FRP) composite materials provide an outstanding means for rehabilitating and strengthening existing reinforced and pre-stressed concrete bridges, buildings and other structures.

Nikita Gupta et al. [3] made an effort to elaborate the procedure of providing concrete jacketing to the column as per guidelines of IS 15988: 2013.

Catalinand Paricia et al. [4] in first part of paper, briefly presents classic and modern retrofitting technologies for industrial buildings. The second part represents a study case of a single storey industrial building retrofitting, using four different intervention options. All the retrofitting methods presented in this lead to a more resistant structure, reducing the seismic risks, lateral displacements decrease, while ductility, bending moment and shear force capacities significantly increase.

Anusha and Paul [5] studies a school building which has suffered damage on 18th September 2011. Earthquake has been evaluated and retrofitting measures have been suggested to upgrade performance level of the building to make it safer against future earthquakes. The whole school building is modelled in SAP2000 and analysed for the seismic activity. From the results the required strength in different regions of the structure is calculated and the techniques that can be used for the retrofitting of the structure are mentioned.

Pavan et al. [6] describes the various causes of structural failures and the principles of rehabilitation of structures. It also describes various techniques in repair and rehabilitation of structures. Major repair that are to be carried out in brick walls, plaster walls and RCC members are explained in detail and an in-depth analysis into reinforced cement concrete repair options like concrete method (guniting) and form and pump method.

Chandar[7] describes the process of rehabilitation, retrofitting characteristics and technical aspects of the major intervention methods.

III. Details of Industrial Building

The structure considered for the case study is an industrial building, with G + 2 storey, which is located in Hyderabad and comes under the seismic zone of II. The building is initially designed a decade back without considering the earthquake loads. The details of the existing building are mentioned in Table I and corresponding STAAD. Pro models are shown in Figs. 1&2.

TABLE I
Details of Industrial Building.

Building type	Industrial building
Building dimensions	34 m x 35 m
Live load	5 kN/m^2
Floor finish	1 kN/m^2
Thickness of slab	180 mm
Size of concrete beam	230 mm x 450 mm
Size of concrete column	600 mm x 230 mm
Damping ratio	5% (0.05)
Thickness of wall	230 mm
Inner plaster	12 mm
Outer plaster	15 mm
Height of floor	3.5 m
Height of roof truss	1.5 m
Truss element size	100 mm X 100 mm
Grade of concrete	M 20
Grade of Steel	Fe 415

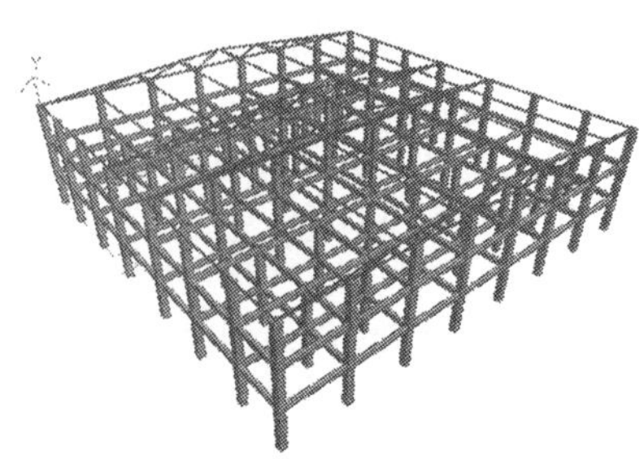

Fig. 1 3D rendered view of the industrial building

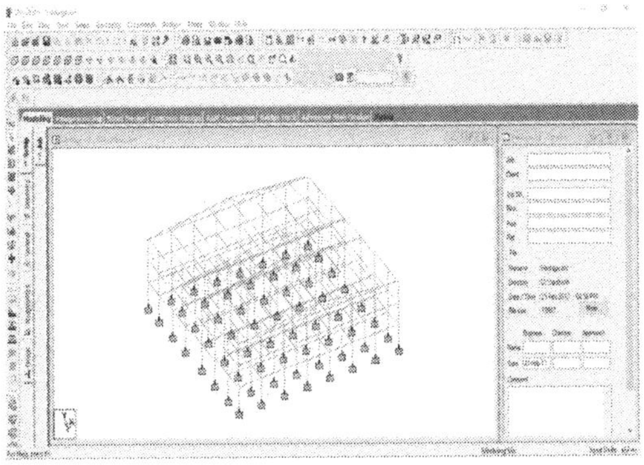

Fig. 2 STAAD Pro. Model of industrial building

A. *Loads on the Structure*

The dead load of the structure is directly calculated by the STAAD. Pro when used self weight by a factor 1.0. Since there are no extra equipments on the structure initially, self weight of the structure is the dead load acting on the structure. The total dead load on the structure can be calculated by multiplying the volume of the structure with density of the RCC i.e., 25 kN/m3.

The structure is initially subjected to the dead load of 4.625 kN/m2 (Fig. 3 shows the assigned dead load), and after installation of new machinery, the dead load is increased to 15 kN/m2 (224% increased), and same is assigned to the structure with and without jacketing as shown in Fig. 4. For roof truss it was calculated as 14.83 kN on intermediate panels and on end panels it was 7.42 kN and assigned on the roof truss.

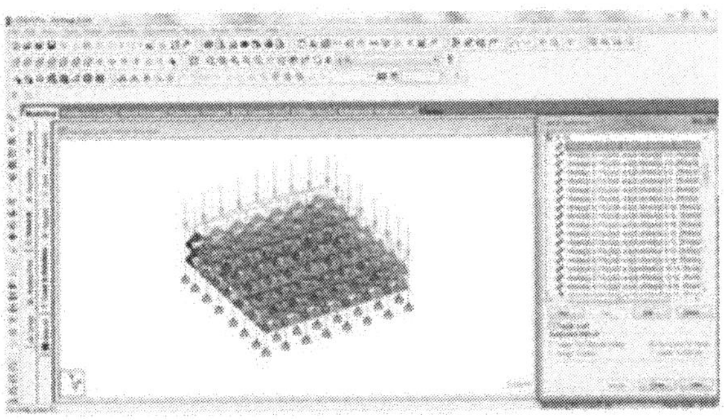

Fig. 3 Assigned Dead Load

Live load of the structure is taken from code IS 875 (Part 2): 1987 for the industrial building it is 5 kN/m2. For the structure with and without additional loads (dead load and earthquake load is increased), live load is considered to be constant (no increase in live load)

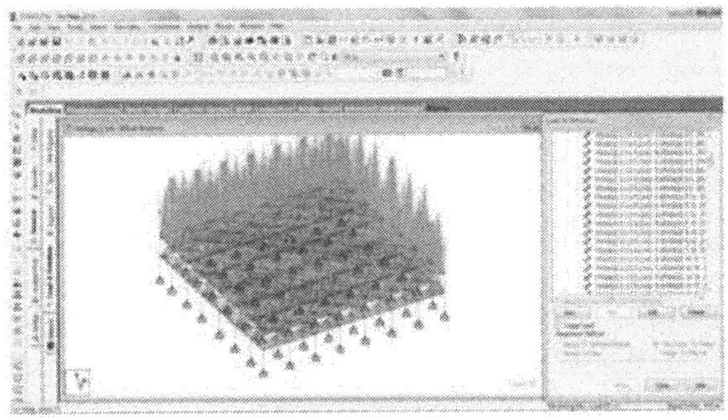

Fig. 4 Assigned Additional Dead Load

Wind load of the structure is considered from the code IS 875 (Part 3): 1987 and is defined in the STAAD. Pro, using the tool wind load definitions, with the exposure factor of 1 for both the cases. Since there is no increase in height of the structure the wind load acting in both the cases (with and without additional loads) will be same in all the four directions

Building is initially not designed for earthquake loads, but for new design earthquake loads are considered. Earthquake load is defined with the parameter (Zone factors, damping ratio, and medium type soil) for both cases (with and without additional dead load). In present case study zone factor is considered as 0.1 (Zone II), and other parameters considered are, damping ratio of 0.05 (5%), response reduction factor as 5, importance factor 1.5, type of structure 3, and rock and soil site factor as 2. All the parameters are considered as per the code IS 1893 2002. As the dead load on the structure is increased (from 4.625 kN/m^2 to 15 kN/m^2), the earthquake load on the structure will also increase the parameters that are assigned on STAAD. Pro model

The different limit state of strength load combinations are considered according to Indian Codal provisions.

IV. Results and Discussion

A. *Non-Destructive Test Results*

No pattern of visual cracking is observed during visual inspection. The compressive strength of 64 columns is recorded with the help of rebound hammer. From those results it is observed that out of 64 columns only ten columns (1, 22, 25, 29, 34, 46, 48, 52, 55, 58) have compressive strength less the 20 MPa and remaining all have more than 20 MPa. The same results are given as an input to the model in STAAD.Pro for further analysis. As mentioned in earlier, that the grade of concrete is M 20 for the whole structure. Columns having compressive strength less than the desired strength (20 MPa) are needed to be strengthened. But out of those ten columns six columns are subjected to jacketing (25, 34, 46, 48, 52, 55), hence no need for separate rehabilitation, but for other four columns (1, 22, 29, and 58) jacketing is not proposed. Hence the four columns should be strengthened by considering appropriate rehabilitation technique.

The quality of concrete of 64 columns is recorded with the help of ultra-sonic pulse velocity test results. Readings are taken at different heights on each column, average of those readings are recorded. From those results it is observed that out of 64 columns only four columns have poor quality of concrete and 24 columns have medium quality of concrete remaining 36 columns have good quality of concrete. Out of 64 columns four columns (1, 22, 29, and 58) are found to be of poor quality, hence these four columns need to be rehabilitated for strength as well as for quality. The column numbers of the structure are shown in the Fig. 5.

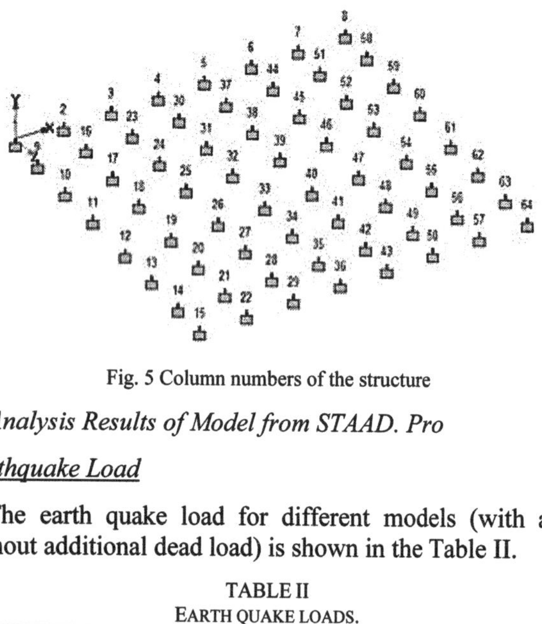

Fig. 5 Column numbers of the structure

B. Analysis Results of Model from STAAD. Pro

Earthquake Load

The earth quake load for different models (with and without additional dead load) is shown in the Table II.

TABLE II
EARTH QUAKE LOADS.

	Earthquake load (kN)			
	EQ + X	EQ - X	EQ + Z	EQ - Z
Existing load condition	577.66	-577.66	577.66	-577.66
Additional load condition	904.76	-904.76	904.76	-904.76

From Table III the existing structure is initially subjected to 577.66 kN of lateral load due to earthquake. Because of 224.3% increase in dead load, the lateral load on the structure is increased about 57%.

Grouping of Columns and Footings

For the design of footings, grouping of columns are made with respect to the load range in F_y and moment range in M_x and M_z. Grouping of columns are shown in the Table 3 with a maximum F_y of 1760 kN on 25, 26, 46 and 47 nodes, and a minimum F_y of 396 kN on nodes 15 and 64.

TABLE III
GROUPING OF COLUMNS AND FOOTINGS WITH EXISTING LOADS.

Group number	Column numbers	Load range (kN)	Column size(mm^2)	Pedestal height(m)	Footing size(m^2)	Depth of footing(mm)
I	1, 2, 3, 4, 5, 6, 7, 8, 15, 22, 29, 36, 43, 50, 57, 64.	< 800	230 x 600	0.7	2 x 2	400
II	9, 10, 11, 12, 13, 14, 58, 59, 60, 61, 62, 63.	800 - 1000	230 x 600	0.7	3 x 3	500
III	16, 17, 18, 19, 20, 21, 23, 24, 25, 26, 27, 28, 30, 31, 32, 33, 34, 35, 37,38, 39, 40, 41, 42, 44, 45, 46, 47,	1000 - 1800	230 x 600	0.7	4 x 3	500

Grouping of columns for additional load condition is worked similarly but with a maximum Fy of 3185 kN on 25, 26, 46 and 47 nodes, and a minimum Fy of 760 kN on nodes 1, 8, 15, and 64.

Stress Observations

After complete analysis, in the STAAD. Pro post processing mode the compressive stresses induced in the columns observed for both the loading cases and for each load case the maximum compressive stress induced in each column is given as input for comparison. The variation of compressive stresses is shown in the Fig. 6.

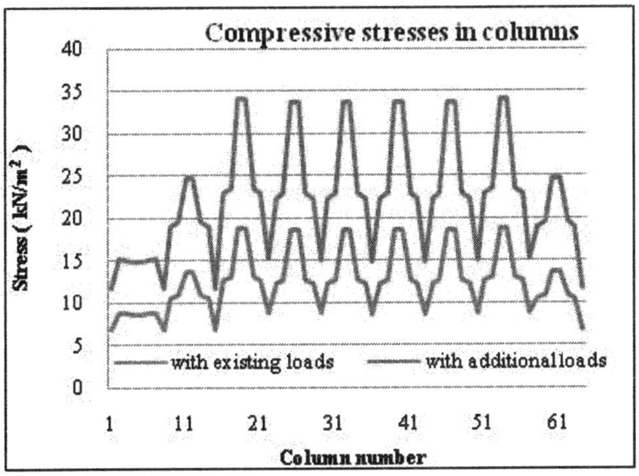

Fig. 6 Variation of compressive stress in columns before jacketing

Necessity of Retrofitting Structure

Necessity of retrofitting the structure is due to the following reasons:

The column design loads for Group-I with additional dead load and earthquake load increased by 550 kN (68.75%), for Group-II with additional dead load and earthquake load increased by 750 kN (75%) and for Group-III with additional dead load and earthquake load increased by 1400 kN(77.8%). Due to the increase in the loads many of the structural members are failed. Hence there is a necessity to strengthen the existing columns against the additional dead load and earthquake load on the structure.

Due to the additional dead load, the earthquake loads are increased about 56.6%. Because of this, many structural elements are getting failed. In order to ensure the safety of those structural elements need to be strengthened.

From non-destructive test results four columns (1, 22, 29 and 58) are to be strengthened because of poor quality and less compressive strength.

C. Strengthening of Members

Since there is a requirement to strengthen the structural members the following strengthening techniques (RCC jacketing, FRP jacketing and SFRC jacketing) are carried out on one of the selected column having the no. 23 confined to Group-III and comparison is made as shown in Table IV. Best economical method is selected from the comparison, and the elaborated procedure of the selected member is provided in the following sections.
Properties of jacket will match with the concrete of existing structure and compressive strength greater than that of the existing structures by 5 kN/m2 or at least equal to that of the existing structure in case of RCC jacketing, where as FRP jacketing material is completely different with that of existing structure and having compressive strength is greater than that of existing structures by 5 N/mm2 or equal to that of the existing structure. But in SFRC jacketing, material match with that of RCC as well as FRP jacketing because concrete, reinforcement, and steel fibre are used for jacketing.

Column Strengthening

The main purpose of jacketing the columns is

i. To increase in shear capacity and load carrying capacity of columns (strong column-weak beam design)
ii. To improve the column's flexural strength.

After carrying out the detailed analysis of the existing building, deficient members are identified. A list of provided and required reinforcements is tabulated and highlighted. All these members require strengthening in order to increase their ductile strength. Hence, retrofitting of these members is carried out using Jacketing.

TABLE IV
COMPARISON OF RCC, FRP, SFRC JACKETING

	RCC Jacketing	FRP Jacketing	SFRC Jacketing
Minimum width of jacketing	Width of jackets used is100 mm which will reduce carpet area of building.	Width of jackets used is 0.66 mm which is very less and will not pose any changes in carpet area of building.	Width of jackets used is 150 mm which is even more than RC jacketing
Cost of jacket	INR 13300 per column	INR 26726 per column	INR 9520 per column
Factored load and moment	Factored load is only used for the design of RCC jacketing	Neither Factored load nor moment is used for the design of RCC Jacketing	Factored load as well as moment is only used for design of RCC Jacketing.

From Table IV the following observations are made:

i. In RCC jacketing, sizes of the sections are increased and the free carpet area becomes less and also huge dead mass is added.
ii. RCC retrofitting technique gives significant improvement in moment resisting capacity, shear

strength capacity in beam and axial load carrying capacity in column.

iii. FRP jacketing is costlier as compared to RCC and SFRC jacketing but provides more free carpet area than that of RCC and SFRC jacketing.

In the present case study RCC jacketing is adopted, as FRP jacketing is costlier, and SFRC jacketing has 150 mm thickness which reduces the carpet area more than that of RCC jacketing.

D. RCC Jacketing

Design of RCC jacketing of column No. 23

Column strengthening is done using the concrete jacketing for acquiring the desire strength by following IS 15988:2013.

The details of existing column number 23 are as follows:

Height of the column = 3500 mm
Cross - section = 230 mm x 600 mm
Effective cover = 30 mm
Grade of concrete = 20 N/mm^2
Grade of steel = 415 N/mm^2
Load P_u = 2512.6 kN
Moment M = 33.935 kN.m
Reinforcement provided = 16 mm Ø bars

Procedure:

$$P_u = 0.4 \times F_{ck} \times A_c + 0.67 \times F_y \times A_{sc}$$

According to the provisions provided in to clause 8.5.1.2 (a) of IS 15988: 2013, concrete strength shall be at least 5 MPa greater than the strength of the existing concrete.
Thus, taking value of F_{ck} = 25 N/mm^2 and assuming
$A_{sc} = 0.8\% A_c$
2512.6 x 103 = 0.4 x 25 x A_c + 0.67 x 415 x (0.8 % A_c) or
A'_c = 205539.9 mm^2
According to 8.5.1.1 (e) of IS 15988:2013, $A_c = 1.5 A'_c$
Thus, A_c = 308309.9 mm^2 assuming the cross sectional details as: B = 450 mm,
D = 308309.9 /450 = 685.133 mm.
Jacketing details of cross section:
B = (450-230)/2 = 110 mm, D = (685.133 - 600)/2
D = 42.567 mm

However, according to the code specified above, minimum jacket thickness shall be 100 mm as per 8.5.1.2 (c) of IS 15988:2013

Thus, new size of the column:
B = 230 + 100 + 100 = 430 mm
D = 600 + 100 + 100 = 800 mm
New concrete area = 450 x 800 = 360000 mm^2>A_ci.e 308309.9 mm^2

Area of steel, A_c = 0.8% x 450 x 800 = 2880 mm^2
But according to 8.5.1.1 (e) IS 15988:2013, A_s = (4/3) A's
A_s = (4/3) x 2880 = 3840 mm^2
Assuming 16 mm Ø bars,
Thus, number of bars, N = 3840 x 4/ (π x 162) = 19 bars
Provide 19 numbers – 16 mm Ø or 5 number – 32 mm Ø bars for jacketed section.
Therefore, revised jacketed section will be 450 mm x 800 mm.

Design of Lateral Ties:

As per clause 8.5.1.2 (e) of IS15988: 2013, minimum diameter of ties shall be 8 mm and not less than one third of the longitudinal bar diameter.

Diameter of bar =1/3 of Ø of largest longitudinal bar = 6 mm, .assume 8mm

Spacing of ties as per clause 8.5.1.1 (f) of IS 15988:2013- The code suggests that the spacing, S of ties to be provided in the jacket in order to avoid flexural shear failure of column and provide adequate confinement to the longitudinal steel along the jacket is given as :

$$s = \frac{F_y d_h^2}{\sqrt{F_{ck}} t_j}$$

where,

F_y = yield strength of steel,
F_{ck} = cube strength of concrete,
d_h = diameter of stirrup, and tj = thickness of jacket

$$s = \frac{415 \ x \ 16^2}{\sqrt{25} \ 200}$$

s = 110 mm

Provide 8mm Ø @110 mm c/c.

However, for columns where extra longitudinal reinforcement is not required, a minimum of 12φ bars in the four corners and ties of 8φ @100 mm c/c should be provided with 135° bends and 10φ leg lengths.

TABLE V
FINAL SIZES OF JACKETING

Group	B (mm)	D (mm)	Jacketing (mm)		Minimum Jacketing size (mm)	Final Size of column (mm)	
			B_j	D_j		B_j	D_j
I	350	326.2	60	0	100	Not Required	
II	350	432.4	60	0	100	Not Required	
III	450 - 550	688 - 740	110	44 - 70	100	450 - 550	800

The jacketing details of Group-III columns are calculated and tabulated in Table VI.

TABLE VI
FINAL SIZES OF JACKETING OF GROUP III COLUMNS

Column	F_y (kN)	M_x (kNm)	M_z (kNm)	Jacketing Section		Jacket Reinforcement	Lateral Ties of 8mm dia. at a spacing in mm c/c
				B_f(mm)	D_f(mm)		
16	2526.6	13.2	38.2	450	800	5-32 Ø	100
17	2708.5	9.7	38.7	450	800	5-32 Ø	100
18	3126.3	25.1	38.4	550	800	6-32 Ø	100
19	3126.3	9.5	38.4	550	800	6-32 Ø	100
20	2708.5	25.2	38.7	450	800	5-32 Ø	100
21	2526.0	19.3	38.2	450	800	5-32 Ø	100
23	2512.6	13.1	33.9	450	800	5-32 Ø	100
24	2689.2	9.6	34.1	450	800	5-32 Ø	100
25	3129.0	25.6	34.1	550	800	6-32 Ø	100
26	3129.0	9.4	34.1	550	800	6-32 Ø	100
27	2689.2	25.3	34.1	450	800	5-32 Ø	100
28	2512.6	19.4	33.9	450	800	5-32 Ø	100
30	2512.9	13.1	32.6	450	800	5-32 Ø	100
31	2688.4	9.6	32.7	450	800	5-32 Ø	100
32	3124.0	25.6	32.9	550	800	6-32 Ø	100
33	3124.0	9.4	32.9	550	800	6-32 Ø	100
34	2688.4	25.3	32.7	450	800	5-32 Ø	100
35	2512.9	19.4	32.6	450	800	5-32 Ø	100
37	2512.9	13.1	32.1	450	800	5-32 Ø	100
38	2688.4	9.6	32.1	450	800	5-32 Ø	100
39	3124.	25.6	32.3	550	800	6-32 Ø	100
40	3124.	9.4	32.3	550	800	6-32 Ø	100
41	2688.4	25.3	32.1	450	800	5-32 Ø	100
42	2512.9	19.4	32.1	450	800	5-32 Ø	100
44	2512.6	13.1	31.2	450	800	5-32 Ø	100
45	2689.2	9.6	31.3	450	800	5-32 Ø	100
46	3129.0	25.6	31.6	550	800	6-32 Ø	100
47	3129.0	9.4	31.6	550	800	6-32 Ø	100
48	2689.2	25.3	31.3	450	800	5-32 Ø	100
49	2512.6	19.4	31.2	450	800	5-32 Ø	100
51	2526.0	13.2	28.6	450	800	5-32 Ø	100
52	2708.5	9.7	28.5	450	800	5-32 Ø	100
53	3126.3	25.5	29.1	550	800	6-32 Ø	100
54	3126.3	9.5	29.1	550	800	6-32 Ø	100
55	2708.5	25.2	28.5	450	800	5-32 Ø	100
56	2526.0	19.3	28.6	450	800	5-32 Ø	100

From Table V jacketing required for the Group-I and Group-II is about 60 mm in shorter direction only, where in the other direction jacketing width works out to be negative. Hence existing section is enough to resists the stresses due to additional deal load. And no jacketing is required for Group-I and Group-II. But in the case of Group-III jacketing width is of 110 mm in shorter direction and 44 mm to 70 mm required in longer direction, according to IS 15988 2013, minimum jacketing width should be of 100 mm. Hence the column jacketing should be required for Group-III columns with a jacketing width of 100 mm in both directions. Final increased column sizes for Group-III columns are shown in Table VI.

Footing Strengthening

The footing design for the existing structure is designed as per the code and the details of the footing and the design details are given in Table VII.

In Table VII reinforcement and size of footing in initial condition found to be sufficient for the additional load in the case Group-I and Group-II, but in Group-III size, depth and reinforcement required resisting the additional dead load and earthquake load is more than the provided. Hence, Group-III members should be strengthened according to the jacketing technique. The jacketing data calculated as - jacketing width 500 mm on both sides of the footing, jacketing in the direction of depth required is 100 mm. The additional reinforcement required is of 100 mm c/c on shorter and longer side of the column.

TABLE VII
FOOTING DESIGN COMPARISON

Group number	Existing load		Additional load		Reinforcement details as of existing condition	Reinforcement details required for the increased load	Check
	Footing size (m^2)	Depth of footing (mm)	Footing size (m^2)	Depth of footing (mm)			
I	2 x 2	400	2 x 2	400	16 dia. bars at 140 mm c/c in both the directions	16 dia. bars at 150 mm c/c in both the directions	OK
II	3 x 3	500	3 x 3	500	16 dia. bars at 150 mm c/c in both the directions	16 dia. bars at 150 mm c/c in both the directions	OK
III	4 x 3	500	5 x 4	600	16 dia. bars at 255 mm c/c in shorter direction and 16dia. bars at 100 mm c/c in longer direction	16 dia. bars at 100 mm c/c in short direction and long direction	Strengthening is required

The compressive stress variation in the columns after jacketing is shown in Fig. 7, from figure it is observed that the compressive stresses in all columns are less than 6.3 MPa, i.e with in the permissible bending compression of concrete (7 MPa in case of M 20 concrete). Hence, the stresses are brought back in to the limits by RCC jacketing technique.

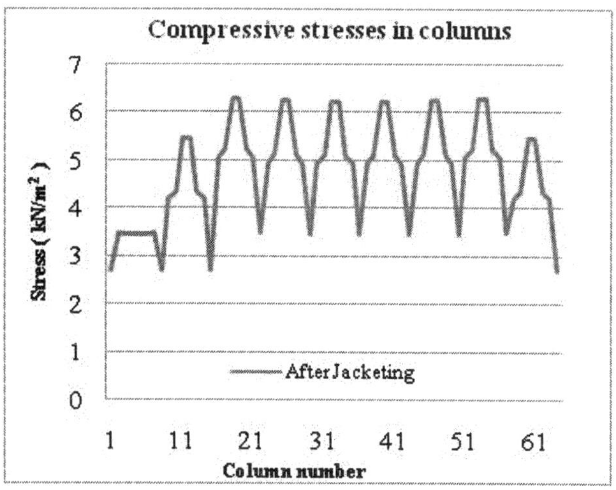

Fig. 7 Variation of compressive stress in columns after jacketing

V. CONCLUSIONS

From the limited analytical studies carried on a case study industrial building, the following conclusions are made:

1. As the machines used are changed the dead load on the structure is changed. In the case study the dead load is increased from 4.625 kN/m^2 to 15 kN/m^2(around 224%).
2. The live load on the structure remained same and used as per code.
3. The wind load remained same as there is no increase in the height of the building.
4. Since the dead load on the structure is increased, there is an increase in seismic loading as well (around 57%).
5. From non-destructive test results, four columns (1, 22, 29, and 58) are found to be strengthened, as they are of poor quality and less compressive strength. The increase in percentage area for these columns is around 52%.
6. The compressive stresses induced in the columns are increased to a minimum of 72% and a maximum of 81%, due to the additional dead load and earthquake load.
7. Group-I and Group-II columns and footings are found to be sufficient for the additional dead load and earthquake load.
8. From cost analysis, RCC jacketing technique is adopted, while FRP jacketing is costlier and SFRC having less carpet area than RCC.
9. In the present study the size of the existing Group-III columns are increased to 161% and the size of footings are increased to 67% using RCC jacketing technique.
10. The percentage of increase in reinforcement in Group-III columns is 139% and in Group-III footings is 96%.

11. The case study building for the modified loadings (dead and earthquake loading) is rehabilitated and retrofitted.

References

[1] PranayRanjan, Poonam Dhiman, "Retrofitting of Columns of an Existing Building by RC, FRP and SFRC Jacketing Techniques", *IOSR Journal of Mechanical and Civil Engineering*, e-ISSN: 2278-1684, p-ISSN: 2320–334X, Special No. AETM'16, 2016, pp. 40 - 46.

[2] Uma Shankar K,Arun Prakash K and Pradeep kumar S, "Rehabilitation and Retrofitting of Building Structures", *International Journal of Management and Information Technology and Engineering*, ISSN 2348-0513, Vol. 3, No. 1, 2015, pp. 1 - 6.

[3] Nikita Gupta, Poonam Dhiman, Anil Dhiman, "Design and Detailing of RC Jacketting for Concrete Columns", *IOSR Journal of Mechanical and Civil Engineering, National Conference on Advances in Engineering*, Technology & Management, Vol. 3, No. 1, 2015, pp. 54 - 59.

[4] CatalinBaciu, PariciaMurzea, "The Retrofitting of Reinforced Concrete Columnsi",*Knowledge-Based Organization Conference*, Vol. XXI, No. 3, 2015, pp. 776 - 781.

[5] Anusha Rani, Paul D.K., "Seismic Retrofitting of a Damaged School Building", *International Journal of Research in Engineering and Technology*, Vol. 03, No. 6, 2014, pp. 22 - 28.

[6] Pavan D, Tikate, Tande S.N, "Repair and Rehabilitation of Structures", *International Journal of Engineering Sciences and Research Technology*, ISSN 2277-9655, Vol. 3, No. 10, 2014, pp. 511 - 515.

[7] Chandar S.S, "Rehabilitation of Buildings", *International Journal of Civil Engineering Research*, ISSN 2278-3652, Vol. 5, No. 4, 2014, pp. 98 – 105.

[8] IS 15988:2013, "Seismic Evaluation and Strengthening of Existing Reinforced Concrete Buildings", *Guidelines, Bureau of Indian Standards*, New Delhi, 2013.

[9] IS 456:2000, "Plain and Reinforced Concrete, Bureau of Indian Standards", *Guidelines, Bureau of Indian Standards*, New Delhi, 2000.

[10] IS 1893:1987(Part 2), "Code of Practice for Design Loads for Buildings and Structures (earthquake)", *Guidelines, Bureau of Indian Standards*, New Delhi, 2002.

[11] IS 13311(Part 1), "Non-Destructive Testing on Concrete-Methods of test, Ultra Sonic Pulse Velocity", *Guidelines, Bureau of Indian Standards*, New Delhi, 1992.

[12] IS 13311(Part 2), "Non-Destructive Testing on Concrete – Methods of test, Rebound Hammer", *Guidelines, Bureau of Indian Standards*, New Delhi, 1992.

Influence of Modeling Aspects on the Seismic Performance of A Tall Building – Numerical Study on a Twenty Storeyed RC Framed Building

Mounika Lakshmipathi[1], Sreenivas Sarma Paraitham[2]

[1]Former post-graduate student,Civil Engineering Department,CBIT,Hyderabad-75(TS)
[2]Professor,Civil Engineering Department,CBIT,Hyderabad-75(TS)
[1]moni.lakshmipathi@gmail.com, ph.9550990331
[2]sreenivassarma.p@cbit.ac.in, ph.9391016066

***Abstract*—Reinforced concrete framed buildings are the most commonly found forms of tall buildings in Indian scenario. The damages that these buildings suffered during the recent earthquakes in India revealed the role of certain secondary structural elements, in the performance of such buildings. Thus, they also indicated the need for modeling these secondary structural elements and consider their effect in the analysis and design. Some such elements are, infill walls, stair cases , Lift cores , Water Tanks etc.,.**

This work presents a case study of a twenty storeyed RC framed tall building, analysed for zone-III seismic forces, using response spectrum method of analysis. Effect of modeling infill walls, stair case, Lift core and water tank is investigated in terms of the response of the building. The responses observed are bending moments, shear forces, displacements of chosen beams and columns (corner, intermediate and interior). Further, the mode shapes and time periods of the building are also observed. Results obtained are discussed and an attempt is made to quantify the effect of these elements independently, in combinations and finally the integrated effect of all the elements modeled in the buildings.

Keywords: influence of modeling, RC framed buildings, Secondary structural elements, Seismic performance

I. INTRODUCTION

The locations of the tallest buildings in the world, as well as the function of the buildings and the materials used to construct these buildings, are rapidly changing. Only 20 years ago, 75% of the 100 tallest buildings in the world were located in North America and as of 2014; this figure is less than 25%, with the shift occurring predominantly to Asia and the Middle East. Preferences and the economic viability of the different structural materials that are used in tall buildings'construction are also changing. In 1970, 90% of the 100 world tallest buildings were all-steel buildings. Today, all-steel buildings account for less than 15% in favour of concrete or composite structures. The cost ofthe material, technological expertise and the way that tall buildings are being built all influence this change in material selection of tall buildings.

The worldwide use of reinforced concrete construction stems from the wide availability of reinforcing steel as well as the concrete ingredients. Unlike steel, concrete production does not require expensive manufacturing mills. Concrete construction, does, however, require a certain level of technology, expertise, and workmanship, particularly in the field during construction. The extensive use of reinforced concrete construction, especially in developing countries, is due to its relatively low cost compared to other materials such as steel. Frequently, reinforced concrete construction is used in regions of high seismic risk, such as Latin America, southern Europe, North Africa, the Middle East, and Southeast Asia. The construction of reinforced concrete buildings with brick masonry infill walls has been a very common practice in urban India for the last 25 years.

II. SEISMIC PERFORMANCE OF RC FRAMED BUILDINGS

In several instances, seismic performance of RC frame buildings has been quite poor, even when subjected to earthquakes below the design level prescribed by code. One of the underlying reasons is the absence of an effective mechanism for code enforcement in some countries. This deficiency in governmental oversight is linked to several related factors, such as the lack of technical control and supervision, problems with the legal framework, low engineering fees, and improper regional construction practices. When one or more such factors are present during construction, the built structure does not comply with many aspects of the design. As a result, its seismic resistance becomes inadequate, with the consequence that unpredictable damage or failure results when subjected to loads below the code-prescribed levels. The key deficiencies identified in the RC frame construction practice include the following:

- Alteration of the member sizes during the construction phase from specifications in the design drawings
- Noncompliance of the detailing work with the design drawings
- Inferior quality of building materials and improper concrete-mix design
- Modifications in the structural system performed by adding/removing components without engineering input
- Reduction in the amount of steel reinforcement as compared to the design specifications
- Poor construction practice

Besides these reasons, an important one appears to be the lack of consideration for the contribution of certain secondary structural elements in the building, during the modeling of the building .

An easy way to comply with the conference paper formatting requirements is to use this document as a template and simply type your text into it.

III. MODELING PRACTICES IN VOGUE

It is a common practice to model tall buildings as bare frame structures where the loads for structural design are supported by beams and columns [1]. Besides, primary structural system, some elements also contribute to lateral load resistance. These elements fall in the category of secondary systems. Secondary system can be structural secondary like infill walls, staircase, structural partition, storage tanks, machinery etc [2]. Intrinsically, the structural strength provided by the walls and slabs are neglected. As the building height increases, the effect of lateral loads on multi-storey structures increases considerably. Design provisions for nonstructural elements in Indian seismic code IS 1893 are either non-existent or too primitive. In usual design practice, Non structural elements are not modeled, because they are assumed to not carry any forces by being a part of the load path. However, some elements, assumed to be non-structural, could significantly influence the seismic behaviour of the building by inadvertently participating in the lateral force transfer[3]. It is a practice in India to neglect a number of items in the process of structural design of buildings, assuming that these items are "non-structural" elements.

An attempt is made in the present work to understand the influence of modeling aspects on the seismic performance of a RC framed multi storeyed building by modeling several secondary structural elements for a G+19 multi storeyed building , such as infill walls, stair case, slabs, lift shaft, roof top water tank.

IV. NUMERICAL STUDY

Keeping in view the various issues related to non structural and structural aspects of modeling, a typical representative RC building is considered in the study, the details of which are given here under. STAAD Pro.V8i software is used to create the models for which response spectrum analysis is carried out to study the performance under seismic loads.

Details of Building:

Building Type : Residential, Exterior walls : 230 mm
No. of storeys : 20,Gr. of Concrete M 30
Size of plan : 25.2m X 25.2m , Gr.of steel : Fe-500
Storey height : 3m, Live load : 2 kN/m^2
Size of columns : 0.65m X 0.65 m, Floor finish: 1.25 kN/m^2
Size of beams : 0.23mX 0.45m
Slab thickness : 125mm

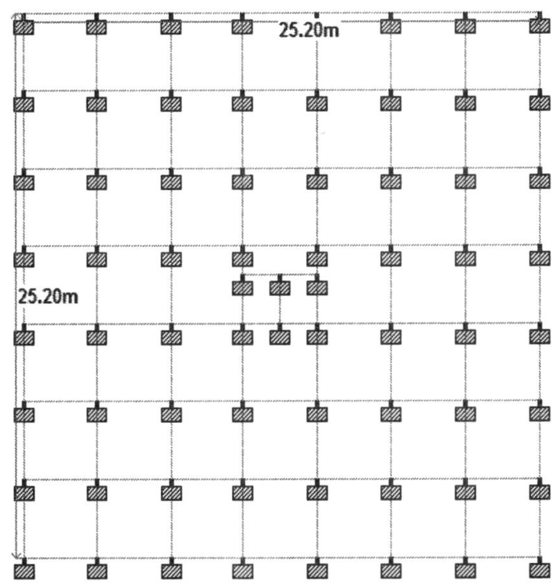

Figure 1: Plan showing the Column locations

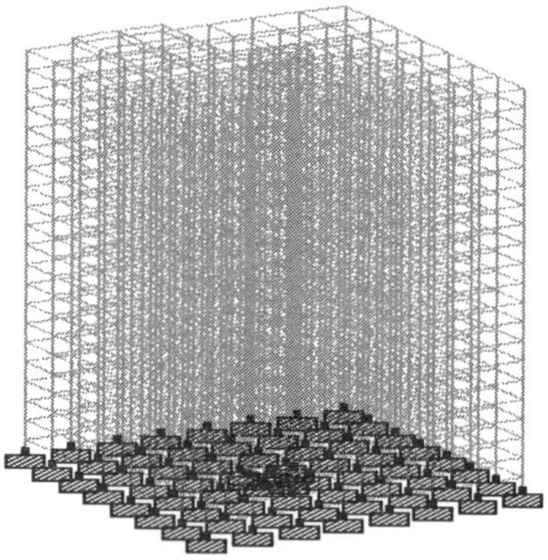

Figure 2: Typical space frame model of G+19 RC framed building

Model 1 [M1] : Bare Frame model
Model 2 [M2] : Bare frame+ masonry infill wall
Model 3 [M3] : Bare frame+slab
Model4 [M4] : Bare frame +stair case
Model 5 [M5] : Bare frame +lift core as brick wall
Model6 [M6] : Bare frame +lift core as shear wall
Model7[M7] : Bare frame +roof top water tank
Model8 [M8] :Bare frame +roof top water tank with sloshing effect
Model9 [M9] :Bare frame +infill wall+slab+staircase+lift core(brick wall)+water tank

Responses Studied

Models are created using STAAD Pro software and dynamic analysis is carried out using Response Spectrum method. Shear forces, Bending Moments, Displacements, Time Period, Frequency and Mode shapes for corner, internal and intermediate columns and beams for every 5 floors are observed in order to study the dynamic behavior of RC framed multi storeyed buildings under dynamic loads.

V. RESULTS

The responses of the models in terms of shear force, bending moment, displacement, time period and mode shapes are presented in Tables 1 to 2 and the variations are depicted through graphs / figures 3 to 25 .

Table 1 : Bending moments (kN-m) in columns

Modelcorner column interior column intermediate column						
ist 5th 10th 15th 20th ist 5th 10th 15th 20th ist 5th 10th15th 20th						
M1 98.77	42.49 68.26 62.815	38 57.83 64.928	33.42 24.92	26.94 114	120 74.23	83.23 68.547
M2	194.39 40.55 13.057	19.084 38.553 7.389	14.649 33.2 1.714	9.309 34.976	2.687 196.	125.93 16.75
M3	117.681 141.926 86.13	54.109 106.091 79.972	43.564 94.132 72.803	39.158 81.463 62.279	42.793 33.021	105.
M4	138.818 122.993 96.659	56.784 100.972 76.212	49.501 85.395 74.731	42.552 24.753	27.226 165.	177.6 99.76
M5	144.71 78.128 93.617	65.996 68 86.796	62.038 54.34 80.073	57.88 32.449	35.989 164.	118.41 102.8
M6	124.308 71.815 90.054	55.189 76.728 83.131	51.659 71.196 69.474	51.822 69.565	29.239 153.	73.641 97.829
M7	96.3 119.794 93.158	41.455 82.522 90.054	34.548 71.124 85.885	32.738 60.88 67.33	30.358 26.402	118.
M8	99.618 120.146 70.622	43.119 82.817 63.599	37.968 70.085 54.668	33.943 57.848 32.553	30.852 21.797	
M9	146.629 21.722 20.249	26.943 25.947 15.297	20.472 27.793 7.028	13.451 28.712	6.134 146.	132 23.72

Table 2 : Storey level Displacements (mm)

FLO OR	M1	M2	M3	M4	M5	M6	M7	M8	M9
1	2.4 22	3.0 27	2.7 45	3.3	3.4 45	3.3	2.4 74	2.3 68	2.7 15
5	13. 726	6.8 05	15. 03	19. 4	19. 51	30. 556	14. 09	13. 4	7.0 13
10	26. 356	10. 728	28. 793	37. 512	37. 347	36. 916	27. 029	25. 826	11. 485
15	35. 634	13. 539	38. 637	50. 952	50. 779	51. 635	36. 678	34. 963	14. 892
20	40. 694	15. 187	45. 006	58. 206	58. 279	59. 433	42. 079	39. 908	17. 089

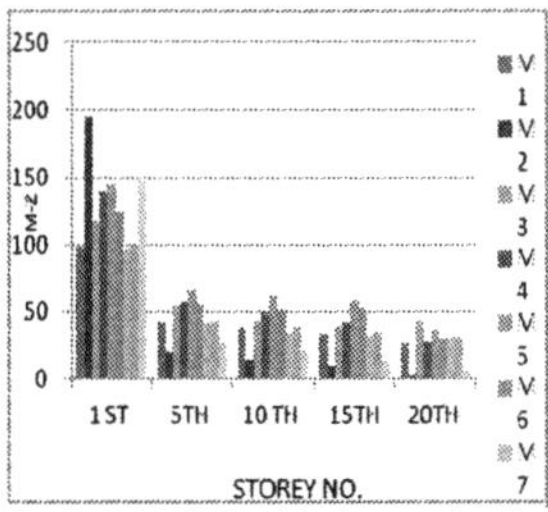
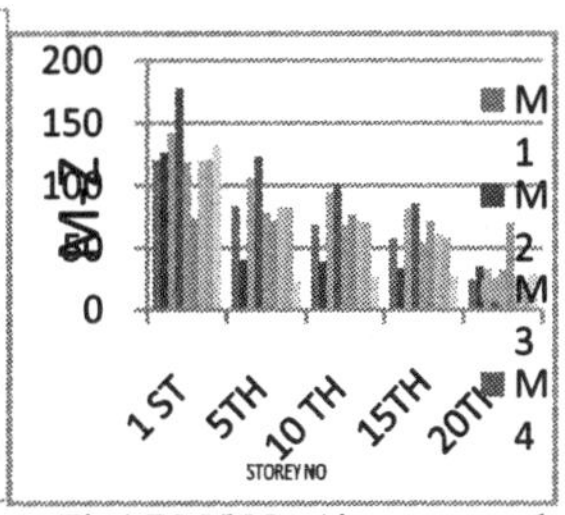

Fig 3: BM(kN-m)in internal columnFig4:BM(kN-m)in corner column

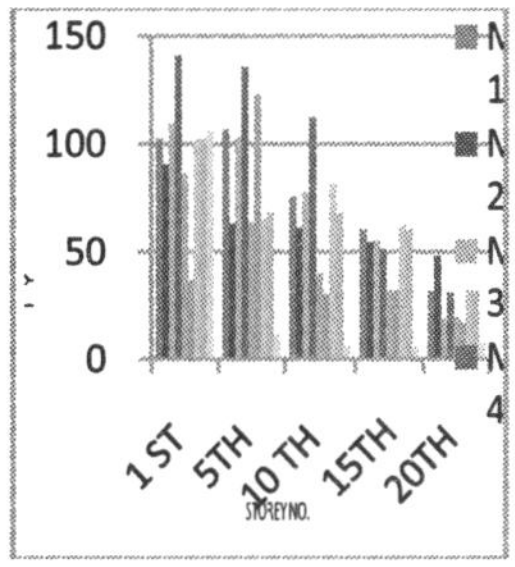
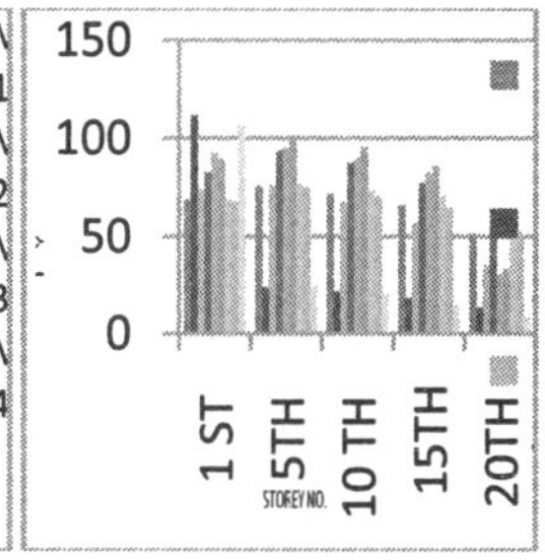

Fig13 Shear(kN) in internalbeam Fig14 Shear(kN)intermedate beam

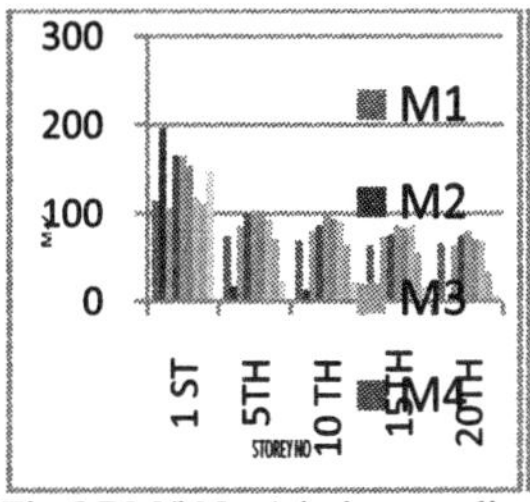
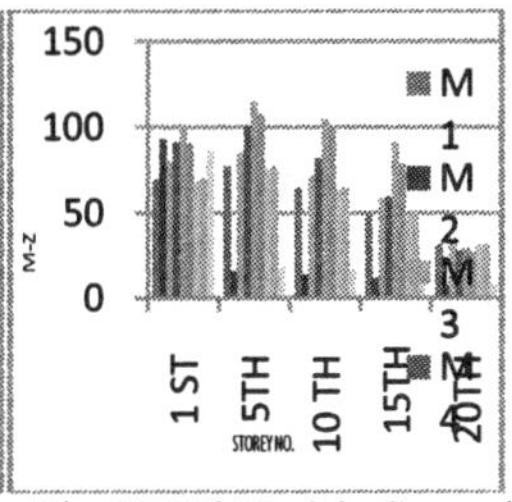

Fig 5 BM(kN-m) in intermediate Fig 6:BM(kN-m) in Corner beam column

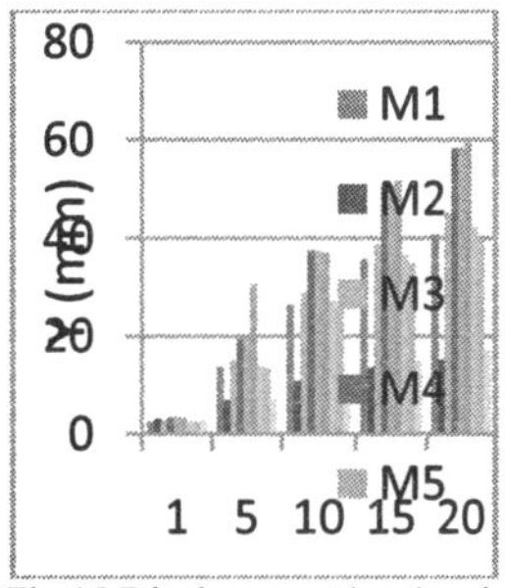
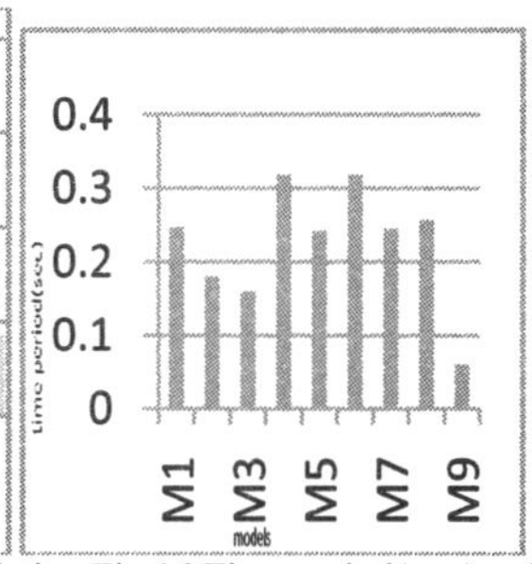

Fig 15 Displacement(mm)variation Fig 16 Time period(sec.)variation

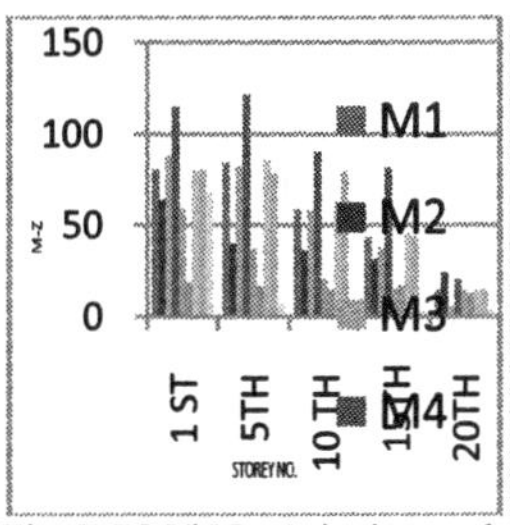
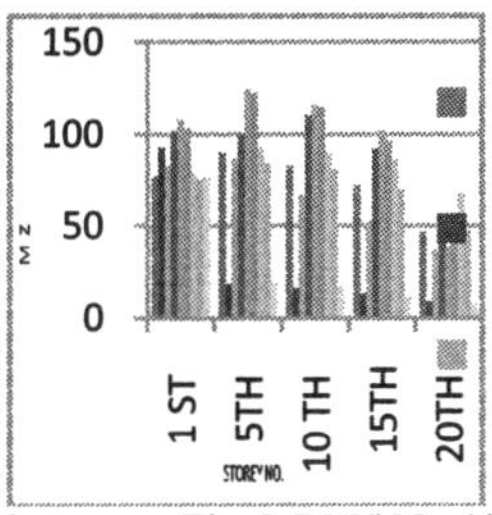

Fig 7 BM(kN-m) in internal beam Fig 8 BM(kN-m)in intermediate beam

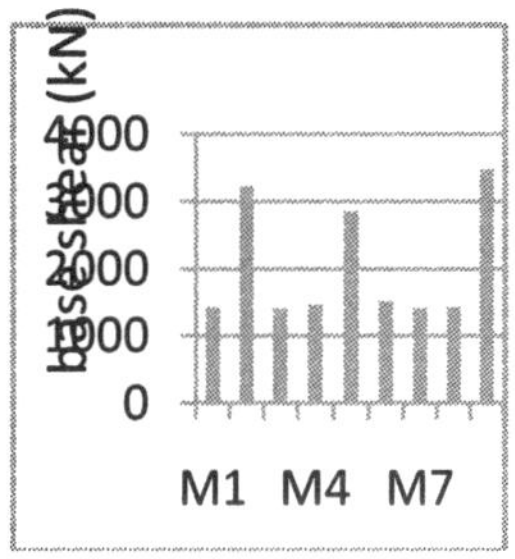
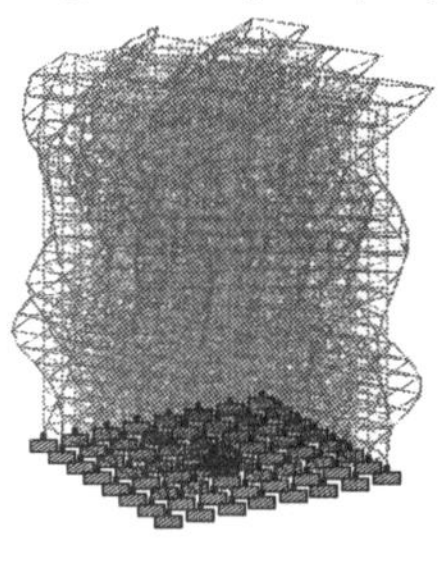

Fig 17 Base Shear(kN) variation Fig 18 Mode shape (Bareframe)

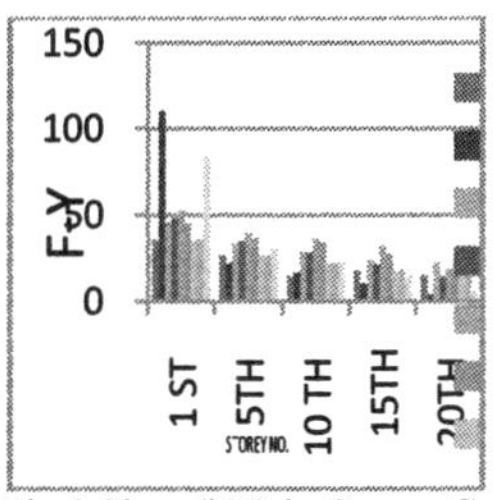
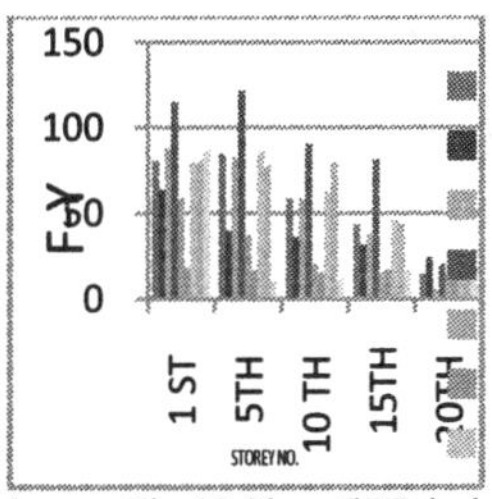

Fig 9 Shear(kN) in Corner Column Fig 10 Shear(kN) in internal column

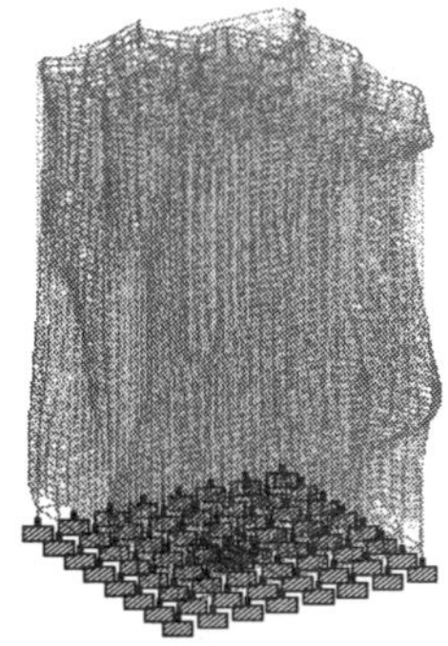
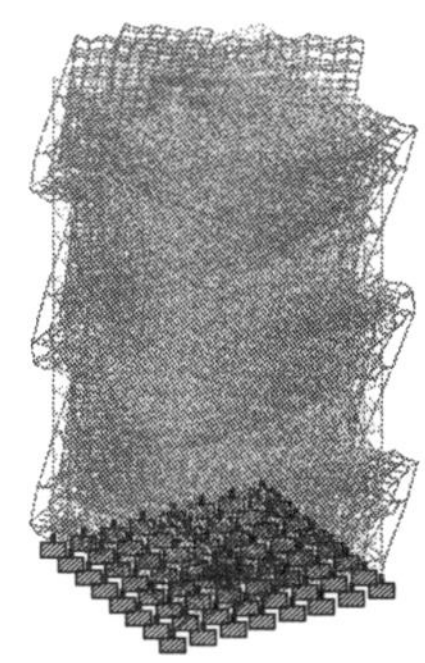

Fig 19 Mode shape(with infill walls) Fig 20 Mode shape (with slabs)

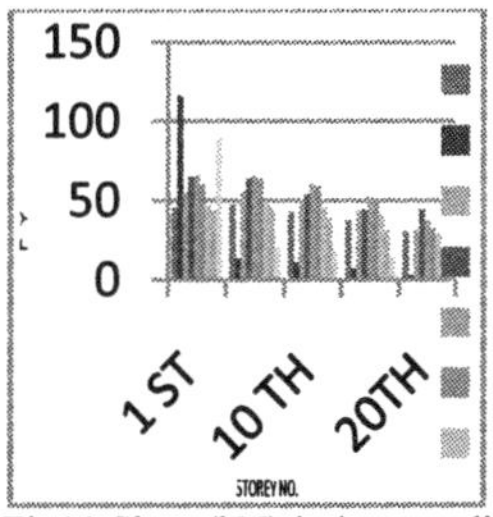
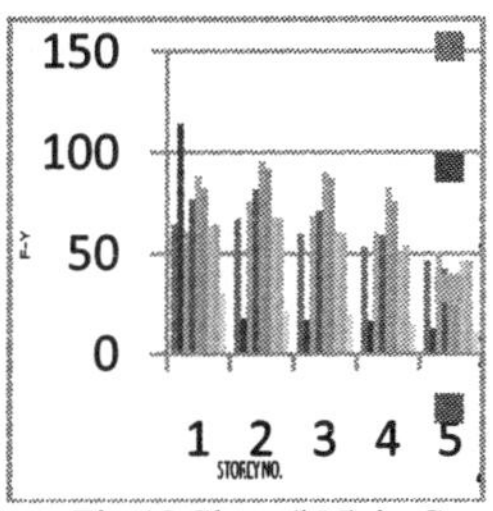

Fig11 Shear(kN) in intermediate Fig 12 Shear(kN) in Corner beam column

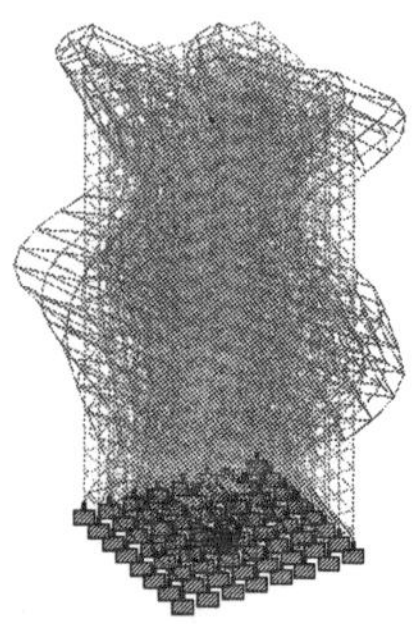
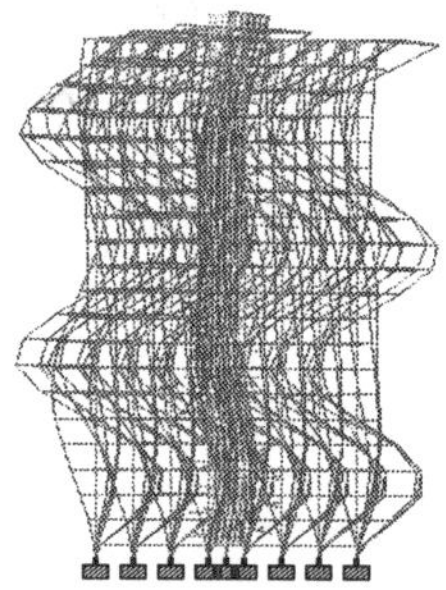

Fig 21 Mode shape(with staircase) Fig 22 Mode shape(with lift core)

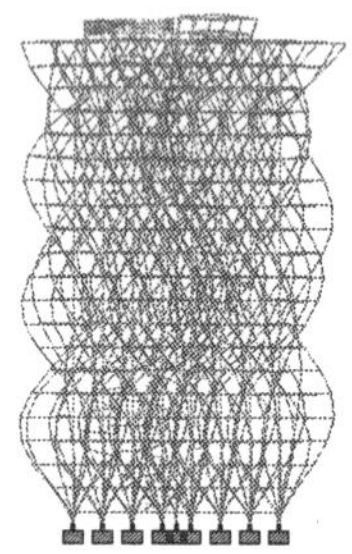
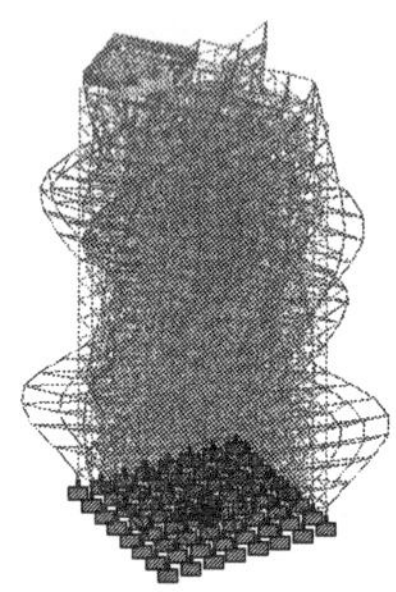

Fig23Modeshape(with water tank) Fig 24 Mode shape(withWT+sloshing)

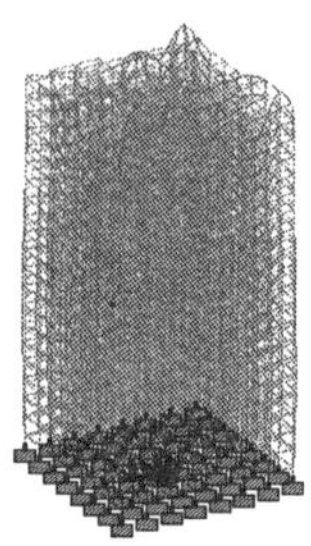

Fig 25 Mode shape (with all Secondary structural elements modelled)

VI. DISCUSSION

Effect of modeling masonry infill wall (model M2 compared with bare frame model M1):

Bending Moments

For corner columns, there is an abrupt increase in bending moment of all most 77% at floor level 1 and a decrease of 55%, 60%,70% and 90% in 5th, 10th,15th and 20th floors respectively and for corner beams it is observed that there is an increase of 75 to 80% for 5th to 20th floors and an increase of 33% at floor level 1 .

For internal columns, which are not surrounded by infill wall, the bending moment reduced by about 40% for 5th, 10th and 15th floors and for 20th floor there is an increase of 40%. For internal beams bending moment got reduced by 20%, 53%, 38% and 27% at 1st, 5th, 10th and 15th floors and increased by 66% at top storey.

For intermediate columns at floor level 1 due to the presence of open storey an increase in bending moment of 72% is observed and for 5th, 10th, 15th, and 20th floors a decrease of 77%, 80%, 88% and 97% respectively is observed. For intermediate beams an increase of 20% in bending moment at first storey has been observed but for all the upper floors bending moment got reduced by 80%.

Shear Force

In corner columns it increased by 211% for 1st floor and then decreased by 16% at 5th floor, again increased by 12% at 10 th floor and then decreased by 40% and 74% for 15th and 20th floors respectively. For corner beams an increase of 77% at 1st floor and a decrease of about 70% for upper floors is observed.

For internal columns a decrease of about 40-60% in shear force is observed for 5th,10th and 15th floors and an increase of about 50% in shear force at 1st and 20th floor is observed. For internal beams a decrease of 40% at 5th floor and an increase of 53% is observed. for other floors not much variation is seen.

For intermediate columns an increase of 156% in shear is observed at 1st floor and a decrease of about 70-90% is observed for the upper floors. for intermediate beams an increase of about 60% in shear force at 1st column and a decrease of about 70% in shear is observed for upper floors.

Displacement

From the results of displacement for model M2 when compared to model M1 ,it is observed that the displacement got increased by 25% at 1st floor level and got reduced by 50-60% for upper levels.

Time period

The time period got reduced by 34% for model M2 when compared to model M1.

Base Shear

For model M2 when compared to model M1 base shear got increased by 144%.

Mode Shape

As the floors above ground floor have become stiffer, the model reflected shear deflection upto ground level and predominant flexure mode in upper floors.

Effect of modeling slab

Bending Moment

From the results of bending moment for model M3 when compared to model M1,there is an increase of about 15% in bending moment upto 15 floors and an increase of 58% at 20th floor for corner columns. in corner beams an increase of about 15% in bending moment is observed.

For internal columns, bending moment increased upto 20% For 1st and 5th floors and around 30-40% for 10th ,15th and

20th floors. for internal beams not much variation is seen upto 15 floors but for 20th floor the bending moment got decreased by 60%.

For intermediate columns the bending moment got increase around 15% and for intermediate beams the bending moment got decreased by 15-20%.

Shear Force

For corner columns, shear force got increased by around 25% at 1st and 5th floors. at 10th floor level bending moment got increased by 92% and at 15th and 20th floors shear force got increased by 35% and 47% respectively. For corner beams the shear force is increased by 10-15% at all floor levels.

For internal columns, an increase of about 25% in shear force is observed at floor level 1 and at 5th floor it got reduced by 17% and at 10th ,15th and 20th floors shear force got increased by 40%.

For internal beams, shear force got decreased by 40% at 20th floor and for other floors not much variation is observed.

For intermediate columns an increase of about 15% in shear is observed at all floor levels except for 20th floor and for intermediate beams a decrease of 30% is observed at 20th floor and not much variation is observed at other floors.

Displacement

There is an increase of 10% in displacement at every floor level for model M3 when compared to model M1.

Time Period

For model M3 when compared to model M1, there is a decrease of 35% in time period.

Base Shear

Not much variation is observed in base shear for model M3 when compared to model M1.

Mode Shapes

The inplane stiffness of slabs provided local rigidity at storey levels and the structure demonstrated rigid movements at storey levels clearly.

Effect of modeling stair case

Bending Moment

From the results of bending moment for model M4 when compared to model M1, the bending moment for corner column got increased by 40% at 1st floor level and about 30% at 5th, 10th and 15th floor levels and no significant variation is observed at 20th floor level. for corner beams an increase of about 30% in bending moment is observed except for 20th floor(decreased by 11%).

For internal column an increase of about 40% in bending moment is observed except for 20th floor level. for internal beams the bending moment got increase by 30-40% at 1st, 5th, 10th and 20th floor levels and at 15th floor level the increase in bending moment is about 87%.

For intermediate columns the increase in bending moment for 1st, 5th, 10th, 15th and 20th floor levels are 45%, 34%, 26%, 21% and 15% respectively. For intermediate beams an increase in bending moment of about 30% is observed at 1st, 10th and 15th floors and for 5th and 20th floors an increase of 10% in bending moment is observed.

Shear Force

From the results of shear force for model M3 when compared to model M1,the shear force at 10th floor got increased by 92% and for floor levels 1,5 and 15 , increase in shear is about 20% to 30%.for 20th floor the shear got reduced by 8%. for corner beams ,an increase in shear of about 15-20% is observed at floor levels 1,5,10 and 15.for 20th floor corner beams a decrease in shear of about 8% is observed.

For internal columns at floor levels 1, 5 and 15 an increase in shear of about 40% is observed. at floor levels 5 and 20 not much variation is observed. For internal beams at floor level1, 5, 10 there is an increase in shear of about 30-40% is observed.

For intermediate columns, an increase of about 40 % in shear at floor levels 1, 5 and 20 is observed and floor levels 10 and 15 shear increased around 20%. For intermediate beams an increase of about 20% in shear is observed.

Displacement

An increase of 40% in displacement is observed with modeling of staircase when compared to bareframe model

Time Period

Time period got increased by 28% for model M3 when compared to model M1.

Base Shear

No significant variation in base shear is observed with modeling of stair case when compared to bare frame model

Mode Shape

As the stair case is in the centre part of the building it is acting as a braced frame at the centre of the building restricting the moments. However, the peripheral structure of the building is experiencing greater flexural moments.

Effect of modeling lift core

Bending Moment

For corner columns, when lift core is modeled as brick wall bending moment got increased by 50-70% at floor levels 1, 5, 10 and 15 and at 20th floor level bending moment got increased by 33% and when lift core is modeled as shear wall the increase in bending moment is around 30-50% for floor levels 1, 5, 10 and 15 and for 20th floor increase in bending moment is about 8% at floor level. For corner beams the bending moment got increased by 50-80% at floor levels 1, 5, 10 and 15 and at 20th floor bending moment got reduced by 8% when lift core modeled as brick wall and when lift core modeled as shear wall the bending moment in corner beams got increased by 40-50% for floor levels 1, 5 10 and 15 and for 20th floor bending moment got reduced by 14%.

For internal columns in M5, bending moment increased by 30% at 20th floor and for M6 there is an increase of 179% at 20th floor. For other floors there is no considerable change in bending moment. For internal beams bending moment for M5 got reduced by 50 to 60% at 5, 10, 15 floor levels and for 20th floor level there is no significant change in bending moment. Similarly for model M6 bending moment got reduced by 60-80% at floor levels 1, 5, 10 and 15 and for 20th floor level a decrease of 13% is observed.

For intermediate columns and beams, in model M5 an increase of 40% in bending moment at all floor levels is observed and for model M6 an increase of about 30% is observed but at 20th floor in models M5 and M6 bending moment in intermediate beams got reduced by around 15 %.

Shear Force

For models M5 and M6, in corner column shear force got increased by 146% and 131% at 10th floor respectively and for 1 and 5 floor levels the increase in shear is about 48% and 30% for M5 and M6 models respectively. For corner beams increase in shear is around 40-50% for models M5 and M6 .For internal columns, shear is reduced upto 30 and 50% at 5th floor level for models M5 and M6 respectively. At 20th floor shear got increased by 60% and 154% for models M5 and M6 models respectively. For internal beams shear got reduced by 50-60% for models M5 and M6.For intermediate columns, in model M5 ,an increase of 40% in shear is observed and for model M6 an increase of 30-40% is observed. For intermediate beams, at 20th floor shear reduced by 30-40% for models M5 and M6.

Displacement

For models M5 and M6, the displacement got increased by 40% when compared to bare frame model.

Time Period

Time period got reduced by 28% when lift core modeled with shear wall and for lift core modeled with brick wall there is no significant variation in time period when compared to bare frame model.

Base Shear

When lift core modeled with brickwall base shear became almost twice and when lift core modeled with shear wall there is no significant change in base shear.

Mode Shape

The mode shapes of lift core are similar to that of stair case experiencing greater flexure moments at peripheral of the structure.

Effect of roof top water tank

Modeling the roof top water tank does not influence the bending moments and shear forces of columns and beams significantly when compared to bare frame model but when sloshing effect is included in the model there is a considerable decrease of 50% in bending moment at 20th floor in intermediate columns and beams and no significant variation in base shear, displacement, time period is observed.

Mode shape

A torsional mode of vibration is evidenced in the case of model M7 where sloshing effect is not considered. This could be due to a concentration of eccentric load caused by the water tank located at the corner of the building. For model M8 when sloshing effect is considered a trend of increasing moments in the top storey is observed.

Effect of combination of all parameters

Bending Moment

For corner columns, bending moment got increased by 48% at 1st floor level and decreased by 36%, 46% 60% and 77% for 5, 10, 15 and 20 floor levels respectively. For corner beams an increase in bending moment of 23% at 1st floor level and a decrease of about 70% in bending moment is observed at other floor levels. For internal columns bending moment got increased by 10% at first floor and a decrease of 50-70% is observed for floor levels 5, 10 and 15. At 20th floor level an increase of 15% is observed. For internal beams a decrease of 70-90% is observed for floor levels 5, 10, 15 and 20. At floor level 1 a decrease of 15% in bending moment is observed. For intermediate columns a decrease of around 60-80% is observed for all upper floors except for 1st floor.

Shear Force

An increase of shear of 137% is observed in corner column at 1st storey, and for 5th and 10th floors shear increased by 13% and 52% respectively. For 15th floor a decrease of 19% is observed and at 20th floor shear decreased by 61%. For corner beams a decrease of 50-70% in shear is observed at the floor levels considered.

For internal columns the shear force increased by 64% at floor level 1 and for floors 5, 10 and 15 shear reduced by 50-80% at 20th floor shear increased by 27%. For internal beams shear reduced by 80-90% except for floor level 1. For floor level 1 there is no significant variation.

For intermediate columns shear increased by 95% at floor level 1 and for other floor levels considered, shear force got reduced by 60-80%.similarly for intermediate beams shear force increased by 55% at 1st floor level and decreased by around 70-80% at upper floor levels.

Displacement

The displacement for model M9 got reduced by around 60% when compared to bare frame model.

Time Period

The time period for model M9 when compared to model M1 got reduced by 77%.

Base Shear

An increase of 161% in base shear is observed for model M9 when compared to model M1.

Mode shapes

As the entire structure has become stiff particularly in periphery and central core due to the presence of infill walls along with the central lift core surrounded by a stair case, the structure demonstrated very less storey drifts. however lot of vertical movements was seen in structure in places where neither infill walls exist nor the lift core or staircase.

VII. Conclusions

Based on the results obtained for the study conducted on the chosen building the following conclusions are drawn.

General Conclusions

When compared with bare frame model the infill wall model has in general performed better resulting in reduced bending moment, shear forces and displacements in all the elements and storeys (with the exception of 1st floor level deformations). Similarly the model with staircase and lift core has resulted in greater bending moments, shears and displacements.

Specific Conclusions

- From the results of bending moment and shear force, it is observed that in the presence of masonry infill wall the bending moment and shear force is almost becoming twice at 1st floor level due to the presence of open storey. For upper floors the bending moment and shear force got reduced by 70-90% and displacement got reduced by 40-50% .Base shear got increased by144%. This is due to the presence of infill wall in the upper floor levels which adds stiffness to the structure.
- The inplane stiffness of slabs provided local rigidity at storey levels and the structure demonstrated rigid movements at storey levels clearly.
- When stair case and lift core are modeled grater moments of about 40-50% are observed at the peripheral of the structure.
- Modeling the roof top water tank does not influence the bending moments and shear forces of columns and beams significantly when compared to bare frame model but when sloshing effect is included in the model there is a considerable decrease of 50% in bending moment at 20th floor in intermediate columns and beams .
- A torsional mode of vibration is evidenced in the case of model M7 where sloshing effect is not considered. This could be due to a concentration of eccentric load caused by the water tank located at the corner of the building. For model M8 when sloshing effect is considered a trend of increasing moments in the top storey is observed.

In all, the performance of the model considering all the parameters has shown considerable variation for bending moment and shear force with a reduction of 70-80% at all floor levels except for 1st floor level. Displacement got reduced by 60% as the building got more stiffer due to the presence of infill wall, stair case, lift core etc. Base shear is increased by 161% and time period got reduced by 77% when compared to the bare frame model[4].

Therefore, due consideration is to be given for modeling the secondary structural elements which are the otherwise considered as non structural elements.

REFERENCES

[1] Mohammed Jameel et.al, "Optimum Structural Modelling For Tall Buildings" ,The Structural Design Of Tall Buildings And Special Buildings,wiley online library 2012

[2] Haroon Rasheed Tamboli and Umesh.N.Karadi, "Seismic Analysis of RC Frame Structure with and without Masonry Infill Walls," Indian Journal Of Natural Sciences, Vol.3 / Issue 14/ October2012

[3] C.V.R Murty et.al , "Introduction to Earthquake Protection of Non-Structural Elements in Buildings" ,Gujarat State Disaster Management Authority

[4] Mounika Lakshmipathi "investigations on the influence of modeling aspects on the seismic performance of a tall building – numerical study on a twenty storeyed rc framed building" A dissertation submitted to Osmania University ,Hyderabad, July, 2017

Seismic Performance of a Retrofitted Building Using Various Numerical Models – A Comparative Study

Anil Kummitha[1], Sreenivas Sarma Paraitham[2]

[1]*Former Post-graduate student, Civil Engineering Department,CBIT,Hyderabad-75(TS)*
[2]*Professor,Civil Engineering Department,CBIT,Hyderabad-75(TS)*

[1]anilcbit.in@gmail.com
[2]sreenivassarma.p@cbit.ac.in

***Abstract*—More often, the actual practices adopted in local or global retrofitting procedures are not reflected in modeling a retrofitted structure. Realising this need of the practicing structural engineering field, a comparative study is taken up in the present work on a five storeyed RC framed building, using the popular ETABS software and adopting response spectrum method of analysis. The building is assumed to be in zone -3 and the members were so designed that some/all of those in the ground floor fail due to the possible up gradation of the building to resist zone-4 forces, requiring retrofitting. One local retrofitting measure (Column Jacketing) and one global retrofitting measure (Braces) are chosen for the study and in each of these cases, representative models reflecting the practices adopted in design offices were tried and compared with those incorporating the executional aspects. Response of each model was observed in terms of Bending moments, shears , axial forces , displacements and mode shapes for the identified columns (corner, intermediate and interior) and in identified floors (1st , 3rd and 5th). Results indicate that there is considerable difference in the axial forces between various models while differences were revealed in moments and shears also in some cases. Small differences were noted even in displacements and mode shapes.**

Keywords: Seismic retrofitting, Seismic Performance, Retrofitted building, NumericalModels, Response spectrum method, Column jacketing, Bracing.

I. INTRODUCTION

Indian subcontinent has suffered some of the greatest earthquakes[8], in the world with magnitude exceeding 8.0. For instance, in a short span of about 50 years, four such earthquakes occurred: Assam earthquake of 1897 (magnitude 8.7) (Oldham, 1899), Kangra earthquake of 1905 (magnitude 8.6) (Middlemiss, 1910), Bihar-Nepal earthquake of 1934 (magnitude 8.4) (GSI, 1939), and the Assam-Tibet earthquake of 1950 (magnitude 8.7) (CBG, 1953). The most tragic earthquakes of last 50 years in India are, the Latur earthquake (which caused about 8000 deaths) and the Bhuj earthquake of 2001 (about 25000 deaths). While the former caused an intensive damage to masonry buildings in many rural areas, the latter struck in a widespread area causing extensive damage to many RC framed buildings besides grounding many villages to debris.

RC framed buildings are the most commonly found in Indian scenario[2], constituting to a major percentage among the total buildings in the country. This may be due to the ease in construction and vertical expansion of such buildings, in addition to the superior seismic performance as compared to the masonry buildings. Even in the rural parts of India, RC construction is clearly on the rise due to the increased awareness and access to raw materials.

However, these RC buildings are also suffering extensive damages during earthquakes in India, raising concern over their safety and the safety of the incumbents as well. Poor workmanship (defective concreting and wrong detailing) is identified as themain reason of failure of RC buildings during the past earthquakes in India. Added to this, the large gap between what is perceived at the modeling stage during analysis and what is practiced during field execution, also appears to be the main reason. This aspect is glaringly ignored in many design offices, particularly while suggesting retrofitting measures for a damaged building.

Seismic retrofitting strategies for buildings could be global or local [3,4]. Column jacketing and bracing are two very commonly adopted techniques among local and global[3], respectively. During the execution stage, the existing structure is strengthened with additional elements, by linking properly. However, this aspect is often ignored by the design offices, Realising this need of the practicing structural engineering field, a comparative study is taken up in the present work on a five storeyed RC framed building, using the popular ETABS software[1] and adopting response spectrum method of analysis.

Fig.1 Column Jacketing

Fig. 2 Steel x- cross bracing

II. BUILDING DETAILS

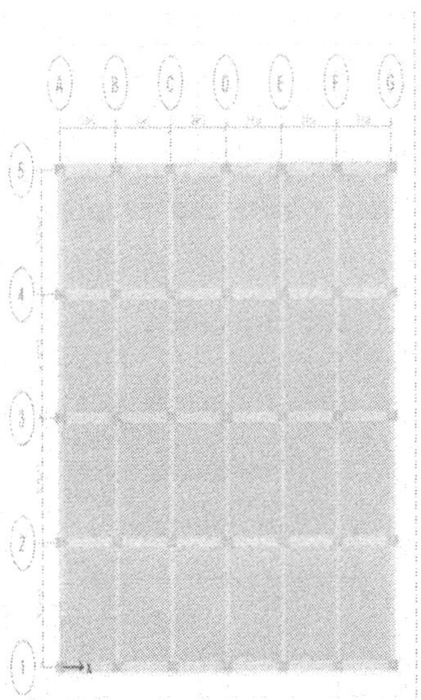

Fig. 3 PLAN

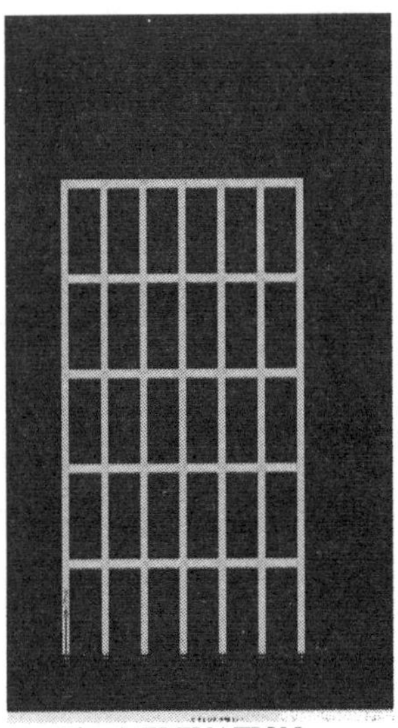

Fig. 4 ELEVATION

Table 1: Building details and common data used

Structure	OMRF
No. of stories	G + 4
Storey height	3.00 m
Type of building used	Residential
Foundation type	Isolated footing
Seismic zone	III
Material Properties	
Young's modulus of M20 concrete, E	22.36 x 10^6kN/m2
Grade of concrete	M20
Grade of steel	Fe 415
Density of reinforced concrete	25 kN/m3
Modulus of elasticity of brick masonry	3.50 x 10^{6kN}/m2
Density of brick masonry	19.20 kN/m3
Member Properties	
Thickness of slab	0.125 m.
Beam size	0.23 x 0.30 m.
Column size	0.23 x 0.60 m.
Thickness of wall	0.23 m.
Live Load Intensities	
Floor and Roof	3kN/m^2

Bay width in x-direction – 3m

Bay width in y-direction – 3m

III. PARAMETERS VARIED

The building was assumed to be in zone-3 and upgraded to zone-4. Two types of retrofitting, one each of local and global were adopted. Column jacketing is chosen as the local measure, while braces were chosen as the global measure[3].

For local retrofitting using column jacketing three types of models were tried viz., old column replaced by a single new column of bigger size, old column designed in section designer and old column surrounded by a new column as jacket pieces stitched together with connectors[1] as is normally practiced in the field.

For global retrofitting three models were tried; one is the brace rigidly connected to the beam – column junctions as a single element, the other is with connection joining the brace to beam and column, as is normally practiced in the field and building with peripheral x-braces [6,9], in ground floor modeled as single element with releases at ends.

Models considered for the study

Model 1 - Building with failure columns .

Model 2 - Building with old column replaced by a single new column of bigger size.

Model 3 - Building with old column replaced by as new one in section designer.

Model 4 - Building with old column jacketted around by a new section using connectors.

Model 5 - Building with peripheral x-braces[6], in ground floor connected rigidly to the beam – column junctions as a single elements.

Model 6 - Building with peripheral x-braces in ground floor modeled as forked elements[1], at the beam column junctions .

Model 7 - Building with peripheral x-braces[1], in ground floor modeled as single element releases at ends.

IV. Parameters Studied

For each model seismic analysis was performed using ETABS software[1] and adopting Response spectrum method of analysis[3,4]. The following responses were studied for three types of columns viz., corner, Intermediate and interior (see figure). 1. Bending moment 2. Shear force 3. Displacements 4. Axial loads 5. Mode shapes.

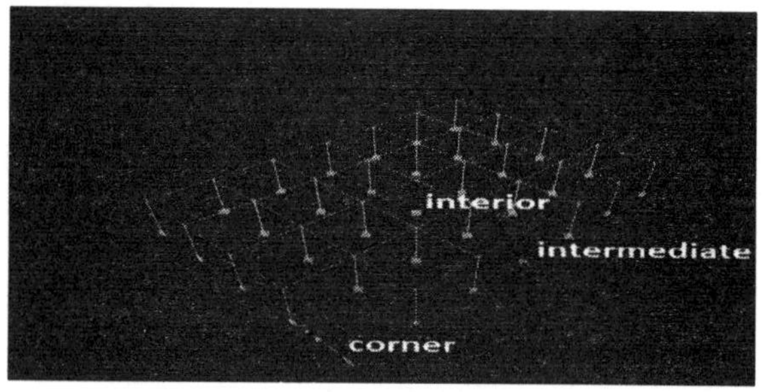

Fig.5: Representation of columns.

V. Results and Discussion

Based on the results obtained from the analysis of various models of the chosen building and the results obtained there on, an attempt is made in this chapter to compare the results of various models[1], discuss and identify the trends.

Bending Moments

Maximum bending moments that have occurred (for any load combination) in the chosen columns in the direction of applied earthquake force were compared. Figure 11 to 13 gives comparison of the same. It may be noted from the figure that the maximum moments in all the three types of columns are comparable in model 2 and 3 and are very high (about 5 to 6 times) when compared to those in model-4 which represents closely the actual field conditions of retrofitting. This trend is understandable as the columns of both models 2 and 3 are more stiffer as compared to those in model-4. Among the braced models (5 to 7) model-7 gives higher values for corner (1.15 times) and interior (2.25 times) columns in lower floor.

The variation in upper stories reflect that model-7 gives higher values, for all the three types of columns viz. corner (1.75 times) intermediate (1.2 times) and interior (1.17 times).

Table 2: Bending moments (kN-m) in corner columns

B.M	CORNER COLUMN		
	1ST	3ND	5TH
MODEL 1	163.4	73.5	48.3
MODEL 2	270.3	89.9	48.6

Contd...

MODEL 3	275.5	89.9	48.5
MODEL 4	63.4	74.0	49.3
MODEL 5	26.3	69.3	47.4
MODEL 6	26.3	69.3	47.9
MODEL 7	30.0	134.3	63.4

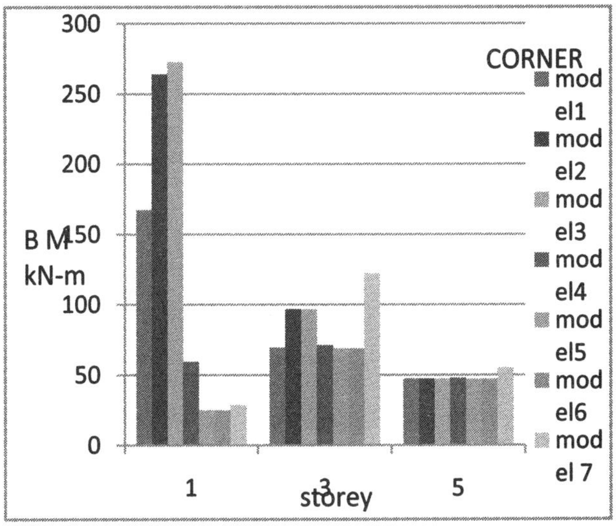

Fig.6 variation of bending moment in cornercolumn, in various models.

Table 3: Bending moments (kN-m) in interior columns

B.M	INTERIOR COLUMN		
	1ST	3ND	5TH
MODEL 1	177.3	125.5	61.2
MODEL 2	245.4	122.3	61.2
MODEL 3	245.4	122.3	61.5
MODEL 4	73.6	130.5	61.8
MODEL 5	14.5	124.4	59.2
MODEL 6	14.5	124.4	59.1
MODEL 7	25.7	148.2	68.6

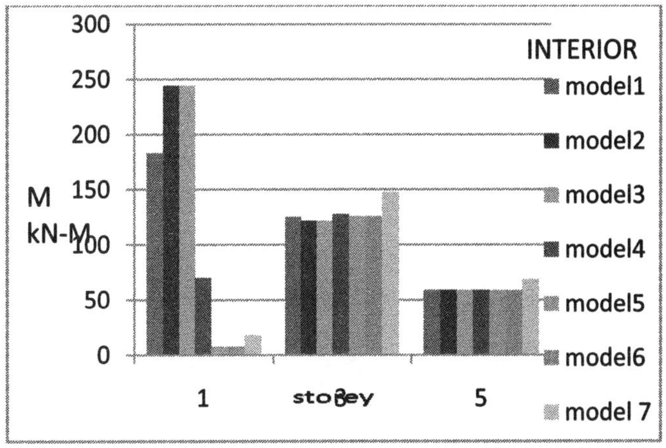

Fig.7 variation of bending moment in interior column, in various models.

Table 4: Bending moments in intermediate columns

B.M	INTERMEDIATE COLUMN		
	1ST	3ND	5TH
MODEL 1	157.3	83.2	53.4
MODEL 2	275.4	90.4	55.3
MODEL 3	283.2	90.4	55.3
MODEL 4	48.3	85.3	51.8
MODEL 5	25.4	82.9	51.9
MODEL 6	25.4	82.9	52.0
MODEL 7	19.3	162.3	69.3

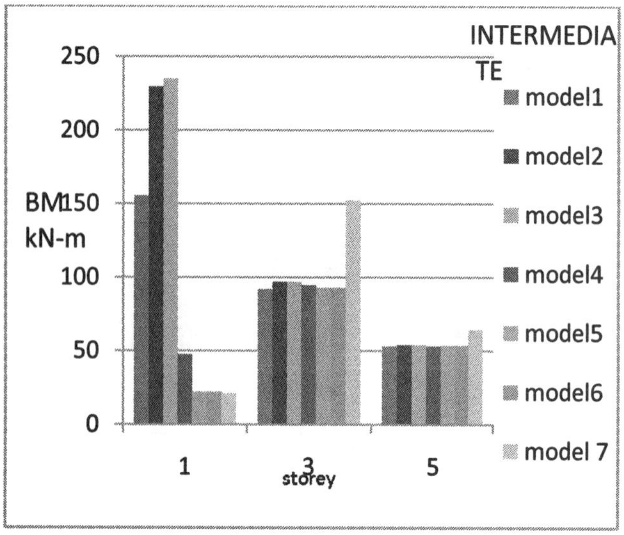

Fig.8 variation of bending moment in intermediate column, in various models

SHEARS IN COLUMNS:

Fig14 to16 show the variation in shears in the three different types of columns. There is a similar trend followed in shear as seen in the case of moments. Again the shears in ground floor column for models 2&3 were comparable. However the shear in model-4 considerably reduced (by about 3 times) in lower floor for corner columns while the same increased in lower floors (by about 1.5 times) for intermediate and interior columns. The variation of shear was negligible in upper floors for all the three types of columns, in models 2&3 and 5&6. Models 4&7 were showing considerable variation in upper floors when compared to their other corresponding models (2&3 or 5&6 as the case may be). Model-4 has reduced the shear by about 15 times in the 3rd storey and maintained almost same shear in the 5th storey, for corner columns. For intermediate columns this model has shown increased shear in the 1st storey(by about 1.45 times) and 5th storey (about 1.1 times) while a decreased shear in the 3rd storey (about 1.2 times). For interior columns, the model has shown an increase in shear of about 1.5 times in the first storey and about 1.2 times in 3rd and 5th stories. Model-7 gave higher values (1.1 times) in all the floors and in all the columns, when compared to models 5&6.

Table 5: Shears (KN) in Corner Columns

SHEAR FORCE(V)	CORNER COLUMN		
	1ST	3ND	5TH
MODEL 1	70.6	52.3	43.4
MODEL 2	109.9	60.01	40.8
MODEL 3	115.4	60.01	40.8
MODEL 4	38.4	11.3	43.9
MODEL 5	25.3	49.9	44.0
MODEL 6	25.3	49.91	44.0
MODEL 7	30.5	57.9	50.4

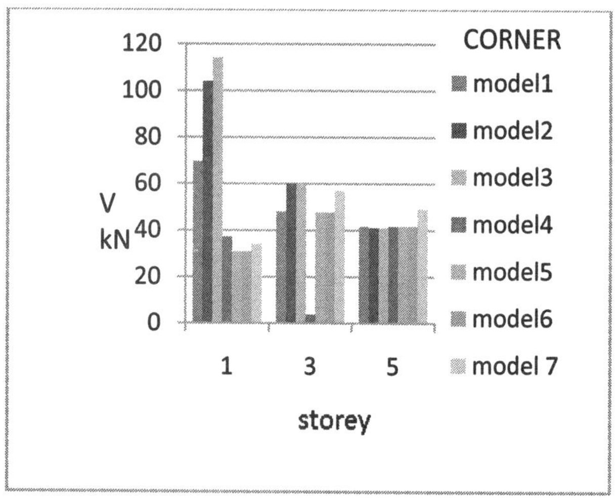

Fig.9 Variation of shear in corner column, in various models

Table 6: Shears (KN) in intermediate columns

SHEAR FORCE(V)	INTERMEDIATE COLUMN		
	1ST	3ND	5TH
MODEL 1	73.4	64.3	36.2
MODEL 2	69.8	62.1	38.4

Contd...

MODEL 3	77.3	62.1	38.4
MODEL 4	110.6	54.2	39.6
MODEL 5	25.3	63.9	37.0
MODEL 6	25.3	63.9	37.0
MODEL 7	30.4	70.6	43.7

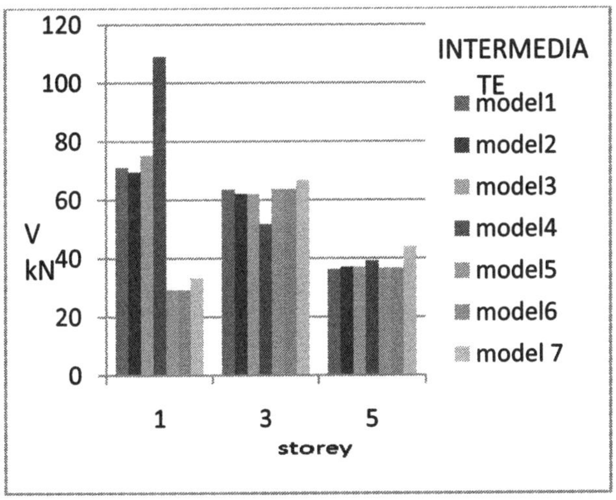

Fig.10 Variation of shear in intermediate column, in various models

Table 7: Shear (KN) in interior columns

SHEAR FORCE(V)	INTERIOR COLUMN		
	1ST	3ND	5TH
MODEL 1	89.3	88.9	57.9
MODEL 2	88.2	60.1	56.3
MODEL 3	88.2	60.1	56.3
MODEL 4	131.2	79.6	62.9
MODEL 5	49.6	84.3	57.0
MODEL 6	49.6	84.3	57.0
MODEL 7	57.3	99.6	70.3

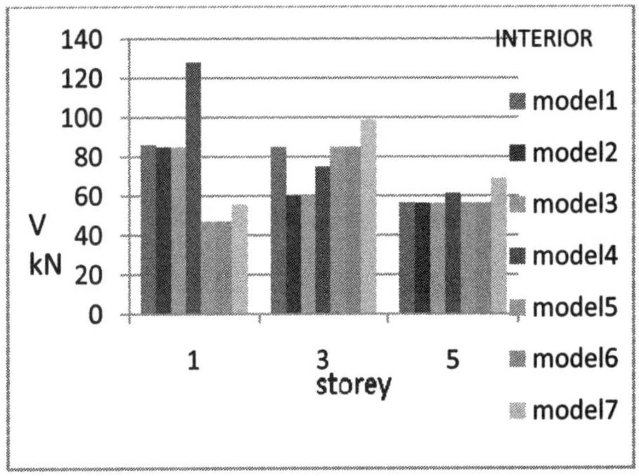

Fig.11 Variation of shear in interior column, in various models

AXIAL LOADS IN COLUMNS:

It was quite conspicuous from the figures 12 to 14 that there is huge variation in axial loads in all the

Three types of columns, for all the models, in the lower story. Model-2 and model-3 differed hugely in axial loads. Model-4 which is a closer representation of field condition, has shown highest axial load in lower storey for corner column, while model-3 has shown highest values for intermediate and interior columns. Model-2 is giving lowest values of axial loads in lower storey for all types of columns. For the 3rdstorey model-4 has given higher values in all types of columns. In the 5th storey there is not much of difference in the values of axial loads in all the columns, among the models 2, 3 and 4.

Among the braced models i.e., 5, 6 and 7, model-7 has consistently shown higher values of axial loads for all the stories and all types of columns. This could be because of the release given to the brace to simulate the field execution of connecting the brace with beam-column junction by same fastenings such as plates with nut-bolt system.

The absolute maximum values of axial loads occurred for model-4 in lower storey and for model -3 in 3rd and 5th stories

Table 8 : Axial forces(kN) in Corner columns

AXIAL FORCE(P)	CORNER COLUMN		
	1ST	3ND	5TH
MODEL 1	843.9	100.0	102.1
MODEL 2	177.3	106.3	100.0
MODEL 3	770.2	106.3	100.0
MODEL 4	854.3	110.2	102.0
MODEL 5	353.2	99.8	100.0
MODEL 6	353.2	99.8	100.0
MODEL 7	421.2	501.2	111.3

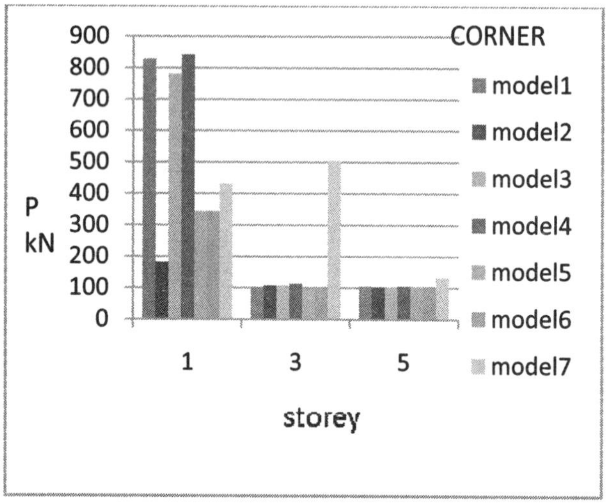

Fig.12 variation axial force in corner column, of various models.

Table 9: Axial forces (kN) in intermediate columns

AXIAL FORCE(P)	INTERMEDIATE COLUMN		
	1ST	3ND	5TH
MODEL 1	1103.5	600.3	174.3
MODEL 2	183.2	98.9	173.9
MODEL 3	1121.3	98.9	173.9
MODEL 4	752.4	608.2	102.3
MODEL 5	179.9	611.1	173.9
MODEL 6	179.9	611.1	173.9
MODEL 7	216.8	701.9	189.2

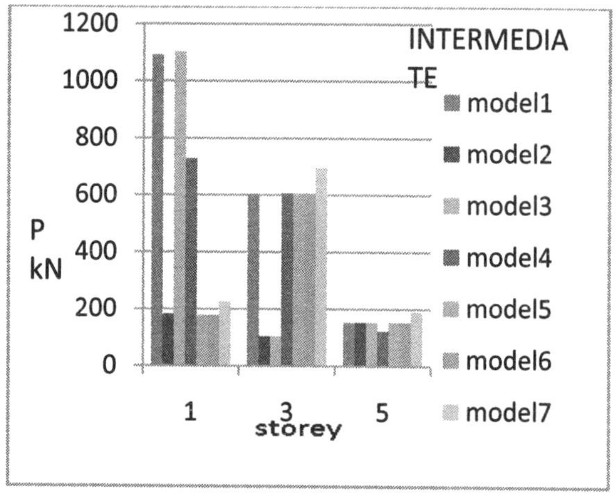

Fig.13 variation of axial force in intermediate column, of various models.

Table 10 : Axial Forces(kN) in interior columns

AXIAL FORCE(P)	INTERIOR COLUMN		
	1ST	3ND	5TH
MODEL 1	1051.6	654.2	50.3
MODEL 2	242.3	623.9	49.9
MODEL 3	1113.2	623.9	49.2
MODEL 4	963.1	648.1	53.2
MODEL 5	208.2	102.8	49.4
MODEL 6	208.2	102.8	49.4
MODEL 7	215.6	734.2	52.3

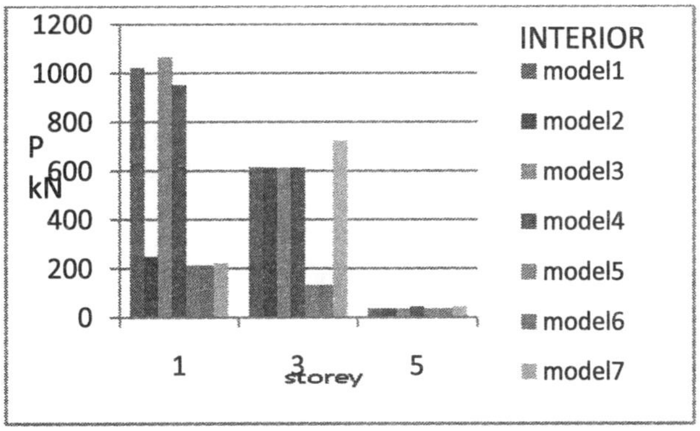

Fig.14 variation of axial force in interior column, of various models.

DISPLACEMENTS

Models 4 and 7, which are close to field implementations of local (column jacketing) and global (bracing), have notably shown higher values of displacements in all the upper floors. When compared to the 1st floor level displacement. The top storey displacement is increased by 11 times in model-4.

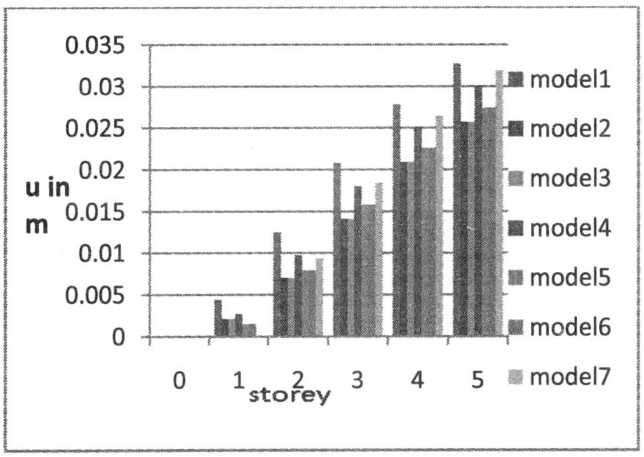

Fig.15 Displacements in direction of application of earthquake forces

5.5 MODE SHAPES

Critical mode shapes for all the models are extracted and on comparison, the following observations are made.

Models 2 & 3 have shown similar mode shapes (predominantly in flexure mode) quit understandable as these are modeled in the a similar way except for the use of a section designer in model-3. Critical mode shapes occurred for both the models at 12th mode, with a time period of 0.078. Model-4 also has shown a similar mode shape but with increased displacements. The critical mode shape has occurred at 10th mode, with a time period of 0.142.

Among the braced models, 5 and 6 have shown similar behavior with predominant flexural mode in lower story, while the upper storey movements were very less. The trend is particularly slowing in internal columns compared to the external columns. This is because the exterior columns are braced in the lower story by which their movements are restricted and interior columns are relatively free to move. Critical mode shapes for both the models have occurred at 13th mode with time period of 0.12. for model-7, though releases were given no change in mode shapes and time periods was noted.

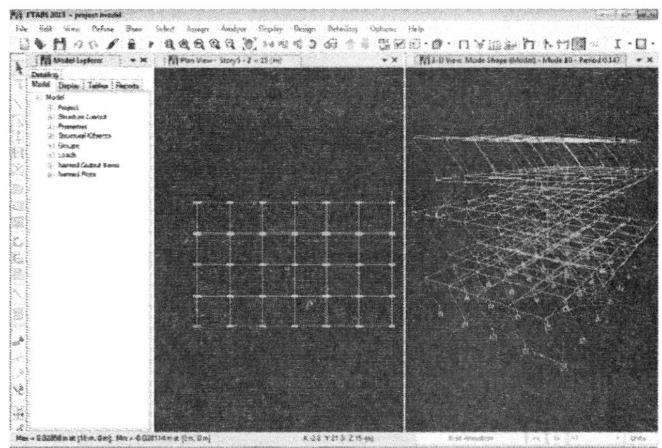

Fig.16 Mode shape for model 1 at mode10.

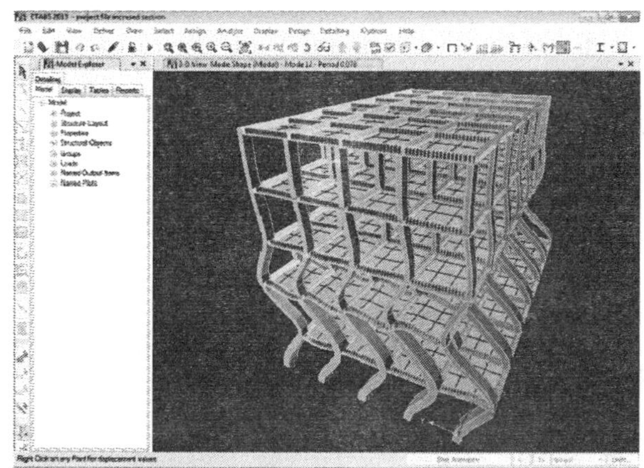

Fig.17 Mode shape for model 2 at 12th mode.

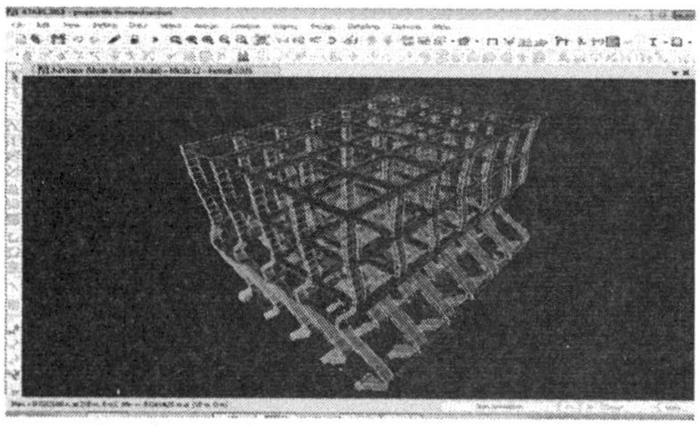

Fig.18 mode shape for model 3 at 12th mode

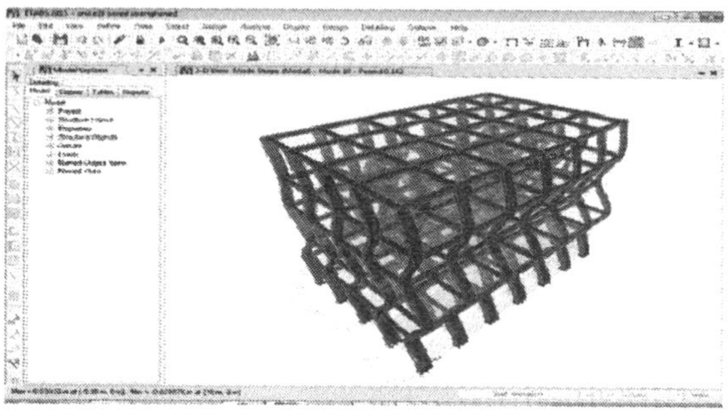

Fig.19 mode shape for model 4 at 10th mode

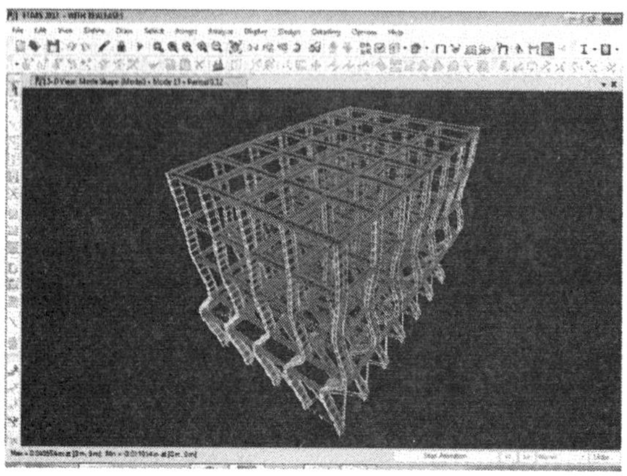

Fig. 20 mode shape for models 5,6 and 7 @ 13th mode.

CONCLUSIONS

Based on the study conducted on the chosen five storied RC framed building , the following general and specific conclusions were drawn .

General Conclusions:

1. Model-2 (increased new section) and model-3 (using section designer) have exhibited similar flexural behavior while considerable change was noted in the shear and axial load behaviour.
2. Model -4 (jacket stitched to the old one using connectors) [1]differed largely with models 2 and 3,in terms of flexural behavior while a comparable behavior was noted in axial load and shear behaviours, with respect to that of model 3.
3. Model-5 (normal brace model) and model-6 (Brace modeled with rigid connectors at the junctions) have demonstrated almost identical influence in the flexure, shear and axial load behavior of all the three types of columns in all the floors. However, when compared with other models , their influence was quite conspicuous in reducing the bending moments , shears and axial loads.
4. Model -7 has shown a consistant increase in moments, shear and axial loads in all the three types of columns, at all the floor levels.
5. Among the models used used for local retrofitting (jacketing), models 2 and 3 have shown similar critical mode shapes, while model-4 has slightly differed with greater displacements. Among the models used for global retrofitting (bracing), all the models (5, 6 and 7) have shown similar critical mode shapes.

Specific conclusions:

1. Bending moments in all the three types of columns were reduced by about 5 times in model-4 when compared with those in models 2 and 3, in the lower floor of the building. The introduction of braces has further decreased these moments by about 2 times in the corner and intermediate columns while the decrease was about ten times in the interior columns, all being in the ground floor again. model-7 has increased bending moments in the upper floors in all the three types of columns viz. corner(1.75 times) intermediate (1.2 times) and interior (1.17 times).
2. Shears reduced in the lower floor of corner columns by about three times in model-4, which closely represents the retrofitted structure, while they increased by about 1.5 times in intermediate and interior columns. Model-7 gave higher values (1.1 times) in all the floors and in all the columns, when compared to models 5 & 6.
3. Axial loads were maximum for corner columns in model-4, and for intermediate & interior columns

in model -3. Model-2 has consistently shown lower values of axial loads (around 200 kN) while the introduction of braces (models 5 and 6) has reduced the axial loads by about 2.5 times in lower floors of corner columns and about 5.5 times in lower floors of intermediate and interior columns. model-7 has consistently shown higher values of axial loads for all the stories and all types of columns,when compared to models 5 and 6.

4. Critical modes and corresponding time periods for various models are as follows :
   Model 1 – mode 10, 0.0147, Model 2- mode 12 , 0.078 , Model 3 – mode 12 ,0.078 ,Model 4 – mode 10 , 0.142 , Model 5,6 and 7– mode 13, 0.12.
5. Models 4 and 7, which are close to field implementations of local (column jacketing and global (bracing), have notably shown higher values of displacements in all the upper floors. When compared to the 1st floor level displacement. The top storey displacement is increased by 11 times in model-4.

REFERENCES

[1] Anil Kummitha (2017) ," Seismic performance of various numerical models used for modeling the behaviour of a retrofitted RC framed building – A comparative study ", a diisertation submitted to Osmania University

[2] Massumil and A.A. Tasnimi(2008). Strengthening of low ductile reinforced concrete frames using steel x-bracings with different details,World Conference on Earthquake Engineering October 12-17, 2008, Beijing, China.

[3] Viswanath K.G (2010). Seismic Analysis of Steel Braced Reinforced Concrete Frames, international journal of civil and structural engineering,ISSN 0976 – 4399

[4] IS 1893(part 1) – 2002, "Criteria for earthquake resistant design of structures, part 1-general provisions and buildings", fifth revision, Bureau of Indian Standards, New Delhi, India.

[5] Maheri M R, Akbari R, (2003). Seismic behaviour factor, R, for steel X-braced and knee-braced RC buildings, Engineering Structures, 25:1505-1513.

[6] Massumil and A.A. Tasnimi(2008). Strengthening of low ductile reinforced concrete frames using steel x-bracings with different details,World Conference on Earthquake Engineering October 12-17, 2008, Beijing, China.

[7] IS 456:2000, "Plain and Reinforced Concrete - Code of Practice", Bureau of Indian Standards, New Delhi, 2000.

[8] Sudhir K. Jain, Indian Earthquakes : An Overview, The Indian Concrete Journal, Vol. 72, No. 11, November 1998.

[9] T. D. Bush, E. A. Jones, Associate Members, ASCE, and J. O. Jirsa, Member, ASCE (1991). Behavior of RC frame strengthened using structural steel bracing, 117(4): 1115-1126.

Influence of Modelling on the Effectiveness of Column Jacketing in the Seismic Performance of Arc Framed Building – A Comparitive Study Using Three Alternative Materials (RCC, Steel, FRP)

Kolli Pavan[1*], SreenivasSarma Paraitham[2]

[1]*Former post-graduate student,Civil Engineering Department,CBIT,Hyderabad-75*
[2]*Professor,Civil Engineering Department,CBIT,Hyderabad-75*

**Corresponding Author mail:[1]pavankolli29@gmail.com*
[2]sreenivassarma.p@cbit.ac.in

***Abstract*—Column jacketing is one of the most common methods practiced as a part of seismic retrofitting strategies. Different materials are in use for strengthening the columns and among them RCC, Steel and FRP are more popular. The choice of any of these three materials has so far been notional and is left most of the times to the discretion of practicing engineers and execution teams, giving priority to the availability of the materials and skills of field force. However, much depends on the actual interaction of these materials with the existing materials of columns, which is often ignored in the design offices while modelling the structures. RC framed buildings of five to six storeys are most commonly found in all the seismic zones, in Indian scenario. Therefore, there is a strong need to look into the lapses and ignorances in modelling the retrofitting aspects such as column strengthening, in these types of buildings.**

Realising this need, a six(G+5)storeyed reinforced concrete framed building is taken up as a case study in the present work. The building is assumed to be originally in a location in zone 3 which is upgraded to zone 4, requiring retrofitting of columns. Three alternative materials are tried for column strengthening viz., RCC, Steel and FRP. For each of these materials two models are tried; one normally adopted in the design offices and the other proposed in the present work to go closer to the actual practice. Response spectrum method of analysis is adopted using ETABS software.

Results indicate that there is considerable influence of proper modelling in case of steel and concrete jacketing. With the proposed modelling, moments are hugely coming down in the concrete jacketing. Although shears and axial forces are increasing in concrete jacketing with the proposed modelling, they are found to be still less than those found in steel and FRP jacketing. Hence, the study revealed that reinforced concrete jacketing, if properly modelled, yields good results.

***Keywords*—Column jacketing, Seismic retrofitting, RC framed building, RCC, Steel, FRP.**

I.INTRODUCTION

There has been an increase in the occurrence of the natural disasters globally, in the recent past. Earthquakes are leading among these in terms of loss of life, property and extensive damages to structures. As such, seismic retrofitting has evolved as a subject of modern context and engineering importance [1].

The mosttragic earthquakes of last 50 years in India are, the Latur earthquake (which caused about 8000 deaths) and the Bhuj earthquake of 2001(about 25000 deaths). While the former caused an intensive damage to masonry buildings in many rural areas, the latter struck in a widespread area causing extensive damage to many RC framed buildings. RC framed buildings of five to six storeys are most commonly found in all the seismic zones, in Indian scenario. Therefore, retrofitting of these buildings can be viewed as a subject of national importance [2].

Column jacketing is one of the most common methods practiced as a part of seismic retrofitting strategies. Different materials are in use for strengthening the columns and among them RCC, Steel and FRP are more popular [3]. The choice of any of these three materials has so far been notional and is left most of the times to the discretion of practicing engineers and execution teams, giving priority to the availability of the materials and skills of field force. The fact that much depends on the actual interaction between the existing structural elements and the proposed new jacketing elements / materials, is often ignored in the design offices[4].

II. MATERIALS FOR COLUMN JACKETING

The most common materials used for jacketing the column are RCC, Steel and FRP. Each of these materials have their own advantages and disadvantages. For example, RCC is cheaper but less stronger and hence greater sectional area is required to strengthen the column. Steel is much stronger but costlier. It is also more susceptible for corrosion. FRP on the other hand provides great flexural rigidity for the column besides giving the advantage of protecting the reinforcing steel from corrosion [4]. When judiciously used it can become a viable solution. However, there are many unresolved issues in the understanding and implementation of this retrofitting strategies.

III. FIELD PRACTICES AND UNRESOLVED ISSUES

Quite often the retrofitting strategy for an a existing building consists of strengthening the existing structure elements by either extending the sections on one side or by jacketing [3]. In either case the new section has to be joined with the old sections, requiring proper modelling of the interaction at the interfaces by the designer [2].It is observed that this aspect is mostly ignored by the designers while the effectiveness of a retrofitting strategy such as column jacketing. Further, the choice of the material for retrofitting is mostly decided based on its availability, skill of the labour in using it and such other factors rather than based on the behaviour of the materials used, their interaction and effectiveness in performing.Therefore, it is felt that there is strong need to investigate in to these unresolved issues and quantify their effects.

Realising this need, a detailed numerical investigation is taken up in this work on a six (G+5) storied RC framed building, for

Fig. 1 (top)Concrete Jacketing Actual field practice(bottom)ETABS models simulating office and field practices [1]

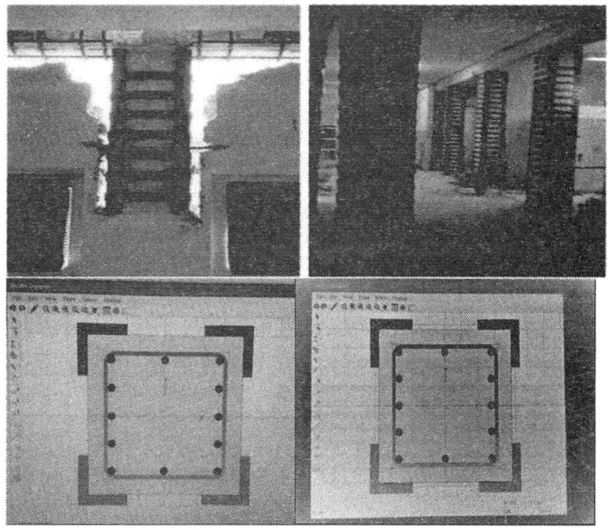

Fig. 2 (top) Steel Jacketing of Columns – Field practices (bottom) ETABS models simulating office and field practices [1]

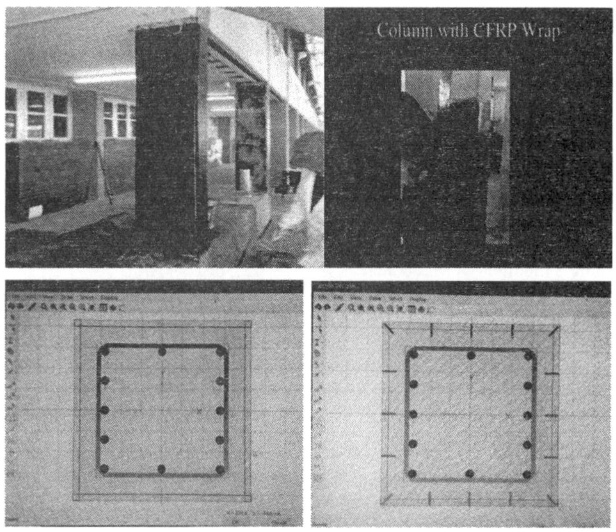

Fig.3 (top) FRP jacketing – Field practice (bottom) ETABS models simulating office and field practices [1]

Seismic zone-3.The effectiveness of 3 types of column jacketing viz., RCC, STEEL and FRP, in contributing for better seismic performance of the building is checked in terms of bending moments, shears, axial forces developed in the columns in various locations and various stories of the building. For each material, two models are tried [1]. One similar to that normally used in design offices and the other closer to the field practice where the jacket is given connections with the existing column in the form of shear connectors, welds etc.

IV. DETAILS OF THE BUILDING CHOSEN

Keeping in view the most commonly constructed buildings, an RC framed building with six(G+5)storeys is chosen for study, with the following details.

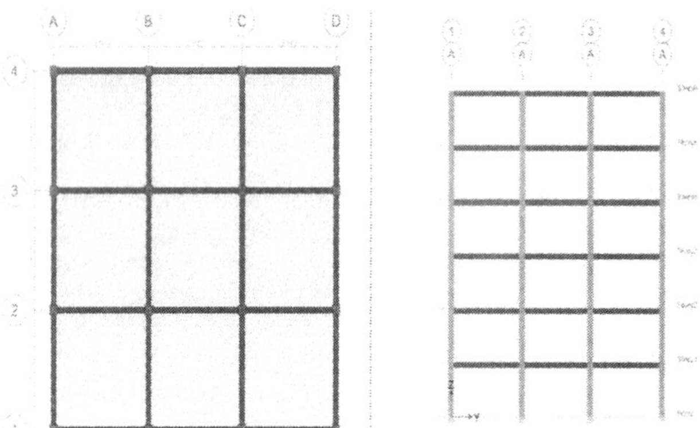

Fig. 4 PLAN and ELEVATION of building

Table 1: Building details and common data used

Structure	OMRF
No. of stories	G+5
Storey height	3.00m
Type of building used	Residential
Foundation type	Isolatedfooting
Seismic zone	III, upgraded to IV
Material Properties	
Young's modulus of M20concrete, E	22.36x106kN/m2
Grade of concrete	M20,M30
Grade of steel	Fe415
Density of reinforced concrete	25kN/m3
Modulus of elasticity of brick masonry	3.50x106kN/m2
Density of brick masonry	19.20kN/m3
Member Properties	
Thickness of slab	0.125m.
Beam size	0.23x0.30m.
Column size	0.40x0.40m.
Thickness of wall	0.23m.
Dead Load Intensities	
Floor finishes	1.0kN/m2
Live Load Intensities	
Roof and Floor	3.0kN/m2
Earthquake LL on slab as per Cl.7.3.1 and 7.3.2 of IS1893 (part1)-2002	
Roof	0kN/m2
Floor	0.25x3.0=0.75kN/m2

Description of figures that drawn in ETABS were explained in following:

1. For Reinforced Concrete jacketing, the each columns were assigned alround 100mm for the existing columns (400mmx400mm).
2. For Steel jacketing, steel plate of L angle of size 100mm (in height and width) and 25mm thickness was taken in all four corners of columns. The height, width and thickness of l shaped angle were obtained by calculating equivalent area.
3. For FRP jacketing, alround the column 15mm thickness of wrapping was done as shown in figure 4.3. The 15mm thickness obtained by calculating equivalent area.

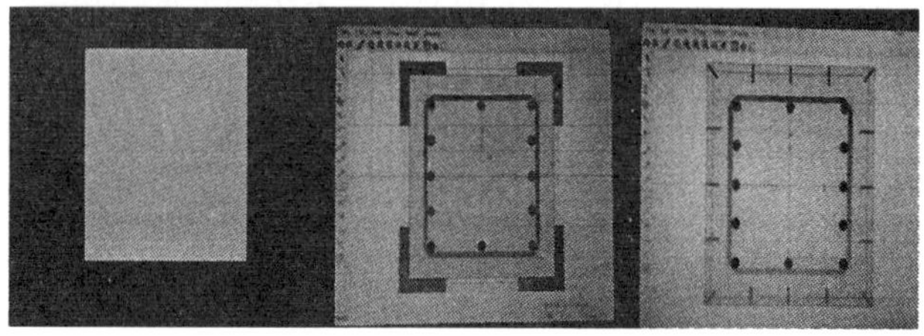

Fig.5 ETABS modelsnear to field practice, for Concrete, Steel and CFRP jacketings with overall sizes of 600mmx600mm, 450 mm x 450 mm, 430 mm x 430 mm respectively

V. MODELS CONSIDERED

All together seven models are considered in the present work.The details are as follows,

MODEL-I: Normal RCC column (400mmX400mm) for zone-3.
MODEL-II:Retrofitted model with increased column size (RCC column 600mmX600mm)
MODEL-III: Retrofitted model with RC jacketing modelled closer to field practice (400mmX400mm existing column with a RC jacket of 100mm alround).
MODEL-IV: Retrofitted model with steel jacketing modelled normally.
MODEL-V: Retrofitted model with FRP jacketing modelled normally.
MODEL-VI: Retrofitted model with steel jacketing closer to field practice
MODEL-VII: Retrofitted model with FRP jacketing closer to field practice.

VI. PARAMETERS VARIED

Three types of column jacketing were considered viz., RCC, Steel and FRP. For each of these three, two models are used. One similar to that normally adopted in design offices [1]. The other is closer to the field practice, duly considering the connection between the old and new portions of the column.

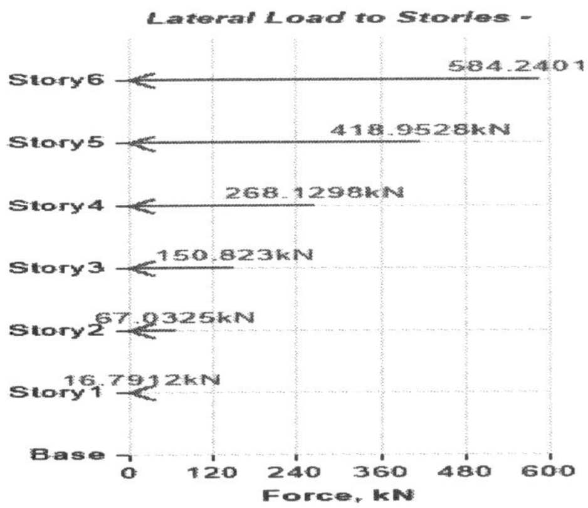

Fig 6: Lateral loads on stories

VII. RESPONSES STUDIED

For each model the response of the columns is observed in various locations and at various floors. Response of columns were increased in terms of Bending moment(M), Shear(V) and Axial forces(P). At the same time the response of entire building in terms of top storey displacement, mode shapes and time periods [1]. The following responses were studied for three types of columns viz., Corner, Intermediate and Interior columns (see figure).

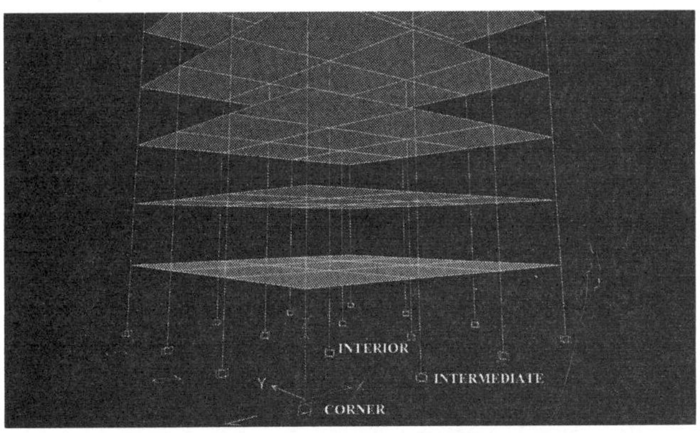

Fig. 7 Representation of corner, intermediate, interior columns

VIII. RESULTS AND DISCUSIONS

Based on the results obtained from the response spectrum analysis of a six(G+5) storey RC framed building, trends in the responses of columns are observed for three types of column jacketing and are presented here in term of bending moments (absolute maximum, Mx and My), shears and axial forces. Besides these, the response of the total building in terms of top storey displacements, time periods, base shears and mode shapes, is observed and presented.

Responses in columns(MODEL II TO MODEL VII):

MODEL II: Retrofitted model with increased column size(RCC column 600mmX600mm).

(a) Bending moments:

(i)Absolute maximum moments(M): For all the floors viz.,1st, 3rd,5[th]the absolute maximum moments occurred for intermediate and interior columns while the least for corner columns. The absolute maximum moments decreased drastically from 1st to 3rd stories (about 60% for interiorand intermediate and 35% for corner)and gradually from 3rd story to 5th storey(about 33% for interior and intermediate and 15% for corner columns).

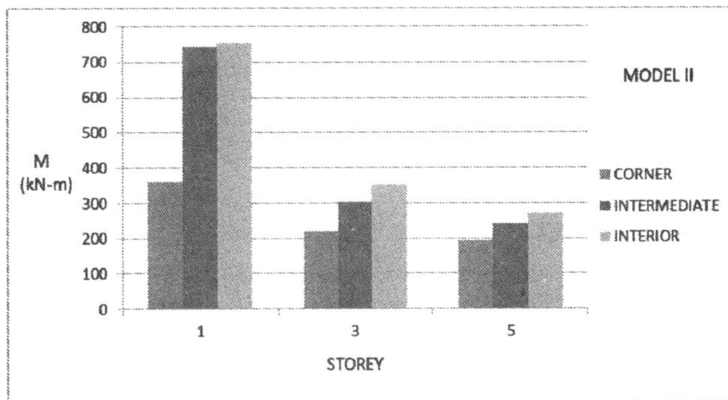

Fig. 8 Variation of Absolute maximum moments

(ii) Moments in X-direction(Mx):For all the floors viz.,1st,3rd,5th floors, absolute maximum moments occurred in X-direction only. Hence, the trends remained same as explained earlier.

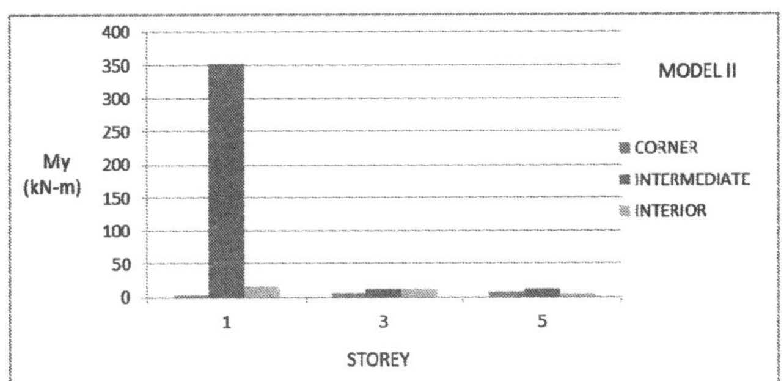

Fig. 9 Variation of Moments in X-direction

(iii) Moments in Y-direction(My): Moments in all the columns and all storeys were almost negligible except for intermediate columns in 1[st]storey. The moments in Y-direction decreased 95% for the intermediate columns while corner and interior columns have minor variations from 1st to 3[rd]storey.

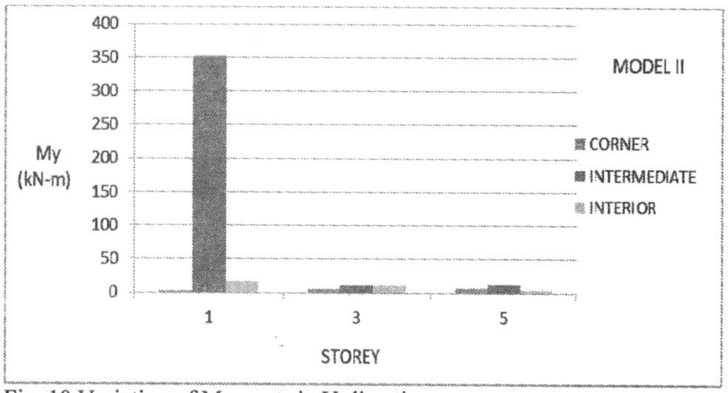

Fig. 10 Variation of Moments in Y-direction

(b) SHEARS(V): Absolute maximum shear occurred in corner column in the ground floor(1ststorey).However, the values decreased by about 60% in the 3rd and 5thstoreys. Shears in interior columns were negligible while shears in the intermediate columns did not vary much.

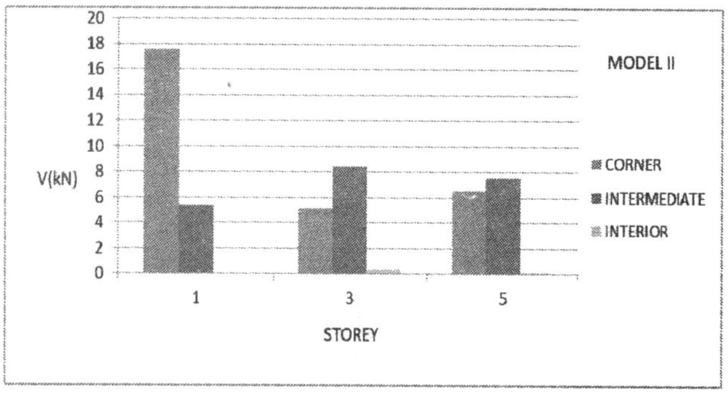

Fig. 11 Variation of Shear

(c) AXIAL LOADS(P): Absolute maximum value has occurred for a corner column in the 1ststorey. Interior and intermediate columns have shown a consistent trend of uniformly decreasing by about 33% from 1st to 3rdstorey and about 50% from 3rd to 5thstorey.However, the corner columns have shown a drastic variation with absolute maximum in the 1ststorey to absolute minimum in the 5thstorey.

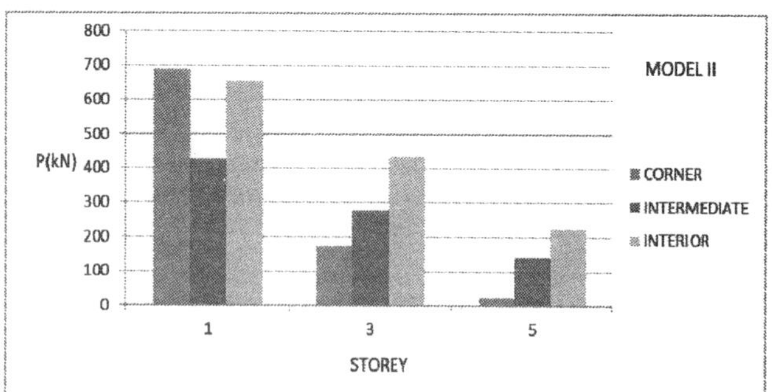

Fig. 12 Variation of Axial forces

MODEL III: Retrofitted model with RC jacketing modelled closer to field practice (400mmX400mm existing column with a RC jacket of 100mm alround).

(a)BENDING MOMENTS

(i) Absolute maximum moments(M): For all the columns, absolute maximum moments occurred in the 3rdstorey, while the minimum occurred the 1ststorey. The moments increased from 1st to 3rdstorey in all columns on an average of 380% and decreased there onwards from 3rd to 5thstoreys, on an average of 27%.

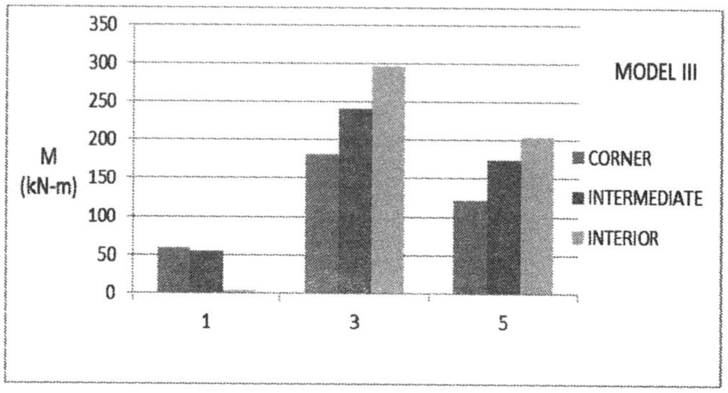

Fig.13Variation of Absolute maximum moments

(ii) Moments in X-direction(Mx): When compared to the variation of absolute maximum moments,the trend almost remained same, except that the moments in 1ststorey differed. They were very minimal for interior and intermediate columns.

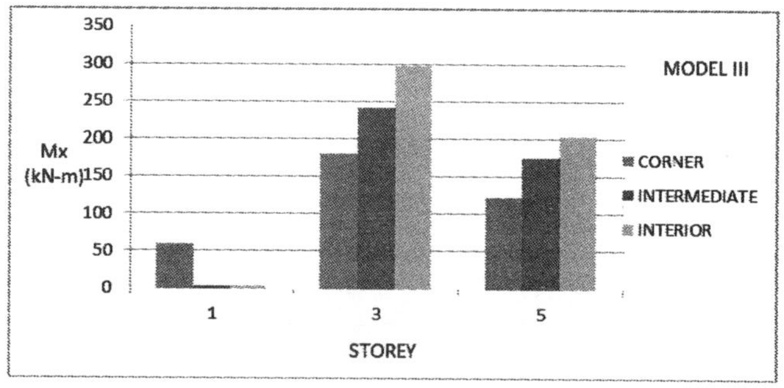

Fig.14 Variation of Moments in X-direction

(iii) Moments in Y-direction (My): In all storeys intermediate column have high moments followed by corner columns and then the interior columns.The moments in intermediate columns decreased gradually from 1st to 3rdstorey(9%) and drastically from 3rd to 5thstoreys(80%).In corner and interior column,they increased drastically from 1st(5 kN-m) to 3rd(40 kN-m)storeys and also decreased drastically from 3rd to 5thstorey(87.5%).

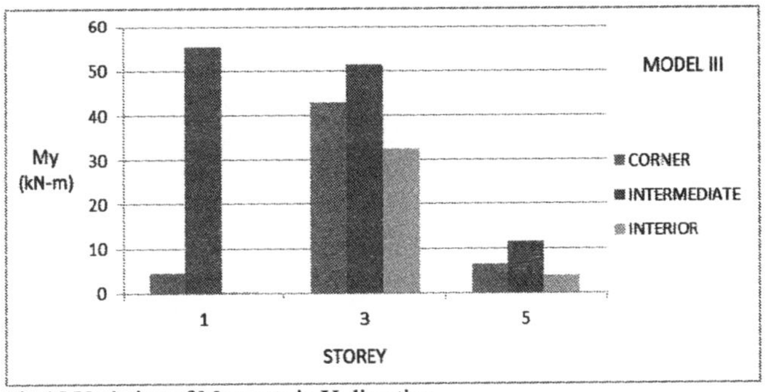

Fig.15 Variation of Moments in Y-direction

(b) SHEARS(V): Interior columns at storey3 have high shear(190kN) but having least shears in 1st and 3rdstorey. The corner and intermediate columns have least shear values.

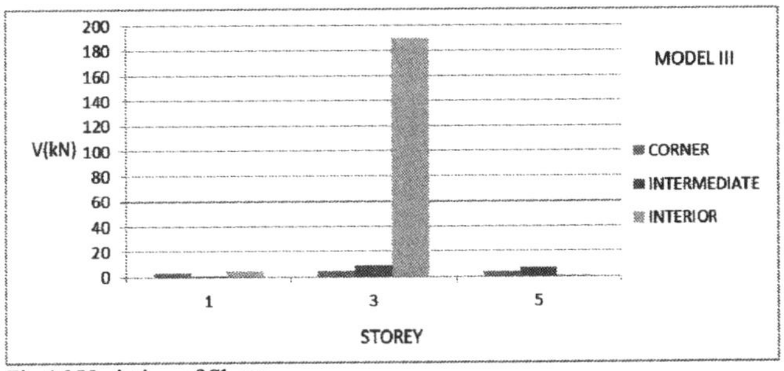

Fig.16 Variation of Shear

(c) AXIAL FORCES(P): For all the columns, axial forces were high in 3rdstorey while axial forces are low in both 1st and 5thstoreys. Corner, intermediate and interior columns decreased axial force by 93%, 95% and 88% respectively from 3rdstorey to 5thstorey.

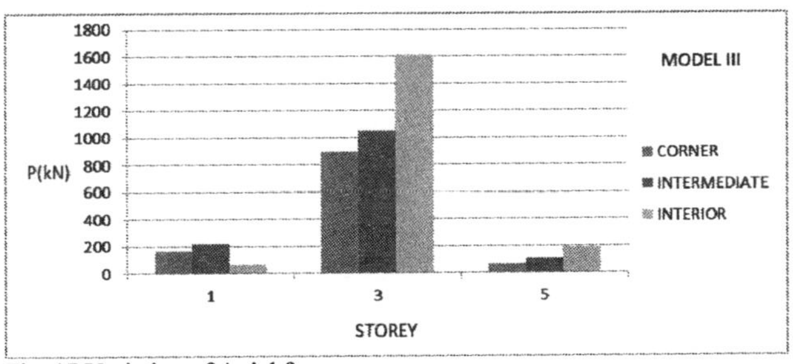

Fig. 17 Variation of Axial forces

MODEL IV: Retrofitted model with steel jacketing modelled normally.

(a) BENDING MOMENTS

(i) Absolute maximum moments(M): At 3rd and 5thstoreys, all the columns having absolute maximum moments are almost negligible while at 1ststoreyallthecolumn has absolute maximum moments approximately (600KN).

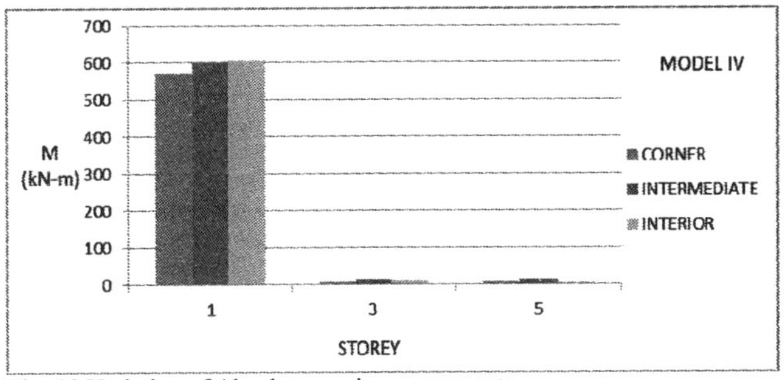

Fig. 18 Variation of Absolute maximum moments

(ii) Moments in X- direction(Mx): At 3rd and 5thstoreys, all the columns are having moments negligible (simillar to absolute maximum moments variations) while at 1ststorey corner and interior column has higher moments in X-direction.

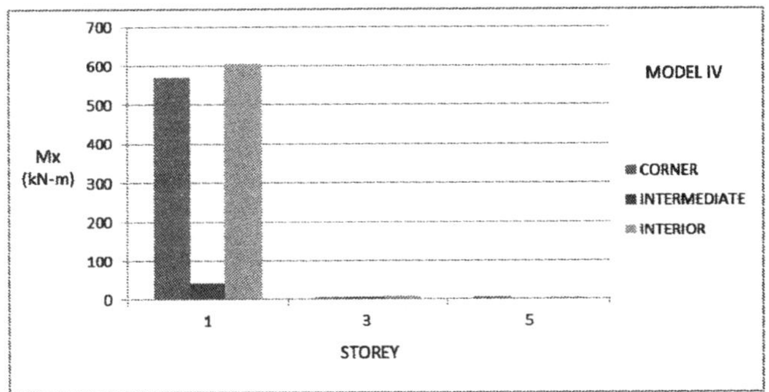

Fig. 19 Variation of Moments in X-direction

(iii) Moments in Y-direction(My): Simillar to moments in X-direction at 3rd and 5thstorey have least moments while at 1ststorey, intermediate column have high moment(600KN).In all the storeys, intermediate columns having higher moments.

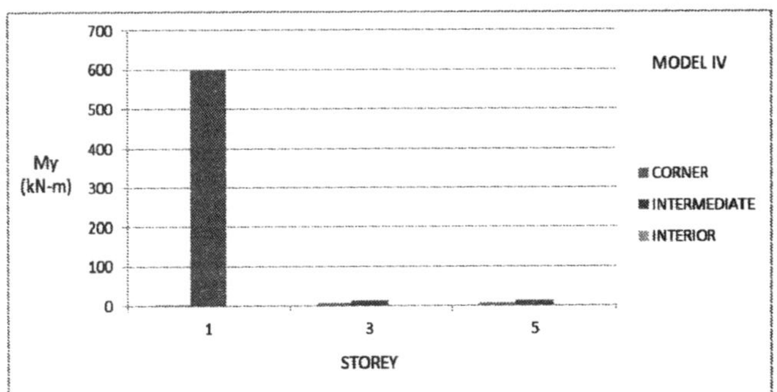

Fig. 20Variation of Moments in Y-direction

(b) SHEAR(V): Interior column at 3rdstorey has high shear(180KN) while they are negligible in 1st and 5thstoreys. Corner and intermediate columns are increased gradually from 1st to 5th storeys.

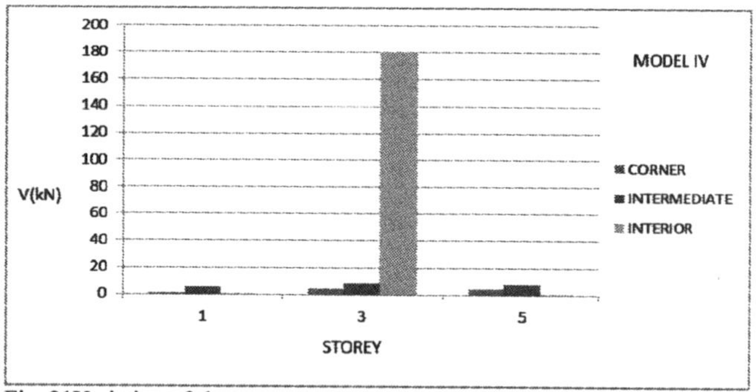

Fig. 21Variation of shear

(C) AXIAL FORCES(P): In all the storeys, axial force decreased gradually for all the columns viz., corner, intermediate, interior columns. Interior columns having high axial forces while the corner columns having least in all the storeys(i.e.,1st to 5thstorey).

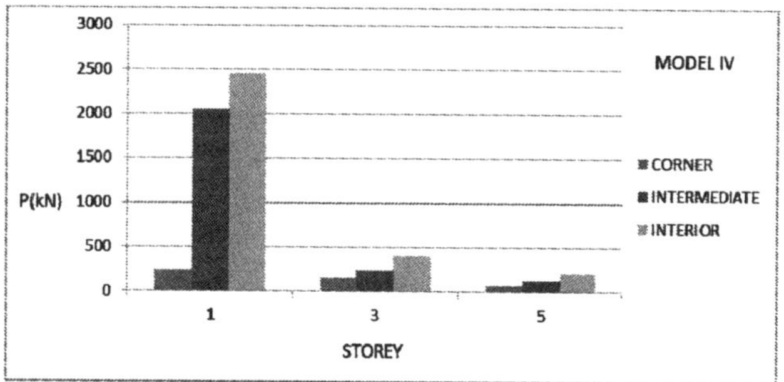

Fig.22Variation of Axial forces

MODEL V: Retrofitted model with FRP jacketing modelled normally.

(a) BENDING MOMENTS:

(i) Absolute maximum moments (M): In all the storey levels, interior columns have shown absolute maximum moments while corner columns the least.There was a decrease in these moments in interior and intermediate columns of 41% from 1st to 3rdstorey and 20% from 3rd to 5thstorey. In corner columns, there was a sudden decrease of about 68% from 1st to 3rdstorey and then a gradual increase of 10% from 3rd to 5thstorey.

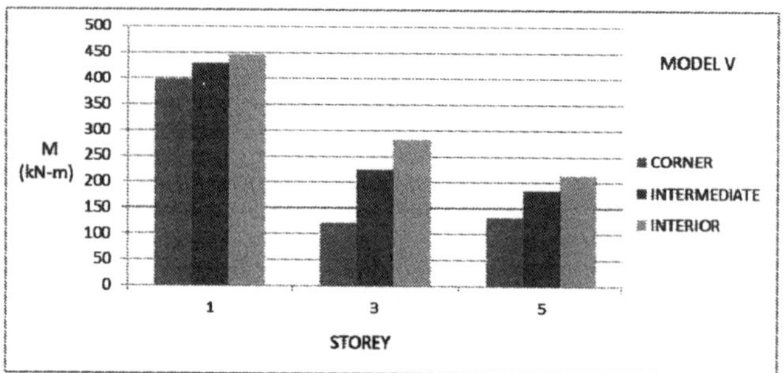

Fig. 23 Variation of Absolute maximum moments

(ii) Moments in X-direction (Mx): For all the floors viz., 1st,3rd,5th floors, absolute maximum moments occurred in X-direction only. Hence, the trends remained same as explained earlier.

(iii) Moments in Y-direction(My): Intermediate columns have high moments in Y-direction at storey1 which are 50% more than 3rd and 5thstorey respectively. Interior columns have shown decreased moments 79% from 1st to 3rdstorey and 82% from 3rd to 5thstorey while the corner columns have minor variation in all the stories.

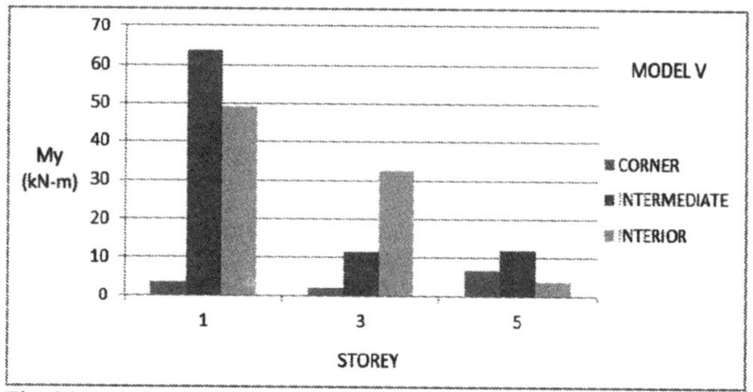

Fig. 24 Variation of Moments in Y-Direction

(b) SHEARS(V): The shears in all the columns at all storeys were very nominal. However, the variation of those were shown in figure.

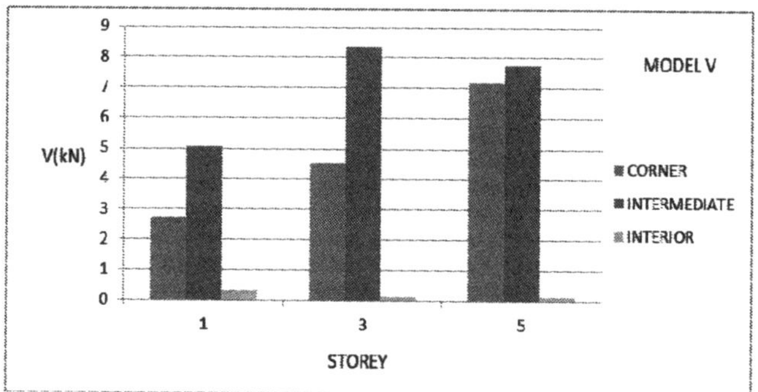

Fig. 25 Variation of Shear

(c) AXIAL FORCES(P): Interior columns have attracted high axial forces and they decreased by about 50% from 1ststorey to 3rdstorey and 86% from 3rd to 5thstorey. Similarly, corner and intermediate column decrease of 10% and 80% respectively from 1ststorey to 3rdstorey and they have minor variations from 3rd to 5thstorey.

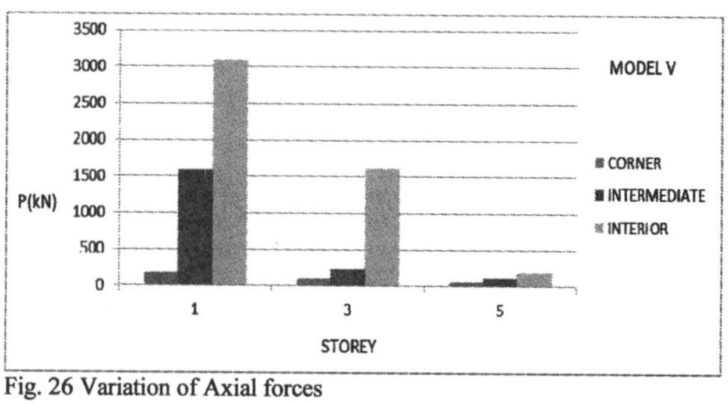

Fig. 26 Variation of Axial forces

MODEL VI: Retrofitted model with steel jacketing closer to field practice.

(a) BENDING MOMENTS:

(i) Absolute maximum moments(M): Moments for all the columns, at 3rd and 5thstorey are negligible while at 1ststorey all the columns having high absolute maximum moments (~600 kN-m).There were, of cause, slight differences in the magnitudes of these moments.

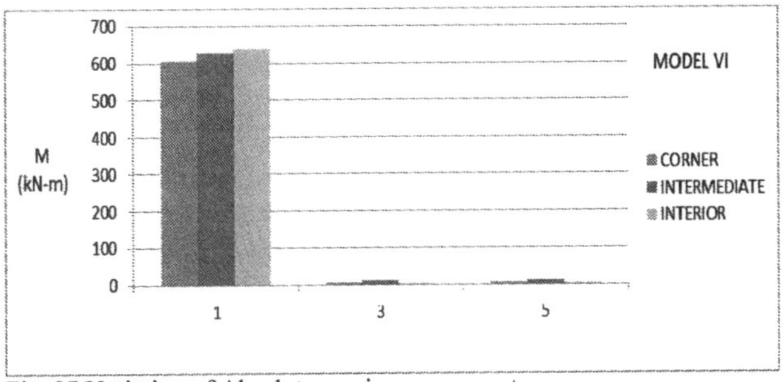

Fig. 27 Variation of Absolute maximum moments

(ii) Moments in X-direction(Mx): For all the floors viz.,1st,3rd,5th floors, absolute maximum moments occurred in X-direction only. Hence, the trends remained same as explained earlier. There are minor variations in the 1ststorey moments in all columns.

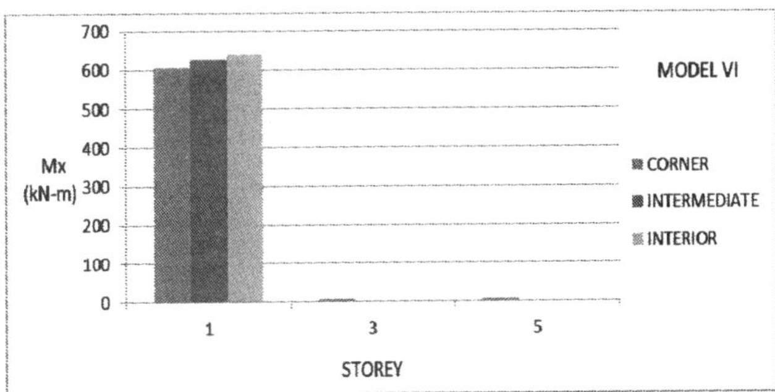

Fig. 28 Variation of Moments in X direction

(iii) Moments in Y-direction(My): Intermediate columns are showing higher moment values in all the stories while interior columns are having least moments. Moments in corner columns increased by 50% from 1st to 3rdstorey and remained same in 3rd and 5thstorey.

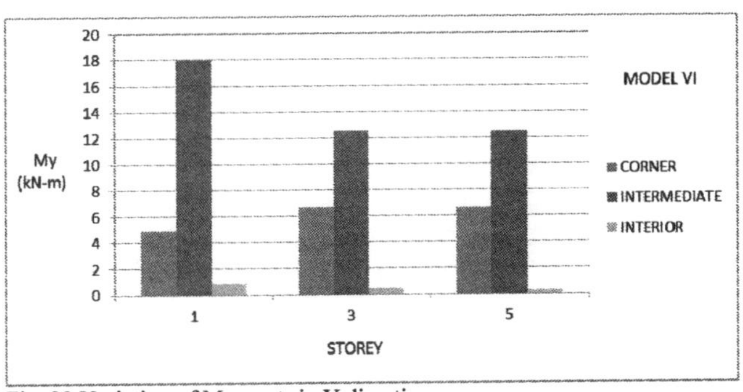

Fig. 29 Variation of Moments in Y direction

(b) SHEARS(V): Intermediate columns are having high shears in all storeys (viz.,1st,3rd,5th storeys)while the interior columns, the least. Corner column increased 25% from 1st to 3rdstorey and 35% from 3rd to 5thstorey.

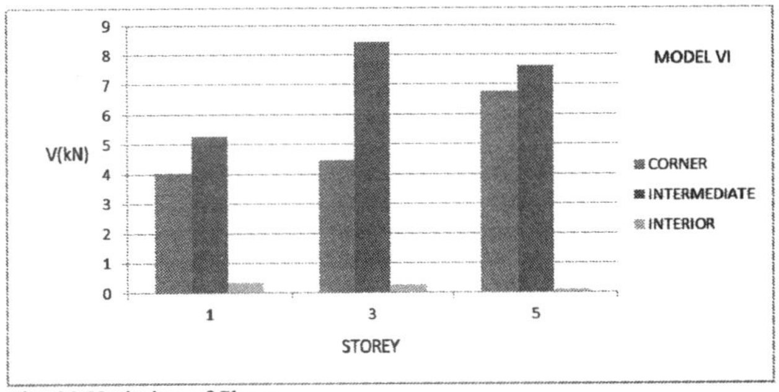

Fig. 30 Variation of Shear

(c) Axial forces(P): Interior columns are having higher axial forces in all storieswhile the corner columns have lower values in all stories. Intermediate columns have shown decrease of 86% from 1st to 3rdstorey and 50% from 3rd to 5thstorey.

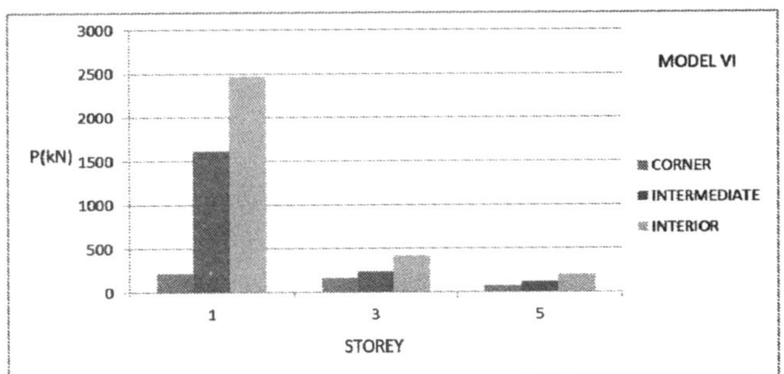

Fig. 31 Variation of Axial forces

MODEL VII: Retrofitted model with FRP jacketing closer to field practice(150 spacing with 16 connectors alround).

(a) BENDING MOMENTS:

(i) Absolute maximum moments(M): Interior columns have high absolute maximum moments in all stories. Intermediate and interior column showing a decrease in moments of approximately 44% from 1ststorey to 3rdstorey and 20% from 3rd to 5thstorey. Corner column have shown a decrease of 62% from 1st to 3rdstorey and 83% from 3rd to 5thstorey.

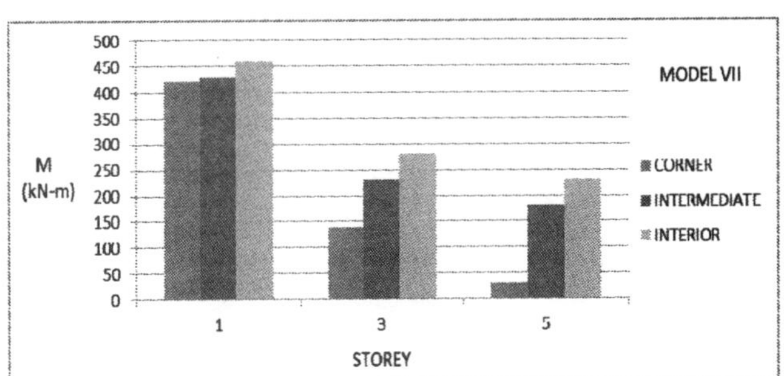

Fig. 32 Variation of Absolute maximum moments

(ii) Moments in X-direction(Mx): For all the floors viz.,1st,3rd,5th floors, absolute maximum moments occurred in X-direction only. Hence, the trends remained same as explained earlier.

(iii) Moments in Y-direction(My): Intermediate columns are having higher moments while corner columns the least moments in all the stories. Moments in interior column decreased by 30% from 1st to 3rdstorey and 88% from 3rd to 5thstorey.

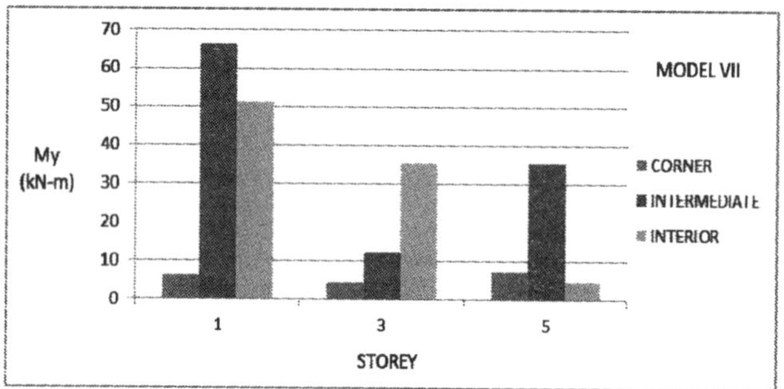

Fig. 33 Variation of Moments in Y-direction

(b) SHEARS(V): Interior columns are having least shears and intermediate columns have shown highest values. Corner columns have shown gradual increase in shear from 1st to 5thstorey.

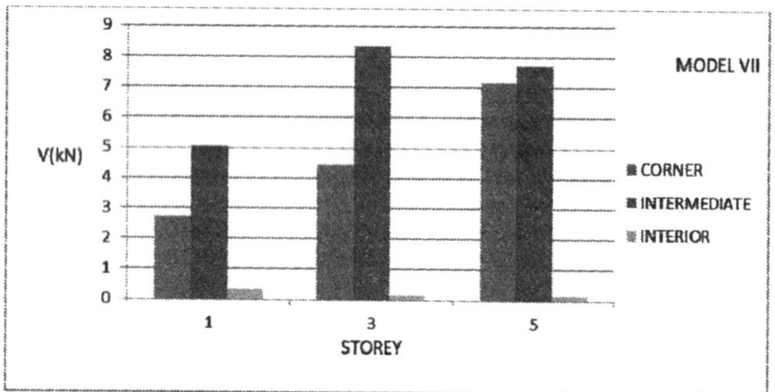

Fig. 34 Variation of Shears

(c) AXIAL FORCES (P): Interior columns are having higher axial forces in all stories while corner columns the least. Axial force decreased by 86% for intermediate column and 50% for interior column from 1st to 3rdstorey. The values were negligible for all the columns in the 5thstorey.

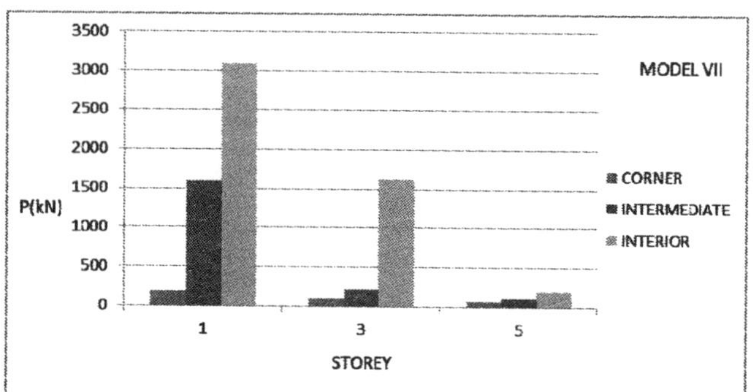

Fig. 35 Variation of Axial forces

RESPONSE OF THE BUILDING:

It is seen that the steel jacketing model IV is quite influencing in controlling the response of the total building. The time period was maximum for this model (0.11 sec), with the critical mode occurring in the 14th mode. The top storey displacement was also minimumfor this model indicating the better dynamic performance. FRP jacketing (model V) was least performing with highest top storey displacement (105.7mm) and time period values(0.15 sec) [1].

IX. COMPARISION OF VARIOUS MODELS FOR ELEMENT RESPONSE(CORNER COLUMNS)

(a) Bending moments:

(i) Absolute maximum moments (M): Among all models the model 2(column size increase model) have higher values for the corner columns at 1st and 5thstoreys. Steel jacketing gave the least values in all floors. This graph is drawn for corner column(C1).It shows that model 6(steel jacketing modelled closer to field practice) increased absolute maximum moment about 83% compared to model 3(steel jacketing modelled normally) at storey 1.Model 7 (Retrofitted model with FRP jacketing closer to field practice) have absolute maximum moments increased 5% compared with model 5 (Retrofitted model with FRP jacketing modelled normally).

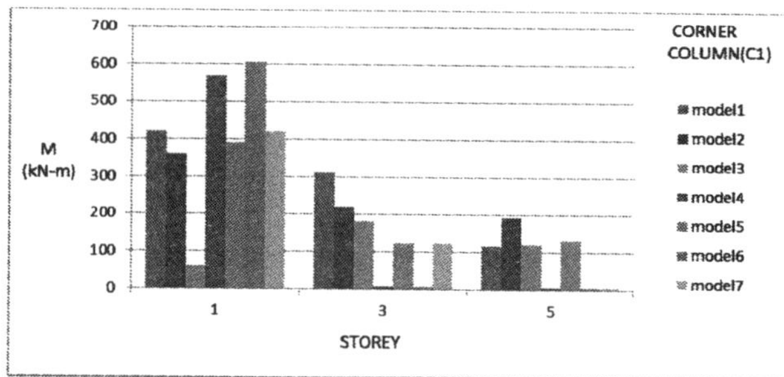

Fig. 36Variation of Absolute maximum moments

(ii) MOMENT (Mx): Again for moments in X-direction, second model has attracted greater moments with the maximum occuring in the 1st floor and reducing about 60% in the 3rd floor and 67% in the 5th floor. Model 4(steel jacketing modelled normally) has less moments than the model 6(steel jacketing modelled closer to field practice). All the other models are having moments similar to absolute maximum moments that explained earlier.

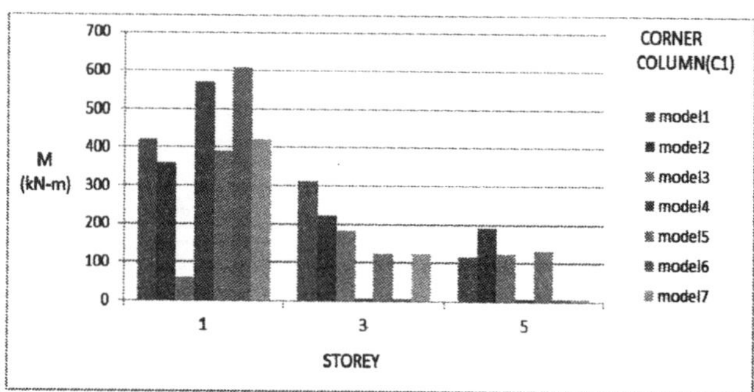

Fig. 37 Variation of Moments in X direction

(iii) MOMENT(My): Model 5(i.e. FRP model)has attracted greater moments in Y-direction, the absolute maximum occurring in the 3rd floor for the model 1. Model 3 at 3rd floor has more moments than at that occurred in 1st floor. At 5thfloor, for all models are having almost same moments.

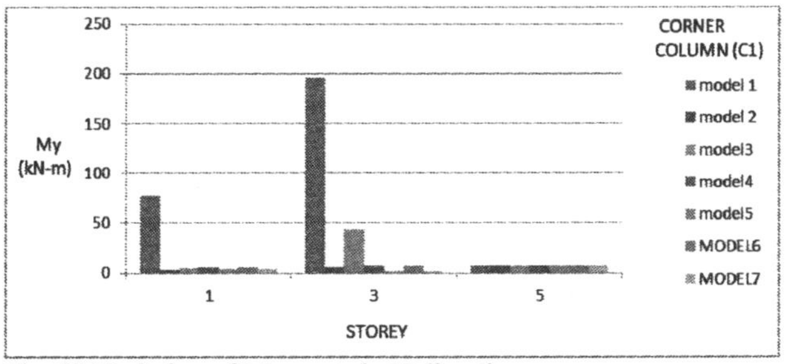

Fig. 38 Variation of Moments in Y direction

(iv) SHEAR(V): More or less a uniform trend was shown for all floors in all models except for the 2nd model(RC column m increased size)which has shown greater moments in the 1st floor(~18 kNm)in all other floors the value was drastically reduced and remained more or less uniform.

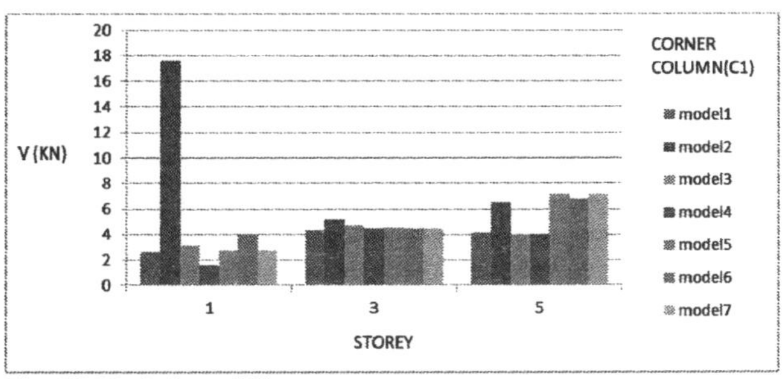

Fig. 39 Variation of Shear

(v) AXIALFORCES(P): For model 1 the shear force has higher value(1400KN) at storey1 while the model 1 and model 3 has higher values at 3rd storey. At 5thstorey, all the models are least compare to 1st and 3rdstoreys. Model 3(RC jacketing modelled closer to field practice) at 3rdstorey has highly increased axial force compared to at storey 1.It seen that model 2(retrofitted model with increased column size) has axial forces gradually decreasing from 1st to 5thstorey respectively.

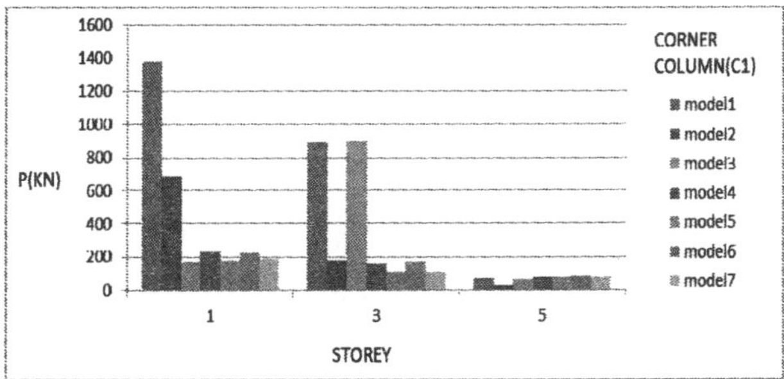

Fig. 40 Variation of Axial forces

MODE SHAPES

In the normal RCC column model in which the columns of ground storey failed and indicated the requirement for retrofitting, the structure was showing greater time period(0.168) while the same got reduced in model-II (0.09) in which the columns were modelled with increased cross section. This could be due to the increased stiffness of the structure in model-II. Again the time period increased to 0.11 due to the increased flexibility of the structure, modelled closer to actual practice in model-III. For models showing steel jacketing (model-IV and model-VI), also the time period increased from 0.104(for model-IV) to 0.134(for model-VI).However, there was not much difference shown in time periods for model-V(0.152) and model-VII(0.154),used for FRP jacketing [1].

In all, an comparision of models for Concrete, Steel and FRP jacketing, it is observed that the dynamic characteristics of the structure greatly varied in steel jacketing while it remained almost same in Concrete and FRP jacketing. However, critical mode shape shifted for concrete jacketing from mode 10 to mode 14, for steel jacketing from mode 11 to mode 12 and for FRP jacketing mode 10 to mode 12.

MODEL I: Normal RCC column(400mmX400mm) for zone-III.

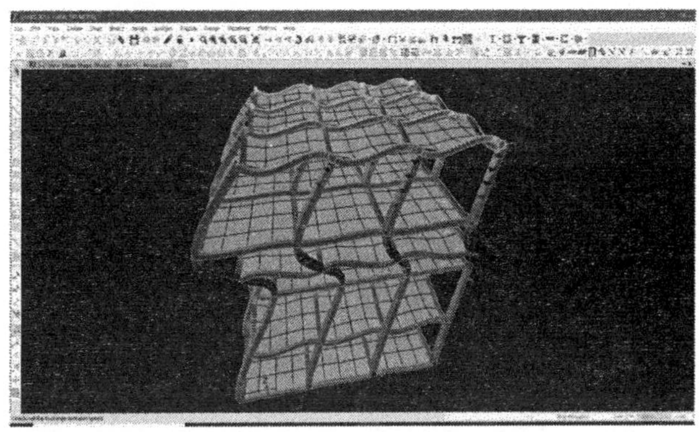

Fig. 41 Mode shape for model I at mode 11-Time Period 0.168

MODEL II: Retrofitted model with increased column size(RCC column 600mmX600mm).

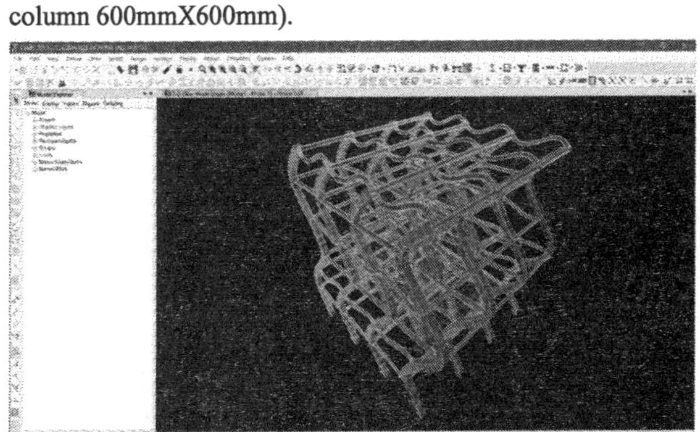

Fig. 42 Mode shape for model II at mode 11-Time Period 0.09

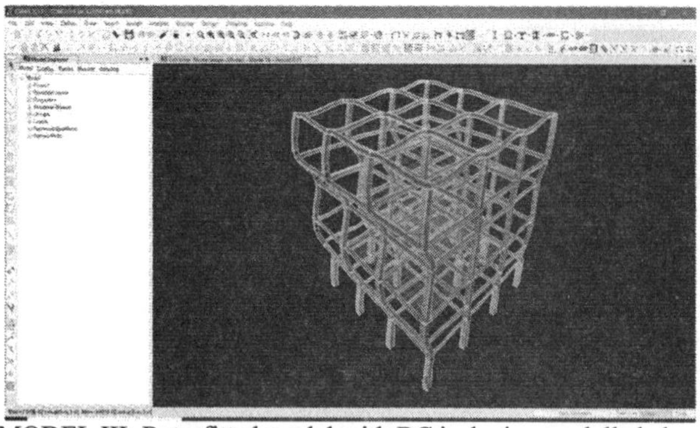

MODEL III: Retrofitted model with RC jacketing modelled closer to field practice (400mmX400mm existing column with a RC jacket of 100mm alround).

Fig. 43 Mode shape for model III at mode 14-Time Period 0.11

MODEL IV: Retrofitted model with steel jacketing modelled normally.

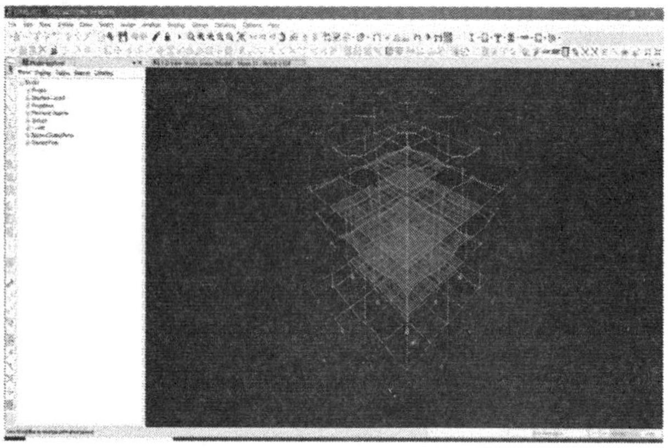

Fig. 44 Mode shape for model IV at mode 11-Time Period 0.104

MODEL-V: Retrofitted model with FRP jacketing modelled normally.

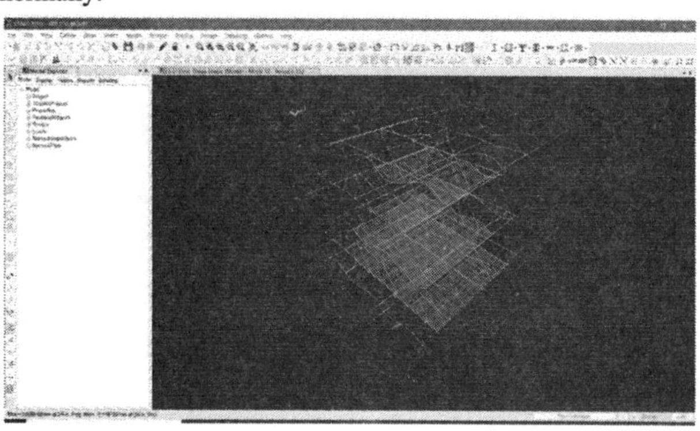

Fig.45 Mode shape for model V at mode 10-Time Period 0.152

MODEL-VI: Retrofitted model with steel jacketing closer to field practice.

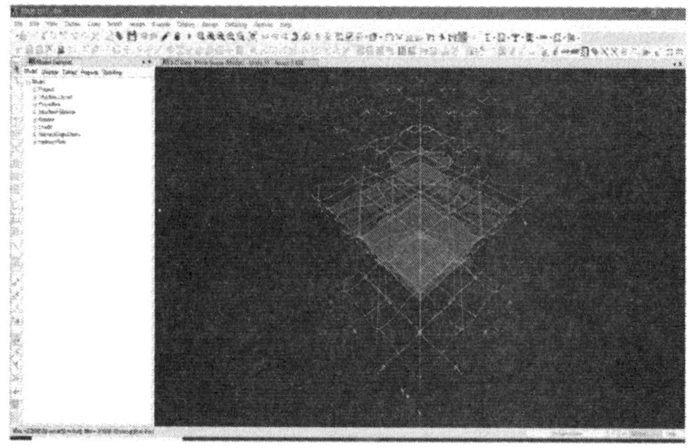

Fig. 46 Mode shape for mode VI at mode 12-Time Period 0.134

MODEL-VII: Retrofitted model with FRP jacketing closer to field practice.

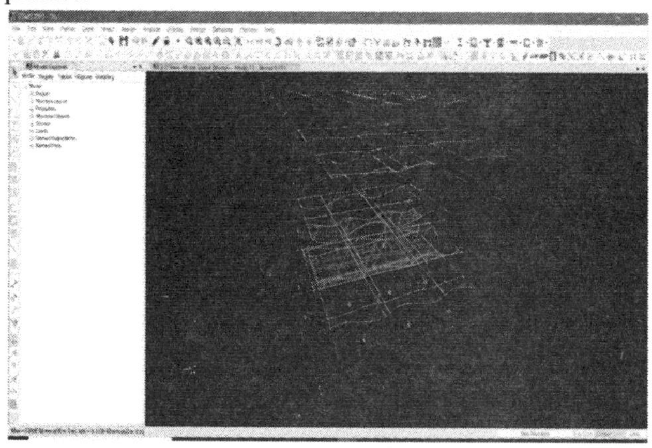

Fig. 47 Mode shape for model VII at mode 12-Time Period 0.154

X. CONCLUSIONS

Based on the study conducted in this work with the limited scope mentioned, the following conclusions could be drawn.

(1) In all the models the absolute maximum moments were occurring in 1st storey (Ground floor) columns.

(2) Among all the three materials chosen, the influence of modeling was found to be very prominent in RC jacketing and nominal in FRP jacketing.

(3) In RC jacketing, moments drastically reduced in the columns with proposed modeling while shears and axial loads increased. In steel jacketing, shears reduced and axial forces remained almost same. For FRP jacketing the influence of modeling was negligible.

(4) Comparing the normally adopted model with the proposed model for all the three materials

(a) For RCC jacketing: Absolute maximum bending moments were reduced by 60% while the maximum axial forces increased from 700kN(for corner columns) to 1600(for an interior column).Max shear got increased from 18kN(for corner) to 180kN(for interior column).

(b) For Steel jacketing: Absolute maximum, Bending moment and maximum axial force remained same while the max shears reduced from 180kN to 8kN.

(c) For FRP jacketing: The maximum moments, shear and axial forces almost remained same for normal modeling and proposed modeling(with 150 mm spacing of ties and 8 connectors). However, using 16 connectors, for the same spacing of ties, there was a marginal increase (about 4%) in the moments, shears and axial loads.

(5) Although the axial loads increased in RC jacketing with the proposed modeling method, they are still very much less than those found in Steel and FRP jacketing. Hence, it can be said that the seismic performance of RC jacketing is bettering with proper modeling.

REFERENCES:

[1] PavanKolli (2018)"Influence of modelling on the effectiveness of column jacketing in the seismic performance of a RC framed building –A comparative study using three alternative materials(RCC, Steel and FRP)", A dissertation submitted to Osmania University.

[2] Gnanasekaran, k. (2008) Seismic Retrofit of Reinforced Concrete Columns in Buildings using Concrete Jacket. Ph.D. Thesis, Department of Civil Engineering, Indian Institute of Technology Madras, Chennai, India.

[3] Li, J., Gong, J., and Wang, L.(July 01, 2009). Seismic Behaviorof Corrosion-damaged Reinforced Concrete Columns Strengthened Using Combined Carbon Fiber-reinforced Polymer and Steel Jacket. Construction and Building Materials, 23, 7, 2653-2663.

[4] Niroomandi A, Maheri A, Maheri, MR, Mahini SS, (2010). Seismic performance of ordinary RC frames retrofitted at joints by FRP sheets, Engineering Structures,32(8):2326-2336.

Application of 3D Printing for Building Prototype Model of Osmania University Arts College – A Case Study

L.Siva Rama Krishna[1], Aravind Reddy.G[2],Bhaskar Sudhakanth.V[3], Sriram Venkatesh[4]

[1,2,3,4]*Dept. of Mechanical Engineering, University College of Engineering, Osmania University, Hyderabad – 500 007*

[1]lsrkou@gmail.com
[2]aravindreddy1993@gmail.com
[3]bhaskar9295@gmail.com
[4]venkatmech@yahoo.com

***Abstract—3D printing* or additive manufacturing is the process of adding one layer over the other to build complex three dimensional solid objects from a 3D CAD model data, CT or MRI scan data, or by a model data created from a 3D object digitizing systems. According to the McKinsey Global Institute report of 2013, it was recognized as one of the most important disruptive technology among the twelve technologies that will transform life, business, and the global economy. It, has wide range of applications starting from small conceptual models like toys manufacturing to making a very big complex parts of an aircraft. The diversified fields of application include biomedical field, arts,defence, aerospace, automobile, archaeology, forensic, fashion industry, entertainment industry, architecture etc. This paper aims to present the application of 3D Printing Technology in civil engineering field. As a case study this paper discusses the methodology adopted for printing prototype model of the Iconic Osmania University(OU) Arts college building.**

***Keywords*—3D Printing, Process Chain, .STL file, Additive Manufacturing.architecture**

I. Introduction

3D printing or additive manufacturing is a manufacturing technology that build complex three dimensional objects by adding layer-by-layer rather than through molding or subtractive techniques such as machining. The input for building the model may be a 3D CAD model or a CT or MRI Scan data or a model data obtained by scanning a 3D object by digitizing systems. The process chain of 3D printing involves 3D Modeling, Data Conversion and Transmission, Checking and Preparing, Building and Post processing.

In the first step, the 3D Model is created by using any 3D CAD modelling package like Creo, Unigraphics, CATIA, SOLID WORKS etc or CT and MRI scan data or model data obtained by scanning 3D object using digitizing systems. In the next step, the 3D model is converted into STL (STereoLithography) file format. The STL file format approximates the surfaces of the model into tiny triangles. The STL file is then transferred to the additive manufacturing System's Computer. In the third step, the errors in the STL files like holes, gaps, cracks, shell-puncture etc. are eliminated by specialized software. Once the STL files are verified to be error-free the required part is built in the additive manufacturing machine. The final step involves cleaning, excess elements adhered with the part by sanding, polishing or painting for better surface finish or aesthetic appearance.

According to The McKinsey Global Institute (MGI) report [1] 3D Printing is one of the most prominent disruptive technologies among the twelve technological advances that will transform life, business, and the global economy in the near future. The reason for 3D Printing to be called a disruptive technology is because it has diversified applications in many fields like in automobile, aerospace, biomedical, Forensic, Film industry, archeology and architecture. Krishna et.al.[2] discussed the application of 3D printing in biomedical field for Zygomatic fractures. VivekManoharan et.al. [3] presents the application of 3D printing in faster prototype development for design visualisation, performance studies and personalisation in the sports footwear industry. Dina R. Howeidy and Zaina Arafat [4] discussed the impact of in the discipline of Architecture and Interior Design.Sunil and Abdullah A. Sheikh [5] in their paper presents the application of 3D printing processes in aerospace. They discussed the materials developed specially for aerospace applications. Alyson Vanderploeg et.al. [6] discussed the application of 3D printing technology in the fashion industry. They presented five types of 3D printing technologies i.e. stereolithography, selective laser sintering, fused deposition modelling, PolyJet, and binder jetting that have great potential in the fashion industry.

II. Problem Statement

The aim of this paper is to present the application of 3D printing in civil engineering field for developing prototype models of complex building structures, stadiums, city planning etc. This helps the civil engineers to explain clearly the details of the entire project to the clients before it is actually executed on the field. As a case study this paper presents the application of 3D Printing for building prototype model of Iconic Osmania University arts college building.

III. Research and Methodology

Fig. 1. Illustrates the research methodology adopted to solve the problem defined in the earlier section.

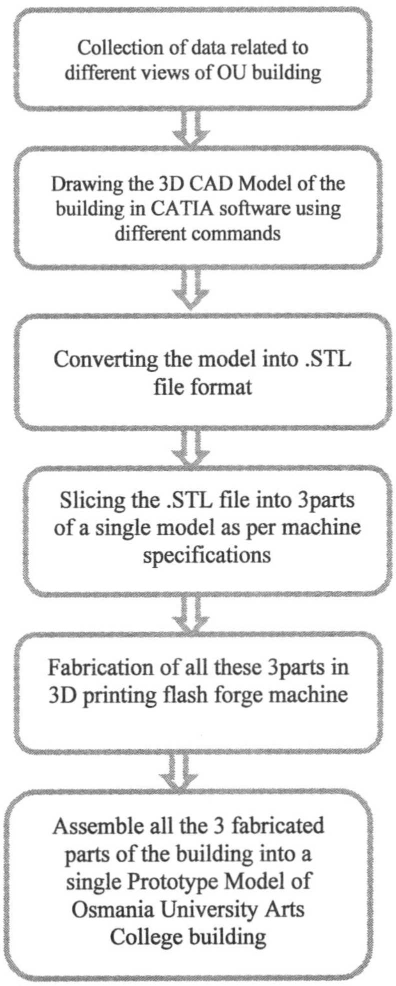

Fig.1. Flow chart showing the research methodology

A. Collection of data

Collection of data from different views of the building has been captured and the outline of the building is seen from google earth. Fig 2 shows the front portion of the building which could help in understanding the detail structure and the projection and it also helps in the view of the dome with a draft followed by a connecting the two end as seen.

Fig 2: Front view of OU Arts College

Fig 3 shows the side view of the building sculpture which gives an idea to develop conceptualize design of the product.

Fig 3: Side view of OU Arts College

Fig 4 shows the top view of the OU arts college from google earth which helps in the outline view of the building

Fig 4: Top view of OU Arts College Captured from google earth

These views help in better understanding of the product design to develop a drafting model. From this the approximate data related to the shape of the building is obtained.

B. Developing 3D CAD model in Catia software

Using the above data dimensions of the building are assumed and then the 3D CAD model of the building is built in CATIA software using different modules like sketcher and part design modules.

First the sketch is to be done to define the axis of plane by using commands such as profile, operation, view, and constraint. Fig 5 describes the sketch based command used for this operation.

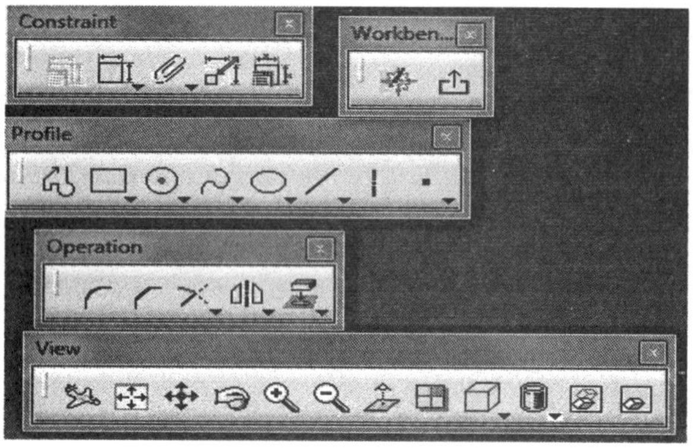

Fig 5: Sketch based commands

Next the sketched part is to be extruded by using a pad command in the part design module by exiting the sketcher work bench. The pad can be defined in sketch based features where pad and pocket can be specified under the pad specification dialogue box which helps in specifying the length to pad and the same procedure is followed for the pocket. Fig 6 shows the command used for this operation.

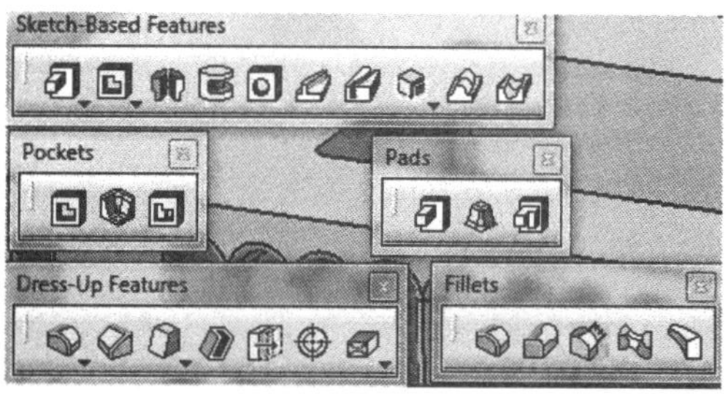

Fig 6 (a): Commands used in pad operation

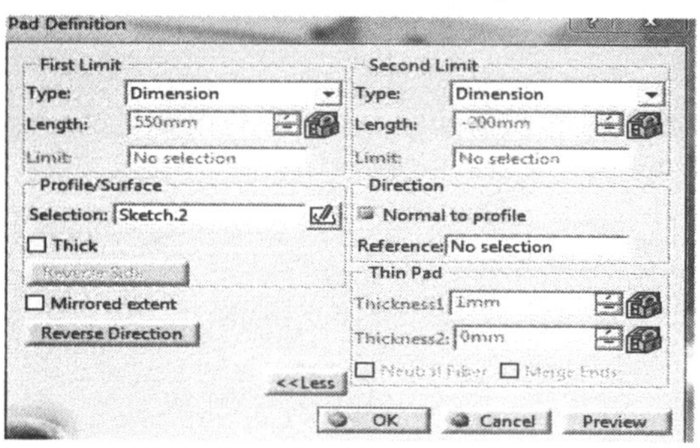

Fig 6 (b): Pad Definition

By applying transformation and mirror features to the model more number of pockets and pads can be added to the model which helps in decreasing the time for modeling. Fig 7 shows the commands used for transformation feature.

Fig 7: Transformation Features

By applying the draft angle command to the centre portion of the building the feature highlighted with blue colour showing the main entrance of the building can be created. Fig 8 shows the application of draft angle to the center portion of the building

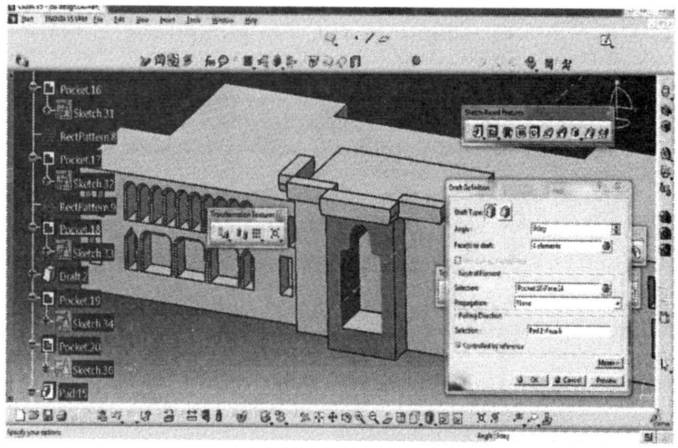

Fig 8: Application of draft angle to the center portion

After the Majority of the design is completed fillet and chamfer commands are applied to the corners and edges of the main portion of the building where ever required to obtain the desired CAD Model. Fig 9, 10 and 11illustrates the structure of the developed building of OU Arts College in different view in CATIA v5 software.

Fig 9: OU Arts College in CATIA v5 software in front view

Fig 10: Side view of OU Arts College in CATIA v5 software

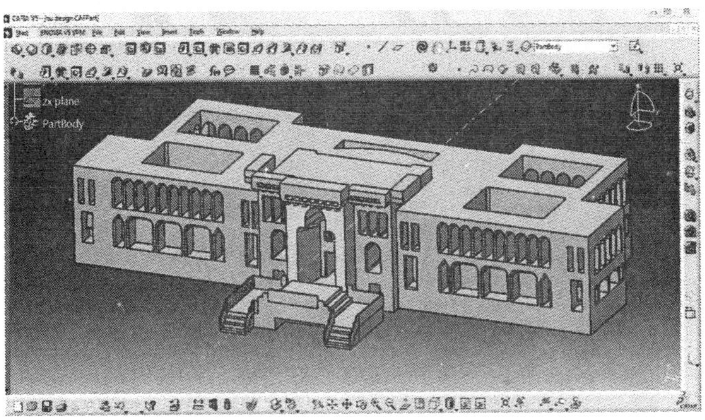

Fig 11: Isometric view of OU Arts College in CATIA v5 software

C. Conversion of CAD Model into .STL File format

After the CAD Model is developed, the file is saved in the. STL file format using save as command in CATIA software. STL file format is the defacto standard accepted by most of the 3D printing machines to build the prototypes. Fig. 12 illustrates the .STL file format of the Osmania University Arts college building opened in Flash Print software, which is the Flash Forge 3D printer machine software.

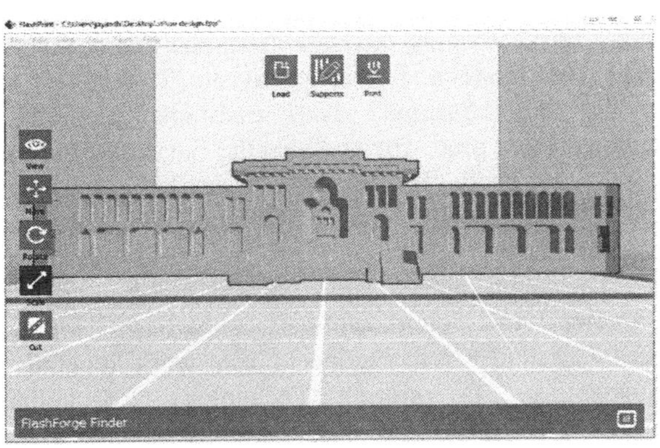

Fig 12: STL file to be printed

As the build volume of the machine is 140 x 140 x 140 mm, it can be seen from the above figure that the developed model is out of the platform hence it has to be sliced.

D. Slicing the Model

The .STL file which has been loaded into flash forge 3d printer software knows as flash print has been sliced into 3 different blocks. Fig 13 shows the slicing of the model

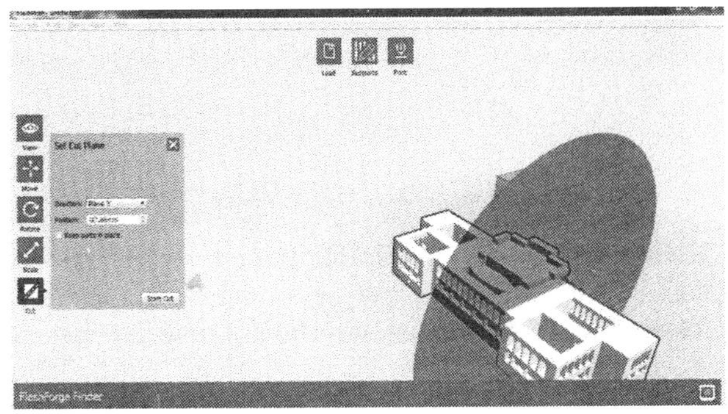

Fig 13: Sliced model

E. Fabrication of the parts

After Slicing the model into 3 different blocks, three different blocks have been fabricated according to the specification given in flash forge software with a layer thickness of 0.18mm, infill density as 15% and fill pattern as hexagonal and additional raft is been provided for better support of the design as shown in Fig 14 represents the fabrications specifications whereas Fig. 15 shows the supports generated in the software before it is sent for building the blocksin green color.

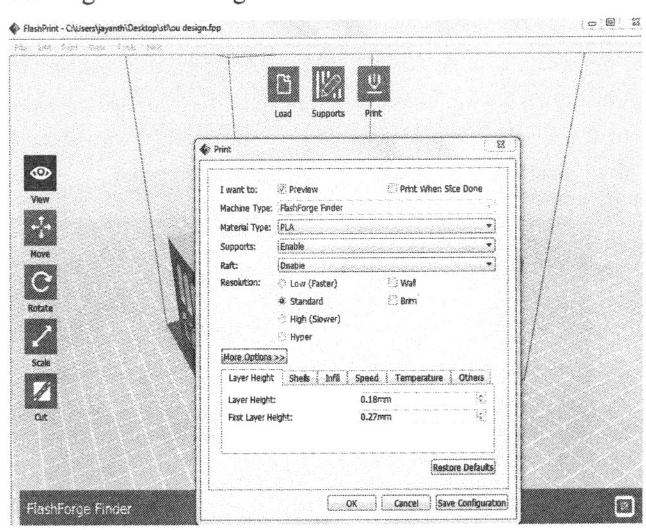

Fig 14: Fabrication specifications

Fig 15: Supports Structures for a Part

Before printing the blocks the print time and the raw material to be consumed can be estimated in flash print software. Fig. 16 shows the estimation of time and material consumed for building the centre block of the building, which is found to be 7 hours 5 minutes and 36.27 meters of wire respectively. The material used for fabrication is PolyLactic Acid (PLA).

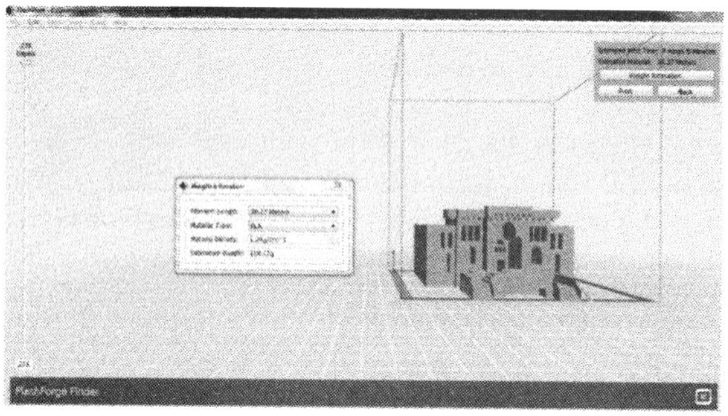

Fig: 16 Time and material Estimation

Once the above process is completed the g-code file is sent to the Flash Forge 3D printing machine. Fig.17 illustrates the block being built in the Flash Forge 3D printer.

Fig: 17 Building the part in Flash Forge 3D printer

The same procedure is adopted for building the remaining two blocks i.e. left and right blocks. For building the right and left blocks the time consumed for each block is 6 hours 50 minutes and the material consumed is 35.07 meters of wire. Hence the total time taken and material consumed for building the three blocks is 21 hours 15 minutes and 107.42 meters of wire. Once the three parts are built then as a post process they are painted and then glued together using fevikwik adhesive to obtain the final Iconic Osmania University Arts College Building. Fig. 18 shows the prototype model of the Iconic Osmania University Arts College Building.

Fig.18. Prototype Model of the OU Arts College Building

IV. CONCLUSIONS

3D Printing or Additive Manufacturing is an emerging innovative technology which has potential applications in diversified fields. The present paper focused on its application in civil engineering for developing the prototype model of complex Osmania University Arts college building structure. It was found from this case study that the prototype model of such a complex structure can be built approximately in 21 hours 15 minutes i.e. within a day excluding the time consumed for developing the 3D CAD model and other field visits. This is very less than the time consumed using traditional methods of manufacturing a prototype and also the finish and accuracy is also very good. This type of technology helps civil engineers to physically visualize the final 3D model of their structures before they actually execute the project on the field. The main aim of this work is to highlight the importance of interdisciplinary approach wherein, Mechanical and Civil Engineers can work together in implementing 3D printing Technology for building complex structures and also in city planning thus contributing to the societal needs. The present work can be further extended by exactly measuring the entire dimensions of the buildings in the Osmania university campus with the help of drones, so that the miniature model of the entire university campus can be developed with more accuracy.

References

[1] Mckinsey Global Institute Report, Disruptive technologies: Advances that will transform life, business and the global economy, May 2013

[2] L. Siva Ramakrishna, BhaskarSudhakanthVemulakonda, AbhinandPotturi, "Evaluation of Zygomatic Complex Fractures Based on Three Point Fixation Technique using Additive Manufacturing", International Journal of Scientific Research in Science and Technology(IJSRST),Print ISSN : 2395-6011, Online ISSN : 2395-602X, Volume 4, Issue 2, pp.1092-1100, January-February 2018.

[3] VivekManoharan, SiawMeng Chou, Steph Forrester, Gin Boay Chai &PuiWah Kong(2013), "Application of additive manufacturing techniques in sports footwear,Virtual and Physical Prototyping",8:4,249-252,DOI: 10.1080/17452759.2013.862.

[4] Dina R. Howeidy and Zaina Arafat," "The Impact of Using 3D Printing on Model Making Quality and Cost in the Architectural Design Projects" International Journal of Applied Engineering Research ISSN 0973-4562 Volume 12, Number 6 (2017) pp. 987-994

[5] Sunil C. Joshi & Abdullah A. Sheikh, "3D printing in aerospace and its long-term sustainability", Journal of Virtual and Physical Prototyping,
10:4,175-185, 2015DOI: 10.1080/17452759.2015.1111519

[6] Alyson Vanderploeg, Seung-Eun Lee & Michael Mamp, "The application of 3D printing technology in the fashion industry",International Journal of Fashion Design, Technology and Education,10:2,170-179, 2016, DOI: 10.1080/17543266.2016.122335.

Development of Artificial Neural Network Model for Geopolymer Concrete

G.Sushma[1], D.Annapurna[2]

[1]*M.E scholar, Civil Engineering Department, UCE (A), Osmania University*

[2]*Assistant Professor,, Civil Engineering Department, University College of Engineering, Osmania University, Hyderabad- 07*

[1]sushmagudepu@gmail.com
[2]annapurna_ouce@yahoo.com

***Abstract*—Environmental pollution is the major problem faced in today's world. Concrete made using geopolymer technology is environmental friendly material and could be considered as part of the sustainable development. Even though aggregate constitutes major volume in geopolymer concrete, only limited study related to this parameter influence on geopolymer concrete has been reported. The present study is carried out to understand the influence of different parameters on the strength of geopolymer concrete. Also an effort has been made to develop mathematical model with the help of data techniques, namely, Artificial Neural Networks (ANNs) model. The data for analysis and model development was collected at 7 and 28-day curing periods through experiments conducted in the laboratory under standard controlled conditions. These parameters were then input into Mat lab, along with their measured compressive strength, to create artificial neural networks (ANNs) model. The comparison for the actual strength values and predicted values is done to obtain minimum percentage error. Results show that ANN is a suitable model to predict the compressive strength of geopolymer concrete with varying parameters of molarity, fly ash, GGBS and aggregate.**

Key words – Artificial neural network, Compressive strength, Fly ash, Geopolymer concrete, Ground granulated blast furnace slag

I. Introduction

To produce environmental friendly concrete, the cement should be replace with the industrial by products such as fly-ash, GGBS (Ground granulated blast furnace slag) etc. In this respect, the new technology geo-polymer concrete is emerging as a promising technique. The term geo-polymer was first coined by Davidovits [1] to represent a broad range of materials characterized by chains or networks of inorganic molecules. Geo-polymers are chains or networks of mineral molecules linked with co-valent bonds. Geopolymer is produced by a polymeric reaction of alkaline liquid with source material of geological origin or by product material such as GGBS. Geo-polymers have the chemical composition similar to zeolites, but they can be formed an amorphous structure. For the binding of materials, the silica and alumina present in the source material are induced by alkaline activators. The most common alkaline liquid used in the geo-polymerization is the combination of Sodium hydroxide/ Potassium hydroxide and Sodium silicate/ Potassium silicate. This combination increases the rate of reaction. All the Al-Si minerals are more soluble in NaOH solution than in KOH solution. The geo-polymer concrete has two limitations such as the delay in setting time and the necessity of heat curing to gain strength. These two limitations of geo-polymer concrete mix was eliminated by replacing of fly ash by GGBS on mass basis with alkaline liquids resulted in Geo-polymer Concrete Composition. Ground granulated blast furnace slag (GGBS) is a by-product from the blast-furnaces used to make iron. During the process, slag was formed and it is then dried and ground to a fine powder.

This study presents an effort to apply neural network-based system identification techniques to predict the compressive strength of concrete based on concrete mix proportions. For this aim, a computer program is developed using neural network design (NND) toolbox in MATLAB from the Math Works.

Artificial neural network (ANN) docs not need a specific equation form; instead it needs sufficient input-output data. It can continuously retrain the new data, so that it can conveniently adapt to new data. Modeling with ANN is much simpler because, although a neural network captures the mathematical relationships in its collection of interconnections between its nodes, no formal mathematical rule or formulae are used or observed within the model.

Using this program, a neural network model with two hidden layers is constructed, trained, and tested using the available test data of different sets gathered from the laboratory [2]. The data used in ANN model are arranged in a format of input parameters that cover the GGBS content, aggregates ratio and molarities. The proposed ANN model predicts the 7th and 28th day compressive strength of geopolymer concrete.

II. Experimental Program

The experimental program was designed to study the effect of different input parameters on compressive strength of geopolymer concrete and to predict the experimental value in MAT LAB software using artificial neural networks and theoretical results are compared with the experimental values to obtain minimum percentage error. In the total mix cases alkaline liquid to fly ash ratio is maintained as 0.5. As per the literature the parameters such as percent GGBS variation, molarity of NaOH, total aggregate percentage will have influence on geopolymer concrete[3,4,5,6,7]. As the geopolyemer concrete strength is influenced by various parameters, a mathematical model is prepared with four input parameters and one output parameter. Details of specimen and test conducted in the study are shown in Table I.

TABLE I
DETAILS OF SPECIMEN

Size of specimen	Type of test	Total no. of specimens casted for each mix
100 x 100 x100 mm	Compression test	12

A. Materials Used

The following materials are used to produce geopolymerconcrete

- Fly Ash (FA)
- Ground Granulated Blast Furnace Slag (GGBS)
- Fine aggregate
- Coarse aggregate
- Sodium hydroxide
- Sodium silicate
- Super-plasticizer

The properties of the materials used are given in the Table II and Table III.

TABLE II
PROPERTIES OFFLY ASH ANDGGBS

S. No	Test conducted	Fly ash	GGBS
1.	Specific gravity	2.08	2.88
2.	Bulk density(gm/cc)	1.16	1230
3.	Fineness(m^2/kg)	290	375
4.	Initial and final setting time(minutes)	30 & 240	170 & 308

TABLE III
PROPERTIES OF FINE ANDCOARSE AGGREGATE

S.No	Test conducted	Fine aggregate	Coarse aggregate
1.	Specific gravity	2.5	2.6
2.	Fineness modulus	2.12	6.9
3.	Water absorption	4.6%	0.03%
4.	Density in compacted state(gm/cc)	1.78	1.58
5.	Density in loose state(gm/cc)	1.62	1.5

B. Procedure for Mixing of Materials

The first step is to mix the alkaline solution a day before casting the specimen. The next step is to gather all of the dry materials required for each mix. All of the dry materials are then mixed together for one minute in pan mixer. After this, the alkaline mix and extra water were added tothe mixer and mixed together until all of the dry materials were combined into the wet mixture. A slump test and compaction factor is performed on fresh mix. The fresh concrete was then cast into specimens, compacted using vibrating table, as shown in Figure 1.

Figure 1 Specimens on vibrating table

The specimens were tested for 7 and 28 days compressive strength as per IS 516: 1959. The specimens were cleaned and weight of each specimen was recorded. The specimen were kept in compression testing machine and loaded till fail as shown in Figure 2.

Figure 2 Specimen in compression testing machine

III. Artificial Neural Network Model

This model is prepared using a soft computing technique composed of simple elements which can be replaced with the customary computations which cannot solve the problems precisely. Basically, ANN consists of an input layer, one or more hidden layer(s), connected by neurons and an output layer. Each neuron receives weighted inputs from other neurons and communicates its output to other neurons through an activation function. The goal of any training algorithm is to minimize the mean square error (MSE) between predicted and observed outputs and to maintain the good generality of the network.

In the first step the data is collected through the experimental results conducted in the laboratory. The data is imported into the MATLAB workspace in the matrix format with the input parameters as input data matrix and experimental values as the target matrix. Configuration of the network is done to create the network in neural network fitting tool. The fitting tool in neural network is used to map between a dataset of numerical inputs and a set of numerical targets. The Neural Network Fitting Tool will help to select data, create and train a network, and evaluate its performance using mean square error and regression analysis[8,9,10]. Table IV shows the ranges for the input parameters given in ANN model.

TABLE IV
RANGE OF PARAMETERS

Sl.No	Parameters	Range
1.	Fly ash	100-60
2.	GGBS	0-40
3.	Aggregate	72-80
4.	Molarity	8-16

Total 162 numbers of sample data is used to prepare ANN model. Inputs 'input' is a 4x27 matrix, representing static data, i.e.27 samples of 4 elements. Targets 'target' is a 6x27 matrix, representing static data, i.e. 27 samples of 6 elements. The 27 samples data is randomly divided into three kinds of samples.

Training: Out of the 27 samples 70% of samples i.e.19 samples are given for training of the network. In the training process the network is trained for the given samples. These are presented to the network during training and the network is adjusted according to its error.

Validation: For validation 15% of the samples i.e.4 samples are used for the validation of the network. These are used to measure network generalization, and to halt training when generalization stops improving.

Testing: The testing of the network is done to 15% of the samples i.e. 4 samples are used. The samples used for the training process should not repeat during the testing process as testing is done to evaluate the network. These have no effect on training and so provide an independent measure of network performance during and after training. After selecting the data for training, validation and testing the number of hidden layers are given to train the neural network. The numbers of neurons can be changed if the network does not perform well after training. Later the network is trained to fit the inputs with the targets. The network will be trained with Levenberg-Marquardt back propagation algorithm (trainlm), unless there is not enough memory, in which case scaled conjugate gradient back propagation (trainscg) will be used.

IV. Results

A. Experimental Results

In this section the results obtained through the experiments studies and model studies are represented. Some of the results are shown in tabular format and some are shown through graphical format for better understanding. The average compressive strength with varying parameters obtained in the laboratory through the experimental studies.

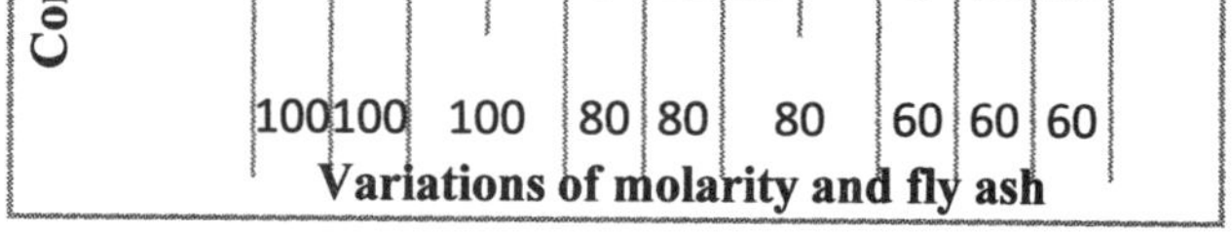

Figure 3 Variations of Molarity and Fly ash on Compressive strength

7 days compressive strength:

The influence of each individual parameter with 72%, 76% and 80% usage of aggregates are shown in figure 3, 4 and 5 respectively for compressive strength of GPC.

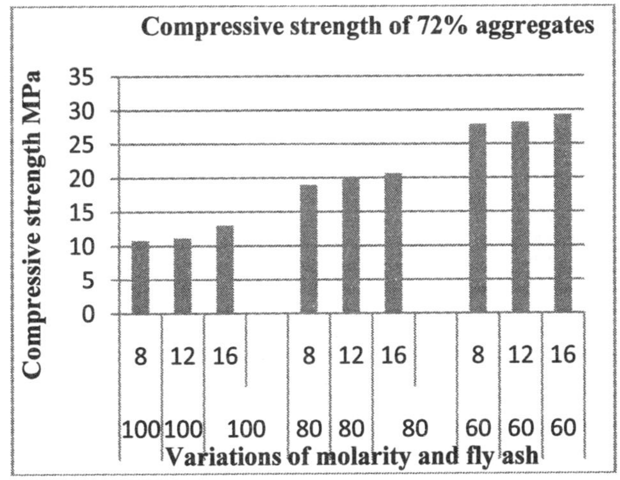

Figure 4 Variations of Molarity and Fly ash on Compressive strength

From the figure 3 to 5 depicting 7 days compressive strength with varying percentage of aggregates from 72 to 80, it has been observed that with increase in the molarity there is an increase in the strength of the GPC, as fly ash percentage decreases i.e. increase in the GGBS percentage there is an increase in the strength of GPC. For increase in the molarity with increase in the GGBS percentage the compressive strength has been increased by 1.3% for aggregates of 76%, when compared with 80% aggregate the strength has been increased by 0.9% only. So 76% aggregates has given better increase in strength for different molarities and fly ash percentages.

28 days compressive strength:

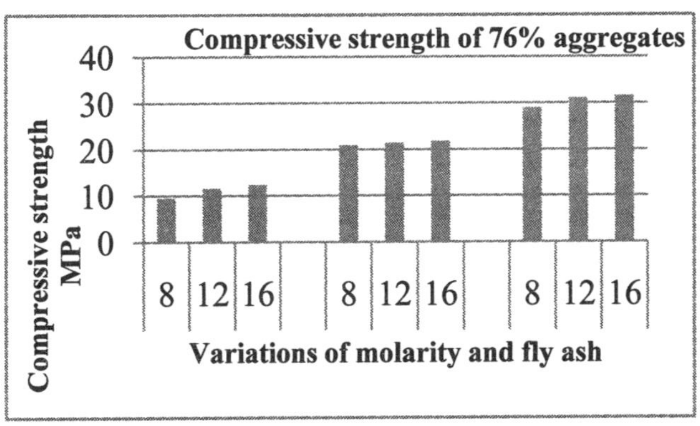

Figure 5 Variations of Molarity and Fly ash on Compressive strength

The figure 6, 7 and 8 respectively are shown for the 28 days compressive strength with varying percentages of aggregates from 72 to 80

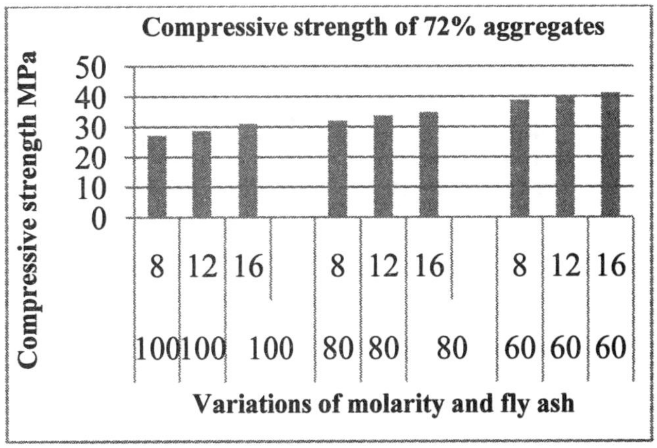

Figure 6 Variations of Molarity and Fly ash on Compressive strength

From the Figure 6 to 8 for 28 days compressive strength with varying percentage of aggregates from 72 to 80, it has been observed that with increase in the molarity there is an increase in the strength of the GPC, as fly ash percentage decreases i.e. increase in the GGBS percentage there is an increase in the strength of GPC. For increase in the molarity with increase in the GGBS percentage the compressive strength has found to be increased by 1.58% for aggregates of 76%, when compared with 80% aggregate the strength has been increased by 0.37% only. So 76% aggregates has given better increase in strength for different molarities and fly ash percentages.

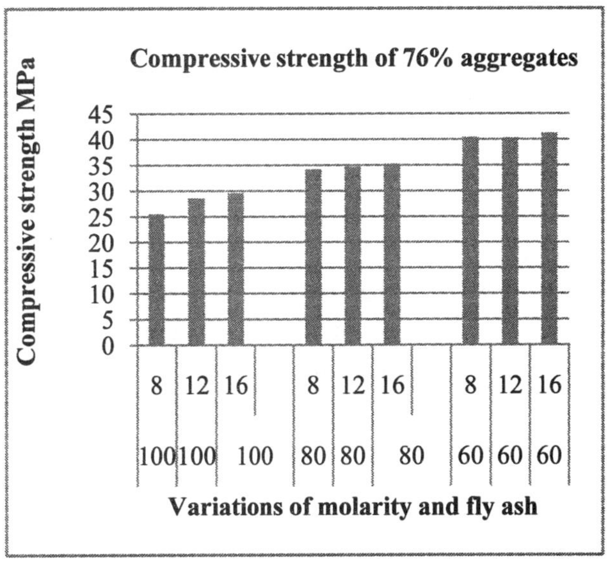

Figure 7 Variations of Molarity and Fly ash on Compressive strength

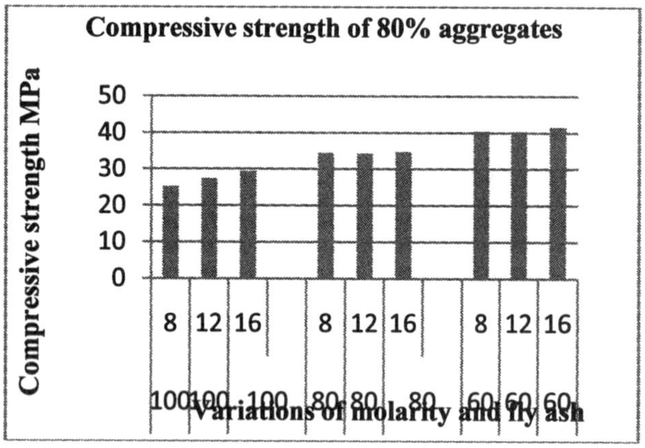

Figure 8 Variations of Molarity and Flyash on Compressive strength

B. Theoretical/Model Results

Theoretical 7 days compressive strength:

The data available for the model is imported into the MATLAB in matrix format 4x27 with four varying parameters for 27 samples as input and matrix 6x27 is imported as the targets with 6 target values for each varying parameter for 27 samples. In ANN model the data set was divided into three subsets of training and validation which contains 70% of total data (i.e. 19 samples), and the validation data which contains 15% of total data (i.e. 4 samples) and test data which contains 15% of total data (i.e. 4 samples). This division is due to increase in the generalization capacity of the ANN model and overcome over-fitting. Various algorithms were used in this study and finally, LM which is the short term of Levenberg-Marquardt was selected as the most efficient one. In addition, only one hidden layer and one output layer have been used in organizing the network, however, the number of hidden neurons in the hidden layer was selected as 12. The network architecture is trained during modeling process for the given hidden layer is shown in figure 9 for 7 days of strength. It has been observed that training is done for 12 iterations since 12 times inputs have been trained and it has been compared with the samples and an output is given.

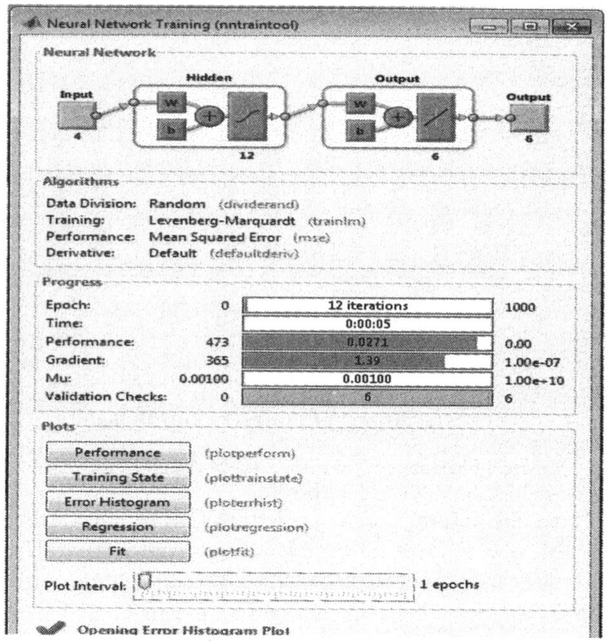

Figure 9 Neural network training

Figure 10 presents the validation performance and mean squared error of the network starting at a large value and reducing to a small value for 7 days compressive strength. The plot consists of three lines for three different steps of training, validation, and test. Training process on the training vectors continues until the model gets to the point that the training reduces the error of network on the validation vectors which would lead to avoiding the over-fitting of the data sets. As it is shown in the Figure 10, the best validation performance is happened at epoch 6, and after 6 error repetitions, the process is stopped at epoch 12.The best validation is obtained at 4.669 at epoch 6.

Figures 11 illustrate the coincidence between the target and output variables for training, and validation steps, respectively. The Target values imply the Measured Compressive Strength and the Output values imply the Predicted Compressive Strength by Matlab Software. The term R (Regression) is obtained by Matlab Software which demonstrates the model efficiency. Mean Squared Error (MSE) is the average squared difference between outputs and targets. Lower values are better. Regression R Values measure the correlation between outputs and targets. An R value of 1 means a close relationship, 0 a random relationship. The MSE and R value for Training validation and testing is given in Table V. The overall Rvalue for 7days compressive is 0.96.

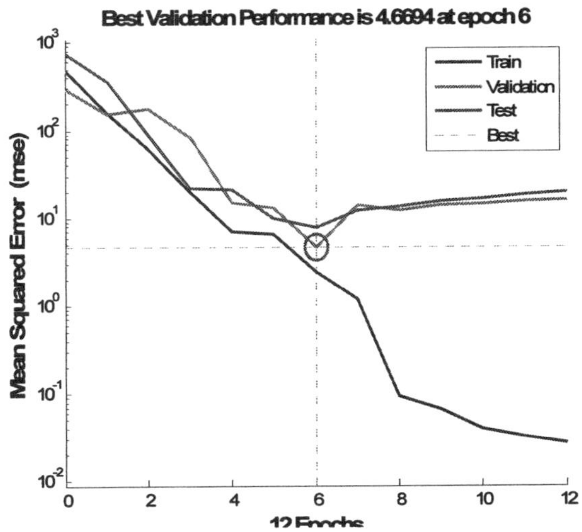

Figure 10 Best Validation Performance in Artificial Neural Network Model

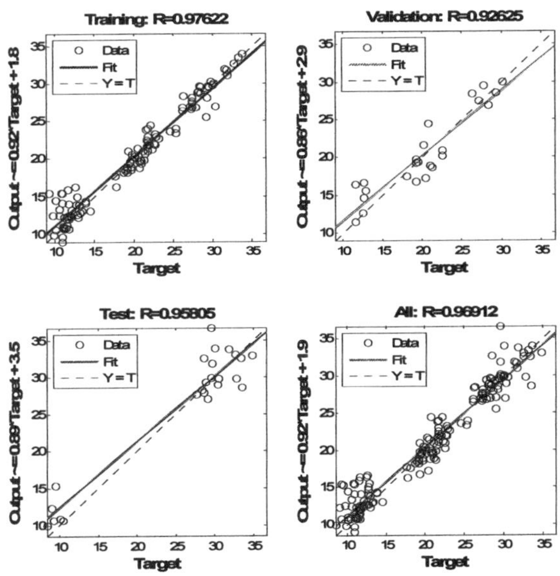

Figure 11 Training, validation and testing set in ANN model

Theoretical 28 days compressive strength

For the 28 days compressive strength a model is developed based on the experimental values of the compressive strength. The data available for the model is imported into the matlab in matrix format 4x27 with four varying parameters for 27 samples as input and matrix 6x27is imported as the targets with 6 targets for each varying parameter for 27 samples. Out of the total available data in ANN model the data set was divided into three subsets of training and validation which contains 70% of total data (i.e. 19 samples), and the validation data which contains 15% of total data (i.e. 4 samples) and test data which contains 15% of total data (i.e. 4 samples). This division is due to increase in the generalization capacity of the ANN model and overcome over-fitting. Various algorithms were used in this study and finally, LM which is the short term of Levenberg- Marquardt was selected as the most efficient one. In addition, only one hidden layer and one output layer have been used in organizing the network, however, the number of hidden neurons in the hidden layer was selected as 10. The network architecture is trained during modeling process for the given hidden layer is shown in Figure 12 for 28 days of strength. It has been observed that training is done for 9 iterations since 9 times inputs have been trained and it has been compared with all the samples and an output is given.

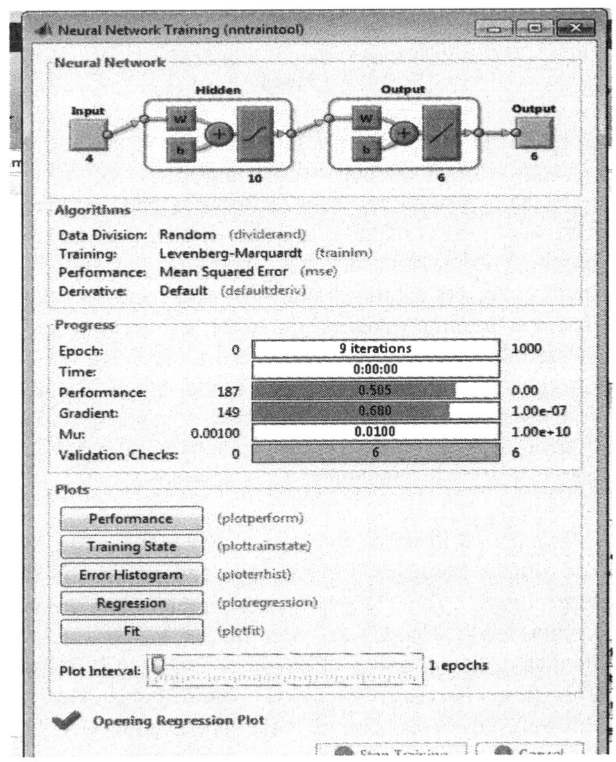

Figure 12 Neural network training

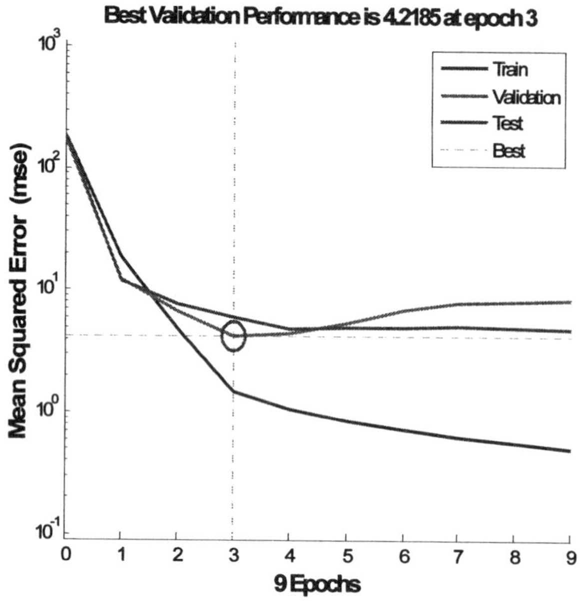

Figure 13 Best Validation Performance in Artificial Neural Network Model

Figure 13 presents the validation performance and mean squared error of the network starting at a large value and reducing to a small value for 28 days compressive strength. The plot consists of three lines for three different steps of training, validation, and test. Training process on the training vectors continues until the model gets to the point that the training reduces the error of network on the validation vectors which would lead to avoiding the over-fitting of the data sets. As shown in the Figure 13, the best validation performance has happened at epoch 3, and after 3 error repetitions, the process is stopped at epoch 9.The best validation is obtained at 4.218 at epoch 3.

Figures 14 illustrate the coincidence between the target and output variables for training, and validation steps, respectively. The Target values imply the Measured Compressive Strength and the Output values imply the Predicted Compressive Strength by MATLAB Software. The term R (Regression) is obtained by MATLAB Software which demonstrates the model efficiency. Mean Squared Error (MSE) is the average squared difference between outputs and targets. Lower values are better. Regression R values measure the correlation between outputs and targets. An R value of 1 means a close relationship, 0 a random relationship. The Rand MSE value for Training validation and testing is given in Table V. The overall Rvalue for 28 days compressive is 0.96.

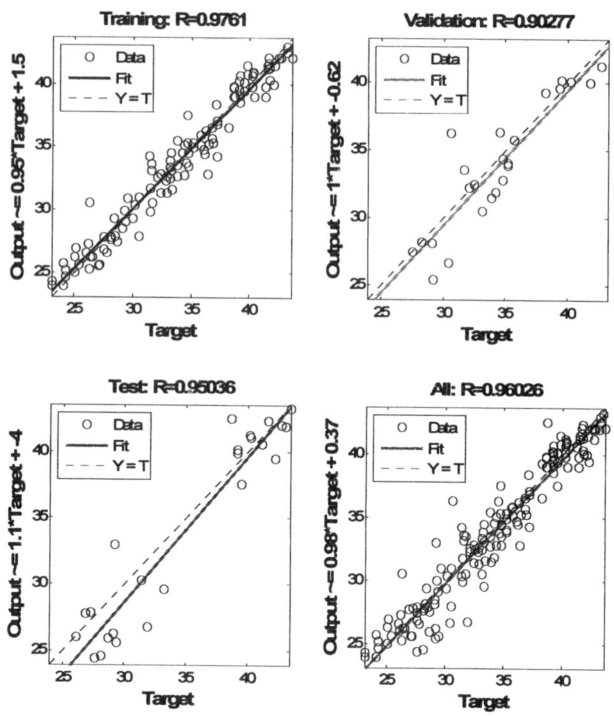

Figure 14 Training, validation and testing set in ANN model

TABLE V
MSE ANDR VALUES

	Samples	MSE for 7 days	MSE for 28 days	R for 7 days	R for 28 days
Training	19	0.38	0.766	0.97	0.97
Validation	4	1.33	0.723	0.92	0.90
Testing	4	0.73	2.49	0.95	0.95

A graph is plotted between the model results and the experimental results and an equation is proposed to check the efficiency of the model and also to obtain the minimum value of coefficient of multiple regressions R^2.

In the figure 15 the actual experimental values are plottedon x- axis and the predicted values are plottedon the y-axis. A scatter graph is obtained for the actual and the predicted data. The accuracy of the artificial neural network model might be due to the fact that, in the ANN the linear relation between the input variables is involved.

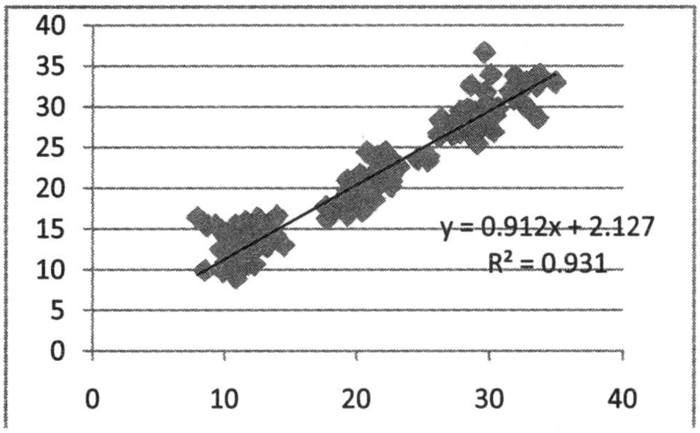

Figure 15 Comparison between the actual and predicted 7 days Compressive Strength by ANN model.

The term$\mathbf{R^2=0.931}$ which implies efficiency of the model. The linear relation is given by an equation **Y=0.912x+2.127**. Here in this equation X is the actual compressive strength and Y is the predicted compressive strength. It was observed that the percentage error obtained through the actual and predicted values are less. Therefore, the ANN is a reliable method for predicting the 7days compressive strength of concrete and can be widely used.

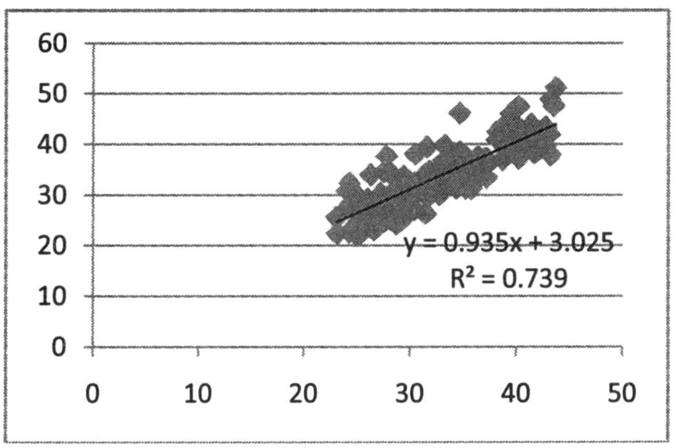

Figure 16 Comparison between the actual and predicted 28 days Compressive Strength by ANN model.

In the figure 16 the term$\mathbf{R^2=0.739}$ which implies efficiency of the model. The linear relation is given by an equation **Y=0.935x+3.025**. Here in this equation X is the actual compressive strength and Y is the predicted compressive strength. It was observed that the percentage error obtained through the actual and predicted values are less. Therefore, the ANN is a reliable method for predicting the 28 days compressive strength of GPC and can be widely used.

V. Discussions

Based on the experimental results the following conclusions are drawn:

- As the molarity increases from 8 to 16 the 7days compressive strength increases by 2.89% and 28 days compressive strength increases by 4.21%.
- As the aggregates percentage increase from 72 to 80, 7days compressive strength of GPC increases by 2.16% and for 28 days the compressive strength increases by 2.19%.
- As the GGBS percentage increases from 0 to 40 i.e. the fly ash percentage decreases from 100 to 60 the 7 days compressive strength increases by 19.54% and 28 days strength increases by 15.23%.
- Therefore GGBS is the most critical parameter which influences the compressive strength of the geopolymer concrete.
- The Mean square error (MSE) value for the 7days is 0.81 and for 28 days compressive strength it is 1.32.
- The coefficient of correlation (R) obtained during ANN modelling process is 0.96 for 7days compressive strength and 0.96 for 28days compressive strength during training, validation and testing process.
- Finally based on the above observations, it can be concluded that the prepared model is efficient in development of ANN model for 7days and 28 days compressive strength.

References

[1] Davidovits, J. "Geopolymers: Inorganic Polymeric New Materials" Journal of Thermal Analysis 37: 1633-1656, 1991.

[2] Wankhade M W and Kambekar A R "Prediction of Compressive Strength of Concrete using Artificial Neural Network" International Journal of Scientific Research and Reviews ISSN: 2279–0543, 2013

[3] Parthasarathi deb, PradipNath, Prabirkumarsarker "The effects of ground granulated blast-furnace slag blending with fly ash and activator content on the workability and strength properties of geopolymer concrete cured at ambient temperature"Article in materials and design 62:32–39 · October 2001

[4] Madheswaran,C.K, Gnansundar,G, Gopalkrishnan., "Effect of molarity in Geopolymer concrete", International Journal of Civil and Structural Engineering, Vol. 4(2) 2013

[5] Ravindra N. Thakur, somnathghosh, " effect of mix composition on compressive strength and micro structure of fly ash based geopolymer concrete", APRN journal of engineering and applied sciences, vol no 4, june 2009, ISSN 1819-6608

[6] Supraja, M. Kanta Rao "Experimental study on Geo-Polymer concrete incorporating GGBS" International Journal of Electronics, Communication & Soft Computing Science and Engineering ISSN: 2277-9477, Volume 2, Issue 2, 2016

[7] Vinay Prasad K S, Ms. Laxmi G Gandage "Effect of Gradation of Coarse Aggregate onStrength Properties of Geopolymer Concrete" IJIRSET Vol. 5, Issue 8, August 2016

[8] Vijay Pal Singh, Yogesh Chandra Kotiyal "Prediction of Compressive Strength Using Artificial Neural Network" International Journal of Civil, Environmental, Structural, Construction and Architectural Engineering Vol:7, No:12, 2013.

Effect of Slope Combination on Dynamic Analysis of RCC Chimney

K. Chaithanya Varada Prasad[1], P. Anuradha[2], K.L. Radhika[3], B. Santhosh Reddy[4]

[1,4]Master's scholar, Civil Engineering Department, University College of Engineering (A), Osmania University, Hyderabad–500007, T.S., India

[2]Associate Professor, [3]Assistant Professor, Civil Engineering Department, University College of Engineering (A), Osmania University, Hyderabad–500007, T.S., India

[1]chaithanyavarada@gmail.com
[3]anuradhaouce@gmail.com
[2]radhikaou@yahoo.com
[4]santhoshreddy6446@gmail.com

***Abstract*—Chimneys are the structures that are highly slender and lightly damped structures which are prone to wind-exited vibration and seismic excitation. Since they are highly slender even a little disturbance of the structure causes more deflections and enormous damage to the stability of the structure. Geometry of a chimney plays an important role in its structural behavior like stability. This is because geometry is primarily responsible for the stiffness parameters of any structure. However, basic dimensions of a RCC chimney, such as height, diameter are generally derived from the associated environmental conditions.**

In the present investigation the main objective is to calculate the maximum deflection of chimney and to find the slope combination which generates the least deflection for a chimney height of 310m. The slope combinations considered in the present work is bottom 2/3rd slope being 1 in 30 to 1 in 100 and top 1/3rd slope being 1 in 20 to 1 in 100 with an increment of 10. The cross section, bottom diameter and thickness of the chimney is maintained constant. The loads are calculated as per code IS 4998 (part-1):1992 and CED38 (7892): 2013 WC. The analysis is done using the STAAD-Pro.the deflections are observed checked whether they are under the limiting value as mentioned in the code. A total of 71 models with different slope combinations are generated and analyzed. The deflections and stresses at respective levels are observed and the best slope combination that gives least deflection is concluded.

Keywords: RCC Chimney, Slope combinations, Deflections , Stresses.

I. Introduction

A chimney is a means by which waste gases are discharged at a high elevation so that after dilution due to atmospheric turbulence, their concentration and that of their entrained solid particles is within the acceptable limits on reaching the ground. A chimney achieves simultaneous reduction in concentration of a number of pollutants such as sulphur dioxide, fly ash etc and being highly reliable it does not require a standby. A chimney also helps in decreasing the particulate matter such as fly ash and pond ash emitted from burning coal in the thermal power plants and helps in proper bifurcation of the particles when collected at a particular place. The main objectives of this paper are: To study various factors that influence the behaviour of the chimney, To study the impact of tapering on the behaviourof the chimney, To study the effect of wind loads and the seismic loads on the structure and to determine the loads that are more effective on the dynamic behaviour of the structure, To propose the best tapering which gives more stiffness and less deflections. Dynamic wind analysis is done for along winds because no vortex shedding resonance condition is taken in generating the model. The analysis process is completely done by using software STAAD.

II. Details Of Chimney

In the present study a RCC chimney of 310m height subjected to the wind loads imposed due to the mean hourly wind speed of 55m/sec in the seismic zone III is considered for the analysis. Single flue of structural steel is provided to discharge the flue gases and is hung from the liner support platform near the chimney top. The shell rests on R.C.C. mat foundation of circular shape.

The following are the details of the chimney considered:

Self weight of the structure	–	25KN/ m^3
Height of chimney	–	310 m
Outer diameter at bottom	–	30 m
Outer diameter at top (minimum)	–	3.0m
Thickness of shell at bottom	–	1.4 m
Thickness of shell at top	–	0.4 m

Grade of concrete	–	M30
Exit velocity of gas at top	–	25.0 m/sec
Flue gas volume from the flue	–	340 cum/sec
Maximum flue gas temperature	–	135^0C
Basic wind Speed	–	55 m/sec
Foundation Type	–	RCC circular mat

Single flue of structural steel is provided to discharge the flue gases and is hung from the liner support platform near the chimney top. The shell rests on R.C.C. mat foundation of circular shape. From the dynamic wind analysis the fluctuating load component on the structure is calculated and the analysis is made with the obtained loads. The calculation of moments and the loads is done using the expressions given in the code IS 4998 (part-1):1992 and CED38 (7892): 2013 WC. For finding the initial parameters like thickness at the bottom and top of the chimney the tapering of 1 in 50 is considered throughout. Taking these parameters constant for different tapering the change in stress and deflections in the chimney is studied. A total of 8 models are generated using different slopes in STAAD

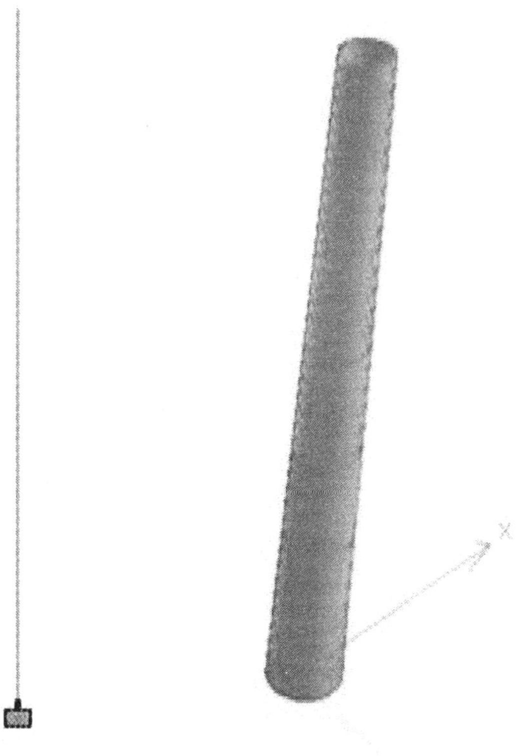

Fig. 1 Column model generated in STAAD

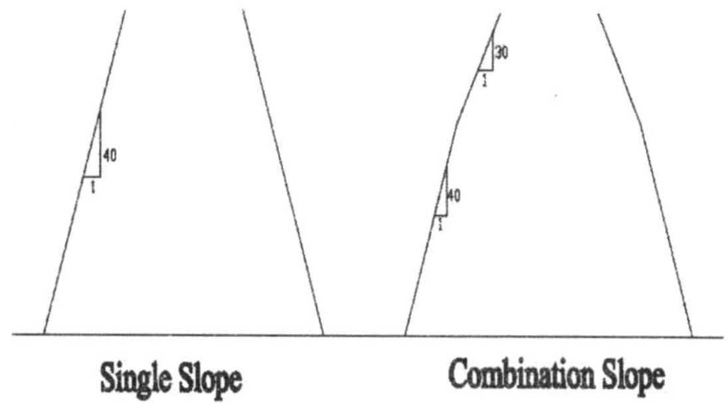

Fig 2 Differentiation of single slope and combination slope

The chimneys are modelled using tapering 1 in 30, 1 in 40, 1 in 50, 1 in 60, 1 in 70, 1 in 80, 1 in 90, 1 in 100. The stresses and deflections at regular intervals is observed and a optimum slope for the design is concluded. The stresses and deflections at regular intervals is observed and a optimum slope for the design is concluded.

III. Literature Review

M.R. Tabeshpour[1], "Nonlinear Dynamic Analysis of Chimney-Like Towers" In this study the most important problem i.e. earthquake behaviour of the structures, hysteric behaviour of material and section properties are studied. The significance of this study is mainly concentrated on model simplification that provides sufficient accuracy based on a nonlinear discrete model. To us power plant chimney is investigated numerically as an example. The nonlinear dynamic analysis essentially needed for seismic assessment in evaluation of actual performance of complicated structures during earthquakes than the damage indices of structure had to be calculated using appropriate damage models. K.R.C. Reddy [2], "Along Wind Analysis of Reinforced Concrete Chimneys", the analysis is done by random vibration approach and codal methods of India, America are presented in this paper. For the analysis based on random vibration approach the RC chimney is modelled as multi degree of freedom system subjected to static load due to mean component of wind velocity and dynamic load due to fluctuating component of velocity. The fluctuating component of wind velocity at a point is considered as temporal random process. Present codal methods of a long - wind analysis are found simplistic and are not equipped to estimate the deflection of chimneys. Different codes are giving different results though basic parameters are same.Jisha S. V, et al [3], "Across Wind Response of Tall Reinforced Concrete Chimneys Considering the Flexibility of Soil", in this experiment a three dimensional soil structure interaction (SSI) analysis of tall slender reinforced concrete chimneys with annular raft foundation subjected to across wind load is carried in the present study. Different ratios of external diameter to thickness of the annular raft and different ranges of height of the chimneys were selected for the parametric study. The integrated chimney foundation soil system was analyzed by finite element software ANSYS based on direct method of SSI assuming linear behaviour. In this study the maximum deflection in chimney increase with increase in raft-thickness ratio and the base moment of chimney decreases due to the effect of soil structure interaction. T Saran Kumar, R. Nagavinothini[4], "Wind Analysis and Analytical Study on Vortex Shedding Effect on Steel Chimney Using CFD"is the study of vortex shedding effect on steel chimney. Vortex shedding means at certain velocities air or fluid past a cylindrical body forms an oscillating flow, which depends on the size and shape of the body. Reynolds number used to predict fluid flow pattern fast a body is steady are turbulent. In this study, five models of chimneys with different heights and diameters at top and bottom, were designed as per IS 6533-1989(part 2) and wind load was calculated as per IS 875 (part 3)-1987.The study on the vortex shedding effect on different chimney models reveals that the wind induced vibration in the tall chimneys varies with respect to height.

IV. Loads Calculation

Generally wind does not blow at fixed rate. It blows at gusts. So this requires that the effects are taken in terms of equivalent loads. Here chimney is analysed as a bluff body having turbulent flow for the computation of along wind loads. Equivalent static procedure is used in codes known as gust factor method. Currently stipulated in all building codes and also in Draft Code CED 38(7892):2013 (third revision of IS 4998(part 1):1992). In this method wind pressure which is assumed to be acting on face of the chimney, due to this wind pressures are considered as static wind loads. This is then improved using the gust factor to make sure of the dynamic effects. The following codes used in estimation of along wing loads are: 1) IS875 (part 3): 1987 - code practice for design loads for building and structures. 2)Draft Code CED 38(7892):2013 (third revision of IS 4998(part 1):1992). The following equations help us to calculate the fluctuating component of wind loads due to gust:

$$f_l = 0.2 * \left(\frac{d_0}{H^2}\right) * \sqrt{\frac{E_{ck}}{\rho_{ck}}} * \left(\frac{t_0}{t_h}\right)^{0.3}$$

$$S = \left\{1 + 5.78 * \left(\frac{f_1}{\overline{V(10)}}\right)^{1.14} * H^{0.98}\right\}^{-0.88}$$

$$E = \frac{\left\{123 * \left(\frac{f_1}{\overline{V(10)}}\right) * H^{0.21}\right\}}{\left\{1.578 * \left(\frac{f_1}{\overline{V(10)}}\right)^{1.14} * H^{0.98}\right\}^{-0.88}}$$

$$B = \left\{1 + \left(\frac{H}{265}\right)^{0.63}\right\}^{-0.88}$$

$$r_t = (0.622 - 0.178 \log_{10} H)$$

$$\nu T = \frac{3600 f_1}{\left(1 + \frac{B\beta}{SE}\right)^{0.5}}$$

$$g_f = \left(\sqrt{2 * \ln(\nu T)} + \frac{0.577}{\sqrt{2 * \ln(\nu T)}}\right)$$

$$G = 1 + g_f * r_t \sqrt{B + \left(\frac{SE}{\beta}\right)}$$

$$F'_z = 3 * \frac{(G-1)}{H^2} * \left(\frac{Z}{H}\right) * \int_0^H \bar{F}_z * Z * dZ$$

where

f_l= natural frequency of unlined chimney in first mode of vibration (hz)

t_0 = thickness of the shell at the bottom (m)

t_h = thickness of the shell at the top (m)

d_0 = centre line diameter of the shell at the bottom (m)

E_{ck} = dynamic modulus of elasticity of the concrete (N/m^2)

ρ_{ck}= mass density of the concrete (Kg/m^3)

S = size reduction factor

$\overline{V(10)}$ =mean hourly wind speed at 10m height above the ground level (m/s)

H = total height of the chimney.

E = available energy in the wind at the natural frequency

B = background factor

r_t = twice the turbulence intensity at the top of the chimney

ν = the effective cycling rate

T = the sample period taken as 3600 sec

β = structural damping as a fraction of critical damping (0.016)

g_f= peak factor

G = gust response factor

The dead load and seismic load calculations are also calculated using the appropriate codes but not mentioned in this paper as the predominant forces is wind loads.

The various loads acting on the chimney are calculated and applied on the models generated in STAAD. The manually calculated values are being verified by the values originated when defined in STAAD.

The graphs which describe the values of loading in various models is given below:

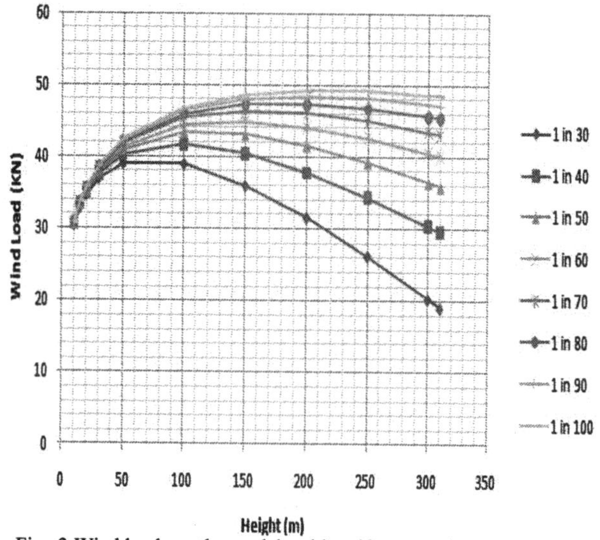

Fig 3 Wind loads on the models with uniform tapering and throughout

Fig 3 describes the graph showing the wind load pattern on the structure at different heights for different slopes. Fig 4 describes the graph showing the seismic loads on the structures for different slopes. After applying the loads analysis of the structure is done in STAAD. The pattern of loading is shown in the figure given below:

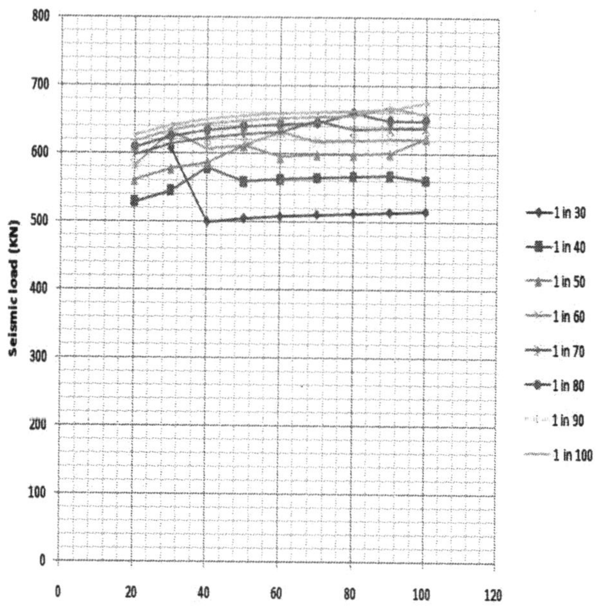

Fig 4 seismic loads on all models

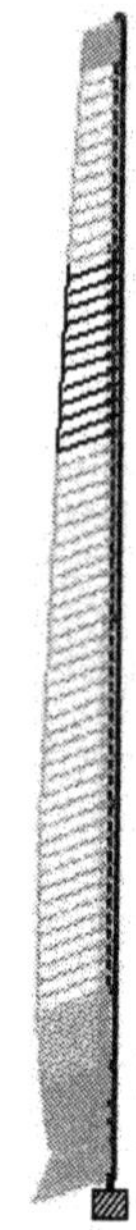

Fig 5 Wind load acting on the model

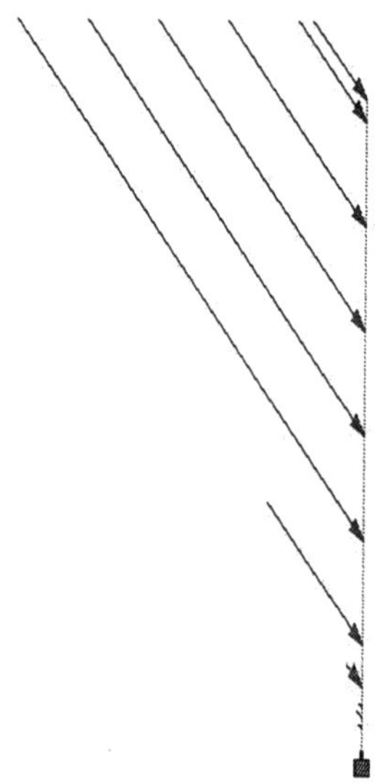

Fig 6 Seismic load on the model

V. Results and Discussion

After the analysis the deflections and stresses generated at different levels can be observed using the post processing mode. The stresses generated in a structure determine the reinforcement design on the structure. More the stresses more will be use of reinforcement at that joint. The graph given below shows the stress variation with respect to height for the models having constant slope throughout the height.

The Table I shows the percentage of reduction in stresses in models with respect to the models having constant slope throughout.

From the graph in Fig 7 it is seen that the stresses are more in the members having least tapering when compared with other tapering. It is also seen that higher stress are seen at the height of 20m from the bottom of the chimney in all the models. More reinforcement and the thickness of chimneys are necessary at the bottom till a height of 20m.

From the models analyzed it has been proved that there is definitely a reduction in stresses at least to the minimum of 3%.

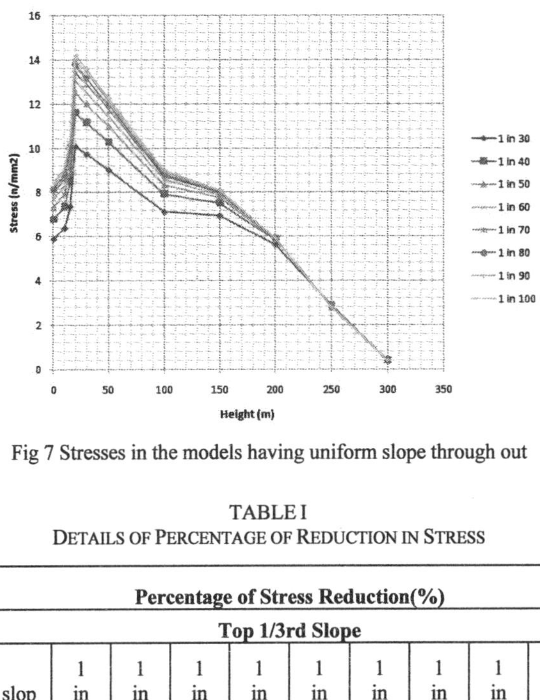

Fig 7 Stresses in the models having uniform slope through out

TABLE I
DETAILS OF PERCENTAGE OF REDUCTION IN STRESS

	Percentage of Stress Reduction(%)									
	Top 1/3rd Slope									
Bottom 2/3rd Slope	slope	1 in 20	1 in 30	1 in 40	1 in 50	1 in 60	1 in 70	1 in 80	1 in 90	1 in 100
	1 in 30		0.	11	9	7	6	5	5	4
	1 in 40	19	13	0	7	6	5	4	4	3
	1 in 50	17	11	8	0	5	4	4	3	3
	1 in 60	16	7	8	6	0	4	4	3	3
	1 in 70	16	10	8	6	5	0	4	3	3
	1 in 80	15	10	7	6	5	4	0	3	3
	1 in 90	15	10	7	6	5	4	3	0	3
	1 in 100	15	10	7	6	5	4	3	3	0

The maximum stress is observed in the member having uniform slope throughout when compared to its combinations. From the models analyzed it has been proved that there is definitely a reduction in stresses with the increase in the slope.

In the post processing mode of STAAD the deflections at respective nodes will be generated. More deflections affect the service ability of the structure. Hence the deflections should be checked whether are under the limit as mentioned in the code. As per code IS 4998 (part-1): 1992 the deflection should not exceed H/500 for an RCC Chimney of circular cross section. The graph in the Fig 8 gives the deflection variation with respect to height in various models having the same tapering throughout the height. From the graph it is seen that the deflections are more in the members having least tapering when compared with more tapering. The maximum deflection is observed at the top of chimney and is observed highest in the chimney tapered with 1 in 100 through out.

In the post processing mode of STAAD the deflections at respective nodes will be generated. The values of these deflections are mentioned in the Table II for different models. More deflections affect the serviceability of the structure. Hence the deflections should be checked whether are under the limit as mentioned in the code. As per code IS 4998 (part-1): 1992 the deflection should not exceed H/500 for an RCC Chimney of circular cross section.

From the Table II it can inferred that thereby the use of slope combination in the place of single slope throughout the deflections can be reduced for sure. A minimum reduction of 5% to the maximum reduction of 30% is being observed from the models generated.

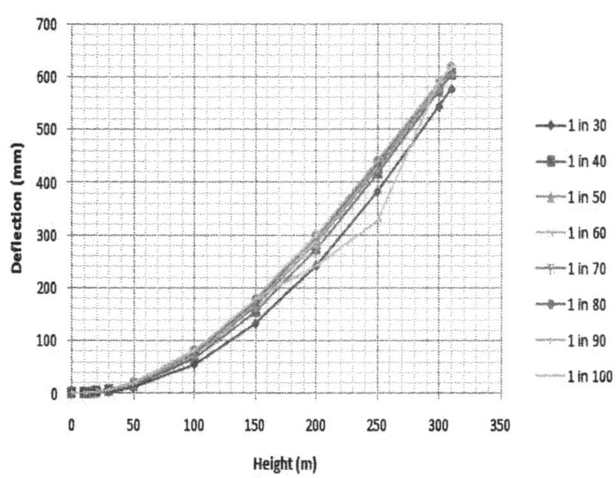

Fig 8 Graph showing deflection variation in various models

TABLE III
DETAILS OF PERCENTAGE OF REDUCTION IN DEFLECTION

	Percentage of Reduction in Deflection (%)									
	Top 1/3rd Slope									
	slope	1 in 20	1 in 30	1 in 40	1 in 50	1 in 60	1 in 70	1 in 80	1 in 90	1 in 100
Bottom 2/3rd Slope	1 in 30		0	18	15	12	10	8	7	6
	1 in 40	30	22	0	13	11	9	8	7	6
	1 in 50	29	20	15	0	10	9	7	6	6
	1 in 60	27	21	14	11	0	8	7	6	5
	1 in 70	26	17	13	10	9	0	6	6	5
	1 in 80	25	17	13	10	8	7	0	5	5
	1 in 90	25	16	12	10	8	7	6	0	5
	1 in 100	24	16	12	10	8	7	6	5	0

VI. CONCLUSIONS

From the observations of Pre-analysis and Post-analysis the following conclusions are made:

1. As the tapering increases the volume of the chimney is decreased due to this the self weight of the structure is also decreased. In this way dead load on the structure is decreased
2. As the tapering increases the projected area decreases due to this the wind load acting on the structure is also decreased.
3. With increase in tapering the volume of the chimney is decreased due to this the weight of the chimney is decreased. As the weight of the body is decreased, the seismic excitation is also decreased.
4. From the observations made in the Post-analysis the stresses in the structure also decreases with the increase in tapering. The magnitude of deflections also decreases with the increase in tapering.
5. This above table shows that when the chimneys are constructed with the combination tapering, a minimum of 3% reduction stresses can be achieved. From the observed model when the chimney is constructed with bottom 2/3rd tapering of 1 in 40 combined with top 1/3rd tapering of 1 in 20 gave a stress reduction of up to 19.55%.
6. A stress reduction from 3% to 19% has been achieved by using combination tapering of the chimney.
7. By using a slope combination the reduction in deflections from 5% to 30 % has been achieved. The chimney in which least stresses are observed has the highest deflection reduction of about 30.72%.
8. From the above observations we can conclude that
    - The chimneys constructed with more tapering have high resistance to the loading compared to the chimneys constructed with less tapering.
    - The chimney constructed with combination tapering has more resistance when compared to the chimneys constructed with constant tapering throughout the height.

References

[1] M R Tabeshpour, "Non linear Dynamic Analysis of Chimney-like towers", Asian Journal of Civil Engineering (Building and Housing), vol.13, NO.1 (2012), pp.97-112.

[2] K.R.C. Reddy, "Along Wind Analysis of Reinforced Concrete Chimneys", IJRET, volume-4 special issue 13, Dec-2015, pp.361-367.

[3] Jisha S V, Dr B R Jayalekshmi, Dr R Shivashankar, "Across Wind Response of Tall Reinforced Concrete Chimneys Considering the Flexibility of Soil" International Journal of Engineering Research and Technology (IJERT) Volume-1, issue-8, october-2012, pp.1-8.

[4] T. Saran Kumar, R. Nagavinothini, "Wind Analysis and Analytical Study on Vortex Shedding Effect on Steel Chimney using CFT" IJSETR, vol 4, issue 4, April 2015, pp.715-718.

[5] Victor bochicchio, "Design of chimney with GRP liner for low and high temperature operation", Vol-22, no-1, pp-1-5.

Development of Mathematical Model for Geo-Polymer Concrete

V.Bhikshma[1], T. Naveen Kumar[2]

[1]*Professor, Department of Civil Engineering, University College of Engineering, Osmania University, Hyderabad, India 500 007*

[2]*Research Scholar, Department of Civil Engineering, University College of Engineering, Osmania University, Hyderabad, India 500 007*

[1]v.bhikshma@yahoo.co.in
[2]naveenkumart1p@gmail.com

***Abstract*- In view of environmental issues, concrete industry is exploring new type of construction and alternative materials. In this process, the development of Geo-Polymer concrete is an important mile stone in concrete world. Geo-polymer concrete produced with environmental-friendly ingredients. Geo-polymer concrete formed by alkali activation of fly ash (FA), ground granulated blast furnace slag (GGBS). Several studies have already established Geo-polymer concrete have significant mechanical characteristics in compared to conventional concrete. But not many studies on stress-strain behavior of Geo-polymer concrete have been carried out. Therefore, in this paper an attempt is made to study the stress-strain behavior and development of mathematicalmodel for Geo-polymer concrete. A series of compression test were conducted on cylinder specimens 150 mm dia and 300mm long with five different grades of concrete viz., M20, M30, M40, M50 and M60. Based on the available existing modelsan empirical stress–strain equation is proposed. The theoretical values were compared with cylinder test results. Good correlation exists between experimental and theoretical values validating model.**

***Keywords* - Geo-polymer concrete, Fly ash, GGBS, Modulus of Elasticity, Saenz Mathematical-model, Stress-Strain behavior.**

I. Introduction

Geo-polymer concrete has become core area to explore the alternative solution to conventional concrete. Studies established an excellent sustainable concrete. Geo-polymer concrete is produced without cement. The term Geo-polymer was introduced by Davidovits [1]. Geo-polymerization is the process of inorganic alumina silicate polymers resulting from reaction of amorphous alumina silicates with alkali hydroxide and silicate solutions. Fly ash is a pozzolanic material contains Silica (Si) and Alumina (Al). When these compounds are activated by highly alkaline solution under heat curing yields binders Si-O-Al(Geopolymers) similar to C-S-H bond of conventional concrete.The commonly alkaline solutions used are mixture of sodium silicate & sodium hydroxide. The concentration of sodium hydroxide can be varied from 8M to 16M. For effective Geo-polymerization process both curing time & temperature plays important role in addition to type of concentration of NaOH. Studies reveal that improved Geo-polymerization process results higher strengthdevelopment [2-4]. Several investigationshave been carried in assessing workability and strength characteristics of Geo-polymer concrete [5-7]. Temperature curing is main hindrance in practical application of Geo-polymer concrete. To overcome this issue present research has been emphasized on the use of ground granulated blast furnace slag (GGBS) for partial replacement of fly ash. GGBS which contains substantial amount of calcium imparts necessary heat of hydration required for Geo-polymerization process. Geo-polymer concrete with fly ash and GGBS has shown encouraging results (in the absence of temperature curing) in terms of mechanical strengths and flexural capacities[8-10].Thispaper is a part of research programmeaimed at stress-strain behavior of Geo-polymer concrete.

II. Research Significance

Inflexural analysis of reinforced concrete beams, stress-strain characteristicis important parameter. Based on this characteristics of stress-block parameters can be evaluated. Hence, understanding of complete stress-strain curvesof concrete is essential from a structural consideration. Research available till date on stress-strain behavior of Geo-polymer concrete is not conclusive.The purpose of this study is a) to present mathematical model for stress-strain curve b) to validate developed model.

III. Experimental Programme

In the present investigationdifferent grades of concrete viz., M20, M30, M40, M50 and M60 have been considered. Based on the previous studies,the percentagereplacement of GGBS 9%, 20%, 27.5%, 38% and43% were fixed and considered for the above concrete grades respectively [11].Fly ash used in the experimental work was a low-calcium fly ash. The silica and alumina are constitutes about 85% of the total mass and its ratio is about 1.5. Properties of fly ash and GGBS are presented in Table I.

Locally available river sand was used as a fine aggregate (Fineness modulus-2.65, Specific gravity-2.62) confirming to zone-II of IS: 383-1970. Similarly well graded coarse aggregates having size 4.75 mm to 20mm were used. A mixture of Sodium hydroxide (NaOH) and Sodium silicate (Na_2SiO_3) was used as alkali activator. Sodium hydroxide is in the form pellets having purity 98%. Commercial grade Sodium Silicate with Na_2O 13%-15% and SiO_2 28% -34% was considered.

TABLE I
PROPERTIES OF FLY ASH AND GGBS

S.No	Characteristics	Percentage by Mass	
		Fly Ash	GGBS
1	Loss on Ignition	1.9	2.6
2	Silica, Sio_2	52.16	34.4
3	Alumina,Al_2O_3	31.97	12.9
4	Calcium, CaO	4.67	42.5
5	Iron, Fe_2O_3	9.32	1.12

To improve the workability, poly carboxyl ether based high performance super plasticizeri.eGleniumB233 was used. The dosage of super plasticizer is taken as 0.5% by mass of fly ash and GGBS.Based on the mix design guidelines proposedby B.V. Rangan, Curtain University, Australia [12] several trial mixes were conducted [12]. Finally, a standard design mix has been adopted in the present experimental work. In the mix design, combined aggregate (Coarse and Fine aggregate) taken as 70% of total mass concrete.Molarity of sodium hydroxide (NaOH) was considered as 8M in the present investigation. Alkaline activator to binder (Fly ash + GGBS) ratio was kept constant 0.5. Also ratio of sodium silicate to sodium hydroxide solution was taken as 2.5.The mix proportions are presented inTable II.

TABLE II
MIX PROPORTIONS OF GEO-POLYMER CONCRETE (kg/m3)

S.No	Item	Grade of Geo-Polymer Concrete				
		M20	M30	M40	M50	M60
1	Molarity	8	8	8	8	8
2	GGBS (%)	9	20	27.5	38	43
3	Fly ash	437	384	348	298	274
4	GGBS	43	96	132	182	206
5	F.Agg	740	749	756	763	767
6	C Agg	915	926	933	943	948
7	Na_2O SiO_2	171	171	171	171	171
8	NaOH	18	18	18	18	18
9	Water	51	51	51	51	51

The sodium silicate solution and the sodium hydroxide solution were mixed together prior to 24 hours of casting. Standard mixing procedurewas adopted for making Geo-polymer concrete. The coarse aggregates in saturated surface dry condition and fine aggregates were first mixed with the flyash & GGBSabout 2 to 3 minutes. At the end of this mixing, the alkaline solution together was added to the dry materials and the mixing continued for another four minutes.The workability was measured by means of conventionalslump test and compaction factor tests.Immediately after mixing, the fresh concrete was transferred in to moulds.15 No's standard cylinders (150mm diameter& 300mm long) have been considered in the present investigation. After 24hours specimens were demoulded and kept under air dry at 27^0Cin laboratory until day of testing i.e., at 28 days. The cylinders are tested in 1000 kNuniversal testing machine as per the provision laid in IS 516-1999 [13]. Loading and strain measurements were carefully controlled. Readings were obtained up to failure state.

IV. STRESS-STRAIN CURVE AND MATHEMATICAL MODEL

The study of stress-strain relationship is an important parameter to understand the behavior of concrete. It is an internal change at micro level that concrete experiences viz., deformation, crack development, damage accumulation, and residual properties. The shape of the stress–strain curve is influenced by the several factors. It is mainly depends up on the testing conditions i.e., type of testing machine, rate & duration of loading, number of load repetitions, size and location of the strain gauges. Interestingly, shape of stress-strain for individual concrete ingredients is straight line, whereas for concrete it is a curve. In view of complexity, only analytical equations are available for the approximation of stress-strain curve of concrete. Number of empirical equations has been developed earlier for describing the stress-strain characteristics of normal concrete. Also recent studies have been carried for evaluating stress-strain behavior of high performance concrete, permeable concrete, bacteria concrete, high volume fly ash concrete[14 – 17].

Number of empirical equations for stress-strain curve are proposed for conventional concrete. Early work are done byHognestad (1955) &Desayi and Krishnan (1964) and proposed a simple model for stress-strain of ordinary concrete [18,19]. Later Saenz (1964) has proposed model duly overcoming the limitation in the model of Desayi and Krishnan [20].Popovics(1973) proposes numerical approach to the complete stress-strain curve of concrete.Carriera and Chu (1985) extended the empirical equation proposed by Popovics [21]. Further, Loov(1991) extended the early work by Carriera and Chu who proposed a model that can be validate experimental values [22]. Collins and et.al (1993) also extended the early work by Thorenfeldt and et.al (1987) who examined the relation between compressive stress at any strain to peak stress [23]. Models proposed by theseauthors enumerated below.

A.Hognestad Model

Stress-strain curve for ordinary concrete defined by

$$\sigma_c = f_c\,[\,2\varepsilon/\varepsilon_o - (\,\varepsilon/\varepsilon_o)^2\,]$$

Where

σ_c= Peak stress in concrete,
ε_o = Strain at peak stress,
f_c = Compressive Strength of concrete
ε = Strain in concrete.

B.Desayi and Krishnan Model

They propose simple model describing stress-strain concrete as

$$f_c / f'_c = (\varepsilon/\varepsilon_o)\,A \,/\, 1 + B\,(\,\varepsilon/\varepsilon_o)^2$$

C. Modified Saenz Model

Desayi and Krishnan has proposed model for ascending portion of stress-strain curve only. In view of this limitation Saenz proposed a model by considering both ascending and descending portion of the stress –strain curve.

$$f_c / f'_c = (\varepsilon/\varepsilon_o)\,A \,/\, 1 + B\,(\varepsilon/\varepsilon_o) + C\,(\,\varepsilon/\varepsilon_o)^2$$

D.Wang et al Mode

The model used by Wang et. al in the form

$$f_c = f'_c\,[\,(\varepsilon/\varepsilon_o)\,A + B(\,\varepsilon/\varepsilon_o)^2 \,/\, 1 + C\,(\varepsilon/\varepsilon_o) + D\,(\,\varepsilon/\varepsilon_o)^2\,]$$

E)Carriera and Chu Model

The following general equation represents the stress-strain behavior proposed by Carreira& Chu [22].

$$f_c = f'_c\,[\,\beta\,(\varepsilon/\varepsilon_o) \,/\, \beta - 1 + (\,\varepsilon/\varepsilon_o)^{\beta}\,]$$

Material parameter, $\beta = 1/\,[\,1 - (f'_c \,/\, E_o\varepsilon_o)\,]$

Where $E_o$is Initial Tangent Modulus of Elasticity. Indian Standard IS456:2000 allows assumption of suitable relationship between the compressive stress distribution in concrete and strain to be rectangular, trapezoidal, parabola or any other shape which results in prediction of strength in substantial agreement with experimental results [24]

V. Mathematical Model for Geo-Polymer Concrete

In the present investigation only ascending portion of curve considered. Out of existing, modified Saenz's model isselected which seem to be valid for ascending portion of curve. The proposed equation is in the form of

$$Y = Ax / 1 + Bx + Cx^2$$

Where Y is the Normalized stress (σ / σ_u) and X is the Normalized strain ($\varepsilon / \varepsilon_u$). A, B, C are the constants. Similarly, the equation for non-dimensional stress-strain curve can be written as

$$(\sigma / \sigma_u) = \frac{A'(\varepsilon / \varepsilon u)}{1 + B'(\varepsilon / \varepsilon u) + C'(\varepsilon / \varepsilon u)^2}$$

The assumed shape of stress-strain curve for Geo-Polymer concrete and non–dimensional stress-strain is shown in figure 1 and 2.

Fig 1. General Stress- strain curve for Geo-Polymer concrete

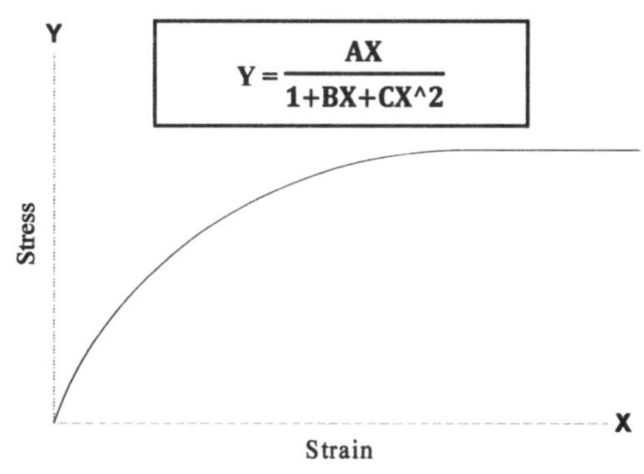

Fig 2. Non-dimensional Stress-strain curve for Geo-Polymer concrete

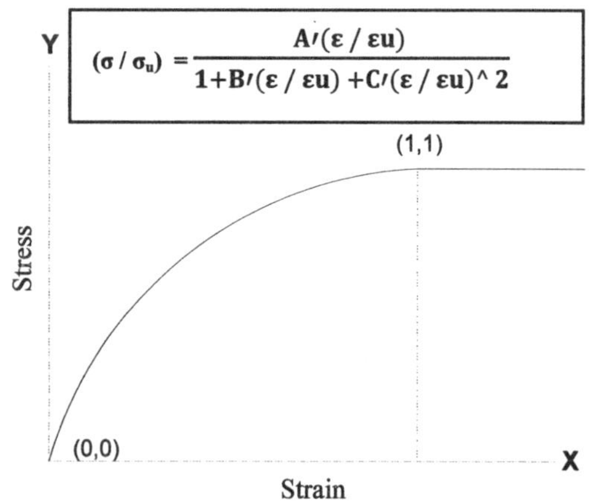

The constants A', B', C' are determined from the boundary conditions of the non–dimensional stress-strain curve. The boundary conditions are as follows.

1) At the origin, $\sigma = 0$ & $\varepsilon = 0$, Slope of the stress-strain curve is maximum
2) Stress-strain ratio of non–dimensional curve is unity at the ultimate
3) Slope of the stress-strain curve at failure is zero

The constants A, B & C for theoretical stress–strain curve are evaluated using following equations.

$A = A' (\sigma / \varepsilon)$, $B = B'(1 / \varepsilon)$ & $C = C'(1 / \varepsilon)2$

Finally, substituting the above constants, theoretical equation for the stress-strain curve is obtained for each grade of concrete. Theoretical stresses are calculated for corresponding strains using developed equation. These theoretical stresses are compared with experimental results for each grade of Geo-Polymer concrete.

VI. Results and Discussions

A. Strain at Peak stress

The test indicates that strain increases with compressive strength increased.

TABLE III
PEAK STRESS AND STRAIN

S.No	Grade of Concrete	Stress σ (N/mm²)	Strain ε x 10⁻⁴
1	M20	20.30	25.75
2	M30	27.92	27.10
3	M40	36.66	28.30
4	M50	45.40	29.74
5	M60	58.09	31.10

Table III provides values corresponding strain at peak stress. Earlier authors reported linear relationship between peak cylinder compressive stress and corresponding strain [25,26].

Popovics proposed a relationship between stress & strain as

$$\varepsilon_o = 0.000875 \, (f_o)^{0.25}$$

Carreria&Chu defined the stress & strain relationship as

$$\varepsilon_o = (7.1 \, f_c + 1680) \, 10^{-6}$$

Almusallam&Alsayed stress& strain relationship stated as

$$\varepsilon_o = (0.398 \, f_c + 18.147) \, 10^{-4}$$

M.K.Hussain, et al. proposed function in the form of

$$\varepsilon_o = 0.0008 + (2 \, f_c) \, 10^{-5}$$

In the present investigation following linear relationship similar to that of Carreria& Chu is proposed.

$$\varepsilon_o = (13.471 \, f_c + 2270) 10^{-6}$$

B. Modulus of Elasticity

The value of Modulus of Elasticity is obtained from the stress-strain curve. The slope of the stress-strain gives modulus of Elasticity. The modulus of elasticity of Geo-polymer concrete was determined as the initial tangent modulus measured at stress level about 40% of the average compressive strength of concrete cylindersthe values of experimentalmodulus of elasticity are shown in the TableIV. As expected the value of modulus of elasticity is increases with increase in compressive strength. The value found to be less than the 6% less than value of conventional concrete. The marginal reduction in the value may be due to the type of curing condition being adopted. As reported by earlier researchers that air cured concrete gives lowerstrength values than the values of moist cured concrete due to changes in the microstructure. Indian Standard IS 456-2000, relation is proposed as $5000\sqrt{f_{ck}}$. The values are in comparable with conventional concrete.

TABLE IV
TEST RESULTS OF MODULUS OF ELASTICITY

S.No	Grade of Concrete	Modulus of Elasticity (GPa)
1	M20	21.07
2	M30	24.78
3	M40	28.89
4	M50	32.68
5	M60	35.55

C. Stress – Strain & Mathematical Model

The behavior of the cylinders under axial loads was similar to that of conventional concrete. Generally there are three failure modes for cylinders under compressive loading viz., shear, splitting or columnar fracture and combination of shear & splitting failure. Geo-polymer concrete cylinders fail in in axial splitting parallel to the applied load. Splitting taken place with gradual development hairline cracks. Prior to failure low cracking noises were observed and cylinders fails gradually after reaching its peak load. Also the crack patterns of both conventional and geo-polymer concrete cylinders are observed to be similar. Cracks are initiated through the aggregate by forming smoother cracked surface due to greater cement-matrix strength.

From the experimental stress-strain values of the corresponding normalized stress-strain values are calculated by dividing each stress value by the peak stress and dividing each strain value by strain at peak strain. The experimental values of stress and corresponding strains for each grade of concrete are shown in Table V to IX

TABLE V NORMALIZED EXPERIMENTAL STRESS – STRAIN VALUES FOR M20 GRADE

σ		ε	
Stress	**Normalized Stress**	**Strain**	**Normalized Strain**
6.20	0.30	2.56	0.10
11.28	0.55	5.13	0.20
13.53	0.66	7.68	0.30
15.22	0.75	10.39	0.40
16.35	0.80	12.72	0.49
17.48	0.86	15.56	0.60
18.33	0.90	18.09	0.70
19.17	0.94	21.05	0.82
19.74	0.97	23.28	0.90
20.30	1.00	25.75	1.00

TABLE VI . NORMALIZED EXPERIMENTAL STRESS – STRAIN VALUES FOR M30 GRADE

σ		ε	
Stress	**Normalized Stress**	**Strain**	**Normalized Strain**
7.33	0.26	2.68	0.10
14.66	0.52	5.48	0.20
18.04	0.64	8.24	0.30
20.30	0.72	10.82	0.40
22.27	0.79	13.73	0.51
23.68	0.84	16.27	0.60
25.09	0.89	19.29	0.71
26.22	0.93	22.10	0.82
27.07	0.97	24.47	0.90
27.91	1.00	27.10	1.00

TABLE VII NORMALIZED EXPERIMENTAL STRESS – STRAIN VALUES FOR M40 GRADE

σ		ε	
Stress	**Normalized Stress**	**Strain**	**Normalized Strain**
9.02	0.24	2.86	0.10
17.76	0.48	5.64	0.20
22.84	0.62	8.47	0.30
26.22	0.71	11.38	0.40
28.76	0.78	14.20	0.50
30.73	0.83	16.87	0.60
32.43	0.88	19.56	0.69
34.12	0.93	22.67	0.80
35.53	0.96	25.64	0.91
36.66	1.00	28.30	1.00

TABLE VIII NORMALIZED EXPERIMENTAL STRESS – STRAIN VALUES FOR M50 GRADE

σ		ε	
Stress	**Normalized Stress**	**Strain**	**Normalized Strain**
10.43	0.23	2.97	0.10
20.86	0.46	5.95	0.20
28.20	0.62	9.02	0.30
32.14	0.70	11.86	0.40
35.53	0.78	15.00	0.50
38.07	0.83	17.89	0.60
40.32	0.88	20.92	0.70
42.30	0.93	23.99	0.81
43.99	0.96	26.97	0.91
45.40	1.00	29.74	1.00

TABLE IX
NORMALIZED EXPERIMENTAL
STRESS – STRAIN VALUES FOR M60 GRADE

σ		ε	
Stress	**Normalized Stress**	**Strain**	**Normalized Strain**
12.40	0.21	3.11	0.10
24.81	0.42	6.22	0.20
34.12	0.58	9.28	0.30
40.04	0.68	12.51	0.40
44.27	0.76	15.49	0.50
47.94	0.82	18.63	0.60
51.04	0.87	21.79	0.70
53.58	0.92	24.77	0.80
56.11	0.96	28.15	0.91
58.09	1.00	31.10	1.00

From the normalized stress-strain values, normalized stress-strain curves are plotted. Empirical equations are proposed and then theoretical stresses are evaluated and compared with experimental stress values. The constants which are required for analytical curves were determined by the boundary conditions are shown in Table X&XI. Finally theoretical stress are arrived and compared with experimental values which are shown in Table XII to XVI. It is found that there is very little variation which validates the proposed mathematical model.**10^{-4}**

TABLE X

CONSTANTS FOR NON-DIMENSIONAL
STRESS- STRAIN CURVE

Grade of Concrete	**A'**	**B'**	**C'**
M20	3.06	1.06	1
M30	2.65	0.65	1
M40	2.43	0.43	1
M50	2.29	0.29	1
M60	2.13	0.134	1

TABLE XI
CONSTANTS FOR THEORETICAL
STRESS- STRAIN CURVE

Grade of Concrete	**A**	**B**	**C**
M20	24176	414	150819
M30	27350	242	136152
M40	31490	152	124852
M50	35042	100	113000
M60	39861	43	103387

TABLE XII
EXPERIMENTAL AND THEORETICAL
STRESS-STRAIN VALUES FOR M20 GRADE

ε x 10-4	**Experimental 'σ' N/mm2**	**Theoretical 'σ' N/mm2**
2.56	6.20	5.55
5.13	11.28	9.91
7.68	13.53	13.20
10.39	15.22	15.77
12.72	16.35	17.36
15.56	17.48	18.72
18.09	18.33	19.50
21.05	19.17	20.03
23.28	19.740	20.237
25.75	20.304	20.304

TABLE XIII
EXPERIMENTAL AND THEORETICAL
STRESS-STRAIN VALUES FOR M30 GRADE

ε x 10^{-4}	**Experimental 'σ' N/mm2**	**Theoretical 'σ' N/mm2**
2.68	7.33	6.82
5.48	14.66	12.78
8.24	18.04	17.45
10.82	20.30	20.80
13.73	22.27	23.64
16.27	23.68	25.37
19.29	25.09	26.74
22.10	26.22	27.48
24.47	27.07	27.809
27.10	27.918	27.918

TABLE XIV
EXPERIMENTAL AND THEORETICAL
STRESS-STRAIN VALUES FOR M40 GRADE

$\varepsilon \times 10^{-4}$	Experimental 'σ' N/mm2	Theoretical 'σ' N/mm2
2.86	9.02	8.56
5.64	17.76	15.78
8.47	22.84	21.88
11.38	26.22	26.84
14.20	28.76	30.46
16.875	30.73	32.95
19.56	32.43	34.69
22.67	34.12	35.93
25.64	35.53	36.51
28.30	36.66	36.66

TABLE XV
EXPERIMENTAL AND THEORETICAL
STRESS-STRAIN VALUES FOR M50 GRADE

$\varepsilon \times 10^{-4}$	Experimental 'σ' N/mm2	Theoretical 'σ' N/mm2
2.977	10.43	10.03
5.954	20.86	18.98
9.026	28.20	26.76
11.867	32.14	32.55
15.006	35.53	37.45
17.893	38.07	40.71
20.922	40.32	43.05
23.991	42.30	44.50
26.978	43.99	45.21
29.748	45.40	45.40

TABLE XVI
EXPERIMENTAL AND THEORETICAL
STRESS-STRAIN VALUES FOR M60 GRADE

$\varepsilon \times 10^{-4}$	Experimental 'σ' N/mm2	Theoretical 'σ' N/mm2
3.11	12.40	12.12
6.22	24.81	23.26
9.28	34.12	32.77
12.51	40.04	41.03
15.49	44.27	46.96
18.63	47.94	51.61
21.79	51.04	54.81
24.77	53.58	56.71
28.15	56.11	57.82
31.10	58.09	58.09

VII. CONCLUSIONS

Following conclusions can be drawn from the present investigation.

*1)*The values of modulus of elasticity are in the range of 21GPa to 35GPa for concrete grades M20 to M60 respectively. Values found to be 6% - 8.0% less than the conventional concrete which reveals insignificant difference.

*2)*The experimental and theoretical stress-strain curves are developed for Geo-Polymer concrete grades for M20 - M60 and theoretical models are developed for five grades of concrete.

*3)*The experimental stress–strain curve of Geo-Polymer concrete resembles the curve of normal concrete.

4) Theoretically stress-strain curves are compared with experimentally obtained and it revealed close agreement between them which indicated the validation of the theoretically developed mathematical model.

References

[1] Davidovits J., Geopolymers:Inorganic polymeric new materials, *Journal ofThermal Analysis*, 1991, 37, pp.1633–1656.

[2] Divya K and Chaudhary R., Mechanism of geopolymerisation and factors influence its development a review, *Journal of Material Science,* 2007, 42, pp.729-746.

[3] Vijai K. Kumutha R. Vishnuram B.G., Effect of types curing on strength of geopolymer concrete, *International journal of Physical Sciences*, August 2010, Vol. 5, No.9, pp.1419-1423.

[4] Siva Kondareddy B. Naveenreddy K Varaprasad J., Influence of curing conditions on compressive strength of cement added low lime fly ash based geopolymer concrete, *Journal of Engineering research and studies*, October 2011, Vol. 2, Issue IV, pp.103-109.

[5] Raijiwala D.B. Patil H.S., Geopolymer Concrete: A Concrete of Next decade, *Journal of Engineering Research and Studies*, March 2011, Vol.II, Issue I, pp.19-25.

[6] AnupamBhowmick and Somnath Ghosh., Effect of Synthesizing parameters on workability and compressive strength of fly ash based Geo-polymer mortar, *International Journal of civil and structural engineering*, August 2012, Vol.3, No.1, pp.168-177.

[7] Kumar S, Pradeepa J. and Ravindra P.M., Experimental Investigation of optimal strength parameters fly based geo-polymer concrete, *International journal structural and civil engineering research,* May 2013, Vol.2 No.2, pp143-152.

[8] Dattatreya J.K. Rajamane N.P. Sabitha D. Ambily P.S. Nataraj M.C., Flexural behavior of reinforced Geopolymer concrete beams, *International Journal of civil and Structural engineering,* September 2011, Vol 2, Issue 1, pp 138-159.

[9] GanapathiNaidu P. Prasad A.S.S.N. Adiseshu S. Satyanarayana P.V.V., A study on strength properties of Geopolymer concrete with addition of GGBS, *International Journal of engineering Research and development*, July 2012,Vol 2, Issue 4, pp 19-28.

[10] Parthiban K. Saravanarajmohan K. Shobana S. AnchalBhaskar A., Effect of replacement of slag on the mechanical properties of fly ash based geopolymer concrete, *International Journal of*

Engineering and Technology, June 2013, Vol 5, No.3, pp.2555-2559.

[11] Bhikshma. V and Naveen kumar T., Strength Characteristics of Fly ash based geo-polymer concrete with addition of GGBS, *Proceedings of International Conference on Engineering and Applied Science*, November, 2013, pp1192-1199.

[12] Rangan B.V., *Fly ash based Geopolymerconcrete* , Research report GC4, Faculty of Engineering, Curtain University of Technology, Perth, 2008, available at www.geopolymer.org.

[13] Indian Standard for Method of tests for strength of concrete, IS 516 :199. Bureau of Indian Standards, New Delhi.

[14] Sureshbabu T. Seshagiri Rao M.V. Rama Seshu D., Mechanical properties and stress-strain behavior of self compacting concrete with and without glass fibers, *Asian Journal of Civil Engineering (Building and Housing,)*, 2008, Vol. 9, No.5, pp. 457-472.

[15] BjanSamali, Mario M, Attard,Chongamin song, *From material to structures : Advancement through innovation*, Taylor & Francis Group London, 2013, pp.293-298.

[16] Srinivasa Reddy V. Rajaratnam V. Seshagiri Rao M V. Sasikala Ch., Mathematical model for predicting stress –strain behavior of bacterial concrete, *International Journal of engineering Research and development*, February 2013, Vol. 5, Issue 11, pp. 21-29.

[17] SuvaranLathaKakara and Seshagiri Rao M.V, Study on stress strain behavior of hardened concrete with HVFA,GGBS and GBS as partial replacement materials, *International Journal of engineering and advancement technology*, April 2013, Vol.2, Issue 4, 813-820.

[18] Hognestad E, Hanson N.W, McHenry D, Concrete stress distribution in ultimate strength design, *ACI Journal*, December 1955, Proceeding 52, pp. 455-479.

[19] [19] Desayi, P. and Krishnan, S., Equation for the Stress-Strain Curve of Concrete," ACI Journal, March 1964, Proceedings 61, No.3, pp.345-350.

[20] Saenz, L.P., Discussion of Equation for the Stress-Strain Curve of Concrete - by Desayi and Krishnan, *ACI Journal*, June 1964, Proceeding No.61, No.6, pp.1229-1235.

[21] Carreira, D.J. and Chu K.D., Stress-Strain Relationship for Plain Concrete in Compression, *ACI Journal*, 1985, Proceeding No.82 No.6, pp.797-804.

[22] Loove, R.E., A General Stress-Strain Curve for Concrete: Implications for High Strength Concrete Columns, Annual Conference of the Canadian Society for Civil Engineering, May 29,1991, pp. 302-311.

[23] Collins, M.P., Mitchell D. and MacGregor, J.G., Structural Consideration for High-Strength Concrete, *Concrete International*, May 1993, Vol.15, No.5, pp. 27-34.

[24] Indian Standard for Code of Practice for plain and reinforced concrete, IS 456 :1978. Bureau of Indian Standards, New Delhi.

[25] Popovics S., A numerical approach to the complete stress-strain curve of concrete, *Cement and Concrete Research*, 1973, Vol. 3, No. 5, pp. 583-99.

[26] Almusallam T.H.and Alsayed S.H., Stress-strain relationship of normal, high and lightweight concrete, *Magazine of Concrete Research*, 1995, Vol. 47, No. 170, pp. 39-44.

A Comparative Study on Seismic Analysis of Irregular Framed Structure with Bare Frame, Open Ground Storey and Infilled Frame

Sirigiri Sowmya[1], K. L. Radhika

[1]*Associate Professor, Civil Engineering Department, University College of Engineering(A), Osmania University, Hyderabad-07*

[2] *M.E scholar, Civil Engineering Department, University College of Engineering, Osmania University, Hyderabad- 07*

sowmyasirigiri@gmail.com

radhikaou@yahoo.com

***Abstract*: One of the most frightening and destructive phenomena of a nature is a severe earthquake and its terrible effect after occurring. Masonry infill walls are known to provide stiffness and strength to the building. These are considered as non-structural elements according to IS 1893:2002 and the code allows analysis of open ground storey buildings without considering infill stiffness but with a multiplication factor 2.5 in compensation for the stiffness discontinuity irrespective tonumber of storeys, number of bays, type and number of infill walls present, number of irregularities and is independent of all the above factors from zone to zone. Structurally these unbalances are unhealthy. This paper is about comparative study on various performances of irregular bare frame, infilled frame and open first storey frame for five and eight storey structure considering medium soil using SAP2000 software. Analysis is carried over using response spectrum method located in II, III, IV and V zones and pushover and time history methods located in V Zone. The primary aim is to study the effect of infill strength in the seismic analysis of soft storey frame. Multiplication factor,base shear, forces, ductility demand, storey drift is calculated and compared for all models. The result shows that infill walls reduce displacements, time period and increases base shear, forces, ductility demand in the ground storey and multiplication factor is also being increased with respect to zones and storeys compare to bare and soft storey frames. So it is essential to consider the effect of masonry infill for the seismic evaluation of moment resisting reinforced concrete.**

***Keyword*: Performance point, Multiplication factor (MF), Response spectrum analysis, Pushover analysis, Time history analysis.**

I. Introduction

Typical masonry infilled frames contain infill walls throughout the building in all storeys uniformly. Although infill walls are known to provide the stiffness and strength to the building globally, these are considered as 'non-structural' by design codes and are commonly ignored in the design practice for more convenience. The presence of infill walls in a framed building not only enhance the lateral stiffness in the building, but also alters the transmission of forces in beams and columns, as compared to the bare frame. In a bare frame, the resistance to lateral force occurs by the development of bending moments and shear forces in the beams and columns through the rigid jointed action of the beam-column joints. In the case of infilled frame, a substantial truss action can be observed; contributing to reduced bending moments but increased axial forces in beams and column.

The assessment of the seismic vulnerability of structures is a very complex issue due to the nondeterministic characteristics of the seismic action and the need for an accurate prediction of the seismic responses for levels beyond conventional linear behavior. The major developments in earthquake engineering have occurred in last four decades. This has been possible as a result of combination of factors such as installation of strong motion instruments world over in active seismic areas, as a result sizeable amount of ground motion data is available, development of basic principles of seismic design, design for strength and ductility, and basic concepts of design response spectrum, developments in mathematical modeling and dynamic analysis-linear and non linear, shake table testing, quasi-static and pseudo dynamic testing, response control, seismic isolation and energy dissipating devices. The availability of high-speed digital computers has played a vital role in these developments. Besides, study of behavior of structures and their performance in past earthquakes have provided a wealth of information on earthquake protection and safety.

II. Research Significance

The infill walls are considered as a non- structural element from the convenience design practice as per IS code. But in the actual practice the presence of infill walls create a strut compressive action acting diagonally in the direction opposite to the application of the lateral force that may try to counter act the lateral force that causes less deflection. Assessment of the multiplication factor (MF) requires accurate analysis of OGS buildings considering infill stiffness and strength. The presence of infill walls in upper storeys of OGS buildings accounts for the following issues:

- Increases the lateral stiffness of the building frame
- Decreases the natural period of vibration
- Increases the base shear.
- Increases the shear forces and bending moments in the ground storey columns.
- Increases the storey drift of first storey than the upper storeys

Inelastic analysis procedures help to demonstrate how building really performs by identifying the failure modes and the potential for progressive collapse. For this there should be a clear need to assess the design guidelines recommended by the code, as existing recommendations for the design of OGS buildings do not depend on the factors such as number of storeys, number of bays, type and the number of infill walls present, etc.

A. *Objectives of the Study*

Based on the previous discussions, the objective of the present study has been identified as follows.

- To study the seismic performance of different floor heights with bare frame, infilled frame, open ground storey frame, comparing their relative performance using response spectrum analysis, pushover analysis and time history analysis.
- To find the response of structure in terms of storey drifts.
- To develop displacement curves for the considered frames.
- To study the effect of infill strength, stiffness in the seismic analysis of open ground storey building and calculating multiplication factor.
- To conduct time history analysis for the evaluation of dynamic structural response under loading which may vary according to specified time function.

III. LITERATURE REVIEW

Raghavendra and Deshpande (2014)have stated that theLateral displacement of bare frame model is higher than other models because of less lateral resistance and stiffness of storey, due to absence of masonry infill walls.First storey displacement of soft first storey model is maximum than other models due to absence of infill in the first storey.In soft first storey frame, there is sudden change in drift between first and second storey. Second storey drift is only 18.28% of first storey.By providing infill at specific locations in first storey and stiffening the first storey columns by increasing the size, there is significant increase in the stiffness, reduction of lateral drift demand, in the first storey column. Infill increases lateral resistance and initial stiffness of the frames, so they appear to have a significant effect on the reduction of the lateral displacement. The use of equivalent diagonal struts at specific positions significantly increases the first storey stiffness. The first storey stiffness comes out to be 36.93% of second storey stiffness. It considerably reduces the lateral displacement and shows the smooth drift profile. Inclusion of infill reduces the fundamental time period of building.

DharmeshVijaywargiya et.al (2014) has shown results that the effect of infill's stiffness on structural response is significant under lateral loads. The magnification factor of 2.5 is high to be multiplied to column forces of the ground storey of the given mid-rise open ground storey building. It is found that the infill panels increases the stiffness of the upper storeys of the structure, thereby increasing the forces, displacement, drift and ductility demand in the soft ground storey. This could become the cause of failure of open ground storey buildings during earthquake.

Saurabh Singh et.al (2014) shown that the MF based on linear and non linear analysis is in the range 1.106-1.1084 for a four storied OFS building, 1.806-1.858 for seven storied OFS building and 1.959-2.193 for ten storied OFS building. The MF increases with the h0eight of the building, primarily due to the higher shift in the time period.

Tamboli and Karadi,(2012) – studied that seismic analysis has been performed using Equivalent Lateral Force Method for different reinforced concrete (RC) frame building models that include bare frame, infilled frame and open first storey frame. He concluded that seismic analysis of bare frame structure leads to under estimation of base shear which may lead to collapse of structure during earthquake shaking. Therefore it is important to consider the infill walls in the scismic analysis of structure.

IV. METHODOLOGY

Modeling masonry structures is a task that involves a detailed description of materials. Masonry is a material that exhibits distinct directional properties due to mortar joints which act as planes of weakness.

In present study infill wall in storeys are modeled as equivalent diagonal strut (proposed by Hendry in 1998) and its equivalent width (W) of a strut is given as,

$$W=\frac{1}{2}\sqrt{\alpha_h^2+\alpha_l^2}$$

To determine α_h and α_l which depends on the relative stiffness of the frame and on the geometry of the panel.

$$\propto_h = \frac{\pi}{2}\left[\frac{4E_f I_c h}{E_m t \sin 2\theta}\right]^{\frac{1}{4}}$$

$$\propto_l = \frac{\pi}{2}\left[\frac{4E_f I_b l}{E_m t \sin 2\theta}\right]^{\frac{1}{4}}$$

Where,

E_f and E_m=elastic modulus of the frame material and masonry wall, respectively

t, h, l = thickness, height and length of the infill wall, respectively

I_c, I_b= moment of inertia of the column and the beam of the frame, respectively

$\theta = \tan^{-1}\left(\frac{h}{l}\right)$

A. Storey Stiffness

(1) Column stiffness of each storey,

Column stiffness = (12EI)/L^3

(2) Infill stiffness of each storey,

Stiffness of infill wall = $(AE_m \cos^2\theta)/l_d$

A = Area of diagonal strut

E = elastic modulus of the concrete

E_m = elastic modulus of the masonry wall

$$\theta = \tan^{-1}\left(\frac{h}{l}\right)$$

l_d = diagonal length of strut

L = length of the column

The modulus of elasticity for the bricks is calculated as per Masonry Institute of America, (1998)

E_m= 750f_m, 20GPA (Max)

Where f_m = compressive strength of masonry and it has been taken (from the table no. E-1, page no -8 and fig no. E-10 page no 8 of SP 20)

B. Methodologies for the Study

1) Linear Dynamic Analysis – Response Spectrum Analysis as per IS 1893 -2002
2) Non Linear Static Analysis –Pushover Analysis
3) Non linear dynamic Analysis – Time History Analysis

TABLE 1DETAILS OF THE PROPOSED STRUCTURAL MODELS ARE AS GIVEN BELOW

1	Type of structure	Multi-storey rigid plane frame (SMRF)
2	Number Of Stories	Six (G+5) ,Nine (G+8)
3	Floor Height	First Floor-3.8m Above Floor-3.5m
4	Infill Wall	250mm thick
5	Size Of Column	450mmX450mm
6	Size Of Beam	400mmX300mm
7	Depth Of Slab (RCC)	120mm
8	Live Load	3KN/m^2
9	Terrace Water Proofing	1.5KN/m^2
10	Floor Finishes	0.5KN/m^2
11	Material	M 30 Grade of concrete Fe 415 HYSD bars
12	Unit weights	a) Concrete=25KN/Cum b) Masonry=20KN/Cum
13	Modulus Of Elasticity Of Concrete	22360.67N/mm^2
14	Modulus Of Elasticity Of Masonry	6975KN/mm^2
15	Total Height Of Building	21.3m for G+5,31.8m for G+8 and 38.8m for G+10
16	Clear Cover Of Beam	25mm
17	Clear Cover Of column	40mm

The Plan configuration consists of

Model I - Five storey structure with bare frame, infilled frame and open first storey frame.

Model II - Eight storey structure with bare frame, infilled frame and open first storey frame.

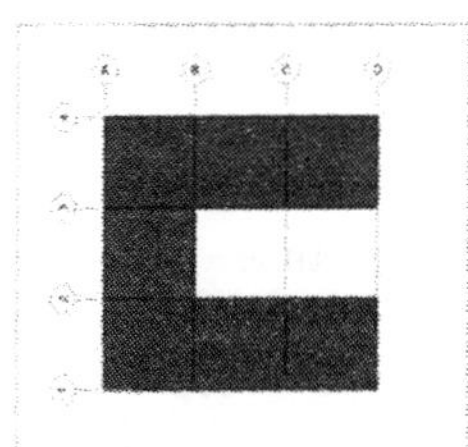

Fig 1. Plan of irregular building (4.5m longitudinal direction and 4m transverse direction)

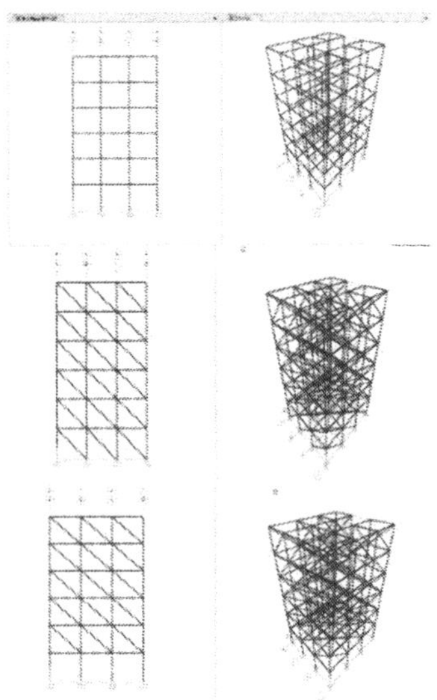

Fig 2.Elevation and Isometric View of Bare, Infilled and OGS Frame

Similarly eight storey structure with bare, OGS and infilled frames are modelled

TABLE 2 SEISMIC DATA ASSUMED FOR THE ANALYSIS

S No.	Design Parameter	Value
1	Seismic Zone	V
2	Zone factor (Z)	0.36
3	Response reduction factor (R)	5
4	Importance factor	1
5	Soil type	Medium soil
6	Damping ratio	5%

V. Results and Discussions

A comparative study is made on various performances of irregular bare frame, infilled frame and open first storey frame for five and eight storey structure considering medium soil using SAP2000 software. Analysis is carried over using response spectrum method located in II, III, IV and V zones and pushover and time history methods located in V Zone.The Results obtained are of different parameters such as Storey drifts, Shear Force, Bending Moment, Base shear, performance point and multiplication factor. Firstly the results are obtained by carrying out Response Spectrum Analysis, secondly by Pushover and Time History Analysis. Subsequent Discussions are made about the Results Obtained based on the different parameters.

A. Results of Five Storey RC Frame Building

Results of Response Spectrum Analysis:

TABLE 3 STOREY DRIFT OF G+5 BUILDING IN ZONE V

Storey no	Bare Frame (mm)	OGS (mm)	Infill Walls (mm)
6	0.0155	0.0028	0.003
5	0.0256	0.004	0.004
4	0.0354	0.005	0.0047
3	0.0393	0.0056	0.0052
2	0.048	0.0082	0.0053
1	0.033	0.0502	0.0051

TABLE 4 STOREY DRIFT OF G+5 BUILDING IN ZONE IV

Storey no	Bare Frame (mm)	OGS (mm)	Fully Infill Walls (mm)
6	0.0103	0.0019	0.002
5	0.0171	0.0027	0.0026
4	0.0232	0.0035	0.0032
3	0.0281	0.0038	0.0035
2	0.0301	0.0056	0.0035
1	0.022	0.0337	0.0034

TABLE 5 STOREY DRIFT OF G+5 BUILDING IN ZONE III

Storey no	Bare Frame (mm)	OGS (mm)	Infill Walls (mm)
6	0.0069	0.0013	0.0013
5	0.0114	0.0018	0.0018
4	0.0154	0.0022	0.0021
3	0.0188	0.0026	0.0023
2	0.02	0.0038	0.0023
1	0.0147	0.0224	0.0023

TABLE 6 STOREY DRIFT OF G+5 BUILDING IN ZONE II

Storey no	Bare Frame (mm)	OGS (mm)	Infill Walls (mm)
6	0.0043	0.0007	0.0007
5	0.0071	0.0011	0.0011
4	0.0097	0.0013	0.0012
3	0.0117	0.0015	0.0013
2	0.0125	0.0021	0.0013
1	0.0092	0.0138	0.0012

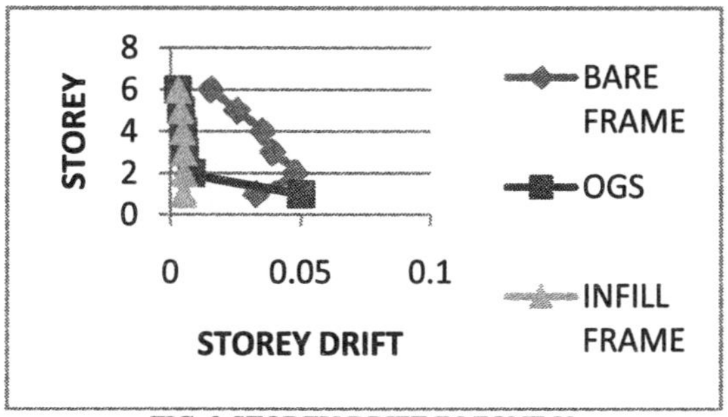

FIG. 3 STOREY DRIFT IN ZONE V

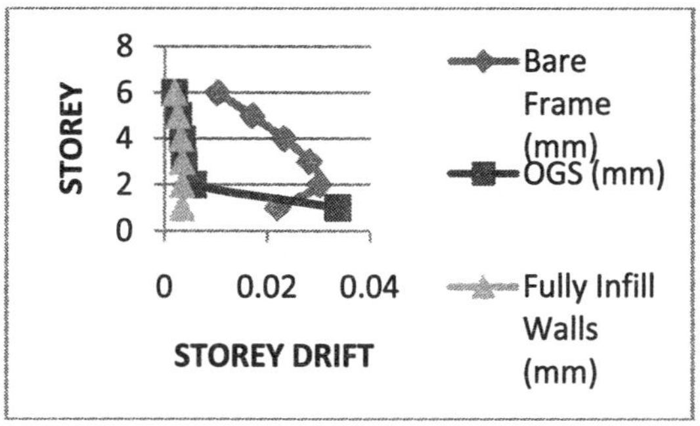

FIG. 4 STOREY DRIFT IN ZONE IV

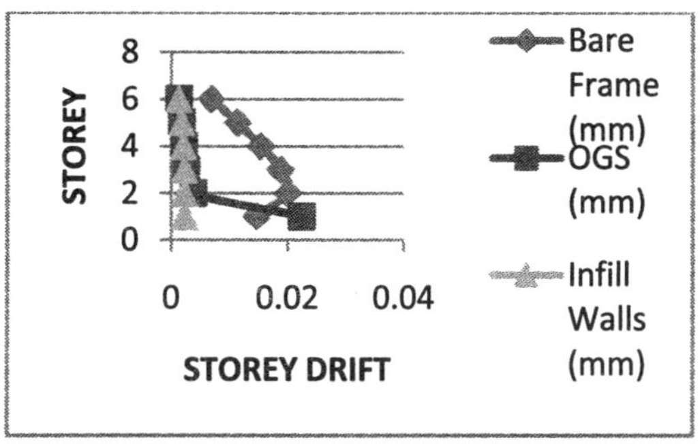

FIG. 5 STOREY DRIFT IN ZONE III

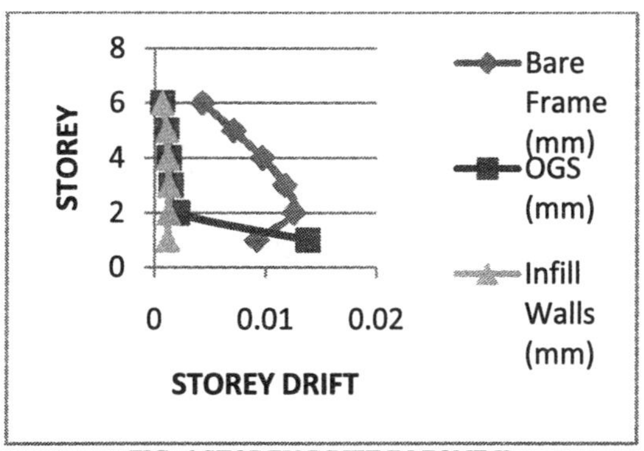

FIG. 6 STOREY DRIFT IN ZONE II

From Tables 3-6 and Figs 3-6 it is observed that for five storey structure the storey drift of first storey of OGS frame is very large than the upper storeys, this is because of the absence of infill walls in the first storey. However in the infilled frame the storey drift of first storey is less because of the presence of infill wall in the first storey (ground storey). Variation in OGS at the first storey is 34.26% more than bare and 89.84% more than infilled frame in V zone; similarly it is varying in all the zones.

TABLE 7 RESPONSE SPECTRUM ANALYSIS FOR B.M. RESULT OF G+5 BUILDING MODEL

Model	Zone	Bare Frame	OGS	Infill Frame
Max B.M. In the Ground Storey Column	V	742.97	1462.85	141.3001
	IV	495.318	1005.1383	82.53
	III	330.212	670.092	75.0154
	II	206.382	406.3476	28.64

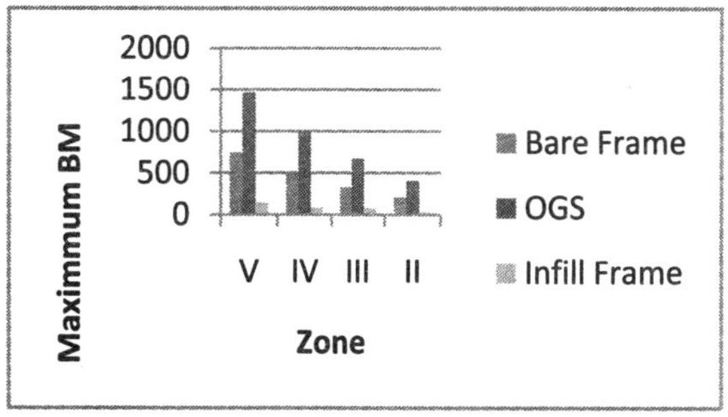

Fig. 7 MAX B.M. IN ALL THE ZONES

TABLE 8 RESPONSE SPECTRUM ANALYSIS FOR S.F. RESULT OF G+5 BUILDING MODEL

Model	Zone	Bare Frame	OGS	Infill Frame
Max S.F. In the Ground Storey Column	V	254.376	659.190	51.586
	IV	169.584	458.248	30.9
	III	113.056	305.499	28.445
	II	70.66	183.108	10.335

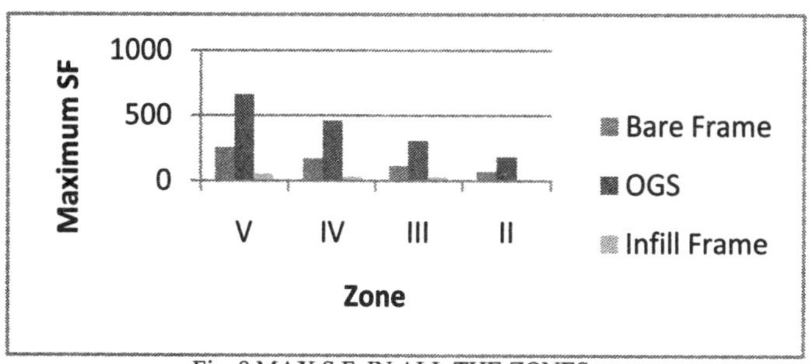

Fig. 8 MAX S.F. IN ALL THE ZONES

From Tables 7-8 and Figs 5-6 it is observed that for five storey structure the bending moment and shear force values of OGS frame is very large than bare frame and infill frame and it is getting decreased from zone V to zone II in all the frames. Variation of BM in OGS is 49.21% more than bare and 90.34% more than infilled frame and of SF is 61.41% more than bare and 92.17% more than infilled frame in V zone. Open first storey frame have more bending moment and shear force than infilled and bare frame resulting that this structure cause more failure than infilled and bare frame.

Results of Pushover Analysis:

Pushover analysis of all the building models is carried out to find the maximum shear force, maximum bending moment, Multiplication Factor (MF) and performance point.

TABLE 9 PUSH OVER ANALYSIS RESULT FOR G+5 BUILDING MODEL

Frame Type		Bare Frame (KN)	OGS (KN)	Infill Frame (KN)
Column(ground storey)	Max B.M.	945.1379	1523.69	302.26
	Max S.F.	352.729	874.29	113.355

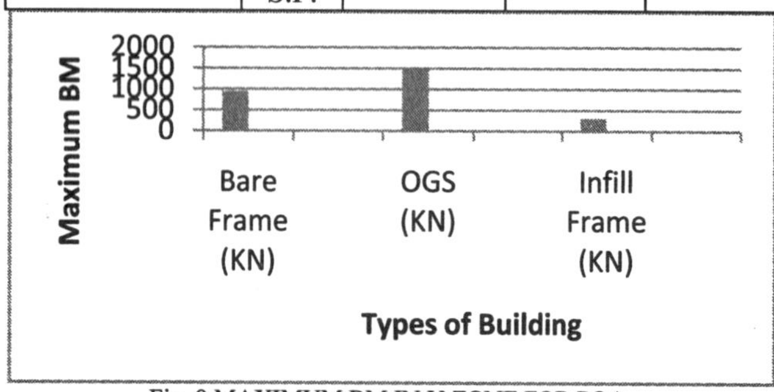

Fig. 9 MAXIMUM BM IN V ZONE FOR POA

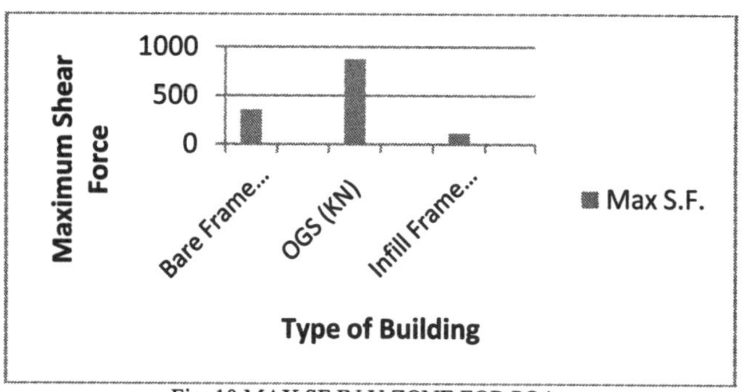

Fig. 10 MAX SF IN V ZONE FOR POA

By non linear analysis from Table 9 and Fig. 7-8, BM is varying in OGS as 80.16% more than infilled frame and 37.97% more than bare frame and SF as 87.03% more than infilled frame and 59.69% more than bare frame in Zone V medium soil condition.

Multiplication factor:

TABLE 10 MULTIPLICATION FACTORS FOR BENDING MOMENT AND SHEAR FORCE OF G+ 5 MODELS

Model	Analysis method	Seismic zone	Bare frame	OGS	Multiplication factor
Maximum bending moment in ground storey(KN m)	RES	II	206.382	406.3476	1.96
	RES	III	330.212	670.092	2.02
	RES	IV	495.318	1005.1383	2.02
	RES	V	742.97	1462.85	1.96
	POA	V	945.1379	1523.69	1.61
Maximum shear force in ground storey(KN m)	RES	II	70.66	183.108	2.59
	RES	III	113.056	305.499	2.7
	RES	IV	169.584	458.248	2.7
	RES	V	254.376	659.190	2.59
	POA	V	352.729	874.29	2.47

*Multiplication factor values for bending moment & shear force are obtained by dividing with the Corresponding values for the bare frame.

From the Table 10, the MF based on linear and non linear analysis with respect to different zones from the Table. 10 is in the range of 1.61-2.02 for BM and 2.47-2.7 for SF. The MF increases with the height of the building, primarily due to the higher shift in the time period. Therefore multiplication factor is varying with respect to zones, storeys and method of analysis which is not specified in code.

Performance Point:

For G+5 RC building frames the non linear static pushover analysis is performed to investigate the performance point of the building frame in terms of base shear and displacement. For pushover analysis the various pushover cases are considered such as push gravity, push X (i.e. loads are applied in X direction), push Y (i.e. loads are applied in Y direction). After pushover analysis the demand curve and capacity curves are obtained to get the performance point of the structure. The performance point is obtained as per ATC 40 capacity spectrum method.

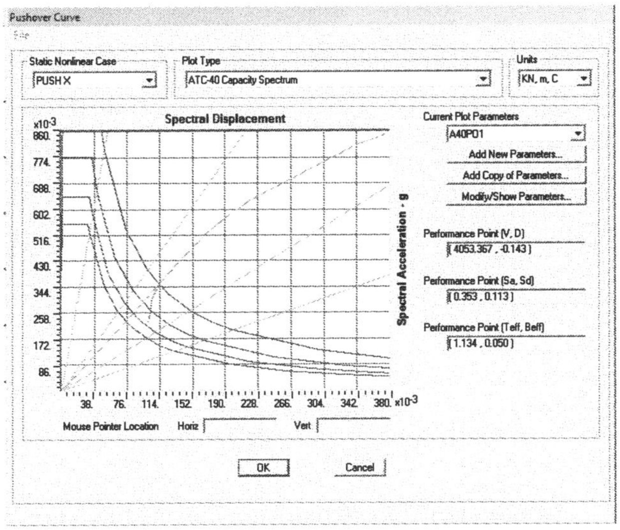

Fig. 11 PERFORMANCE POINT FOR G+5 (BARE FRAME)

Fig. 11 shows the Performance point for five storey bare frame structure for load case PUSHX is 4053.367KN.

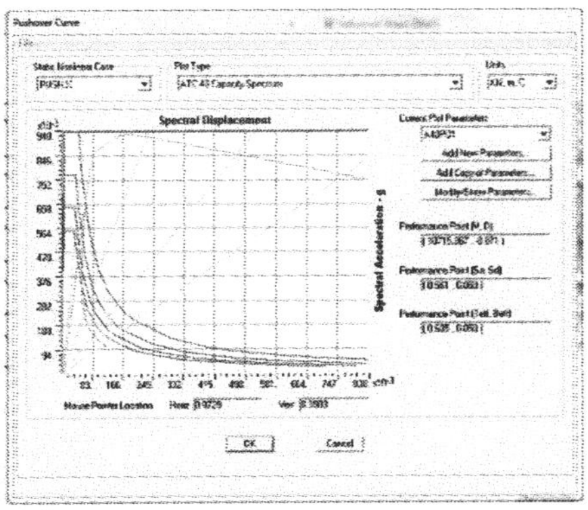

Fig. 12 PERFORMANCE POINT FOR G+5 (OGS)

Fig. 12 shows the Performance point for five storey OGS frame structure for load case PUSHX is 10715.367KN.

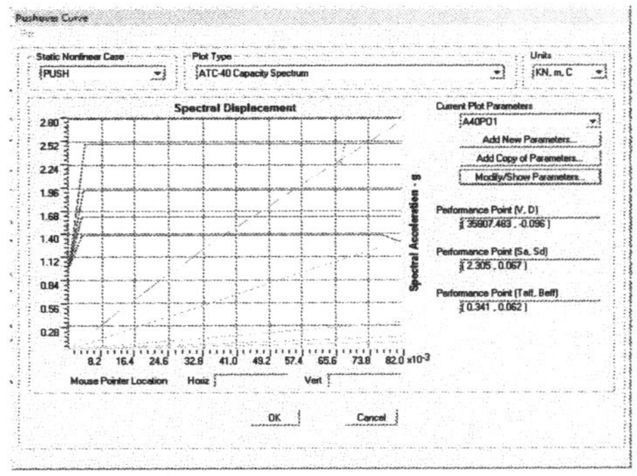

Fig. 13 PERFORMANCE POINT OF G+5 (INFILL)

Fig. 13 shows the Performance point for five storey infill frame structure for load case PUSHX is 35807.483KN.

TABLE 11 PERFORMANCE POINT OF G+ 5 MODELS

Frame Type	Bare Frame (KN)	OGS (KN)	Infill Frame (KN)
Performance Point	4053.367	10715.367	35807.483

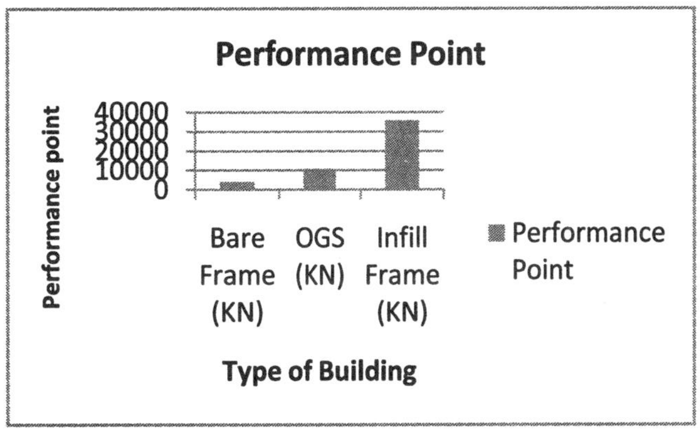

FIG. 14 PERFORMANCE POINT OF G+5 FOR ALL FRAMES

From the Table 11 and Fig.14 performance point of G+5 building models, it is clear that bare frame is having lesser lateral load capacity (Performance point value) compare to infill frame and open first storey. Performance point of infilled frame is varying as 70.07% more than OGS frame and 88.68% more than bare frame.

Results of Time History Analysis:

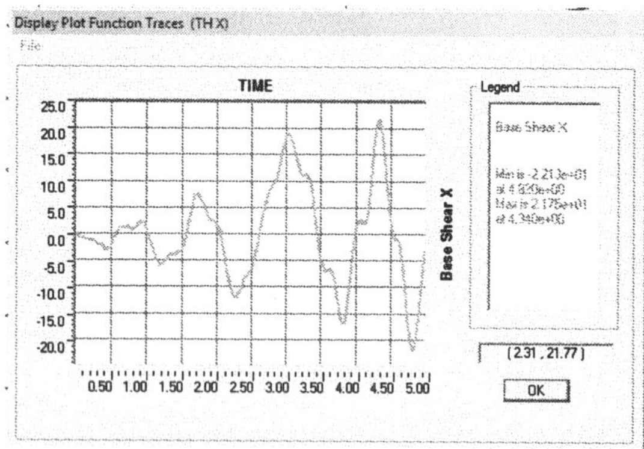

FIG. 15 TIME VS BASE SHEAR –X FOR G+5 (BARE FRAME)

Fig. 15 shows the Base shear time history for five storey with bare frame structure for load case THX is maximum at 21.77 KN

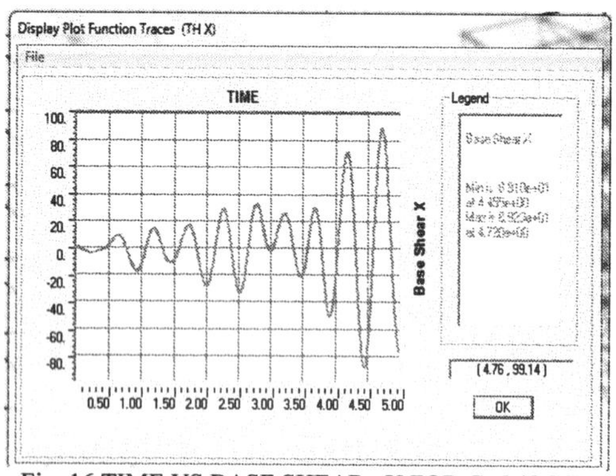

Fig. 16 TIME VS BASE SHEAR –X FOR G+5 (OGS)

Fig. 16 shows the Base shear time history for five storey with open first storey frame structure for load case THX is maximum at 89.66 KN.

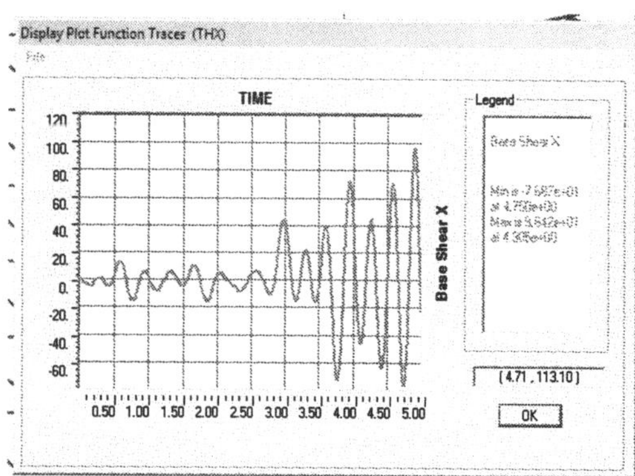

Fig 17 TIME VS BASE SHEAR –X FOR G+5 (INFILL)

Fig. 17 shows the Base shear time history for five storey with infill frame structure for load case THX is maximum at 96.72KN.

TABLE 12 BASE SHEAR OF G+5 BUILDING

Frame Type	Bare Frame (KN)	OGS (KN)	Infill Frame (KN)
Base shear	21.77	89.66	96.72

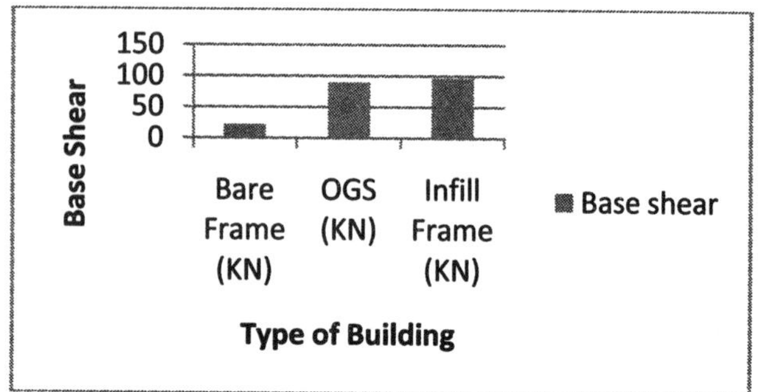

Fig. 18 BASE SHEAR COMPARISON FOR FIVE STOREY STRUCTURE FOR LOAD CASE THX

From the Table1 2 and Fig. 18, the base shear of infilled frame is more than bare and open first storey frame. Percentage decrease in base shear of bare frame is 77.4% and open first storey is 7.29% compare to infilled frame.

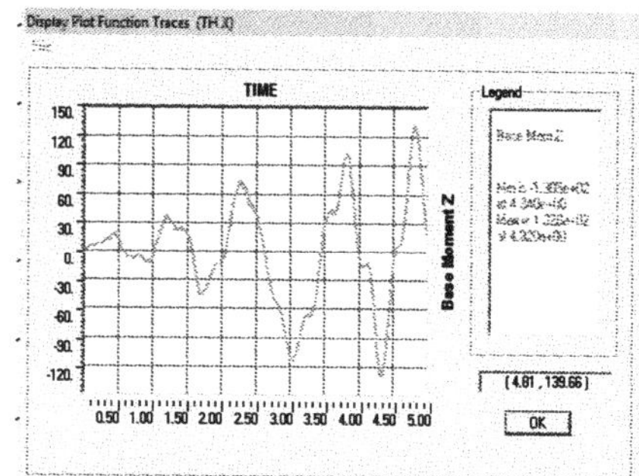

Fig. 19 TIME VS BASE MOMENT–Z FOR G+5 (BARE FRAME)

Fig. 19 shows the Base moment time history for five storey with bare frame structure for load case THX is maximum at 132.86KN

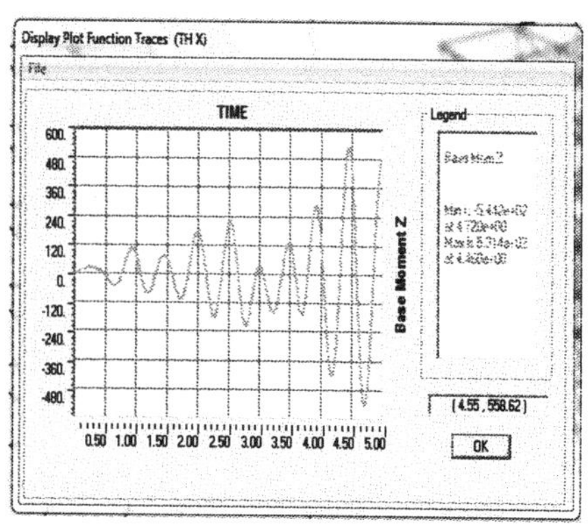

Fig. 20 TIME VS BASE MOMENT–Z FOR G+5 (OGS)

Fig. 20 shows the Base moment time history for five storey with open first storey frame structure for load case THX is maximum at 531.42KN

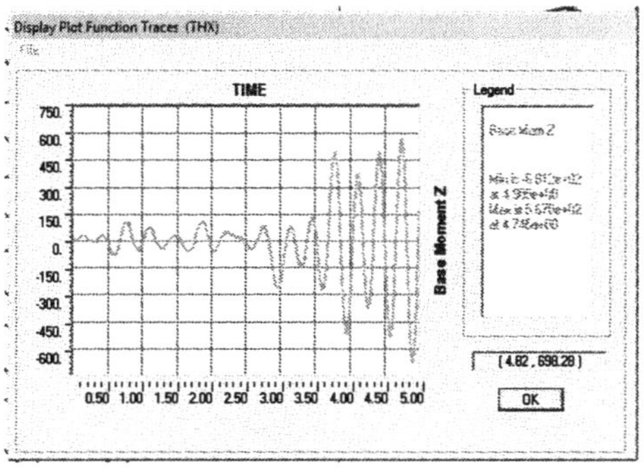

Fig. 21 TIME VS BASE MOMENT –Z FOR G+5 (INFILL)

TABLE 13 BASE MOMENT OF G+5 BUILDING

Frame Type	Bare Frame (KN)	OGS (KN)	Infill Frame (KN)
Base moment	132.86	531.42	567

From the Table 13, the base moment of infilled frame is more than bare and open first storey frame. Percentage decrease in base shear of bare frame is 76.56% and open first storey is 6.27% compared to infilled frame.

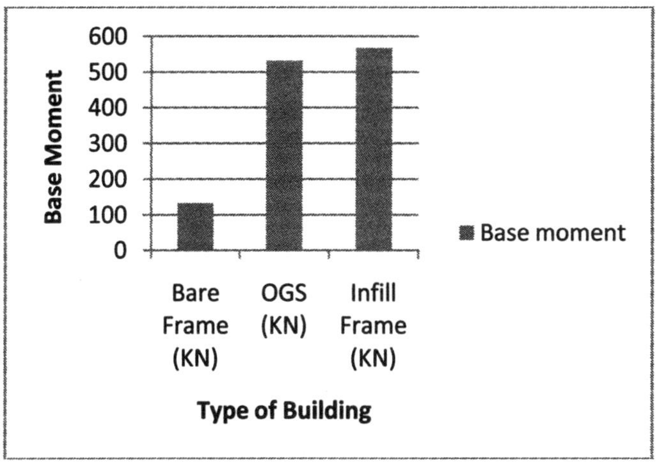

Fig. 22 BASE MOMENT COMPARISON OF FIVE STOREY STRUCTURE FOR LOAD CASE THX

Fig. 22 shows the Base moment time history for five storey with infill frame structure for load case THX is maximum at 567 KN

B. Results of Eight Storey RC Frame Building

TABLE 14 STOREY DRIFT OF G+8 BUILDING IN ZONE V

Storey no	Bare Frame (mm)	OGS (mm)	Infill Walls (mm)
9	0.0106	0.0053	0.0076
8	0.017	0.0055	0.0089
7	0.0229	0.0055	0.0102
6	0.0281	0.0055	0.0110
5	0.0329	0.0052	0.0116
4	0.0373	0.0048	0.0119
3	0.0409	0.004	0.0116
2	0.0415	0.0043	0.0112
1	0.0294	0.0604	0.0106

TABLE 15 STOREY DRIFT OF G+8 BUILDING IN ZONE IV

Storey no	Bare Frame (mm)	OGS (mm)	Infill Walls (mm)
9	0.007	0.0037	0.0049
8	0.0113	0.0039	0.0057
7	0.0153	0.0041	0.0064
6	0.0188	0.0041	0.0069
5	0.0219	0.0042	0.0072
4	0.0249	0.004	0.0072
3	0.0272	0.0037	0.007
2	0.0277	0.0039	0.0066
1	0.0196	0.0419	0.006

TABLE 16 STOREY DRIFT OF G+8 BUILDING IN ZONE III

Storey no	Bare Frame (mm)	OGS (mm)	Infill Walls (mm)
9	0.0047	0.0025	0.0033
8	0.0075	0.0026	0.0038
7	0.0102	0.0027	0.0043
6	0.0125	0.0028	0.0045
5	0.0146	0.0027	0.0048
4	0.0166	0.0027	0.0048
3	0.0182	0.0024	0.0047
2	0.0184	0.0027	0.0044
1	0.0131	0.0279	0.004

TABLE 17 STOREY DRIFT OF G+8 BUILDING IN ZONE II

Storey no	Bare Frame (mm)	OGS (mm)	Infill Walls (mm)
9	0.003	0.0015	0.0019
8	0.0047	0.0017	0.0023
7	0.0063	0.0016	0.0025
6	0.0078	0.0018	0.0027
5	0.0092	0.0017	0.0028
4	0.0103	0.0017	0.0027
3	0.0114	0.0015	0.0026
2	0.0115	0.0017	0.0024
1	0.0082	0.0174	0.0021

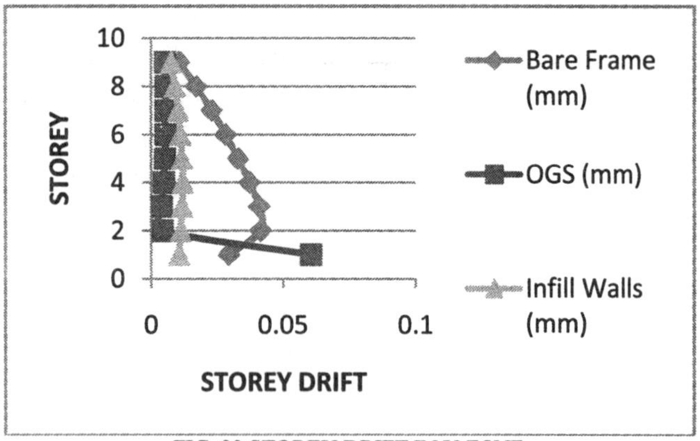

FIG. 23 STOREY DRIFT IN V ZONE

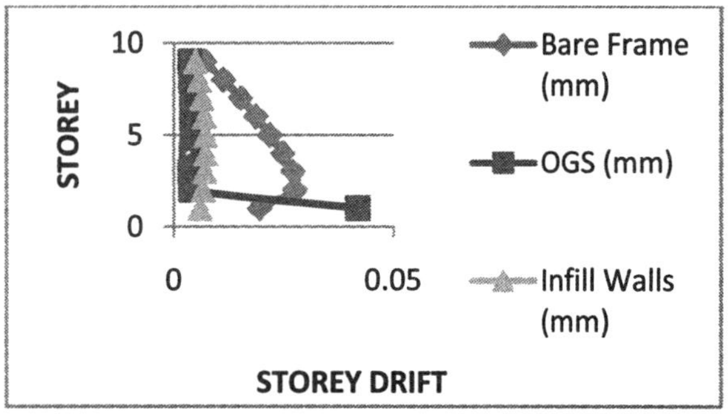

Fig. 24 STOREY DRIFT IN IV ZONE

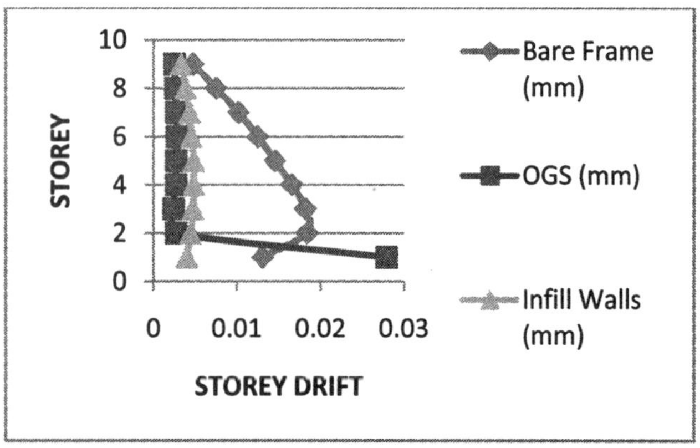

Fig. 25 STOREY DRIFT IN III ZONE

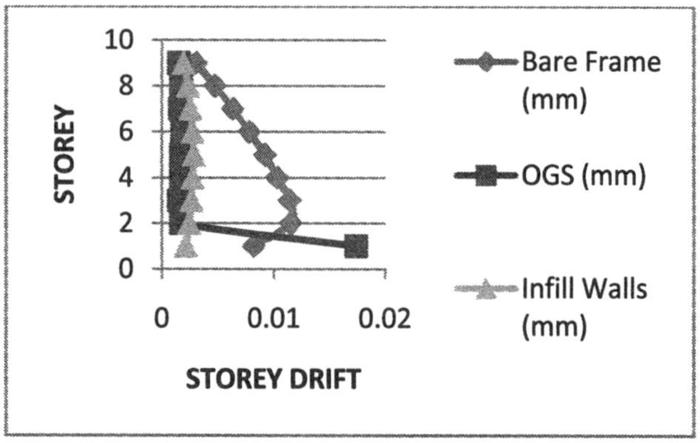

Fig. 26 STOREY DRIFT IN II ZONE

From Tables 14-17 and Figs 23-26 it is observed that for eight storey structure the storey drift of first storey of OGS frame is very large than the upper storeys, this is because of the absence of infill walls in the first storey. However in the infilled frame the storey drift of first storey is less because of the presence of infill wall in the first storey (ground storey). Variation in OGS at the first storey is 51.32% more than bare and 87.41% more than infilled frame in V zone; similarly it is varying in all the zones

TABLE 18 RESPONSE SPECTRUM ANALYSIS FOR B.M. RESULT OF G+8 BUILDING MODEL

Model	Zone	Bare Frame	OGS	Infill Frame
Max B.M. In the Ground Storey Column	V	865.48	1994.07	210.8017
	IV	585.629	1329.38	140.53
	III	409.355	886.255	80.1886
	II	244.01	553.9103	50.1178

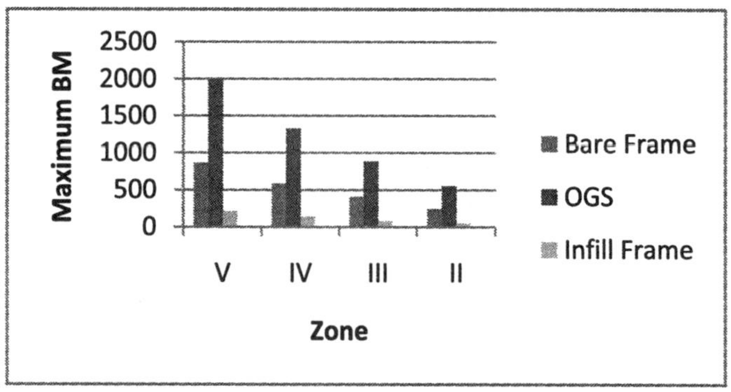

Fig. 27 MAXIMUM BM BY RSA IN ALL ZONES

TABLE 19 RESPONSE SPECTRUM ANALYSIS FOR S.F. RESULT OF G+5 BUILDING MODEL

Model	Zone	Bare Frame	OGS	Infill Frame
Max S.F. In the Ground Storey Column	V	313.808	950.840	75.145
	IV	209.205	633.893	50.097
	III	145.72	422.596	29.161
	II	94.3	264.122	50.117

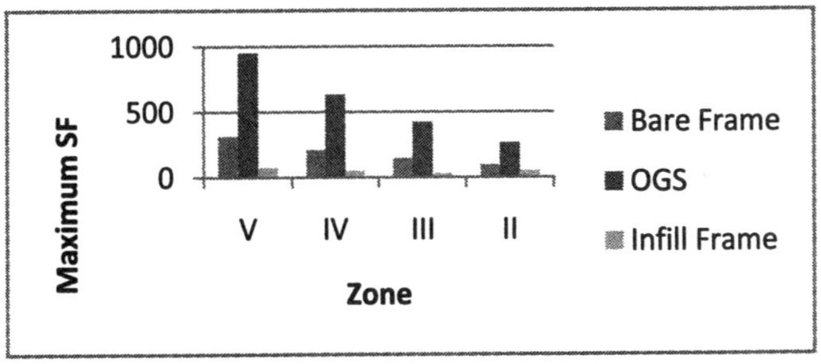

Fig. 28 MAXIMUM SF BY RSA IN ALL ZONES

From Tables 18-19 and Figs 27-28 it is observed that for eight storey structure the bending moment and shear force values of OGS frame is very large than bare frame and infill frame and it is getting decreased from zone V to zone II in all the frames. Variation of BM in OGS is 56.59% more than bare and 89.42% more than infilled frame and of SF is 66.96% more than bare and 92.09% more than infilled frame in V zone. Open first storey frame have more bending moment and shear force than infilled and bare frame resulting that this structure cause more failure than infilled and bare frame.

Results of Pushover Analysis:

TABLE 20 PUSHOVER ANALYSIS RESULT FOR G+8 BUILDING MODEL

Model		Bare Frame (mm)	OGS (mm)	Infill Walls (mm)
Column(ground storey)	Max B.M.	1084.101	1864.655	300.032
	Max S.F.	357.538	912.413	111.653

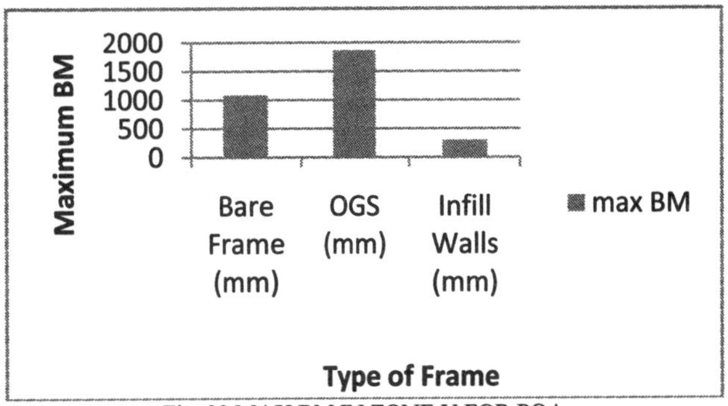

Fig. 29 MAX BM IN ZONE V FOR POA

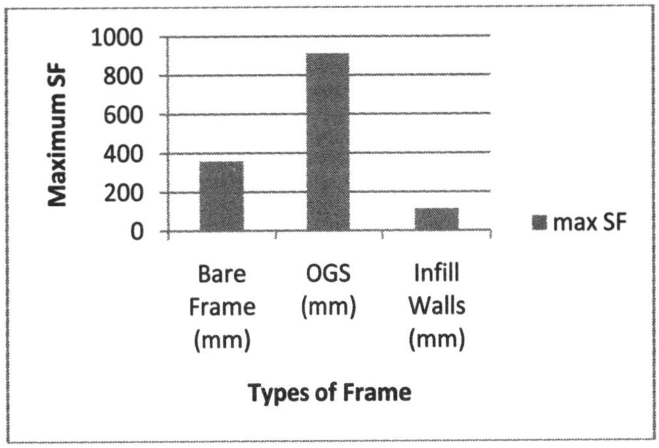

Fig. 30 MAX SF IN V ZONE FOR POA

By non linear analysis from Table 20 and Fig. 29-30, BM is varying in OGS as 83.90% more than infilled frame and 41.86% more than bare frame and SF as 87.76% more than infilled frame and 60.81% more than bare frame in Zone V medium soil condition.

Multiplication factor:

TABLE 21 MULTIPLICATION FACTORS FOR BENDING MOMENT AND SHEAR FORCE OF G+ 8 MODELS

Model	Analysis method	Seismic zone	Bare frame	Open first storey frame	Multiplication factor
Maximum bending moment in ground	RES	II	244.01	553.9103	2.27
	RES	III	409.355	886.255	2.165
	RES	IV	585.629	1329.38	2.27

storey(K Nm)	RES	V	865.48	1994.07	2.304
	POA	V	1084.101	1864.655	1.72
Maximum shear force in ground storey(K Nm)	RES	II	94.3	264.122	2.8
	RES	III	145.72	422.596	2.9
	RES	IV	209.205	633.893	3.03
	RES	V	313.808	950.840	3.03
	POA	V	357.538	912.413	2.55

The MF based on linear and non linear analysis with respect to different zones from Table 21 is in the range 1.72-2.304 for BM and 2.55-3.03 for SF for a eight storey frames. The MF increases with the height of the building, primarily due to the higher shift in the time period. Therefore multiplication factor is varying with respect to zones, storeys and method of analysis which is not specified in code.

Performance Point:

For G+8 RC building frames the non linear static pushover analysis is performed to investigate the performance point of the building frame in terms of base shear and displacement.

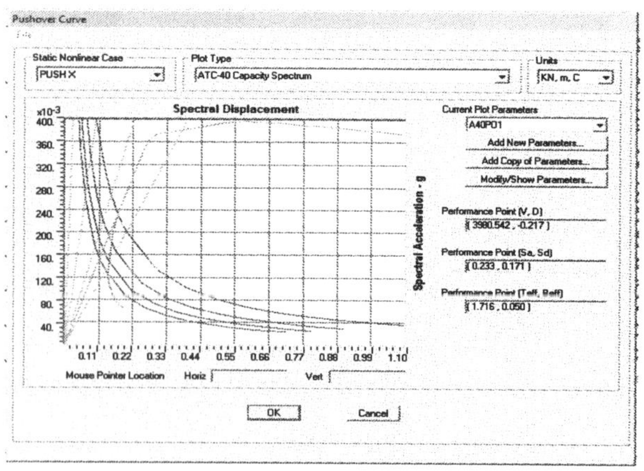

Fig. 31 PERFORMANCE POINT FOR G+8 (BARE)

Fig.31 shows the Performance point for eight storey bare frame structure for load case PUSHX is 3980.542KN.

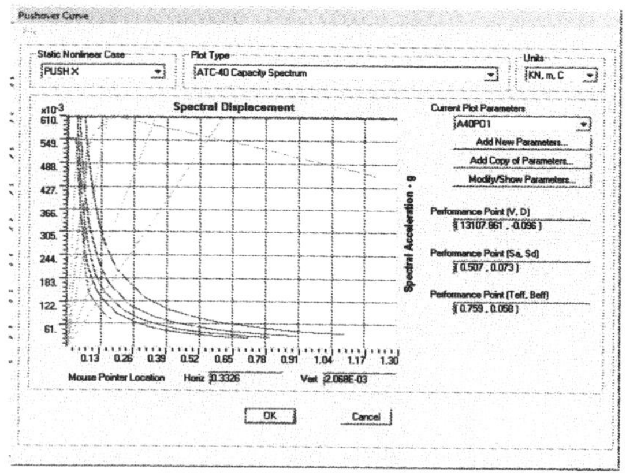

Fig. 32PERFORMANCE POINT FOR G+8 (OGS)

Fig. 32 shows the Performance point for eight storey OGS frame structure for load case PUSHX is 13107.861KN.

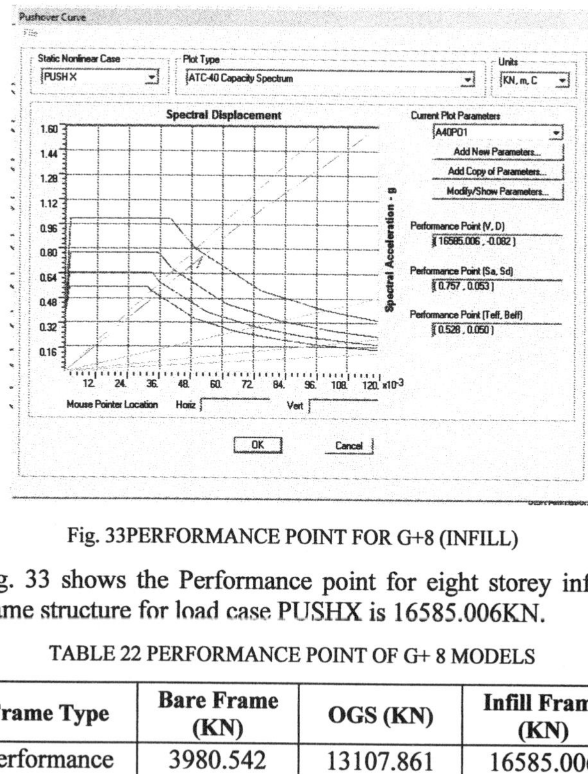

Fig. 33PERFORMANCE POINT FOR G+8 (INFILL)

Fig. 33 shows the Performance point for eight storey infill frame structure for load case PUSHX is 16585.006KN.

TABLE 22 PERFORMANCE POINT OF G+ 8 MODELS

Frame Type	Bare Frame (KN)	OGS (KN)	Infill Frame (KN)
Performance Point	3980.542	13107.861	16585.006

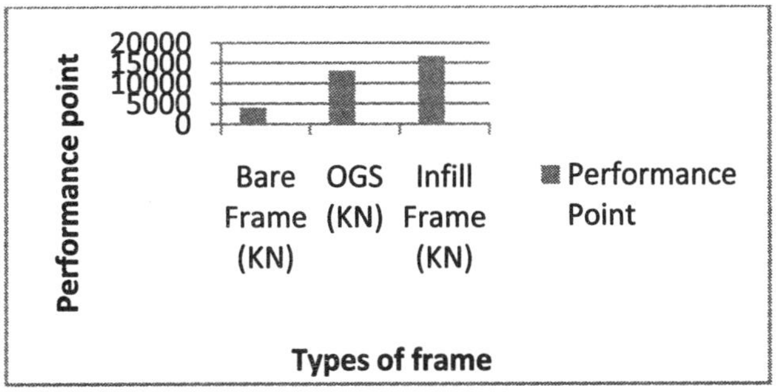

Fig. 34 Performance point for G+8

From the Table 22 and Fig. 34 performance point of G+8 building models, it is clear that bare frame is having lesser lateral load capacity (Performance point value) compare to infill frame and open first storey. Performance point of infilled frame is varying as 20.96% more than OGS frame and 75.99% more than bare frame.

Results from Time History Analysis:

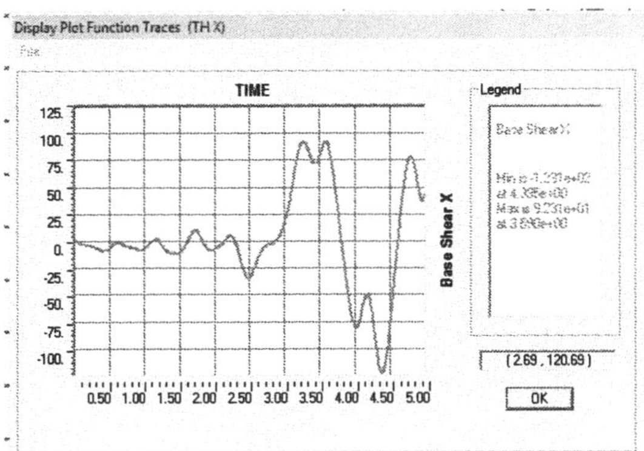

Fig. 35TIME VS BASE SHEAR –X FOR G+8 (BARE FRAME)

Fig. 35 shows the Base shear time history for eight storey with bare frame structure for load case THX is maximum at 92.31 KN

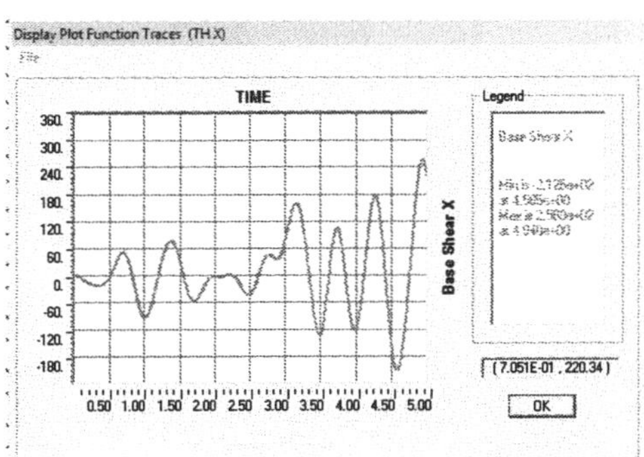

Fig. 36TIME VS BASE SHEAR –X FOR G+8 (OGS)

Fig. 36 shows the Base shear time history for eight storey with open first storey frame structure for load case THX is maximum at 256.97 KN

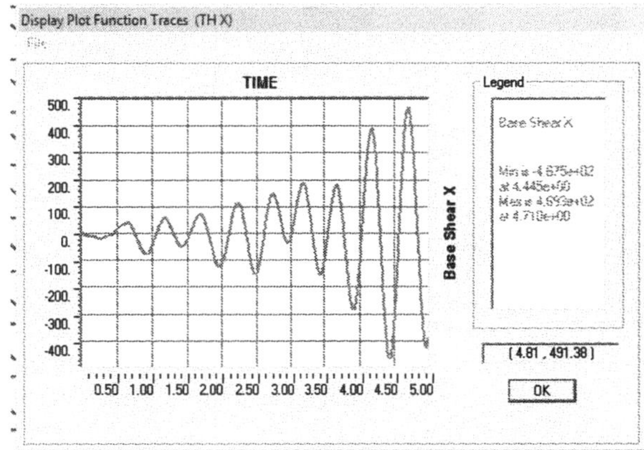

Fig. 37 TIME VS BASE SHEAR –X FOR G+8 (INFILL)

Fig. 37 shows the Base shear time history for eight storey with infill frame structure for load case THX is maximum at 469.39 KN.

TABLE 20 BASE SHEAR OF G+8 BUILDING

Frame Type	Bare Frame (KN)	OGS (KN)	Infill Frame (KN)
Base shear	132.86	531.42	567

From the Table 23 and Fig. 38, the base shear of infilled frame is more than bare and open first storey frame. Percentage decrease in base shear of bare frame is 76.56% and open first storey is 6.27% compare to infilled frame.

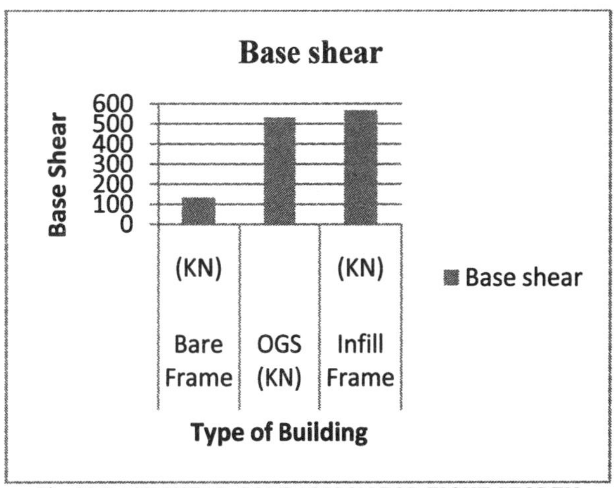

Fig. 38 BASE SHEAR COMPARISON FOR EIGHT STOREY STRUCTURE FOR LOAD CASE THX

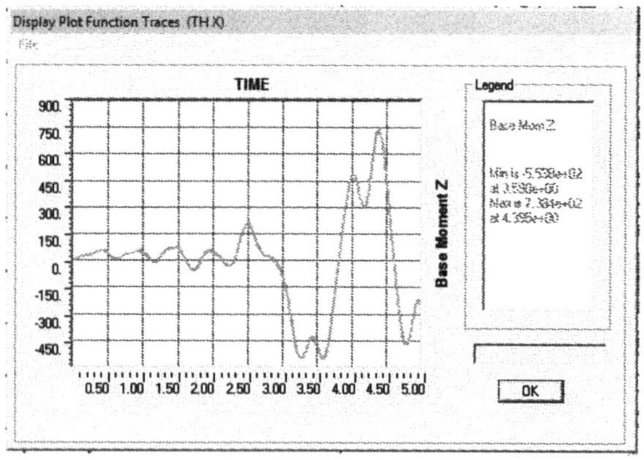

Fig. 39 TIME VS BASE MOMENT –Z FOR G+8 (BARE FRAME)

Fig. 39 shows the Base moment time history for eight storey with infill frame structure for load case THX is maximum at 738.43 KN

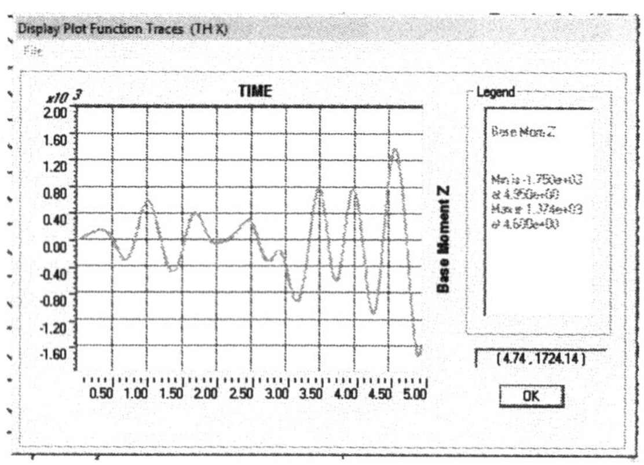

Fig. 40 TIME VS BASE MOMENT –Z FOR G+8 (OGS)

Fig. 40 shows the Base moment time history for eight storey with infill frame structure for load case THX is maximum at 1374.07KN

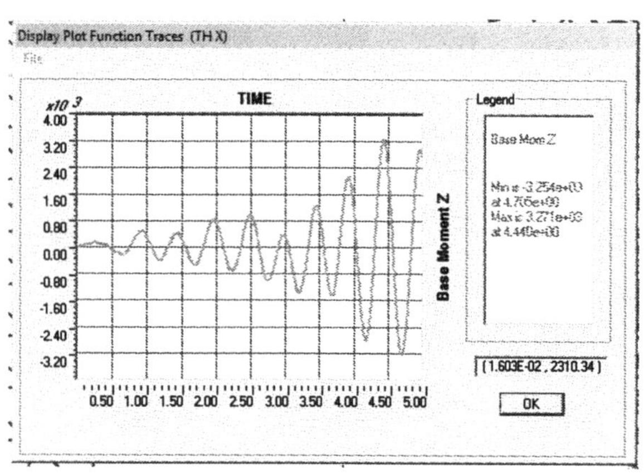

Fig. 41 TIME VS BASE MOMENT –Z FOR G+8 (INFILL)

Fig. 41 shows the Base moment time history for eight storey with infill frame structure for load case THX is maximum at 3271.81 KN.

TABLE 24 BASE MOMENT OF G+8 BUILDING

Frame Type	Bare Frame (KN)	OGS (KN)	Infill Frame (KN)
Base shear	738.43	1374.07	3271.81

From the Table 24 and Fig. 42, the base moment of infilled frame is more than bare and open first storey frame. Percentage decrease in base shear of bare frame is 77.43% and open first storey is 58% compared to infilled frame.

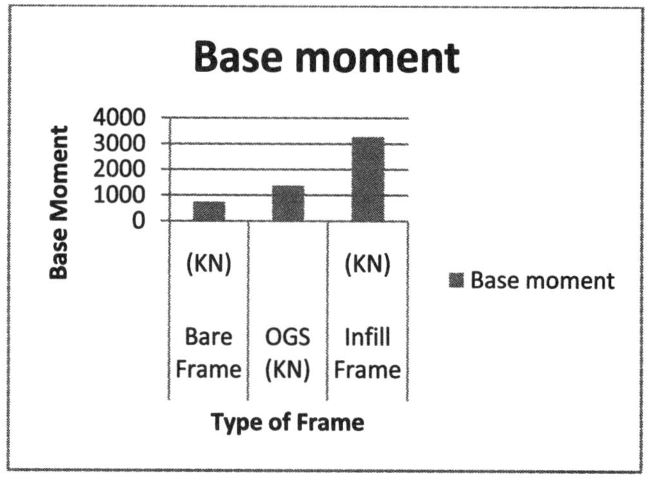

Fig. 42 BASE MOMENT COMPARISON FOR FIVE STOREY STRUCTURE FOR LOAD CASE THX

VI. Conclusions

In this paper seismic analysis of irregular RC frame models has been studied that includes bare frame, infilled frame, and open ground storey frame. From the seismic analysis of RC frames following conclusions are drawn

1. The MF based on linear and non linear analysis with respect to different zones is in the range 1.61-2.02 for BM and 2.47-2.7 for SF for a five storied OGS building, 1.72-2.304 for BM and 2.55-3.03 for SF for a eight storied OGS building. The MF increases with the height of the building, primarily due to the higher shift in the time period. Therefore multiplication factor is varying with respect to zones, storeys and method of analysis which is not specified in code.
2. From the analysis the performance point of G+5 building models, it is clear that bare frame is having lesser lateral load capacity (Performance point

value) compare to infill frame and open first storey. Performance point of infilled frame is varying as 70.07% more than OGS frame and 88.68% more than bare frame, similarly of G+8 building models, infilled frame is varying as 20.96% more than OGS frame and 75.99% more than bare frame. Also conclude that as the no of storey increases lateral load carrying capacity increased with corresponding displacement.

3. The base shear of infilled frame is more than bare and open first storey frame and hence there will be a considerably difference in the lateral force along the height of the building. Percentage decrease in base shear of bare frame is 77.4% and open first storey is 7.29% compare to infilled frame for five storey structures, similarly decrease in base shear of bare frame is 76.56% and open first storey is 6.27% compare to infilled frame for eight storey structures
4. There is a reduction in the base torsion moment. The base moment of infilled frame is more than bare and open first storey frame. Percentage decrease in base shear of bare frame is 76.56% and open first storey is 6.27% compared to infilled frame for five storey structure, similarly decrease in base shear of bare frame is 77.43% and open first storey is 58% compared to infilled frame for eight storey structure. So negligible of infill walls in analysis of structure may lead to mislead of safety in earthquake prone areas.
5. The structural member forces, deformations do vary with the different parameters associated with the infill walls. Such variations are not considered in current codes and thus the guidance for the design of buildings having infill walls is incomplete and specifically for buildings with soft ground storey it is imperative to have design guidelines in detail.
6. The seismic analysis of RC (Bare frame) structure leads to under estimation of base shear. Therefore other response quantities such as storey drift, base shear, shear force, bending moment and performance point are not significant. The underestimation of base shear may lead to the collapse of structure during earthquake shaking. Therefore it is important to consider the infill walls in the seismic analysis of structure.
7. Since the behaviour of the soft storey is very different during a quake, the construction undergoes damage and it increases costs. For this reason, in regions where the risk of quake is high, we should not produce soft storeys, if necessary quake controls should be done starting from design stage through the stage of occupancy.

A. Scope For Further Work

1. The present study is limited to reinforced concrete multi-storey framed buildings that are irregular in plan and regular in elevation. It can be extended to buildings having irregularity in elevation. Also, similar studies can be carried out on steel framed buildings.
2. Another field of wide research could be the design of the infill walls considering the door and the window openings which has not been considered in this research work with different soil conditions.
3. Plan irregular buildings with basement, shear walls and plinth beams are not considered in this study. The present methodology can be extended to such buildings also.
4. Soil -structure interaction effects are neglected in the present study. It will be interesting to study the response of the irregular buildings considering the soil -structure interaction.

References

[1] **CSI**. SAP2000 V-15 2010 Integrated finite element analysis and design of structures basic analysis reference manual. Berkeley (CA, USA)": *Computersand Structures Inc...*

[2]DharmeshVijaywargiya, Abhay Sharma and Vivek Garg, (2014), Seismic Response of a Mid Rise RCC Building with Soft Storey at Ground Floor, *ISSN: 2348-4098*, Vol. 02 (06).

[3]Haroon Rasheed Tamboli and UmeshKaradi N., (2012),Seismic Analysis of RC Frame Structure with and without Masonry Infill Walls, *Indian Journal Of Natural Sciences* Vol.3 / Issue 14/ October2012 ISSN: 0976 – 0997 © IJONS.

[4]IS 1893 Part 1 (2002) Criteria for *Earthquake Resistant Design of Structures*, Bureau of Indian Standards, New Delhi.

[5]Patel S., (2012), Earthquake Resistant Design Of Low-Rise Open Ground Storey Framed Building, M. Tech Thesis, *National Institute of Technology*, Rourkela.

[6]Raghavendra and Deshpande S., (2014), Seismic Analysis of Reinforced Concrete Building with Soft First Storey, *International Journal of Scientific & Engineering Research*Vol. 5 (5), May-2014.

[7]Saurabh Singh, Saleem Akhtar and GeetaBatham, (2014), Evaluation of Seismic Behavior for Multi-storeyed RC Moment Resisting Frame with Open First Storey, *International Journal of Current Engineering and Technology*E.

A Study on Skew Effect of Prestressed Concrete Bridges

Rupesh Kumar D[1]., Venkateswarlu R[2].
[1]*Associate Professor,*
[2]*Masters' Scholar*
Civil Engineering Department, University College of Engineering(A), Osmania University, Hyderabad – 500007, T.S., India.
[1] rkdhondy@gmail.com
[2]rv113878@gmail.com

***Abstract* - The present study is to investigate the shear forces and bending moments for skew bridge deck slab with longitudinal girders of different spans of 15 m, 20 m, 25 m and 30 m with the different skew angles from dead load, moving load and combined dead load and moving load cases using Staad Pro V8i (select series 6) software by considering IRC class 70 R and IRC class AA standards . The results are presented in terms of shear forces and bending moments.**

***Keywords*—Aspect ratio, PSC skew deck slab, skew angle, span length.**

I. INTRODUCTION

The supports for bridge deck slabs are sometimes not orthogonal for traffic direction necessitated by alignment constraints, land acquisition problems, short space etc. Such bridge decks are defined as skew bridge decks. The structural response of skewed bridge to stresses in slab and reactions on abutments can be significantly altered by the skew angle of the substructure. Several practices exist in reducing the skew effects, as there are many apprehensions about the correct prediction of the behavior and proper designs of the skew bridges especially if the skew angle is very high.

For skew slabs the force flow is through the strip of area connecting the obtuse angled corners and the slab primarily bends along the line joining the obtuse angled corners. The width of primary bending strip is a function of skew angle and the ratio between the skew span the width of deck (aspect ratio). The areas on either side of the strip do not transfer the load to the supports directly but transfer the load only to the strip cantilever[1]. Hence the skew slab is subjected to twisting moments. Because of this, the principal moment direction also varies and it is the function of skew angle. The deflection of the slab also is not uniform and symmetrical as it is right deck. There will be warping leading to higher deflection near obtuse angled corner areas and less deflection near acute angled corner areas The free edge deflection profile is becoming unsymmetrical, the maximum deflection moves towards obtuse angled corners [2-5].As skew angle increases, the maximum deflection is maximum very near the obtuse angled corners and near acute angled corners there could be negative deflection resulting in` S' shaped deflection curve with associated twist. Increase in skew angle results in decrease in bending moments but increase in twisting moments, the total strain energy remaining the same.

II. MODELING AND ANALYSIS

The pre-stressed concrete skew bridge deck slab of 12 m wide and different spans from 15 m ,20m 25m and 30 m and skew angle is varied from 15° to 45° at 5° interval, with the depth of deck slab 220 mm for all spans. Longitudinal girder of depth 2080 mm, thickness of web at support 750 mm and at mid span 300 mm is considered in the present study. The bridge decks are analyzed for dead loads, moving loads and combined dead loads and moving loads for IRC class 70 R and IRC class AA [6-10] using Staad.pro V8i (select series 6) software by considering IRC class 70 R and IRC class AA is depicted in Fig.1.

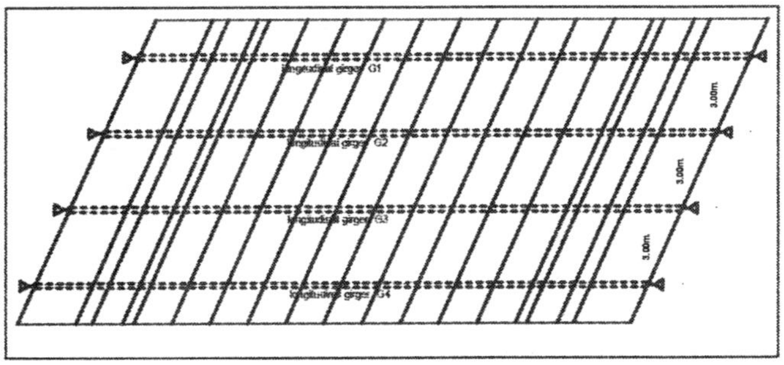

Figure1. Plan of bridge

Section properties of the longitudinal grillage beams

Geometry:

Carriageway width	= 7.50 m
Overall width	= 12.00 m
Width of footway	= 2.25 m
Thickness of wearing coat	= 75 mm
No. of longitudinal girders	= 4
c/c of longitudinal girders	= 3.00 m
cantilever overhang	= 1.50 m
Depth of girder	= 2.08 m
Depth of deck slab	= 0.22 m
Total depth of super structure	= 2.30 m
Thickness of web at support	= 0.75 m
Thickness of web at mid span	= 0.30 m
Flange width of L-girder	= 1.00 m
Bulb width of L-girder	= 0.75 m
Bulb thickness of L-girder	= 0.25 m
Tappering portion of bulb	= 0.20 m
Thickness of end girder	= 0.50 m

Projection of L-Girder beyond c/l of bearing= 0.40 m

Material properties:

Grade of concrete	= M40
Grade of steel	= Fe500

The cross section of longitudinal girder of a model of the present study is considered and shownin Fig.2.

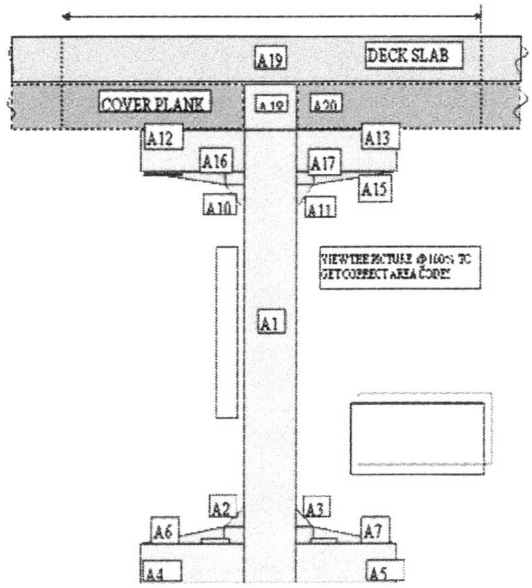

Figure 2. Cross section of longitudinal grillage beams

The support section and mid section properties of grillage beams of shapes of I and T are shown in table I and table II respectively.

TABLE I

I AND T SECTIONS – SUPPORT SECTION PROPERTIES

Sl.No	Description of components	Area code	Breadth (mm)	Depth (mm)
1	Web (Total height)	A1	750	2080
2	Bottom-Left-Rectangle1	A4	0	250
3	Bottom-Right-Rectangle1	A5	0	250
4	Bottom-Left-Tapper1	A6	0	200
5	Bottom-Right-Tapper1	A7	0	200
6	Bottom-Left-Rectangle2	A8	0	150
7	Bottom-Right-Rectangle2	A9	0	150
8	Top-Left-Rectangle1	A12	125	150
9	Top-Right-Rectangle1	A13	125	150
10	Top-Left-Tapper1	A14	125	35
11	Top-Right-Tapper1	A15	125	35
12	Top-Left-Rectangle2	A16	0	100
13	Top-Right-Rectangle2	A17	0	100
14	Deck slab	A19	3250	220

Sl.No	Description of components	Unit	Precast	Total
1	Area of L-Girder	M^2	1.6019	2.3169
2	C.G - Y_{bot}	M	1.065	1.4122
3	C.G - Y_{top}(Girder)	M	1.0150	0.6678
4	C.G - Y_{top}(Deck)	M	-	0.8878
5	Moment of Inertia – Ixx	M^4	0.5998	1.2283
6	Section Modulus - Z_{bot}	M^3	0.5632	0.8698
7	Section Modulus - Z_{top}(Girder)	M^3	0.5909	1.8393
8	Section Modulus - Z_{top}(Deck)	M^3	-	1.3835

TABLE II

I AND T SECTIONS – MID SECTION PROPERTIES

Sl.No	Description of components	Area code	Breadth (mm)	Depth (mm)
1	Web (Total height)	A1	300	2080
2	Bottom-Left-Rectangle1	A4	225	250
3	Bottom-Right-Rectangle1	A5	225	250
4	Bottom-Left-Tapper1	A6	225	200
5	Bottom-Right-Tapper1	A7	225	200
6	Bottom-Left-Rectangle2	A8	0	150
7	Bottom-Right-Rectangle2	A9	0	150
8	Top-Left-Rectangle1	A12	350	150
9	Top-Right-Rectangle1	A13	350	150
10	Top-Left-Tapper1	A14	350	100
11	Top-Right-Tapper1	A15	350	100
12	Top-Left-Rectangle2	A16	0	100
13	Top-Right-Rectangle2	A17	0	100
14	Deck slab	A19	3250	220

Sl.No	Description of components	Unit	Precast	Total
1	Area of L-Girder	M^2	0.9215	1.6365
2	C.G – Y_{bot}	M	1.0355	1.5399
3	C.G – Y_{top} (Girder)	M	1.0445	0.5401
4	C.G – Y_{top} (Deck)	M	-	0.7601
5	Moment of Inertia – Ixx	M^4	0.4671	1.0066
6	Section Modullus – Z	M^3	0.4511	0.6537
7	Section Modulus – Z	M^3	0.4471	1.8637
8	Section Modulus – Z	M^3	-	1.3243

Section properties of the transverse grillage beams

Inner Girder:

Effective width of flange , bf = 0.720 m

Depth of deck slab = 0.220 m

Depth of girder (1.630+0.220) = 1.850 m

ThickNess of web = 0.300 m

Area= 0.6474 m2

Distance of c.g. from bottom fibre, Y = 1.0413 m2

Moment of inertia, Iz = 0.2113 m4

End girder:

Effective width of flange , bf = 0.920 m

Depth of deck slab = 0.400 m

Depth of girder (1.450+0.400) = 1.850 m

ThickNess of web = 0.500 m

Area = 1.093 m2

Distance of c.g. from bottom fibre, Y = 1.0364 m2

Moment of inertia, Iz = 0.3408 m

III. RESULTS AND DISCUSSIONS

The detailed analysis and design of skew deck slabs of different spans with varying skew angles from 0° to 45° are performed and results obtained are presented in terms of shear forces and bending moments.

Variation of bending moment and shear force for different spans for varying skew angles for dead loads is shown in Table III.

Table III

VARIATION OF BENDING MOMENT AND SHEAR FORCE FOR DIFFERENT SPANS FOR VARYING SKEW ANGLES FOR DEAD LOADS

Skew angle	Maximum shear force (kN)				Maximum bending moment (kN-m)			
	15 m	20 m	25 m	30 m	15 m	20 m	25 m	30 m
0°	506.374	650.544	1251.06	945.073	1766.00	3048.00	9126.00	6677.00
15°	552.504	652.206	1285.503	947.114	2719.00	3054.00	9172.00	6684.00
20°	515.721	653.403	1252.102	948.754	1776.00	3060-.00	9000.00	6696.00
25°	503.074	659.990	1273.596	950.909	1768.00	3067.00	9202.00	6710.00
30°	504.360	657.01	1261.090	953.746	1773.00	3075.00	9202.00	6729.00
35°	506.669	659.54	1243.759	957.380	1784.00	3086.00	9187.00	6752.00
40°	506.643	662.648	1221.980	962.210	1776.00	3098.00	9151.00	6780.00
45°	528.372	666.445	1196.992	968.289	1876.00	3112.00	9086.00	6814.00

Variation of bending moment and shear force for different spans for varying skew angles for moving loads is given table IV.

TABLE IV

VARIATION OF BENDING MOMENT AND SHEAR FORCE FOR DIFFERENT SPANS FOR VARYING SKEW ANGLES FOR MOVING LOADS

Skew angle	Maximum shear force (kN)				Maximum bending moment (kN-m)			
	15 m	20 m	25 m	30 m	15 m	20 m	25 m	30 m
0°	847.794	213.300	361.914	254.433	844.800	929.795	2520.902	1727.262
15°	261.310	211.331	360.503	252.432	1248.618	930.205	2523.289	1732.904
20°	277.001	211.356	358.598	251.479	855.675	934.151	2522.486	1731.759
25°	191.955	211.476	355.943	251.228	675.665	939.703	2523.112	1728.336
30°	190.998	210.867	353.517	250.562	681.696	947.478	2522.917	1722.109
35°	190.974	211.644	353.581	251.477	687.751	955.396	2521.983	1712.008
40°	189.007	209.836	353.049	249.589	688.455	959.578	2511.215	1696.761
45°	210.255	233.670	370.704	267.107	697.784	975.195	2504.506	1672.610

Shear force

Variation of bending moment and shear force for different spans for varying skew angles for combined dead load and moving loads is shown in Table V.

TABLE V

VARIATION OF BENDING MOMENT AND SHEAR FORCE FOR DIFFERENT SPANS FOR VARYING SKEW ANGLES FOR COMBINED DEAD LOAD AND MOVING LOADS

Skew angle	Maximum shear force (kN)				Maximum bending moment (kN-m)			
	15 m	20 m	25 m	30 m	15 m	20 m	25 m	30 m
0°	1354.16	863.844	1612.974	1199.506	2610.80	3977.795	11646.902	8404.262
15°	813.81	863.537	1646.700	1199.546	3967.61	3984.205	11695.289	8416.904
20°	792.72	864.759	1610.700	1200.233	2631.67	3994.151	11522.486	8427.759
25°	695.02	871.466	1629.539	1202.137	2443.66	4006.703	11725.112	8438.336
30°	695.35	867.877	1614.607	1204.308	2454.69	4022.478	11724.920	8451.109
35°	697.64	871.184	1597.34	1208.857	2471.75	4041.396	11708.983	8464.000
40°	695.65	872.484	1575.029	1211.799	2464.45	4057.578	11662.215	8476.761
45°	738.62	900.115	1567.696	1235.396	2573.78	4087.195	11590.506	8486.610

Variation of shear force for different spans for varying skew angles for different loads is depicted in Fig.3.

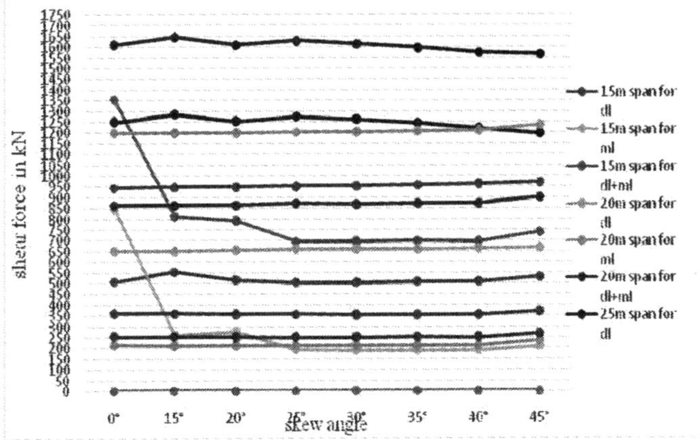

Figure 3. Variation of shear force for different spans for varying skew angles for different loads.

Variation of bending moment for different spans for varying skew angles for different loads is shown in Fig.4.

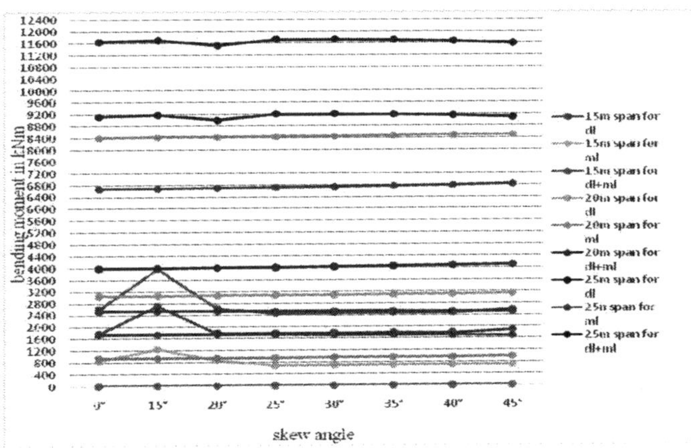

Figure 4. Variation of bending moment for different spans for varying skew angles for different loads

Shear force

In dead loads, for 15m span of skew bridge, the shear force increases by 9.1% at 15° and 4.34% at 45°. In 20m span of skew bridge, shear force gradually increases by 0.26% at 15° and 2.44% at 45°. In 25m span of skew bridge, it increases by 2.75% at 15° and gradually decreases up to 4.32% at 45°. In 30m span of skew bridge, it increase by 0.2% at 15° and gradually increases by 2.45% at 45°. In moving loads, the shear force in 15m span of skew bridge gradually decreases by 69.78% at 15° to 75.20% at 45°. In 20m span of skew bridge, it gradually decreases by 0.92% at 15° to 1.62% at 40° and suddenly raises 9.55% at 45°. In 25m span of skew bridge, it decreases by0.39% at 15° and gradually decreases2.45% at 40° and suddenly rises by 2.43% at 45°. In 30m span of skew bridge, it is decreases by 0.78% at 15° and further gradually decreases1.90% at 40° and suddenly rises by 4.98%. In combined dead load and moving loads, the shear force in 15m span of skew bridge decreases by39.90% at 15° and gradually increases by 48.48% at 45° and then decreases by43.73% at 45°. In 20m span of skew bridge, it decreases by0.03% at 15 m and gradually increases by 4.20% at 45°. In 25m span of skew bridge, it increases by 2.05% at 15° and gradually decreases by 2.80% at 45°. In 30m span of skew bridge, it gradually increases by 2.99% at 45°.

Bending moment

The bending moment in dead loads, in 15m span of skew bridge is abnormally increases by 53.96% at 15° and gradually decreases by 6.23% at 45°. In 20m span of skew bridge, it gradually increases by 0.19% at 15° to 2.10% at 45°. In 25m span of skew bridge, it slightly increases by 0.50% at 15° and gradually decreases to 0.44% at 45°. In 30m span of skew bridge, 0.10% slightly increases at 15° and gradually increases by 2.05% at 45°. In moving loads, the BM in 15m span of skew bridge abnormally increases by 47.80% and decreases by 17.40% at 45°. In 20m span of skew bridge, it gradually increases by 0.04% at 15° to 4.88% at 45°. In 25m span of skew bridge, it gradually increases by 0.09% at 15° to 0.65% at 45°. In 30m span of skew bridge, it gradually increases by 0.32% at 15° to 3.16% at 45°. In combined dead load and moving loads, the BM in 15m span of skew bridge abnormally increases by 51.97% at 15° and gradually decreases by 1.42% at 45°. In 20m span of skew bridge, it is increases by 0.16 at 15° to 2.75% at 45°. In 25m span of skew bridge, it is increases by 0.41% at 15° and gradually decreases by 0.48% at 45°. In 30m span of skew bridge, it gradually increases by 0.15% at 15° to 0.98% at 45°.

Shear force in main girders
15m span of skew bridge

In dead loads, the shear force is drastically decreases by 57.61% at 15°, increases by 1.84% at 20° and gradually decreases by 2.50% at 45°in G1. It increases by 26% at 15°, decreases by 1.42% at 20° and gradually decreases by 4.41% at 45° in G2. In G3, it increases by 24.67% at 15°, decreases by 2.13% at 20° to 2.08% at 45°. In G4, it abnormally decreases by 60.11% at 15° and gradually increases by 4.34% at 45°.In moving loads, it drastically decreases by 59.15% at 15° and gradually increases by 38.70% at 45° in G1. In G2, it decreases by -21.24% at 15° and gradually decreased 36.62% at 45°. In G3, it is decreased 22.63% at 15° and gradually decreased 37.42% at 45°. It is drastically decreased 58.11% at 15° and decreased -2.33% at 45° in G4. In combined dead load and moving loads, it is drastically decreased 57.81% at 15°, gradually decreases by 2.23% at 40° and increases 4.72% at 45° in G1.In G2, it increases by 5.65% at 15° and gradually decreases by -18.29% at 45°. It increases by 4.29% at 15° and gradually decreases by 17.30% at 45° in G3. In G4, it drastically decreases by 59.76% at 15° and gradually increases by 3.17% at 45°.

20m span of skew bridge

In dead loads, the shear force increases by 0.25% at 15° and gradually increases by 2.44% at 45° in G1. In G2 and G3, it increases by 0.10% at 15° and gradually increases by 1.28% at 45°. It increases by 0.17% at 15° and gradually increases at 45° in G4. In moving loads, it is decreases by 1.96% at 15° and gradually increases8.77% at 45° in G1. In G2, it decreases by 1.57% at 15° and it further decreases by 3.82% at 40° and increases by 9.54% at 45°. It decreases by 0.92% at 15° and gradually increases by 8.19% at 45° in G3. In G4, it increases by 1.27% at 15°, decreases by 0.65% at 40° and increases by 1.06% at 45°. In combined dead and moving loads, it decreases by 0.21% at 15°, further decreases by 0.45% at 40° and increases by 3.58% at 45° in G1. In G2, it decreases 0.34% up to 40° and increases by 3.50% at 45°. It decreases by 0.17% at 15° and gradually increases by 3.13% at 45°in G3. In G4, it increases by 0.37% at 15° and gradually increases by 2.19% at 45°.

25m span of skew bridge

In dead loads, the shear force increases by 1.61% at 15° and gradually increases by 49.68% at 45° in G1. In G2, it increases by 2.75% at 15° and gradually increases by 0.8% at 30° and gradually decreases by 4.32% at 45°. It increases by 2.86% at 15° and gradually decreases by 3.41 at 45° in G3. It gradually increases by 9.77% at 15° further increases by 61.22% at 45° in G4. In moving loads, it increases by 2.09% at 15° and gradually increases by 209.58% at 45° in G1. In G2, it decreases by 0.38% at 15° and it further decreases by 0.25% at 40° and increases by 2.42% at 45°. It decreases by 2.19% at 15° and gradually decreases by 4.36% at 45° in G3. In G4, it increases by 11.16% at 15° and gradually increases by 77.70% at 45°. In combined dead and moving loads, it increases by 1.68% at 15°, gradually increases by 71.36% at 45° in G1. In G2, it increases by 2.04% at 15° and decreases by 2.8% at 45°. It increases by 1.71% at 15° and gradually decreases by 3.63% at 45° in G3. In G4, it increases by 9.97% at 15° and gradually increases by 63.63% at 45°.

30m span of skew bridge

In dead loads, the shear force increases by 0.16% at 15° and gradually increases by 2.42% at 45° in G1. In G2, it increases by 0.13% at 15° and gradually increases by 1.62 at 45°. It increases by0.17% at 15° and gradually decreases by 1.62 at 45° in G3. It gradually increases by 0.21% at 15° further increases by 2.45% at 45° in G4. In moving loads, it decreases by 1.82% at 15° and gradually decreases by 2.53% at 45° in G1. In G2, it decreases by 1.48% at 15° and it further increases by 2.17% at 45°. It decreases by 0.78% at 15° and gradually increases by 4.98% at 45° in G3. In G4, it increases by 1.38% at 15° and gradually increases by 5.32% at 45°. In combined dead and moving loads, it decreases by 0.08% at 15°, gradually increases by 1.61% at 45° in G1. In G2, it decreases by 0.24% at 15° and increases by 1.75% at 45°. It decreases by 0.05% at 15° and gradually increases by 2.39% at 45° in G3. In G4, it increases by 0.40% at 15° and gradually increases by 2.92% at 45°.

Bending Moment in main girders

15m span of skew bridge

In dead loads, the bending moment drastically decreases by 80.36% at 15°, and gradually decreases by 5.20% at 45°in G1. It drastically increases by 63.47% at 15°, decreases by 7.09% at 45° in G2. In G3, it is abnormally increases by 65.78% at 15°, decreases by 2.32% at 45°. In G4, it abnormally by decreases by 86.20% at 15° and gradually increases by 7.63% at 45°. In moving loads, it drastically decreases by 85.76% at 15° and further gradually decreases by 32.43% at 45° in G1. In G2, it increases by 47.80% at 15° and gradually decreases by 20.35% at 25° and further decreases by 18.57% at 45°. In G3, it increases by 45.53% at 15° and decreases by 20.02% at 25° and further decreases by 17.48% at 45°. It drastically decreases by 85.99% at 15° and gradually decreases by 34.38% at 45° in G4. In combined dead load and moving loads, it drastically decreases by 81.81% at 15° and decreases by 12.55% at 45° in G1. In G2, it increases by 58.16% at 15° and gradually decreases by 10.98% at 45°. It drastically increases by 58.90% at 15° and gradually decreases by 7.47% at 45° in G3. In G4, it drastically decreases by 586.14% at 15° and gradually decreases by 3.81% at 45°.

20m span of skew bridge

In dead loads, the bending moment gradually increases by 0.21% increases by 2.10% at 45°in G1. It increases by 0.05% to 0.58% at 45° in G2. In G3, it increases by 0.05% at 15°, increases by 0.58% at 45°. In G4, it increases by 0.21% at 15° and gradually increases by 2.07% at 45°. In moving loads, it decreases by 1.36% at 15° and gradually decreases by 9.80% at 45° in G1. In G2, it increases by 0.04% at 15° and gradually increases by 4.88%at 45°. In G3, it decreases by 0.76% at 15° and increases by 1.57% at 45°. It decreases by 1.54% at 15° and gradually decreases by 11.01% at 45° in G4. In combined dead load and moving loads, it decreases by 0.13% at 15° and decreases by 0.53% at 45° in G1. In G2, it increases by 0.05% at 15° and gradually increases by 1.63% at 45°. It decreases by 0.14% at 15° and gradually increases by 0.82% at 45° in G3. In G4, it decreases by 0.17% at 15° and gradually decreases by 0.82% at 45°.

25m span of skew bridge

In dead loads, the bending moment decreases by 17.28% at 15°, and gradually increases by 148.27% at 45° in G1. It decreases by 0.95% to 2.44% at 45° in G2. In G3, it increases by 0.94% at 15°. In G4, it increases by 39.46% at 15° and drastically increases by 70.42% at 45°. In moving loads, it increases by 2.63% at 15° and gradually increases by 119.43% at 45° in G1. In G2, it increases by 0.09% at 15° and decreases by 0.65%at 45°. In G3, it decreases by 1.06% at 15° and further decreases by 3.89% at 45°. It increases by 21.30% at 15° and gradually increases by 123.00% at 45° in G4. In combined dead load and moving loads, it decreases by 13.80% at 15° and gradually increases b y143.22% at 45° in G1. In G2, it gradually decreases by 0.72% to 2.05% at 45°. It gradually decreases by 0.50% to 0.84% at 45° in G3. In G4, it drastically decreases by 35.90% to 80.73% at 45°.

30m span of skew bridge

In dead loads, the bending moment gradually increases by 0.19% to increases by 1.95% at 45°in G1. It increases by 0.12% to 1.14% at 45° in G2. In G3, it increases by 0.96% to 1.85% at 45°. In G4, it increases by 0.10% to 2.05% at 45°. In moving loads, it increases by 0.32% at 15° and gradually decreases by 3.16% at 45° in G1. In G2, it decreases by 0.20% at 15° and decreases 0.16%at 45°. In G3, it gradually decreases by 0.94% at 45°. It decreases by 0.75% at 15° and gradually decreases by 5.71% at 45° in G4. In combined dead load and moving loads, it increases by 0.22% at 15° and gradually increases 0.88% at 45° in G1. In G2, it increases by 0.06% at 15° and gradually increases by 0.95% at 45°. It decreases by 0.05% at 15° and increases by 0.61% at 45° in G3. In G4, it decreases by 0.07% at 15° and increases by 0.45% at 45°.

IV. CONCLUSIONS

Shear force and bending moment decreases for increase in span of bridges for varying skew angles from 0° to 45°.The maximum shear force and bending moment is observed in combined dead load and moving load case.

Maximum variation in shear force for dead load, moving load and combined dead load and moving load cases is observed at 15° and thereafter the variation of shear force is not significant for further skew angles. Similarly, maximum bending moment for dead load, moving load and combined dead load and moving load cases is observed at 15° and thereafter the variation of bending moment is not significant for further skew angles.

Maximum shear force and bending moment at the end girders is observed in dead load case at the end of girders G1 and G4 and least in the middle girders G2 and G3,where as the maximum shear force and bending moment is noted in middle girders G2 and G3 and minimum at the end girders G1 and G4 in moving loads. Similarly, in combined dead load and moving load case the maximum shear force and bending moment is noted at the middle girders G2 and G3 and minimum at the end girders G1 and G4.

References

[1] Trilok Gupta and Anurag Misra, "Effects of support reaction of T-beam skew bridges, *ARPN Journal of Engineering and Applied sciences*, Vol. 2, No. 1, 2007, pp.1-8.

[2] C. Menassa; M. Mabout; K. Tarhini; and G. Frederick, "Influence of skew angle on reinforced concrete slab bridges, □ *Journal of Bridge Engineering(ASCE)*,Vol. 12, No. 2, 2007, pp.205-214.

[3] A. Aziz Saber, J. Toups, L. Guice and A. Tayebi, "Continuity diaphragm for skewed continuous span precast pre-stressed concrete girder bridges-LTRC Project No. 01-1ST and State Project No. 736-99-0914. Baton Rouge, LA: *Louisiana Department of Transportation and Development and Louisiana Transportation Research Center,* 2007.

[4] Ibrahim S. I. Harba, "Effect of skew angle on behaviour of simply supported R.C.T-beam bridge decks,□ *ARPN Journal of Engineering and Applied Sciences*, Vol. 6, 2011, pp.1-14.

[5] Iman Mohsen and A. Khalim Rashid,"Transverse load distribution of skew cast-in- place concrete multicell box- girder bridges subjected to traffic condition,□ *Latin American Journal of Solids and Structures*, Vol.10, 2011, pp. 247-262.

[6] IRC 6:2014, Standard Specifications and Code of Practice for Road Bridges, Section –II Loads and Stresses □, Indian Road Congress, New Delhi.

[7] IRC: 21-2000, Standard specifications and code of practice for road bridges –Section III Cement concrete (Plain and Reinforced), Indian Roads Congress, New Delhi.

[8] IRC: 112-2011, Code of practice for Concrete Road Bridges, Indian Roads Congress, New Delhi.

[9] N. Krishna Raju, "Design of Bridges,□ Oxford & IBH Publishing Co. Pvt. Ltd, New Delhi,1996.

[10] N. Rajagopalan, "Pre-stressed Concrete, □ Narosa Publishing House Pvt. Ltd, New Delhi, 2005.

Stream II: Water Resources Engineering

Estimating Runoff Using SCS Curve Number Method

ZeenatAra, Mohammad Zakwan

Assistant Professor, MANUU, Hyderabad

zeenatiitd@rediffmail.com

zakwancivil@gmail.com

***Abstract*—Rainfall and runoff are significant constitute the sources of water for recharge of ground water in the watershed. Rainfall is a major the primary source of recharge into the ground water. Use of remote sensing and GIS technology can be useful to overcome the problem in conventional methods for estimating runoff. In this paper, modified Soil Conservation System (SCS) CN method is used for runoff estimation that considers parameter like slope, vegetation cover, area of watershed. The Land cover map developed for the study region was used in analyzing the runoff generated over the command area. Rainfall data and soil map for the region was acquired to calculate the antecedent moisture condition (AMC) and hydrological soil group (HSG) map respectively. SCS curve number model was employed to determine the runoff. The computation was carried out on a GIS platform to accommodate the spatial variability. Total runoff generated over the study region during the year 2007 was computed as 17.98 mm. The peak runoff was observed in the month of July which contributed 39.85% of the total.**

***Keywords*—Remote Sensing;Runoff; Soil Conservation Service Curve Number; Watershed.**

I. Introduction

Runoff generated in a river basin contributes significantly to the river discharge [1,2]. River basin characteristic such as length, slope, land use and basin shape have significant impact on the runoff generated from the river basin [3]. There are number of methods available for rainfall runoff modeling such as hydrologic models, empirical equations and data driven techniques to correlate rainfall and runoff [4]. Soil Conservation Services and Curve Number (SCS–CN) technique is one of the primogenital and simplest method for rainfall runoff modelling. Land cover information is used in hydrologic modeling to estimate the value of surface roughness or friction as it affects the velocity of the overland flow of water [5,6]. It may also be used to determine the amount of rainfall that will infiltrate into the soil [7]. Mockus [8] used data on soil, land use, antecedent rainfall, storm duration, and average annual temperatureto estimate surface runoff in ungaged catchments.NEH [9] developed "SCS-CN method". The method requires numeric catchment characteristics which are the basis of catchment runoff determination. The objective of the method is to determine the accurate curve number of the catchment of interest that defines the runoff potential. Hydrologic soil group number, land use type, vegetation cover, soil conservation measures, antecedent soil moisture conditions are the basic catchment characteristics used for curve number calculations. Sharma et al. [10] studied the hydrologic response of a watershed to land use changes based on Geographical Information System (GIS) and Remote Sensing (RS) approach. Gangodagamage and Agarwal [11] carried out hydrological Modeling using remote sensing and GIS. Accurate modeling will require estimation of the spatial and temporal distribution of the water resources parameters. The present work aims to prioritize watershed of Sone canalbased on runoff generated, expressed as yield, due to existing land use conditions, and to evaluate the hydrologic response of these measures on runoff.

II. Study Area and Data Used

The study area selected for this paper is eastern Sone canal originating on Sone river, India. The total catchment area of the river is about 70,196 km^2. Monsoon season sets in June accompanied by a fall in temperature and increase in humidity. The basin experiences maximum rains during the months of July and august. The average rainfall, in the normal conditions, recorded in these months is in the proximity of 300mm. The study area is bounded by latitude $24^{0}12'0''$ to $25^{0}14'0''$ and longitude $84^{0}30'0''$to $85^{0}0'0''$. The study area is as shown in Figure 1. Satellite image of LANDSAT 7 ETM+ of 30 m resolution and Land use data of the year (2005-2006) was used to generate the land use/land cover map. The soil map of the study area was obtained from Soil Conservation Department, Patna while rainfall data for study area was obtained from Statistic and Monitoring Department, Patna.

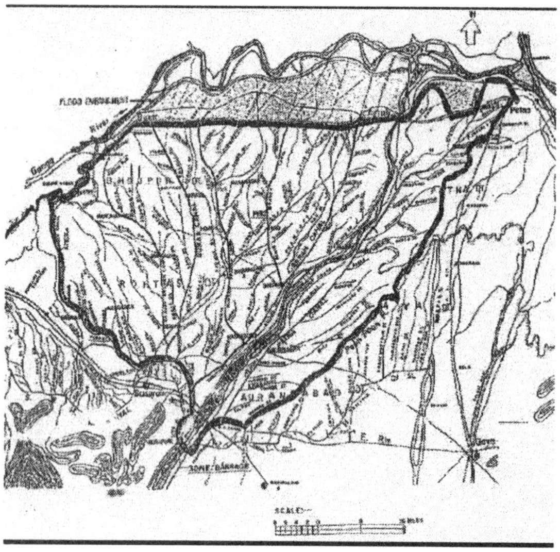

Figure 1 Sone canal command

III. Methodology

Direct runoff from a watershed produced by a given precipitation, may be estimated using various models. Out of these models, SCS-CN model is widely used for estimating runoff on small to medium sized ungauged drainage basins. The SCS method of estimating runoff from storm rainfall was developed by USDA scientist. The SCS approach involves the use of simple empirical formula, tables and curves. The empirical equations require the rainfall and watershed coefficient as inputs. The watershed coefficient called as curve number (CN)is an index that represents the combination of hydrologic soil group and land use and land treatment classes. SCS model enables the hydrologist to stimulate the various design alternatives and compare the result. The parameter defined by land use allow the user to experiment with alternative form of land development and management and to assess the impact of the proposed changes. The soil map of study area was scanned and then registered with the help of geo-referenced SOI topographical map. The registered soil map was digitized, and different soil attributes were assigned to the different soil groups as described in Table 1. Hydrologically soils are assigned into four groups based on intake of water on bare soil when thoroughly wetted. The hydrological soil group classification is based on texture of soil as presented in Table 2. The expression used in SCS method for estimating runoff may be presented as

$$Q = \frac{(P - I_a)^2}{\{(P - I_a) + S\}} \qquad (1)$$

Where, Q=Accumulated storm runoff, m; P=Accumulated storm rainfall, mm, S=potential maximum retention of water by the soil, Ia= initial quantity of interception, depression and infiltration. To simplify the above equation empirical relationship between the variables S and I_a was developed from data collected from various watersheds in U.S.A resulting in following equation.

I_a= 0.3S for AMC I, I_a= 0.2S for AMC II, I_a= 0.1S for AMC III

The central soil and water conservation Research and Training institute (ICAR) Dehradun has suggested some of the empirical relation for Indian condition which suggests that forBlack soil region AMC-II and III, I_a=0.1S, Black soils region AMC I, I_a=0.3S, all other region, I_a=0.3S, S value is derived from curve number (CN) using following formulae

$$S = \frac{25400}{CN} - 254 \qquad (2)$$

Where CN= function of watershed hydrologic land use/land cover units hydrologic soil groups antecedent moisture condition. CN values can be obtained for different land uses and hydrologic condition from the standard Table CN values for AMC-I and II can be obtained using the following empirical equation:

$$CNI = \frac{4.2 \times CNII}{10 - 0.058 \times CNII} \qquad (3)$$

$$CNIII = \frac{23 \times CNII}{10 + 0.13 \times CNII} \qquad (4)$$

ILWIS software and ERDAS IMAGINE software were used for preparing the land use /land cover map. ILWIS comprise a complete package of image processing, spatial analysis and digital mapping.

IV. Results and Discussions

The different parameters required to compute the runoff were computed and presented in this section. Precipitation data was used to calculate the antecedent moisture condition for the study period. Soil map was converted into hydrological soil group map and the land use map derived from the satellite data was combined with it to extract the curve number value.

A. Computation of AMC

Daily Rainfall data of the study area has been taken from the Statistics and Monitoring Department of Patna. The lowest rainfall recorded in the year 2007 was during the month of April (1.36cm) whereas the highest was during the month of July (45.8 cm). The monthly rainfall value is depicted by bar chart, shown in Figure 2. The total annual rainfall for the command area was computed as 118.19 cm. Daily rainfall value for the study region during the 2007 shown in Figure 3. The precipitation value is the most important component in the runoff modeling and influences all other parameters of the equation. The daily rainfall value was used to compute the antecedent moisture condition by adding up previous five-day rainfall. The antecedent moisture condition is used to determine the AMC class which in turn would decide the curve number. The AMC class was computed on the basis of five day accumulated moisture for the dormant and growing season separately. May, June, July, August, September, October and November was taken as growing period whereas the rest of the months were considered as dormant period. The AMC class for dormant and growing season presented in Table 2 and were used in the present study.

TABLE I
HYDROLOGICAL SOIL GROUP

Group	Infiltration Rate (mm/hr)		Soil Texture
A	High	>25	Sand, Loamy sand, or Sandy loam
B	Moderate	12.5-25	Silt loam or loam
C	Low	2.5-12.5	Sandy clay laom
D	Very Low	<2.5	Clay loam, Silty clay loam, Sandy clay, Silty clay or clay

TABLE II
ANTECEDENT MOISTURE CONDITION CLASSES

AMC- Class	Dormant season(mm)	Growing Season	Condition
I	< 12.7	<35.6	Dry soil but not the wilting point
II	12.7-27.9	35.6-53.3	Average conditions
III	>27.9	>53.3	Saturated soils, heavy rainfall or light rainfall

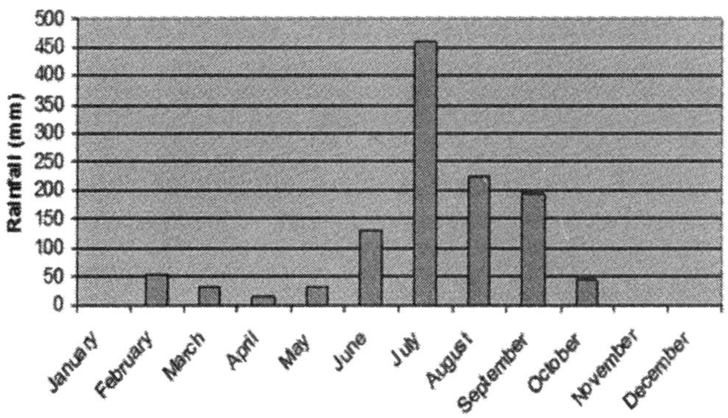

Figure 2. Monthly rainfall during the year2007.

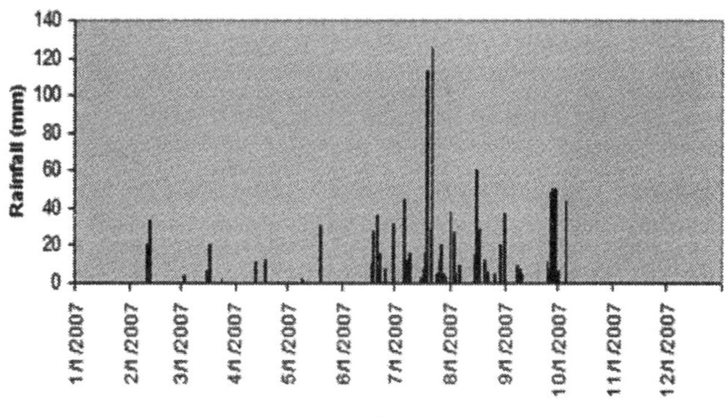

Figure 3. Daily Rainfall for the study period 2007

B. Development of HSG Map

Soil map was used to develop the hydrological soil group map by assigning appropriate values for different types of soil. The study area consisted of Heavy alluvium soil, Old alluvium soil, Recent alluvium soil, Sandy clay loam. Based on the infiltration characteristics of the soil the present study area soil was placed under different hydrological soil group. Figure 4 showsthe different soil types of the hydrological soil group assigned and map was developed. Figure 5 shows the hydrological soil group map for the study region.The major soil type in the study area is

Recent alluvium soil which occupies around 37.43% of the region as shown in Figure 6.

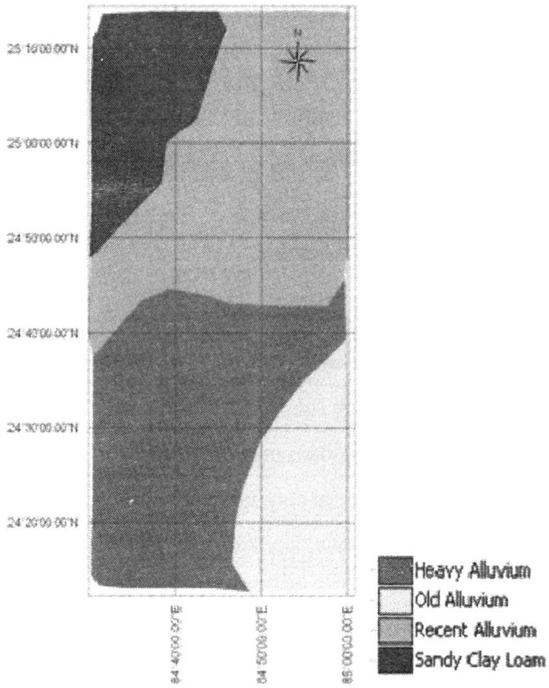

Figure 4 Soil class map used for deriving the Hydrological Soil group

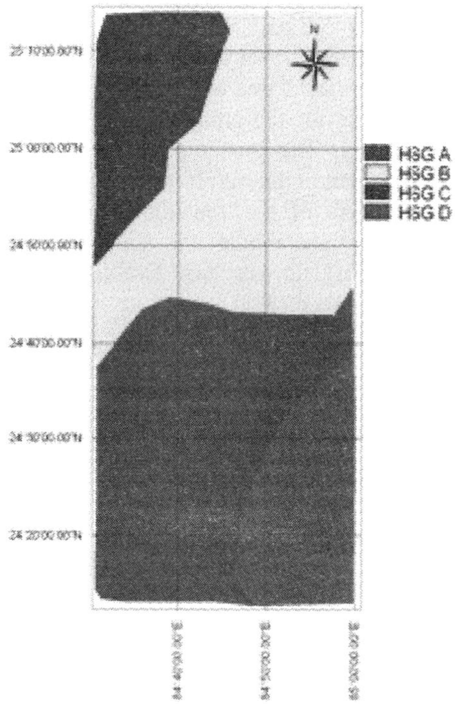

Figure 5 Hydrological Soil Group map for the different soil types of the study area.

C. Computation of Curve Number (CN) from Land use and HSG Map

The curve number is a function of antecedent moisture condition and land use-HSG conditions. Land use map prepared [5] was crossed with the hydrological soil group map to extract twenty-eight classes of different combinations. The weighted average value of CN was calculated as

$$CN\ II = (\sum CN_i \times NP_i)/\sum(NP_i) \quad (5)$$

CN II = Weighted curve number, CN_i = Curve number from 1 to any no. N., NP_i = Number of Pixel from 1 to any no. N. CN I and CN III was calculated as a function of CN. CN I, CN II and CN III was computed as 52.58, 72.53.and 85.86 respectively. For calculating the runoff discharge appropriate value of CN was selected based on the antecedent moisture condition.

D. Estimation of Runoff Discharge for the study area.

The runoff was estimated by knowing the antecedent moisture condition and the curve number. Using the SCS rainfall-runoff relation the daily runoff was computed. The calculation was done on excel spreadsheet. Weighted Curve Number Map of the study area is as shown in Figure 7. Figure 8 represents the Cross map of land use and HSG Map of study area. Runoff discharge would occur only if the precipitation would exceed the value 0.3S. Using this condition the runoff generated on different dates was computed. Calculated monthly runoff values are shown in Figure 9 which shows highest runoff occurs in July.

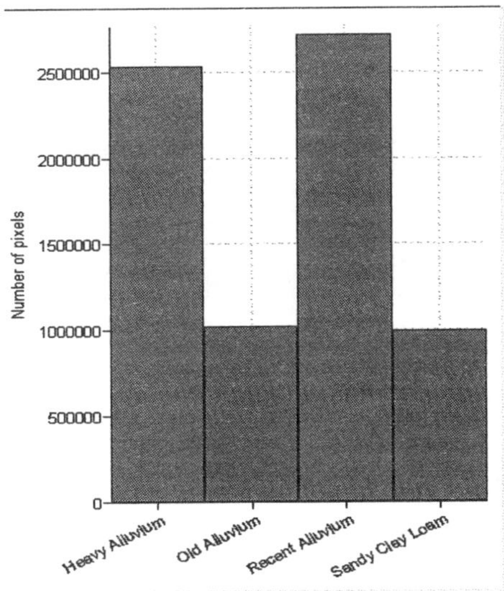

	npix	npixpct	pctnotund
Heavy Alluvium	2533648	32.72	34.86
Old Alluvium	1020916	13.18	14.04
Recent Alluvium	2721035	35.14	37.43
Sandy Clay Loam	993319	12.83	13.67
Min	993319	12.83	13.67
Max	2721035	35.14	37.43
Avg	1817230	23.47	25.00
StD	938627	12.12	12.91
Sum	7268918	93.87	100.00

Figure 6 Area occupied by different type of soils

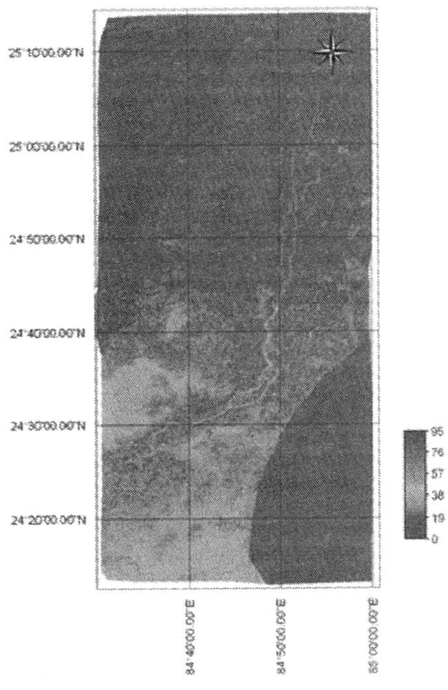

Figure 7. Weighted curve number map

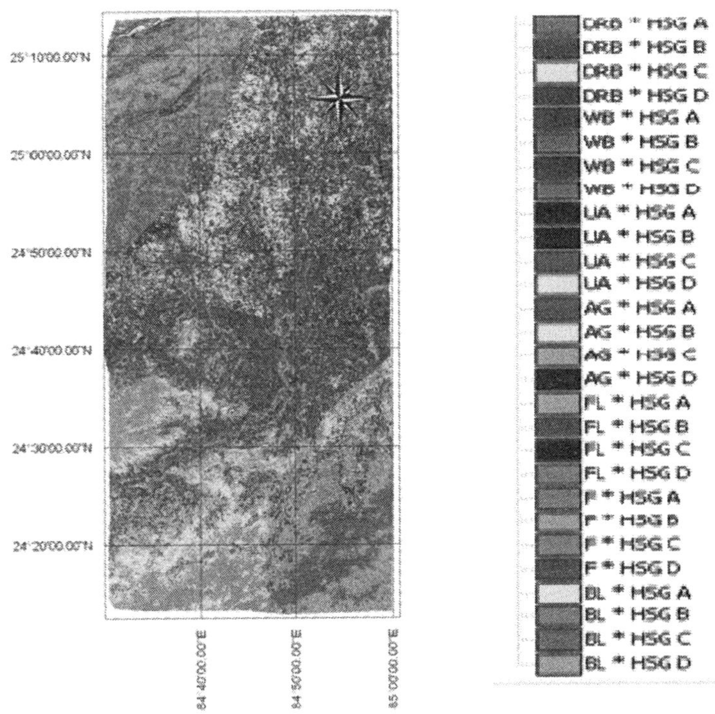

Figure 8. Land use-HSG Map of the study area.

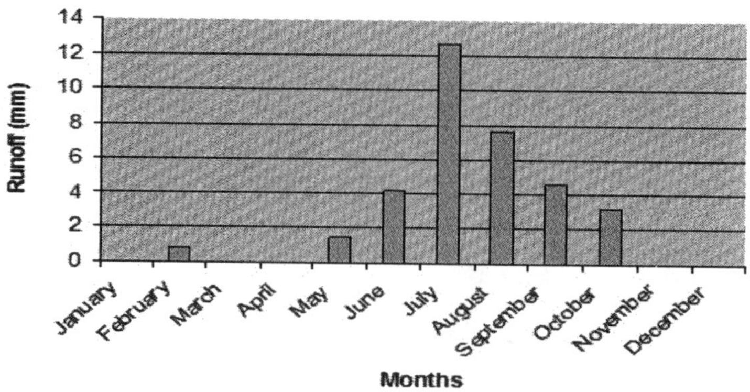

Figure 9 Monthly Runoff value during the year 2007 computed from SCS curve number model

V. CONCLUSIONS

The present work shows that remote sensing satellite images are very useful to determine runoff distribution of the study area. Thus, it has become inevitable to determine rainfall/runoff model by using remote sensing and GIS technologies. In the present study SSC-CN model was used to compute runoff in Sone canal command area. Curve number was determined based on land use/cover from classified Landsat images and hydrological soil groups. There are four type of soil in Sone canal command areawhich include heavy alluvium, old alluvium, recent alluvium and sandy clay loam, each soil has different hydrological soil group and respond differently to rainfall. Overall runoff from the study region for the year 2007 was computed to be 17.98mm with maximum contribution from the monsoon month.

References

[1] Muzzammil, M., Alam, J., & Zakwan, M. 2015. An optimization technique for estimation of rating curve parameters. Proceedings of National Symposium on Hydrology (pp. 234-240).

[2] Zakwan, M., Muzzammil, M., &Alam, J. 2017. Developing Stage-Discharge Relations using Optimization Techniques. Aquademia: Water, Environment and Technology, 1(2), 05.

[3] Zakwan, M. 2016. Estimation of runoff using optimization technique. Water and Energy International, 59(8), 42-44.

[4] Zakwan, M. 2016 Equation Solvers as an Alternative to Conventional Regression. Proc. 3rd Nat. Con. on Sustain. Water Resour. Dev. and Manag., Aurangabad, 139-143.

[5] Ara, Z. 2018 Land Use Classification Using Remotely Sensed Images A Case Study of Eastern Sone Canal-Bihar. STIWM-2018, IIT Roorkee, Roorkee.

[6] Zakwan, M., & Muzzammil, M. 2016. Optimization approach for hydrologic channel routing. Water and Energy International, 59(3), 66-69.

[7] Zakwan, M. 2017. Assessment of Dimensionless Form of Kostiakov Model. Aquademia: Water, Environment and Technology, 1(1), 01.

[8] Mockus, V. 1949. Estimation of Total (and Peak Rates of) Surface Runoff for Individual Storms. *Interim Survey Report*, Grand (Neosho) River Watershed, Exhibit A of Appendix B, USDA, Lincoln, Nebraska

[9] NEH, 1985. National Engineering Handbook section 4-Hydrology, U.S. Department of Agriculture, Washington, D.C

[10] Sharma, T., Kiran, P.V.S., Singh, T.P., Trivedi, A.V. and R. R. Navalgund R.R., 2001, Hydrologic response of a watershed to land use changes a remote Sensing and GIS approach, International Journal of Remote Sensing, Vol.22, 2095-2108.

[11] Gangodagamage, C. and Agarwal, S.P., 2001, Hydrological Modeling using remote sensing and GIS, Asian Conference on remote sensing 5-9 November 2001

Daily River flow Modeling using Artificial Neural Networks

C.S.V. Subrahmanya Kumar[1], G.K.Viswanadh[2]

[1] *Professor, Department of Civil Engineering, MVSR Engineering College, Nadergul, Hyderabad, Telangana*
[2] *Professor of Civil Engineering & OSD to VC, JNTU College of Engineering, Kukatpally, Hyderabad, Telangana*

[1] csvs.kumar1@gmail.com
[2]gorti_gkv@yahoo.co.in

Abstract— **River flow prediction is useful in water resources development, planning and management. This paper demonstrates the application of Artificial Neural Networks in forecasting the River flows. Neural network model is formulated and evaluated to predict daily river flows in River Sabri at Konta using Gradient descent back propagation algorithm. To study the performance of the model developed, various statistical performance indices namely correlation coefficient, normalized root mean square error, coefficient of efficiency, average absolute relative error are computed during training and testing phases. The results indicate that Artificial Neural Networks can be effectively used to model streamflows in a river.**

***Keywords*—Streamflow, Modeling, Artificial Neural Networks, Statistical Performance Indices. Back propagation algorithm**

I. Introduction

Prediction of river flows help in optimal use of water resources. A wide variety of models have been developed and used for flood forecasting. Soft computing techniques such as Artificial Neural Networks, fuzzy logic have emerged to model the river flows. Notable contributions in streamflow modeling are Poff et al. [14], Muttiah et al. [12], Tawfik et al. [23], Karunanithi et al. [11], Thirumalaiah and Deo [24], ,Jain et al. [10]), Jagadeesh et al. [9], Amin et al. [1], Birikundavyi et al. [4], Ozgur Kisi [13], Wu et al. [26] , Francois et al. [6], and Subrahmanya Kumar CSV et al.,[18]-[22].

II. Artificial Neural Networks Based Modeling Approach:

An ANN is a massively parallel distributed information processing system that has certain performance characteristics resembling biological neural networks of the human brain, (Haykin, [7]). ANN plays an important role in the field of hydrology, since the analysis of hydrologic systems deals with high degree of empiricism and approximation. As large number of publications has appeared in the recent past, to avoid duplication, the main concepts are highlighted in this section.

An ANN is composed of many non- linear and densely interconnected processing elements or neurons. In ANN architecture, neurons are arranged in groups called layers. Each neuron in a layer operates in logical parallelism. Information is transmitted from one layer to another in serial operations (Hecht- Nielsen, [8]). A network can have one or several layers. The basic structure of a network usually consists of three layers- the input layer, where the data are introduced to the network, the hidden layer(s), where the data are processed, and the output layer, where the results for the given input are produced. The neurons in the hidden layer(s) are connected to the neurons of a neighboring layer by weighing factors that can be adjusted during the model training process. The networks are organized according to training methods for specific applications. Figure. 1 illustrates a three layer artificial neural network. The most distinctive characteristic of an ANN is its ability to learn from examples. Learning or training of an ANN model is a procedure by which ANN repeatedly processes a set of test data (input – output data pairs) , changing the values of its weights. In the training or learning process, the target output at each output node is compared with the network output, and the difference or error is minimized by adjusting the weights and biases through some training algorithm. In the present study, the training of ANNs was accomplished by Gradient descent algorithm with back- propagation.

In Back-Propagation, each input pattern of the training data set is passed through the network from the input layer to the output layer. The network output is compared to the desired target output, and an error is computed. The error is propagated backward through the network to each node and correspondingly the connection weights are adjusted. Thus back propagation algorithm consists of two phases: a forward pass, during which the processing of information occurs from the input layer to the output layer; and a backward pass, when the error from the output layer is propagated back to the input layer and the interconnections are modified based on equation (1).

$$\Delta W_{ij}(n) = \alpha \Delta W_{ij}(n-1) - \eta (\partial E / \partial W_{ij}) \quad (1)$$

where $\Delta W_{ij}(n)$ and $\Delta W_{ij}(n-1)$ are the weight increments between nodes i and j during the n th and (n-1) th steps. 'α' is the momentum factor, used to speed up the training in flat regions of the error surface and to prevent oscillations in the weights. 'η' is the learning rate used to avoid the chance of being trapped in local minimum instead of global minima (ASCE Task Committee, [2,3]). In the present study the initial learning rate is taken as 0.01 and the momentum term as 0.9. Low value of learning rate takes more time for error convergence. Thus, a back propagation algorithm consists of two phases: a forward pass, during which the processing of information occurs from the input layer to the output layer; and a backward pass, when the error from the output layer is propagated back to the input layer and the interconnections are modified.

The back propagation algorithm was originally developed by Werbos [25] in 1974. Rumelhart et al.[15] rediscovered the algorithm and made it popular by demonstrating the training of hidden neurons for complex mapping problems. The algorithm is given by Fausett [5] (Source: ASCE Task Committee, 2000).

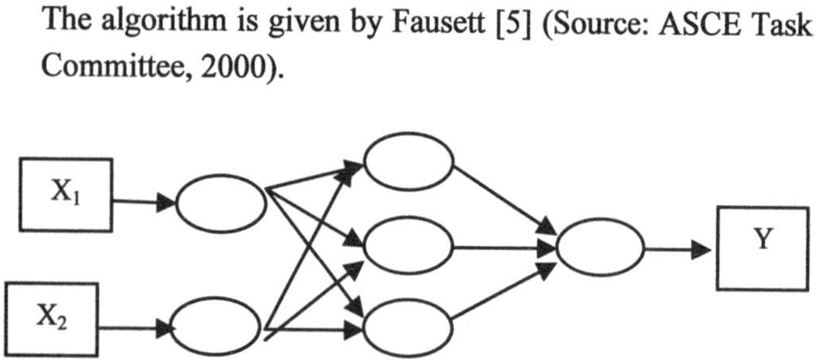

Fig.1 : A Typical Three Layer Feed forward ANN Configuration

III. STUDY AREA

To demonstrate the methodology for modeling daily streamflow using ANN technique, Konta gauging station on River Sabari is considered. The basin lies in the Deccan Plateau and is situated between latitude 16° 16'N and 22° 43'N and longitude 73° 26'E and 83° 07'E. The schematic representation of Godavari catchment plan with gauging stations is shown in Fig.2.

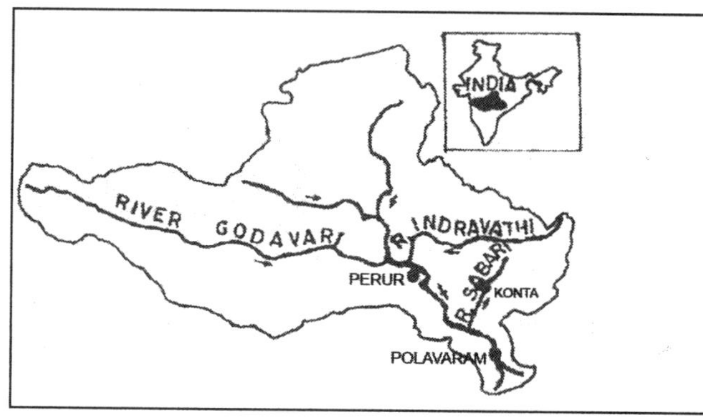

Fig: 2 Schematic representation of Godavari Catchment Plan

IV. EVALUATION METHODOLOGY

The steps involved in the present study in the formulation of the river flow model are as follows:

(1) Selection of data sets for calibration and validation of the model.
(2) Normalization of the selected data.
(3) Formulation of the model by the identification of the input and output vectors.
(4) Determination of the structure of the Artificial Neural Network i.e., number of neurons in the input layer, hidden layer and the output layer.
(5) Training the Artificial Neural Network model using Gradient Descent Back Propagation algorithm.
(6) Validation of the model by presenting the test data to the developed ANN model.
(7) Computation of the statistical performance indices for both training and validation phases.

The steps involved in the present study in the formulation of River flow prediction model is shown in Fig.3.

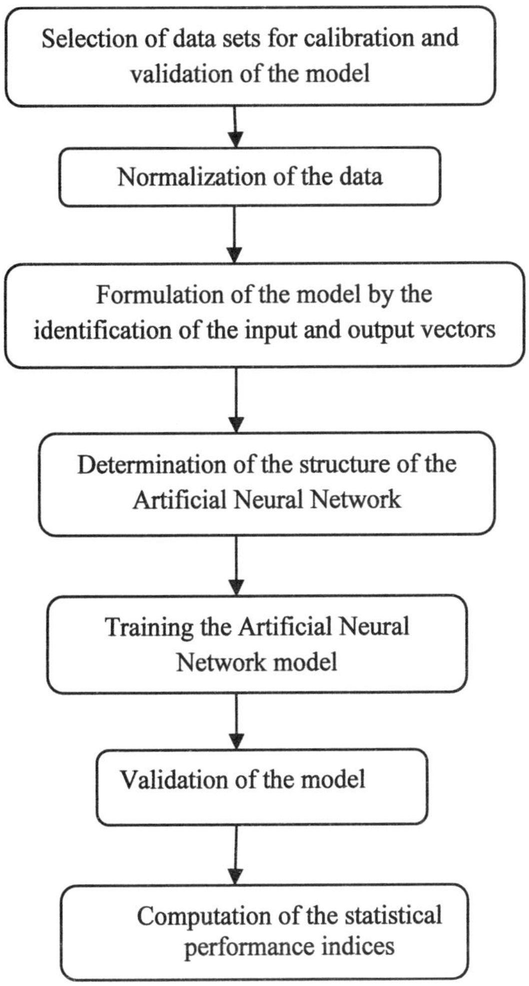

Fig: 3 Flow chart showing Evaluation Methodology

V.DAILY RIVER FLOW MODEL FORMULATION

The varying degree of influence of individual variables on the output hydrograph can be comprehended by the physical behavior of the system. The flow hydrograph consists of various components that result from different physical processes in a watershed. The rising limb of a stream flow hydrograph is the result of the gradual release of water from various storage elements of a watershed due to gradual increase in the storage due to the rainfall input. Also, the rising limb of the hydrograph is influenced by varying infiltration capacities, watershed storage characteristics, intensity and duration of the rainfall and less so by climatic factors such as temperature and evapotranspiration etc. (Zang and Govindaraju, 2000). Conversely, the falling limb of a watershed is the result of the gradual release of water from various storages of the watershed after the rainfall has ceased and is influenced more by the storage characteristics of the watershed and climatic characteristics to some extent. Further, the falling limb of a hydrograph can be divided into three parts: initial portion just after the peak, middle portion, and the final portion. The initial portion of the falling limb of a flow hydrograph is influenced more by the quick flow or interflow, the middle portion of the falling limb is more dominated by the delayed surface flow, and the final portion of the falling limb of smaller magnitudes is dominated by the base flow. Hence it can be concluded that the trained ANN certainly represents the physical behavior of the system through its input variables.

Daily stream flow data is available for the period 1996 to 2006. The model is trained using data for 7 years (1996-2002) and validated on 4 years (2003-2006). The input vector to the model is identified using the procedure outlined by Sudheer et al. (2002). The historical river flow series was normalized between 0 and 1 using equation (2).

$$(x_i)nor = \frac{(x_i)act - (x_i)min}{(x_i)max - (x_i)min} \quad (2)$$

Where, $(x_i)_{nor}$ is the normalized value of the variable under consideration, $(x_i)_{act}$ is the actual value of the variable, $(x_i)_{max}$ and $(x_i)_{min}$ are the maximum and minimum values in the data series of a variable under consideration.

The statistical analysis carried out indicated that, the most appropriate input vector includes antecedent flows upto a lag of 6 days. Thus the functional form of the ANN stream flow model is,

$$Q_t = f(Q_{t-1}, Q_{t-2}, Q_{t-3}, Q_{t-4}, Q_{t-5}, Q_{t-6}) \quad (3)$$

Where Q_t represents the river flow at time t and Q_{t-1}, Q_{t-2}, Q_{t-3}, Q_{t-4}, Q_{t-5}, Q_{t-6} are river flows at time periods (t-1), (t-2), (t-3), (t-4), (t-5), and (t-6) respectively. Thus the input layer consists of six neurons and the output layer had one neuron for the current flow Q_t.

A three layer ANN model was employed to develop river flow model. The number of neurons in the hidden layer is finalised by trial and error. The configuration that gives the minimum MSE and maximum correlation coefficient was selected for each of the options. Sigmoid function is used as the activation function in the network training process. The final ANN architecture arrived consists of one hidden layer with six neurons.

To assess the potential of all the models developed, the first three statistical moments namely, mean, standard deviation and skewness are determined for training and testing phases. The values of the first three moments for the historic and computed flow series are presented in Table 2 and Table 2. The analysis reveals that the mean of the historical flow series are preserved by the models developed, both during training and testing.

To test the robustness of the model developed the performance criteria such as Correlation coefficient, Average absolute relative error (AARE), Nash coefficient of efficiency, Normalized Root Mean Square Error (NRMSE), are evaluated during training and testing and is presented in Table 3.

STATISTICAL PERFORMANCE INDICES:

(1)Correlation Coefficient (R): The correlation coefficient is given as,

$$R = \frac{[y_o(t) - y'_o(t)] * [y_p(t) - y'_p(t)]}{\sqrt{\Sigma[y_o(t) - y'_o(t)]^2} * \sqrt{[y_p(t) - y'_p(t)]^2}} \quad (4)$$

Where $y_o(t)$ and $y_p(t)$ are the observed and computed values of a variable and $y'_o(t)$, $y'_p(t)$ are the mean of the observed and computed values.

(2) Average Absolute Relative Error (AARE):

Average Absolute Relative Error gives average error prediction. It is the average of the absolute values of the relative errors in forecasting. Mathematically AARE is calculated using the following equations.

$$RE(t) = \frac{y_o(t) - y_p(t)}{y_o(t)} * 100 \quad (5)$$

$$AARE = \frac{1}{n}\sum |RE(t)| \quad (6)$$

where $y_o(t)$ and $y_p(t)$ are the observed and computed values of a variable at time t, $RE(t)$ is the relative error in predicting the variable at time t and n, the number of observations. Smaller the value of *AARE* better is the performance of the model.

(3) Nash- Sutcliffe coefficient of efficiency (η):

The Nash coefficient of efficiency (Nash- Sutcliffe, 1970) compares the computed and the observed values of the variable and evaluates how far the model is able to explain the total variance in the data set.

The Nash coefficient of efficiency is calculated as,

$$\eta = \frac{[\Sigma y_o(t) - y'_o(t)]^2 - y_p(t) - y_o(t)^2}{\Sigma[y_o(t) - y'_o(t)]^2} * 100 \quad (7)$$

where $y'_o(t)$ is the mean of observed values and all other variables are same as explained earlier. Higher the value of efficiency better is the model performance.

(4)Normalised Root Mean Square Error (NRMSE):

The Normalised Root Mean Square Error is computed using the following equation.

$$NRMSE = \frac{1/n\sqrt{\Sigma[y_p(t) - y_o(t)]^2}}{1/n\,\Sigma y_o(t)} \quad (8)$$

Better model performance is indicated by lower value of NRMSE.

VI.RESULTS AND DISCUSSION

In the river flow prediction model it is found that the model with architecture, 6 input neurons, 6 hidden neurons, 1 output neuron is the most suitable model. The correlation coefficient is found to be 0.871, 0.850 and the Mean square error is 0.000654, 0.001149 during training and testing phases at 1000 epochs. With increase in epochs beyond 1000, the correlation coefficient was observed to decrease during testing indicating over training.

Based on the performance evaluation criteria, it can be concluded the model using Gradient descent algorithm performed well. The linear scale plot of the observed and modeled flows v/s time during training and testing phases is shown in Fig. 4 and Fig. 5. The graphs show a good match between modeled and observed flow values. The scatter plots of the modeled flow versus observed flows for the training and testing phases are shown in Fig. 6 and Fig. 7.

Table 1 Summary Statistics for River flow Model (Training)

Statistical Parameter	Observed	Modeled
Mean (m^3/sec)	444.82	442.47
Standard deviation (m^3/sec)	509.89	441.14
Skewness coefficient (m^3/sec)	4.05	3.10

Table 2 Summary Statistics for River flow Model (Testing)

Statistical Parameter	Observed	Modeled
Mean (m^3/sec)	399.41	382.55
Standard deviation (m^3/sec)	611.26	436.23
Skewness coefficient (m^3/sec)	6.47	4.01

Table. 3 Statistical Performance Indices during Training & Testing for 6-6-1 configuration

Phase	R	η (%)	NRMSE	AARE (%)
Training	0.871	75.77	0.564	18.15
Testing	0.850	70.36	0.832	23.51

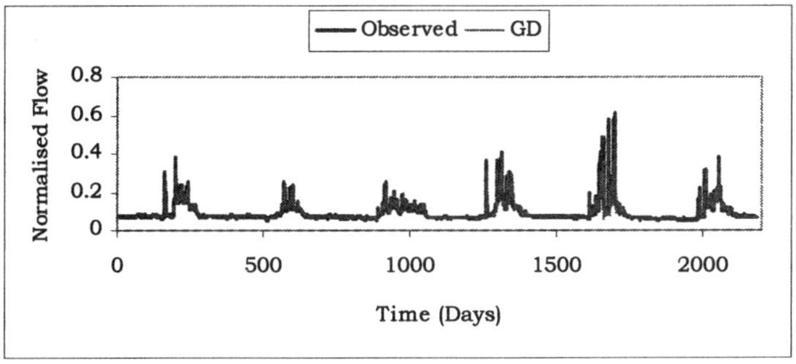

Fig. 4 Hydrographs for River flow model during training

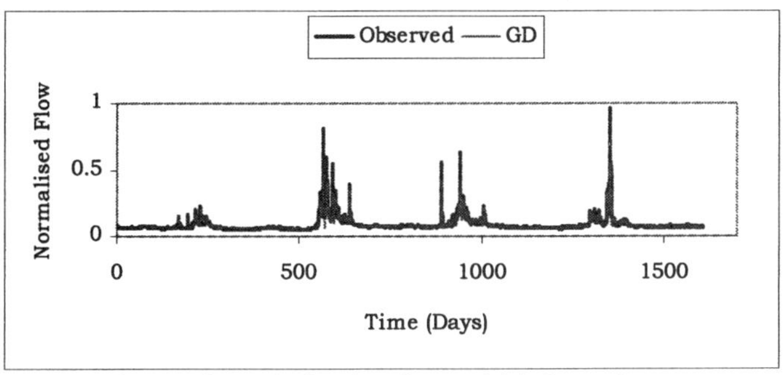

Fig. 5 Hydrographs for River flow model during testing

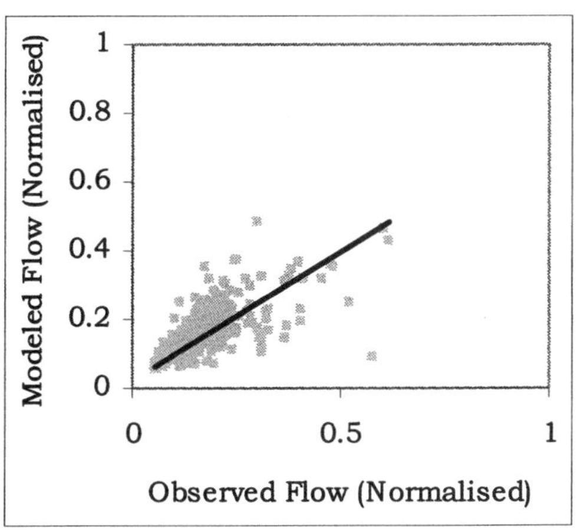

Fig. 6 Scatter plot comparing the modeled and observed flows during training

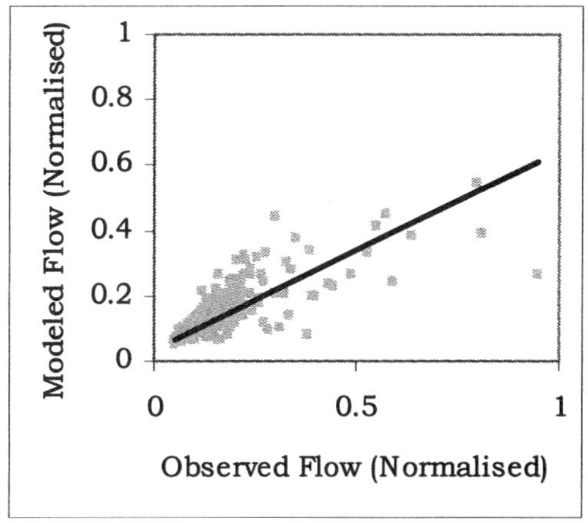

Fig. 7 Scatter plot comparing the modeled and observed flows during testing

REFERENCES

[1]. Amin Elshorbagy., Simnovic, S.P., Panu, U.S. (2000). "Performance Evaluation of Artificial Neural Networks for Runoff Prediction." Journal of Hydrologic Engineering, 4(5), 424-427.

[2]. ASCE Task Committee (2000a). "Artificial Neural Networks in Hydrology I Journal of Hydrologic Engineering, 5(2), 115- 123.

[3]. ASCE Task Committee (2000b). "Artificial Neural Networks in Hydrology II, Journal of Hydrologic Engineering, 5(2), 124- 132.

[4]. Birikundavyi,S., Labib,R., Trung,H.T., Rousselle.J. (2002). "Performance of Neural Networks in Daily Streamflow Forecasting." Journal of Hydrologic Engineering, 5(7), 392- 399. [5]. Cigizoglu., (2005). "Application of Generalized Regression Neural Networks to Intermittent Flow Forecasting and Estimation." Journal of Hydrologic Engineering, 4(10), 336-341.

[5]. Fausett,L. (1994). "Fundamental of Neural Networks." Prentice Hall, Englewood Cliffs,N.J.

[6]. Francois Anctil, Alexandre Rat. (2005). "Evaluation of Neural Network Streamflow Forecasting on 47 Watersheds." Journal of Hydrologic Engineering, 1(10), 85-88.

[7]. Haykin, S. (1994). "Neural networks: A Comprehensive Foundation." Mac Millan, New York.

[8]. Hect- Nielson, R.(1991). "Neuro Computing." Addison-Wesley, New York.

[9]. Jagadeesh Anmala, Bin Zhang, Rao S. Govindaraju. (2000), "Comparison of ANNs and Empirical Approaches for Predicting Watershed Runoff." Water Resources Planning and Management, 3(126), 156-166.

[10]. Jain.S.K., Das.A., Srivastava.D.K. (1999). "Application of ANN for Reservoir Inflow Prediction and Operation." Water Resources Planning and Management, 5(125), 263-271.

[11]. Karunanithi,N., Grenney,W.J., Whitley,D., and Bovee,K. (1994). " Neural Networks for River flow Prediction." J. Comp. in Civil Engg., ASCE, 8(2), 201- 220.

[12]. Muttiah,R.S., Srinivasan,R., and Allen,P.M. (1997). "Prediction of two- year Peak Stream Discharges using Neural Networks." Journal of American Water Resources Association, 33(3), 625-630.

[13]. Ozgur Kisi. (2007). "Development of Streamflow-Suspended Sediment Rating Curve using a Range Dependent Neural Network." International Journal of Science and Technology, 1(2), 49-61.

[14]. Poff,L.N., Tokar and Johnson. P.A (1996). "Stream Hydrological and Ecological Responses to Climatic change assessed with an Artificial Neural Network." Limnol and Oceanogr., 41(5), 857-863.

[15]. Rumelhart,D.E., Hinton,G.E., and Williams,R.J. (1986). "Learning Representations by Back-Propagating Errors" Nature, 323, 533-536.

[16]. Subrahmanya Kumar. C.S.V & Viswanadh G.K (2018) "Development of Sediment Transport Model Using Artificial Neural Networks" Journal of Emerging Technologies and Innovative Research, pp 274- 280, Vol. 5, Issue 3, March 2018.

[17]. Subrahmanya Kumar. C.S.V & Viswanadh G.K (2017) "Performance Evaluation of Neural Networks in Daily Streamflow Forecasting" Journal of Emerging Technologies and Innovative Research, pp 177- 183, Vol. 4, Issue 7, July 2017.

[18]. Subrahmanya Kumar. C.S.V & Viswanadh G.K (2017) "Rainfall Runoff Relationship using Neural Networks and Fuzzy Logic" Journal of Emerging Technologies and Innovative Research, pp 212- 220, Vol. 4, Issue 3, March 2017.

[19]. Subrahmanya Kumar. C.S.V & Viswanadh G.K (2017) "Study of Performance of Daily Rainfall-Runoff Model Using Neural Networks, International Journal of Creative Research Thoughts, pp 2393-2402, Vol 5, Issue 1, February 2017.

[20] Subrahmanya Kumar. C.S.V., (2009), Ph.D Dissertation on "Performance Evaluation and Comparison of Different types of Hydrological Models using Artificial Neural Networks", JNTU, Hyderabad.

[21]. Subrahmanya Kumar. C.S.V & Viswanadh G.K (2009), "Performance Evaluation of Rainfall-Runoff Modeling using Artificial Neural Networks", International Journal of Scientific Computing, pp 245-250, Vol 3, No.2, July – December, 2009.

[22]. Subrahmanya Kumar. C.S.V & Viswanadh G.K (2008) "Artificial Neural Network Approach for Reservoir Stage Prediction", International Journal of Applied Mathematical Analysis and Applications, pp 13- 19, Vol 3, No.1, Jan - June 2008.

[23] Tawfik,M., Ibrahim,A., and Fahmy,H. (1997) "Hysteresis Sensitive Neural Network for Modeling Rating Curves" Journal of Comp. in Civil Engineering, 11(3), 206- 211.

[24]. Thirumalaiah,K., and Deo,M.C. (1998) "River Stage Forecasting using Artificial Neural Networks" Hydrologic Engineering, 3(1), 26-32.

[25]. Werbos,P. (1974). "Beyond Regression: New Tools for Prediction and Analysis in the behavioral Sciences" Ph.D dissertation, Harvard University, Cambridge.

[26]. Wu., Jun Han., Shastri Annambhotla., Scott Bryant. "Artificial Neural Networks for Forecasting Watershed Runoff and Stream Flows" Journal of Hydrologic Engineering, 3(10), 216-222.

Performance Evaluation of Daily Sediment Yield Transport Model Using Artificial Neural Networks

C.S.V. Subrahmanya Kumar[1], G.K.Viswanadh[2]

[1]*Professor, Department of Civil Engineering, MVSR Engineering College, Nadergul, Hyderabad*
[2] *Professor of Civil Engineering & OSD to VC, JNTU College of Engineering, Kukatpally, Hyderabad*

[1] csvs.kumar1@gmail.com
[2]gorti_gkv@yahoo.co.in

***Abstract*—** The assessment of the volume of sediment transported by a river is of vital interest in hydraulic engineering due to its importance in the design and management of water resources projects. Neural Network model is formulated to predict daily suspended sediment yield in river Sabari at Konta using Gradient Descent back propagation algorithm. To test the robustness of the model formulated, statistical performance indices namely, Correlation coefficient (R), Nash coefficient of efficiency (η), Normalized Root Mean Square Error (NRMSE) and Average Absolute Relative Error (AARE) are computed as 0.913, 83.39%, 0.0009, 30.80% during training and 0.877, 76.65%, 0.0013 and 55.58% during testing. The results indicate that ANN can be effectively used to model daily suspended sediment yield.

***Keywords*—** Suspended sediment yield, catchment, Atrificial Networks, Gradient descent back propagation algorithm

INTRODUCTION

Soil erosion occurring in different forms on the earth surface is an unavoidable phenomenon that is deteriorated by human activities. Knowledge of the erosion status and its prediction has always been a general concern. Correct estimation of sediment yield or sediment concentration carried by a river is very important for many water resources projects. The assessment of the volume of sediment transported by a river is of vital interest in hydraulic engineering. Its assessment is important in the design of life of the reservoirs.

There are many parameters like rainfall, moisture content of the soil, land use pattern, slope of the catchment, soil characteristics etc. that affect the sediment load. Although it is possible to identify sophisticated models taking into consideration the hydrological hydro meteorological variables, it is economically preferable to have a model that can simulate the sediment variations on the basis of flow discharge and sediment records (Ozgur Kisi, [11]).

A plethora of models and procedures have so far been adopted for sediment computations. These models are mostly derived from statistical methods and therefore lack the required accuracy. The earlier studies (Ozgur Kisi, [11]), carried out on sediment predictions indicated that ANN based models performed better when compared to the regression based methods. Chang et al. [6] studied total bed- material discharge relation in Alluvial Channels. Ackers and White [1] developed Sediment Transport models. The works by some investigators using the regression techniques for sediment prediction coefficients are those by Shen and Hung [13], Brownlie [5], Karim and Kennedy [10], Ariffin [2] developed Sediment Transport Models for Selected Rivers in Malaysia using Regression Analysis and Artificial Neural Network. Subrahmanya Kumar et al., developed various hydrological models using Artificial Neural Networks [14] – [20].

The present study forecasts the daily sediment yield using Artificial Neural Networks in River Sabari at Konta station.

ARTIFICIAL NEURAL NETWORKS BASED MODELING APPROACH

An ANN is a massively parallel distributed information processing system that has certain performance characteristics resembling biological neural networks of the human brain (Haykin, [8]). ANN plays an important role in the field of hydrology, since the analysis of hydrologic systems deals with high degree of empiricism and approximation. As large numbers of publications have appeared in the recent past, to avoid duplication, the main concepts are highlighted in this section.

An ANN is composed of many non- linear and densely interconnected processing elements or neurons. In an ANN architecture, neurons are arranged in groups called layers. Each neuron in a layer operates in logical parallelism.

Information is transmitted from one layer to another in serial operations (Hecht- Nielsen, [9]). A network can have one or several layers. The basic structure of a network usually consists of three layers- the input layer, where the data are introduced to the network, the hidden layer(s), where the data are processed, and the output layer, where the results for the given input are produced. The neurons in the hidden layer(s) are connected to the neurons of a neighbouring layer by weighing factors that can be adjusted during the model training process. The networks are organized according to training methods for specific applications. Fig. 1 illustrates a three layer Artificial Neural Network The most distinctive characteristic of an ANN is its ability to learn from examples. Learning or training of an ANN model is a procedure by which ANN repeatedly processes a set of test data (input – output data pairs), changing the values of its weights. In the training or learning process, the target output at each output node is compared with the network output, and the difference or error is minimized by adjusting the weights and biases through some training algorithm. In the present study, the training of ANNs was accomplished by Gradient descent algorithm with back- propagation.

In Back-Propagation, each input pattern of the training data set is passed through the network from the input layer to the output layer. The network output is compared to the desired target output, and an error is computed. The error is propagated backward through the network to each node and correspondingly the connection weights are adjusted based on the equation,

$$\Delta W_{ij}(n) = \alpha \Delta W_{ij}(n-1) - \eta(\partial E / \partial W_{ij}) \qquad (1)$$

where $\Delta W_{ij}(n)$ and $\Delta W_{ij}(n-1)$ are the weight increments between nodes i and j during the n th and (n-1) th steps. 'α' is the momentum factor, used to speed up the training in flat regions of the error surface and to prevent oscillations in the weights. 'η' is the learning rate used to avoid the chance of being trapped in local minimum instead of global minima (ASCE Task Committee, [3,4]). Thus, a back propagation algorithm consists of two phases: a forward pass, during which the processing of information occurs from the input layer to the output layer; and a backward pass, when the error from the output layer is propagated back to the input layer and the interconnections are modified. In the present study the initial learning rate is taken as 0.01 and the momentum term as 0.9.

The back propagation algorithm was originally developed by Werbos [21] in 1974. Rumelhart et al., [12] (1986, reported in Haykin, 1994) rediscovered the algorithm and made it popular by demonstrating the training of hidden neurons for complex mapping problems. The algorithm is given by Fausett [10] (Source: ASCE Task Committee, 2000).

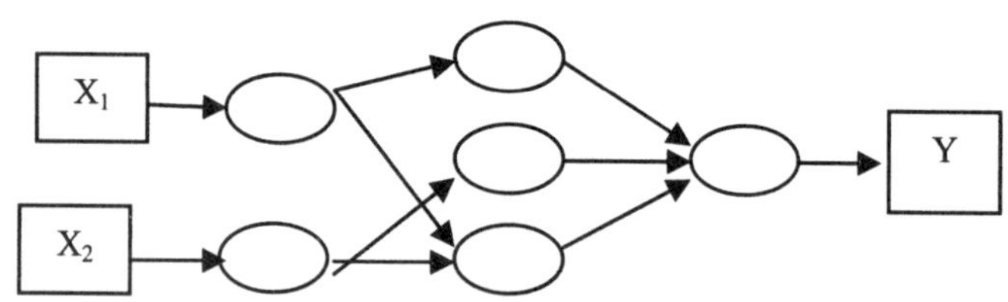

Fig.1 : A Typical Three Layer Feed forward ANN Configuration

STUDY AREA

To demonstrate the methodology for modeling daily sediment yield using ANN technique, Konta gauging station on River Sabari is considered. The basin lies in the Deccan Plateau and is situated between latitude 16° 16'N and 22° 43'N and longitude 73° 26'E and 83° 07'E. The schematic representation of Godavari catchment plan with gauging stations is shown in Fig. 2.

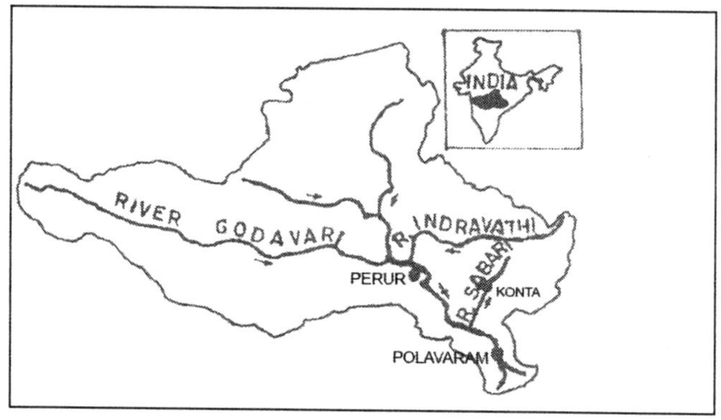

Fig: 2 Schematic representation of Godavari Catchment Plan

EVALUATION METHODOLOGY

The steps involved in the present study in the formulation of various hydrological models are as follows:

(1) Selection of data sets for calibration and validation of the model.
(2) Normalization of the selected data.
(3) Formulation of the model by the identification of the input and output vectors.
(4) Determination of the structure of the Artificial Neural Network i.e., number of neurons in the input layer, hidden layer and the output layer.

(5) Training the Artificial Neural Network model using Gradient Descent Back Propagation algorithm.
(6) Validation of the model by presenting the test data to the developed ANN model.
(7) Computation of the statistical performance indices for both training and validation phases.

DAILY SUSPENDED SEDIMENT YIELD PREDICTION MODEL

Daily suspended sediment data is available for the period 1996 to 2006. The model is trained using data for 7 years (1996-2002) and validated on 4 years (2003-2006). The historical flow series was normalised between 0 and 1 using equation (2). Observed values of the river flow are used in model formulation.

$$(x_i)nor = \frac{(x_i)act - (x_i)min}{(x_i)max - (x_i)min} \quad (2)$$

Where, $(x_i)_{nor}$ is the normalized value of the variable under consideration, $(x_i)_{act}$ is the actual value of the variable, $(x_i)_{max}$ and $(x_i)_{min}$ are the maximum and minimum values in the data series of a variable under consideration.

The study was focused on sediment predictions using the past discharge and sediment records at station Konta. A network involving 3 input nodes of suspended sediment and stream flows at Konta and one output node corresponding to the sediment yield forecast at time t was developed. The functional form of the sediment yield ANN model is,

$$S_t = f[Q_t, Q_{t-1}, Q_{t-2}, S_{t-1}, S_{t-2}] \quad (3)$$

Where S_t represents the sediment yield at time t , Q_t, Q_{t-1}, Q_{t-2} are stream flows at time periods t, (t-1), (t-2) and S_{t-1}, S_{t-2} are the sediment yields at time (t-1) and (t-2).

A three layer ANN model was employed to develop daily sediment yield model. The number of neurons in the hidden layer is finalised by trial and error. The configuration that gives the minimum MSE and maximum correlation coefficient was selected for each of the options. Sigmoid function is used as the activation function in the network training process.

To test the robustness of the model developed the performance criteria such as Correlation coefficient, Average absolute relative error (AARE), Nash coefficient of efficiency, Normalised Root Mean Square Error (NRMSE), are evaluated during training and testing.

STATISTICAL PERFORMANCE INDICES

(1)Correlation Coefficient (R): The correlation coefficient is given as,

$$R = \frac{[y_o(t) - y'_o(t)] * [y_p(t) - y'_p(t)]}{\sqrt{\sum[yo(t) - y'o(t)]2} * \sqrt{[y_p(t) - y'_p(t)]2}}$$

(4)

Where $y_o(t)$ and $y_p(t)$ are the observed and computed values of a variable and $y'_o(t)$, $y'_p(t)$ are the mean of the observed and computed values.

(2) Average Absolute Relative Error (AARE): Average Absolute Relative Error gives average error prediction. It is the average of the absolute values of the relative errors in forecasting. Mathematically AARE is calculated using the following equations.

$$RE(t) = \frac{y_p(t) - y_o(t)}{y_o(t)} * 100 \quad (5)$$

$$AARE = \frac{1}{n}\sum |RE(t)| \quad (6)$$

where $y_o(t)$ and $y_p(t)$ are the observed and computed values of a variable at time t, RE(t) is the relative error in predicting the variable at time t and n, the number of observations. Smaller the value of AARE better is the performance of the model.

(3) Nash- Sutcliffe coefficient of efficiency (η):

The Nash coefficient of efficiency (Nash- Sutcliffe, 1970) compares the computed and the observed values of the variable and evaluates how far the model is able to explain the total variance in the data set.

The Nash coefficient of efficiency is calculated as,

$$\eta = \frac{[\sum y_o(t) - y'_o(t)]^2 - y_p(t) - y_o(t)]^2}{\sum [y_o(t) - y'_o(t)]^2} * 100$$

(7)

where $y'_o(t)$ is the mean of observed values and all other variables are same as explained earlier. Higher the value of efficiency better is the model performance.

(4)Normalised Root Mean Square Error (NRMSE)

The Normalised Root Mean Square Error is computed using the following equation (8).

$$NRMSE = \frac{\left(\frac{1}{n}\sum [y_p(t) - y_o(t)]^2\right)^{1/2}}{\frac{1}{n}\sum y_o(t)}$$

(8)

Better model performance is indicated by lower value of NRMSE.

RESULTS AND DISCUSSION

In the sediment yield prediction model, it is found that the model with architecture, 5 input neurons, one hidden layer with 16 neurons, 1 output neuron is the most suitable model. The correlation coefficient is found to be 0.905, 0.874 and the Mean square error is 0.001144, 0.004125 during training and testing phases at 1000 epochs. With increase in epochs from 1000 to 4000, the correlation coefficient has increased to 0.913 during training and to 0.877 during testing phase. The MSE has further decreased to 0.001049 during training and to 0.001702 during testing. The summary statistics for sediment yield models during training and testing is presented in Table 1 and Table 2. The statistical parameters are nearly preserved.

For the selected models, the computed sediment yield values are denormalised and the performance criteria such as correlation coefficient, NRMSE, AARE, Nash coefficient of efficiency are evaluated during training and testing and are presented in Table 3.

The values of the performance criteria namely R and coefficient of efficiency are good for the sediment yield model both during and testing.

The linear scale plot of the observed and modeled values v/s time during training and testing phases is shown in Fig. 3 & Fig. 4. The graphs show a good match between modeled and observed values both during training and validation periods. The scatter plots of the modeled versus observed sediment yield for the training and testing phases are shown in Fig. 5 and Fig. 6.

Table. 1 Summary Statistics for Sediment Yield Model (Training)

Statistical Parameter	Observed	Predicted
Mean (gm/l)	0.162	0.166
Standard Deviation (gm/l)	0.212	0.195
Skewness Coefficient (gm/l)	2.417	1.708

Table. 2 Summary Statistics for Sediment Yield Model (Testing)

Statistical Parameter	Observed	Predicted
Mean (gm/l)	0.125	0.128
Standard Deviation (gm/l)	0.228	0.187
Skewness Coefficient (gm/l)	4.146	2.605

Table.3 Statistical Performance Indices during Training & Testing.

Phase	ANN Configuration			R	η (%)	NRMSE	AARE (%)
	I	H	O				
Training	5	16	1	0.913	83.39	0.0009	30.80
Testing				0.877	76.65	0.0013	55.58

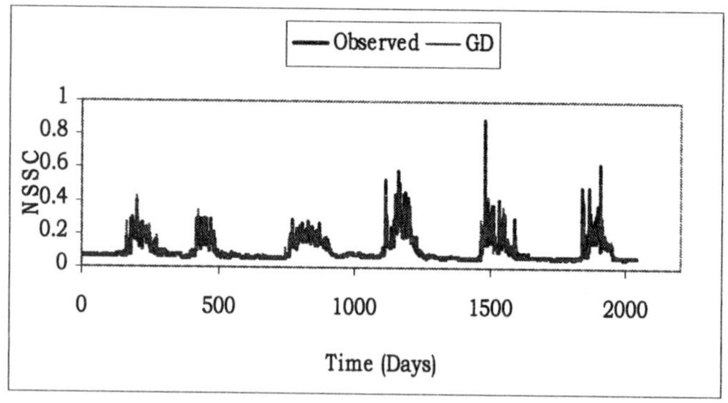

Fig 3: Daily Predicted Sediment Yield during Training

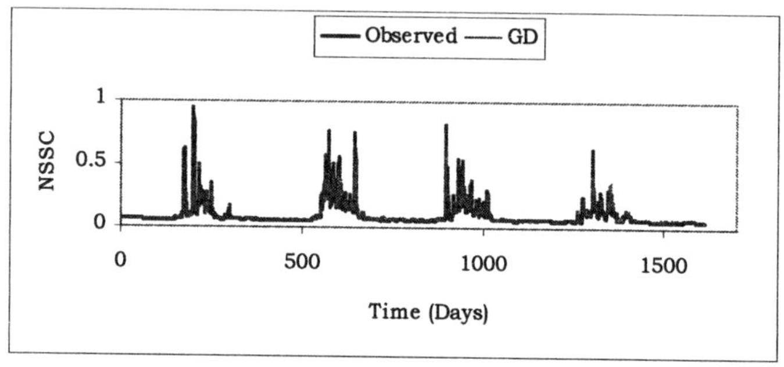

Fig 4: Daily Predicted Sediment Yield during Testing

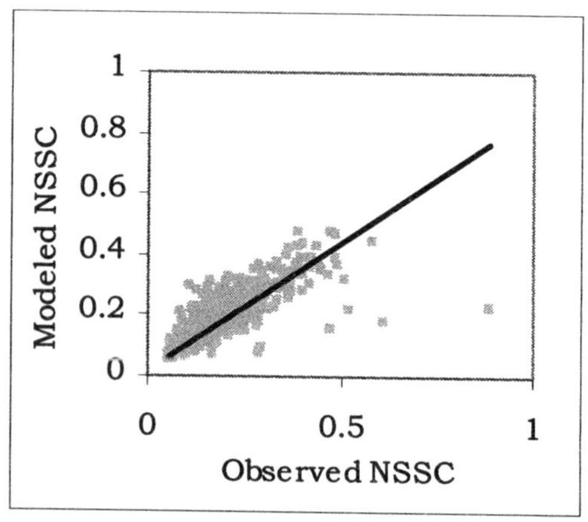

Fig: 5 Scatter Plots comparing Modeled & Observed Sediment Yield during Training

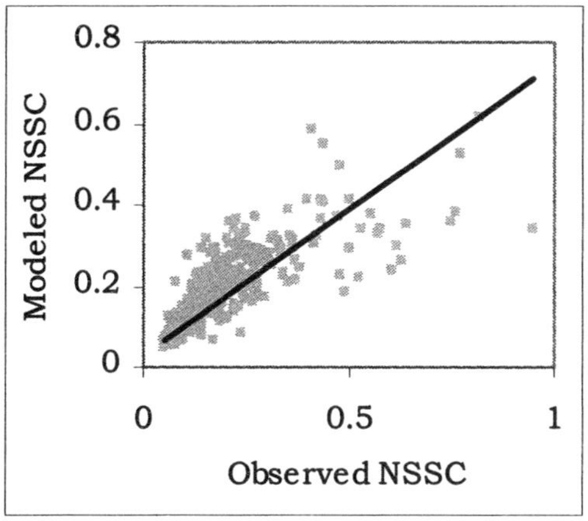

Fig: 6 Scatter Plots comparing Modeled & Observed Sediment Yield during Testing

References

[1] Ackers, P., and White, W.R. (1973). "Sediment Transport: New Approach and Analysis." Journal of the Hydraulics Division, ASCE, 2041- 2060

[2]. Ariffin, J. (2004). "Development of Sediment Transport Models for Selected Rivers in Malaysia using Regression Analysis and Artificial Neural Network." Ph.D Thesis, University of Science Malaysia, Penang, Malaysia.

[3]. ASCE Task Committee (2000a). "Artificial neural networks in Hydrology I Journal of Hydrologic Engineering, 5(2), 115- 123.

[4] ASCE Task Committee (2000b). "Artificial neural networks in Hydrology II, Journal of Hydrologic Engineering, 5(2), 124- 132.

[5]. Brownlie,W. (1982). "Prediction of Flow Depth and Sediment Discharge in Open Channels." Reports of the California Institute of Technology, Pasadena, Report No. NSF/CEE-82090, 73- 154.

[6]. Chang,F.M., Simons, D.B., and Richardson, E.V. (1965). "Total Bed Material Discharge in Alluvial Channels." U.S. Geological Survey Water Supply Paper 1498-I.

[7] Fausett,L. (1994). "Fundamental of Neural Networks." Prentice Hall, Englewood Cliffs,N.J.

[8]. Haykin, S. (1994). "Neural networks: A comphrensive foundation." Mac Millan, New York.

[9]. Hect- Nielson, R.(1990). "Neuro Computing." Addison-Wesley, New York.

[10]. Karim,M.F., and Kennedy,J.F. (1990). "Menu of Coupled Velocity and Sediment-Discharge Relationship for River." Journal of Hydraulic Engineering, 116(8), 987- 996.

[11]. Ozgur Kisi. (2007). "Development of Streamflow- Suspended Sediment Rating Curve using a Range Dependent Neural Network." International Journal of Science and Technology, 1(2), 49-61.

[12]. Rumelhart,D.E., Hinton,G.E., and Williams,R.J. (1986). "Learning Representations by Back- Propagating Errors." Nature, 323, 533-536.

[13]. Shen,H.W., and Hung, C.S. (1972). "An Engineering Approach to Total Bed Material Load by Regression Analysis." Proceedings Sedimentation Symposium, Chapter14, 14.1-14.7.

[14] Subrahmanya Kumar. C.S.V & Viswanadh G.K (2018) "Development of Sediment Transport Model Using Artificial Neural Networks" Journal of Emerging Technologies and Innovative Research, pp 274- 280, Vol. 5, Issue 3, March 2018.

[15].Subrahmanya Kumar. C.S.V & Viswanadh G.K (2017) "Performance Evaluation of Neural Networks in Daily Streamflow Forecasting" Journal of Emerging Technologies and Innovative Research, pp 177- 183, Vol. 4, Issue 7, July 2017.

[16]. Subrahmanya Kumar. C.S.V & Viswanadh G.K (2017) "Rainfall Runoff Relationship using Neural Networks and Fuzzy Logic" Journal of Emerging Technologies and Innovative Research, pp 212-220, Vol. 4, Issue 3, March 2017.

[17]. Subrahmanya Kumar. C.S.V & Viswanadh G.K (2017) "Study of Performance of Daily Rainfall- Runoff Model Using Neural Networks, International Journal of Creative Research Thoughts, pp 2393- 2402, Vol 5, Issue 1, February 2017.

[18] Subrahmanya Kumar. C.S.V., (2009), Ph.D Dissertation on "Performance Evaluation and Comparison of Different types of Hydrological Models using Artificial Neural Networks", JNTU, Hyderabad.

[19] Subrahmanya Kumar. C.S.V & Viswanadh G.K (2009), Performance Evaluation of Rainfall-Runoff Modeling using Artificial Neural Networks, International Journal of Scientific Computing, pp 245-250, Vol 3, No.2, July – December, 2009.

[20]. Subrahmanya Kumar. C.S.V & Viswanadh G.K (2008) Artificial Neural Network Approach for Reservoir Stage Prediction, International Journal of Applied Mathematical Analysis and Applications, pp 13- 19, Vol 3, No.1, Jan - June 2008.

[21]. Werbos,P. (1974). "Beyond Regression: New Tools for Prediction and Analysis in the behavioral Sciences." Ph.D dissertation, Harvard University, Cambridge.

Assessment and Evaluation of Groundwater Quality due to Landfill Leachate Using Fuzzy Logic

[1]C.S.V. Subrahmanya Kumar [2]G.K.Viswanadh [3]S.Ramesh Kumar [4]P.Jyothi Sree

[1]*Professor, Department of Civil Engineering, MVSR Engineering College, Nadergul, Hyderabad, Telangana*

[2] *Professor , Department of Civil Engineering & OSD to VC, JNTU College of Engineering, Kukatpally, Hyderabad*

[3]*Associate Professor, Department of Civil Engineering, MVSR Engineering College, Nadergul, Hyderabad* [4]*Graduate student, ACE Engineering College, Ghateskar, Hyderabad*

[1] csvs.kumar1@gmail.com

[2]gorti_gkv@yahoo.co.in

[3]rksonikar@gmail.com

***Abstract*— Groundwater is considered as an important water source due to its relatively low susceptibility to pollution. Determination of groundwater quality has become a serious problem in recent years due to indiscriminate disposal of waste water from various sources and municipal solid waste disposal. One of the major problems associated with dumping of municipal solid waste landfill is the release of leachate and its impact on groundwater.**

In the present study an attempt is made to measure the impact of municipal solid waste landfill on groundwater quality around Nagole, a solid waste dumping site in Hyderabad, Telangana State, India.

Groundwater samples were collected from wells, 2km radius around the solid waste dumping site and physico-chemical parameters of water samples were analysed. The various parameters analyzed are Chlorides, Calcium, Magnesium, Potassium, Sodium, p^H, Nitrate, Total Hardness, Alkalinity, Total dissolved solids, Dissolved Oxygen and BOD.

The Groundwater quality index was determined in the study area using Fuzzy logic to assess the overall quality of groundwater. The study revealed that the groundwater contained pollutants at a level beyond the permissible limit set by Bureau of Indian standards

***Keywords*—Groundwater quality, water quality parameters, leachate, fuzzy logic, fuzzy value**

I. Introduction

Groundwater quality determination assumes significance in the field of water quality management because of its inconsistent variation with groundwater table, geological and soil conditions and contamination through percolation etc. Periodic estimation of groundwater quality is highly necessary in order to ascertain the quality of water to use for human consumption. The pollution parameters monitored for the assessment of the quality of any system gives an idea of pollution status with respect to those particular parameters. The representation of all water quality parameters in a single form is called quality index that facilitates to get composite inference of all the quality parameters on that system and also helps to compare overall quality of water with a unit value.

Solid wastes are being produced since the beginning of civilization. With the advent of industrialization and urbanization, the problems of waste disposal increased. High population density, intensive land use for residential, commercial and industrial activities led to adverse impact on the environment. The problem of waste generation and management is fast becoming a global problem. According to a recent United Nations report, by 2025, it is estimated that there will be a five-fold increase in global waste generation. On the basis of available data, it is estimated that the nine major metropolitan cities in India are presently producing 34,000 tons of solid waste per day. As per recent estimates, Hyderabad and Secunderabad generate about 3,400 tonnes per day.

II. Area of Study

Hyderabad, the capital city of Telangana, is one of the most populated city in India. Municipal solid waste generated in the city is around 3000 metric tonnes per day. The solid waste generated from twin cities, Hyderabad and Secunderabad is partly disposed at Nagole landfill site. The landfill site lies in latitude N17°22'23.4" and longitude E78°33'33.5". Type of climate in Hyderabad is semi-arid. Hydro-geological features of the area: pink and granite of Archaeans age, intruded at places by dolerite dykes, pegmatite and quartz veins.

In the present study, an attempt is made to study Ground Water Quality around municipal landfill site at Nagole. Groundwater samples are collected and various chemical parameters such as Calcium, Magnesium, Potassium, Sodium, p^H, Nitrate, Total Hardness, Alkalinity, Total dissolved solids, Chlorides, Dissolved Oxygen, BOD were analyzed and later used to identify the degree of pollution using Fuzzy logic.

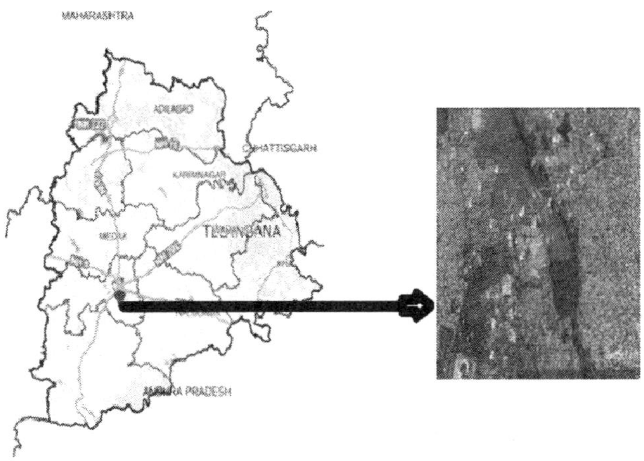

Fig 1 Location of water samples collected from the bore wells

III. Evaluation Methodology

1. The wells near the dumping site in a distance of 2 km radius were identified.
2. Ground water samples were collected from 20 wells.
3. The water samples were analyzed for the parameters, Calcium, Magnesium, Potassium, Sodium, p^H, Nitrate, Total Hardness, Alkalinity, Total dissolved solids, Chlorides, Dissolved Oxygen and BOD.
4. Membership functions were developed for all the water quality parameters considering the permissible and excessive limits of drinking water as shown in Fig. 2 to Fig.13.
5. For the known values of chemical parameters, the fuzzy values are read from the membership functions.
6. Net fuzzy value is determined using equation (1).
7. Groundwater quality was determined using the net fuzzy values and water quality rating.

IV. Fuzzy Logic

Fuzzy logic approach is a mathematical method used to characterize and propagate uncertainty and inaccuracy in data and functional relationships. The idea of Fuzzy Logic was first proposed by Dr. Lotfi A. Zadeh [5] of the University of California in his paper [1965]. The capability of Fuzzy logic to express gradual transitions from membership to non-membership has broad utility. It provides us not only with a more meaningful and powerful representation of vague concept expressed in natural language. The main concept of Fuzzy theory is that the membership function for a variable represents numerically the degree to which an element belongs to a set.

Since the transition from member to non-member appears gradual rather than abrupt, the Fuzzy set introduces vagueness by eliminating sharp boundary dividing members of the class from non-members. Notable contributions are Akinbile C.O. and Yusoff, M.S. [1], Amadi, A. N., et al., [2], Bhide A.D. & Muley V.U. [3], Ashwani, K.T. and Abhay, K.S [4] and so on.

To study ground water pollution, membership functions were developed for all the chemical parameters. From the known values of chemical parameters, fuzzy value was determined from membership function. Lastly Net Fuzzy value was computed using equation (1)..

V. Membership Functions

Fig 2: Membership function of alkalinity

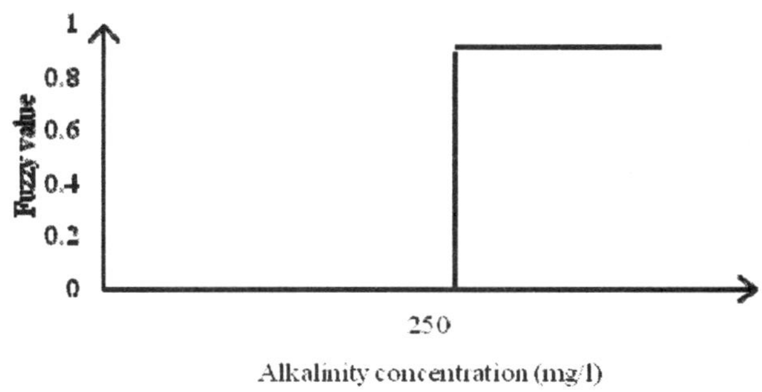

Fig, 3 Membership function for Chloride

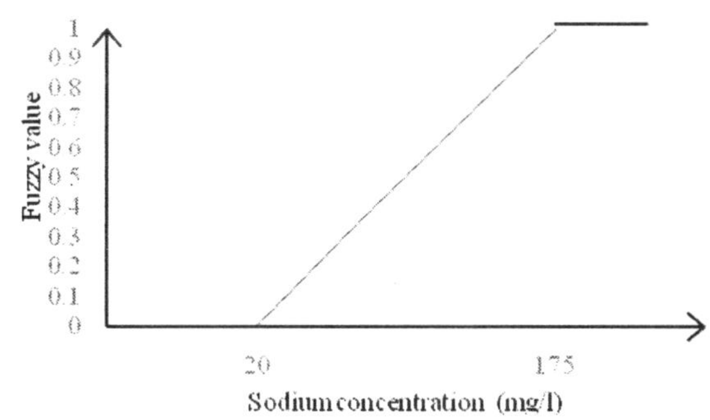

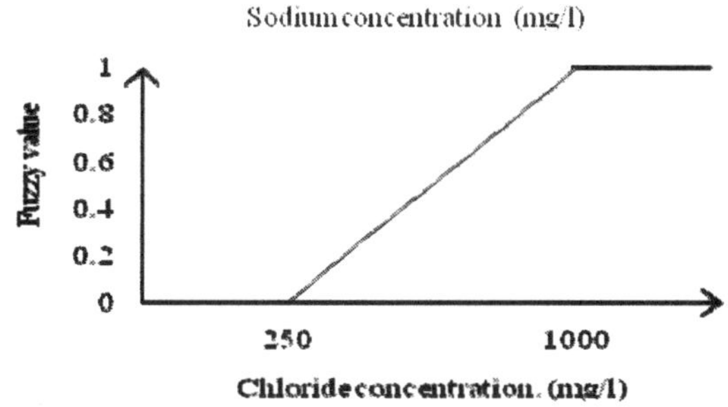

Fig.4 Membership function for Calcium

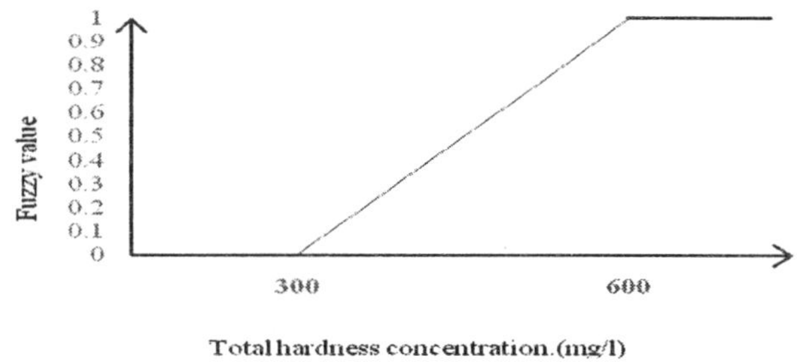

Fig. 5 Membership function for Total Hardness

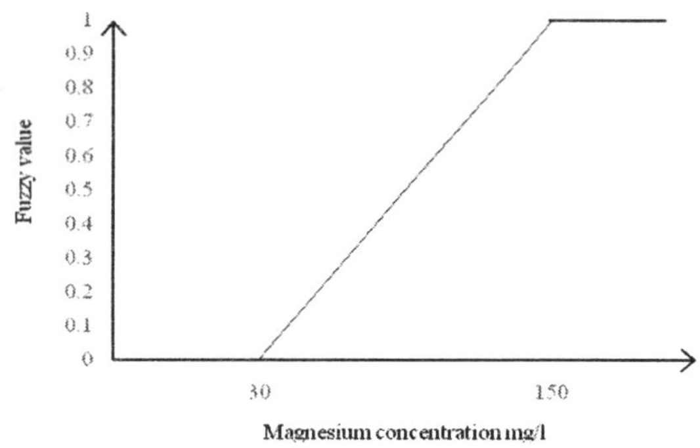

Fig.6 Membership function for Magnesium

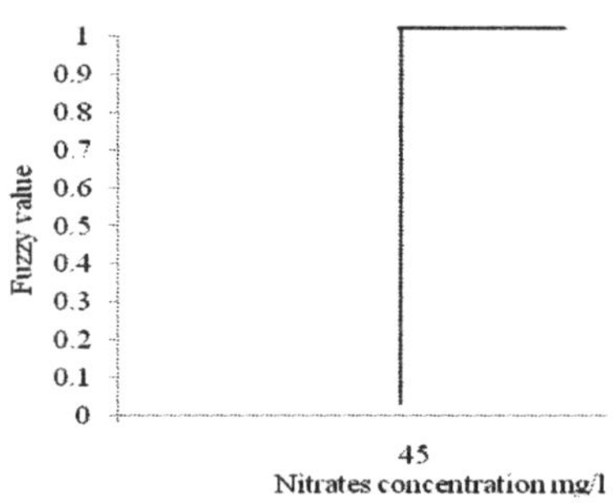

Fig.7 Membership function for Nitrates

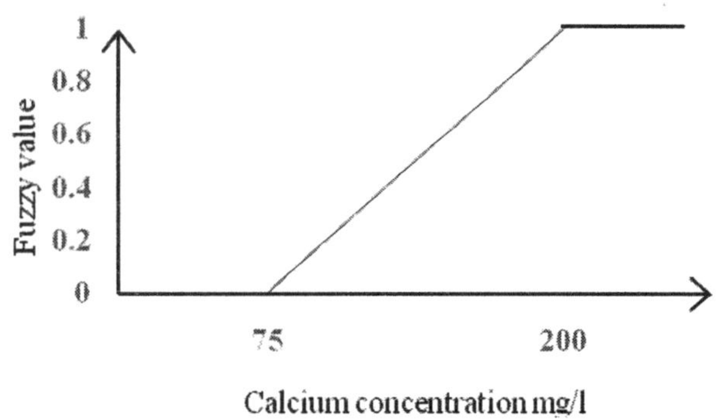

Fig. 8 Membership function for sodium

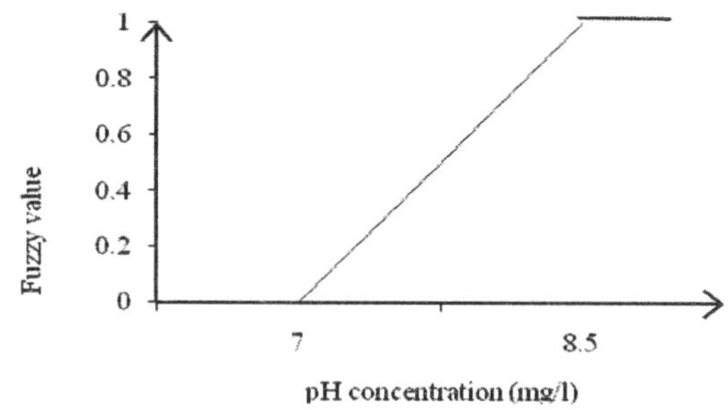

Fig.9 Membership function for p^H

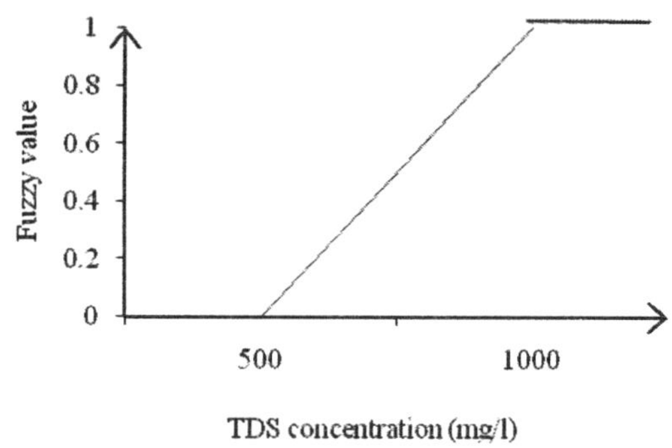

Fig. 10 Membership function for TDS

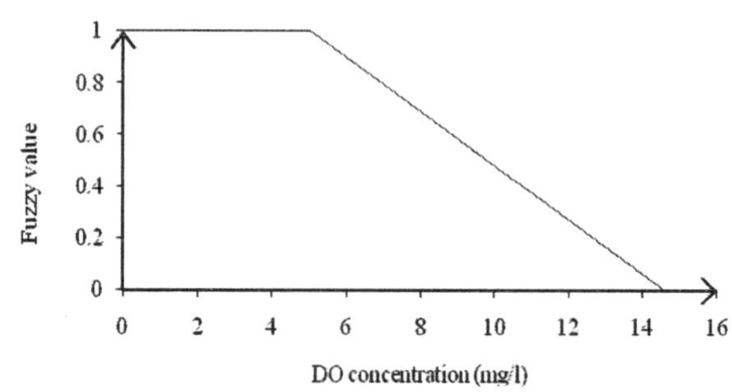

Fig. 11 Membership function for DO

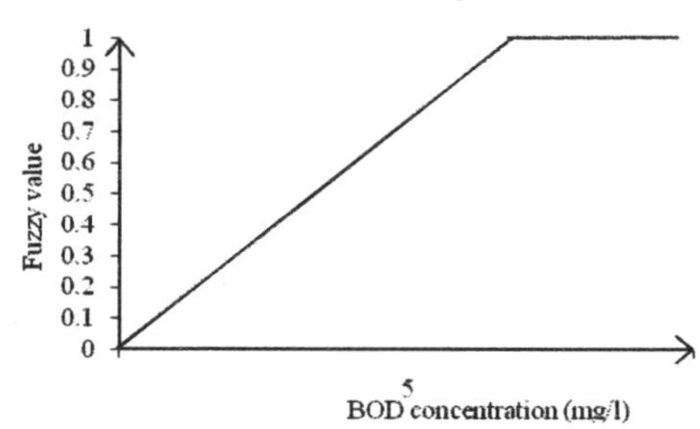

Fig.12 Membership function for BOD

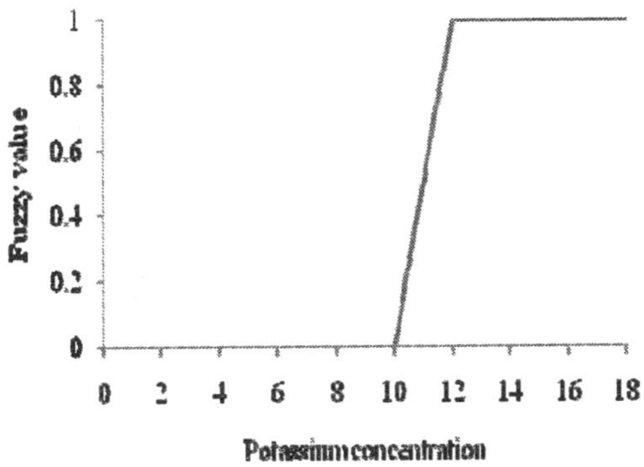

Fig.13 Membership function for Potassium

To find out the net fuzzy value, it is necessary to combine all the fuzzy values for various chemical parameters. The major advantage with the Fuzzy Logic approach is that the final result of this method gives a single unique value for each site that can precisely confirm the extent of ground water pollution. This unique distinct value is called as the net fuzzy value.

The net fuzzy value for any site can be calculated using the weightage and the fuzzy values for each chemical parameter. This calculation is done by using the formula.

Net fuzzy value, $F_i = \sum_{i=1}^{n} W_i C_i / \sum_{i=1}^{n} W_i$ (1)

where W_i = Weightage factor and C_i = Fuzzy Value

$W_i = K / s_i$, where $K = \dfrac{1}{(1/s_1)+(1/s_2)+(1/s_3)+\cdots+(1/s_i)}$

s_1, s_2, s_3-----------s_i are standard values of various parameters from 1,2,3,------i.

Chemical Analysis of water gives a concept about its physical and chemical composition by some numerical values but for estimating exact quality of water, it is better to depend on rating the water quality which gives the idea of quality of drinking water. Similar to groundwater quality index rating, the water quality rating is given in Table.1. The net fuzzy values are presented in Table.2 and the variation of water quality is shown in Fig.14.

Table 1 Water Quality rating based on Fuzzy value

Net Fuzzy Value Range	Water Quality Rating
0 – 0.25	Excellent
0.26 –0.50	Good
0.51 – 0.75	Poor
0.75 – 1.0	Unfit

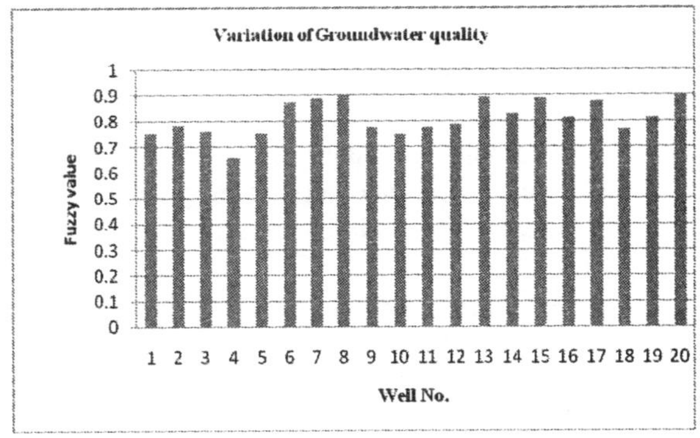

Fig. 14 Variation of groundwater quality

Table. 2 Estimation of Net fuzzy values

Bore Well No.	Net Fuzzy Value	Water Quality Rating
1	0.753	Unfit
2	0.783	Unfit
3	0.762	Unfit
4	0.659	Very Poor
5	0.753	Unfit
6	0.875	Unfit
7	0.891	Unfit
8	0.899	Unfit
9	0.774	Unfit
10	0.750	Unfit
11	0.774	Unfit
12	0.788	Unfit
13	0.894	Unfit
14	0.831	Unfit
15	0.888	Unfit
16	0.811	Unfit
17	0.878	Unfit
18	0.767	Unfit
19	0.812	Unfit
20	0.900	Unfit

VI. Results & Discussions

1. The values of almost all the parameters are above the permissible limits. The wide variation is due to dissolved materials from leachate.
2. p^H values are found to vary from 7.45 – 9.42. Though p^H has no direct effect on human health, all bio-chemical reactions are sensitive to the variation of p^H. The limit of p^H value for drinking water is specified as 6.5 – 8.5.
3. Conductivity is very important parameter for determining the water quality for drinking and

agriculture purpose. The values in the study area are from 0.53 – 4.95 millisimons/cm.

4. Total alkalinity of water is mainly due to presence of bicarbonate contents in water. This is also associated with calcium and magnesium contents in water. The alkalinity of samples is very high and varies between 240 to 500 ppm. The maximum permissible limit is 250 ppm.
5. Total hardness of water is characterized by contents of calcium or magnesium salts or both. The concentration of calcium and magnesium in potable water ranges from 75 - 200 ppm and 30 - 100 ppm respectively. The calcium and magnesium sulphates exert a cathartic action on human beings. It is also associated with respiratory diseases. In the study area calcium and magnesium contents of water vary from 50 to 220 ppm and 255 to 875 ppm respectively. The magnesium content being higher than calcium in the samples indicate the occurrence of magnesium salts in this study area.
6. DO and BOD is very important pollution parameters. The values of DO and BOD indicate degree of contamination. Generally low DO values indicate high pollution nature and high BOD values indicates presence of organic materials in water sources. The observed values of DO and BOD varies from 6.4 to 7.6, 3 to 19 ppm respectively. Water samples with DO values less than 5 ppm and BOD value greater than 5 ppm respectively are polluted.
7. Chlorides are considered to be pollution indicating parameters. They impart salty taste to water. The limiting value for chlorides is 250 ppm at which the water will not taste salty. The range of chlorides in the study area 105 to 779 ppm.
8. Net Fuzzy values were found to be above 0.5, thus indicating degree of pollution is above 50% in the entire area.
9. Thus, the results indicate that ground water is polluted near the landfill site and is unfit for drinking.
10. High values of sulphates and TDS in drinking water are generally not harmful to human beings, but high concentration of these may affect persons suffering from kidney and heart problems.
11. The sanitary landfill site is to be used to dispose the municipal solid waste.

VII. Conclusions

1. The ground water quality near the Municipal solid waste dumping site is of poor quality.
1. The water quality using Fuzzy Logic also revealed that the water is unfit for drinking as the net fuzzy value was above 0.5.
2. The sanitary landfills are to be built with liners to prevent leachate from seeping through soil into aquifers. Leachate collection systems store the liquid away from the water table. Clay caps prevent rainwater runoff from carrying pollutants from the landfill into the groundwater.
3. The municipal solid waste must be managed by adopting composting, incineration and power generation techniques.

References

[1] Akinbile C.O. and Yusoff, M.S., 2011. Environmental Impact of Leachate Pollution on Groundwater Supplies in Akure, Nigeria, International Journal of Environmental Science and Development, 2(1):81-86.

[2] Amadi, A. N., P.I Olasehinde, Okosun, E.A and Yisa, J., 2010. Assessment of the Water Quality Index of Otamiri and Oramiriukwa Rivers. Physics International. 1 (2): 116-123.

[3] Ashwani, K.T. and Abhay, K.S., 2014. Hydro geochemical investigation and Groundwater Quality assessment of Pratapgarh District, Uttar Pradesh. Journal Geological Society of India, 83:329-343.

[4] Bhide A.D.& Muley V.U. 'Studies on Pollution of Ground Water by Solid Wastes'. Proc.Symp. on 'Environmental Pollution', CPHERI, Nagpur, Jan.1973, p.236-243.

[5] Lotfi A. Zadeh (1965) Fuzzy Sets, Information and Control.

Indian Summer Monsoon Rainfall Extremes Projections using Block Maxima Approach under Climate Change

K Shashikanth[1*],M Prashanthi[2]

[1]*Associate Professor, Department of Civil Engineering, University College of Engineering, Osmania University, Hyderabad-7*

[2]*PG Scholar, WRE Division, UCE, OU, Hyderabad*

**Corresponding Author mail:*[1]*kulkarni.shashikanth@gmail.com*
[2]*mandala.prashanthi92@gmail.com*

***Abstract*—the extreme rainfall projections under future climate are assessed by General Circulation Models (GCM) and these GCMs represent poorly at regional scale. The modified Statistical methodology (MSD) has been used to project extremes for the Indian summer monsoon rainfall at 0.25 degree spatial resolution. The extremes are assessed by two conventional extreme value theory approaches such as Block Maxima (BM) and Peak over Threshold (PoT). However, in the present study Block or Annual Maxima approach is used to assess 30 year return period. The extremes projections have been significantly improved with implementation of Kernel Regression. The rainfall projections are carried out three different time windows 2020, 2050 and 2080 using IPSL GCM from CMIP5 suite. Here we find spatial non uniform increase in rainfall for future time slices and results are in line with mean rainfall Indian summer monsoon Rainfall (ISMR) projections as observed from previous studies.**

***Keywords*—Modified Statistical Downscaling, GCMs, Extreme Value Theory (EVT)**

I. INTRODUCTION

Modeling of extremes is a major research challengefacing the hydrologicalcommunity considering the complexities involved into it. As the factors affecting the extreme excesses are not clearly understood and methods for evaluation are still under developmental phase. Therefore, proper scientific study of extremes is necessary for proper planning and management of extremes events. Recent studies indicates occurrence of extremes have increased due to global warming/ anthropogenic activities [IPCC, (1)]. Although much progress in understanding the science of extremes modeling has been witnessed since the last two to three decades but still extremes are causing havoc to human life, infrastructure, industry, agriculture, ecosystem etc. at an unprecedented scales e.g. Mumbai floods in India 2005, Kedarnath (Uttarakhnad) floods in India 2013, Chennai floods (2015).

General Circulation Models (GCMs) have emerged credible models for understanding the variability and projections of rainfall under climate change scenario. [1, 2]. However, GCMs poor skills to model extremes pose serious challenge [3], asGCMs operate at coarse resolution.Many researchers have established that observations and climate models also reveal increases for extremes under warming climate. Therefore, accurate projections/predictions of future changes of extremes at local/regional scales are critical for policy formulations and policy decisions [3]. At present two downscaling approaches are popular for regional studies. Viz. Dynamic downscaling and statistical downscaling, however, they possess low skill for extremes projections. Here, we use statistical downscaling methodology proposed by Shashikanth et al [3] for the current study.

II. DATA AND METHODOLOGY

In the current study, the data required for statistical downscaling (SD) are obtained from IPSL GCM from CMIP5 suite from PCMDI. In SD model, predictors play a very crucial role [4]. Here, we use NCEP/NCAR reanalysis data [5] as predictors and gridded rainfall provided by APHRODITE as predictand for establishing the relationship between predictors and predictand. The predictors are air temperature, wind velocities (U and V) at surface and 500 hpa pressure level and specific humidity 500hpa at pressure field and Mean sea level Pressure (MSLP).

GCM used for current work is IPSL_CM5A_LR Institut Pierre Simon Laplaceand observed rainfall data is provided by APHRODITE [6]

III. Methodology

The projections of extremes in the present study are carried out by two steps. In the step one, we apply Kernel Regression based SD model for the simulation of rainfall projections [7, 8]. In the second step, 95 percentile values of rainfall series are segregated from the downscaled projections and on these; again Kernel Regression (KR) employed to model extremes. Later, on modeled rainfall extremes, the return periods are assessed by Block Maxima or Annual Maxima (BM/AM) [9, 10]

Statistical Downscaling

The philosophy of Statistical Downscaling is to obtain local to regional (10 to 50 km) projections from the large scale climate predictors. In this method, the statistical relationship is established between large scale climate predictors from reanalysis data (NCEP/NCAR) (Predictors) to regional-scale predictand variable (Predictands in this case rainfall). Later, the same relation is applied on GCM outputs to obtain predictands under the impacts of climate change for future. The present method utilizes the following methods to obtain the projections viz. Bias correction, K- mean clustering, classification and Regression trees [CART] and Kernel Regression [7, 8]. K-means clustering algorithm coupled with CART, is employed to for the generation of rainfall states using large scale synoptic scale circulation patterns. Conditional on the derived rainfall state, the kernel regression is employed for modeling the multisite rainfall [7, 8].

Extreme Value Theory

The Extreme Value theory (EVT) is a statistical tool used for assessing the hydrologic extremes [10]. The return periods are evaluated using Block Maxima (Annual Maxima) approach by applying the Generalized Extreme Value (GEV) distribution. The block maxima approach of EVT theory mainly consists of isolatingthe data into non-overlapping periods of equal size (monsoon days from June-September) andselecting the maximum data in each period. The new data series thus constitute extreme values. Parametric statistical GEV method is employed for the evaluation of return period. The Kolomogorov - Smirnov (K-S) [5%level significance] is used to obtain the goodness of fit on those fitted parameters and if the test fails an empirical distribution is fit in place of GEV.Further information can be obtained from the research papers of Ghosh et al 2011 [9] and Coles, 2001 [10]. The major disadvantage of the Block or Annual Maxima is that it does not consider the multiple occurrences of impactful extremes events [11].

The probability density function of GEV mentioned below:

Suppose 'x' represents the annual/block maxima of daily precipitation in a given series, then the GEV distribution is defined by [10]

$$F(x;\mu,\alpha,\xi) = \begin{cases} \exp\left\{-\left[1-\frac{\xi(x-\mu)}{\alpha}\right]^{-\frac{1}{\xi}}\right\} \\ 1+\xi(x-\mu)/\alpha > 0 \quad \xi \neq 0 \\ \exp\left\{-\exp\left[-\frac{(x-\mu)}{\sigma}\right]\right\} \quad \xi = 0 \end{cases} \quad (1)$$

GEV distribution has three parameters namely location (μ), scale parameter (α) and shape parameter (ξ). In the present work the maximum likelihood estimation (MLE) technique is used to estimate the parameters.

The return period or intensity is defined as a particular value exceedingonce in every N year (here, 30 year) with probability of 1/N in any given year

$$F^{-1}(1-p;\mu,\alpha,\xi) = \begin{cases} \mu-(\alpha/\xi)\{1-[-\ln(1-p)]^{-\xi}\} \quad \xi \neq 0 \\ \mu-\alpha\ln[-\ln(1-p)] \quad \xi = 0 \end{cases} \quad (2)$$

A nonparametric Gaussian kernel distribution was fitted to those grids where KS test was failed for GEV.

IV. Results and Discussions

The statistical downscaling model developed by Kannan and Ghosh [7] and Salvi et al [8] is used for the multisite rainfall projections on daily scale. The mean rainfall projections are very well modeled by the present method. Since all statistical downscaling models fail to model day to day variability that well and hence extremes are not well simulated by them. Therefore slight modifications are suggested for modeling of extremes (Fig 1)

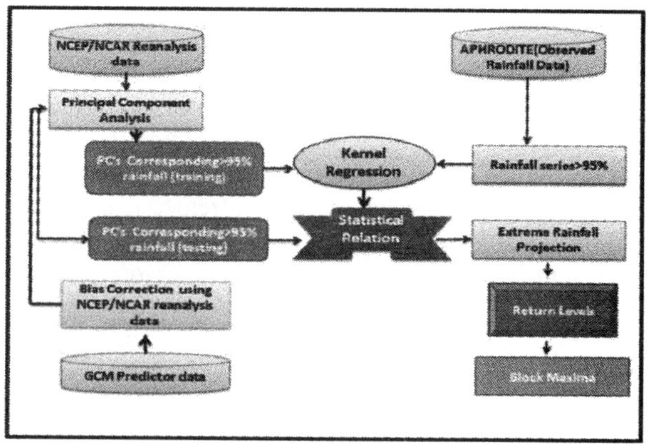

Fig 1: The Flowchart for Statistical Downscaling for extremes using Block Maxima approach.

The spatial distribution of observed mean rainfall, NCEP/NCAR simulated mean rainfall and IPSL simulated average rainfall (Figure 2) and standard deviation is very well modeled by the Kannan and Ghosh [7] method.

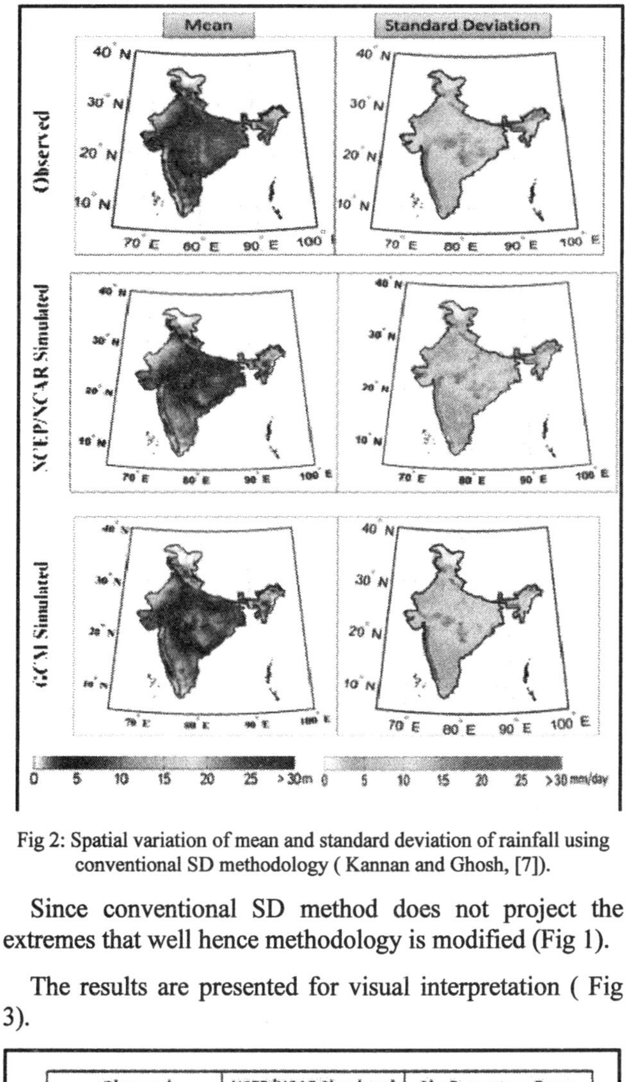

Fig 2: Spatial variation of mean and standard deviation of rainfall using conventional SD methodology (Kannan and Ghosh, [7]).

Since conventional SD method does not project the extremes that well hence methodology is modified (Fig 1).

The results are presented for visual interpretation (Fig 3).

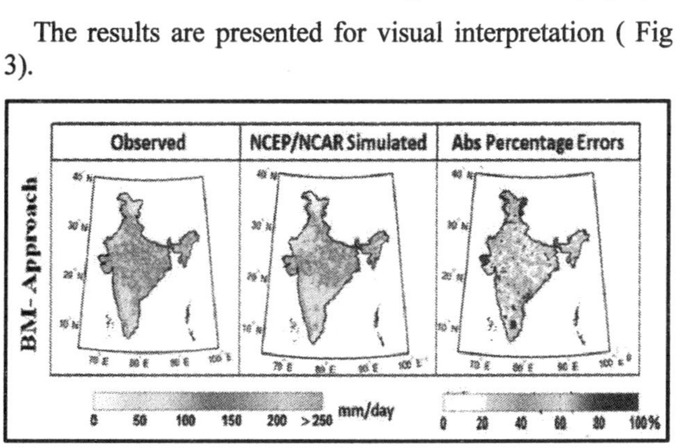

Fig. 3: Extreme rainfall projections of ISMR with 30 year return period.

The rainfall intensity using Block maxima approach is assessed and for future RCP 8.5 scenario is used to know the impacts of climate change on extremes for ISMR. Based on the same approach the future extremes for ISMR is evaluated for different time windows viz. 2010-2040 (2020s), 2041-2070 (2050s) and 2071-2100 (2080s). The results are presented in Fig 4.

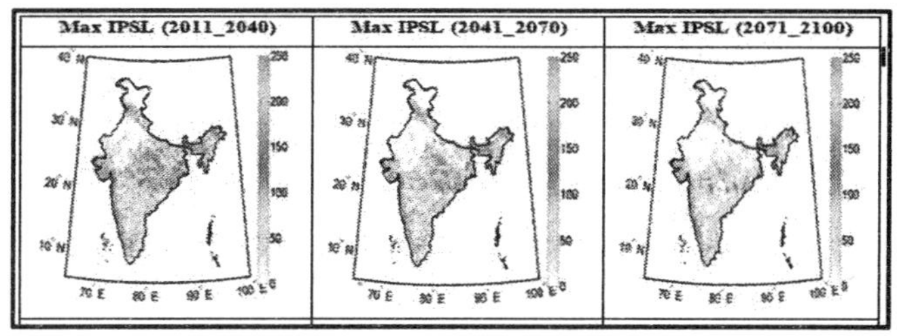

Fig 4: variation of extremes of IPSL for the three future windows 2020s,2050s, 2080s.

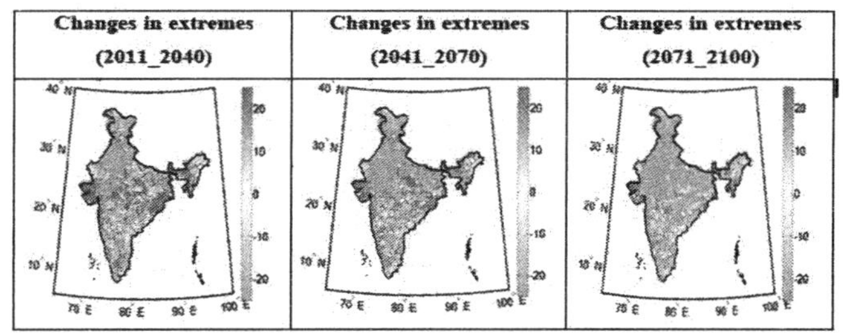

Fig 5: The changes in extremes at 30 year return period with respect to base line period (1981-2000).

The projected changes in return levels as obtained with block maxima exhibit spatially non uniform changes .The extreme projections for different time windows 2020s (2010-2040),2050s (2041-2070), 2080s (2071-2100) ,as they show decrease of changes in extremes .Although with increase in global warming, no doubt extremes are increase but are limited to few regions in India, but non uniform changes increases are found in the current study.

V. Conclusions

Projections of rainfall extremes are a major research challenge in climate science considering the challenges it poses and still it is even more complex for ISMR. The results from the present work can provide some basic strategies in countering the menace of extremes. In the downscaling of the extremes, the local factors such as urbanization and deforestation which play significant role have not been considered and would form the future scope of study from the present work.

The results show that in the future the extremes are heterogeneously poised across Indian region and this will form a valuable input to study the impact of climate change on local hydrology for the management of extremes.

VI. Limitations of Present Study

Since the usage of single GCM in climate trajectory projections may sometimes produce misleading information [12]. Therefore for more reliability and acceptance more number GCMs should be used for better representation of ISMR extremes.

The main weakness of block maxima method is that it does not consider multiple occurrences of an extreme event over a particular threshold. Therefore Peak over Threshold (PoT) method should be applied for better improvements in the projections.

VII. Acknowledgement

We acknowledge the World Climate Research Programme's Working Group on Coupled Modelling, which is responsible for CMIP, and we thank the climate-modelling groups for producing and making available their model output. For CMIP, the U.S. Department of Energy's Program for Climate Model Diagnosis and Intercomparison provides coordinating support and leads the development of software infrastructure in partnership with the Global Organization for Earth System Science Portals. We would like to thank APHRODITE, Japan for making available observed 0.25 degree resolution data. I profusely thank TEQIP Phase –II for sponsoring the project. I extend my sincere thanks to Prof. Subimal Ghosh of IITB for his help and support.

References

[1] IPCC, 2013: Summary for Policymakers. In: Climate change 2013: The Physical Science Basis. Contribution of Working Group I to the Fifth Assessment Report of the Intergovernmental Panel on Climate Change [Stocker, T.F., D. Qin, G.-K. Plattner, M. Tignor, S. K. Allen, J. Boschung, A. Nauels, Y. Xia, V. Bex and P.M. Midgley (eds.)]. Cambridge University Press, Cambridge, United Kingdom and New York, NY, US

[2] Kharin VV and Zwiers FW (2005), Estimating extremes in transient climate change simulations, J. Clim., 18, 1156–1173.

[3] Shashikanth, K., Ghosh, S., Vittal H, S Karmakar (2017) Future projections of Indian summer monsoon rainfall extremes over India with statistical downscaling and its consistency with observed characteristics , Climate Dynamics, DOI 10.1007/s00382-017-3604-2.

[4] Wilby et al. (2004) Guidelines for use of climate scenarios developed from statistical downscaling methods. http://www.narccap.ucar.edu/doc/tgica-guidance-2004.pdf accessed on 719 10/08/2013.

[5] Kalnay et al. (1996), The NCEP/NCAR 40-years reanalysis project, Bull. Amer. Meteor. Soc, 77(3), 437471

[6] Yatagai et al. (2012) APHRODITE: constructing a long-term daily gridded precipitation dataset for Asia based on a dense network of rain gauges. Bull. Am. Meteor. Soc. 939 (1401–1415), 727. http://dx.doi.org/10.1175/BAMS-D-11-00122.1.

[7] Kannan S, and Ghosh S (2013) A nonparametric kernel regression model for downscaling multisite daily precipitation in the Mahanadi basin, Water Resour. Res., 49, doi:10.1002/wrcr.20118.

[8] Salvi K, Kannan S, Ghosh S (2013) High-resolution multisite daily rainfall projections in India with statistical downscaling for climate change impacts assessment. J. Geophys. Res. Atmos 118, DOI: 10.1002/jgrd.50280

[9] Ghosh S, Das D, Kao SC., and Ganguly AR (2011), Lack of uniform trends but increasing spatial variability in observed Indian rainfall extremes, Nat. Clim. Change,2(2), 86–91, doi:10.1038/nclimate1327

[10] Coles S (2001) An Introduction to Statistical Modeling of Extreme Values Springer Series in Statistics.

[11] Vittal H, Karmakar S, and Ghosh S (2013) Diametric changes in trends and patterns of extreme rainfall over India from pre-1950 to post-1950, Geophys. Res. Lett., 40, 3253–3258, doi: 10.1002/grl.50631

[12] Ghosh S and Mujumdar PP (2006) Future Rainfall Scenario over Orissa with GCM Projections by Statistical Downscaling Current Science, 90(3), Feb 10, 2006, pp. 396-404.

ANFIS Model for Reservoir Operation

A. Saraswati Hiranmayi[1] and M. Anjaneya Prasad[2]

[1]*Research Scholar, Department of Civil Engineering, College of Engineering, O.U*
[2]*.Professor,Department of Civil Engineering, College of Engineering, O.U*

[1]smarad2002@gmail.com
[2]mprasad2016@gmail.com

***Abstract*—The operation of a reservoir can be divided into three categories viz., Analogous model, Experimental Model and Mathematical model. In the Analogous or Analogical model, the method uses the properties of the reservoir similar to target reservoirs to predict the reservoir performance. In Experimental model, the various physical properties of the reservoirs are measured in the laboratories. The reservoir operation has been modeled in several ways by the researchers to understand to improve the reservoir operation. Several models have been developed and are being developed using various models viz. stochastic modeling, Artificial Neural Networks, Fuzzy based expert modeling, Modeling based on Genetic Algorithms and Real time modeling with forecasting.In this paper soft computing model using Adoptive Neuro Fuzzy Information System (ANFIS) is used to effectively model and predict the reservoir operation. The model developed successfully mimicked the reservoir operation based on historical operation.**

***Keywords*— Reservoir, Optimization, Neural Network, ANFIS, Storage of Water and Releases.**

I. INTRODUCTION

A reservoir (etymology from French *réservoir* a "storehouse") is an artificial lake used to store water. The demand for water has increased due to higher standards of living, depletion of water resources of acceptable quality and excessive water pollution due to agricultural and industrial expansions [1].Although progress has improved the quality of life, it has caused significant environmental destruction in such a magnitude that could not be predicted [2]. As one of the three vital elements of air, soil, and water, the role of water in the conservation of the environment is receiving increased global attention [3].Determination of efficient operating policy of the existing multi reservoir system is extremely important to meet the pressing needs of the developing countries such as food and energy [4,5]. Reservoirs may be created in river valleys by the construction of a dam or may be built by excavation in the ground or by conventional construction techniques such a brickwork or cast concrete [6]. There are several research operation models adopted by researchers to understand and improve the reservoir operation system.Since the beginning of the 19th century, the population of the world has tripled, nonrenewable energy consumption has increased by a factor of 30 and the industrial production has multiplied by 50 times. Water is a precise resource, and the need for sustainable and integrated management is on the agenda of every state.

II. NEED FOR RESERVOIR OPTIMIZATION

In large scale water storage projects, attention is focused on improving the operational effectiveness efficiency. Reservoirs serve many needs including water supply for domestic and industrial needs, flood controls etc. The reservoir system deals with the severe restrictions from water tribunals, interstate contracts and handling other such complex legal agreements [7]. Optimization methods attempt to prevail over the high dimensional, dynamic and non-linear characteristics of the reservoir systems Heuristic programming methods using Genetic algorithms, neural networks and Fuzzy logic are being adopted for effective operation of reservoirs system's in the development of countries [8].

In this paper, Nagarjuna Sagar reservoir has been selected as a case study for mimicking the reservoir operation based on historical data base. The Nagarjuna Sagar project was constructed during the period 1956-1967 on Krishna river This project has a catchment area of 215,185 Square Kilo Meters and has gross storage capacity of 11,553 mm^3.It has a total catchment at dam site as 215,285 Square Kilo Meters and the average rainfall is 889 mm.

III. ANN AND FUZZY LOGIC MODEL

An artificial neural network (ANN) is an information processing system that roughly replicates the behavior of the human brain by emulating the operations and connectivity of biological neurons. Research in this area started during 1950's but useful applications are reported from 1980's. Mathematically ANN is a complex non-linear function with many parameters that are adjusted or trained in such a way that the ANN output becomes similar to the measured output on a known data set. Many models were used in the field, each defined at a different level of abstraction and trying to model different aspects of neural systems. They range from models of the short-term behavior of individual neurons, through models of how the dynamics of neural circuitry arise from interactions between individual neurons, to models of how behavior can arise from abstract neural modules that represent complete subsystems. These include models of the long-term and short-term plasticity of neural systems and its relation to learning and memory, from the individual neuron to the system level. The origin of Fuzzy Logic approach dates back to 1965 since Lotfi Zadeh introduced *fuzzy-set theory* and applications. The Fuzzy logic begins with the concept of a fuzzy-set. The fuzzy-set is viewed as a generalization of classical sets. Classical sets and their operations are useful in expressing classical logic and they lead to Boolean logic. Fuzzy sets and fuzzy operations on the other hand are useful in expressing the ideas of fuzzy logic leading to applications such as fuzzy optimization.

IV. ANFIS MODEL

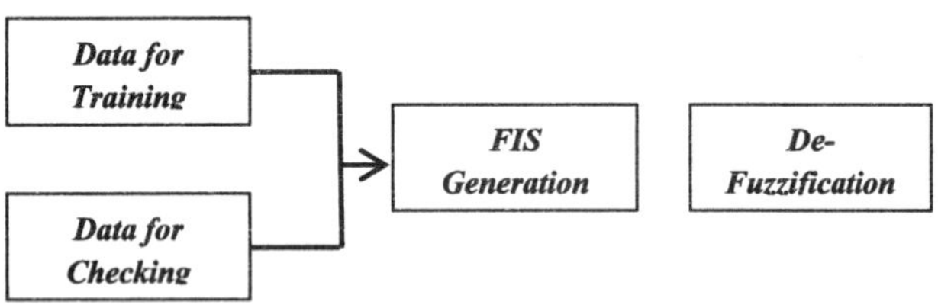

Figure 1: Steps involved in the proposed Modeling

The Neuro-adaptive learning method works similarly to that of neural networks. Neuro-adaptive learning techniques provide a method for the fuzzy modeling procedure to learn information about a data set. Fuzzy Logic Toolbox software computes the membership function parameters that best allow the associated fuzzy inference system to track the given input/output data. The Fuzzy Logic Toolbox function that accomplishes this membership function parameter adjustment is called ANFIS. The ANFIS function can be accessed either from the command line or through the ANFIS Editor GUI. Because the functionality of the command line function ANFIS and the ANFIS Editor GUI is similar, they are used somewhat interchangeably in this discussion, except when specifically describing the GUI. The Figure 1shows various steps involved in the proposed modeling.

The data used for this project has been taken from Nagarjuna Sagar project. The variables taken are initial storage, Inflows and Release of the project for thirty two years i.e. from 1967 to 2005. The model is fed with Storage and Inflows as inputs and the output taken is the releases from reservoir for training the model. The data selected for training is tested for different input membership functions like Triangular, Trapezoidal, GumBell and Gauss functions. The selected trial models were trained for a maximum 15000 epochs and the results were compared. The training is stopped when either the maximum number of epochs is reached or the maximum amount of time is exceeded. The equations used for the different membership functions are given in equations (1) to (4). The training error variations with number of epochs for different input membership functions considered in Figure 2.

$$f(x:a,b,c) = \max\left(\min\left(\frac{x-a}{b-c},\frac{c-x}{c-b}\right),0\right) \ldots..(1)$$

$$f(x:a,b,c,d) = \max\left(\min\left(\frac{x-a}{b-a},\frac{d-x}{d-c}\right),0\right) \ldots..(2)$$

$$f(x,\sigma,c) = e^{\frac{-(x-c)^2}{2\sigma^2}} \ldots\ldots\ldots..(3)$$

$$f(x,a,b,c) = \frac{1}{1+\left|\frac{x-c}{a}\right|^{2b}} \ldots\ldots\ldots.(4)$$

Equation (1) is a Triangular membership function, (2) a Trapezoidal membership function, (3) is a Gaussian Membership function and (4) is GBell Membership function. The equation (5) gives the calculation of error function.

$$ErrorFunction = \sum (HistoricalRelease - ReleaseModel)^2 \ldots..(5)$$

Figure 3 shows the editor menu screen shots adopted for the model of ANFIS editor screenshot. Figure 4 indicates the screenshot FIS editor of the model and Figure 5 shows membership from editor adopted in the present study for a typical month. The load data has two input parameters, reservoir storage and inflow to the reservoir. The output parameter is the release from the reservoir to the canals. The input membership function is selected as combination of ***trapezoidal*** membership on either side and ***triangular*** membership in the middle input membership functions. The Figure 5 shows the screen shot for this selection. The model starts by reading the data from file for testing. It checks for the year and month for which it has to validate, corresponding month model is selected for testing. The release for the given inputs storage and inflow for a particular month is calculated as per the trained FIS model. Storage for the next month is calculated using the mass balance equation shown in equation 6.

$$S_{t+1} = S_t + I_t - E_t - R_t - O_t \text{-------------} (6)$$

where
S_{t+1}=Storage of next month
S_t=Storage of the month

I_t=Inflow of the month

E_t=Evaporation loss of the month

R_t=Releases of the month including seepage losses

O_t=Spill of the month.

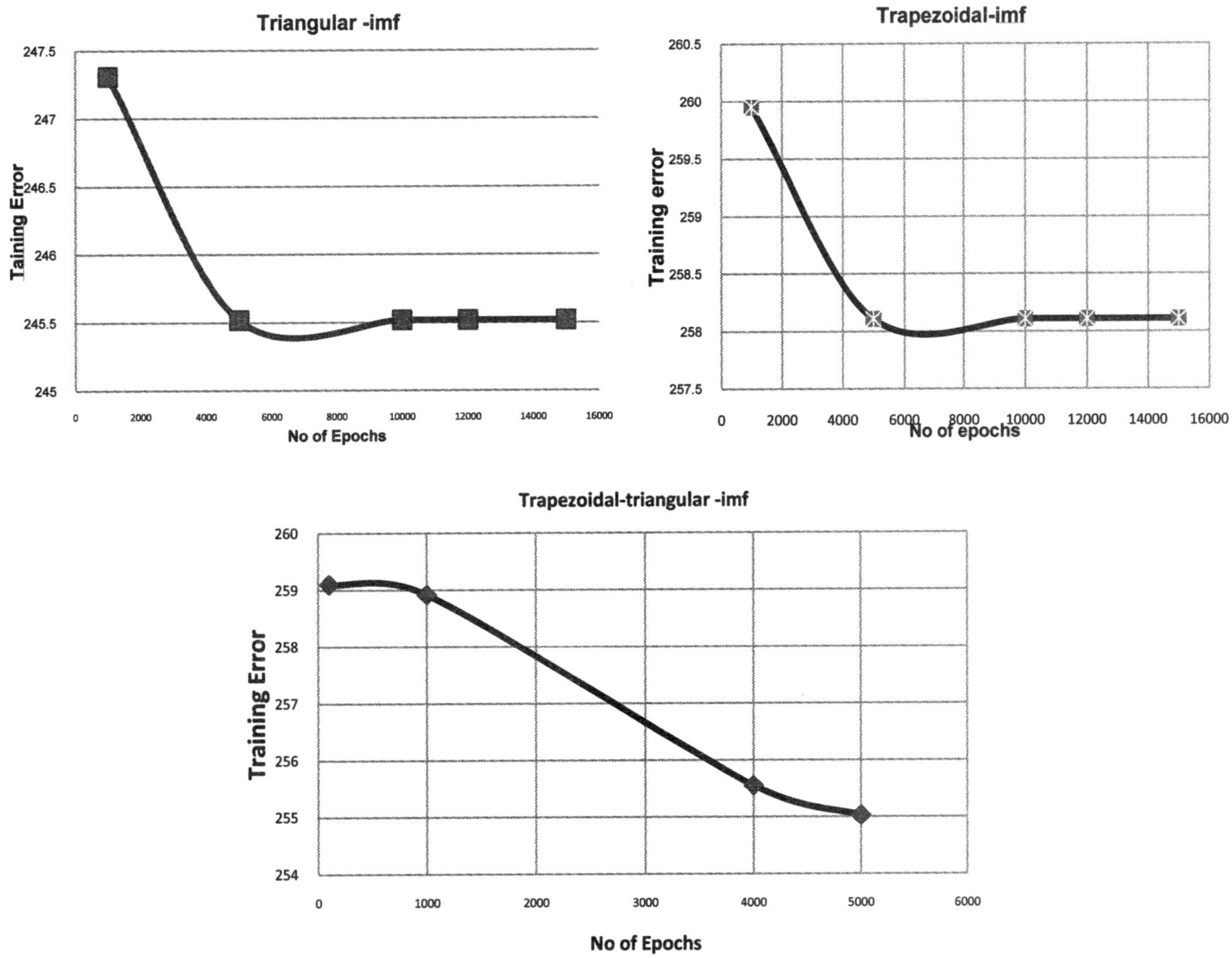

Figure 2: Training Error vs. Number of Epochs

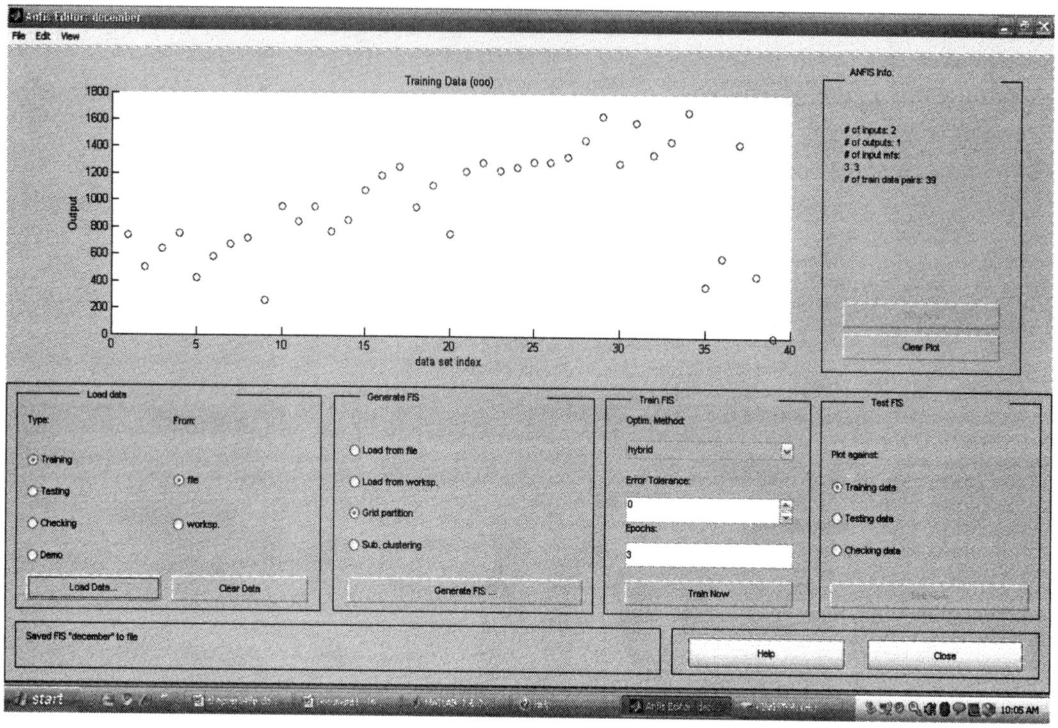

Figure 3: Screen Shot of ANFIS Editor for Selected Month

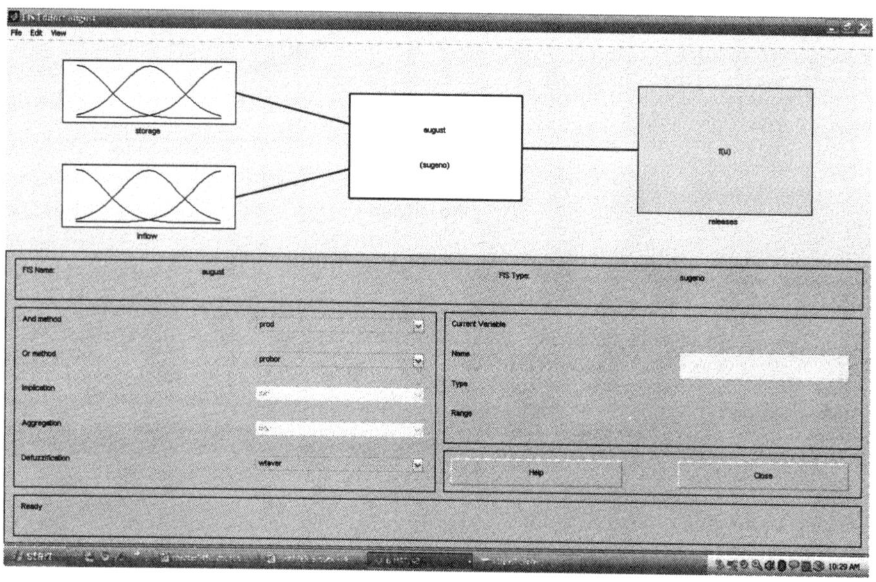

Figure 4: FIS editor for the ANFIS Model

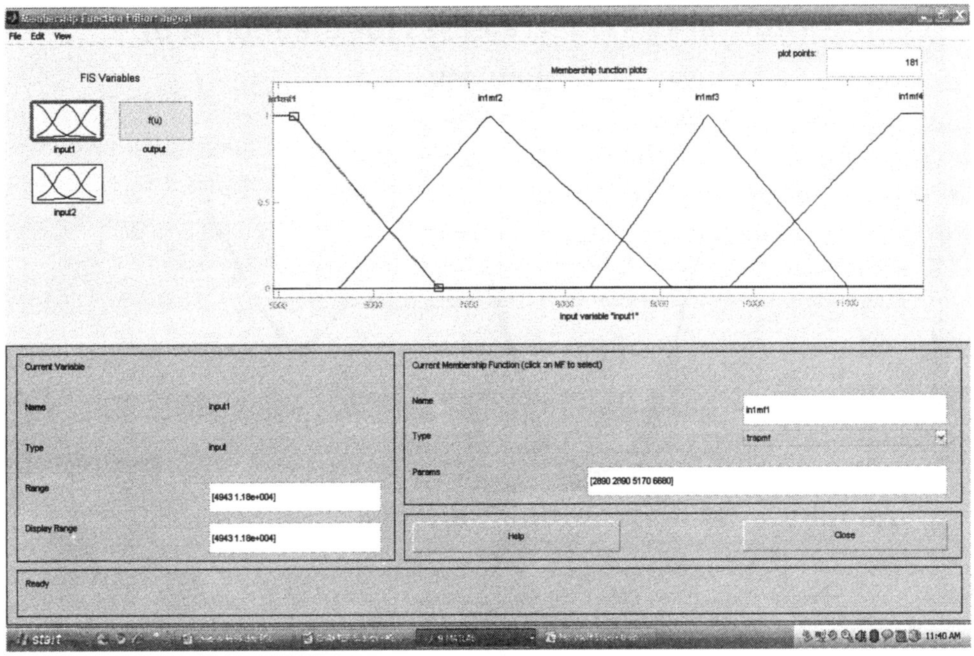

Figure 5: Membership Function Editor

The calculated storage was taken as one of the input parameter and the inflow for the next month was invoked by reading the corresponding inflow for that month. This process will get repeated for all twelve months of a year, and is tested for all the years. The output from the model was stored in an output file. The results thus obtained were compared with the historical values. Simulation model in ANFIS is validated for testing years and the releases are compared with actual historical values. Model results are found to be satisfactory. However during some years, there is a variation in testing period data with training period data. This variation may be due to variation in operational polices occurred in actual practice. This variation in operational policy has been noticed in the actual data. This variation in results is found to be more practically during the periods of zero releases during zero inflows. The developed model has been successful to mimic the historical operations for eight months out of twelve months fairly well.

V. RESULTS

It has been found that the training with Triangular-Trapezoidal membership with four membership functions has given good results when compared with the other type of membership functions. It has been observed that this membership function has got stabilized when the number of epochs was 5000. The training error has been found to be 173.4 for a combination of trapezoidal and triangular memberships with four input membership functions. The results have been tested for all the months of the year for the combination of trapezoidal and triangular memberships with four input membership functions. The comparison between the available historical data and the results obtained from the model developed for the month of January and May is shown in Figure 6 and Figure 7.

The figure shows the comparison between the model and Historical releases for the month January and it can be seen in the years 2006 and 2007 historical releases were higher than model releases. This may be because due to less rain fall or policy issues might be responsible for releasing more water. Similarly the comparison of the historical releases and the model releases for the month of October is in Figure 8. In the year 2006 and 2007 historical releases were small than model. This may be because due to high rain fall due to floods. The developed model referred in this paper has been validated with the available historical data for the years 2001 to 2008. As seen the model developed was able to mimic the actual historical data reasonably with the trends. However there is scope for improvement and these results are shown in Figure 8. Comparison of results of the developed model and the historical release data is shown in Figure 9. As seen from the figure the developed model water releases are more than the historical release data the first four years. For the next four years of validation period it has been found that the predicted water releases of the model are less than the actual historical

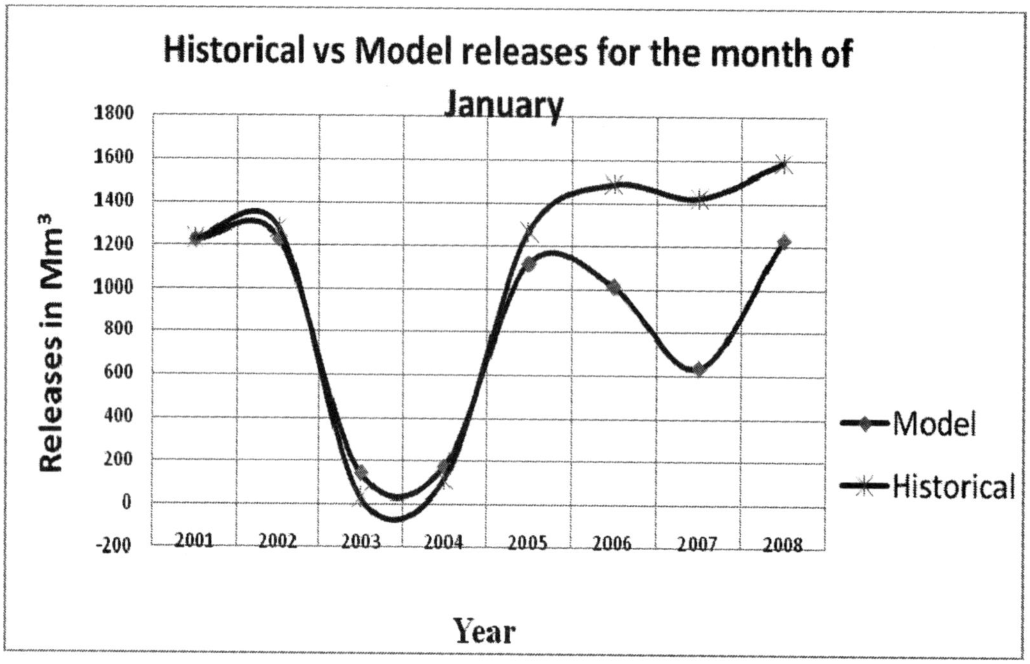

Figure 6: Historical and Model releases for the month of January

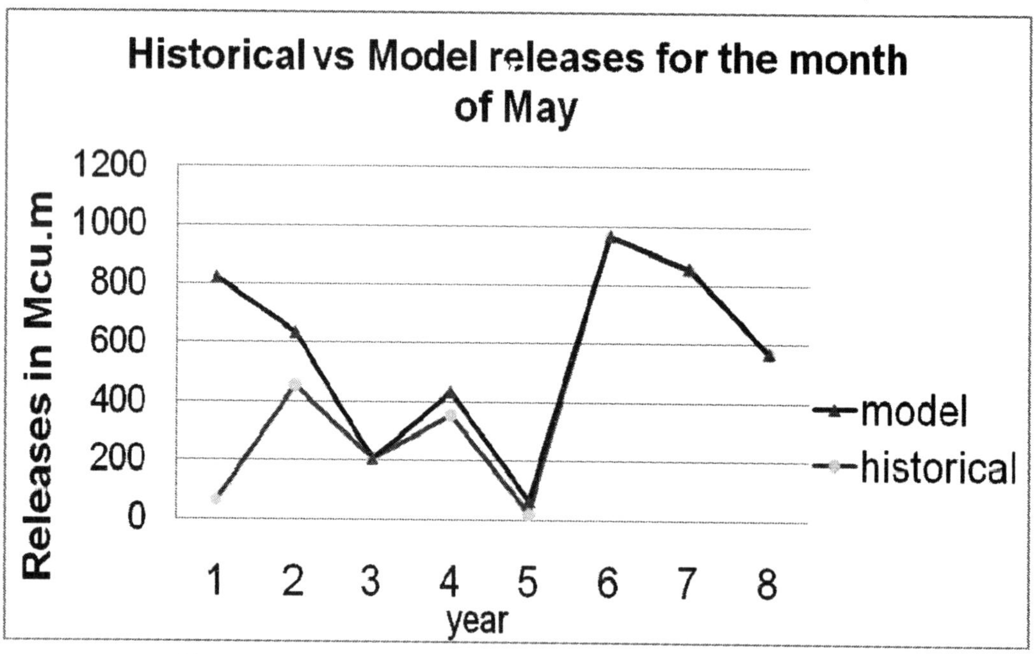

Figure 7: Historical and Model releases for the month of May

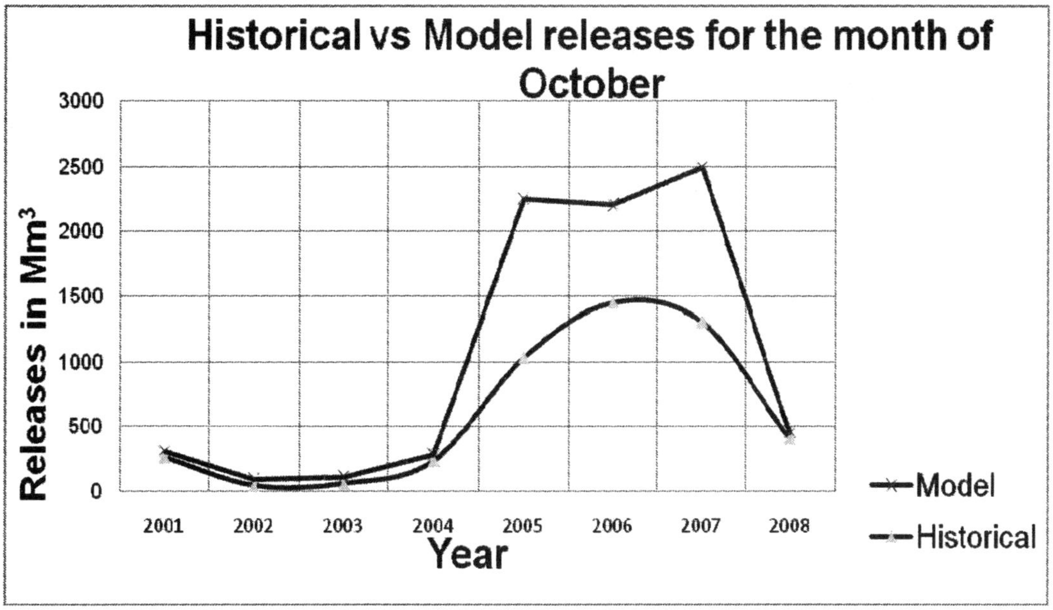

Figure 8 Historical and Model releases for the month of October

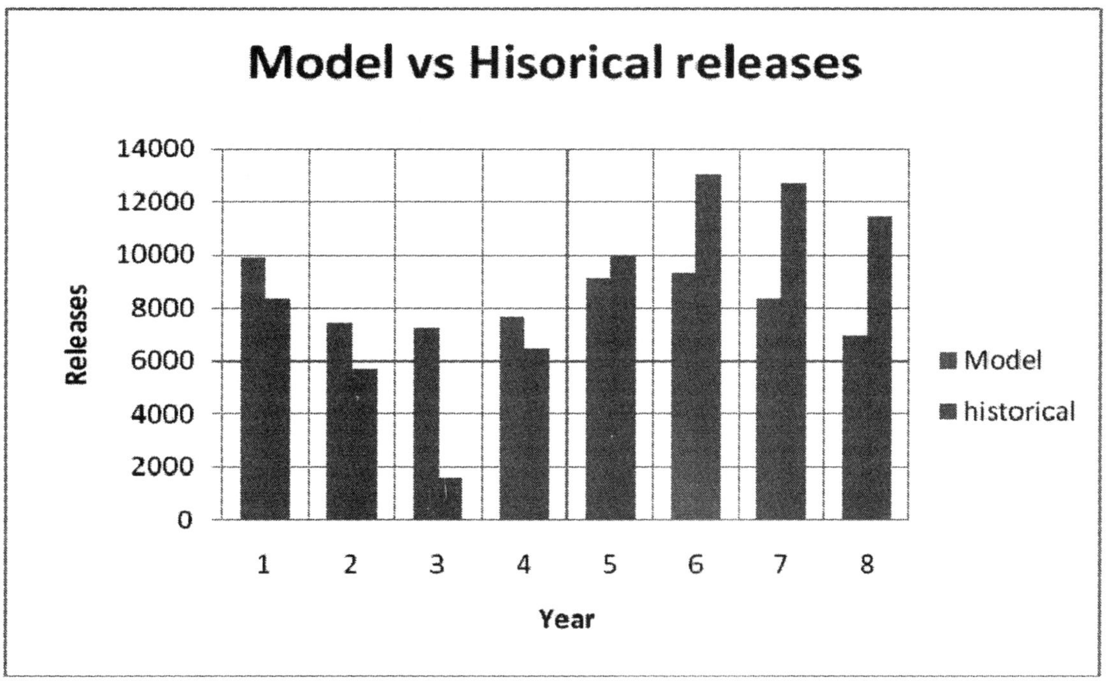

Figure 9: Model releases with historical releases

release data. These variations are due to the operational policies that occur in actual practice. These variations in operation policy are noticed during the actual release data of water. It has been observed that the variations in results are found particularly more during the periods of zero inflows.

VI. Conclusions

An ANFIS model has been successfully developed for reservoir operation and the model was tested with historical data of the reservoir. It has been observed that the triangular and trapezoidal membership functions with four different intervals have yielded good results. The developed model has been successful in mimicking the historical operations for eight months out of twelve months fairly well. The developed model performance has an average deficiency of 25.7% when compared with the historical data during the validation phase

References

[1] P.T. Anju and Sheena Hassan, *Rainfall frequency analysis using parametric methods and artificial neural network,* 10th National conference on technical trends (NCTT09), pp.110-115, Nov. 2009.

[2] D.C.Bisht, M.Mohan Raju and M.C. Joshi, *Simulation of water table elevation fluctuation using Fuzzy-logic and ANFIS,* Computer modeling and new technologies, Vol.13, No. 2, pp. 16-23,2009

[3] Y.-M. Chiang, L.-C. Chang, M.-J. Tsail, Y.-F. Wang and F.-J. Chang, *Auto control of pumping operations in sewerage systems by rule-based fuzzy neural networks,* Hydrology and Earth Systems. Sciences Discussion, pp.6725-6756, 2010.

[4] M.Erol Keskin and E.Dilek Taylan, *Artificial intelligent models for flow prediction: A case study on Alara stream,*Journal ofEngineering Science and Design, Vol. 1, No.1, pp. 8-13, 2010.

[5] Emad A. El-Sebakhy, *Flow regions identification and liquid-holdup prediction in horizontal multiphase flow based on Neuro-Fuzzy inference systems,* Elsevier publications, May 2007.

[6] Ehsan Khadangi, Hossein Riahi Madvarand Mohammad Mehdi, *Comparison of ANFIS and RBF models in daily stream flow forecasting,* Amirkabir Univ of Tech.

[7] M. Figueiredo, R. Ballini, S. Soares, M. Andrade, and F. Gomide, *Learning algorithms for a class of Neurofuzzy network and application,* IEEE transactions on systems, ma and cybernetics-Part C: Applications and reviews, vol. 34, No.3, pp. 293-301, August 2004

[8] D.K.Goutam and K.P.Holtz, *Rainfall-runoff modeling using adoptive neuro-fuzzy systems,* Journal of hydroinformatics, pp. 3-10, 2001.

Water Distribution Network Model Using EPANET

M. Anjaneya Prasad [1], K. Shashikanth [2], M. RedyaNaik[3] M. Narender Reddy[4]

[1] *Professor Department of Civil Engineering, University College of Engineering, O.U. Hyderabad*

[2] *Associate ProfessorDepartments of Civil Engineering, University College of Engineering, O.U. Hyderabad*

[3]*PG Scholar, Department of Civil Engineering, University College of Engineering, O.U. Hyderabad*

[4]*Executive Engineer, RWS, Govt. of Telangana*

[1]*kulkarni.shashikanth@gmail.com*

[1]maprasad2016@gmail.com

***Abstract*—The demand for water is continuously increasing due to growing population and it is essential to provide the sufficient and uniform quantity of drinking water through the designed network of pipes. The general features of the area and hydraulic distribution about the main water source, population of the area, demand of water, requirement of the pumps, distribution network and water tanks are essential for efficient design of water distribution system. The present work highlights the process carried out on design of water supply system for an area named MUCHERLLA network that has been selected as a case study using EPANET software. Simulations of the study area have been chosen to compute the hydraulic distribution of the selected area. The model has been simulated for several roughness coefficients to compute the impact on hydraulic parameters of the network. The rate of flow has been simulated and pressures at nodal points have been verified. The methodology has been demonstrated with a case study of Mucherla segment in Telangana State. Studies were also carried out to study the impact on hydraulic variables by varying roughness coefficient due to aging of pipes in the network.**

***Keywords*—EPANET, Water Distribution, Network**

I. Introduction

EPANET was developed by the Water Supply and Water Resources Division (formerly the Drinking Water Research Division) of the U.S. Environmental Protection Agency's National Risk Management Research Laboratory. It is public domain software that may be freely copied and distributed with certain limitations. EPANET is a computer based software model that performs extended period simulation of hydraulic and water quality behavior within pressurized pipe networks. EPANET is designed to be a research tool for improving of understanding of the movement and fate of drinking water constituents within distribution systems. The model can be simulated with the varying conditions of hydraulics for getting fruitful results and with local restrictions that can be modeled effectively. Arunkumar and Mariappan (2011) have, examined the water demand analysis of public water supply in municipalities using EPANET software and reported the usefulness with a case study in urbanized areas of Chennai Metropolitan, Tamil Nadu, India. Bwire, Onchiri and Mburu (2015) opined that a well-designed water system is meant to operate optimally such that consumers have access to portable water of sufficient pressure and quality at all times. Their study investigated the operations of Kimilili water supply system in Bungoma County of Kenya in terms of pressure variations from the treatment works to the consumer points. It was reported that pipe failure in water distribution systems disrupts the water supply to consumers and reduces the reliability of the system.

II. Data and Methodology

Through the process of calibrating a model, credibility of the model needs to be established. A calibrated model is known to simulate a network system for a range of operating conditions. Its input data has been examined and adjusted to insure that the model can be used as an accurate predictive tool. Once a network model has been calibrated to a known range of operating conditions, it can be used as a benchmark. Pressure and flow rates computed by this model become the benchmark from which pressure and flow rates computed by subsequent, modified models can be compared. The differences between the two models can then be used to analyze the changes brought about in the modified system. A calibrated model can be used to predict any potential problems due to changes in the system operation. In the process of calibrating a model, collection and analysis of data used to define the model and studying the existing network. The engineer needs to simulate many of the same system settings and operations that a network operator makes in order to calibrate the model to the actual operation of the network system. In addition, by analyzing the system operation, possible improvements to system operation may be determined. Inconsistencies between the model results and the actual field conditions have to be examined, with additional field data being collected and analyzed.

III. Description of Stufy Area

Mucherla is a village located in Kandukur Block of Rangareddy district in Telangana. Placed in rural area of Rangareddy district of Telangana State. The population is 4147 according to census 2011 with overall literacy rate is 44%. The distribution system designed here is tree system or dead end system. By adopting EPANET model data filling of one by number of nodes, demand, elevation, tanks and pipes we design the respective distribution system. The number of nodes designed here are 54 with 10 overhead water tanks and in the entire segment with 41 pipes.

IV. Calculation of Pipe Diagrams

Once the design discharge is known, pipe diameters are assumed in a way that the velocities of flow in pipes remain between 0.6 to 3 m/s. smaller velocity is assumed for pipes of smaller diameter and larger velocity for pipes of larger diameter. The loss of head in the pipes is then calculated using Hazen Williams's formula as given in equation 1

$$V = 0.849 \times C \times R \times 0.63S \times 0.54 \quad \text{-- 1}$$

where:
V = mean velocity of flow in pipe (m/s)
R = hydraulic radius (mean depth) in m
S = hydraulic gradient
C = coefficient of roughness of pipe

In terms of diameter D of the pipe, the above formula reduces as per equation. 2

$$V = 0.354\ C \times D \times 0.63S \times 0.54 \quad \text{-- 2}$$

where, D is the diameter of the pipe in meters. Expressed in terms of head loss hf and the length L of the pipe, the Hazen Williams formula takes the following form given is 3 and 4

$$hf = 6.843(D \times 1.167) \times VC \times 1.852 \quad \text{-- 3}$$

The discharge Q (m3/s) is given by:

$$Q = 0.278C \times D \times 2.63S \times 0.54 \quad \text{-- 4}$$

A steady state simulation is used to calibrate the maximum (peak) hour demand, whereas an extended period simulation is needed to calibrate a maximum day demand. All pipes, pumps, valves, tanks, and reservoirs should be identified, including nodal elevations, pressure zone boundaries, and other important information. Whenever changes occur in the water distribution network, such as operational changes, network configuration, or increases in water consumption, the degree of accuracy for the calibrated model is reduced. If these changes are severe enough, the model will need to be recalibrated. In practice this means that the model should be recalibrated whenever major new facilities are added to the network system, a new record for maximum hour is set, or operational procedures change significantly.

V. Simulation of Model

It is important that the network model accurately represents the physical layout of the system. Pipes and nodes must be accurately located in the model. Pipe Roughness values should be estimated based upon the age of the pipe the consumption values must be defined at the nodes. Initially, EPANET model provides a method of globally applying the total network demand to each of the individual network nodes. An initial simulation is performed to simply determine what the resulting pressures and flow rates are in the pipe network with all the relevant data has been considered for simulation. This simulation may be simplified by using single operational values rather than complete operational data. The flow rates and pressures should be prepared at key locations in the system so that comparisons with the computed analysis results can be quickly performed. A comparison of flow rates and pressures between actual values and computed values is carried out. The differences between the computed and actual measured values need to be determined and adjustments to the model data can be performed to make the computed results match more closely to that of the actual data. The present study has been taken up with the data provided by the Rural Water Supply (RWS) department

VI. Results and Discussions

By the use of EPANET various relations are being found between elevation, velocities, flow, pressure, head, demand, contours, etc. these relations can be understood by analysing the results graphically. The lengths of main links also have been modified by introducing sub nodes in order to modify the diameters in the network with the acceptable pressures and quantities of flow. The network diagram thus considered for the modelling is shown in Figure 1. The simulated results of the network at all the junctions indicated in the figure 2 which shows the distribution of pressure and also flow in the entire network. The elevations at junctions of the network are shown in the Figure 3. It can be seen from the results the elevation varying from 500 mm to 14000 mm. The simulated results for velocity of the network at the junctions indicated in the figure 4 shows the variation of velocity at which is varying from 0.42 m/s to 0.9 m/s at these junctions. The simulated results of the network at all the junctions indicated in the figure 5 shows the variation of pressure at junctions of the network. It can be seeing the results the pressure varying from 18 m to 112 m. The model was simulated for various roughness coefficients due to aging of pipes so as to understand the effect on pressure at various junctions of network. The variation of pressures at few important nodes of the network near Mucherla area were observed is given in Table I which shows nodal pressures are varying from The developed simulation model indicated minimum pressure and maximum pressure of 7.13 m and 53.76 m when roughness Hazen willium coefficient varied from 105 to 140 at Mucherla Junction. The developed simulation model indicated change in velocity of maximum 0.39 m/s and when diameter is varied in the network the obtained velocity of maximum 0.71 m/s and minimum of 0.01 m/s The model has indicated change in flow of maximum 1253 cumecs and minimum of 53cumecs when diameter is varied in the network flow obtained as maximum 656 cumecs and minimum of 24. cumecs.

TABLE I

VARIATION OF PRESSURES DUE TO MODIFIED ROUGHNESS AT NODES NEAR MUCHERLA

ROUGH NESS	NODE 38	NODE 34	NODE 30	NODE 24	NODE 14
105	47.49	41.17	32.26	13.26	43.46
110	48.49	43.27	33.07	14.03	45.48
115	49.37	45.11	33.77	14.71	47.26
120	50.14	46.74	34.4	15.31	48.84
125	50.83	48.18	34.96	15.84	50.23
130	51.44	49.47	35.45	16.32	51.48
135	52	50.63	35.9	16.74	52.6
140	52.49	51.67	36.3	17.13	53.6

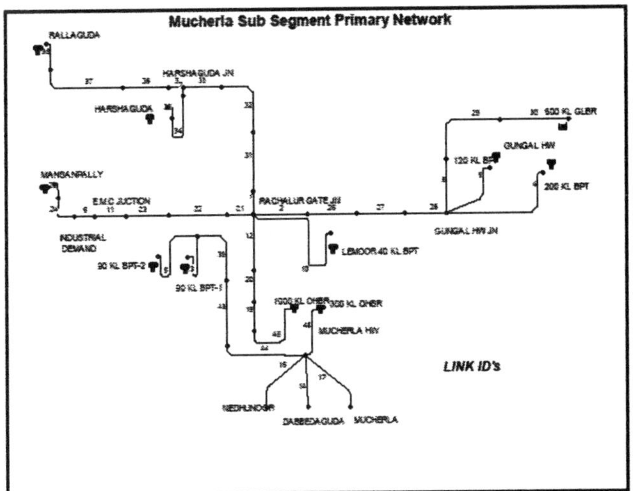

Fig 1: Water distribution system in Mucherla

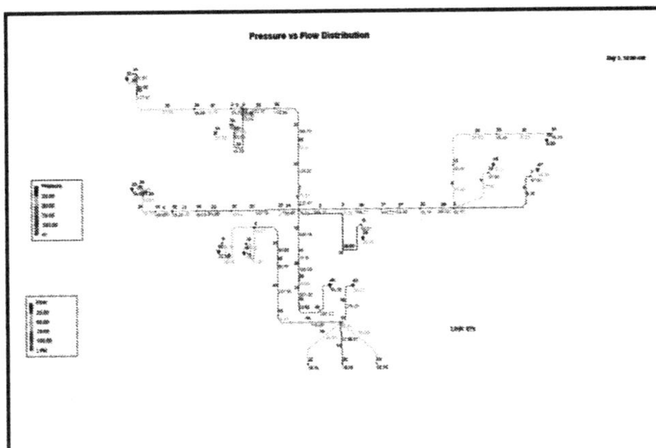
Fig 2: Simulated water distribution for flow and pressure system in Mucherla

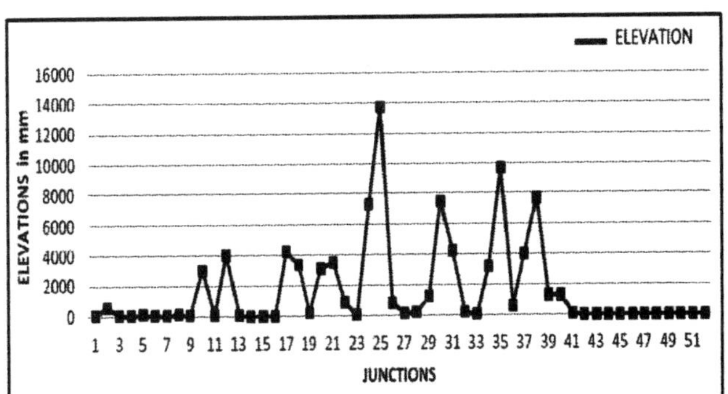

Fig 3: Variation of Elevations across the Junctions

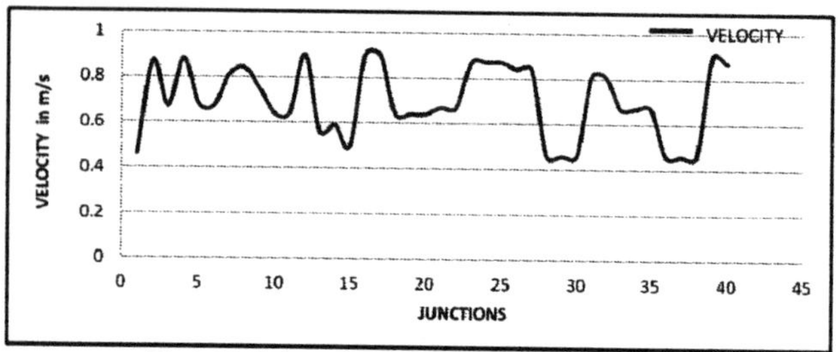

Fig4: Variation of Velocity across the Junctions

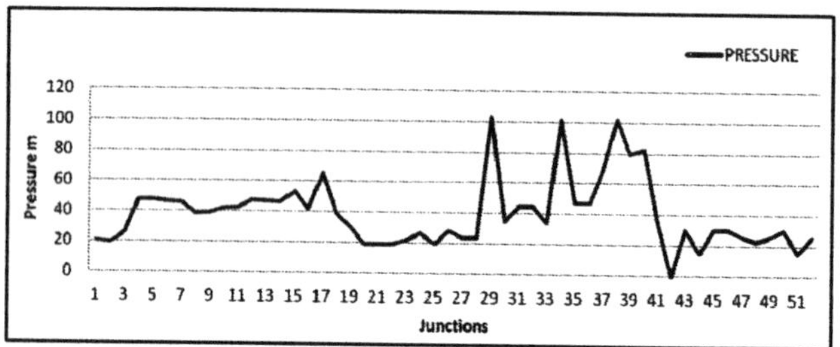

Fig 5: Variation of pressures across the junctions

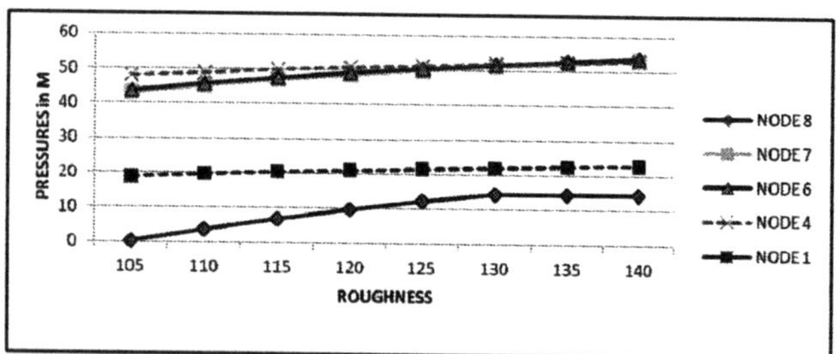

Fig 6: Variation of Pressures due to Modified Roughness at Nodes near Mucherla

References

[1] Arunkumar M. &Mariappan, N.V.E. (2011). Water demand analysis of municipal water supply using EPANET software. International Journal on Applied Bioengineering, 5 (1), 9- 18

[2] Bwire, C., Onchiri, R., Mburu, N. (2015). Simulation of pressure variations within Kimilili water supply system using EPANET.International Journal of Civil Engineering and Technology. 6 (4), 28-38.

[3] M. RedyaNaik (2017) "Water Distribution Model Using EPANET " M.E. Dissertation book submitted to Osmania University, Hyderabad, India

[4] RWS Department, Government of Telangana State, India "Data collected from Department".

Temperature Projections from GCMs Using Quantile Remapping Method

K. Shashikanth[1], RajsekharReddy[2] and M. Anjaneya Prasad [3]

[1]*Associate Professor Department of Civil Engineering, University College of Engineering, O.U. Hyderabad*
[2]PG Student, *Department of Civil Engineering, University College of Engineering, O.U. Hyderabad*
[3]*Professor Department of Civil Engineering, University College of Engineering, O.U. Hyderabad*

[1]kulkarni.shashikanth@gmail.com
[2]rajasekhar.222.reddy@gmail.com
[3]maprasad2016@gmail.com

***Abstract*—General Circulation Models (GCMs) represent the state art of models for simulations of global climate which takes in to changes in circulation patterns through mathematical and Numerical models. The Globalization and rapid Industrialization coupled with change in land use land cover, is altering the CO2 content in the atmosphere ultimately increasing the temperature. The present study deals with projections of temperature across Indian land region using Quantile remapping method from CMIP5 suite under RCP 8.5 scenario. Bias occurs in the GCM model outputs due to various reasons such as incomplete understanding of geophysical processes, subsequent parameterization, assumptions, methods of solutions in the GCM leads to bias in GCM simulated variables. In the present study 10 GCM are used and the Multi model average (MMA) indicate increase in surface temperature, minimum and maximum temperature for future time windows (2020s, 2050s and 2080s). Our study highlights the usefulness of the climate models for future management of temperature.**

***Keywords*—GCMs, Bias Correction method Multimodel Average (MMA)**

I. Introduction

GCMs are widely used for weather forecasting, understanding of the climate system, and projecting climate change for future. These computationally intensive numerical models are based on the integration of variety of fluid dynamical, chemical, and biological equations [IPCC, 1]. Climate is measured by assessing the patterns of variation in temperature, humidity, atmospheric pressure, wind, precipitation, atmospheric particle count and other meteorological variables in a given region over elongatedtime periods nearly for 30 years or so [1]. GCMs exhibit significantskill in simulation of global climate at huge spatial scale. GCMs areat present are the most realistic tools for simulation of climate system to rising greenhouse gas concentration. They are, however, incapable to stand for local sub-grid scale features and dynamics [2, 3]. GCMs are skillful in simulations of climate related variables rather than hydro meteorological variables [4]. However, due to partial understanding of complete geophysics behind the climate system, the outputs from GCMS exhibit systematic error (bias) with that of observed data [3, 5]. Therefore this systematic/logical bias needs to be corrected using various bias correction methods viz. Nested bias corrections method, Quantile remapping method, Multiplicative shift technique, Regression technique, Principal component regression technique [6,7]. Here, we employquantile based transformationmethod of Li et al [5].

II. Data and Methodology

IMD (India Meteorological Department) has provided the observed surface, minimum and maximum temperature at 1^0 spatial resolutions. Here, we use 10 GCMs from CMIP5 suite for analysis and future projections of temperature under 8.5 RCP scenario.

TABLE 1
GCMs used in the Present Study from CMIP5

Model Centre	Model	Institution
CMCC	CMCC-CESM	Euro-Mediterranean Center on Climate Change
CNRM	CNRM-CM5	National Meteorological Research Centre
CSIRO	ACCESS-1	Commonwealth Scientific and Industrial Research Organisation, Australia
INM	INM-CM4	Institute for Numerical Mathematics
IPSL	IPSL-CM5B-LR	Institute Pierre-Simon Laplace
MIROC	MIROC-ESM	Japan Agency for Marine-Earth Science and Technology, Atmosphere and Ocean Research Institute
MPI	MPI-ESM-MR	Max Planck Institute for Meteorology (MPI-M)
MRI	MRI-ESM1	Meteorological Research

		Institute
NCC	NorESM1-M	Norwegian Climate Centre
NIMR	HadGEM2-AO	National Institute of Meteorological Research, Korea

III. Methodology

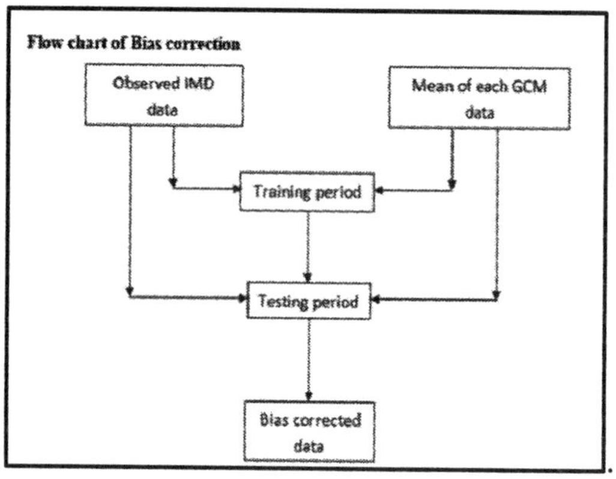

Fig 1: Flow chart for Bias correction method

The Fig 1 shows the broad outline of the bias correction method suggested by Li et al [5]. GCMs data is extracted to Indian portion. After the extraction of required period, GCMs data is interpolated to that of observations.Here, we notice the GCMs original data do not match with observed IMD temperature data. Hence, Bias correction is performed on the GCM simulated data.

The methodology used in the present study is described below:

Li et al. (2010) method is basically a quartile based remapping method wherecumulative distribution functions are fitted to the observed, training and testing data of GCM. The methodology includes the following steps:

1).The observed as well as GCM (XGCM) simulated data, first Cumulative Distribution Functions (CDFs) are fitted to them.

2). GCMs testing period is used to generate new series by making use of GCM train parameters. By finding the difference between new data and test data, climate change signal is obtained.

3). for future/ testing, corresponding to a CDF value, the change is added to GCM test data with observed parameters. For further details refer to Li et al [5] method.

IV. Results and Discussions

The methodology is applied to GCM simulated data with 1969-1984 as training and 1985- 2000 as testing data. All the plots are presented for testing data. The gridded observed temperature data is obtained from India Meteorological Department (IMD). (Fig 2).

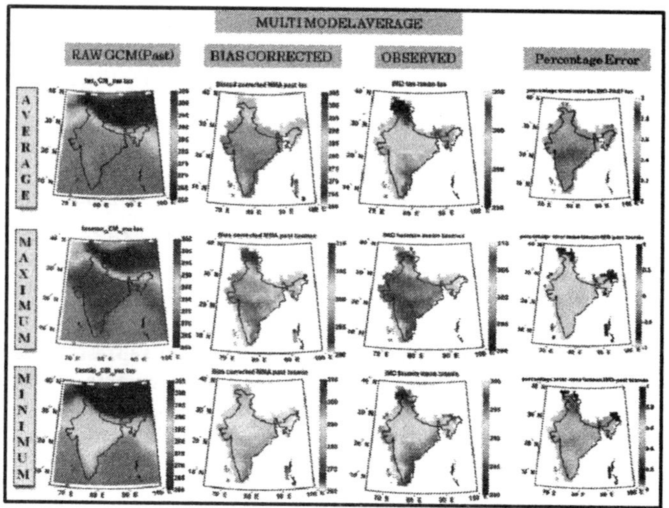

Fig 2: Shows the Multimodel average of original/raw, bias corrected, observed, percentage error for simulated data. (Units are in ^{0}K).

We find from Fig 2 that the percentage errors lies around 4-5% at most of nodes and hence present Bias correction method performs very well. It has captured the spatial variability also well.

V. Future Projections Results (RCP 8.5 Scenario)

The future changes in temperature are carried out for 90 years (2011-2100). These changes are performed in three time scales of 30year time period (2011-2040, 2041-2070, 2071-2100). The changes in temperature are performed with respect to base bias period (1986-2005). There is rise in temperature in central, south, north east of India. The western India do not show significant rise in average temperature.

Average temperature is increases from 2011-2040 to 2071-2100. Minimum and maximum temperatures also show some increase in temperature in three time periods. In 2011-2040 the average temperature is about 298 ^{0}K in north India and 302 ^{0}K in south India and Gujarat, Rajasthan regions. In 2041-2070 the average temperature is increased about 2 to 3 ^{0}K compared to 2011-2040. In 2071-2100 average temperature increases drastically. In all three time periods minimum temperature shows high value about 300 ^{0}K in coastal regions. Maximum temperature shows high values about 306 to 310 ^{0}K in middle Indian regions.

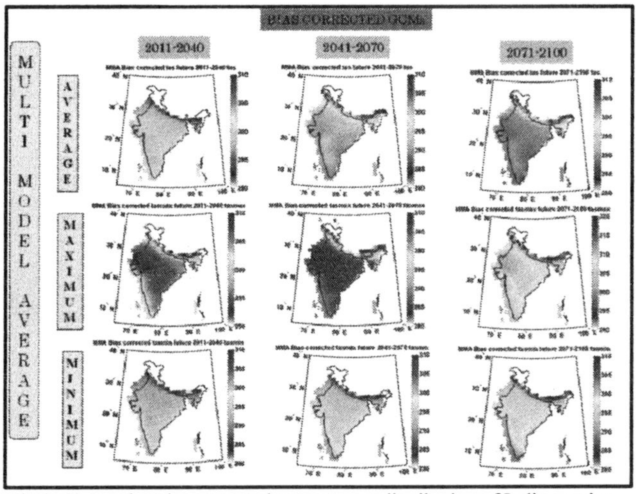

Fig 3: Shows the Bias corrected temperature distribution of Indian region for different time windows 2020s, 2050s and 2080s.

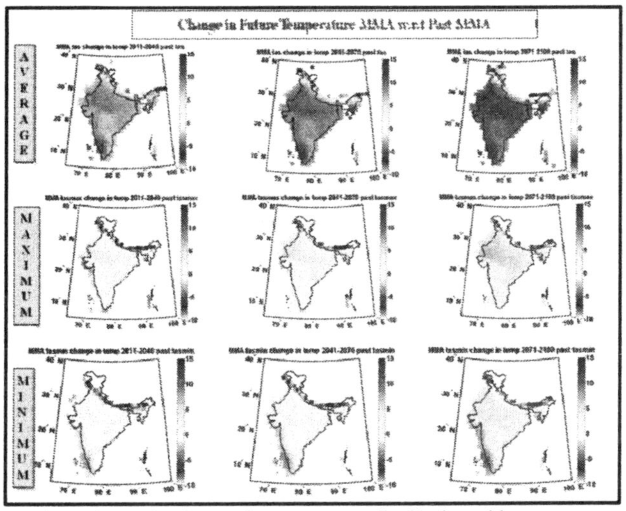

Fig 4: Shows the changes in temperature distribution with respect to historical period (1986-2005).

The fig 4 is an important finding from our research study. Bias corrected future temperatures show increase in temperature with respect to the historical temperatures. Average temperature is increasing in future. Minimum and maximum temperatures are not changing 2011-2040, but increasing up to 5^0C in 2041-2070 and 2071-2100.

VI. Conclusions

The objective of the study is to examine the performance of bias correction on climate models and the estimation of daily temperature projections of India for the future period up to 2100.

The major findings of the present work are as follows:

- The multi model average of all the bias corrected GCMs has better result.
- The future projection for the years (2011-2040, 2041-2070, 2071-2100) indicates that the average temperature is increasing in all three future time scales (2011-2040, 2041-2070, 2071-2100).
- The change in maximum and minimum temperature for the future period 2011-2040 does not show significant change from historical period.
- The changes in maximum and minimum temperature for the future period 2041-2070 and 2071-2100 shows increase in temperature up to 5^0C in most regions of India with respect to historical period. This needs to be thoroughly examined using various regional models for reliability studies.

References

[1] IPCC(2013) Summary for Policymakers. In: Climate change 2013: The Physical Science Basis. Contribution of Working Group I to the Fifth Assessment Report of the Intergovernmental Panel on Climate Change [Stocker, T.F., D. Qin, G.-K. Plattner, M. Tignor, S. K. Allen, J. Boschung, A. Nauels, Y. Xia, V. Bex and P.M. Midgley (eds.)]. Cambridge University Press, Cambridge, United Kingdom and New York, NY, US

[2] Wilby, R.L and T.M.L. Wigley (1996), Downscaling general circulation model output: a review of methods and limitations Progress in physical geography, 21,4, pp 530-548

[3] Salvi, Kaustubh., S. Kannan and Ghosh, S. (2011), Statistical Downscaling and Bias Correction for Projections of Indian Rainfall and Temperature in Climate Change Studies International Conference on Environmental and Computer Science, IPCBEE vol.19, IACSIT Press, Singapore.

[4] Ghosh, S., and Mujumdar, P.P. (2008) Statistical Downscaling of GCM simulations to stream flow using Relevance vector machine. Advances in Water Resources 31(1), pp. 132-146

[5] Li, Haibin., Justin Sheffield, and Eric, F. Wood (2010), Bias correction of monthly precipitation and temperature fields from Intergovernmental Panel on Climate Change AR4 models using equidistant quantile matching, J. Geophys.Res., 2010,doi:10.1029/2009JD012882.".

[6] Johnson, F., and Sharma, A. (2012), A nesting model for bias correction of variability at multiple time scales in general circulation model precipitation simulations. Water Resou.Res.48(1), 1-16. doi:10.1029/2011WR010464 1199, 2003

[7] Mehrotra and Sharma (2012) An improved standardization procedure to remove systematic low frequency variability biases in GCM simulations. Water Resources Research Vol 48, W 12601doi.10.1029/21012WR012446, 2012.

Stream III: Transportation Engineering and Construction Engineering Management

Evaluation of Performance of Isolated Signalized Intersections and Design of a Coordinated Signal System by Using Vissim Software

R. Srinivasa Kumar [1], K. Vinay Kumar[2]

Department of Civil Engineering, University College of Engineering, Osmania University, Hyderabad, India

Abstract—Road intersections in series in urban areas lead to conflict between opposing traffic flows and cause to delays and accidents. To overcome these problems over at intersections, the traffic flows across the intersections are controlled by using signals. The fixed timings and isolated operation of signals at each intersection along a street may cause delays on red duration and also generate vehicular queue during peak hours. When properly timed and the signal timings are coordinated with reference to intersection distance and the average travelling speed of vehicles can enhance traffic handling capacity along the streets even during peak hours.

The aim of coordinating traffic signals in series along a street is to facilitate smooth flow of traffic across the intersections in order to reduce travel time and delay. This research has been carried out to evaluate the existing operating system of traffic signals and also investigate the benefits of these signals coordinated by using micro-simulation software PTV Vissim. Initially, the Vissim simulation was calibrated and the coordinated signals were run for execution based on the prepared model in Vissim. The traffic flow delays and travel times obtained by the simulation were compared to the corresponding values found before coordination.

The output from this research reveals that, a considerable reduction in delays and travel times were observed after coordinating the signals along the study street. Further, it is also expected that the methodology and procedure adopted in this research will be useful for similar traffic coordination studies elsewhere, subjected to the intervals of intersections and traffic flow characteristics are comparable.

Keywords: Delay, Signal coordination, Micro-simulation and Vissim.

I. Introduction

Coordination of signalized intersection is one of the popular concepts in traffic flow management along a street. Signal coordination refers to the interlinking of timings of the signals along the intersections in street so that a platoon of vehicles traveling on the street cross through the intersections at a succession of green lights, without stopping. The objective of signals coordination is to permit the greatest number of vehicles pass through the intersections in series with fewest or without stops.

Change of traffic signals timing and interlinking traffic signal with succession of green times are the most important strategies in signal coordination and thereby to reduce travel time, delay and shorten the queue length before the intersections (ATAC, 2003).

Such improvements in signal timings can avoid the immediate need to expand the existing right of way or build new road infrastructure to cater the ever increasing travel times, delays, congestion and save share of budget allocations in the urban infrastructure sector. However, detailed study of traffic flow and design of signals time plan with coordinated concept can help near future traffic flow delays along the streets.

II. Need for the Study

With the rapid increase of traffic growth, traffic delays and speed reduction are common phenomenon along the streets installed with traffic signals. Coordinating isolated signals along a street can cause reduction in travel time. Coordination traffic signals ensure optimum travel speeds, reduced delays, and minimal stops. Coordinated traffic signals along street intersections are influence by numerous conditions such as corridor speeds, spacing between the traffic signals, pedestrian volumes, cycle length of the traffic signals, number of phases, additional right-turn phases, congestion and traffic flow characteristics.

The coordinated signal operations of adjacent intersections along a corridor can considerably improve traffic flow and reduce delay. However, developing coordinated signal system requires data collection and detailed analysis that would take into consideration traffic flow parameters, spacing between intersections and cost of signal integration which is compared with benefits of reduced delay.

There are several tools available for evaluation of alternative coordination plans along a study street. Such tools may be classified as signal timing optimization tools and traffic flow simulation tools. Optimization tools are used to estimate effectiveness of any time plan of signal operation and compare with before and after studies. Traffic simulation tools particularly, microscopic traffic simulation tools can be used for modeling of observed traffic flow parameters along these signalized interactions. The present research is focused on the traffic flow simulation with the observed traffic parameters and comparison of delays with before and after simulation studies.

This study has been conducted by the Transportation Section, Civil Engineering Department of Osmania University, Hyderabad. The purpose of this study was to develop best practices for traffic signal coordination by conducting a case study and which may be used as a reference model for future signal coordination efforts in Hyderabad City.

Based on the above need, the present study was taken up with the following objectives.

III. Objective and Scope of the Study

The broad objective of this study is to Compute the Cycle times and signal timings of the selected junctions and to design the Signal system which is used for coordinating the three signalized junctions by simple progressive system and comparing the delays by using PTV VISSIM Software. The Scope of the work includes the following:

(a) One way coordination of the three signalized Junctions by using Simple progression system.

(b) Computing the Vehicular delays for present existing signal timings at three signalized junctions by using PTV Vissim.

(c) Computing the Vehicular delays for the designed signal system at three signalized junctions by using PTV Vissim.

(d) Comparison of vehicular delays for present existing and the designed signal system by using PTV Vissim

(e) Recommendations for reducing the delays at these signalized intersections based on the present study.

IV. Literature Review

Review of literature on signal design, signal retiming and signal coordination studies carried out in India and other countries are presented below.

Traffic Signal priority (TSP) is being adopting since more than three decades to reduce delays at intersection queues (Chang, 2002). The TSP can reduce transit delay and travel time for improving overall quality of the transit service.

As a common observation, inefficiency of any urban traffic system can be attributed to the delay experienced at signalized intersections. It was found that the stopped delay of buses at signalized intersections comprises about 20% of overall transit delay (Zhang, 2001).

A cyclically time-expanded network with mixed integer linear programming was formulated for simultaneously optimizing both coordination of signals and traffic assignment in an urban street network. This model can be used for evaluating extensive simulation experiments and establish as a traffic simulation model (Kohler and Strehler, 2010).

A study conducted along 12-intersection corridor on Glades Road in Boca Raton in USA to integrating Vissim, SSAM, and VISGAOST tools for optimizing signal timings to reduce surrogate safety measures and subsequently reduce risks of potential road accidents. In addition to this study, a multiple-objective genetic algorithm was implemented with VISGAOST and identified the relationship between surrogate safety and traffic efficiency. They found that, the optimized signal timings provided both safety and efficiency in traffic operations (Stevanovic et al, 2011).

Coensel1 and Botteldooren (2011) studies on for the Dutch vehicle fleet and investigated studied the influence of traffic signal coordination on vehicle noise and air pollutant emissions by using a microscopic traffic simulation model coupled with emission models. They found that largest potential reduction found when traffic intensities are close to capacity and the green split is low. This methodology can be used to determine the effects of a wide range of intelligent transportation systems which are integrated as coordinated signal system.

Based on the probabilistic model, a practical signal timing guideline was developed according to the percentage of stops on non-coordinated arterials. This model was developed to precisely estimate the number of stops and has been validated through VISSIM simulation of observed traffic parameters along a signalized arterial in Nevada (NDOT, 2012).

Retiming and coordination of traffic signals along a selected section of a road is one of the most cost effective ways to improve traffic flow, mitigate congestion, reduces air pollution, road-accidents and driver frustration. The ability to synchronize multiple intersections that are in series and thereby enhance operation of through and crossing traffic movements in a system is termed as traffic signal coordination (MnDOT, 2013).

V. Methodology

The steps involved and the methodology adopted to conduct this study is presented in Fig.1

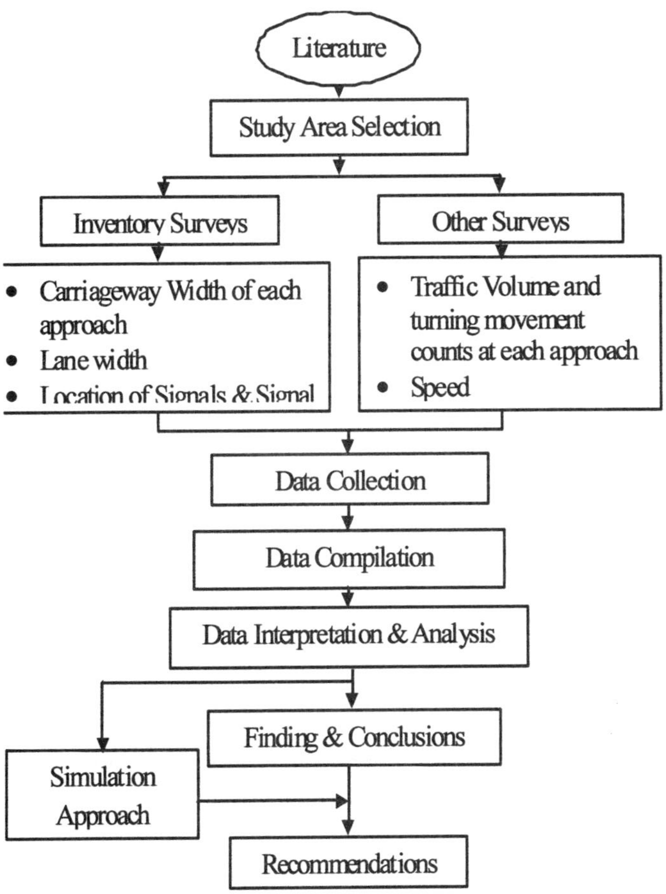

Fig 1. Methodology of present study

VI. The Study Area

The study area considered for this project is in Hyderabad city and the urban arterial street connecting of three signalized 4-legged intersections, RTC X-Roads, Azamabad Junction and VST Junction (Fig.2). These three signalized junctions are spaced apart by 300m and 600m from VST to Azamabad junction and Azamabad to RTC X Roads Respectively.

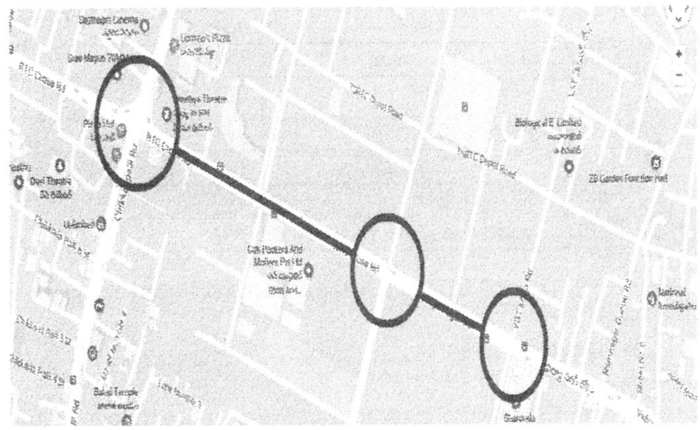

Fig.2 Google Map showing 3 Signal Junctions

A. Data Collection

The data collections at these intersections include traffic volume studies, their turning movements and travel time studies. The traffic volume study was conducted by taking video footages from Cyberabad police Commissionerate, Hyderabad. Classified turning movement volume counts of vehicles of each of each junction are presented in Table 1, 2 and 3.

Table 1 Peak Hour flow rate at RTC X Road Signal junction

Approach	**Direction of flow**	**Peak hour flow(vehicle/hour)**
Ashok nagar	Through	818
	Left	228
	Right	670
Hindi mahavidyalaya	Through	622
	Left	514
	Right	1126
Koti	Through	432
	Left	397
	Right	284
Secunderabad	Through	661
	Left	147
	Right	275

Approach	Direction of flow	Peak hour flow(vehicle/hour)
RTC X road signal junction	Through	1400
	Left	274
	Right	313
Hindi mahavidyalaya	Through	1619
	Left	294
	Right	436
TSRTC Depot road	Through	139
	Left	758
	Right	368
RTC Kalabhavan road	Through	117
	Left	193
	Right	336

Table 2 Peak Hour flow rate at Azamabad Signal junction

B. Travel Time survey

Travel times were measured in these routes by conducting moving car method. The details of the travel times and the details are presented below.

Direction of traffic flow	Trip 1	Trip 2	Trip 3
Azamabad signal junction to VST signal junction (300m)	1m 3sec	1m 2 sec	1m 7sec
RTC X Road signal to VST signal junction (900m)	1m 51sec	1m 56 sec	1m 54sec
Travel time from RTC X Road signal junction to VST signal junction (1200m)	2m 54sec	2m 58sec	3m 1sec
Average speed of travel from RTC X Road signal junction to VST signal junction (1200m)	18.62 km/hr	18.20 km/hr	17.90 km/hr

The Average speed from RTC X Road junction to VST signal junction is 18.54 Kmph.

C. Signal Timings

Approach	Direction of flow	Peak hour flow(vehicle/hour)
Azamabad signal Junction	Through	1117
	Left	589
	Right	332
Hindi mahavidyalaya	Through	1236
	Left	1683
	Right	235
Ramnagar	Through	81
	Left	367
	Right	141
Sri Vaishnavi Enclave road	Through	206
	Left	492
	Right	266

Table 3 Peak Hour flow rate at VST signal junction

The existing signal timings of the three junctions are given below, the green time of all 3 junctions and their four approaches are given. These timings have to be cross checked with the proposed new design and should be optimized based on coordination principles.

Junction	Approach	Green time
RTC X Road Junction	North	30 seconds
	South	30 seconds
	East	20 seconds
	West	20 seconds
Azamabad signal junction	North	24 seconds
	South	22 seconds
	East	15 seconds
	West	15 seconds
VST signal Junction	North	22 seconds
	South	24 seconds
	East	20 seconds
	West	15 seconds

VII. Analysis of Data

The traffic volume data collected at field and geometric data such as road widths are summarized for analysis of signal timings. The details of the inputs considered and the Webster's method of optimum cycle length and the signal timing of these three intersections are presented below:

RTC X Road signal junction

Junction leg	North		South		East		West	
Direction of traffic	Through	Right	Through	Right	Through	Right	Through	Right
(PCU/hr)	547	446	416	753	288	189	442	184
Total (q) (PCU/hr)	993		1169		477		626	
Width (w)	7.75		8.5		6.53		9.46	
Saturation (s)	4069		4463		3428		4967	
y = (q/s)	0.244		0.262		0.139		0.126	

Azamabad signal junction:

Junction leg	North		South		East		West	
Direction of traffic	Through	Right	Through	Right	Through	Right	Through	Right
(PCU/hr)	936	209	1083	293	93	246	77	226
Total (q) (PCU/hr)	1145		1376		339		303	
Width (w)	8.58		9.67		7.05		5.6	
Saturation (s)	4505		5077		3701		2940	
y = (q/s)	0.254		0.271		0.091		0.103	

VST signal junction:

Junction leg	North		South		East		West	
Direction of traffic	Through	Right	Through	Right	Through	Right	Through	Right
(PCU/hr)	742	220	821	156	53	141	136	176
Total (q) (PCU/hr)	962		977		194		312	
Width (w)	8.20		7.55		3.5		5.1	
Saturation (s)	4305		3964		1890		2380	
y = (q/s)	0.223		0.246		0.102		0.131	

A. Traffic signal coordination

After the above signal design, we have to coordinate the stretch of 900m of inbound traffic from south to north by using Vissim (Fig. 3). This simulation model was developed in Germany by PTV AG. It is a microscopic simulation model which is capable of simulating different modes of vehicle operations along the streets. This tool comprises of traffic simulator and also signal state generator. Vissim can also interface to traffic signal controllers type NEMA (ATAC, 2003).

Time space diagram: For the given signal stretch, coordination has to be done, The average travel time in these junctions is taken as 31kmph, the cycle lengths for RTC X Road signal junction, Azamabad signal junction and VST signal junctions are 120 seconds, 103 seconds, and 98 seconds, the green time for south leg is 33seconds, 31seconds and 26seconds. Distance between intersections is 300m and 600m from VST to Azamabad and Azamabad to RTC X Road Respectively.

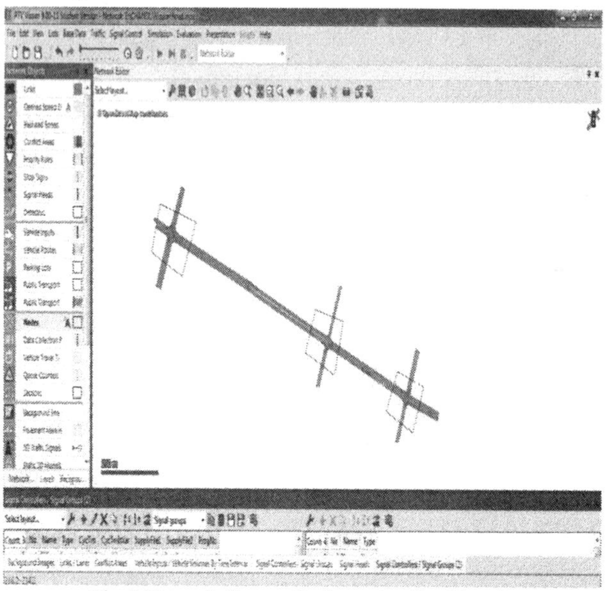

Fig. 3 Network diagram for three signalized junctions

The green time is taken as bandwidth in signal coordination diagram by default and corresponding red, and amber times are indicated. The offset is determined as:

Offset for 300m = 300 / (31*(1000/3600) = 35 seconds.

Offset for 900m = 900 / (31* (1000/3600) = 104 seconds.

The time interval is taken as 20 seconds on x-axis

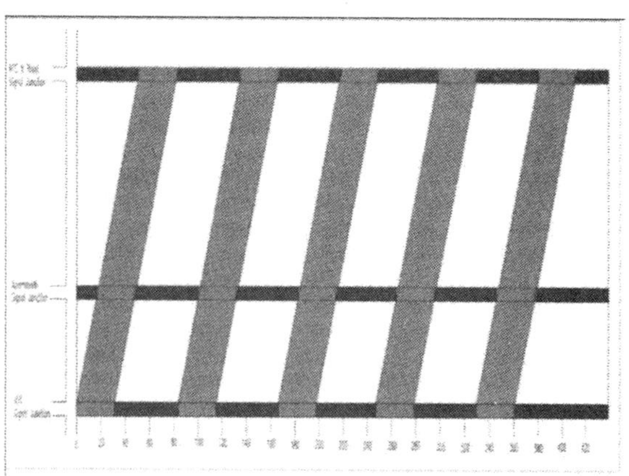

Fig 4 One way coordination diagram for three signalized junctions

B. Presentation One way Coordination Diagram

Presenting one way coordination is very simple than two way coordination. In the above diagram (Fig.5), the x-axis and y-axis is drawn taking x- axis as time interval of 20 seconds till 420 seconds and y-axis as distance between the intersections at 300m marking horizontal line parallel to x axis, and at 600m parallel to Azamabad signal junction. At VST signal junction, at 0 seconds the green time is started marking 26 seconds this is called as bandwidth. After 26 seconds is marked, the red time continues, followed by green time and so on. This bandwidth extends through next signal and till third signal; the through band meets from VST to Azamabad signal junction at offset of 35 seconds. And there the green time is marked of 31 seconds, followed by red time and so on...up to 3 to 4 cycles. And at third signal junction at 900m with offset of 104 seconds, the green time of 33 seconds is drawn followed by red time and so on. The through band indicates the continuous movement of vehicles without any stopping.

(a) Since the cycle length and phases are not equal it will not align the through bands uniformly. Hence is has to be adjusted such that is has at least are always in same position relative to each other.

(b) Since the offsets are different i.e. 0 at first junction, 35 seconds at 2nd junction and 104 seconds at 3rd junction, the signal turns green after some time after it turns green in the first junction. If the offsets has been same or zero, then all the signal would show green at same time.

(c) There are two ways in which coordination can be achieved, one of the ways is to stop the west bound traffic at certain intersection and allow the east bound traffic to flow without any stopping, or allow for west bound traffic to flow but east bound traffic will have to be stopped at one intersection.

(d) Another method is to allow the both the ways to travel without stopping by reducing the bandwidth and due to this the right turn flow has to be stopped while the through flow continuous in both ways. Allowing both ways to travel reduces the bandwidth considerably.

C. Results

The following results are obtained from the above analysis

(a) From the above analysis from the data, it can be seen that the signals has a very less green time for the given traffic volume, the green time of VST signal junction should be increased from 22 seconds to 26 seconds.

(b) The green time of East leg of VST signal junction should be reduced from 20 seconds to 12 seconds, because the traffic flow is meager. This reduced 8 seconds should be added to North leg and South leg approaches

(c) The green time from Azamabad signal junction from VST to RTC X Roads should be increased from 24 seconds to 31 seconds, reducing east leg approach from 15 seconds to 11 seconds.

(d) At RTC X Road signal junction, the green time from Azamabad signal junction to RTC X Roads should be increased from 30 seconds to 33 seconds, reducing east leg approach signal from 24 seconds to 19 seconds

(e) At RTC X Roads signal junction, the green time of south leg approach should be increased from 30 to 35 seconds, reducing west approach signal from 22 seconds to 17 seconds

(f) The one way signal coordination of the three signalized junction are almost possible with progression speed of 31 kmph for the distance of 300m.

The bandwidths of each signal junctions is taken as 26 seconds at VST signal junction, 22 seconds at Azamabad signal junction, and 33 seconds at RTC X Roads signal junction, which are green times of respective intersection.

VIII. SUMMARY AND CONCLUSIONS

The summary of the present study and the conclusions drawn based on the data analysis are presented below:

A.Summary

The above study, data collection, analysis and results carried out are for three signalized junction at one of the busiest vehicular traffic stretch at RTC X Road, VST signal junction, and Azamabad signal junction. These junctions have more traffic volume due to many commercial activities around it. The works carried out are measurement of geometric data of roads, their width, and traffic volume counts and travel time study. As these are the main routes and inbound towards the city of Hyderabad and Secunderabad. HCV and multi axle vehicles are not allowed into these stretches. The types of vehicle considered for the study are 2w, 3w, cars, and buses. All the parameters calculated are for peak hour traffic flow only. Signal design is carried out by Webster method, all the green times and towards north bound towards city should be changed to work more efficiently.
From the above study, the following summary can be drawn, the change in green times for all the three signal junctions is given below, some of the signal timings are changed or increased or decreased accordingly to give more priority to the major corridor

Intersection	Approach	Green time		Improvement (%)
		Before	After	
RTC X Road junction	North	30 seconds	33 seconds	10.00 %
	South	30 seconds	35 seconds	16.67%
	East	24 seconds	19 seconds	20.83%
	West	22 seconds	17 seconds	22.72%
Azamabad signal junction	North	24 seconds	31 seconds	29.16%
	South	22 seconds	33 seconds	50.00%
	East	15 seconds	11 seconds	26.66%
	West	15 seconds	13 seconds	13.33%
VST signal junction	North	22 seconds	26 seconds	18.18%
	South	24 seconds	29 seconds	20.83%
	East	20 seconds	12 seconds	40.00%
	West	15 seconds	15 seconds	0.00%

Table 4 Summary of green times of signals and the delay reductions

All the green times are increased accordingly, the above values after design improves the signal system efficiency.

The traffic signal coordination is done by simple progressive system. The progression speed is taken as 31kmph. Therefore, all the vehicles should strictly limit the speed to 31kmph in order pass the green bandwidth. The distance between junctions is 300m and 600m respectively; the offset is taken as 35 seconds from VST to Azamabad signal junction, and 104 seconds from Azamabad signal junction to RTC X Roads signal junction. The speed of traffic flow is also improved by 40%.

B. Conclusions

The following conclusions can be drawn based on the present work.

(a) Due to traffic signal coordination in this stretch, the speed of the vehicles should be increased by 40%

(b) As the speed of vehicles in the stretch increases, the travel time can be reduced considerably due to coordination.
(c) More delays are occurring at side legs of VST and Azamabad signal junction as the roads are very narrow.
(d) The U turns should not be allowed in middle of the road, at it makes the platoon of vehicles to stop until the vehicle clears the road.
(e) The coordination should be used only during peak hours, during non peak hours it is not useful as it makes other junctions wait which is not efficient during non peak hours.

References

1. MnDOT (2013), "MnDOT Traffic Signal Timing and Coordination Manual", Minnesota Department of Transportation, May. 2013.

2. ATAC (2003),"Signal Coordination Strategies Final Report", Prepared by: Advanced Traffic Analysis Center Upper Great Plains Transportation Institute North Dakota State University Fargo, North Dakota, Prepared for: Grand Forks/East Grand Forks Metropolitan Planning Organization, June.

3. Deshpande V. (2003), "Evaluating the Impacts of Transit Signal Priority Strategies on Traffic Flow Characteristics: Case Study along U.S.1, Fairfax County, Virginia", Thesis submitted to the faculty of the Virginia Polytechnic Institute and State University.

4. Chang J. (2003), "Evaluation of Service Reliability Impacts of Traffic Signal Priority Strategies for Bus Transit", Dissertation, Virginia Polytechnic Institute and State University.

5. Coensel1 B. D. and Botteldooren D. (2011), "Traffic Signal Coordination: A measure to Reduce the Environmental Impact of Urban Road Traffic?", Inter-Noise, Sept., Osaka, Japan.

6. Kohler E. and Strehler M. (2010),"Traffic Signal Optimization Using Cyclically Expanded Networks", 10th Workshop on Algorithmic Approaches for Transportation Modelling, Optimization, and Systems (ATMOS '10). Editors: Thomas Erlebach, Marco Lübbecke; pp. 114–129.

7. NDOT (2012), "Signal Timing and Coordination Strategies Under Varying Traffic Demands", Report No. 236-11-803, Prepared by Rasool A. and Tian Z., Nevada Department of Transportation 1263 South Stewart Street Carson City, NV 89712.

8. Stevanovic A., Stevanovic J. and Kergaye C. (2011), "Optimizing Signal Timings To Improve Safety Of Signalized Arterials", Proc., of the 3rd International Conference on Road Safety and Simulation, September 14-16, Indianapolis, USA.

9. Zhang, Y.(2001), "An Evaluation of Transit Signal Priority and SCOOT Adaptive Signal Control", Master's thesis, Virginia Polytechnic Institute and State University

A Case Study of Mode Choice Analysis in Hyderabad City

S. Ramesh Kumar[1] M. Kumar[2] C.S.V Subrahmanya Kumar[3] Mr. Praveen[4]

[1]*Associate Professor, Department of Civil Engineering, MVSR Engineering College, Nadergul, Hyderabad, Telangana*

[2]*Professor, Department of Civil Engineering, University College of Engineering, Osmania University, Hyderabad*

[3]*Professor, Department of Civil Engineering, MVSR Engineering College, Nadergul, Hyderabad, Telangana*

[4]*Assistant Professor, Department of Civil Engineering, CVR college of Engineering, Ibrahimpatnam, Hyderabad, Telangana*

[1]rksonikar@gmail.com
[2]kumartrans@gmail.com
[3]csvs.kumar1@gmail.com
[4]samardhipraveen@gmail.com

***Abstract*—**With rapid urbanization and increase in population the demand for transportation facilities is ever increasing. In this paper an attempt is made to study the mode choice behavior of people of central zone of Hyderabad. In this connection suitable mode choice model is developed using ALogit software. The mode choice model helps to understand the current trend of mode competition in the study area and the effect of new transportation facility on other modes of transport and mode choice of people. Lastly, probable willingness of people to shift to new transport facility i.e., Metro rail is studied.

***Keywords*—**Alogit software, Model choice, Travel Analysis

I. Introduction

Transport is a key infrastructure of a country. The country's economic status depends upon how well it is served by its roads, rail ways, air ways, ports and shipping. The country's economy growth is very closely linked to the rate at which the transport sector grows.

The planning aspects of transportation engineering relate to urban planning, and involve technical forecasting decisions and political factors. The researchers namely, Mark P. DE Guzman (2005), Shlomo Bekhor, Tim Schwanen (2005), Milimol Philip, Frank S. Koppelman and Chandra Bhat, (2006), Sven Muller,(2008), Bernetti, G. Longo, G. Tomasella, L Violin, L(2008), Gauthier, H. Land Mitchelson, R.L.(1981), Hsieh, S. Joseph, T. Morrison, M. Chang, S. (1993), Limtalakool, N. Dijst and Schwanen, (2006). Southworth F, (1981), Lucas, Y. Archilla and Papacostas C.S (2007), carried out works in Mode choice.

II. Need for the Study and Expected Outcomes

The Hyderabad urban transportation network is tremendously experiencing an increase in growth of vehicular traffic on a regular basis. Hence it is inevitable to study the mode choice behavior of the travelers so that suitable policies may be suggested to improve the transportation system of the area. Some of the factors which greatly influence the demand for urban travel are: 1) Location and intensity of land use, 2) Socioeconomic characteristics of people living in the area and 3) Extent of Cost and Quality of available transportation services.

The expected outcomes from the study are as follows;

- the behavior of the travelers of a particular area
- the current trend of mode competition in the study area
- the effect of new transportation facility on other modes of transport and mode choice of people.
- The percentage of shifting from current available modes to new mode

Objectives:

1) To analyze the travel characteristics of people in the proposed area of study.
2) To identify the factors affecting the mode choice.
3) To develop the mode choice software-based model.
4) To study the effect of introduction of new transportation facility (metro rail) on other modes of transport as well as mode choice of people and their probable willingness to shift to metro.

Data collection is carried out with the help of questionnaire, in the form of responses given by the individuals for the designed questions at the selected places of the study area; mainly targeting the daily travel characteristics of working personnel and students of the study area.

III. Study Area

Study area selected is the central zone of Hyderabad under HMDA, which is sprawling from Kapra to Patancheruvu (East - West) and Jawahar Nagar to Shamshabad (North -

South). Available modes in the study area are 2 wheelers, 4 wheelers, private/institutional buses, auto/paratransit, RTC buses and MMTS.

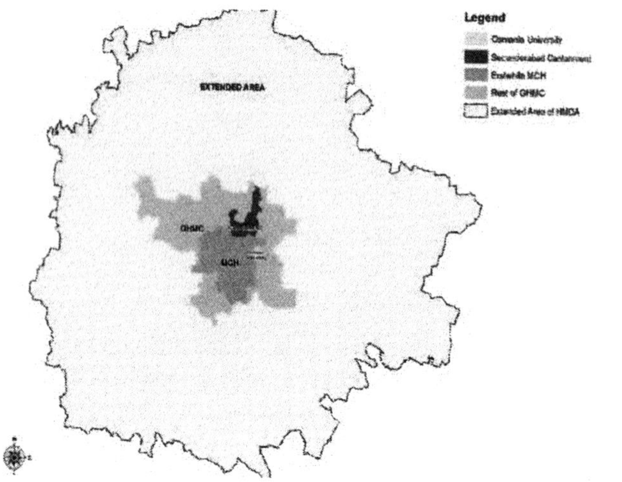

IV. Model Development

Mode Choice Analysis Mode choice analysis allows the modeler to determine what mode of transport will be used, and what modal share results. The flowchart of Mode choice model is shown in figure.

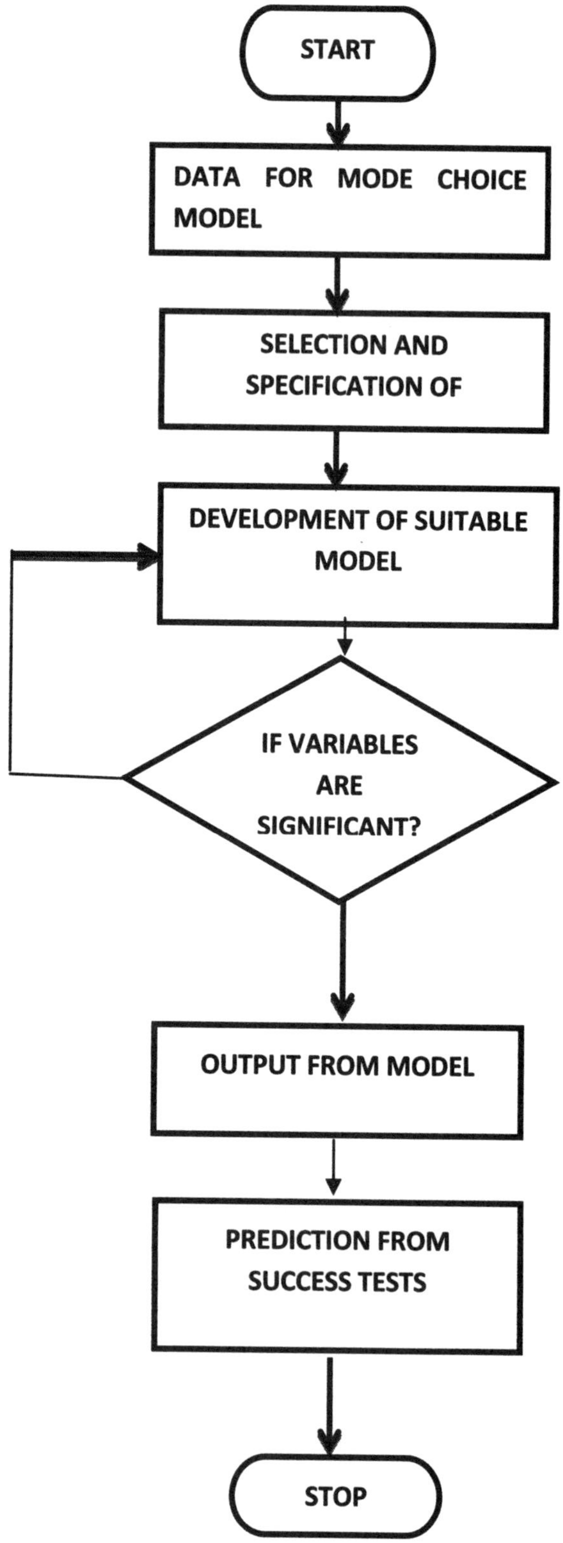

Travel Analysis and their characteristics:

These characters include the personal characters of the passengers who are using different modes to travel from one destination to other destination. The personal characteristics like gender, age, household income, household size, vehicle ownership, purpose of trip, mode used and main mode. From the analysis it is observed that, majority of people prefer travelling by rtc bus (46%) and the second majority preference is to 2 WHEELER (19%) followed by 4 wheelers (15%) for their daily travel activity. while the other modes i.e. MMTS, private/institutional bus, auto/paratransit have a share of 9%, 6%, 5% respectively. Also, most of the people participated in the survey gave more importance to budget over comfort and convenience. It can be inferred that majority of participants of the survey are willing to use metro for their daily travel purpose.

Mode choice analysis is carried out by using ALOGIT (version 3.2, 1992).

Multinomial logit Model (general/present scenario)

MODEL 1

A multinomial logit model has been developed for general/present scenario and the model structure is as shown in the Figure 5.1. The estimated values of variables and others statistics parameters are given in Table. The estimated values of coefficients of defining variables and various statistics are discussed thereafter.

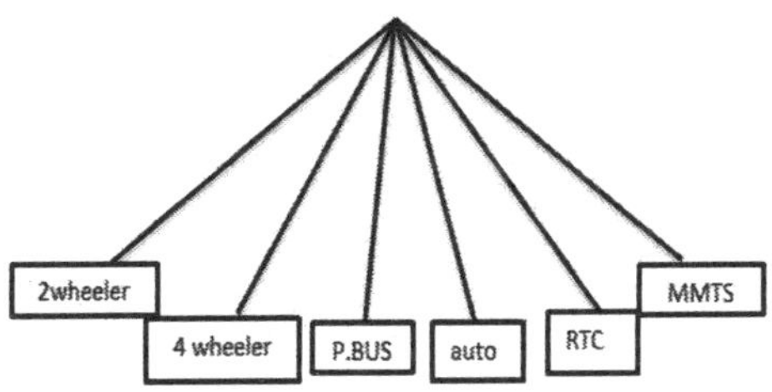

Fig 2 Multinomial logit model (general/present scenario)

Table 1 Statistics for best fit multinomial Logit Model for general/present scenario.

Variables	Coefficient estimate	Relevance of variable
Travel time	$0.3101*10^{-1}$(4.5)	Generic
Travel cost	$-0.1941*10^{-1}$(-2.8)	Generic
gender	0.000	2 wheeler
Vehicle ownership	0.9119(3.1)	4 wheeler
comfort	-2.689(-3.6)	Private/institutional bus(p.bus)
Household size	$-0.2372*10^{-1}$ (-0.1)	Auto/paratransit
Household income	-0.2573(-3.5)	RTC bus
age	1.242(7.1)	MMTS
Structural parameters		
L(0)	-754.3307	
L(c)	-626.7235	
Initial likelihood	-754.3307	
Final likelihood	-560.8217	
ρ^2 with respect to zero	0.252	
ρ^2 with respect to constant	0.1052	

L (0): Likelihood with zero coefficients L(c): Likelihood with constant only

ρ2: Rho-squared statistics

In a Multinomial Model, it is assumed that every available mode has equal preference (i.e. competes individually).

The estimates obtained can be concluded as follows; It can be concluded that the travel time is highly significant than the travel cost and negative value of travel cost indicates that as the travel cost increases utility decreases. It is observed that gender does not have an influence on choice of mode. It is observed that as number of vehicle registrations increases the probability of personal vehicle utility also increases. It is observed that utility of private/institutional bus decreases as more importance is given to budget over comfort. The utility of auto/paratransit increases as the household size decreases. The household income is highly significant as the utility of RTC bus increases as household income decreases. The results of statistical analyses are good. Log likelihood and rho-squared values are indicating goodness-of-fit of the model. (the values of both rho-squared measures lie between 0 and 1, except the difference in log-likelihood values (at convergence) is small $0.1992*10^{-3}$).

Nested logit model (general/present scenario)

MODEL 2

The nested logit structure is the value of the logsum parameter for the nest. The criteria of mode combinations used to define the nested structures is: 1) 2 wheeler, 4 wheeler RTC bus are competing individually. 2) Auto/paratransit, MMTS, private/institutional bus (p.bus) are competing under a nest (i.e they have mutual competion among themselves).

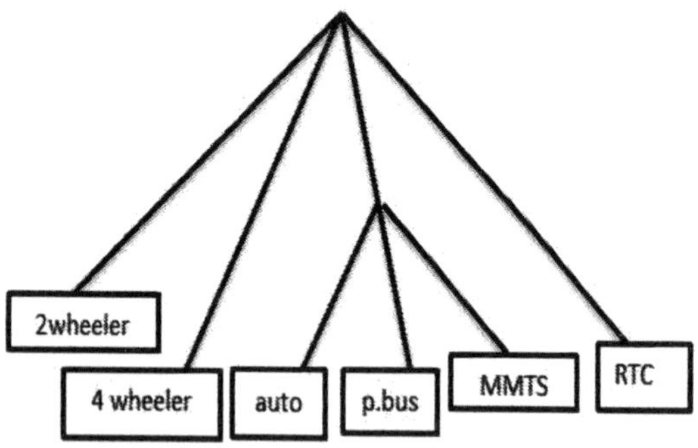

Fig.3 Nested Logit Model

Table 2 Statistics for best fit nested Logit Model for general/present scenario

Variables	**Coefficient estimate**	**Relevance of variable**
Travel time	$0.4527*10^{-1}$(6.7)	Generic
Travel cost	$-0.2524*10^{-1}$(-3.3)	Generic
gender	$0.2491*10^{-1}$(0.1)	2 wheeler
Vehicle ownership	0.8778(2.9)	4 wheeler
comfort	-5.022(-4.9)	Private/institutional bus(p.bus)
Household size	0.2941(0.5)	Auto/para transit
Household income	-0.2619(-3.5)	Rtc bus
age	3.058(5.0)	MMTS
Structural parameters		
L(0)	-754.3307	
L(c)	-626.7235	
Initial likelihood	-560.8217	
Final likelihood	-528.6706	
ρ^2 with respect to zero	0.2992	
ρ^2 with respect to constant	0.1565	
log sum	0.1221(1.9)	

L (0): Likelihood with zero coefficients L(c): Likelihood with constant only
ρ2: Rho-squared statistics

In this model we can observe that gender has shown slight influence on mode choice and suggests that the utility of 2 wheelers is increasing among male respondents. Age is highly significant as the age increases mode choice as MMTS also increases. The log sum value lies between 0.0 - 1.0 which indicates that nested structure is fitting well. This range of values is appropriate for the nested logit model. Log likelihood and rho-squared values are indicating goodness-of-fit of the model. (the values of both rho-squared measures lie between 0 and 1, except the difference in log-likelihood values (at convergence) is small $0.9547*10^{-3}$).

Multinomial model (if Metro is introduced)

MODEL 3

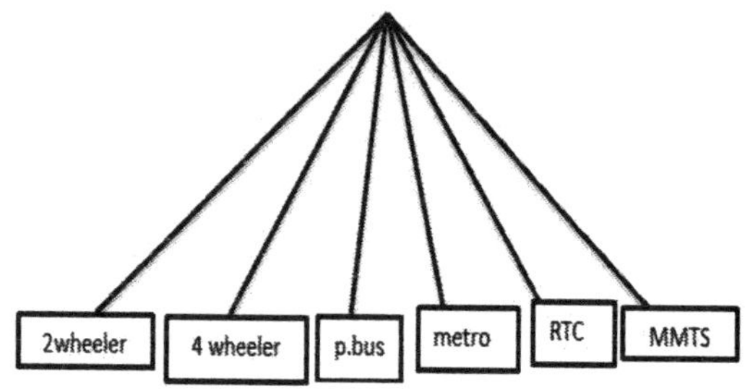

Fig 4 Multinomial logit model(Metro)

Table 3 Statistics for best fit multinomial Logit Model after introduction of metro

Variables	Coefficient estimate	Relevance of variable
Travel time	$0.3542*10^{-1}$(4.9)	Generic
Travel cost	$0.9391*10^{-1}$(0.1)	Generic
gender	0.1138(0.4)	2 wheeler
Vehicle ownership	0.9425(3.2)	4 wheeler
comfort	-2.845(-3.8)	Private/institutional bus(p.bus)
Household income	-0.63874(-3.1)	Metro
Household size	0.4533(4.2)	Rtc bus
Structural parameters		
L(0)	-754.3307	
L(c)	-626.7235	
Initial likelihood	-754.3307	
Final likelihood	-575.588	
ρ^2 with respect to zero	0.237	
ρ^2 with respect to constant	0.0816	

L (0): Likelihood with zero coefficients L(c): Likelihood with constant only
ρ2: Rho-squared statistics
In the above model we are assuming that the utility of auto/paratransit will be completely reduced by introduction of Metro. The estimates obtained show that travel time remains to be significant than travel cost and a smaller value of travel cost indicates that the cost variable no longer influences the mode choice of people. And as the household income decreases the utility of metro is expected to increase. Log likelihood and rho-squared values are indicating goodness-of-fit of the model. (the values of both rho-squared measures lie between 0 and 1, except the difference in log-likelihood values (at convergence) is small $0.5857*10^{-3}$).
Nested logit model (if metro is introduced)
MODEL 4
The criteria of mode combinations used to define the nested structures is: 1) 2 wheeler, 4 wheeler, Metro, private/institutional bus are competing individually. 2) Auto/paratransit, mmtsare competing under a nest (i.e they have mutual competion among themselves).

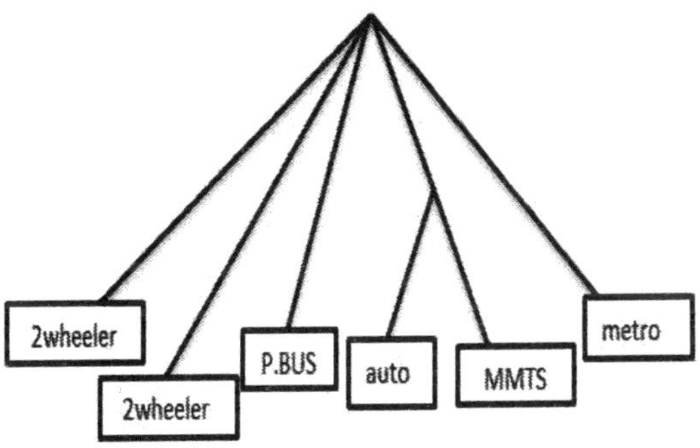

Fig 5 nested logit model (metro)

Table 4 Statistics for best fit Nested Logit Model after introduction of metro

Variables	Coefficient estimate	Relevance of variable
Travel time	$0.4545*10^{-1}$(4.0)	Generic
Travel cost	$-0.8774*10^{-2}$(-0.8)	Generic
gender	$-0.1518*10^{-1}$(-0.1)	2 wheeler
Household income	0.3972(3.4)	4 wheeler
budget	1.436(1.9)	Private/institutional bus(p.bus)
Household size	0.5899(0.8)	Auto
comfort	5.979(7.4)	Metro

Structural parameters		
L(0)	-754.3307	
L(c)	-626.7235	
Initial likelihood	-480.3574	
Final likelihood	-419.5352	
ρ^2 with respect to zero	0.4438	
ρ^2 with respect to constant	0.3306	
logsum	0.1323(4.1)	

L (0): Likelihood with zero coefficients L(c): Likelihood with constant only
ρ2: Rho-squared statistics
In the above model we are substituting the available mode RTC bus by metro. The estimates obtained show that travel time remains to be significant than travel cost and a smaller value of travel cost indicates that the cost variable no longer influences the mode choice of people. And as the desire to have comfortable journey increases among respondents the mode choice as metro also increases. The logsumvalue lies between 0.0 - 1.0 which indicates that nested structure is fitting well. These range of values are appropriate for the nested logit model. Log likelihood and rho-squared values are indicating goodness-of-fit of the model. (the values of both rho-squared measures lie between 0 and 1, except the difference in log-likelihood values (at convergence) is small $0.7183*10^{-2}$).

V. CONCLUSIONS

1. Male participants are more compared to female participants
2. The majority of respondents were fairly spread across age of 19-25yrs.
3. The largest household size of 4 members were participants in the survey.
4. The most popular mode choice for respondents observed from the survey was RTC Bus, with a share of 46%.
5. The use of MMTS for daily travel activity varies, as its availability for respondents is limited and travel time is also more. Only residents close to MMTS network can avail the facility.
6. The willingness to use Metro Rail was highest i.e., 93%.
7. The most preferable access mode to Metro rail station was walk. This implies that most people are willing to have easy access to Metro and are not interested to have multiple shifts to reach Metro station. There is also positive response to special transport facility introduced by metro,

42% of total respondents would prefer to use the facility provided to reach metro station.
8. The travel time is more significant than travel cost and the negative value of travel cost indicates that as travel cost increases utility decreases. When Metro is implemented then the travel cost may become nearly insignificant i.e. the facility is affordable.
9. The mode choice of 2 wheelers for daily travel is high among male respondents,
10. It is observed from model 1,2,4 that, as household size increases, the utility of auto/paratransit increases.
11. It is observed from model 1,2 that as household income decreases the utility of RTC Bus increases and model 4 shows that, as household income increases utility of personal vehicle increases.
12. From model 4, we can infer that metro can be a popular mode choice among small income groups.
13. From model 3, we can infer that the desire to have comfortable journey increases as Metro efficiency increases.
14. The logsum value of Nested Logit Models 2,4 comes out to be less than 1.0 which indicates that nested structure is fitting well.
15. Log likelihood and rho-squared values are indicating goodness-of-fit of the models developed.

VI. Recommendations:

1. Most of the respondents are willing to reach metro station by walk, this implies that residents near to metro network have a higher opportunity to use Metro.
2. For residents away from metro network appropriate awareness of the facilities available to reach Metro station should be given to increase the effectiveness of new transport facility.
3. As majority of people are willing to travel by Metro, increasing the metro capacity and serviceability is advisable.
4.. Incorporating few more factors to modelling process would give a detailed analysis of mode choice behavior.

REFERENCES

[1]. Mark P. DE Guzman (2005)," Analysis of mode choice behavior of students in Exclusive schools in metro manila: the case of Ateneo de manila university & Miriam College" Vol. 5, pp. 1116 - 1131.
[2]. Shlomo Bekhor1," Specification and Estimation of Mode Choice Model Capturing Similarity between Mixed Auto and Transit Alternatives Journal of Choice Modelling", 3(2), pp 29-49,www.jocm.org.uk .
[3]. Tim Schwanen (2005)," What affects commute mode choice: neighborhood physical structure or preferences toward neighborhoods? Journal of Transport Geography", 13 83–99.
[4]. Milimol Philip, "Activity based travel behavioural study and mode choice modelling"
[5]. Frank S. Koppelman and Chandra Bhat, (2006), "A Self Instructing Course in Mode Choice Modeling: Multinomial and Nested Logit Models".
[6]. Sven Muller,(2008), "Travel-to-school mode choice modelling and patterns of school choice in urban areas Journal of Transport Geography" 16 (2008) 342–357.
[7]. Bernetti, G. Longo, G. Tomasella, L Violin, L(2008), "Sociodemographic groups and mode choice in a middle-sized European city", journal of the transportation research Board, Vol.No.2067,17-25.
[8]. Gauthier, H. Land Mitchelson, R.L.(1981), "Attribute importance and mode satisfaction in Travel Mode choice" Economic Geography, Vol.57, 348-361.
[9]. Hsieh, S. Joseph, T. Morrison, M. Chang, S. (1993), "Modelling the Travel Mode Choice of Australian Outbound Travellers" Journal of Tourism studies Vol. 4.
[10]. Limtalakool, N. Dijst and Schwanen, (2006). "The Influence of Socio-Economic Characteristics, land use and Travel time considerations on Mode Choice for Medium and Longer Distance Trips" Journal of transport geography, Vol. 14, 327-341. 59
[11]. Southworth F, (1981), " Calibration of Multinomial Logit Models of Mode and Destination choice", Journal of Transportation Research Board, Vol. 15a, 315-325.
[12]. Lucas, Y. Archilla and Papacostas C.S (2007), "Mode choice Behaviour of Elderly Travellers in Honolulu, Hawaii", Submitted for Presentation at the Transportation Research Board, 86th Annual Meeting (2007) and Publication in the Transportation Research Board.

Evaluation of the Effect of Aggregate Gradation and Binder Parameters on Bituminous Mix Rutting

D.Rajashekar Reddy[1]

[1]*Associate Professor, Civil Engineering Department,*
University College of Engineering, Osmania University, Hyderabad, India
dudipalars@yahoo.com

***Abstract*—Bituminous pavements are composed of three components: aggregate, binder, and air. In the process of plant production and on site construction, the construction quality can vary in the three components and the variability can further affect a pavement's future performance. This research identifies aggregate gradation, binder content, and air voids content as the fundamental parameters. Understanding the fundamental parameters influence on the Hot Mix Asphalt (HMA) mixture's performance properties can provide valuable information on how to improve the current quality practice. The objective of this study is to investigate how mix gradation, air voids and small range binder content deviation from design binder content can affect, individually and collectively, the performance properties (rutting, cracking, and moisture susceptibility) of asphalt concrete in the context of construction variations**

***Keywords*—Hot Mix Asphalt, Rutting, Gradation, Air voids, Bituminous concrete**

I. Introduction

A. Background

India has a road network with 4.23 million km length of roads. (Source: http://en.wikipedia.org/wiki/Indian_road_network). The National Highways Development Project (NHDP), initiated by Indian Government, is a project to upgrade, rehabilitate and widen major highways in India. Recently NHDP (phase III) was taken up to upgrade about 10,000 km of the existing national highway to four lane facility at an estimated cost Rs. 55,000 crores. This project also aimed at providing the connectivity to the state capitals and connectivity to centres of economic importance covering around 2000 km.

Most of the pavements, currently built in India under national highway development program (NHDP), have bituminous layers with dense bituminous macadam (DBM) and bituminous concrete (BC) as binder and wearing courses respectively. Rutting and fatigue cracking are the most common distresses observed on several sections. This indicates that the bituminous mixtures currently being used are inadequate for heavy axle loads, high tire pressures and climatic conditions generally encountered in India. To improve rutting and fatigue performance of bituminous mixes, it is necessary to have a clear understanding of the characteristics of binder and mixes.

Performance of the bituminous mixes can be defined by their ability to resist permanent deformation, fatigue cracking, moisture induced damage, thermal cracking, and the mixture's overall stiffness. Aggregate gradation can affect all these and other properties such as skid resistance, field constructability, and the asphalt binder aging characteristics. Designing a bituminous mixture to meet the needs of a particular paving project requires careful selection of the aggregate and bitumen to be used. An appropriate bitumen grade and content must be selected. A compatible aggregate source and gradation must also be chosen to meet the needs of the project. All four properties will affect the overall performance of the bituminous mixture.

Bituminous mixture is composed of approximately 95%, by weight, or 80%, by volume, mineral aggregate. Therefore it is important to see how aggregate gradation can affect the fundamental properties of bituminous mixture.

Two mechanisms are involved in the formation of rutting: traffic densification and material lateral movement. Densification in a layer occurs in the first few summers after opening to traffic and the degree of densification depends on the initial compaction level. The lateral movement of material is related to the shear resistance of a bituminous mixture material. The rutting performance of a bituminous mixture depends not only on the properties of the aggregates and binder, but also on how these materials interact in the mixture. Rutting in bituminous mixes is controlled by the characteristics of the binder and aggregates and their interaction

B. Problem Statement

Majority of the roadways in India are flexible pavements. Rutting is the most serious concern as it affects the serviceability and safety of the road. Not only that, reducing the potential of rutting development will have enormous economic benefits due to reduction of maintenance costs and extension of the service life of the roadway.In spite of following IRC type pavement design practices and MORTH specifications, many of the bituminous surfaces have started showing premature signs of distresses (MORTH, 2013). And majority of the roadway in India fails by rutting. Superpave uses binder parameter according to rutting susceptibility at high pavement temperatures. National Co-operative Highway Research Program (NCHRP) also uses different mix parameters to control rutting. In this context, it is necessary to recheck the existing rutting controlling parameters and to think of a new parameter which can explain rutting more reliably.

II. Objective

The main objective of the study is evaluation of the effect of aggregate gradation and binder parameters on rutting of bituminous mixes commonly used in India.

1. To evaluate the effect of aggregate gradations on bituminous mix rutting.
2. Evaluation of various rutting parameters for binders to identify the most appropriate binder parameter that can be used to control mix rutting (in India).

III. Literature Review

A. *Literature Background*

Indian road transportation infrastructure is rapidly expanding with the ambitious development of road networks under National Highways Development Programme (NHDP), State Highways Improvement Programmes, etc. The fast growing Indian economy will further demand for road transport network with a high quality pavement structure as the main corridors are required to cater to very heavy traffic-both in terms of number and axle loading. While these road development projects help in adding considerable infrastructural assets, their construction and subsequent maintenance phases require huge amount of suitable pavement materials.

Currently, majority of the Indian roads are flexible pavements since these are less expensive with regard to initial investment and maintenance. Flexible pavements are so named because the total pavement structure deflects, or flexes, under loading. A flexible pavement structure is typically composed of several layers of materials. Each layer receives the loads from the above layer, spreads them out, and then passes on these loads to the next layer below. A typical flexible pavement structure consists of the surface course and the underlying base and sub-base courses. Surface course is the top layer which comes in contact with the traffic. It may be composed of one or several different HMA sub-layers. Base course is the layer directly below the HMA layer and generally consists of aggregates. Subbase course is the layer under the base layer.

There are many kinds of pavement distresses but most of the roads in India fail by rutting and fatigue cracking. Fatigue cracking occurs due to repeated traffic loading. Rutting is surface depression in the wheel path. There are two basic types of rutting: structural or subgrade rutting and non-structural or mix rutting. Mix rutting occurs when the subgrade does not rut yet the pavement surface exhibits wheel path depressions. Subgrade rutting occurs when the subgrade exhibits wheelpath depressions due to loading. In this case, the pavement settles into the subgrade ruts causing surface depressions in the wheelpath.

As the pavement temperature in India goes as high as 60°C, HMA at the top of pavement layer softens and under the wheel load pavement, shows HMA rutting. There are binder parameters (Superpave) as well as mix parameters (NCHRP) to control the rutting phenomenon of HMA. Though flexible pavements are practiced according to existing IRC guidelines and MORTH, pavements are showing failure by rutting at a premature stage indicating problem in mix design. So, to improve rutting performance of bituminous mixes, it is necessary to have a clear understanding of the characteristics of binders and mixes to recheck the existing parameters for controlling rutting and reconfirm in Indian context. In the following sections of this chapter a brief review of literature has been presented on the parameters of both binder and the mix which are used for controlling rutting.

B. *Binder Parameter*

The test carried out for controlling rutting is dynamic shear rheometer (DSR). Two parameters G* (complex shear modulus) and δ (phase angle), are found out from the test conducted at different temperatures and frequencies. Super pave binder specification uses the parameter G*/Sin (δ) to specify binders according to rutting susceptibility at high pavement temperatures. This parameter is measured using a dynamic shear rheometer (DSR), which subjects a sample of binder placed between two parallel plates to oscillatory shear. Tests are performed on both fresh binder and aged binder. The binder parameter G*/Sin (δ) is based on dissipated energy. With each cycle of loading, the work done in deforming an asphalt or an asphalt pavement at high temperatures is partially recovered by the elastic component of the strain and partially dissipated by the viscous flow component of the strain and any associated generation of heat.

A number of researchers have carried out studies on identifying a binder parameter for explaining the rutting behaviour of the binders. Leahy and Quintus (1994) studied the effect of binders on rutting performance of bituminous mixes. The results indicated that the G*/sin (δ) has a weak relationship with the results obtained from the wheel track and shear test. Bahia et al (2001) studied the effect of different rheological parameters for predicting the rutting performance of modified binders. The results indicated that the mixture rutting indicators have a very poor correlation with the G*/sin (δ). Said S. F.(2005) has shown that the stiffness modulus and creep deformation of the bituminous layers can change significantly during the early life of the pavement and this change should be considered in performance specifications and pavement analysis.

D'Angelo et al (2007) has performed the MSCR test on different types of modified binders and correlated it with the rutting observed in the accelerated load facility sections. The G*/sin (δ) has shown very poor correlation with rutting in bituminous mixes as compared to correlation with non-recoverable creep compliance obtained from MSCR test. The non-recoverable creep compliance obtained at 3200 Pa has shown a better correlation with mix rutting as compared to G*/sin(δ) (D□Angelo et al 2007). At high stress level the non-recoverable creep compliance of bitumen has shown a better correlation with the mix rutting. Knowing the PG grade as determined by G*/sin (δ) or with Jnr value at a lower stress level, it does not guarantee that the binder will resist rutting under heavy traffic loading conditions (Reinke, 2010).

Kumar and Veeraragavan (2011) studied the influence of aging on the rheological properties of modified asphalt binders and the influence of temperature and aging on the rutting resistance of modified asphalt mixes. It was observed from aging and rutting indices that rubber modified asphalt binder is more susceptible to aging than unmodified asphalt binder. Modification of asphalt binder and aging has significant influence on the rheological properties and rutting characteristics of asphalt binders and mixes. The non-recoverable creep compliance (Jnr) obtained from MSCRT is a better alternative to replace the G*/sin(δ) for the prediction of rutting since it differentiates binders having penetrations, softening points or G*/sin(d) in the same range (Dreessen et al,2009). G*/sin(d) specifications are based on the testing of unmodified binders, so these are not effective for evaluating the rutting performance of modified binders(D□Angelo,2010). Also studies have shown that compared to zero shear viscosity, the multiple stress creep recovery value of the binder is very useful tool for predicting the creep performance of modified binders (Zoorob et al, 2012)

C. Mix Parameter

Mix. parameter used for rutting is determined from the Simple Performance Test (SPT). For linear viscoelastic material, such as HMA mixes, the stress-to-strain relationship under constant sinusoidal loading is defined by complex dynamic modulus (E*). It relates stress to strain for linear viscoelastic materials subjected to continuous sinusoidal loading in the frequency domain.

The AASHTO new "Mechanistic Empirical Pavement Design Guide" includes a procedure for predicting asphalt pavement permanent deformation (rutting). A joint research study was undertaken to develop rutting resistance criteria for SuperpaveTM (Superpave) and other asphalt mixes. The study used the new Simple Performance Test (SPT) and an accelerated laboratory wheel rutting resistance test. The SPT is included in AASHTO 2002 as a means of asphalt mix characterization. The SPT□s were performed using the University of Waterloo□s Interlaken asphalt and soil testing apparatus.

Vivar and Haddock (2006) studied the pavement performance in term of rutting. The dynamic modulus was used as a measure of HMA performance and durability. HMA mixture samples were tested in both unconditioned and conditioned states. Two types of specimen conditioning were used for the study, moisture and air with varying air void. For moisture conditioning, the samples were partially saturated and placed in a 60°C water bath for 24 hours prior to testing.

Conditioning in air was completed by placing the specimens in an 85°C forced draft oven for 5 days prior to testing. Moisture conditioning tends to promote moisture damage, thereby enabling the decrease in performance and durability due to this damage to be quantified by the dynamic modulus. Rutting was measured by the Purdue laboratory wheel tracking device (PurWheel). In this test, load is applied with a pneumatic tire typically inflated to produce a contact pressure of 0.69 MPa. Prior to testing, the samples were conditioned in the water at the test temperature for 20 minutes. During the test, the computer records the number of wheel passes, the deformation and the elapsed test time. The test ends automatically when a 20 mm rut depth is reached or 20,000 wheel passes are applied, whichever occurs first.

It was found that air voids contents provided the highest differences in dynamic modulus values. Frequency did not appear to be significant. However, in some cases, the change in air voids content does appear to increase the moisture damage. For lower frequency the correlation of stiffness rut factor and rutting was good for air void 4% for air conditioned sample. But for moisture conditioned sample, correlation factor was as low as 0.48.

According to Roberts et al. (1996), rutting can be reduced by increasing the voids in the mineral aggregate, establishing minimum and maximum air voids contents, limiting the amount of natural sand, establishing a minimum percentage of crushed coarse and fine aggregates, using stiffer binder, or by the use of coarser mixture gradations.

Fred (1967) reported that aggregate gradation appeared to have more influence than aggregate type. He also concluded that the temperature susceptibility characteristics of the asphalt appear to have more influence at longer time of loading. Bitumen binders are visco-elastic materials whose resistance to deformation under load is very sensitive to loading time and temperature (Ramond et al., 1999). The bitumen viscosity directly affects the strength of bituminous concrete in compression (rutting) for the practical range of temperatures. The log of pavement resistance and of cohesion varies directly with the log of asphalt viscosity. Modulus of elasticity in compression was influenced by the type of asphalt, temperature and amount of lateral confinement (William et al., 1967). Brown and Snaith (1974) suggested that the increase in deformation is related to the decrease in binder viscosity at high temperatures, thereby leading to a lower interlock between the aggregates. The contribution of the aggregate skeleton towards the behaviour of the mixture becomes more significant at higher temperatures.

IV. SUMMARY

It is seen from the literature that significant amount of research has been carried out on the performance of bituminous pavements and climate parameters on the performance. Bituminous binder, being a key constituent of the mix, has significant influence on the performance of the mix. Parameter obtained from rheological evaluation of the binders using dynamic shear rheometer (DSR) over a wide range of temperature and frequency are being used to study rutting performance of bituminous mix.

Rutting occurring in the bituminous layers has been considered as a major distress in bituminous pavements especially when subjected to high temperatures and heavy axle load. Repeated load test (flow number) is the commonly adopted parameter for evaluation of the permanent deformation characteristics of bituminous mix. From the above literature, it appears that MSCR test better represents the rutting potential of the modified binders compared to other binder parameters. The review of the literature presented in the chapter has been useful in identifying the critical bituminous procedures and understanding the effect of different bituminous mix parameters, traffic loading and climatic parameters on the performance of asphalt pavement. The review is also useful for selecting appropriate test procedures for evaluating the characteristics of binders and mixes.

References

[1] Bahia, H.U., Hanson, D.I., Zeng, Zhai, H., Khatri, M.A., Anderson, R.M (2001), "Charecterization of modified binders in Superpave mix design" Transportation Research Board, Washington D.C

[2] D'angelo J., Kluttz R., Dongre R., Stephens K. and Zanzotto L (2007). "Revision of the Superpave high temperature binder specification: The Multiple Stress Creep Recovery Test", Journal of Association of Asphalt Paving Technologists, Vol. 76, pp. 123-162

[3] D'angelo J. (2010). "New high-temperature binder specification using multiple stress creep and recovery", Transportation Research Circular E-C147, pp. 1-13

[4] Dressen S., Planche J.P.and Gardel V (2009). "A new performance related test method for rutting prediction:MSCRT."Advanced Testing and Characterization of Bituminous Materials-Loizos, Partl, Scarpas and AlQuadi (eds), Taylor and Francis Group, ISBN 978-0-41555854-9.

[5] Kumar, S.A. and Veeraragavan, A.(2011), "Rheological and Rutting Characterization of Asphalt Mixes with Modified Binders", Journal of Testing and Evaluation, vol.40,No.1

[6] Leahy R.B., and Quintus H.V. (1994). "Validation of relationship between Specification Properties and Performance", Report No.A-409, Strategic Highway Research Program, Transportation Research Board,Washington D.C

[7] MoRT&H (2013), *Specification for Road and Bridge Works*, 5thEdition, Ministry of Road Transport and Highways, Indian Roads Congress, New Delhi, India.

[8] Said S.F. (2005). "Aging effect of mechanical characteristics of bituminous mixes", Journal of Transportation Research Board, No. 1901, Transportation Research Board of the National Academies, Washington,D.C., 2005, pp. 1–9.

[9] Vivar, E.D. and Haddock, J.E. (2006), "HMA Pavement Performance and Durability", Publication FHWA/IN/JTRP-2005/14. Joint Transportation Research Program, Indiana Department of Transportation and Purdue University, West Lafayette, Indiana.

[10] Zoorob S.e., Castro-Gomes J.P., Oliveira L. A. and O'Connell J(2012)."Investigating the multiple stress creep and recovery bitumen characterisation test," Construction and Building Materials,Vol. 30, pp 734-745.

Project Success Analysis of Contractor Organization Attributes using Regression Model

Balla Bhavani Shankar[1], Asem Ali Ahmed Alshahethi[2], K.L. Radhika[3]

[1,2]Post Graduation Student, [3]Associate Professor

Department of Civil Engineering, University College of Engineering, Osmania University, Hyderabad, India

Abstract—Project success is somewhat ambiguous in construction industry. Different attributes of different stakeholders play a crucial role for success/failure of the projects. One of the main stakeholder is the contractor. So, it is necessary to study about the influence of contractor on construction projects. This study deals with the contractor's organization attributes influencing project success in Indian construction industry. Among the various attributes, a few attributes which are quite experienced by professionals in Indian construction industry are taken. The attributes picked up for this study aretype of projects completed, size of projects completed, length of time in business, experience in region, failure in completion of project, overrun of contract time, overrun of contract cost, record of conflicts and disputes, company size, image of the company, age in business.The level of impact of each attribute is known using Likert scale from a questionnaire survey. Various statistical tests are done at preliminary stage of analysis. Finally a regression model is developed to identify the attributes affecting project success.Image of the company, record of conflicts and disputes and age in business are the attributes of contractor which influence the project success.

Keywords— Attributes, Project success, Indian construction industry, Factor analysis, Regression

I. Introduction

Construction industry is one of the largest contributor to Indian Economy. Many infrastructure projects are being executed. Most of the projects are not properly executed. This is leading to failure of the projects. The failure is not experience not just the execution stage but also during various stages of construction. The stakeholders play a crucial role in project success or failure. One of the most important stakeholder is contractor. Several studies reveal that the contractor's is a very important part of a project.The projects which are completed on time, in budget, and as per specifications described by customer are known as successful projects. The project success is not just dependent on time, cost, and specifications but there are other criteria to be considered. There are many critical factors which impact the success criteria. The factors may be related to management, stakeholder, resources etc. The critical factors vary with the perception of the viewer (professional). Since they are dependent on perception there are infinite number of factors. In past, many studies were done to identify these factors but no study could identify all the factors. So, the scope of the study in this field (project success) is very high.

The project is said to be successful if it meets the principles of time, cost and quality[1]. The iron triangle represents the most accepted criteria (on time, under budget, according to quality) for project success[2].

The importance of the contractor as a main stakeholder is studied in many previous studies. This importance is seen in studies done in selection criteria of the contactor based on his/ her qualification [3, 4].

<u>*Construction industry in India:*</u>

The construction industry was accorded Industrial Concern Status under the Industrial Development Bank of India. Now, the construction industry is the second largest industry, next only to agriculture. Its contribution to the GDP at factor cost in 2006 to 2007 was rupees 1, 96, 555 crores, which is about 6.9% of the country's GDP. It employed 31.46 million personnel comprising both skilled and unskilled workers, technicians, foremen, clerical staff and engineers.

Some of the factors that go against the Indian construction industry are low productivity, the ratio of skilled to unskilled workers, high cost of finance and complicated tax structure, and the presence of mostly small contractor who lack financial and technological backup, have low Technologies, have negligible investment in research and development, and show little regard for systems.A host of factors such as acute housing shortage, upturn in industrial sector, restructuring of State Electricity boards and expansion of power grid will contribute to the growth of the Indian construction industry. There is a big upturn in commercial production, creating a correspondingly big market forcommercial buildings. Factories are being put up at mask and its implication that have been declared as industrial area by State Governments. The concept of tax holiday has given further Boost to establishing factories. There is also a huge market in building residential units for both the private and public sectors. Real estate investment has shot up in recent times due to the tax benefits announced by the government. A lot of housing projects are being undertaken not only in Metropolitan cities but in other major cities has well.

In road sector, the execution of the Golden Quadrilateral and the north south and east west corridor has created a lot of opportunity. Further, work on Pradhan Mantri Gram SadakYojana proposes an investment to the tune of rupees 60000 crores. This will connect to the rural area with certain Habitat strengths. The operation and maintenance of the huge network will spawn extensive opportunity to work in this sector. Public private partnership initiative build operate transfer (BOT) and build own operate transfer (BOOT) Route is proving to be a blessing in disguise for the upgrade of existing airports in the country. Operation and maintenance of these airports are sure to attract bulk investment.

There are 11 Major ports and 163 minor ports in the country at present. The average ship turnaround time is 6 days in India, and this is very high when we compare it to other better managed ports with high class infrastructure in the developed World. For example, the average ship turnaround time in Singapore it just 6 hours. Traffic is expected to increase further, which will throw up a huge potential for investment and construction. This sector is set to grow since development of small ports and inland waterways is a part of the Prime Minister's investment policy decision.

Water and effluent treatment sector is also bound to grow in near future. Already, there is an increase in investment in improvement of Civic facilities in rural and urban areas, in order to improve water supply and address sanitation related problems as envisaged in the Tenth Five Year Plan. There is a plan to link the major rivers of the country, which will bring huge investments into the construction sector. There are many projects in the planning stages to bring water from river to cities through pipelines. Further, enforcement of stringent norms for discharge from Industries under Environmental and Pollution Act will also spur growth in the effluent treatment sector.

The Restructuring of state electricity board, setting up of new substations And switchyards, implementation of accelerated power development and reforms program, and revamping of Transmission lines to reduce Transmission and distribution losses from 35% to 40% to International norms of 8% to 10% are sure to bring Momentum to electrical projects. Privatisation of Transmission and distribution systems with further increase investments.

India suffers from perennial power shortage and there is a huge potential in the field of power, as new additions in power generation capacity are required. National Hydroelectric Power Corporation (NHPC) and Nuclear Power Corporation of India Limited (NPCIL) have plans for huge capacity building in the hydel power sector and nuclear power sector, respectively. In thermal power, large private investments are in the pipeline and a number of independent power producers (IPPs) are in the final stages of financial closure. Also, there are increased investments in captive power plants by large industries in cement, aluminium, sugar, etc.

India has considerable natural gas reserves. There are plans to invest in pipelines to save on transportation costs. Similarly, there is are plans to lay pipelines from ports to refineries to carry crude and finished products to different destinations, apart from projects for expansion of refineries and LNG storage facilities. All these are bound to throw up opportunities in the hydrocarbon sector.

In addition to the above mentioned opportunities, there are promising prospects in bulk materials handling projects. While development of ports would require investment in port-handling equipment, investment in thermal power sector would call for more coal-handling plants, and increased food production would mean more opportunity for grain-handling plant construction.

Here, it must be noted that the indigenous construction industry is bound to face increasing competition from multinational companies. Already, projects including major portions of Delhi Metro, some high-value hydroelectric jobs such as Uri Project, high-tech projects such as Bangalore Infotech project and Chennai Tidel Park project, and power projects such as Enron have seen a major chunk of construction going into the hands of multinational companies. A number of MNCs such as Skanska, Hyundai, Bechtel, Kumi Gumi, Obayashi and Toyo are now operating in India. The future is going to be quite competitive and the domestic companies who can face the challenges posed by the MNCs will emerge stronger.

II. Literature Review

Cheng et al. [5] developed a framework to establish the critical success factors for partnering projects. Effective communication, conflict resolution, adequate resources, management support, mutual trust, long term commitment and coordination, and creativity were identified as critical success factors in this framework. It is concluded that partnering project success can be determined by objective measures and subjective measures.

Iyer and Jha[6] conducted a questionnaire survey on the attributes of the project success in Indian industry. In this survey, the respondents were asked to scale (1-5) the attributes. The attributes were classified into 3 groups based on the mean values of the attributes. The main groups were success attributes and failure attributes, the other group was neglected. Relative Importance Index (RII) was used to rank the attributes. The success attributes and the failure attributes were classified into success factors and failure factors respectively based on the factor analysis. Another questionnaire survey was conducted based on this success factors and failure factors. The stepwise regression model was developed for these factors. Finally, it was concluded that the factor named coordination between project participants is the factor which influences the cost performance in the Indian construction industry.

Doloi et al. [7] initially identified the key factors affecting the delay in construction industry of India and then established the relationship between the critical attributes by developing prediction models. The critical factors of construction delay as lack of commitment, inefficient site management, poor site coordination, improper planning, lack of clarity in project scope, lack of communication, and substandard contract were identified from factor analysis. Finally it was identified that slow decision from owner, poor labour productivity, architects' reluctance for change, and rework due to mistakes in construction are the reasons that influence the project delay

To rank different critical success factors for construction projects in Lithuania, Analytic Hierarchy Process (APH) was used as a tool. For construction projects in Lithuania various CSFs were ranked [8].

Sinesilassie et al. [9] conducted a questionnaire survey in Ethiopian construction industry. The questionnaire survey was designed to assess the impact of the identified 35 project performance attributes on the cost of the project. Target respondents of the survey were engineers involved in public sector projects. Many statistical tests were carried out to determine the success and the failure factors. Finally, through stepwise multiple regression it is found that success factors namely scope clarity, project manager's competence were affecting cost of the project. It was also found that failure factors namely conflict among project participants and projects manager's ignorance, and lack of knowledge were affecting cost performance of the project in the Ethiopian public construction projects.

Palaneeswaran and Kumaraswamy[10] developed a scoring model to assess contractors selection for design-build projects based on a range of criteria established through a knowledge mining process. The model categorizes design/build projects into either simple or complex projects based on an assessment of project attributes. The developed model is also unsatisfactory since it did not establish a relationship between contractor selection criteria and project outcomes.

In previous studies, many different methods were used to identify the factors influencing the project. The factors considered in the study were general factors, they were not related to a particular stakeholder (contractor, client, employees etc). This paper is based on the contractor related critical success factors affecting the project success. The criteria considered for project success are the cost (budget), the time (schedule), and the quality of the project. This study focuses on Indian construction industry.

III. Methodology

A. Identification of critical success factors affecting project success

Firstly, the attributes related to contractor which affect the project success are to be identified. To identify the attributes many professionals in reputed organizations were interviewed. From these interviews certain number of attributes were concluded. It is seen that the professions who had experience in Indian construction projects were only interviewed. Concluded attributes were as follows:

1. Type of projects completed
2. Size of projects completed
3. Length of time in business
4. Experience in region
5. Failure in completion of project
6. Overrun of contract time
7. Overrun of contract cost
8. Record of conflicts and disputes
9. Company size
10. Image of the company
11. Age in business

B. Development of Questionnaire Survey

The questionnaire was designed to assess the influence of the identified 11 attributes on the project success. The first part of the survey consisted of personal details of the respondents. These questions were asked to ensure that the respondent had enough experience in the construction industry. Second part of the questionnaire was the principal part of the questionnaire, and was designed for rating attributes on a Likert scale of 5 (1-strongly disagree, 2-disagree, 3-neutral, 4-agree, and 5-strongly agree). The respondents were invited to rate the influence of each attribute on project success based on their experience. 11 attributes were listed in the questionnaire. The respondents were requested to add any other missing contractor's attributes which affect the project success. This part also had a question which asks the respondent to rate the contractor's influence on project success on Likert scale of 5.

C. Data Analysis

The survey was targeted on the professionals who had experience in Indian construction industry. It was seen that invalid responses were excluded from the analysis. The invalid responses means repeated respondents and responses from the respondents who had no experience in Indian construction industry. The questionnaire was sent to 500 professionals. Finally, 222 responded for this survey. So, the response rate is 44.4%.

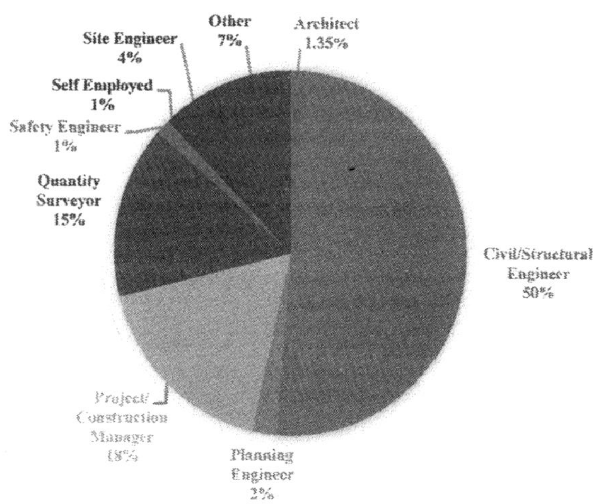

Fig 1. Profile for Profession

In the responses received, highest number of the respondents were of Civil/Structural Engineers category. The second highest percentage of respondents Project/Construction Managers, whose contribution to the survey is 18%. The Quantity Surveyors contributed 15% of the survey. While smaller percentage of respondents were Site Engineers, Planning Engineers, Architects, Safety Engineers, Self Employed and others.Most respondents indicated that they had been in Indian construction industry for a very long time. 34% of respondents were in industry for more than 6 years. Around 50% of the respondents had an industrial experience of 4 years or more.

Most of the respondents were from government organizations. There were respondents even from private organizations. Here, the private organizations include contractors, sub-contractors and consultants.

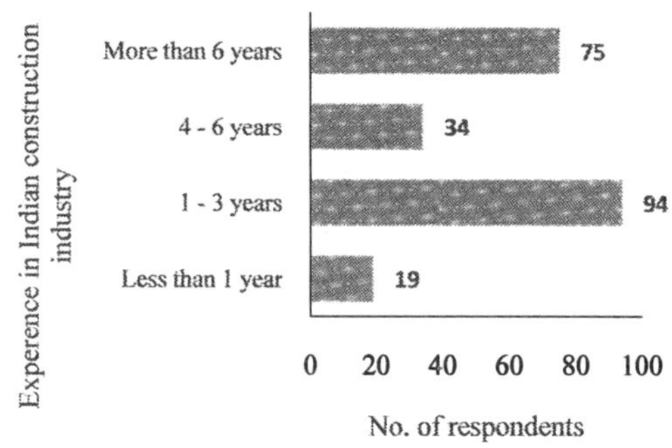

Fig. 2. Profile for Work Experience

In descriptive statistical analysis, there is a need to determine the central tendency or the middle of the distribution. A measure for central tendency for Likert type data is done using mode and median. In this study all the variables were Likert type. So, to measure central tendency mode and median were chosen. The median and mode for many factors were either agree or strongly agree.Since the central tendency was good, it shows that many respondents agree that all the variables considered in the survey are affecting the project success.

Factor Analysis (FA) is a technique which is used to reduce a data set to a more manageable size. In a correlation matrix, the highly correlated factors can be identified. Using FA, variables that are inter correlated can be grouped together so that they can be treated as one combined variable. The Principal Component Analysis can be used to find the factor loadings in the rotated component matrix. If it is found that any variable does not belong to particular group (component) those type of variables can be exempted for further analysis. The factors can also be exempted from analysis if it is found that the factor loadings of the variables in rotated component matrix are not too high.

In this paper, the factor analysis (FA) was done using SPSS 25.0 (Statistical Package for the Social Sciences). Varimax method in factor analysis was used. The Kaiser-Meyer-Olkin Measure (KMO) of Sampling Adequacy and Bartlett's Test results were verified. The KMO measure of adequacy was 0.900 (> 0.5). This shows a good sampling adequacy. The Bartlett's Test of Sphericity showed a low significance which shows that the correlation matrix is not an identity matrix. The determinant of correlation matrix is 0.01. The KMO and Barlett's Test results are shown in

Table I. The Cronbach's Alpha was 0.916. This indicates good internal consistency of the factors.

TABLE I
KMO AND BARTLETT'S TEST

Kaiser-Meyer-Olkin Measure of Sampling Adequacy.		.900
Bartlett's Test of Sphericity	Approx. Chi-Square	1372.699
	df	55
	Sig.	.000

A logistic regression model was developed to determine the most significant attributes influencing the project success. The model was developed in SPSS 25.0. The model was developed with 11 organization attributes as the independent variables and "contractor's influence on project success" as dependent variable.

IV. DISCUSSION OF FACTOR ANALYSIS RESULTS

From factor analysis, the attributes are classified into two factors. The factors are reputation of the organization and past performance of the organization. The total variance explained was 68.623%.

A. *Reputation of the organization*

The variance explained by this factor is 54.506%. There are 7 different attributes in this factor. Reputation is of the important critical success factor in construction projects*[11]*. The image of the firm was an interesting finding that should definitely be considered by the firms in the market*[12]*. However, this factor has attributes image of the company, company size, age in business, size of projects completed, length of projects completed, length of time in business, type of projects completed and experience in region. The image of the company has highest factor loading of 0.820. The experience in the region has the lowest factor loading of 0.698.

B. *Past performance of the organization*

Contractors who completed projects successfully are more likely to achieve project targets in the future[13]. Predictive performance of contractors can be determined by investigating contractors' past performance. High priority should be given to contractors' past time performance since delays in construction projects have significant cost and quality implications[14]. An investigation of past performance might show the owner what a contractor has done in the past. A historical baseline defines an average of past performance [15]. This baseline can be established through the collection of historical data from previous projects. Contractors of high reputation and better past performance will improve client confidence and raise the possibility of future business [16].

TABLE II
FACTOR PROFILE OF CONTRACTOR ATTRIBUTES

Details of factors and attributes	Factor loading	Variance explained
Reputation of the organization		*54.506%*
Image of the company	.820	
Company size	.782	
Age in business	.777	
Size of projects completed	.769	
Length of time in business	.734	
Type of projects completed	.702	
Experience in region	.698	
Past performance of the organization		*14.116%*
Overrun of contract time	.888	
Overrun of contract cost	.881	
Failure in completion of project	.867	
Record of conflicts and disputes	.673	

V. DISCUSSION OF REGRESSION RESULTS

The independent variables used are the attributes resulted from the factor analysis as shown in Table II. Dependent variable is the impact of contractor organization attributes on project success which has been asked separately to every respondent. These attributes are entered into regression model. Thus the stepwise regression model framed to measure the overall impact on project success caused by individual attributes can be expressed generally as

$$Y = a + b_1X_1 + b_2X_2 + \cdots b_mX_m \pm e$$

where Y is dependent variable, a is constant and intercepts at Y axis; b_1 to b_m are estimated regression coefficients; X_1 to X_m are values of predictor or independent variables, e is error.

The final regression model for project success can be expressed as:

$$\textit{Project success due to Contractor Organization Attributes} = 2.025+0.205X+0.178Y+0.162Z$$

where X= image of the company, Y= record of conflicts and disputes and Z= age in business.

The independent variables which are significant in this model are image of the company, record of conflicts and disputes and age in business.

TABLE III
SUMMARY OF STEPWISE REGRESSION MODEL

	Unstandardized Coefficients		Std. Coefficients	t	Sig.
	Estimate	Std. Error			
Constant	2.025	.234		8.638	.000
Image of the company	0.205	.07	.253	2.923	.004
Record of conflicts and disputes	0.178	.062	.204	2.997	.004
Age in business	0.162	.073	.185	2.212	.028

VI. CONCLUSIONS

The organization attributes namely image of the company, record of conflicts and dispute and age in business are the major independent variables (predictors) which influence the project success. Among all these predictors image of the company is the strongest predictor. This predictor's shared and unique contribution to the project success is 4.33% and 3.28% respectively.Record of conflicts and disputes shared and unique contribution is 4.24% and 3.2%. So, the influence of this predictor on the project success is somewhat close to image of the company. Therefore, both the predictors namely image of the company and record of conflicts and disputes have good impact on project success. It is finally the reputation of the contractor's organization which has some good impact on project success in Indian construction industry as 2 out of 3 attributes related to this factor are the most significant ones in the regression model developed.

References

[1] A. Diallo and D. Thuillier, "The success of international development projects, trust and communication: An African perspective," International Journal of Project Management, vol. 23, no. 3, pp. 237-252, 2005.

[2] R. Atkinson, "Project management: cost, time and quality, two best guesses and a phenomenon, it's time to accept other success criteria," International Journal of Project Management, vol. 17, no. 6, pp. 337-342, 1999.

[3] D. Sing and R. L. K. Tiong, "Contractor selection criteria: Investigation of opinions of Singapore construction practitioners," Journal of Construction Engineering and Management, vol. 132, pp. 998-1008, 2006.

[4] Doloi, "Analysis of pre-qualification criteria in contractor selection and their impacts on project success," Construction Management and Economics, vol. 27, pp. 1245-1263, 2009.

[5] E. W. L. Cheng, H. Li and P. E. D. Love, "Establishment of critical success factors for construction partnering," Journal of Management in Engineering, ASCE, vol. 16, no. 2, pp. 84-92, 2000.

[6] K. C. Iyer and K. N. Jha, "Factors affecting cost performance: evidance from Indian construction projects," International Journal for Project Management, vol. 23, pp. 283-295, 2005.

[7] H. Doloi, A. Sawhnew, K. C. I. Iyer and S. Rentala, "Analysing factors affecting delays in Indian construction projects," International Journal of Project Management, vol. 30, no. 4, pp. 479-489, 2012.

[8] N. Gudiene, A. Banaitis, V. Podvezko and N. Banaitene, ", Identification and evaluation of the critical success factors for construction projects in Lithuania: AHP approach," Journal of Civil Engineering and Management, vol. 20, no. 3, pp. 350-359, 2014.

[9] E. G. Sinesilassie, S. Z. S. Tabish and K. N. Jha, "Critical factors affecting cost performance: A case of Ethiopian public cpnstruction projects," International Journal of Construction Management, Taylor & Francis, 2017.

[10] E. Palaneeswaran and M. Kumaraswamy, "Recent advances and proposed improvements in contractor prequalification methodologies," Building and Environment, vol. 36, pp. 73-87, 2001.

[11] V. Sanvido, F. Grobler, M. Parfitt, M. Guvenis and M. Coyle, "Critical success factors for construction projects," Journal of Construction Engineering and Management, vol. 118, no. 1, pp. 94-111, 1992.

[12] M. Egemen and A. N. Mohamed, "Clients' needs, wants and expectations from contractors and approach to the concept of repetitive works in the Northern Cyprus construction market," Building and Environment, vol. 41, no. 5, pp. 602-614, 2006.

[13] G. D. Holt, P. O. Olomolaiye and F. C. Harris, "Evaluating prequalification criteria in contractor selection," Building and Environment, vol. 29, no. 4, pp. 437-448, 1994.

[14] F. Khosrowshahi, "Neural network model for contractors' prequalification for local authority projects," Engineering, Construction and Architectural Management, vol. 6, no. 3, pp. 315-328, 1999.

[15] R. F. Cox, R. R. A. Issa and D. Ahrens, "Management's perception of key performance indicators for construction," Journal of Construction Engineering and Management, vol. 129, no. 2, pp. 142-151, 2000.

[16] H. Xiao and D. Proverbs, "Factors influencing contractor performance: an international investigation," Engineering, Construction and Architectural Management, vol. 10, no. 5, pp. 322-332, 2003.

[17] A guide to the project management body of knowledge (PMBOK guide), Project Management Institute, 2000.

[18] K. Jha and K. Iyer, "Commitment, coordination, competence and the iron triangle," International Journal of Project Management, vol. 25, pp. 527-540, 2007.

Factors Affecting Cost Estimation:A Case from Yemen Construction Projects

Asem Ali Ahmed Alshahethi[1], Balla Bhavani Shankar[2], K.L. Radhika[3]

[1,2]Post Graduation Student, [3]Associate Professor

Department of Civil Engineering, University College of Engineering, Osmania University, Hyderabad, India

[1]first.author@first.edu

[2]second.author@second.com

[3]third.author@third.edu

***Abstract*—This paper presents the findings of a questionnaire survey conducted on the factors affecting cost estimation of Yemen construction projects. The significance of this study lies in its major role in putting the project into action or cancelling it when coming to cost prediction and estimation. Thus, the main aim of this research is to determine the main factors affecting cost estimation of construction projects. Factor analysis of the response on the 39 factors identified through literature review and personal interview extracted twelve factors. The most critical factors obtained by the analysis are: consumer price index, cost of construction materials, type of building, market conditions, structural system, site area, type of slab, other supplementary buildings, location of the project, project size, type of foundation, building closeness, and fluctuation in the currency. Furthermore, analysis indicates a good indicator among project participants as the most significant of all factors having maximum influence on cost estimation.**

***Keywords*—Cost, Factor Analysis, Relative Important Index, Questionnaire survey, Yemen construction projects,**

I. Introduction

Inaccurate prediction of project cost causes overrun cost in the construction. To estimate the cost with high accuracy, traditional methods, Monte Carlo, fuzzy logic, and regressions have done. Due to the disadvantages for using these methods and techniques the error is unacceptable, traditional approach it is difficult and inadequate, fuzzy logic is not primarily empirical models, regression assumes that the relationships between the cost and drivers (inputs) are linear whereas the relationships between the cost of construction and factors influencing the cost is nonlinear, therefore the product is less accurate and far from reality. Genetic algorithm and neural networks have been done to address the demerits and reduce the margin error, stable output and good processing speed, to develop a stable predictive cost models for building works.

Conceptual stage contains estimating the cost and value engineering because they are very important to success the project and overcome the overrun budget. To be able to estimate it requires experience and applying different methodologies such as Magnitude Estimate, Square-Foot Estimate, Assembly or Systems Estimate. If the estimation is prepared carefully, there will not be much difference in the estimated cost and actual cost. Traditional methods are prepared and applied for prediction of the communication projects costs, the result was more error, and lake of precision and uncertainty, regression is offered better result and address the disadvantages[1]. Construction management and cost engineering have made tremendous advances to address overrun and delay, minimizing uncertainties, productivity estimation. Predicting ability despite the non-uniform distribution and incompleteness data[2]. A few techniques such as regression, and traditional methods, artificial neural network technique is utilized for predicting costs in various construction projects, which address the problems to enable the estimator of cost predicting accurate cost in construction building projects.

The resource requirement is obtained, the estimate to complete each of these can be prepared based on the unit cost of the resources and the total units of the resources required. This process is called cost planning and it is a must for project cost management. The essential components of a cost plan are the project schedule and estimates. Cost planning aims at ascertaining cost before many decisions are made related to the design of a facility. It provides a statement of the main issues, identifies the various courses of action, determines the cost implications of each course, and provides a comprehensive economic picture of the project. The planner and the quantity surveyor should be continuously questioning whether it is giving value for money or whether there is any better way of performing the particular function.

At the detailed design stage, final decisions are made on all matters relating to design, specification, construction and others. Every part of the facility must be comprehensively designed and its cost checked. Where the estimated cost exceeds the cost target, either the element must be redesigned or other cost target reduced to make more money available for the element in question – through all this, the overall project cost limit must remain unaltered.

The planner and estimator should be continuously examining the cost aspects throughout the design process, and keep asking certain typical question – "Is a particular feature, material, or component really giving value for money?" Is there a better alternative?" Is a certain item of expenditure really necessary?" Cost planning establishes needs, sets out the various solutions and their cost implications, and finally produces the probable cost of the project while maintaining a sensible balance between cost on one hand and quality, utility and appearance on the other.

II. Literature Review

This section of paper provides a review of relevant literature of predicting the cost in construction projects by using the artificial neural networks method, regression, and genetic algorithm. Several studies have used different techniques for predicting the cost for buildings, highways, productivity, infrastructure and civil construction. Summaries of important conclusions of previous studies.Table Ishows the important factors in the previous studies that affect the construction projects cost [3-9]. This article reviews journals in the field of construction engineering and management.

TABLE I
Summary of Studies in the Factors Affecting Construction Project Cost

Author Name	Summary of the cost factors (cost drivers)
Shehatto [3]	Area of typical floor, number of floors in the building, area of retaining walls type of building, type of used foundation in the building, number of elevators in the building, type of slab (solid, ribbed), length of spans between columns, number of columns, number of rooms, location of project, number of staircases in the building and type of contract.
AL-Zwainy, Rasheed, & Ibraheem [4]	Age, experience, number of the labor, height of the floor, size of the marbles tiles, the security conditions, the health status for the work team, weather conditions, site condition, availability of construction materials
Al-Zwainy & Hadhal [5]	Site area, foundation types, section type, availability of materials variation orders, method of assembling, quality of planning and control experience of contractor, tower high, quality of works, holidays and emergency events, construction method, main cable, market condition, cost of construction materials and efficient of cost management
Aibinu, Dassanayake, & Thien [6]	Class of contractor, project size, project type, client type, working time (8–12) hours, working shifts (12–24) hours, sub-contractor(s) nature firm(s) need for work, auditing process period, labor turnover, percentage of rejected submittals, special construction engineering requirements, wages of labors, type of contract, execution errors, contractor(s) – joint venture new construction techniques
El-Kholy [7]	Financial condition of the owner, cash flow of contractor, method of procurement (open tender or selective tender), material cost increase due to inflation, competition at tender stage (aggressive or not), fluctuations in the currency that the payment will be made, project size (small or large), risk retained by client for quantity variations, delay in design and approval, drawings (detailed or not), inaccurate material estimating
Al-Tabtabai & A. [8]	Changes in owning cost, change in labour price rates, change in material price rates, change in quantity, change in labour productivity, change in operating cost
Alqahtani & Whyte [9]	Roof repair, internal cleaning, laundry, gas expenditure, electricity expenditure fuel oil expenditure, management fees, porterage, rates, insurance, decoration internal

TABLE II
COST FACTORS AFFECTING IN CONSTRUCTION (BUILDING) PROJECTS

Group Name	Number	Cost Factor
General Factors	1	Location of the Project
	2	Site Area
	3	Site Conditions
	4	Type of the Building
	5	Project Size
	6	Building Closeness (Attached, Semi-attached, Separate)
	7	Other Supplementary Buildings (W. Tank, Administration, Warehouse, etc.)
	8	Area of Typical Floor
	9	Weather Conditions (rainy, sunny, cloudy, windy etc.)
	10	Site Accessibility
Engineering related Factors	11	Type of Slab (Solid, Ribbed, Flat, etc.)
	12	Number of Floors
	13	Type of Foundation
	14	Length of span between columns
	15	Construction Methods
	16	Number of columns
	17	Number of Staircase and Elevators
	19	Drawings (detailed or not)
	20	Geo-technical natural of soil
	21	Structural Design Loads
Resource Related Factors	22	Market Conditions
	23	Cost of Construction Materials
	24	Availability of Resources (Human, Financial, Raw Material, Facilities)
	25	Cement Price
	26	Labors Price
	27	Reinforcement Price
	28	Availability of Required Power
Special Factors	29	Type of Contract
	30	Experience of Contractor
	31	Quality of the Work
	32	Time of Completion of the Project
	33	Applying Safety System
External Factors	34	Fluctuation in the Currency
	35	Corruption
	36	General Economy
	37	Import Price
	38	Changing Laws by the Government
	39	Inflation

III. METHODOLOGY

A. Identifying Factors affecting in construction cost

To identify the main parameters affecting cost of building projects in Yemen. The first set of factors was previously concluded in the literature review done and personal interviews as Table II.

B. Questionnaire Survey

A questionnaire is a research instrument consisting of a series of questions and other prompts for the purpose of gathering information from respondents. Although they are often designed for statistical analysis of the responses, this is not always the case. A structured questionnaire in addition to expert interviews were used together in this research, (39) Cost factors were predetermined. The questionnaire was based on a qualitative five-point scale to facilitate the answering process to recipients. Each recipient was asked to determine both "the impact" for each factor, in accordance with their experience-based judgment. This scale varies from "very low to very high". Where, "very low" means that this factor has a very weak effect on cost and the factor existed scarcely or changeability rarely happen, and "low" means that this factor has a weak effect on cost but might be existed or changed. However, "moderate" means that this factor has a medium effect on cost and has 50%/50% to be existed or changed, whilst "high" means that this factor has a huge effect on cost and frequently existed and changeable. Finally, "very high" means that this factor has a drastic effect on cost and there is no doubt of its existence no changeability.

C. Data Analysis

This part illustrates the procedure and results of the analysis the data that aims to identify the most important cost factors, that are expected to affect the construction projects costs in Yemen. A questionnaire survey was prepared and distributed, (192) respondents were replied by online and manual, (47) respondents are rejected due the data and information is uncomplimentary. The data of (145) respondents is used and analyzed throughout a statistical package for the social sciences (SPSS 23) program.. 39 items to be analyzed in five groups namely A, B, C, D, and E, the items shall restrict my discussion to Likert scales. The items on a Likert scale consist of statements with which respondents are expected to differ with respect to the extent to which they agree with them. I have used 5 - points optical scanning responses forms in my research namely, very low, low; moderate, high, and very high.

-Figure 1 shows the classification of one hundred and forty -five to their party. It was found to have 17 project managers, 5 contractors, 109 civil engineers, 12 architecture engineers, 2 electrical and geology engineers. It is obvious that civil engineer's representative the majority and the highest participants due to all civil engineers understand the questionnaire and they have the knowledge more than the other participants. On the other side the project managers were more helpful than contractors, because they know the most factors that affect in construction project costs and they are preparing the bidding and award of the construction projects.

-Figure 2 illustrates the previous experience in construction projects that respondents have. The classification indicates that about 16% recipients have experience above than 20 years, about 26% recipients have experience between 10 to 20 years, about 12% recipients have experience from 6 to 10 years, and about 45% have experience less than 5 years.

Reliability Analysis

-Cronbach's alpha is the most common measure of internal consistency ("reliability"). It is most commonly used when you have multiple Likert questions in a survey/questionnaire that form a scale and you wish to determine if the scale is reliable. Table III shows the Cronbach's alpha is 0.889, which indicates a high level of internal consistency for our scale in a questionnaire.

Relative Importance Index analysis

The Relative Importance Index (RII) was employed. Relative Importance Index or weight is a type of relative importance analyses. RII was used for the analysis because it best fits the purpose of this study. According to Johnson and LeBreton[10], RII aids in finding the contribution a particular variable makes to the prediction of a criterion variable both by itself and in combination with other predictor variables. In the calculation of the Relative Importance Index (RII), the formula below was used.

$$\text{RII} = (W/\,A^*\,N) = \frac{\sum 1*n1+2*n2+3*n3+4*n4+5*n5}{5*N}$$

where w is the weight given to each factor by the respondents and range from 1 to 5, A is the highest weight (i.e., 5 in this case), and N is the total of respondents (i.e., 145 in this case).

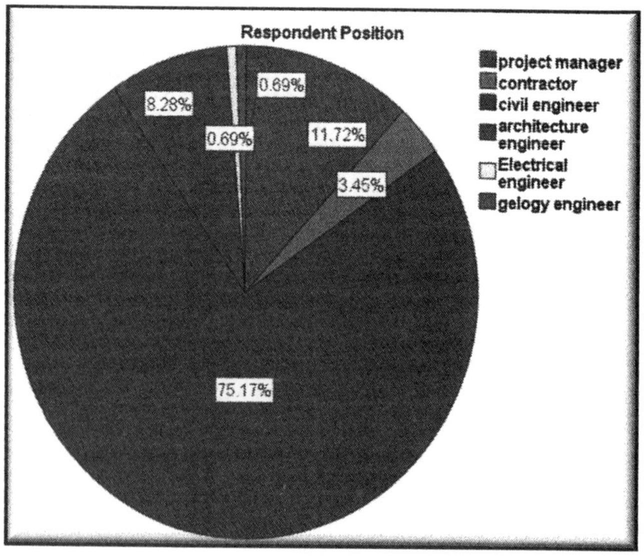

Figure 1: Classifications of Respondents Position

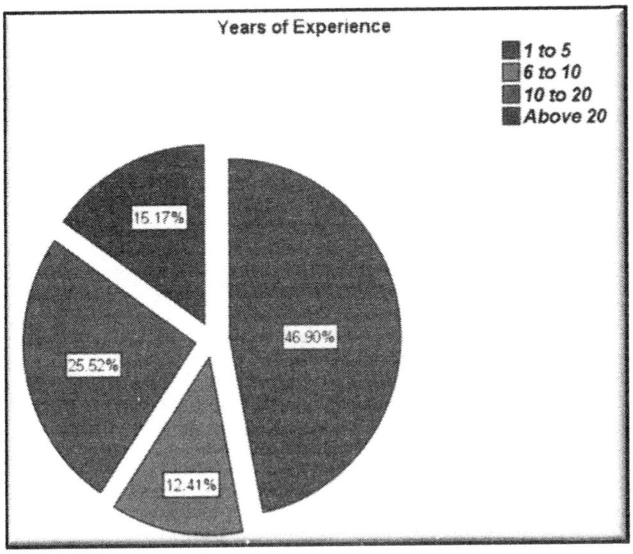

Figure 2: Classification of Respondents Experience

Factor Analysis

The Factor Analysis is an explorative analysis. Much like the cluster analysis grouping similar cases, the factor analysis groups similar variables into dimensions. This process is also called identifying latent variables. Since factor analysis is an explorative analysis it does not distinguish between independent and dependent variables.

Factor Analysis reduces the information in a model by reducing the dimensions of the observations. This procedure has multiple purposes. It can be used to simplify the data, for example reducing the number of variables in predictive regression models. If factor analysis is used for these purposes, most often factors are rotated after extraction. Factor analysis has several different rotation methods—some of them ensure that the factors are orthogonal. Then the correlation coefficient between two factors is zero, which eliminates problems of multicollinearity in regression analysis.

TABLE III
KMO AND BARTLETT'S AND RELIABILITY TEST

KMO and Bartlett's Test		
Kaiser-Meyer-Olkin Measure of Sampling Adequacy		0.774
Bartlett's Test of Sphericity	Approx. Chi-Square	2197.204
	df	741
	Sig.	.000

The KMO and Bartlett's test is shown above in the Table III that measures the adequacy of the 39 samples in this research. The result equals 77.4%, therefore the sample is adequate to be analyzed and factor analysis processing.

IV. RESULTS AND DISCUSSIONS

From descriptive and relative important indices analysis, the factors are classified and ranked as shown in Table IV. Depending upon the mean scores of responses, the factors were then segregated in four groups: the first group ($\mu \geq 4$) that showed very high impact; the second group ($4 < \mu \geq 3.5$) that showed high impact; the third group ($3.5 < \mu \geq 3$) that showed neutral impact; and the fourth group ($\mu < 3$) that showed low and very low impact. The results from descriptive analysis are not suitable to assess the overall rankings because they don't reflect any relationship between the factors, thus the relative important index (RII) used for evaluating and ranking overall factors.

From factor analysis, the principle component analysis generated twelve components with eigenvalues greater than 1 explaining 67.834% of the variance. The factor clustering on varimax rotation is shown in Table V, only factors with loading exceeding 0.40 were selected to evaluate the factors patterns. In figure 3 is shown the distribution of 39 cost factors using Eigenvalue and the result shows the minimum factors are 12 corresponding to 1 in the Eigenvalue. 12 cost factors are extracted and rotated after (58) iteration and 67% accumulative variance. In Table V is shown the 12 factors with extraction sums of squared loadings and rotation sums of squared loadings, also in rotation matrix is explained the relation between the factors and the value that contribute to the factor has been selected to represent other factors.

V. METHODOLOGY

Questionnaire survey on extensive project components that affect the cost estimation of project, a questionnaire has revealed the important factors that associated with the cost and its impact.Depending upon the mean scores and relative important index RII and impact to evaluate and rankings the factors that used in a questionnaire by using SPSS program, the impact of critical factors of the cost estimation was high and very high from mean and relative important index irrespective.• The most important factor among all factors which is obtained from the result of factor analysis namely; Consumer price index, cost of construction materials, type of building, market conditions, structural system, site area, type of slab, other supplementary buildings, location of the project, project size, type of foundation, building closeness, and fluctuation in the currency.

TABLE IV
RESULTS OF CRITICAL COST FACTORS AFFECTING CONSTRUCTION PROJECTS

Number	Cost Factor	Weight	Mean	RII	Rank
1	Location of the Project	556	3.83	76.69	11
2	Site Area	500	3.45	68.97	23
3	Site Conditions	498	3.43	68.69	24
4	Type of the Building	545	3.76	75.17	13
5	Project Size	562	3.88	77.52	9
6	Building Closeness	429	2.96	59.17	37
7	Other Supplementary Buildings	420	2.90	57.93	38
8	Area of Typical Floor	430	2.97	59.31	35
9	Weather Conditions	414	2.86	57.1	39
10	Site Accessibility	557	3.84	76.83	10
11	Type of Slab	497	3.43	68.55	26
12	Number of Floors	532	3.67	73.38	17
13	Type of Foundation	564	3.89	77.79	7
14	Length of span between columns	520	3.59	71.72	21
15	Construction Methods	492	3.39	67.86	27
16	Number of columns	485	3.34	66.90	28
17	Number of Staircase and Elevators	467	3.22	64.41	30
18	Number of Rooms	458	3.16	63.17	32
19	Drawings (detailed or not)	434	2.99	59.86	34
20	Geo-technical natural of soil	564	3.89	77.79	8
21	Design of Structural Loads	529	3.65	72.97	20
22	Market Conditions	570	3.93	78.62	5
23	Cost of Construction Materials	584	4.03	80.55	2
24	Availability of Resources	550	3.79	75.86	12
25	Cement Price	530	3.66	73.10	19
26	Labors Price	513	3.54	70.76	22
27	Reinforcement Price	586	4.04	80.83	1
28	Availability of Required Power	483	3.33	66.62	29
29	Type of Contract	438	3.02	60.41	33
30	Experience of Contractor	535	3.69	73.79	16
31	Quality of the Work	579	3.99	79.86	3

32	Time of Completion of the Project	543	3.74	74.90	14
33	Applying Safety System	430	2.97	59.31	36
34	Fluctuation in the Currency	572	3.94	78.90	4
35	Corruption	565	3.90	77.93	6
36	General Economy	531	3.66	73.24	18
37	Import Price	542	3.74	74.76	15
38	Changing Laws by the Government	461	3.18	63.59	31
39	Inflation	497	3.43	68.55	25

TABLE V
RESULTS OF FACTOR ANALYSIS

Component	Cost Factor	Factor Loading	Variance Explained%
1	General Economy	0.816	*20.485*
	Import Price	0.764	
	Corruption	0.720	
	Inflation	0.640	
	Changing Laws by the Government	0.526	
	Fluctuation in the Currency	0.460	
2	Quality of the Work	0.746	*7.587*
	Drawings	0.596	
	Time of Completion of the Project	0.567	
	Applying Safety System	0.545	
	Experience of Contractor	0.531	
	Type of Contract	0.527	
	Geo-technical natural of soil	0.501	
3	Labors Price	0.816	*6.735*
	Reinforcement Price	0.752	
	Cement Price	0.726	
4	Cost of Construction Materials	0.718	*5.612*
	Availability of Resources	0.657	
	Market Conditions	0.650	
	Number of Floors	0.443	
5	Number of Rooms	0.739	*4.572*
	Number of columns	0.653	
	Length of span between columns	0.606	
	Number of Staircase and Elevators	0.424	

	Structural Design Loads	0.411	
6	Construction Methods	0.757	*3.873*
7	Site Area	0.700	*3.804*
8	Area of Typical Floor	0.841	*3.343*
	Weather Conditions	0.641	
	Other Supplementary Buildings	0.422	
9	Site Conditions	0.742	*3.163*
	Location of the Project	0.720	
10	Type of the Building	0.712	*3.014*
	Project Size	0.709	
11	Site Accessibility	0.770	*2.962*
	Type of Foundation	0.522	
12	Building Closeness	0.788	*2.686*
	Availability of Required Power	0.491	

References

[1] W. J. D. Pico, Estimating Building Costs- for the Residential & Light Commercial Construction Professional, New York, United States: John Wiley & Sons Inc, 2012.

[2] K. N. Jha, Construction Project Management: Theory and Practices, Pearson Education India, 2015.

[3] E. O. M. Shehatto, Cost estimation for building construction projects in Gaza Strip using Artificial Neural Network (ANN), M.Sc. Thesis in Construction Management, The Islamic University of Gaza Strip, 2013.

[4] M. S. AL-Zwainy, H. A. Rasheed and H. F. Ibraheem, "Development of the construction productivity estimation model using artificial neural network for finishing works for floors with marble," APRN Journal of Engineering and Applied Sciences, vol. 7, no. 6, pp. 714-722, 2012.

[5] F. M. S. Al-Zwainy and N. T. Hadhal, "Building a mathematical model for predicting the cost of the communication towers projects using multifactor linear regression technique," International Journal of Construction Engineering and Management, vol. 5, no. 1, pp. 25-29, 2016.

[6] A. A. Aibinu, D. Dassanayake and V. C. Thien, "Use of Artificial Intelligence to predict the accuracy of pre-tender building cost estimate," in Management and Innovation for a Sustainable Built Environment : CIB International Conference of WO55, WO65, WO89, W112, TG76, TG78, TG81, Delft, 2011.

[7] A. M. El-Kholy, "Predicting cost overrun in construction project," International Journal of Construction Engineering and Management, vol. 4, no. 4, pp. 95-105, 2015.

[8] H. Al-Tabtabai and P. A. A., "Prediction of cost performance in construction projects using neural networks," Kuwait Journal of Science and Engineering, vol. 24, no. 2, pp. 226-239, 1997.

[9] A. Alqahtani and A. Whyte, "Artificial Neural Networks incorporating cost significant Items towards enhancing estimation for (life-cycle) costing of construction projects," Australasian Journal of Construction Economics and Building, vol. 13, no. 3, pp. 51-64, 2013.

[10] J. W. Johnson and J. M. Lebreton, "History and use of Relative Importance Indices in organizational research," Organizational Research Methods, vol. 7, no. 3, pp. 238-257, 2004.

A Comparative Study of Different Contractor Selection Methods

S.V.S.N.D.L Prasanna[1], Kalithkar Rakesh[2]

[1]*Assistant Professor,* [2]*Post Graduation Student*

Department of Civil Engineering, University College of Engineering, Osmania University, Hyderabad, India

***Abstract*—Contractors are very important in construction projects for the completion of project andselection of the best contractor for the project is a crucial decision for clients or owner. Selectingthe right contractor for the right project is the most crucial challenge for any construction clients.Selection of the contractor to whom the client can trust and give the responsibility to execute theproject has been primarily on the basis of bid price alone and the lowest price (tender) is usuallydescribed as being the key to win the contract, despite the fact that the tender sum is a majorconsideration because of instability and competitiveness of the construction industry, the selectionof lowest bidder is one of the major reason for project failures. Recently there has been a trendaway from a lowest price wins principle and subjective judgments to a multi criteria selectionapproach.In the present study A Comparative Study of Different Contractor Selection Methods hasbeen done. Multi criteria decision approach considers both price and non-price related criteria's forthe selection of the contractor. Based on the past research done by the professionals the criteria'sare selected. The important criteria's are listed out by survey for the selection of the best contractorand by using those criteria comparative study of different contractor selection methods has beendone. Here I have used Analytical hierarchy process (AHP), TOPSIS (Technique for OrderPreference by Similarity to an Ideal Solution) and Weighted Score Method (WSM) for the selectionof a contractor among the bidders and those methods were compared.**

***Keywords*— Multi criteriaselection approach, Best contractor for project, AHP, TOPSIS, WSM.**

I. Introduction

The contractor selection issue is one of identifying a contractor who can undertake theclient's project and take it to satisfactory conclusion. It is a decisive event for project success. Itcorresponds to an interface between variety arrays of construction companies. As the contractorplays vital role in the overall project performance, selecting the right contractor for the rightproject is the most crucial challenge for any construction client.

Selection of contractor to whom the client can trust and give the responsibility to executethe project has been primarily on the basis of bid price alone and the lowest price (tender) isusually described as being the key to win the contract. Despite the fact that the tender sum is amajor consideration because of instability and competitiveness of the construction industry, theselection of lowest bidder is one of the major reasons for project failures. When the contractorsare faced with shortage of work, wantedly quoted low bid price to win contract and to remain inbusiness. To decrease the project failures multiple criteria□s are to be considered while selectionof contractor so that we can improve the contractor selection process.

Hwong& Yoon [1] describes multiple decisions making as follows: Multiple decisionsmaking is applied to preferable decisions (such as assessment, making priority and choice)between available classified alternatives by multiple attribute. People generally use one of twofollowing methods for making decisions:

1. Trial & Error method
2. Modeling method

In trial & Error method decision maker face the reality so he chooses one of alternativeand witness the results. If decision errors are great and cause some problems, he changes thedecision and selects other alternative. In modeling method decision maker models the realproblem and specifies elements and their effect on each other and get through model analysis andprediction of real problem. Many mathematical programming models have been developed toaddress contractor selection problems. For the selection of best contractor multi criteria decisionmaking models are used. However in recent years, multi-criteria decision making (MCDM)methods have gained considerable acceptance for judging different proposals.

Recently there has been a trend away from lowest price wins principle and subjectivejudgment to a multi criteria selection approach. To assist the owners or clients in making thedecisions, the selection of the contractors for construction projects should be on the basis ofmultiple decision criteria that are both price and non price related. So that we can select the goodcontractor who is well suited for the project work. In the present study first contractor selection criteria's are identified and contractor selection methodologies Analytical Hierarchy Process(AHP), Technique for Order Preference by Similarity to Ideal

Solution (TOPSIS) and WeightedScore Method (WSM) are used for the selection of contractor and then comparative study ofcontractor selection methods have been done. The main scope of the present work is to select thebest contractor suited for the project and compare the different contractor selection methods.

II. Literature Review

Jeffrey S.Russell and MiroslawJ.Skibniewski [2] have done research on Decision Criteria in Contractor Prequalification. Contractor prequalification is a decision making process involving a wide range of criteria for which information is qualitive, subjective and imprecise. Contractor prequalification involves the screening of contractors by project owner, according to given set of criteria in order to determine their competence to perform the work if awarded the construction contract. The criteria considered for the prequalification of contractor in this paper are cost of the project, time required for completion, quality of finished products, safety achieved during construction.

Jose Ramon San Cristobal et.al [3] has done research on Contractor Selection Using Multi criteria Decision-Making Methods. Contractors play vital role in the overall performance of a project. Selecting the right contractor for the right project is the most Crucial challenge for any construction client. Numerous and often conflicting objectives and alternatives, such as tender price, completion Date and experience need to be considered .Recently ,to assist owners in making decisions. Increased project complexity and higher requirements have recently demanded the use of multi criteria decision-making methods for contractor selection. Two multi criteria decision methods ,the technique for order Preference by similarity to ideal solution(TOPSIS) and vlsekriterijumskaoptimizacija I kompromisnoresenje (VIKOR) methods, are applied to the selection of a contractor for the road building project "LaBraguía" undertaken during 2002.

EvangelosTriantaphyllou, Stuart H. Mann [4] applied analytic hierarchy process for decision making in engineering applications. In many industrial engineering applications the final decision is based on the evaluation of a number of alternatives in terms of a number of criteria. This problem may become a very difficult one when the criteria are expressed in different units or the pertinent data are difficult to be quantified.

Saaty, T.L. [5] "Decision making with the analytical hierarchy process" decision involves many tangibles that need to be traded off. To do that they have to be measured alongsidetangibles.AHP is a theory of measurement through which comparisons were made and depend on the judgments given by the decision maker priority scale. It is a scale which measures the intangibles□ in relative terms. The scale represents that the attribute is how much important than the other attributes with respect to a given attribute. The judgment may be inconsistent then how to measure the inconsistency and how improve the judgments when possible to obtain better consistency is the concern of the AHP.

MeghalkumarIzala [6] has done research on an approach of contractor selection by using Analytical Hierarchy Process. This paper suggests AHP technique for contractor selection problem in Indian context. By using this model & with the help of AHP technique one can develop contractor selection approach which can be most useful for the stakeholders. This paper suggests AHP Technique for selection of contractor problem in Indian context. Contractor selection hierarchy model is given and selection criteria's and its importance are given. This explains the limitations of the AHP.

G.R. Jahanshahloo, F. HosseinzadehLotfi, M. Izadikhah [7] developed an algorithmic method to extend TOPSIS for decision-making problems with interval data. In this research, from among multi-criteria models in making complex decisions and multiple attribute models for the most preferable choice, technique for order preference by similarity ideal solution (TOPSIS) approach has been dealt with. In some cases, determining precisely the exact value of the attributes is difficult and that, as a result of this, their values are considered as intervals. Therefore, aim of this research is to extend the TOPSIS method for decision-making problems with interval data. By extension of TOPSIS method, an algorithm to determine the most preferable choice among all possible choices, when data is interval, is presented.

AlirezaAfshari, Majid Mojahed and RosnahMohdYusuff [8] have done researchon Simple Additive Weighting approach to Personnel Selection problem. Selection of qualified personnel is a key success factor for an organization. The complexity and importance of the problem call for analytical methods rather than intuitive decisions. This paper considers a real application of personnel selection with using the opinion of expert by one of the decision making model, it is called SAW method. This paper has applied seven criteria that they are qualitative and positive for selecting the best one amongst five personnel and also ranking them. Finally the introduced method is used in case study. To increase the efficiency and ease-of-use of the proposed model, simple software such as MS Excel can be used. Evaluation of the candidates on the basis of the criteria only will be sufficient for the future applications of the model and implementation of this evaluation via simple software will speed up the process. The limitation of this article is that the decision-making process. Numbers can be used to obtain the evaluation matrix and the proposed model can be enlarged by fuzzy approach.

In previous studies, many different methods were used for selection of contractor for constructionproject. This paper is based on the contractor selection system that is well structured in approach and capable of assisting the owners or clients in making decisions regarding contractor selection in a systematic, consistent and more productive way.

III. Methodology

A. Analytical Hierarchy Process(AHP)

AHP method developed by Saaty[5] is aimed at determining the relativeimportance of a set of criteria describing various activities in a multi-criteria decision problem. Ithelps decision maker find the decision that best suits their understanding of the problem. AHP iswidely applied in various decision problems such as conflict resolution, technological problemsand economic / management problems.This evaluation process is defined as a theory of measurement with a capacity tohandle both tangible and intangible sets of criteria.

In the first step, a sophisticated decision problem is structured as a hierarchy. Thismethod breaks down a sophisticated decision construction problem into the hierarchy ofobjectives, criteria and alternatives.These decision elements make a hierarchy of the structure, including the goal of theproblem at the top, criteria in the middle and the alternatives at the bottom of this hierarchy.

Inthe second step, the comparisons of the alternatives and criteria are made. Pair wise comparisonis adopted in the comparison of alternatives and criteria. A nine point Saaty's[5] scale is adopted inthe pair wise comparison of the elements.

TABLE I
SAATY'S NINE-POINT INTENSITY OF IMPORTANCE SCALE AND ITS DESCRIPTION.

Definition	**Intensity of Importance**
Equally Important	1
Moderately more Important	3
Strongly more Important	5
Very strongly more Important	7
Extremely more Important	9
Intermediate Values	2,4,6,8

Referred from [6]

In the Table I classifications of the points on the scale are given briefly which forms thebase for the respondents to give responses in pair wise comparisons of entities.

Let C = { C_j,j=1,2,3,...,n} be the set of criteria. The result of the pair wisecomparison on criteria can be summarized in an (n×n) evaluation matrix A in whichevery element a_{ij} (i, j=1, 2, 3..., n) is the quotient of weights of criteria as shown below [4]:

$$A = \begin{pmatrix} a11 & \cdots & a1n \\ \vdots & \ddots & \vdots \\ an1 & \cdots & ann \end{pmatrix}, \; a_{ij} = 1, \; a_{ji} = \frac{1}{aij}, \; a_{ij} \neq 0$$

At the third step, the mathematical process commences to normalize and find the relativeweights for each matrix. The relative weights are given by the right eigenvector (w)corresponding to the largest value (λ_{max}) [6].

$$(A - \lambda I)\, w = 0$$

If pair wise comparisons are completely consistent the matrix A has rank 1 and λ_{max} =n.In this case the weights can be obtained by normalizing any of the rows or columns of A. Thequality of the output of the AHP is strictly related to the consistency of the pair wise comparisonjudgments. Consistency is defined by the relation between the entries of A:

$$a_{ij} \times a_{jk} = a_{ik}.$$

The consistency index (CI) [4] is

$$CI = (\lambda_{max} - n) / (n-1)$$

TABLE II
AVERAGE RANDOM CONSISTENCY (RI)

Size of the Matrix	1	2	3	4	5	6	7	8	9	10
Random Consist-ency	0	0	0.58	0.9	1.12	1.24	1.32	1.41	1.45	1.49

Referred from [5]

The final consistency ratio (CR), using which one can conclude whether the evaluations are sufficiently consistent, is calculated as the ratio of the CI to the random index (RI), as indicated below [6]:

$$CR = CI / RI$$

The CR index should be lower than 0.10 to accept the AHP results as consistent. If the final consistency ratio exceeds this value, the evaluation procedure has to be repeated to improve the consistency. The CR index could be used to calculate the consistency of decision makers as well as the consistency of all the hierarchy.

B. Technique for Order Preference by Similarity to an Ideal Solution (TOPSIS)

TOPSIS method was developed by Hwang and Yoon (in 1981) for solving a MultiAttribute Decision Making (MADM) problem. This method is based on the concept that thechosen alternative should have shortest Euclidean distance from the ideal solution and thefarthest from the negative ideal solution. The ideal solution is a hypothetical solution for whichall attributes values correspond to the maximum attribute values in the database comprising thesatisfying solution for which all attribute values correspond to the minimum attribute values inthe database.

TOPSIS thus gives a solution that is not only closest to the hypothetically best, thatis also the farthest from the hypothetically worst. The method is very useful for solving realworld problems and it provides an optimal solution or the alternative's ranking.

TOPSIS method is based on the assumption that m x n decision-making matrix Dincludes m-alternatives and n-criteria and that the attributes expressed by linguistic terms arequantified. It is also assumed that the benefits of each individual criterion are determined andthat relative criteria weights w_i have also been defined.

If m alternatives and n criteria are given for assessment in order to choose the mostacceptable alternative out of the finite alternative group, taking into account all criteriasimultaneously.

$$A = [a_1, a_2, a_3 \ldots.. a_m]$$

Each alternative a_i; i = 1,2,3,........,m is described by attribute values f_j ; j = 1,2,3,.........,nmarked as follows : x_{ij} ; i = 1,2,......,m; j = 1,2,......,n. Criteria f_j may be of profit (benefit) orexpenditure (cost) type. Profit type criteria means that greater value of attribute is preferred tolesser attribute value (herein represented by " max"), while cost type criteria means that lesserattribute value is preferred to greater value of attribute (herein represented by "min"). Theabove is illustrated with the following matrix D [9].

$$D = \begin{matrix} & f1 & \cdots & fn \\ a1 & \left[x11 \right. & \cdots & \left. x1n \right] \\ \vdots & \vdots & \ddots & \vdots \\ am & \left[xm1 \right. & \cdots & \left. xmn \right] \\ & \binom{max}{min} & \cdots & \binom{max}{min} \end{matrix}$$

The elements of the matrix D are real numbers (not negative) or linguisticexpressions from the given group of expressions. Linguistic attributes have to be quantifiedwithin previously determined and agreed value scale. Interval scale represents the suitabletool to be used when performing quantification of qualitative attributes. The mostcommonly used ordinal scale is 1 to 9, since the extremes of attributes for the criteria beinganalyzed are usually unknown.

TABLE III
TRANSLATING THE QUALITATIVE ATTRIBUTES INTO QUANTITATIVE ATTRIBUTES

Qualitative Estimation	Bad	Good	Average	Very good	Excellent
Quantitative Estimation	1	3	5	7	9

Referred from [9]

In order to solve the problem, it is necessary to normalize the attribute values, i.e. toperform the "unification" or "make the attributes non-dimensional", which means that theattribute values would be set within 0-1 interval.After the normalized decision-making matrix R (= $[r_{ij}]$) is made, it is necessary todetermine the coefficients of relative criteria importance w_j; j = 1, 2... n – Which are also beingnormalized, which results in the following [7]:

$$\sum_{j=1}^{n} Wj = 1$$

Relative importance of criteria represents a significant part of multi criteria task setup, since it ensures the relation between criteria which are not of the same value. Relativeimportance of criteria depends on subjective estimation of the DM (Decision Maker) andhas a significant influence on the final result. Multiplication of each normalized matrix'selement r_{ij} with the assigned weight coefficient w_j results in weighted normalized decisionmaking matrix V. The elements of this decision-making matrix are calculated as [7]:

$$V_{ij} = W_j x r_{ij} ; i = 1, 2, \ldots..m; j = 1, 2, \ldots..n$$

TOPSIS method determines the similarity or closeness to ideal solution. Therefore, itintroduces the criteria space in which every alternative A_i is represented by a point in the ndimensionalcriteria space and coordinates of those points are attribute values of decisionmaking matrix V and the Next step is determining of ideal and anti-ideal points and finding theEuclidean alternative distances from the ideal and anti-ideal point.

C. Weighted Score Method (WSM)

WSM is another common approach used for evaluation and selection of the best alternative in multi criteria decision making problem. Consider m alternatives { A_1, A_2,..... A_m} with n deterministic criteria {C_1, C_2,....C_n}. The alternatives are fully characterized by decision matrix {S_{ij}}, where S_{ij} the score that measures how well alternative A_i performs on criterion C_j. The weights { W_1, W_2,.... W_k} accounts for the relative importance of the criteria. The best alternative is the one with highest score. In WSM the final score for the alternative Ai is calculated using the following formulae [10].

$$S(A_i)=\Sigma W_j S$$

Where sum is over j=1,2,..., n; W_j is relative importance of jthcriterion; S_{ij} is score that measures how well alternative A_i performs on criterion C_j.

D. Data Collection and Analysis

From the previous studies the criteria required for contractor selection are identified and the lists of criteria are prepared for the questionnaire survey.The Questionnaire form contains the list of criteria which are collected from the past study and structured in the form of written set of questions, comparisons to which respondent record their answers, usually within rather closely defined alternatives.

Initial lists of 40 criteria are taken for the survey. In order to identify that which of these criteria would be significant for the study, several experienced construction contractors, research scholars and the owner's opinion are taken. Respondents to criteria survey consists 5 contractors, 4 research scholars, 1 engineer, 3 M.Tech Students. Based on the comprehensive and valuable input from 13 respondents, criteria were selected to be included in the contractor selection. Relative Rank Index (RRI) is adopted in the selection of criteria using six-point Likert's scale. Respondents were asked to indicate the degree of relevance or level of importance of these criteria on a six-point Likert's scale.

According to Likert's scale there are six different rankings be given. In this 0 means the criterion is Irrelevant (IR), 1 means the criterion has Very Low Important (VLI), 2 means the criterion has Low Important (LI), 3 means the criterion has Medium Important (MI), 4 means the criterion has Important (I) and 5 mean it is Very Important (VI).

The RRI technique is used for comparison between importance levels of variables and derived from Likert's scales which represent the level of importance of variables chosen by respondents which need to be transformed into a Relative Rank Index that has a value of one or less.

The RRI can be calculated using the following equation [7]:

$$RRI = \frac{1}{nN}(\sum l_i x_i) where\ i=1\ to\ n$$

Where, RRI refers to Relative Rank Index;

n - Maximum Likert's scale value (here 5)

N - Total number of responses:i - 1, 2.....n ;

l_i = Likert's scale (l_1 is the least important and ln is the most important)

x_i = the frequency of the ith response.

TABLE IV
CRITERIA TAKEN AND SURVEY RESULTS OBTAINED FROM RESPONDENTS.

S.No	Description of Criteria	RRI
1	Experience	0.83
2	Financial stability	0.893
3	Past performance	0.8
4	Current Work Load	0.846
5	Management Staff	0.769
6	Manpower resources availability	0.754
7	Contractor organization	0.554
8	Familiarity with the project geographic location	0.662
9	Management Capability	0.723
10	Quality Performance	0.985
11	Equipment resources	0.8
12	Purchase expertise and material handling	0.646
13	Safety consciousness	0.785
14	Planning, scheduling and controlling	0.892
15	Equipment repairing and maintenance yard	0.492
16	Reputation of sub-contractor	0.692
17	Bid or tender price	0.892
18	Quoted project duration	0.846
19	Defect liability period	0.661
20	Advance bank payment	0.846
21	Construction method statement	0.677
22	Balance sheet data of contractor	0.692
23	Black listing in past projects	0.969
24	Work quality in completed projects	0.969
25	Reputation of contractor	0.8
26	Past failures of contractors works	0.892
27	Age and registration of contractors	0.615
28	Human resource management	0.554
29	Relationship with client	0.661
30	Technical capability	0.861
31	Fraudulent activity	0.738
32	Competitiveness	0.631
33	Cycle time	0.6
34	Durability	0.877
35	Ergonomic qualities	0.554
36	Reliability	0.708
37	Environment performance	0.785
38	HR practices	0.492
39	Judicial	0.677
40	Innovativeness	0.661

In this present study, the criteria having 80 % and more RRI value (> 0.80) are considered for the contractor selection process. Based on contractor's data for the particular criterion only eight criteria's are taken for contractor selection.

TABLE V
CRITERIA TAKEN FOR CONTRACTOR SELECTION.

S.No	Description of Criteria	RRI
1	Experience.......................(EXP)	0.83
2	Financial stability............(F.S)	0.89
3	Current workload...... (C.W.L)	0.84
4	Quality performance...........(Q.P)	0.96
5	Equipment resources.........(E.R)	0.80
6	Technical capability.........(T.C)	0.86
7	Quoted project duration.(Q.P.D)	0.84
8	Reputation of contractor...(R.C)	0.80

IV. DISCUSSIONS ONCASE STUDY

The work being dealt with "Construction and Design of Multi Storey Building". The estimated contract value is more than Rs.350 million. Period of completion of work is given as 18 months. Four bidders are participating in the bidding process.

For instance let

Contractor A- B.L.Kashyap&sons Ltd,

Contractor B- JMC Projects (India),

Contractor C- EMAS Engineers &contractors Pvt Ltd,

Contractor D- Consolidated Construction Consortium Ltd.

TABLE VI
CONTRACTORS DATA.

Details of contractors	Contractor A	Contractor B	Contractor C	Contractor D
Type of company	Public	Public	Public	Public
Date of incorporation	08 April 1995	21 January 1994	3 august 1995	17 July 1997
Experience of working on similar projects	5 similar projects	3 similar projects	4 similar projects	3 similar projects
Financial stability	Assets 13.26crores	Assets 96.6 crores	22.51 crores	45.56 crores
Current work load	3 medium projects	3 BP,1MP	3 medium projects	2 BP and 1 MP
Quality performance	Not furnished	ISO-9002	ISO-9002	ISO-9001:2000
Equipment resources	6 batching plants, 10 concrete mixers 2 tower cranes	8 batching plants,10 concrete mixers 4 tower cranes	12 batching plants, 6 concrete mixers 3 tower cranes	12 batching plants, 15 concrete mixers 7 tower cranes
Technical capability	1 PM-10 yrexp 3 GE 4 DE	3 PM-15yr exp. 8 GE 6 DE	1 PM-15yr exp. 6 GE 8 DE	2 PM-5yr exp. 8 GE 8 DE
Quoted project duration	19 months	20 months	18 months	18 months
Reputation of contractor	Good reputation	Average reputation	Average reputation	Good reputation

A. Analysis of Analytical Hierarchy Process Model for Case study

AHP method is one of the best techniques in MultiCriteria Decision Making methods. In this section AHP method was used for analyzing themethod for selection of a contractor. The Eigen Values are found out and thusthe consistency test also done.

TABLE VII
PAIR WISE COMPARISON MATRIX OF ALL CRITERIA:

	EXP	F.S	C.W.L	Q.P	EQ.R	T.C	Q.P.D	R.C	Priority vector	Eigen vector
EXP	1	0.2	0.33	0.14	2	0.2	0.2	3	0.048	0.090
F.S	5	1	3	0.2	5	2	3	5	0.185	0.380
C.W.L	3	0.33	1	0.14	3	0.5	1	3	0.083	0.164
Q.P	7	5	7	1	7	7	7	7	0.391	0.839
EQ.R	0.5	0.2	0.33	0.14	1	0.33	0.5	1	0.036	0.071
T.C	5	0.5	2	0.33	3	1	2	3	0.131	0.267
Q.P.D	5	0.33	1	0.2	2	0.5	1	3	0.090	0.182
R.C	0.33	0.2	0.33	0.14	1	0.33	0.33	1	0.033	0.066

<u>*Consistency check:*</u>

Principal Eigen value (λ max) =8.5817

Size of matrix (n) =9

Consistency index (CI) = $(\lambda_{max}-n)/(n-1)$ =0.0831

Average random consistency index (RI) =1.485

Consistency Ratio (CR) = CI / RI =0.0559

The pair wise comparison matrix is consistent as CR =0.0559<0.1

The pair wise comparison of criteria was done and Eigen values and Eigen vector obtained. The consistency of matrix ischecked and Eigen vector and priority vector of all the criteria were found out.

The same procedure is adopted with respect to pair wise comparison of contractors in the index of all criteria's andEigen Values are found out and thus the consistency test also done. The weights of all the criteria with respect to each contractor are calculated. The values thus obtained are used in the calculation of weights and rankings of contractors.

TABLE VIII
OVERALL PRIORITIES OF ALL CONTRACTORS AND THEIR RANKINGS FOR THE CASE STUDY:

	WEIGHT AGE	Contractor A	Contractor B	Contractor C	Contractor D
EXP	0.0483	0.573	0.109	0.209	0.109
F.S	0.1858	0.088	0.484	0.157	0.271
C.W.L	0.083	0.28	0.1645	0.391	0.1645
Q.P	0.3912	0.0625	0.2263	0.2158	0.4954
EQ.R	0.0367	0.0638	0.1338	0.34715	0.4175
T.C	0.1311	0.0603	0.489	0.162	0.2887
Q.P.D	0.0902	0.1639	0.1405	0.3478	0.3478
R.C	0.0337	0.375	0.125	0.125	0.375
Overall Priorities		0.1294	0.283	0.226	0.36
RANK		4	2	3	1

Overall priorities of contractors A to D are obtained as 0.1294, 0.283, 0.226, 0.36 and corresponding ranking pattern is 4, 2, 3 and 1. From this model for the case study contractor D is selected as best.

B. *Analysis of TOPSIS Model for Case study*

The analysis was done for contractor selection. Table IX showsthe decision matrix for all criteria, while Table X shows the decision matrix between alternatives and criteria.

TABLE IX
DECISION MATRIX FOR ALL CRITERIA:

Criteria	Priorities	Normalized value $(\frac{Pi}{\sum Pi})$
EXP	7	0.1346
F.S	9	0.173
C.W.L	3	0.05769
Q.P	8	0.1538
EQ.R	7	0.1346
T.C	8	0.1538
Q.P.D	7	0.1346
R.C	3	0.05769

TABLE X
DECISION MATRIX BETWEEN ALTERNATIVES AND CRITERIA

	A	B	C	D
EXP	9	7	8	7
F.S	3	7	3	5
C.W.L	5	9	5	7
Q.P	3	7	7	9
EQ.R	6	7	8	9
T.C	6	7	7	8
QP.D	6	7	5	5
R.C	9	5	5	9

The normalized weighted decision matrix (R_{ij}) of criteria Experience for contractor A is calculated as follows [7]:

$$R_{ij} = \frac{x_{ij}}{\sqrt{\sum_{i=1}^{m} x^2 ij}} (j = 1, 2, \dots . n)$$

The weighted normalized score (V_{ij}) of criteria Experience for contractor A is calculated as follows:

$$V_{ij} = w_j \text{ x } R_{ij}$$

TABLE XI
NORMALIZED WEIGHTED DECISION MATRIX BETWEEN ALTERNATIVES AND CRITERIA

	A	B	C	D
EXP	0.07789	0.060615	0.069255	0.060615
F.S	0.054149	0.126117	0.05449	0.090133
C.W.L	0.021634	0.03886	0.021634	0.030218
Q.P	0.033726	0.078694	0.078694	0.101
EQ.R	0.05346	0.06237	0.07128	0.080055
T.C	0.065178	0.076041	0.076041	0.086904
QP.D	0.06966	0.08127	0.05805	0.05805
R.C	0.03523	0.019551	0.019551	0.03523

The ideal alternative (A^+) and the anti-ideal alternative (A^-) correspond to hypothetical alternatives in which all attribute values correspond to the best and worst levels respectively. The ideal and anti - Ideal solutions/ alternatives are computed using the equation.

$A^+ = \{(\max_i V_{ij}, j\epsilon J), (\min_i V_{ij} j\epsilon J')\}$

$A^+ = \{V_1^+, V_2^+, V_3^+, \dots\dots V_m^+\}$ Ideal alternative coordinates

$A^- = \{(\min_i V_{ij}, j\epsilon J), (\max_i V_{ij} j\epsilon J')\}$

$A^- = \{V_1^-, V_2^-, V_3^-, \dots\dots V_m^-\}$ Anti Ideal alternative coordinates

Thus ideal alternative (A^+) and the anti-ideal alternative (A^-) are formed with maximum and minimum values respectively in the rows of normalized weighted decision matrix as follows:

A^+ = {0.07789, 0.126117, 0.021634, 0.101, 0.080055, 0.086904, 0.05805, 0.03523}

A^- = {0.060615, 0.054149, 0.03886, 0.033726, 0.05346, 0.065178, 0.08127, 0.019551}

The separation of each alternative from the ideal alternative (S^+) and the anti-alternative (S^-) are determined in terms of Euclidean distances.Euclidean distance $S_i^+$of each alternative a_i, from the ideal point A^+

$$S+= \sqrt{\sum_{j=1}^{n}(Vij - Vj+)2} \quad , i=1, 2....m.$$

S^+ = {0.10497, 0.04804, 0.078691, 0.040827}

Euclidean distance $S_i^-$of each alternative $a_i$from the anti-ideal point A^-

$$S-= \sqrt{\sum_{j=1}^{n}(Vij - Vj-)2} \quad , i=1, 2....m.$$

S^- = {0.031238, 0.086017, 0.056725, 0.343999}

The alternative contractors have been ranked based on C_i value is computed as follows [7].

$$Ci = \frac{si^-}{s_i^- + s_i^+}$$

TABLE XII

CLOSENESS INDEX OF CONTRACTORS AND THEIR RANKING

	C_i	Rank
Contractor A	0.2293	4
Contractor B	0.64164	2
Contractor C	0.4188	3
Contractor D	0.8939	1

C. *Analysis of WSM for Case study*

The analysis was done for contractor selection. Table VIII shows the decision matrix for all criteria considered for contractor selection. Here we use the same criterion priority values as used for the TOPSIS method above to evaluate the contractors. Table IX shows decision matrix between alternatives and criteria considered for contractor selection. The total score is obtained by sum of product of the criteria weightage and the weightage of the contractor for the particular criteria.

TABLE XIII

TOTAL SCORE OF CONTRACTORS AND RANKING OF THEM.

	A	B	C	D	Weightage of criteria
EXP	9	7	8	7	0.135
F.S	3	7	3	5	0.173
C.W.L	5	9	5	7	0.058
Q.P	3	7	7	9	0.154
EQ.R	6	7	8	9	0.135
T.C	6	7	7	8	0.153
QP.D	6	7	5	5	0.135
R.C	9	5	5	9	0.057
Total Score	5.53	7.00	6.07	7.22	
Ranking	**4**	**2**	**3**	**1**	

V. RESULTS ANDDISCUSSIONS

Ranking Results from all the models for the case study are presented in Table XII. It is observed that from AHP, TOPSIS and WSM method contractor D is given first rankand contractor A has given last rank.It is concluded that the contractor D is best in his performance followed by contractor B&contractor C. The overall performance of contractor A is not good enough with respectto different criteria among all the contractors.

TABLE XIV

RESULTS FROM THREE METHODS

Models used	Contractor A	Contractor B	Contractor C	Contractor D
AHP	4	2	3	1
TOPSIS	4	2	3	1
WSM	4	2	3	1

TABLE XV

SUMMARY OF COMPARISON OF CONTRACTOR SELECTION METHODS

	AHP	TOPSIS	WSM
Consistency	It provides the consistency in judgment considering that the consistency Index (CI) is calculated.	It cannot provide controlled consistency because it is not having the comparative indexes as indicator	It cannot provide controlled consistency because it is not having the comparative indexes as indicator

Problem structure	AHP uses a hierarchical structure by pair wise comparison hence this method becomes complicated for a problem structure with a no of alternatives or criteria.	TOPSIS can solve the selection problem however the process provides numerous alternatives and criterions because of simple mathematical equations and calculations	WSM can solve the selection problem however the process provides numerous alternatives and criterions because of simple calculations
Principle of calculation	Uses the hierarchy principle and pair wise comparison matrix to select the obtained alternatives	TOPSIS calculates the shortest distance of an alternative from the positive ideal solution and longest distance from the negative ideal solution	It applies the principle of weighted average by assigning a scale value to each Alternative
Concept	Focus on model from which a vector of global score is obtained by competing alternatives.	Classified as compromising model with the belief that no ideal solution exists, but a solution with optimal values on all criteria is simultaneously selected.	It focus on model from which a vector global score is obtained by Competing Alternatives
Relative Importance	It will consider the relative importance of criteria.	It uses two reference points using vector normalization but it does not consider the relative importance of the distances.	It will consider relative importance of criteria.

VI. Conclusions

In this study, selection of contractor with multi criteria's for a construction project was made considering AHP, TOPSIS and WSM methods. A real-life project was selected as a case study and the actual data regarding alternative contractors were collected. The main contribution of this study is to propose a multi criteria's decisionmaking, which uses the main criteria (i.e., experience, financial stability, current workload, quality performance, equipment resources, technical capability, quoted project duration, reputation of contractor) of client requirements to select the best suited contractor for each criteria that constitute the entire project simultaneously.The proposed methods enabled the clients to select the optimal contractor who is having more weightage for the criteria is selected as the best contractor. The comparision between contractor selection methods are also taken in consideration which concluded that checking the consistency is done in AHP. It is also observed that AHP, WSM Focuses on model from which a vector of global score isobtained by competing alternatives and relative importance of criteria but whereas TOPSIS is compromising model withoptimal values on all criteria is simultaneously selected and usestwo reference points but it does not consider the relative importance of thedistances.

References

[1] Yoon, K.P., & Hwang, C.L.(1995) Multiple Attribute Decision Making: An introduction (Sage University Paper series on Quantitative Application in the Social Sciences, 07-104). Thousand Oaks, CA: Sage.

[2] Jeffrey S.Russell and MiroslawJ.Skibniewski "Decision Criteria in Contractor Prequalification" Journal of Management Engineering 1988:148 – 164.

[3] José Ramón San Cristóbal "Contractor Selection Using Multi criteria Decision-Making Methods" Journal of Construction Engineering and Management © ASCE /June2012.

[4] EvangelosTriantaphyllou, Stuart H. Mann "Using the Analytic Hierarchy Process for Decision Making In Engineering Applications: Some Challenges" International Journal ofIndustrial Engineering: Applications and Practice, Vol. 2, No. 1, pp. 35-44, 1995.

[5] Thomas L. Saaty "Decision making with the analytic hierarchy process" International Journal Services Sciences, Vol. 1, No. 1, 2008.

[6] Meghalkumar I Zala, Prof. Rajiv B Bhatt "An Approach of Contractor Selection by Analytical Hierarchy Process" National Conference on Recent Trends in Engineering &Technology.

[7] G.R. Jahanshahloo, F. Hosseinzadeh Lot, M. Izadik hah "An algorithmic method to extendTOPSIS for decision- making problems with interval data" International Journal of AppliedMathematics and Computation 175 (2006) 1375-1384.

[8] AlirezaAfshari, Majid Mojahed and RosnahMohdYusuff "Simple Additive Weighting approach to Personnel Selection problem" International Journal of Innovation, Management andTechnology, Vol. 1, No. 5, December 2010 ISSN: 2010-0248.

[9] AsadAsadzadeh, Sujit Kumar Sikder "Assessing Site Selection of New Towns Using TOPSIS Method under Entropy Logic: A Case study: New Towns of Tehran Metropolitan Region (TMR)" Environmental Management and Sustainable Development ISSN 2164-76822014, Vol. 3, No.1.

[10] Patcy Paul "Selection of the most optimal contractor in Indian Construction Industry usingvarious multi criteria decision making methods" M.Tech thesis of Nit Warangal 2013.

Author Index